rsac

JUN 07

Good Eggs

Good Eggs

∽ A memoir ∾

PHOEBE POTTS

HARPER

An Imprint of HarperCollins*Publishers*
www.harpercollins.com

HarperCollins books may be purchased for educational, business, or sales promotional use. For information, please write: Special Markets Department, HarperCollins Publishers, 10 East 53rd Street, New York, NY 10022.

FIRST EDITION

Library of Congress Cataloging-in-Publication Data has been applied for.
ISBN: 978-0-06-171146-6

10 11 12 13 14   OFF/   10 9 8 7 6 5 4 3 2 1

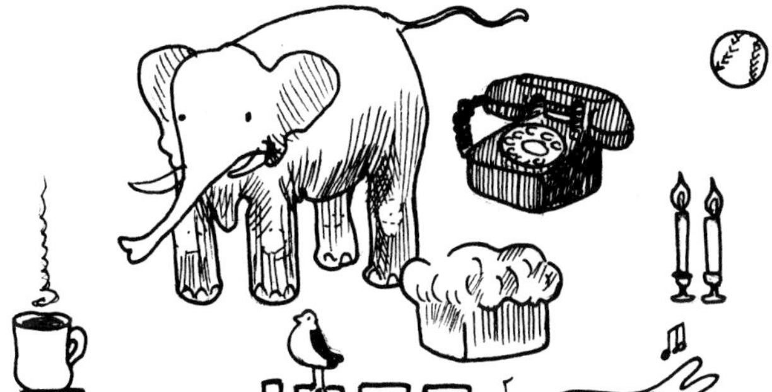

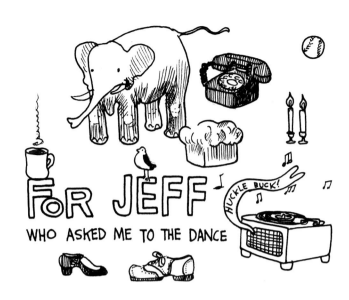

FOR JEFF

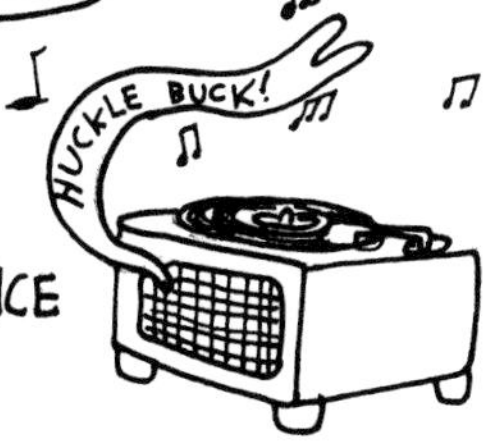
HUCKLE BUCK!

WHO ASKED ME TO THE DANCE

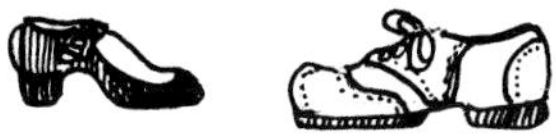

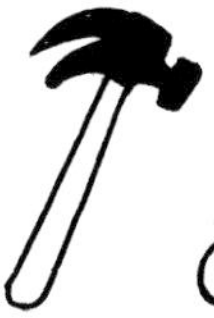

& FOR MY PARENTS

WHO TAUGHT ME THE STEPS

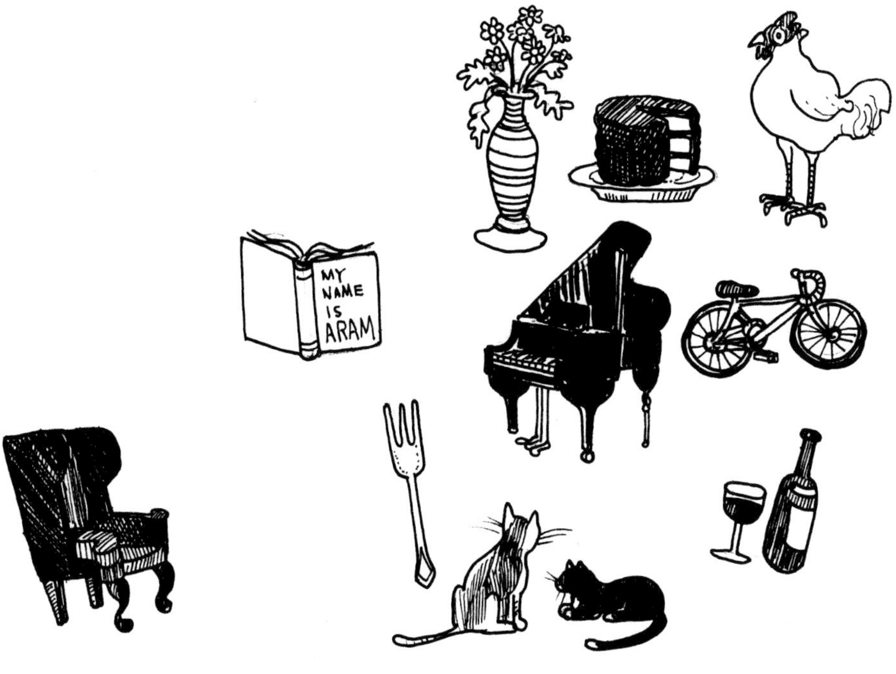
MY NAME IS ARAM

foreword!

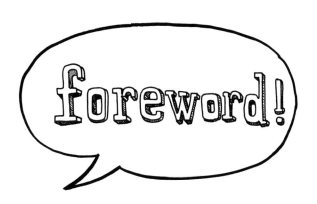

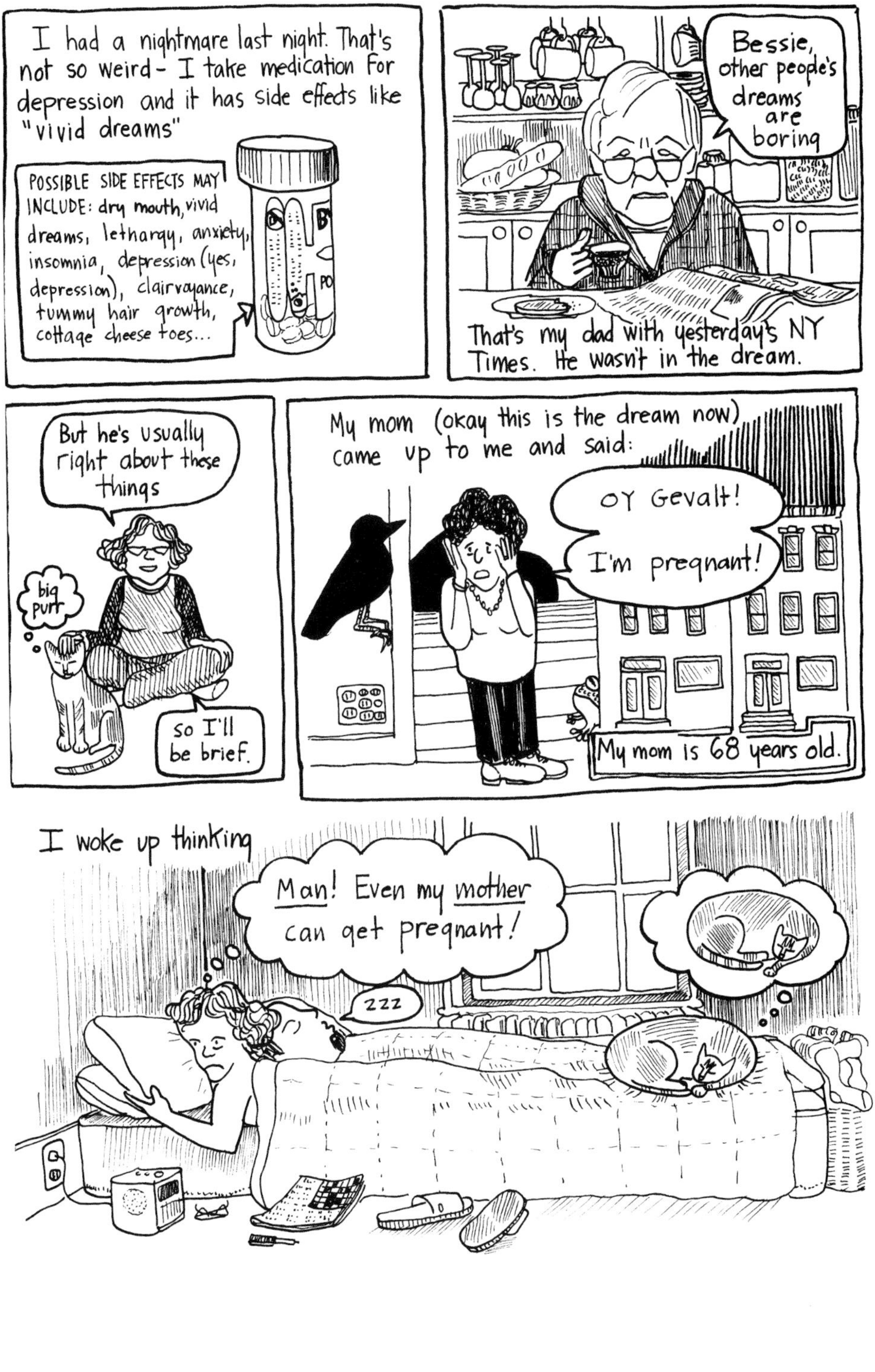

I had a nightmare last night. That's not so weird - I take medication for depression and it has side effects like "vivid dreams"
POSSIBLE SIDE EFFECTS MAY INCLUDE: dry mouth, vivid dreams, lethargy, anxiety, insomnia, depression (yes, depression), clairvoyance, tummy hair growth, cottage cheese toes...
Bessie, other people's dreams are boring
That's my dad with yesterday's NY Times. He wasn't in the dream.
But he's usually right about these things
big purr
So I'll be brief.
My mom (okay this is the dream now) came up to me and said:
OY Gevalt!
I'm pregnant!
My mom is 68 years old.
I woke up thinking
Man! Even my mother can get pregnant!
zzz

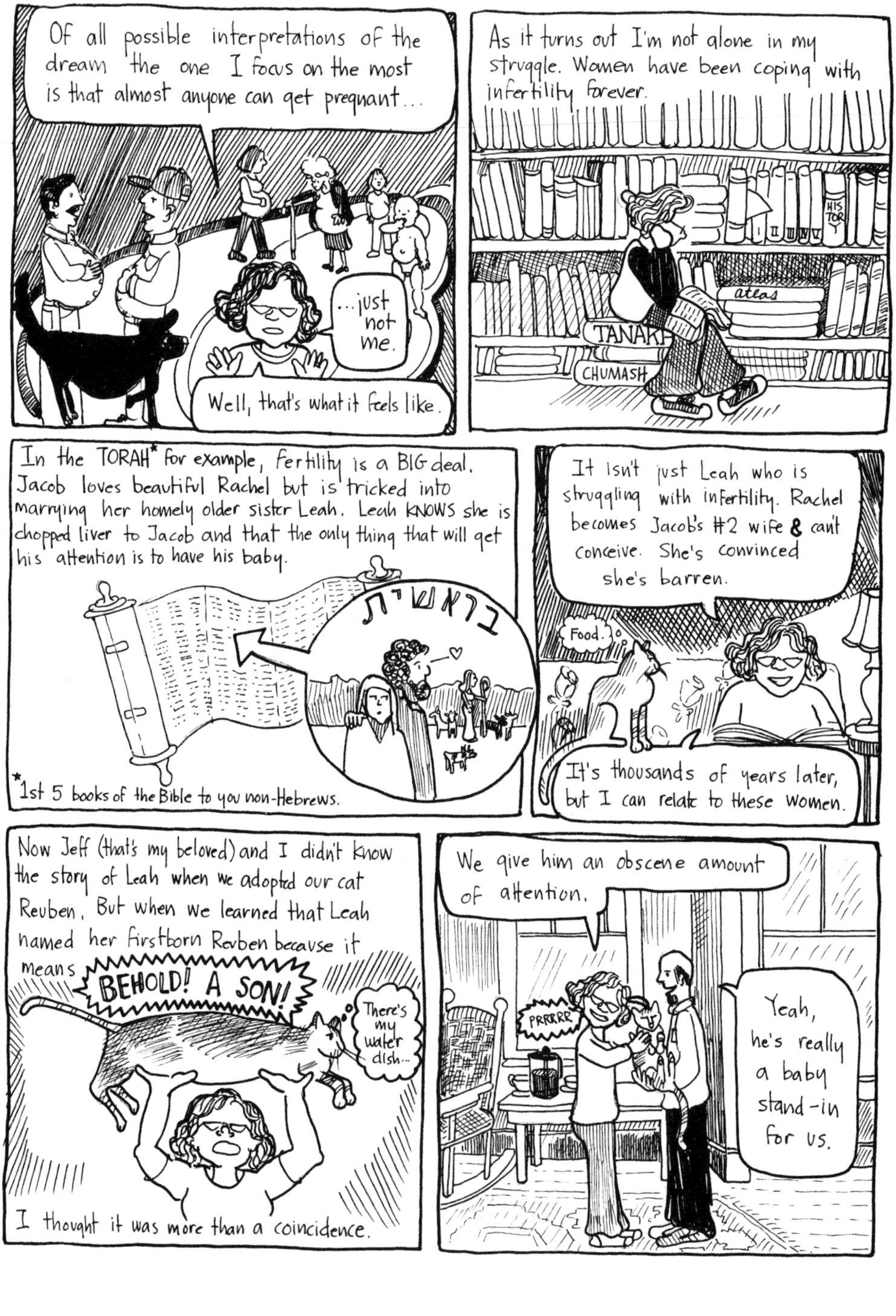
Of all possible interpretations of the dream the one I focus on the most is that almost anyone can get pregnant...
...just not me.
Well, that's what it feels like.
As it turns out I'm not alone in my struggle. Women have been coping with infertility forever.
HISTORY
atlas
TANAKH
CHUMASH
In the TORAH* for example, fertility is a BIG deal. Jacob loves beautiful Rachel but is tricked into marrying her homely older sister Leah. Leah KNOWS she is chopped liver to Jacob and that the only thing that will get his attention is to have his baby.
בראשית
*1st 5 books of the Bible to you non-Hebrews.
It isn't just Leah who is struggling with infertility. Rachel becomes Jacob's #2 wife & can't conceive. She's convinced she's barren.
Food.
It's thousands of years later, but I can relate to these women.
Now Jeff (that's my beloved) and I didn't know the story of Leah when we adopted our cat Reuben. But when we learned that Leah named her firstborn Reuben because it means
BEHOLD! A SON!
There's my water dish...
I thought it was more than a coincidence.
We give him an obscene amount of attention.
PRRRRR
Yeah, he's really a baby stand-in for us.

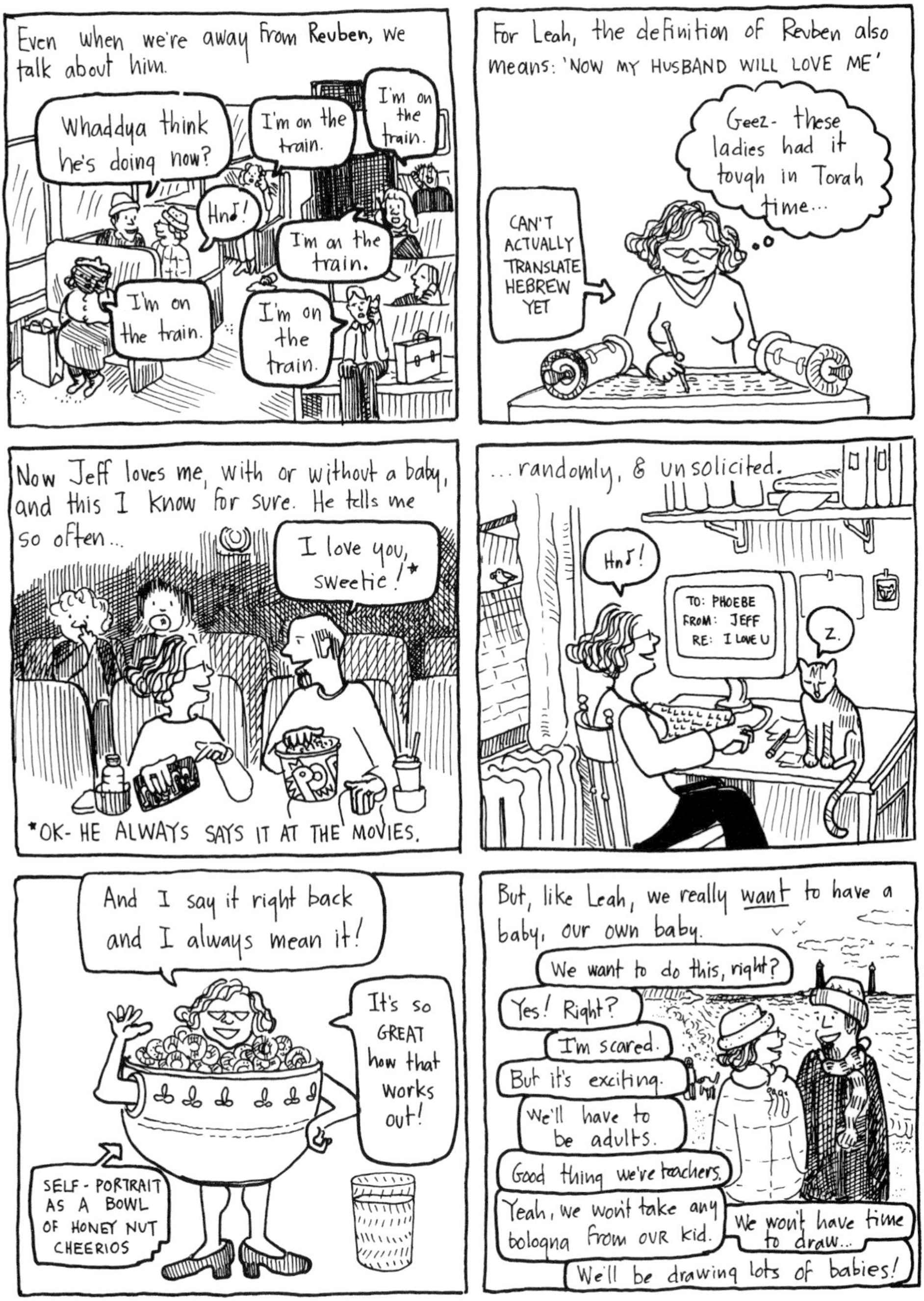

Even when we're away from Reuben, we talk about him.
Whaddya think he's doing now?
I'm on the train.
I'm on the train.
Hnd!
I'm on the train.
I'm on the train.
I'm on the train.
For Leah, the definition of Reuben also means: 'NOW MY HUSBAND WILL LOVE ME'
Geez- these ladies had it tough in Torah time...
CAN'T ACTUALLY TRANSLATE HEBREW YET
Now Jeff loves me, with or without a baby, and this I know for sure. He tells me so often...
I love you, sweetie!*
POP
*OK- HE ALWAYS SAYS IT AT THE MOVIES.
...randomly, & unsolicited.
Hnd!
TO: PHOEBE
FROM: JEFF
RE: I LOVE U
Z.
And I say it right back and I always mean it!
It's so GREAT how that works out!
SELF-PORTRAIT AS A BOWL OF HONEY NUT CHEERIOS
But, like Leah, we really want to have a baby, our own baby.
We want to do this, right?
Yes! Right?
I'm scared.
But it's exciting.
We'll have to be adults.
Good thing we're teachers.
Yeah, we won't take any bologna from our kid.
We won't have time to draw...
We'll be drawing lots of babies!

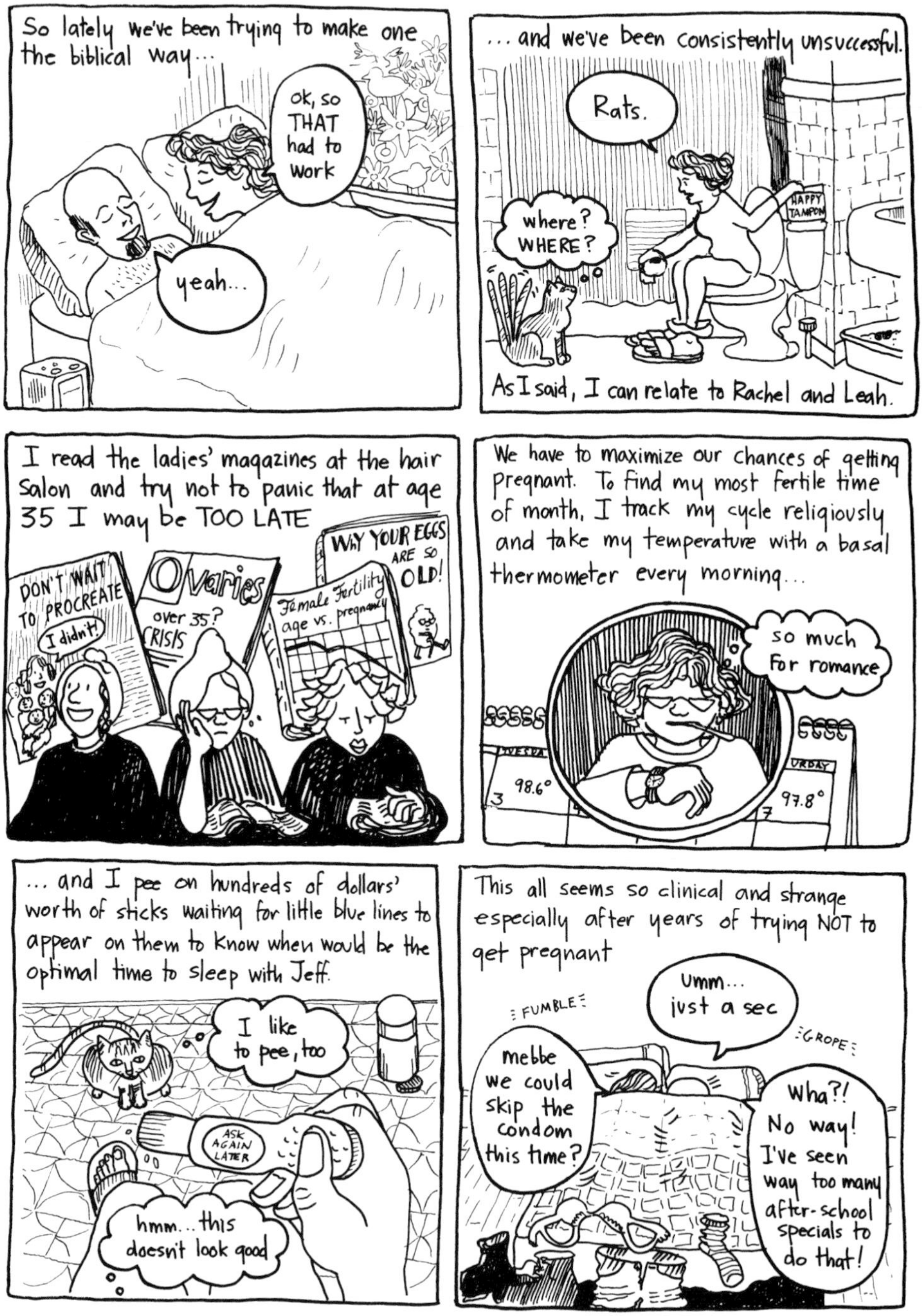
So lately we've been trying to make one the biblical way...
ok, so THAT had to work
yeah...
... and we've been consistently unsuccessful.
Rats.
where? WHERE?
HAPPY TAMPON
As I said, I can relate to Rachel and Leah.
I read the ladies' magazines at the hair salon and try not to panic that at age 35 I may be TOO LATE
DON'T WAIT TO PROCREATE
I didn't!
Ovaries over 35? CRISIS
Female Fertility age vs. pregnancy
WHY YOUR EGGS ARE SO OLD!
We have to maximize our chances of getting pregnant. To find my most fertile time of month, I track my cycle religiously and take my temperature with a basal thermometer every morning...
so much for romance
98.6°
97.8°
... and I pee on hundreds of dollars' worth of sticks waiting for little blue lines to appear on them to know when would be the optimal time to sleep with Jeff.
I like to pee, too
ASK AGAIN LATER
hmm... this doesn't look good
This all seems so clinical and strange especially after years of trying NOT to get pregnant
FUMBLE
Umm... just a sec
GROPE
mebbe we could skip the condom this time?
Wha?! No way! I've seen way too many after-school specials to do that!

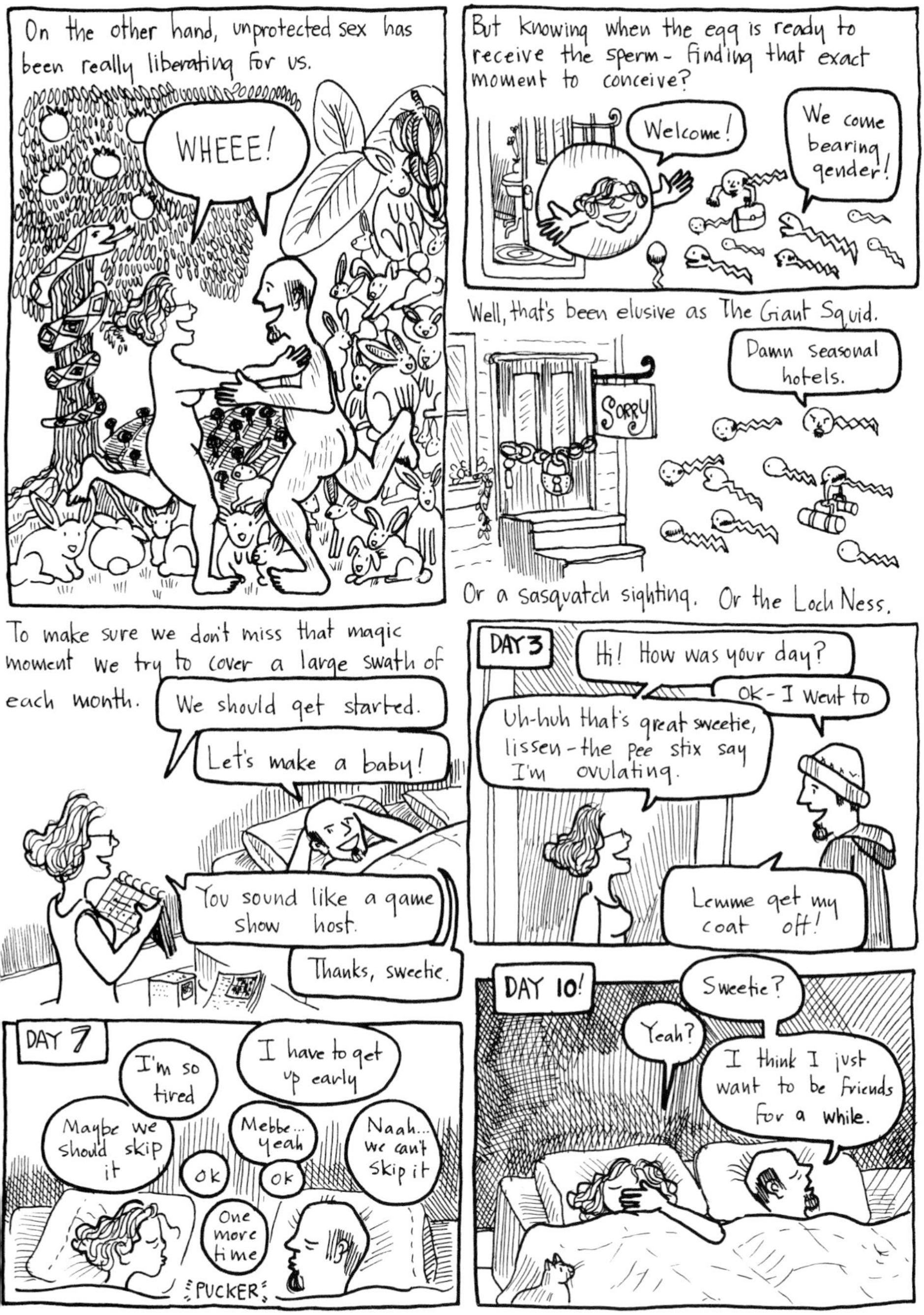
On the other hand, unprotected sex has been really liberating for us.
WHEEE!
But knowing when the egg is ready to receive the sperm - finding that exact moment to conceive?
Welcome!
We come bearing gender!
Well, that's been elusive as The Giant Squid.
SORRY
Damn seasonal hotels.
Or a sasquatch sighting. Or the Loch Ness.
To make sure we don't miss that magic moment we try to cover a large swath of each month.
We should get started.
Let's make a baby!
You sound like a game show host.
Thanks, sweetie.
DAY 3
Hi! How was your day?
OK - I went to
Uh-huh that's great sweetie, lissen - the pee stix say I'm ovulating.
Lemme get my coat off!
DAY 7
I'm so tired
I have to get up early
Maybe we should skip it
Mebbe... yeah
Naah... we can't skip it
ok
ok
One more time
PUCKER
DAY 10!
Sweetie?
Yeah?
I think I just want to be friends for a while.

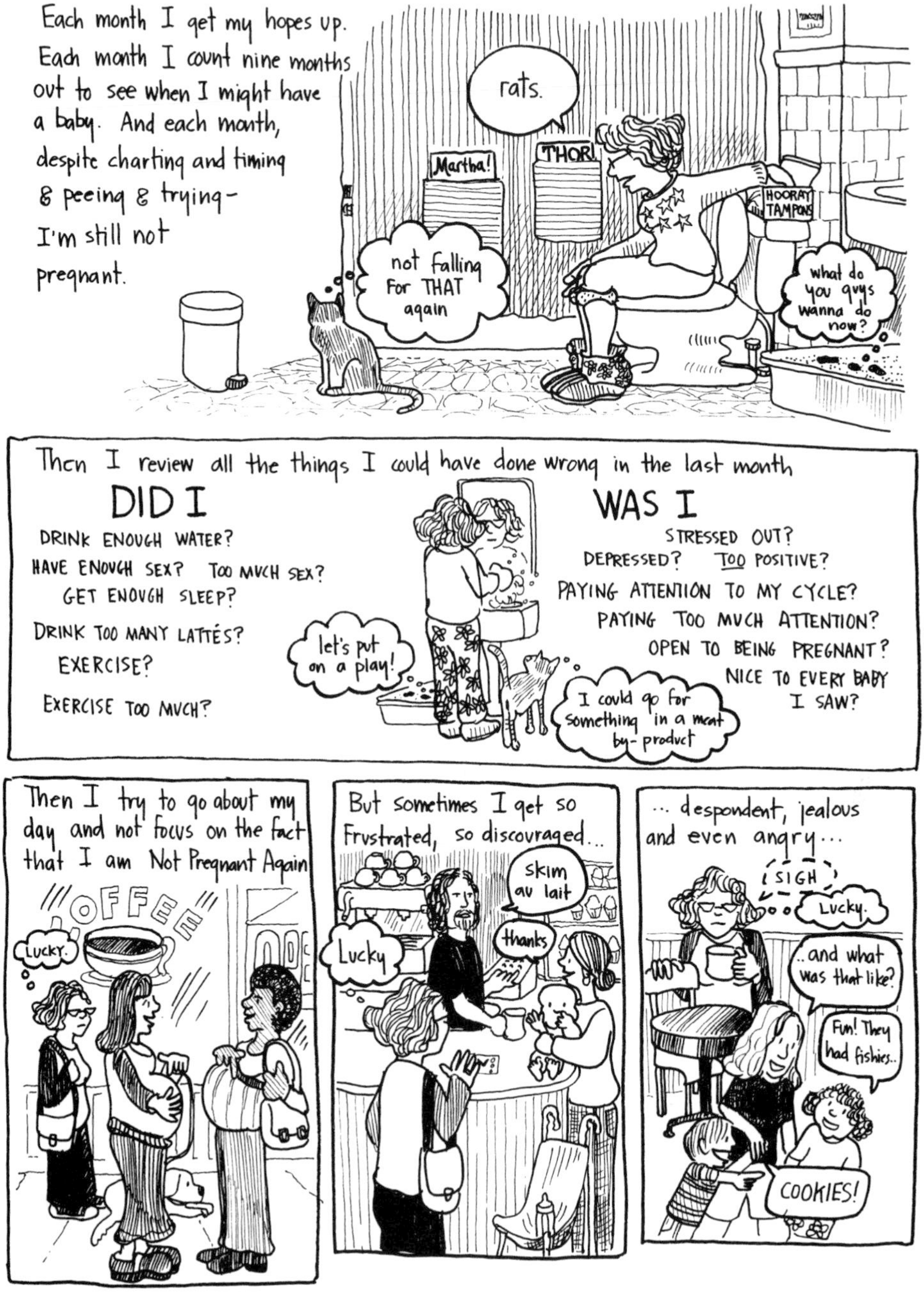

Each month I get my hopes up. Each month I count nine months out to see when I might have a baby. And each month, despite charting and timing & peeing & trying - I'm still not pregnant.
rats.
Martha!
THOR
HOORAY TAMPONS
not falling for THAT again
what do you guys wanna do now?
Then I review all the things I could have done wrong in the last month
DID I
DRINK ENOUGH WATER?
HAVE ENOUGH SEX? TOO MUCH SEX?
GET ENOUGH SLEEP?
DRINK TOO MANY LATTÉS?
EXERCISE?
EXERCISE TOO MUCH?
let's put on a play!
WAS I
STRESSED OUT?
DEPRESSED? TOO POSITIVE?
PAYING ATTENTION TO MY CYCLE?
PAYING TOO MUCH ATTENTION?
OPEN TO BEING PREGNANT?
NICE TO EVERY BABY I SAW?
I could go for something in a meat by-product
Then I try to go about my day and not focus on the fact that I am Not Pregnant Again
COFFEE
Lucky.
But sometimes I get so frustrated, so discouraged...
skim au lait
thanks
Lucky
... despondent, jealous and even angry...
SIGH
Lucky.
..and what was that like?
Fun! They had fishies..
COOKIES!

Sometimes I just want to scream:

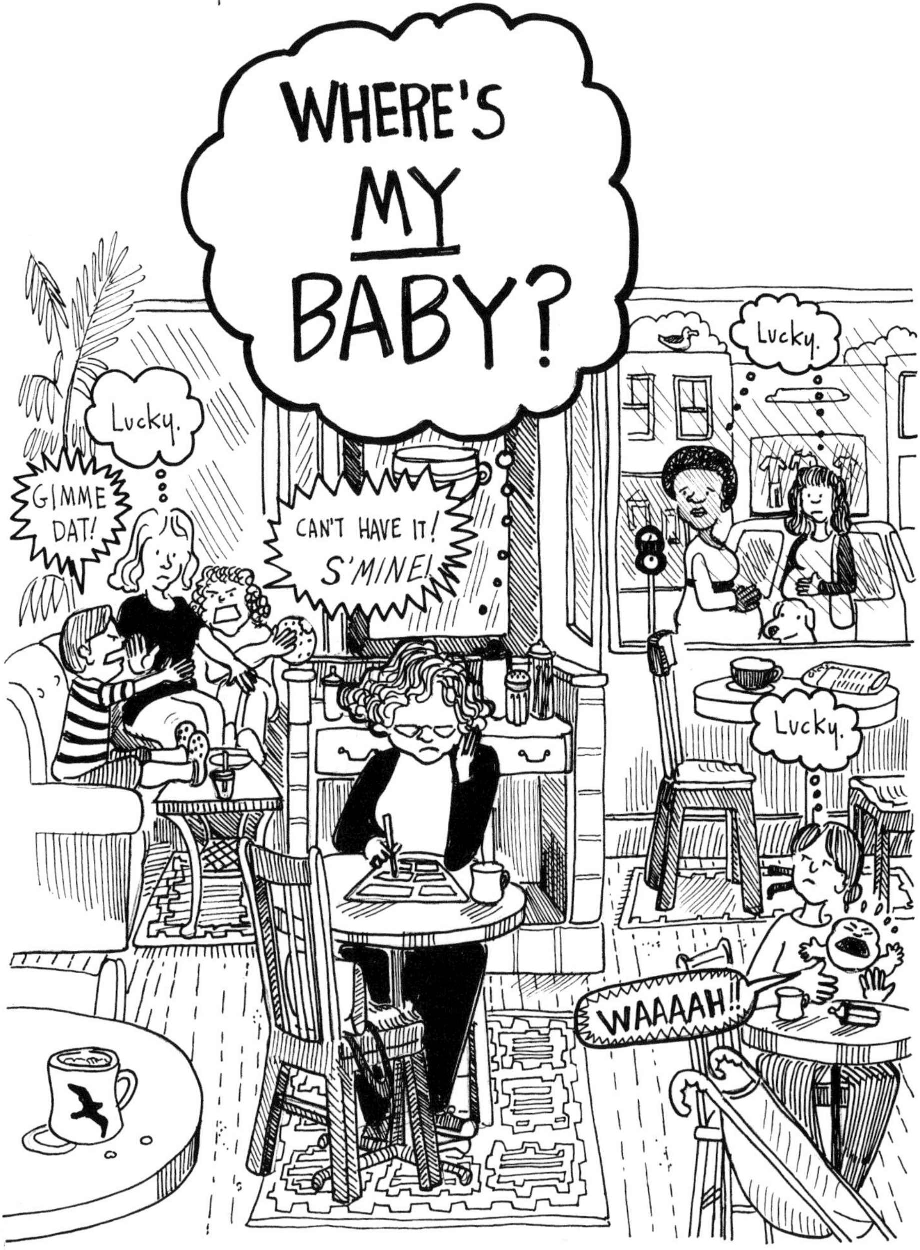
WHERE'S MY BABY?
Lucky.
GIMME DAT!
CAN'T HAVE IT! S'MINE!
Lucky.
Lucky.
WAAAAH!!

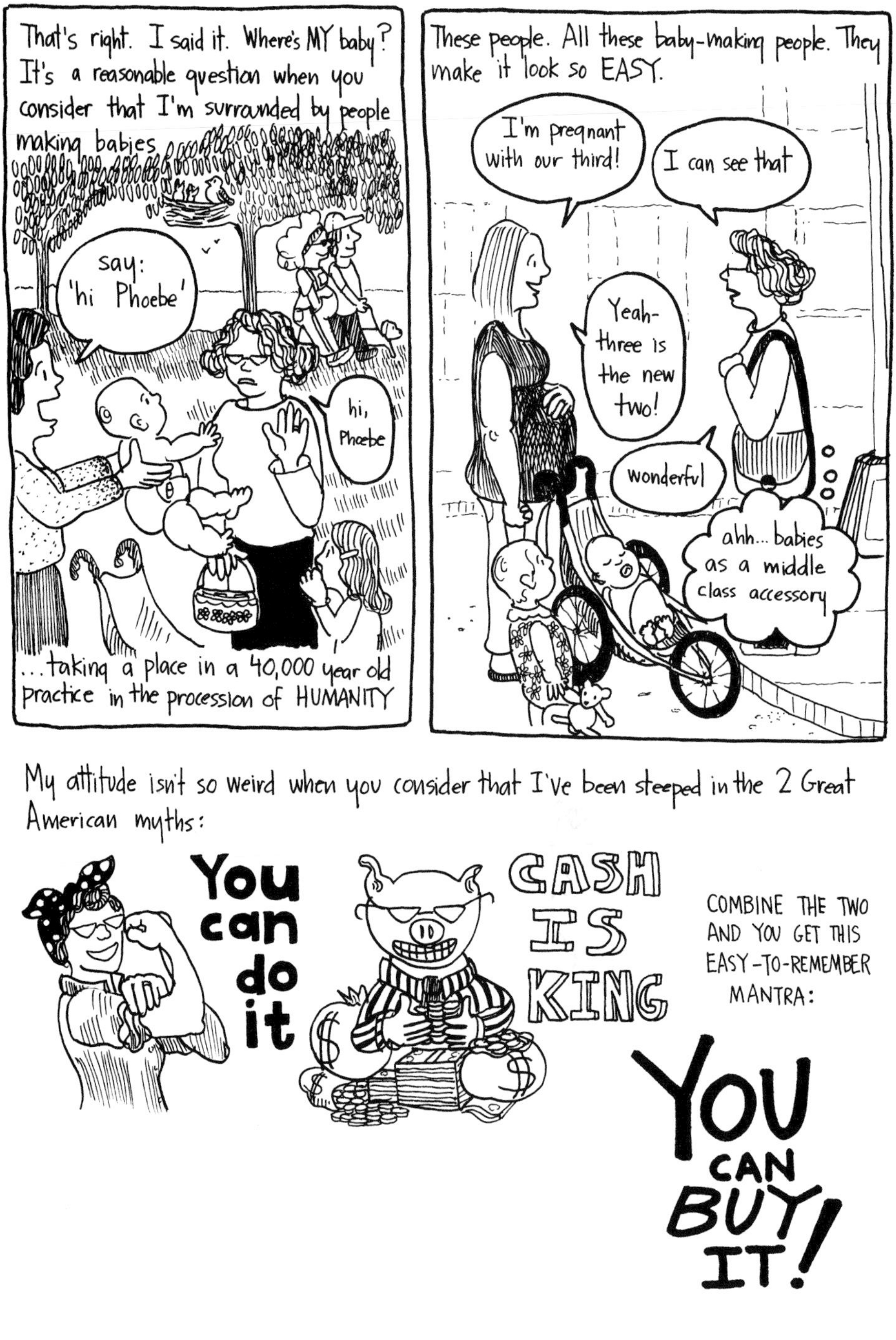
That's right. I said it. Where's MY baby? It's a reasonable question when you consider that I'm surrounded by people making babies
say: 'hi Phoebe'
hi, Phoebe
...taking a place in a 40,000 year old practice in the procession of HUMANITY
These people. All these baby-making people. They make it look so EASY.
I'm pregnant with our third!
I can see that
Yeah- three is the new two!
wonderful
ahh... babies as a middle class accessory
My attitude isn't so weird when you consider that I've been steeped in the 2 Great American myths:
You can do it
CASH IS KING
COMBINE THE TWO AND YOU GET THIS EASY-TO-REMEMBER MANTRA:
YOU CAN BUY IT!

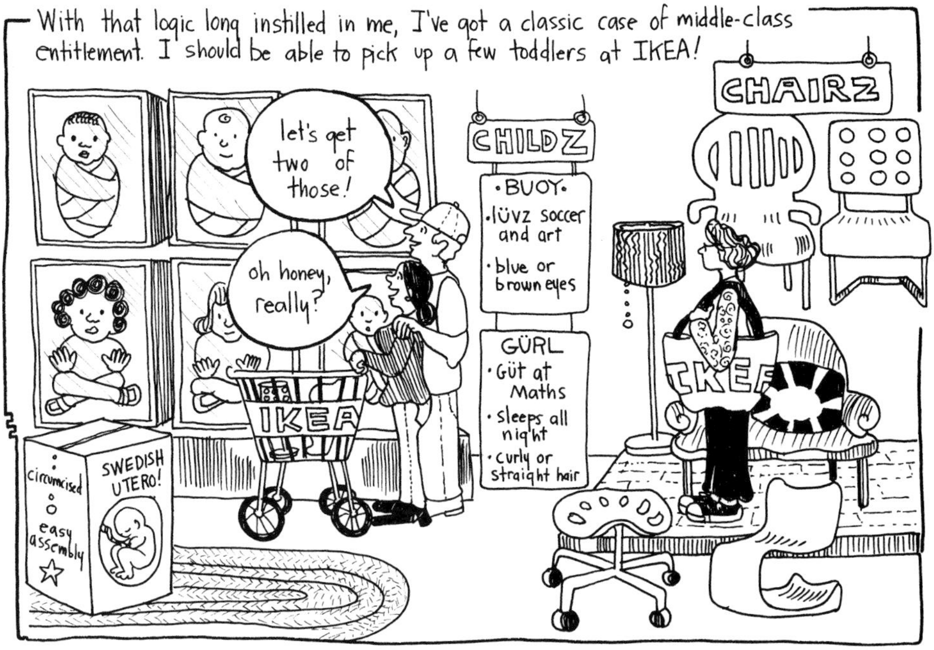
With that logic long instilled in me, I've got a classic case of middle-class entitlement. I should be able to pick up a few toddlers at IKEA!
let's get two of those!
oh honey, really?
CHILDZ
•BUOY•
•lüvz soccer and art
•blue or brown eyes
GÜRL
•Güt at Maths
•sleeps all night
•curly or straight hair
CHAIRZ
SWEDISH UTERO!
circumcised
easy assembly
IKEA
IKEA

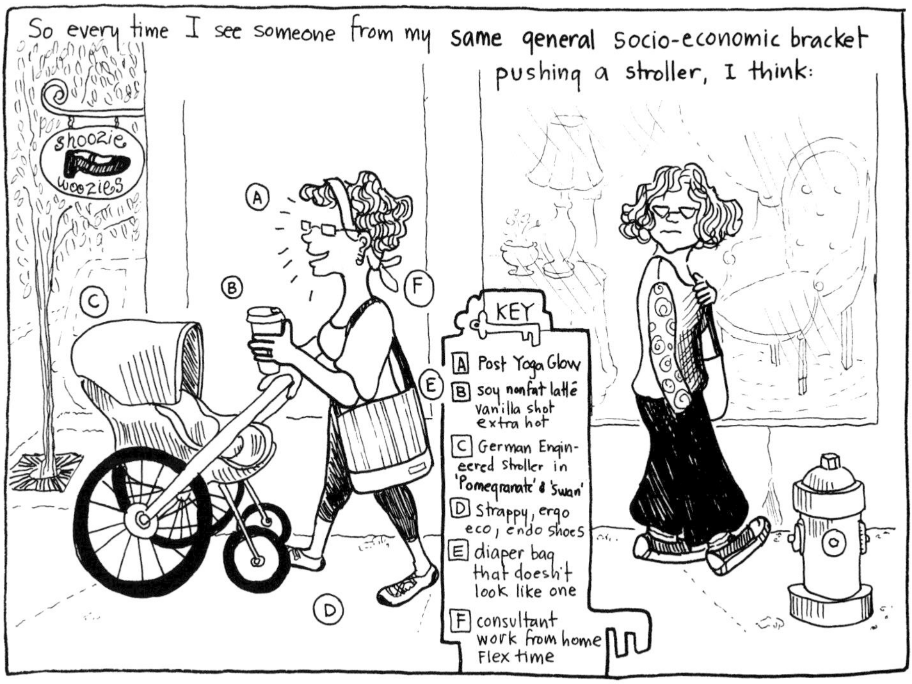
So every time I see someone from my same general socio-economic bracket pushing a stroller, I think:
shoozie woozies
KEY
A Post Yoga Glow
B soy nonfat latté vanilla shot extra hot
C German Engineered Stroller in 'Pomegranate' & 'Swan'
D Strappy, ergo eco, endo shoes
E diaper bag that doesn't look like one
F consultant work from home Flex time

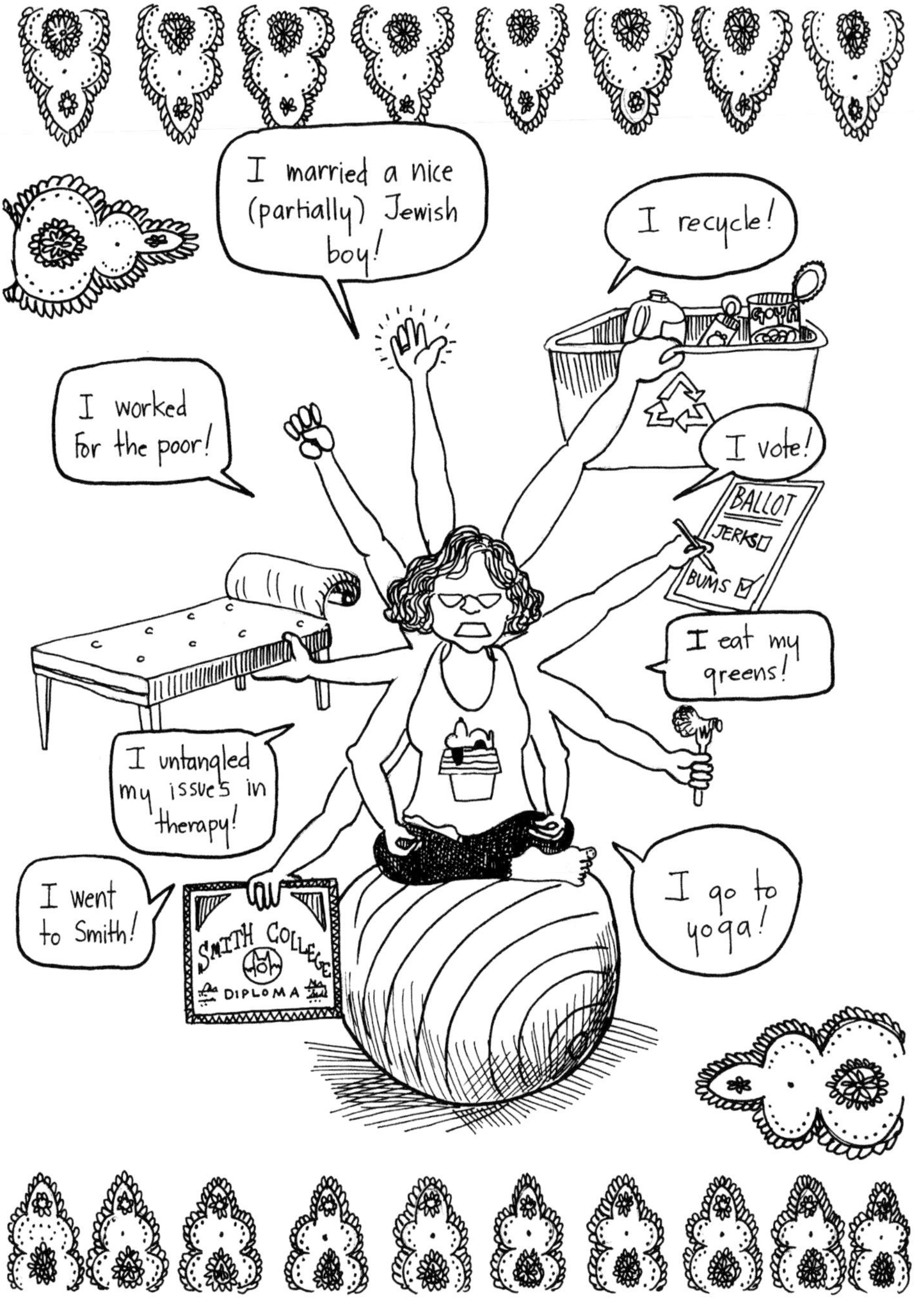
I married a nice (partially) Jewish boy!
I recycle!
GOYA
I worked for the poor!
I vote!
BALLOT
JERKS
BUMS
I eat my greens!
I untangled my issues in therapy!
I went to Smith!
SMITH COLLEGE
DIPLOMA
I go to yoga!

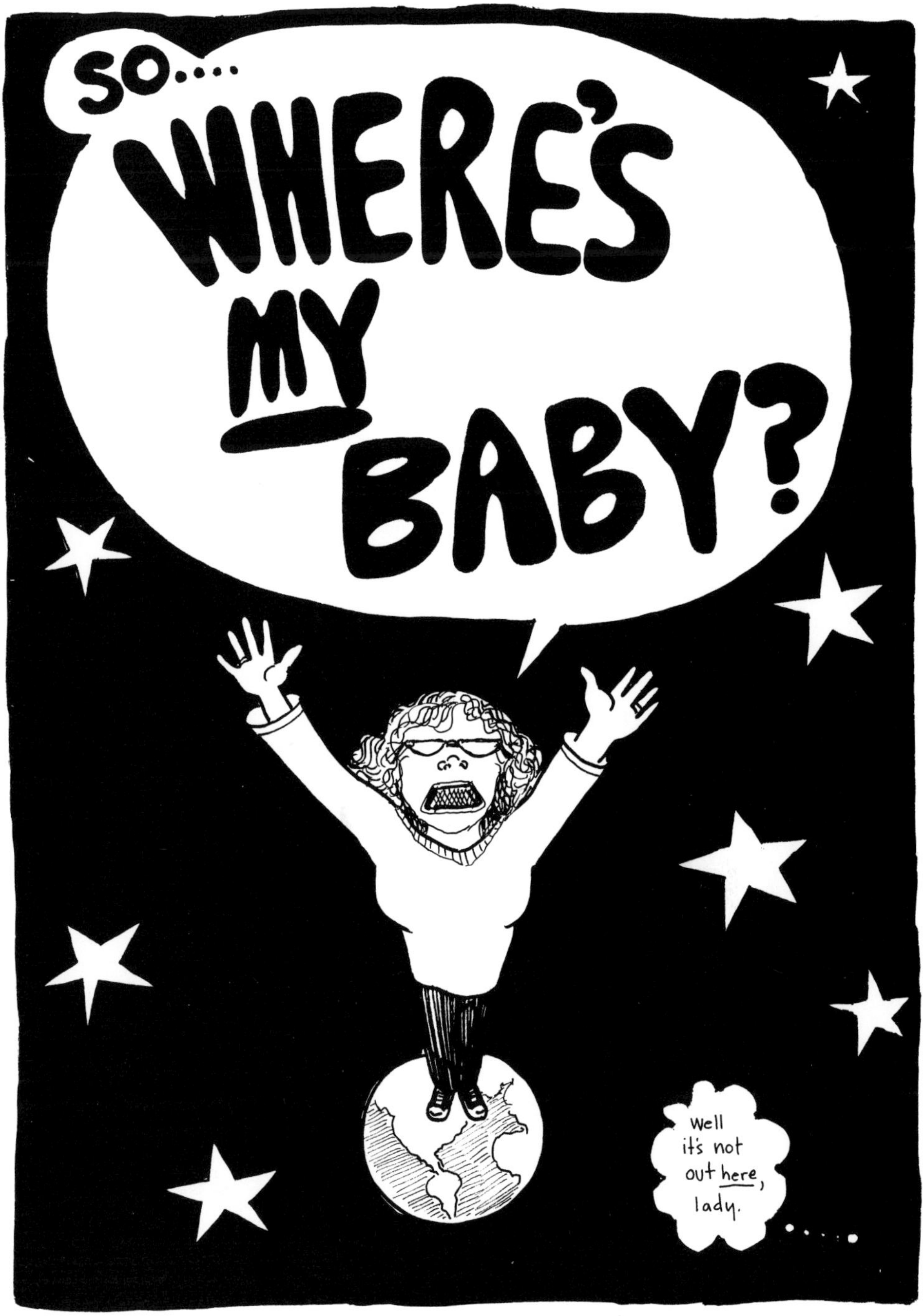
SO....
WHERE'S MY BABY?
Well it's not out here, lady.

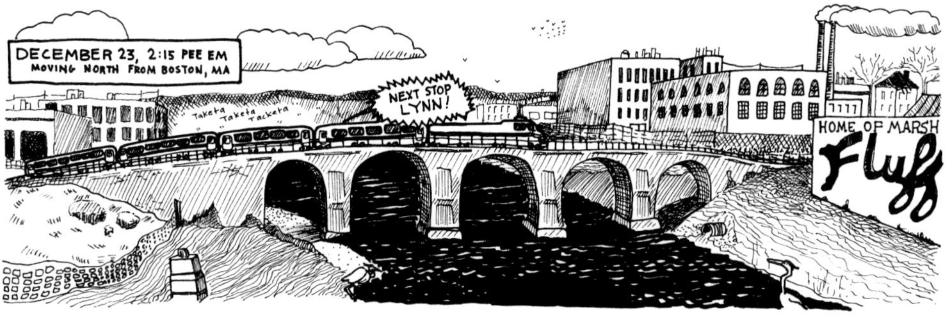
DECEMBER 23, 2:15 PEE EM
MOVING NORTH FROM BOSTON, MA
Taketa Taketa Tacketa
NEXT STOP LYNN!
HOME OF MARSH
Fluff

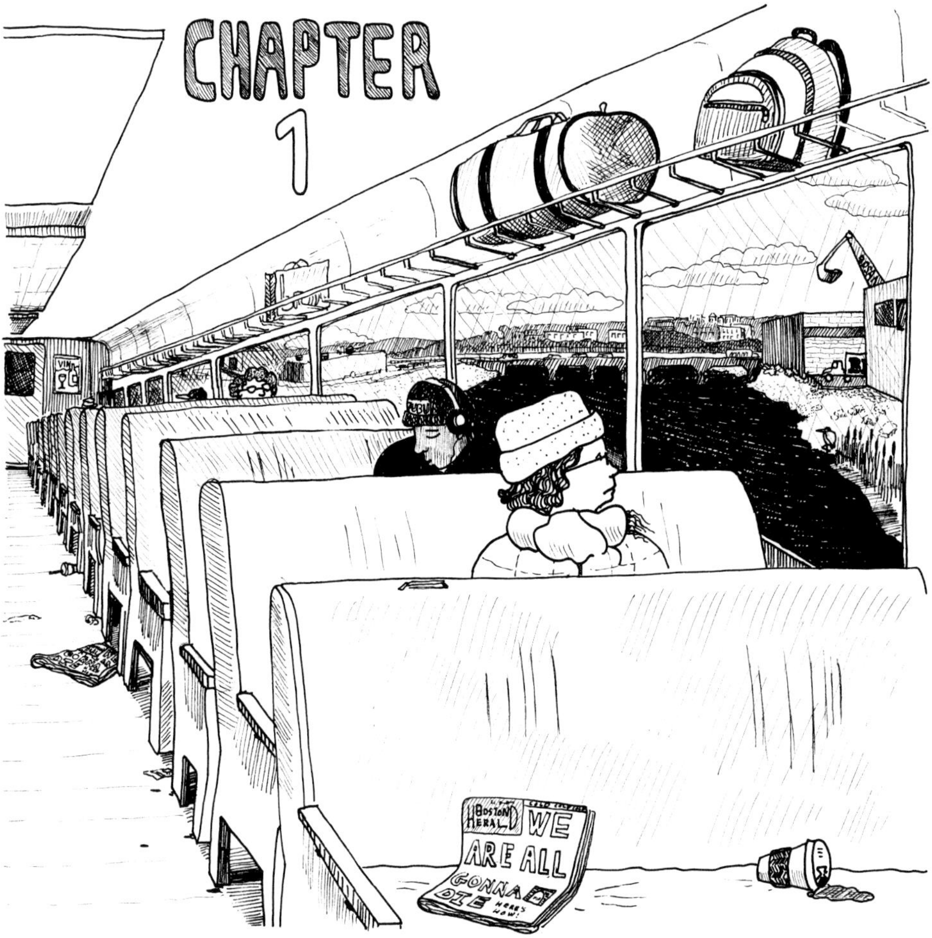
CHAPTER
1
BOSTON HERALD
WE ARE ALL GONNA DIE
HERE'S HOW!

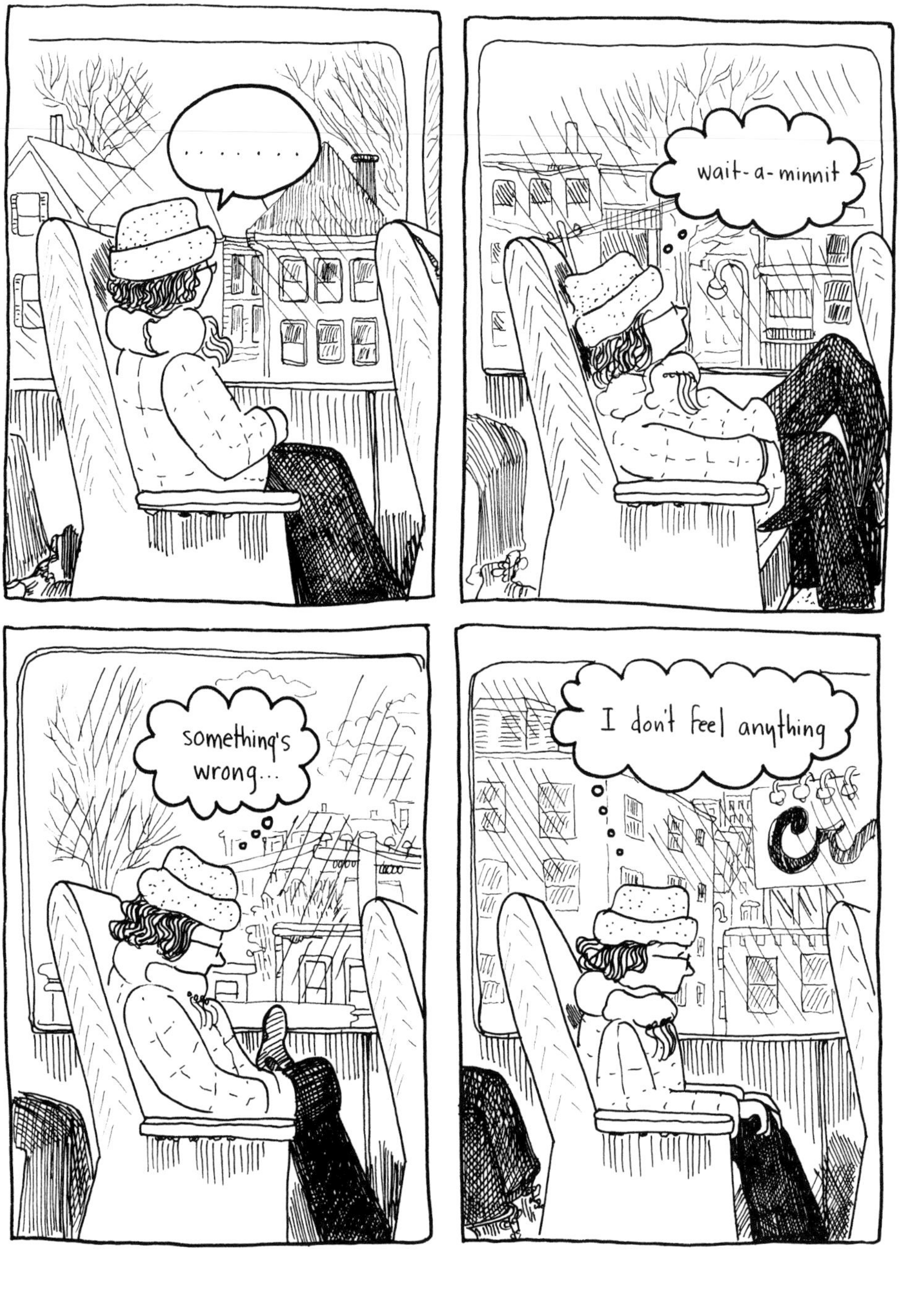
. . . .
wait-a-minnit
something's wrong...
I don't feel anything

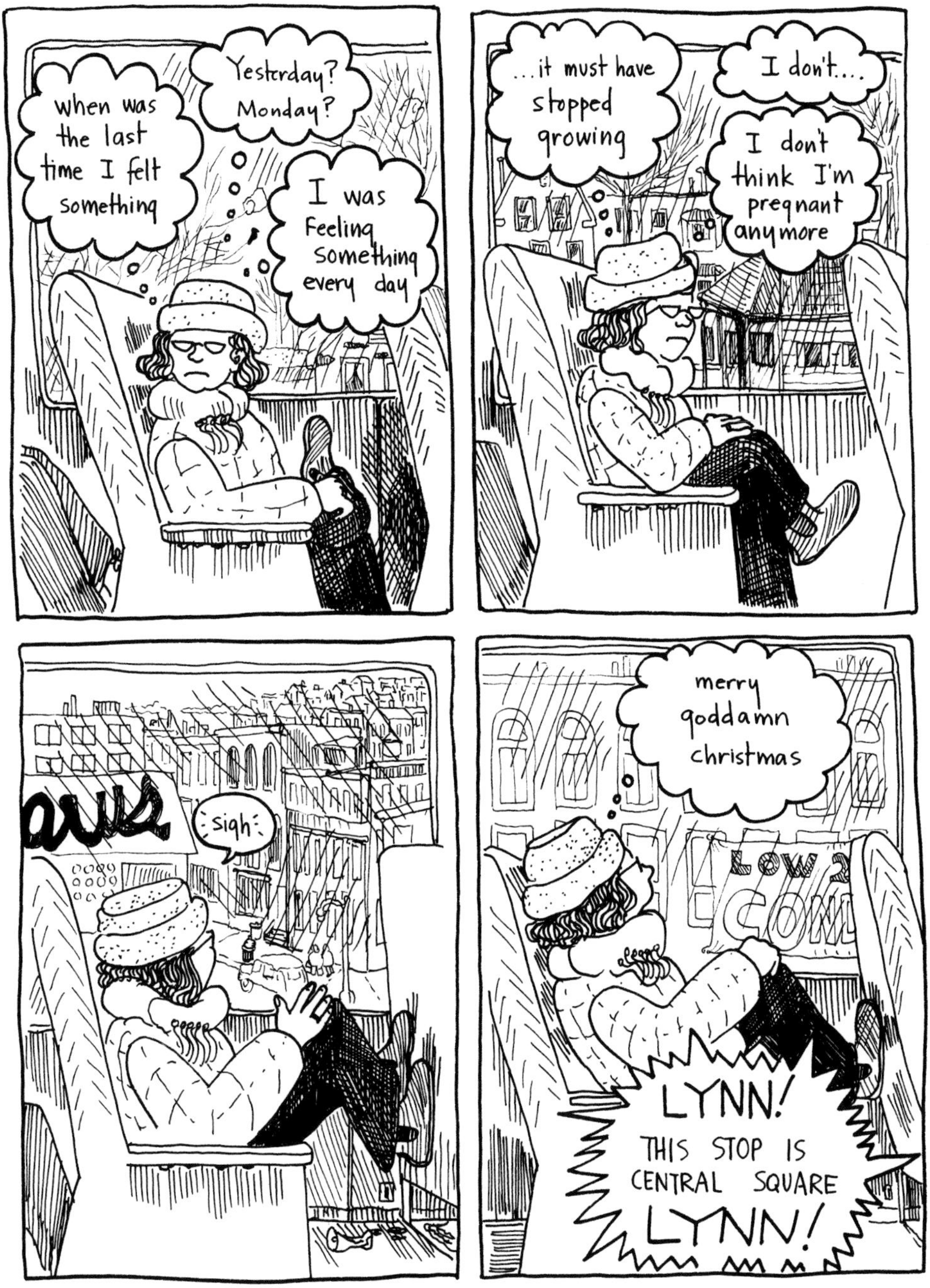
when was the last time I felt something
Yesterday? Monday?
I was Feeling something every day
...it must have stopped growing
I don't....
I don't think I'm pregnant anymore
sigh
merry goddamn christmas
LYNN! THIS STOP IS CENTRAL SQUARE LYNN!

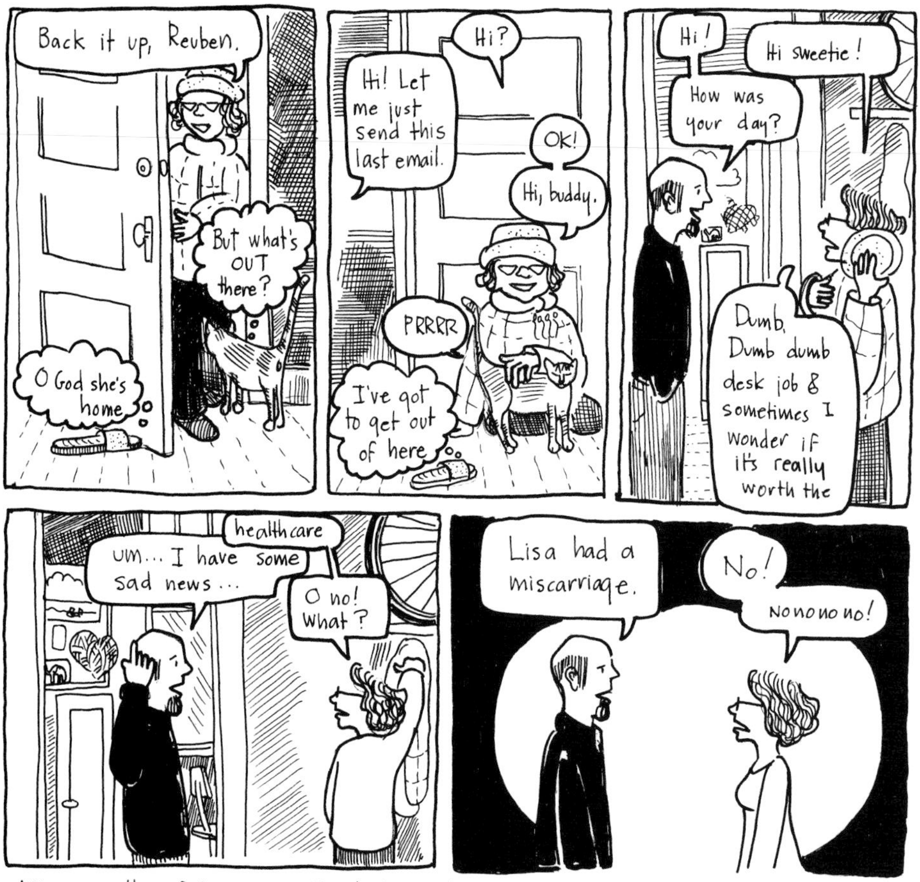
Back it up, Reuben.
But what's OUT there?
O God she's home
Hi! Let me just send this last email.
Hi?
OK!
Hi, buddy.
PRRRR
I've got to get out of here
Hi!
Hi sweetie!
How was your day?
Dumb. Dumb dumb desk job & sometimes I wonder if it's really worth the
healthcare
um... I have some sad news...
O no! What?
Lisa had a miscarriage.
No!
Nonono no!

After months of trying, our friends Lisa & Kelly and Jeff & I had finally gotten pregnant - albeit by different methods.

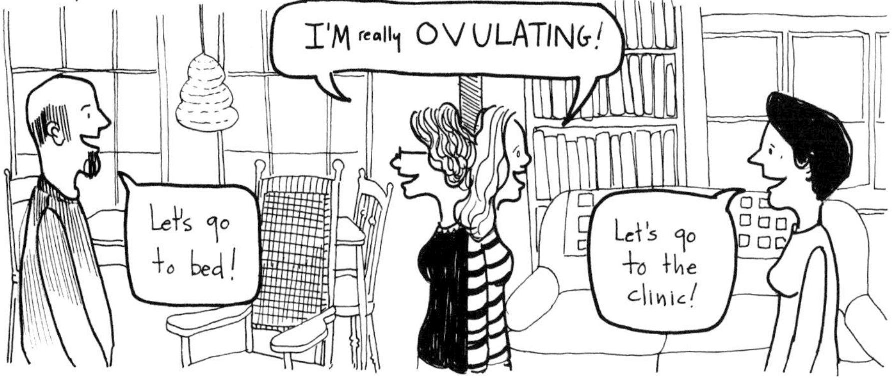
I'M really OVULATING!
Let's go to bed!
Let's go to the clinic!

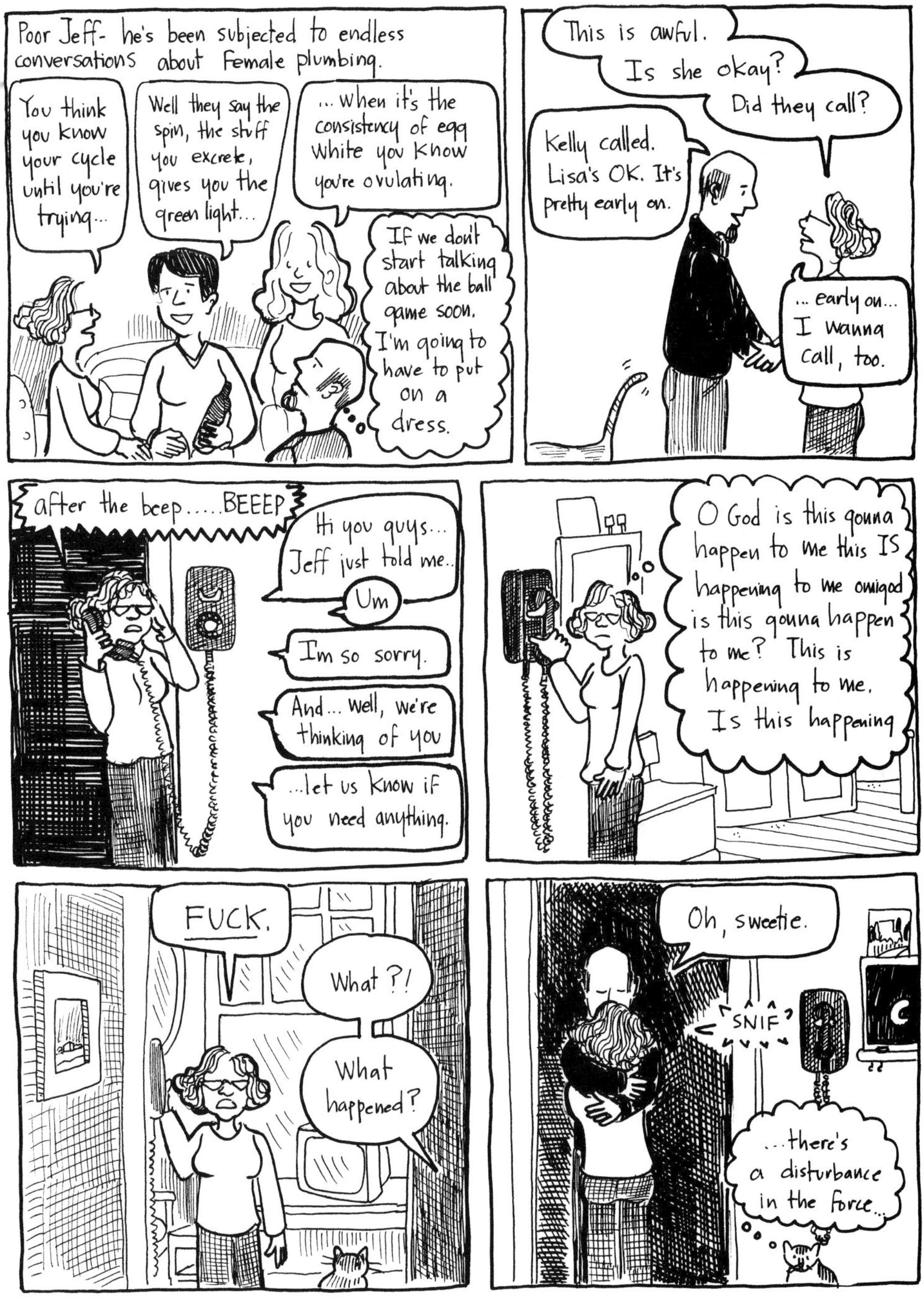
Poor Jeff- he's been subjected to endless conversations about Female plumbing.
You think you know your cycle until you're trying...
Well they say the spin, the stuff you excrete, gives you the green light...
... when it's the consistency of egg white you know you're ovulating.
If we don't start talking about the ball game soon, I'm going to have to put on a dress.
This is awful.
Is she okay?
Did they call?
Kelly called. Lisa's OK. It's pretty early on.
... early on... I wanna call, too.
after the beep.....BEEEP
Hi you guys... Jeff just told me..
Um
I'm so sorry.
And... well, we're thinking of you
...let us know if you need anything.
O God is this gonna happen to me this IS happening to me omigod is this gonna happen to me? This is happening to me. Is this happening
FUCK.
What?!
What happened?
Oh, sweetie.
SNIF
...there's a disturbance in the force...

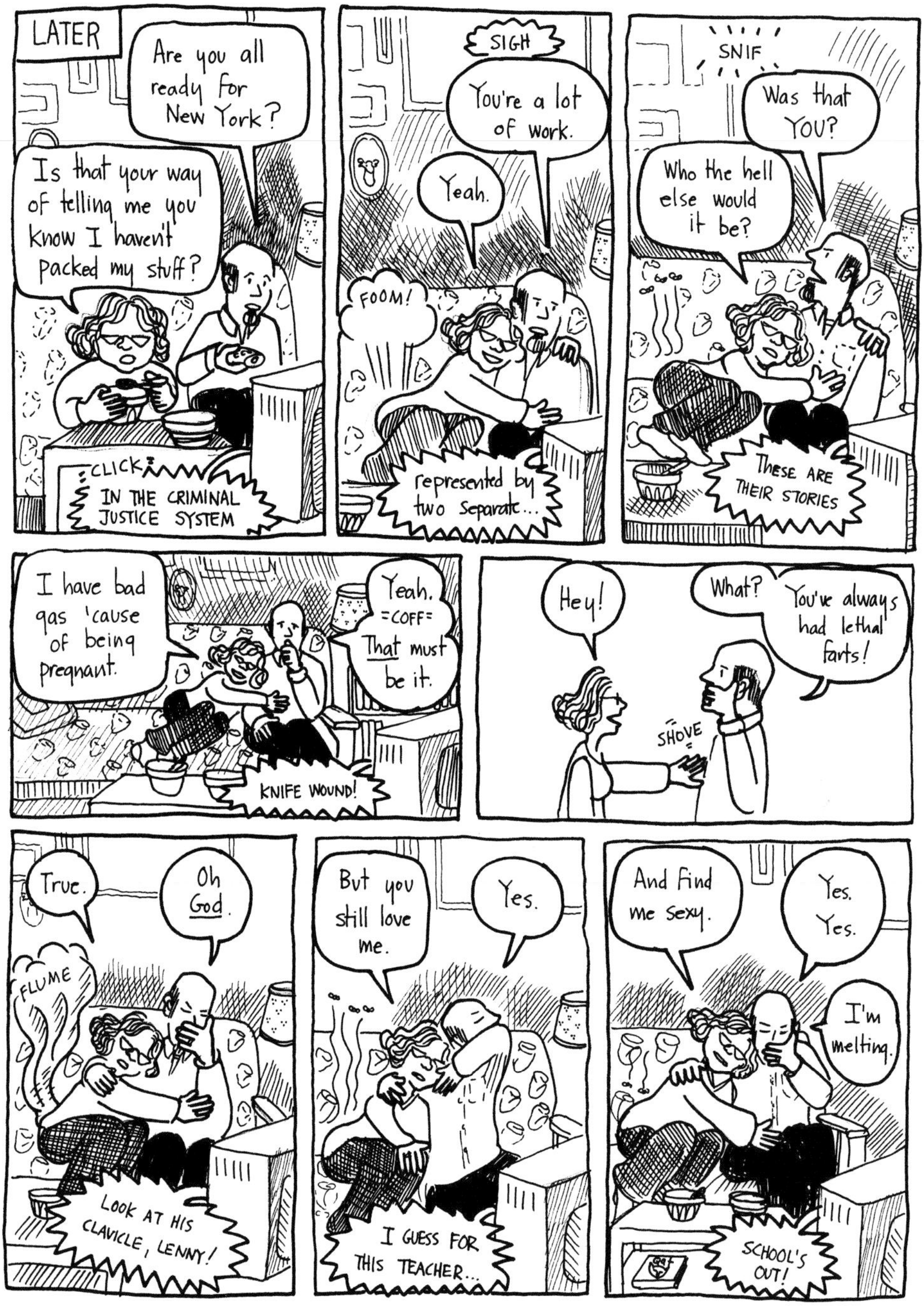
LATER
Are you all ready for New York?
Is that your way of telling me you know I haven't packed my stuff?
CLICK
IN THE CRIMINAL JUSTICE SYSTEM
SIGH
You're a lot of work.
Yeah.
FOOM!
represented by two separate...
SNIF
Was that YOU?
Who the hell else would it be?
THESE ARE THEIR STORIES
I have bad gas 'cause of being pregnant.
Yeah. =COFF= That must be it.
KNIFE WOUND!
Hey!
What?
You've always had lethal farts!
SHOVE
True.
Oh God.
FLUME
LOOK AT HIS CLAVICLE, LENNY!
But you still love me.
Yes.
I GUESS FOR THIS TEACHER...
And find me sexy.
Yes. Yes.
I'm melting.
SCHOOL'S OUT!

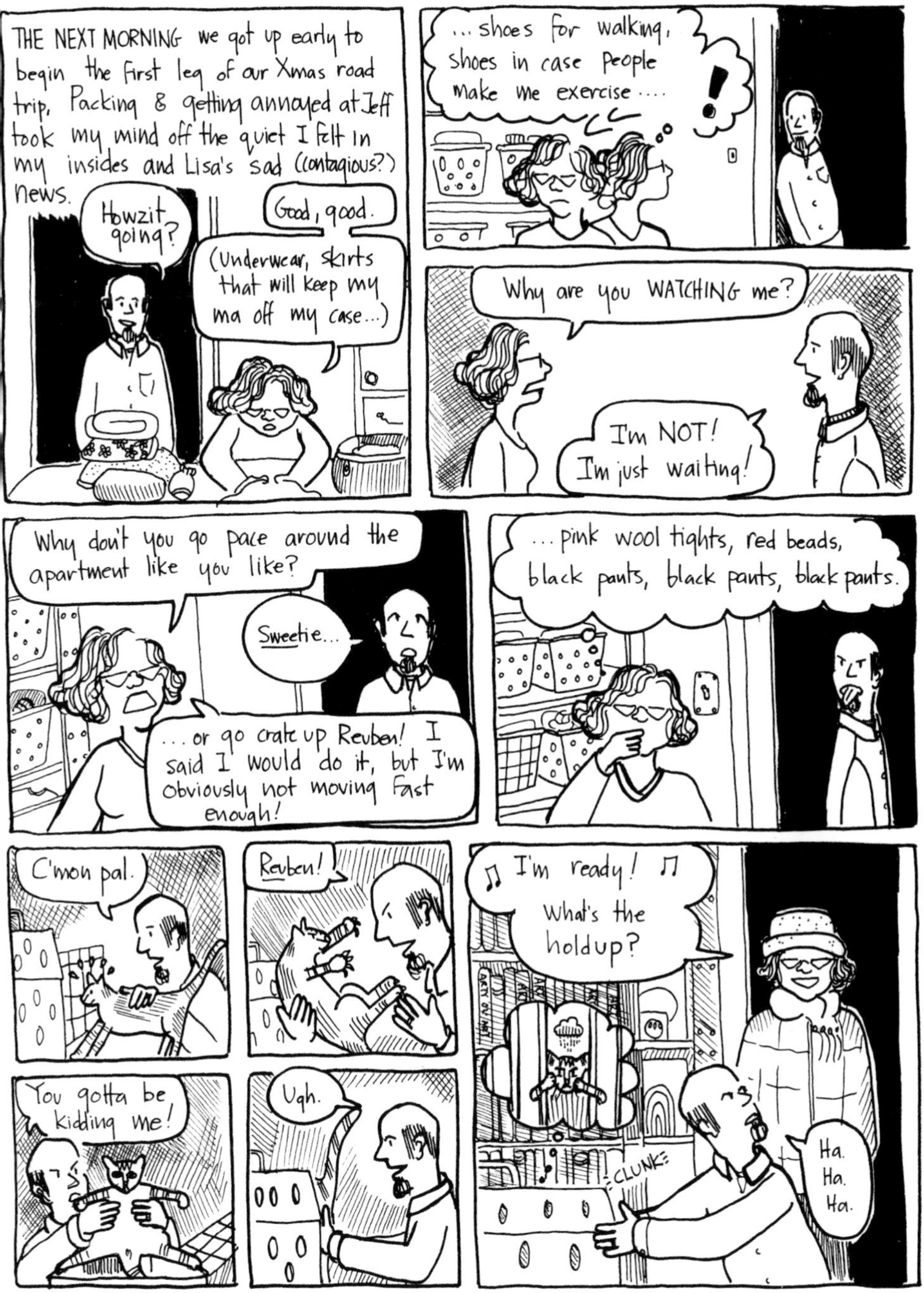
THE NEXT MORNING we got up early to begin the first leg of our Xmas road trip. Packing & getting annoyed at Jeff took my mind off the quiet I felt in my insides and Lisa's sad (contagious?) news.
Howzit going?
Good, good.
(Underwear, skirts that will keep my ma off my case...)
...shoes for walking, shoes in case people make me exercise....
!
Why are you WATCHING me?
I'm NOT! I'm just waiting!
Why don't you go pace around the apartment like you like?
Sweetie...
...or go crate up Reuben! I said I would do it, but I'm obviously not moving fast enough!
...pink wool tights, red beads, black pants, black pants, black pants.
C'mon pal.
Reuben!
You gotta be kidding me!
Ugh.
♫ I'm ready! ♫ What's the holdup?
CLUNK
Ha. Ha. Ha.

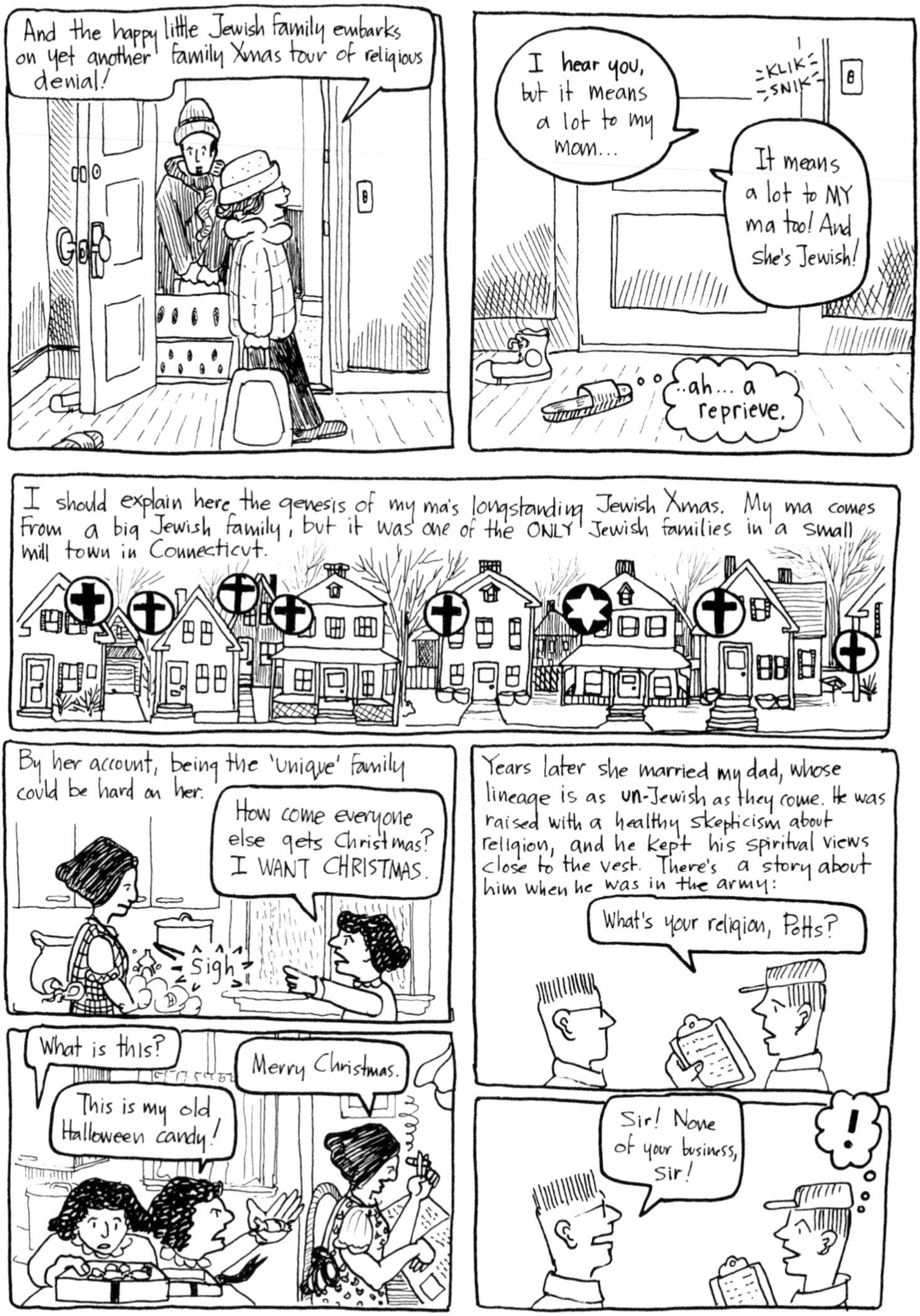
And the happy little Jewish family embarks on yet another family Xmas tour of religious denial!
I hear you, but it means a lot to my mom...
KLIK SNIK
It means a lot to MY ma too! And she's Jewish!
..ah... a reprieve.
I should explain here the genesis of my ma's longstanding Jewish Xmas. My ma comes from a big Jewish family, but it was one of the ONLY Jewish families in a small mill town in Connecticut.
By her account, being the 'unique' family could be hard on her.
How come everyone else gets Christmas? I WANT CHRISTMAS.
Sigh
Years later she married my dad, whose lineage is as un-Jewish as they come. He was raised with a healthy skepticism about religion, and he kept his spiritual views close to the vest. There's a story about him when he was in the army:
What's your religion, Potts?
What is this?
Merry Christmas.
This is my old Halloween candy!
Sir! None of your business, sir!
!

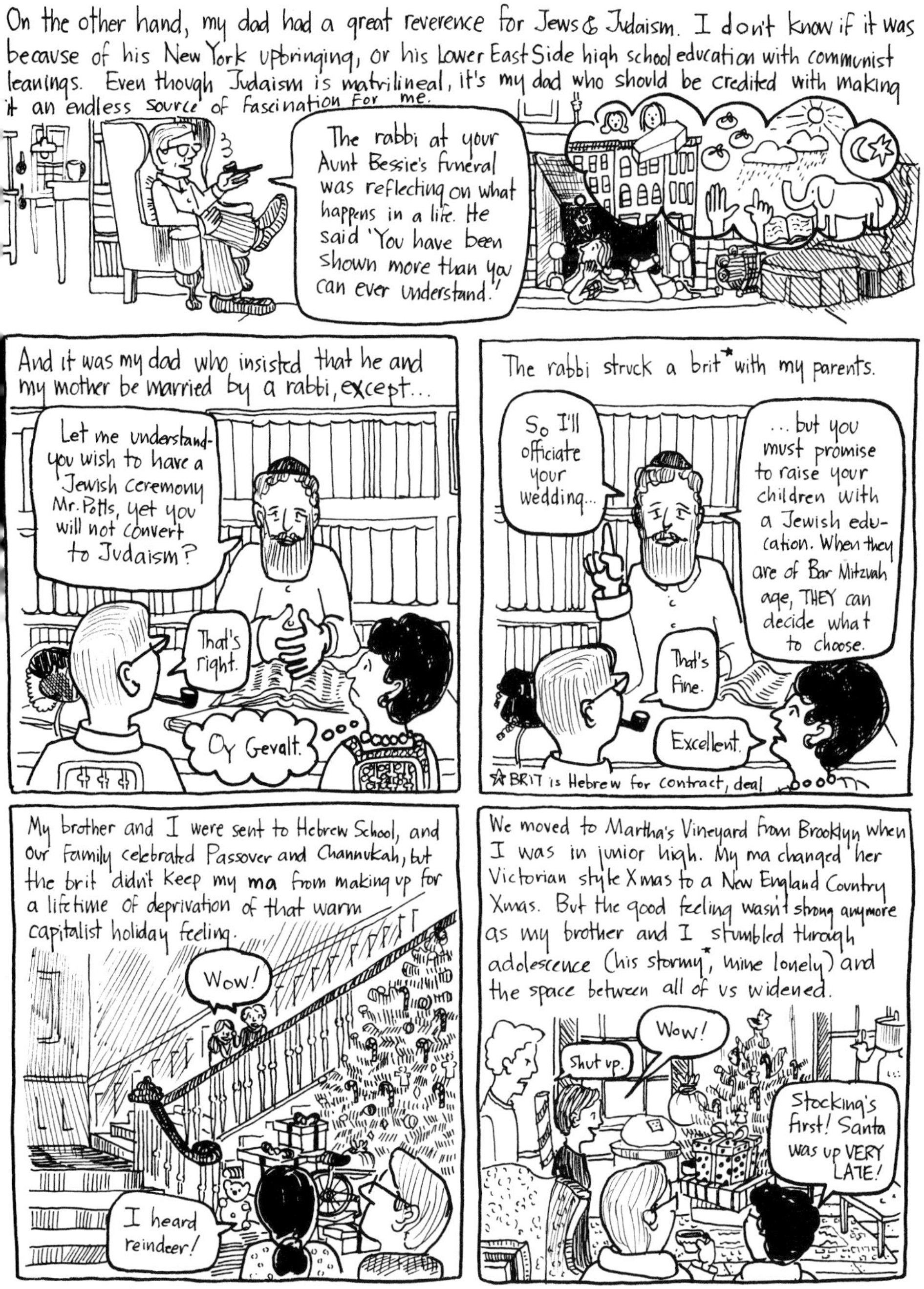
On the other hand, my dad had a great reverence for Jews & Judaism. I don't know if it was because of his New York upbringing, or his Lower East Side high school education with communist leanings. Even though Judaism is matrilineal, it's my dad who should be credited with making it an endless source of fascination for me.
The rabbi at your Aunt Bessie's funeral was reflecting on what happens in a life. He said 'You have been shown more than you can ever understand.'
And it was my dad who insisted that he and my mother be married by a rabbi, except...
Let me understand-you wish to have a Jewish ceremony Mr. Potts, yet you will not convert to Judaism?
That's right.
Oy Gevalt.
The rabbi struck a brit* with my parents.
So I'll officiate your wedding...
...but you must promise to raise your children with a Jewish education. When they are of Bar Mitzvah age, THEY can decide what to choose.
That's Fine.
Excellent.
*BRIT is Hebrew for contract, deal
My brother and I were sent to Hebrew School, and our family celebrated Passover and Channukah, but the brit didn't keep my ma from making up for a lifetime of deprivation of that warm capitalist holiday feeling.
Wow!
I heard reindeer!
We moved to Martha's Vineyard from Brooklyn when I was in junior high. My ma changed her Victorian style Xmas to a New England Country Xmas. But the good feeling wasn't strong anymore as my brother and I stumbled through adolescence (his stormy*, mine lonely) and the space between all of us widened.
Shut up.
Wow!
Stocking's first! Santa was up VERY LATE!

* J.J. CAUCUS, DOONESBURY G. TRUDEAU

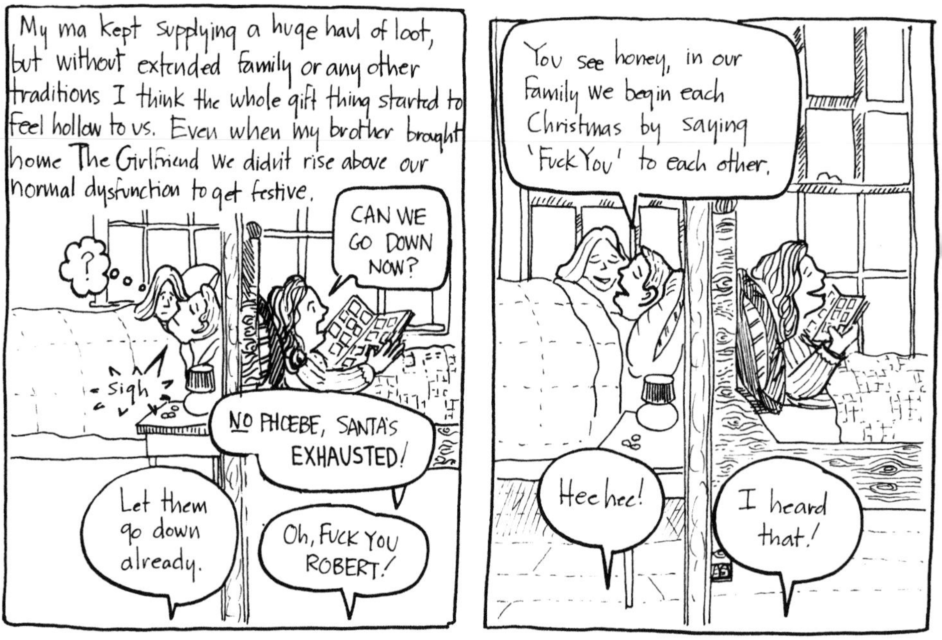
My ma kept supplying a huge haul of loot, but without extended family or any other traditions I think the whole gift thing started to feel hollow to us. Even when my brother brought home The Girlfriend we didn't rise above our normal dysfunction to get festive.
CAN WE GO DOWN NOW?
?
Sigh
NO PHOEBE, SANTA'S EXHAUSTED!
Let them go down already.
Oh, FUCK YOU ROBERT!
You see honey, in our Family we begin each Christmas by saying 'Fuck You' to each other.
Hee hee!
I heard that!

One year my brother called to say that he was spending Xmas with The Girlfriend's family. That made sense, they were Catholic, and let's face it, Baby Jesus has the corner on the market. My ma called in reinforcements. She fired off a dispatch to her co-Matriarch, Elizabeth. Mother of 5, wife of J. Richard, epicenter of Upper West Side politics, Belle of Nebraska, iron-fisted, velvet-gloved Elizabeth. In other words, the big guns.

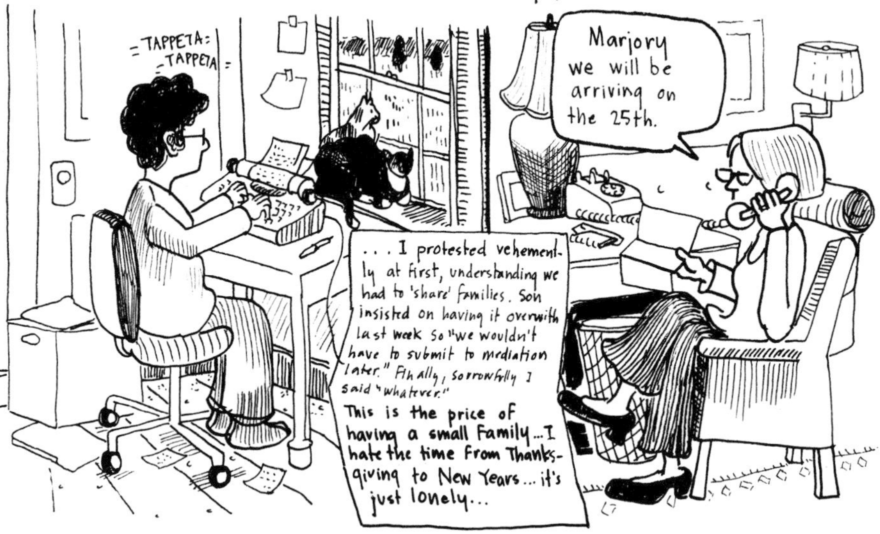
TAPPETA TAPPETA
Marjory we will be arriving on the 25th.
. . . I protested vehemently at first, understanding we had to 'share' families. Son insisted on having it over with last week so "we wouldn't have to submit to mediation later." Finally, sorrowfully I said "whatever."
This is the price of having a small Family... I hate the time From Thanksgiving to New Years... it's just lonely...

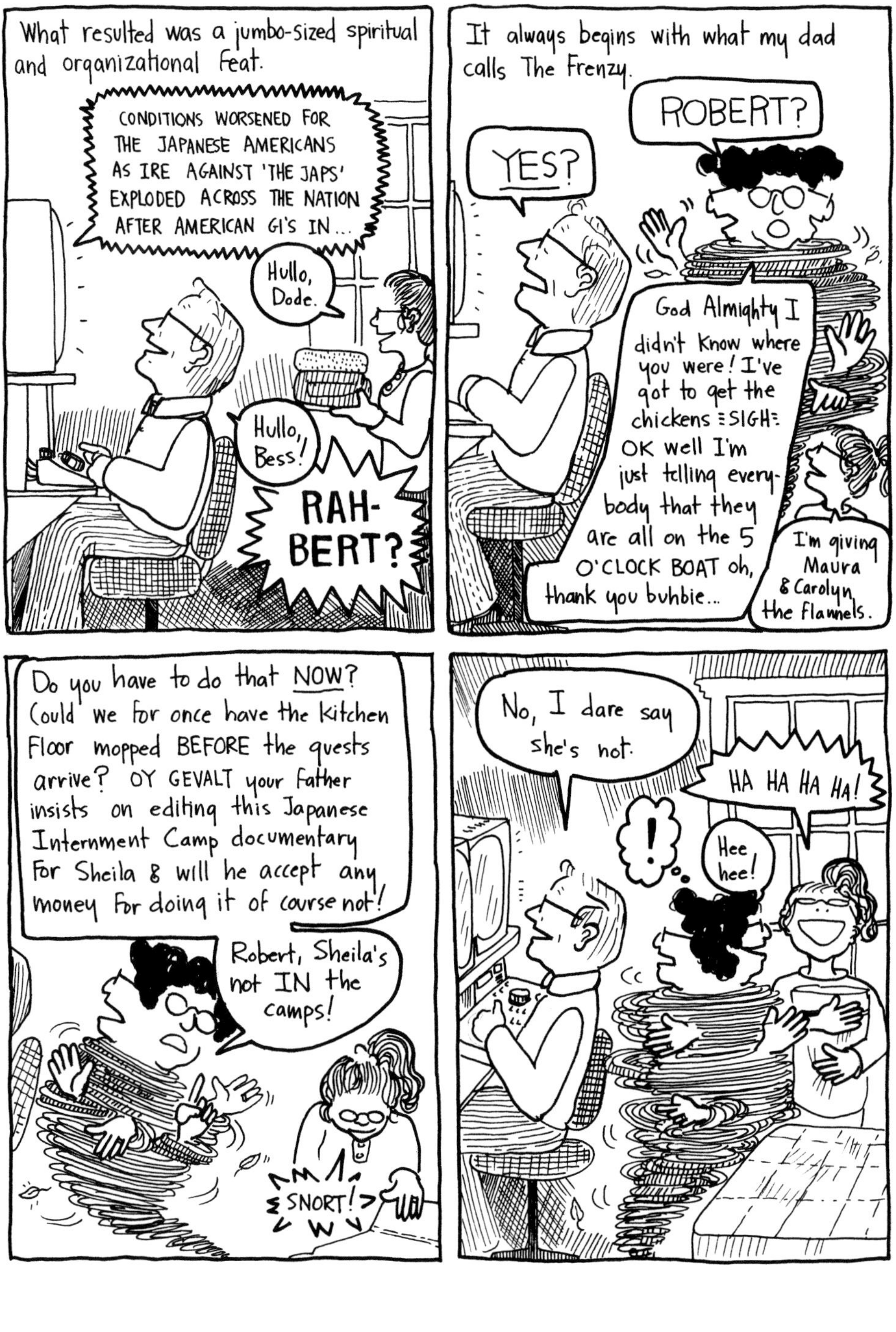
What resulted was a jumbo-sized spiritual and organizational feat.
CONDITIONS WORSENED FOR THE JAPANESE AMERICANS AS IRE AGAINST 'THE JAPS' EXPLODED ACROSS THE NATION AFTER AMERICAN GI'S IN...
Hullo, Dode.
Hullo, Bess!
RAH-BERT?
It always begins with what my dad calls The Frenzy.
ROBERT?
YES?
God Almighty I didn't know where you were! I've got to get the chickens =SIGH= OK well I'm just telling everybody that they are all on the 5 O'CLOCK BOAT oh, thank you buhbie...
I'm giving Maura & Carolyn the flannels.
Do you have to do that NOW? Could we for once have the kitchen floor mopped BEFORE the guests arrive? OY GEVALT your father insists on editing this Japanese Internment Camp documentary for Sheila & will he accept any money for doing it of course not!
Robert, Sheila's not IN the camps!
SNORT!
No, I dare say she's not.
HA HA HA HA!
!
Hee hee!

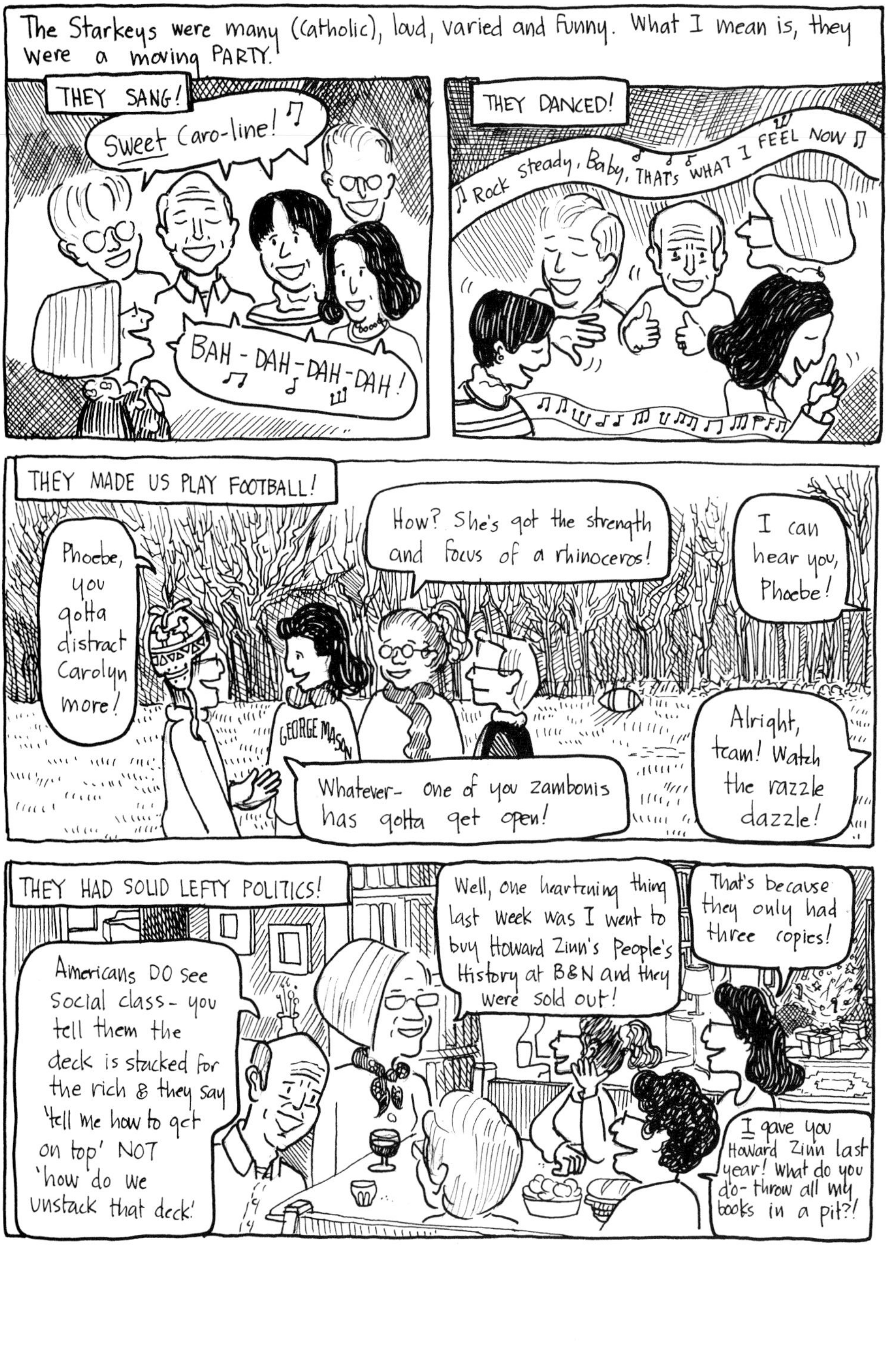
The Starkeys were many (catholic), loud, varied and funny. What I mean is, they were a moving PARTY.
THEY SANG!
Sweet Caro-line!
BAH-DAH-DAH-DAH!
THEY DANCED!
Rock steady, Baby, THAT'S WHAT I FEEL NOW
THEY MADE US PLAY FOOTBALL!
Phoebe, you gotta distract Carolyn more!
How? She's got the strength and focus of a rhinoceros!
I can hear you, Phoebe!
GEORGE MASON
Whatever- one of you zambonis has gotta get open!
Alright, team! Watch the razzle dazzle!
THEY HAD SOLID LEFTY POLITICS!
Americans DO see social class- you tell them the deck is stacked for the rich & they say 'tell me how to get on top' NOT 'how do we unstack that deck'
Well, one heartening thing last week was I went to buy Howard Zinn's People's History at B&N and they were sold out!
That's because they only had three copies!
I gave you Howard Zinn last year! What do you do- throw all my books in a pit?!

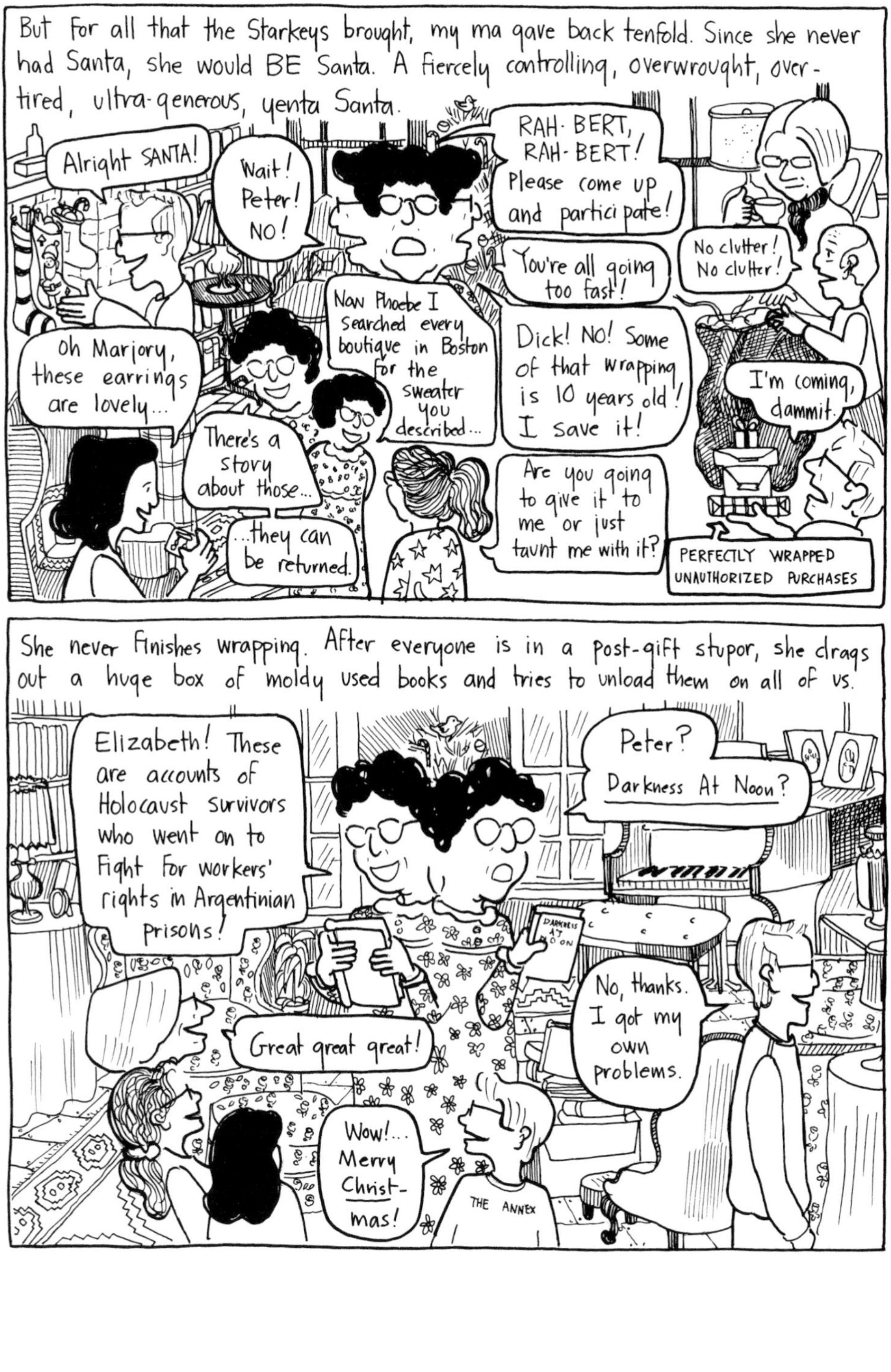
But for all that the Starkeys brought, my ma gave back tenfold. Since she never had Santa, she would BE Santa. A fiercely controlling, overwrought, over-tired, ultra-generous, yenta Santa.
Alright SANTA!
Wait! Peter! NO!
RAH-BERT, RAH-BERT! Please come up and participate!
No clutter! No clutter!
You're all going too fast!
Now Phoebe I searched every boutique in Boston for the sweater you described...
Dick! No! Some of that wrapping is 10 years old! I save it!
I'm coming, dammit.
Oh Marjory, these earrings are lovely...
There's a story about those...
...they can be returned.
Are you going to give it to me or just taunt me with it?
PERFECTLY WRAPPED UNAUTHORIZED PURCHASES
She never finishes wrapping. After everyone is in a post-gift stupor, she drags out a huge box of moldy used books and tries to unload them on all of us.
Elizabeth! These are accounts of Holocaust survivors who went on to fight for workers' rights in Argentinian prisons!
Peter? Darkness At Noon?
DARKNESS AT NOON
Great great great!
No, thanks. I got my own problems.
Wow!... Merry Christ-mas!
THE ANNEX

As I identify myself more and more as a Jew lately, Xmas just becomes a lot of gross commercial static– offensive to the senses. But being with my folks & the Starkeys remains a tradition (15 years!) that anchors me during the whole year. And the way I see it our 'Xmas' is really a JEWISH event, built on the tenets of Judaism: Mitzvot (good deeds, commandments) neuroses & lots of food.

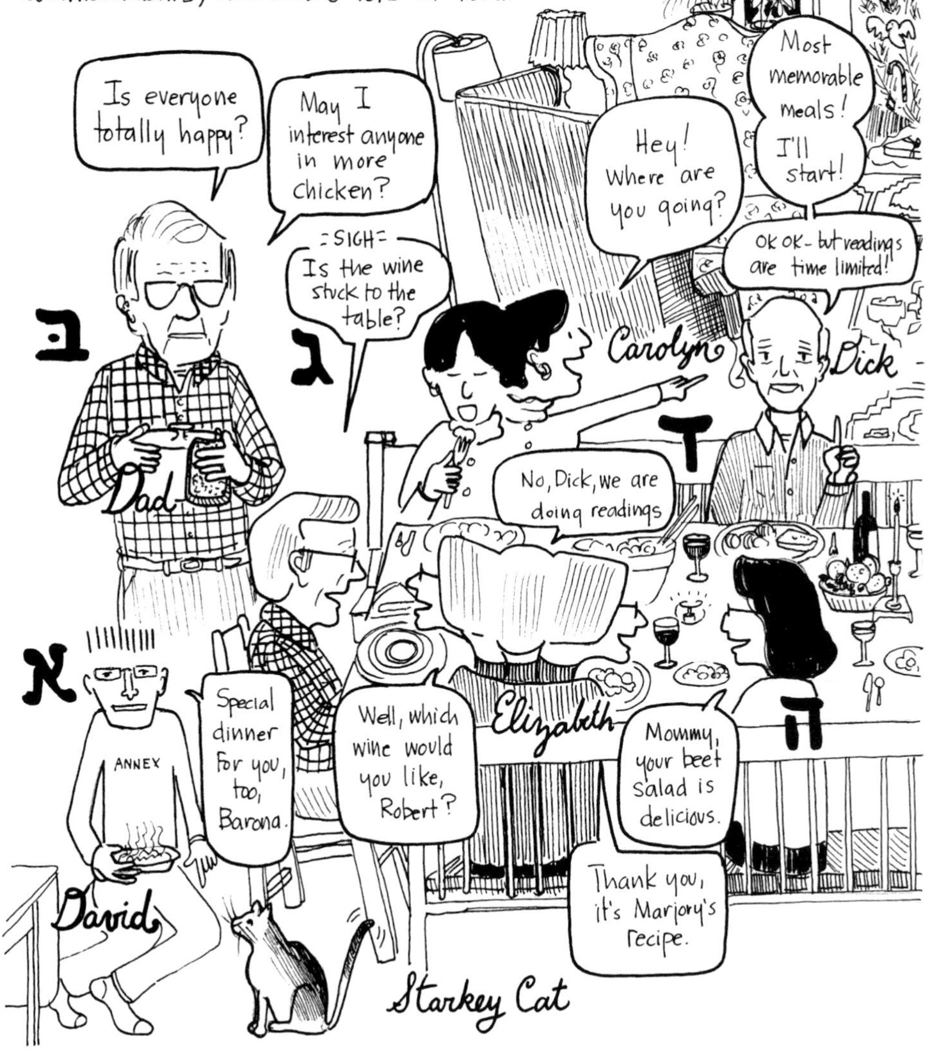

Is everyone totally happy?
May I interest anyone in more chicken?
=SIGH=
Is the wine stuck to the table?
Hey! Where are you going?
Most memorable meals! I'll start!
OK OK– but readings are time limited!
ב
Dad
ג
Carolyn
Dick
ד
No, Dick, we are doing readings
א
David
ANNEX
Special dinner for you, too, Barona.
Well, which wine would you like, Robert?
Elizabeth
ה
Mommy, your beet salad is delicious.
Thank you, it's Marjory's recipe.
Starkey Cat

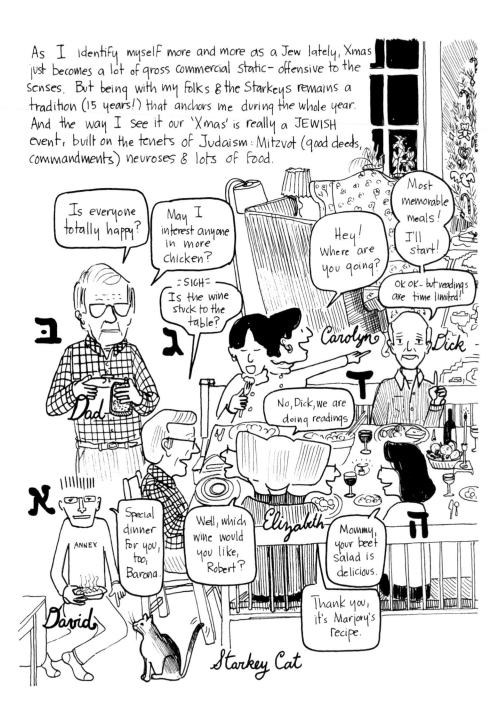

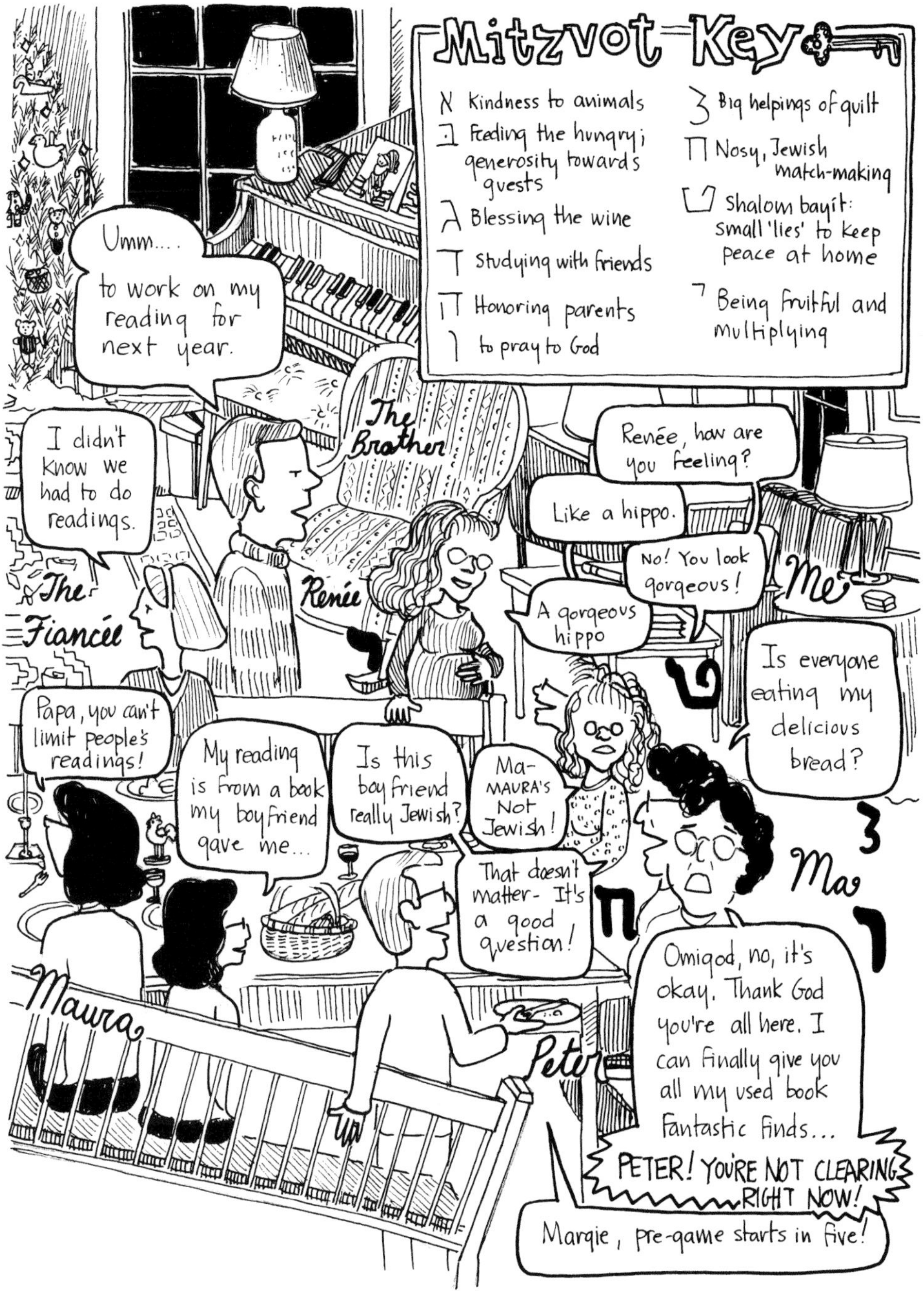
Mitzvot Key
א Kindness to animals
ב Feeding the hungry; generosity towards guests
ג Blessing the wine
ד Studying with friends
ה Honoring parents
ו to pray to God
ז Big helpings of guilt
ח Nosy, Jewish match-making
ט Shalom bayit: small 'lies' to keep peace at home
י Being fruitful and multiplying
Umm.... to work on my reading for next year.
The Brother
I didn't know we had to do readings.
The Fiancée
Renée
Renée, how are you feeling?
Like a hippo.
No! You look gorgeous!
A gorgeous hippo
Me
Is everyone eating my delicious bread?
Papa, you can't limit people's readings!
My reading is from a book my boyfriend gave me...
Is this boyfriend really Jewish?
Ma- MAURA'S NOT Jewish!
That doesn't matter- It's a good question!
Ma
Maura
Peter
Omigod, no, it's okay. Thank God you're all here. I can finally give you all my used book fantastic finds...
PETER! YOU'RE NOT CLEARING RIGHT NOW!
Margie, pre-game starts in five!

SO THAT'S WHY we were on this annual Family Xmas tour - First to NYC to Jeff's folks & then back up to Massachusetts to mine.

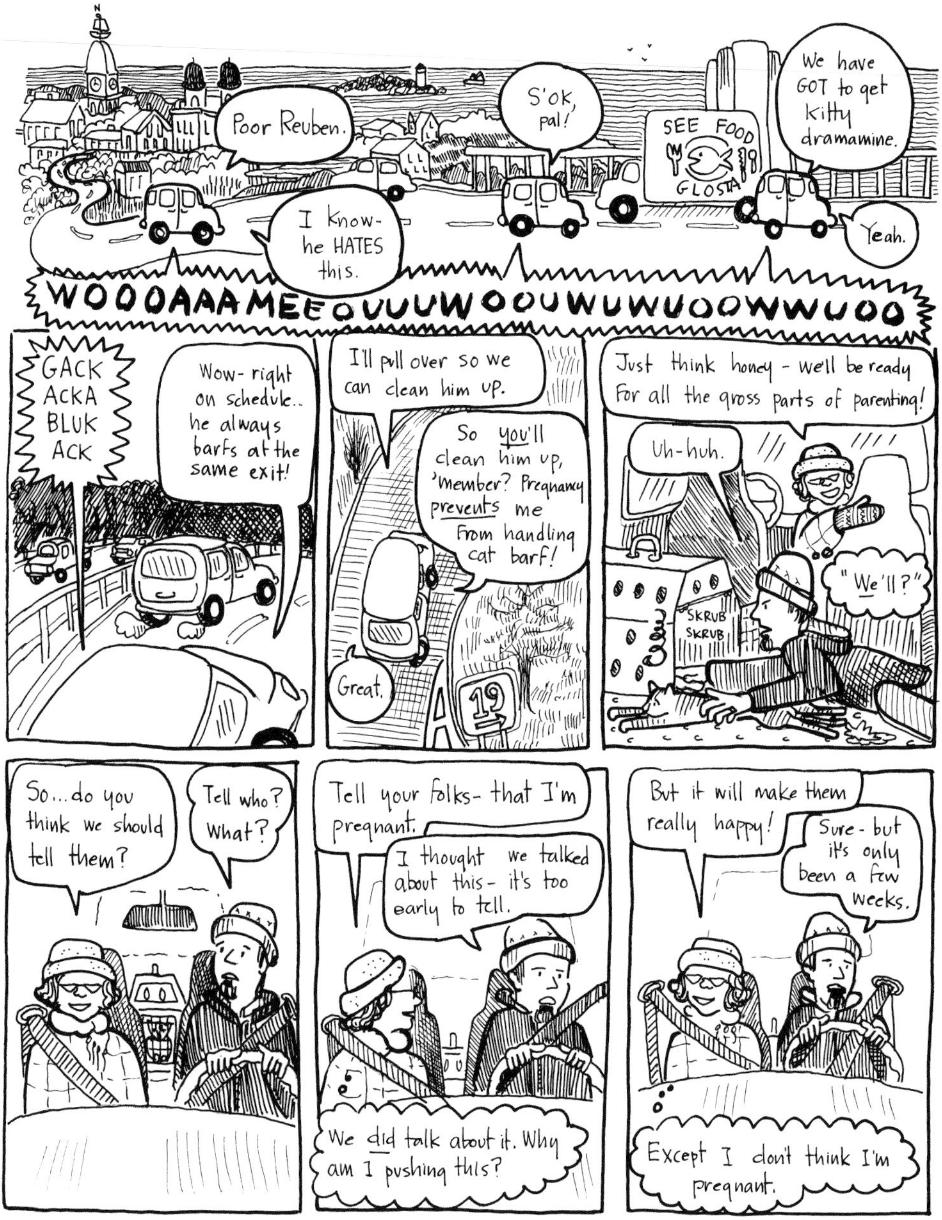
Poor Reuben.
I know- he HATES this.
S'ok, pal!
SEE FOOD
GLOSTA
We have GOT to get kitty dramamine.
Yeah.
WOOOAAAMEEOUUUWOOUWUWUOOWWUOO
GACK ACKA BLUK ACK
Wow- right on schedule.. he always barfs at the same exit!
I'll pull over so we can clean him up.
So you'll clean him up, 'member? Pregnancy prevents me from handling cat barf!
Great.
19
Just think honey - we'll be ready for all the gross parts of parenting!
Uh-huh.
"We'll?"
SKRUB SKRUB
So... do you think we should tell them?
Tell who? What?
Tell your folks- that I'm pregnant.
I thought we talked about this- it's too early to tell.
We did talk about it. Why am I pushing this?
But it will make them really happy!
Sure- but it's only been a few weeks.
Except I don't think I'm pregnant.

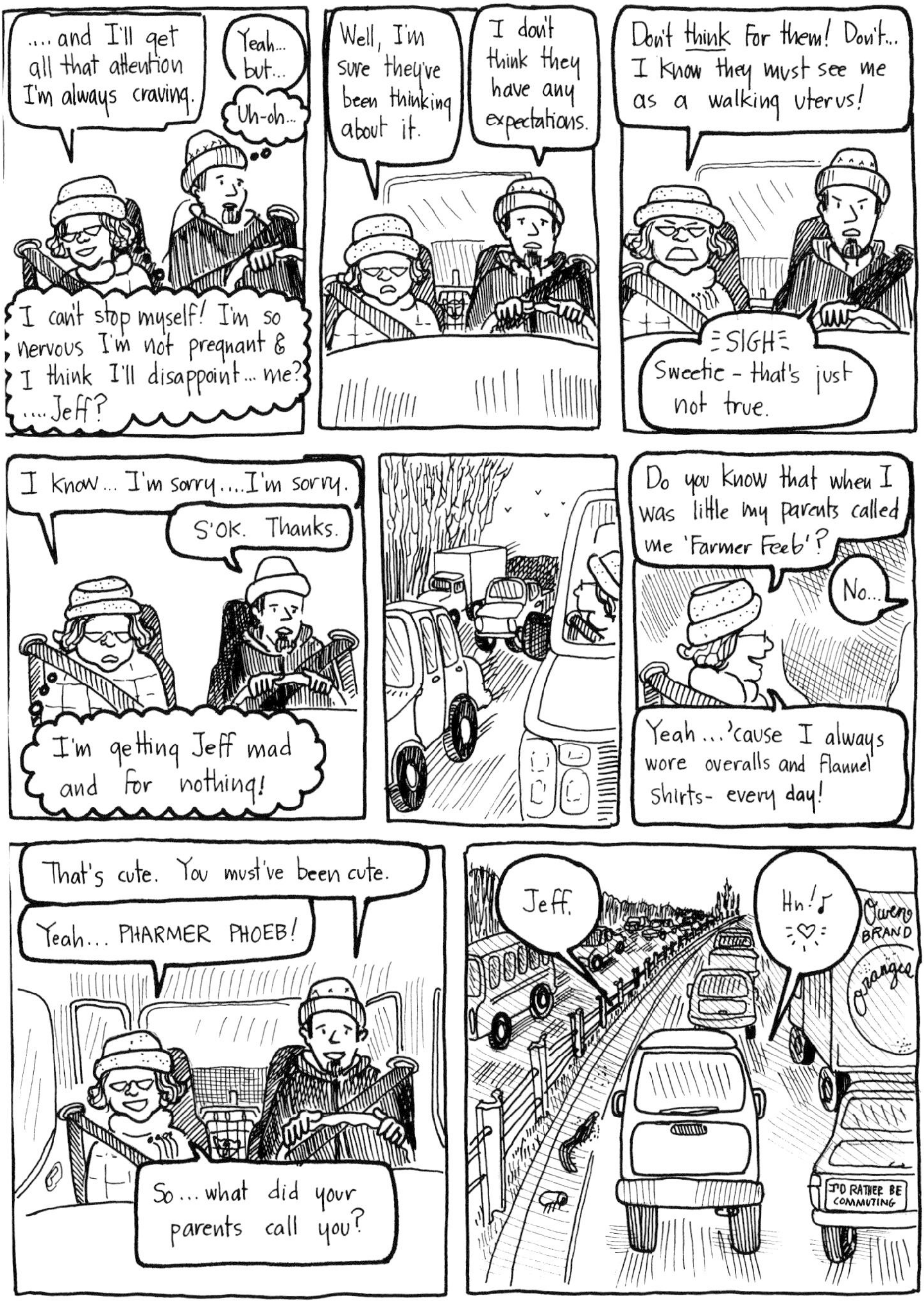
.... and I'll get all that attention I'm always craving.
Yeah... but...
Uh-oh...
I can't stop myself! I'm so nervous I'm not pregnant & I think I'll disappoint... me? .... Jeff?
Well, I'm sure they've been thinking about it.
I don't think they have any expectations.
Don't think for them! Don't... I know they must see me as a walking uterus!
SIGH
Sweetie - that's just not true.
I know... I'm sorry.... I'm sorry.
S'OK. Thanks.
I'm getting Jeff mad and for nothing!
Do you know that when I was little my parents called me 'Farmer Feeb'?
No...
Yeah... 'cause I always wore overalls and flannel shirts - every day!
That's cute. You must've been cute.
Yeah... PHARMER PHOEB!
So... what did your parents call you?
Jeff.
Hn!
Owens BRAND
oranges
I'D RATHER BE COMMUTING

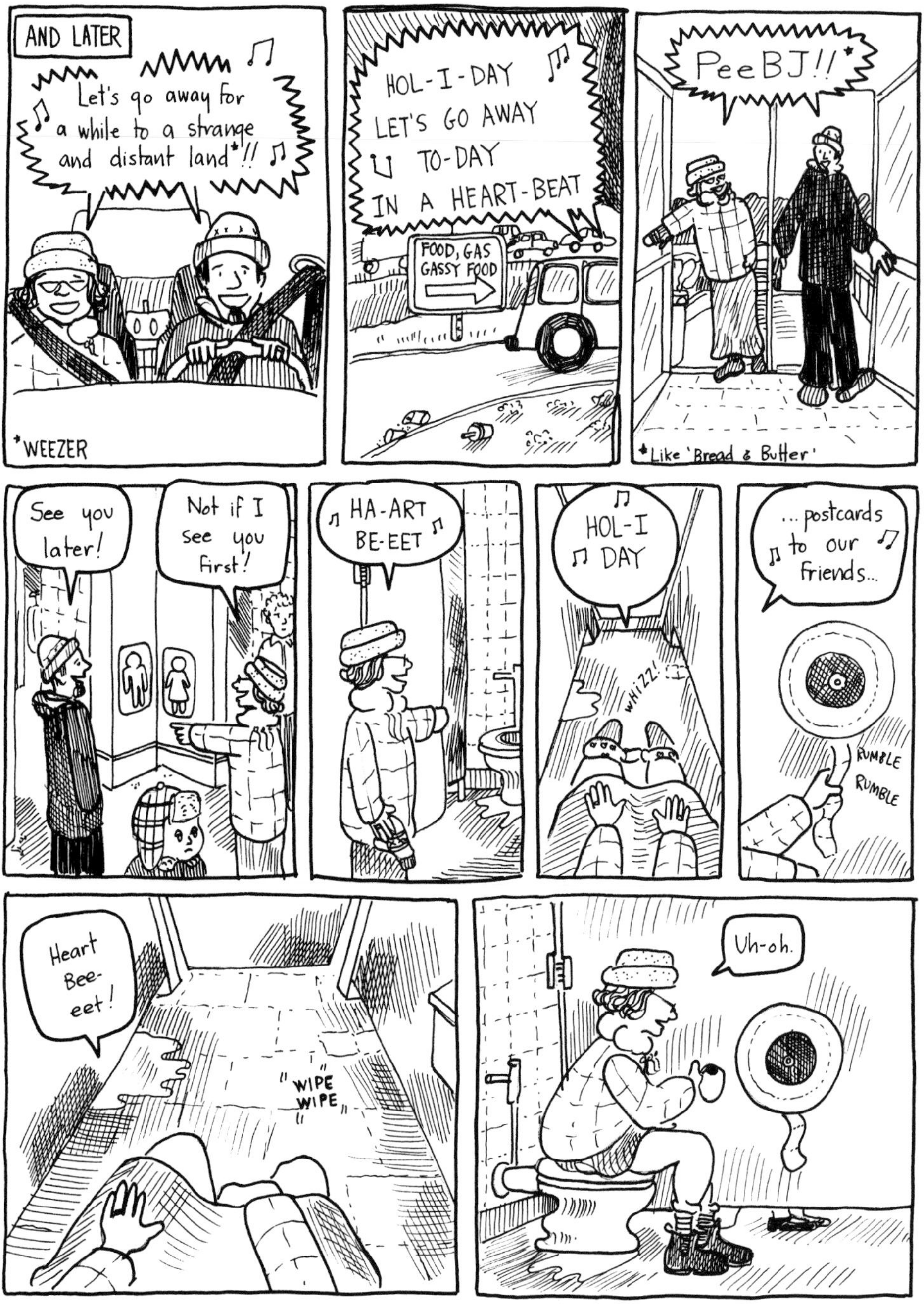
AND LATER
Let's go away for a while to a strange and distant land*!!
*WEEZER
HOL-I-DAY LET'S GO AWAY TO-DAY IN A HEART-BEAT
FOOD, GAS GASSY FOOD
PeeBJ!!*
*Like 'Bread & Butter'
See you later!
Not if I see you first!
HA-ART BE-EET
HOL-I DAY
WHIZZ!
...postcards to our friends...
RUMBLE RUMBLE
Heart Bee-eet!
"WIPE WIPE"
Uh-oh.

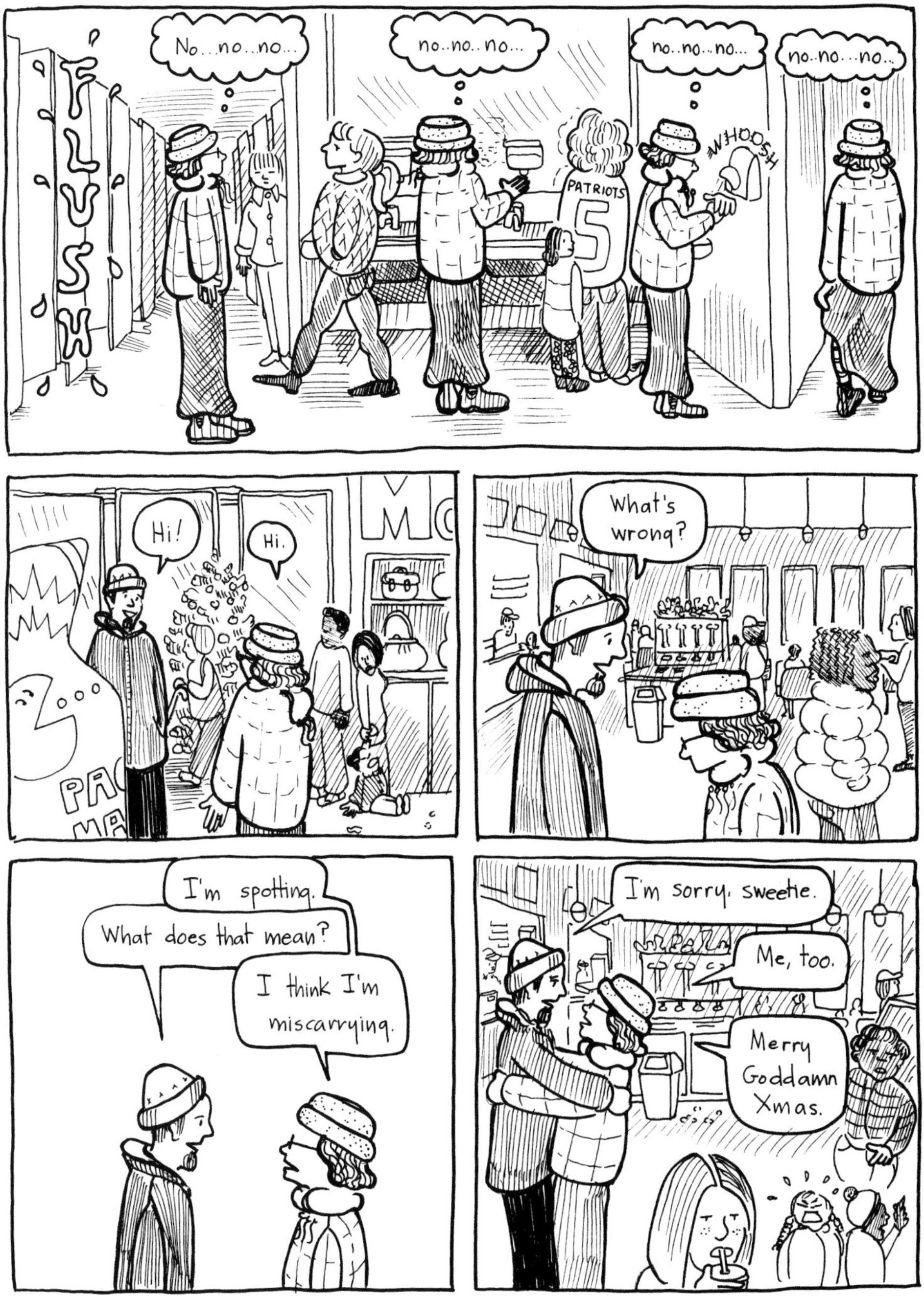
FLUSH
No...no...no...
no..no..no...
no..no...no...
WHOOSH
no..no...no..
PATRIOTS
5
Hi!
Hi.
What's wrong?
I'm spotting.
What does that mean?
I think I'm miscarrying.
I'm sorry, sweetie.
Me, too.
Merry Goddamn Xmas.

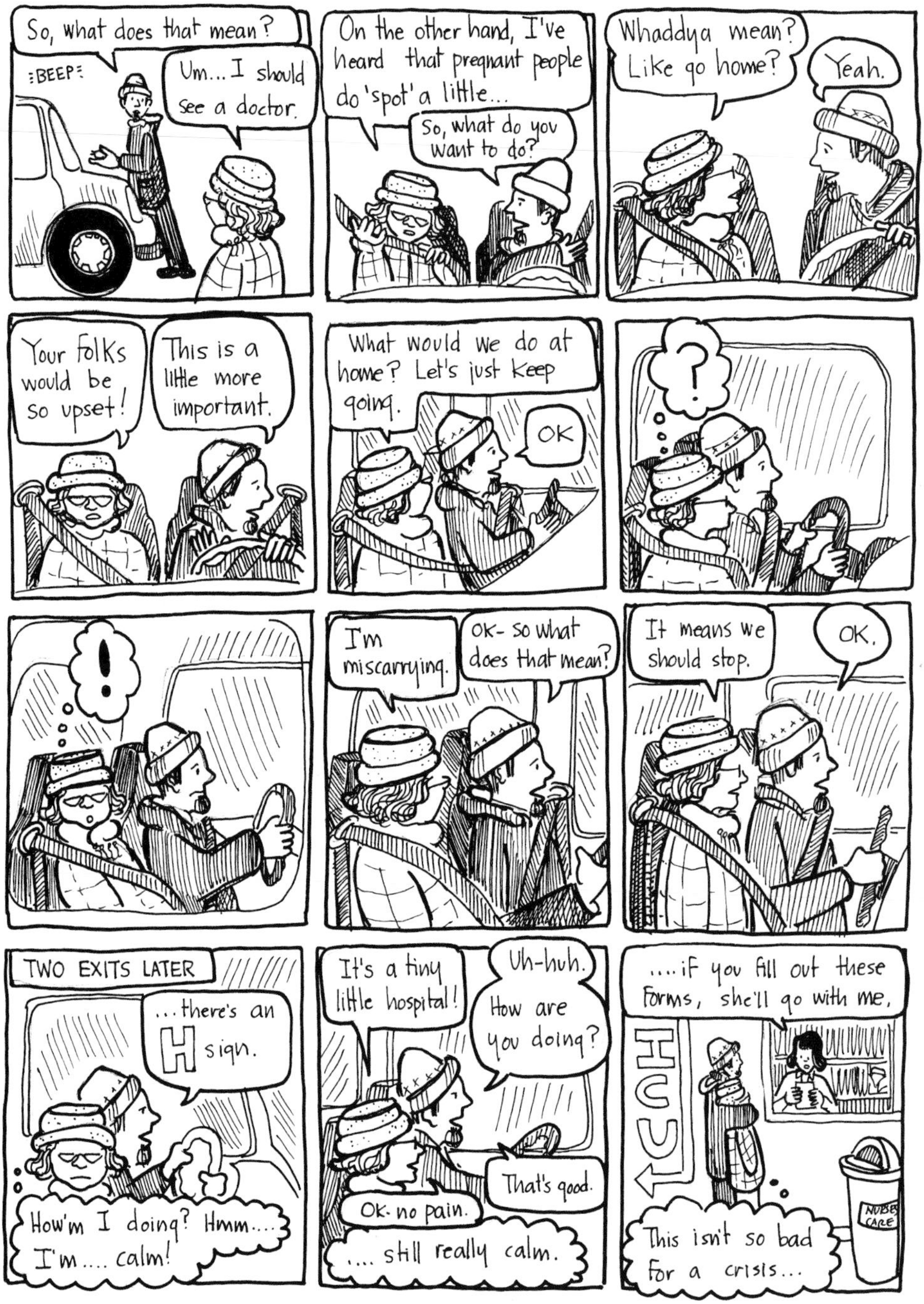

So, what does that mean?
BEEP
Um... I should see a doctor.
On the other hand, I've heard that pregnant people do 'spot' a little...
So, what do you want to do?
Whaddya mean? Like go home?
Yeah.
Your folks would be so upset!
This is a little more important.
What would we do at home? Let's just keep going.
OK
?
!
I'm miscarrying.
OK- so what does that mean?
It means we should stop.
OK.
TWO EXITS LATER
...there's an H sign.
How'm I doing? Hmm.... I'm.... calm!
It's a tiny little hospital!
Uh-huh. How are you doing?
That's good.
OK. no pain.
.... still really calm.
....if you fill out these forms, she'll go with me.
ICU
This isn't so bad for a crisis...

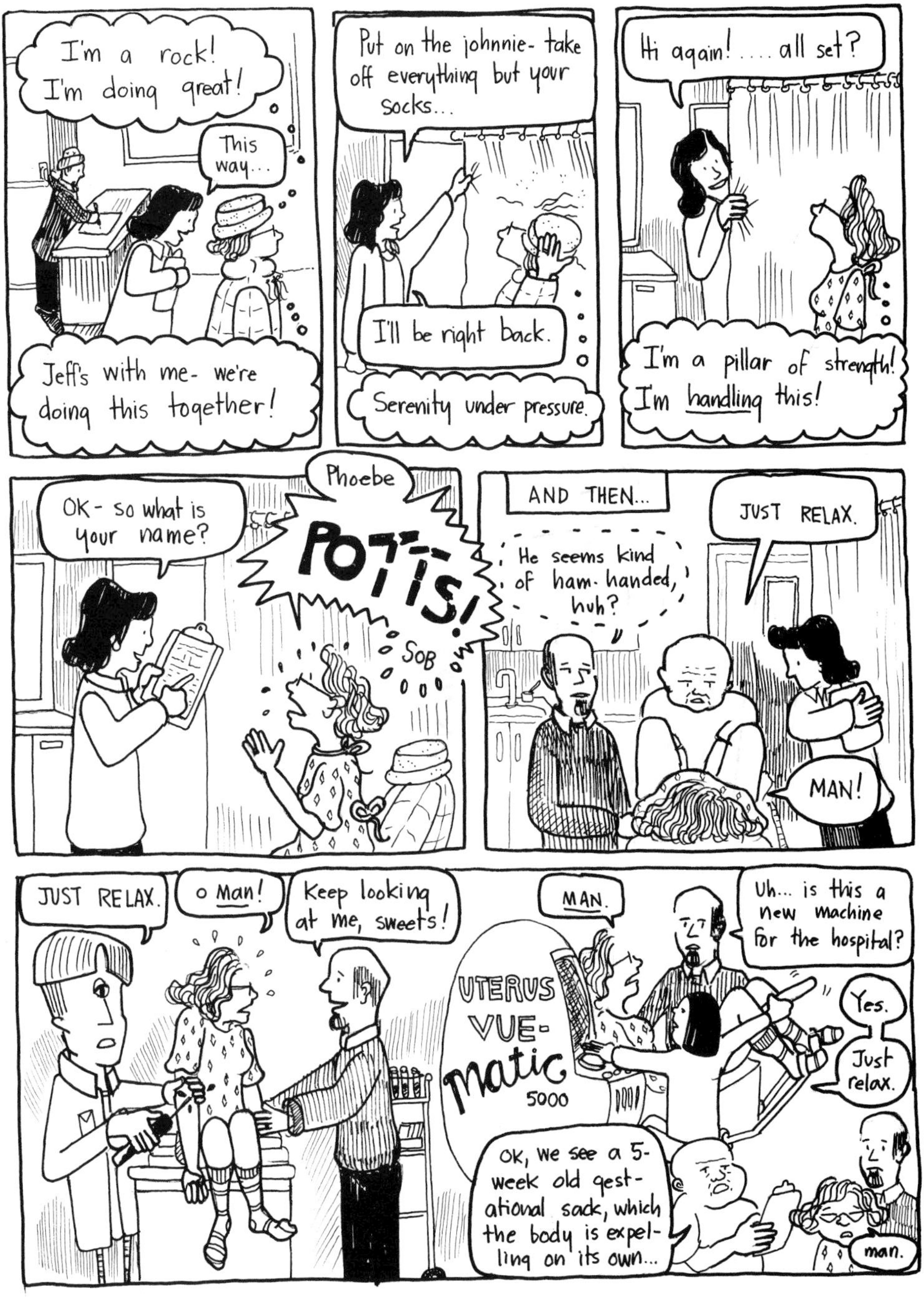
I'm a rock! I'm doing great!
This way...
Jeff's with me- we're doing this together!
Put on the johnnie- take off everything but your socks...
I'll be right back.
Serenity under pressure.
Hi again! .... all set?
I'm a pillar of strength! I'm handling this!
OK- so what is your name?
Phoebe
POTTS!
SOB
AND THEN...
He seems kind of ham-handed, huh?
JUST RELAX.
MAN!
JUST RELAX.
o Man!
Keep looking at me, sweets!
MAN.
Uh... is this a new machine for the hospital?
Yes.
Just relax.
UTERUS VUE-matic 5000
OK, we see a 5-week old gestational sack, which the body is expelling on its own...
man.

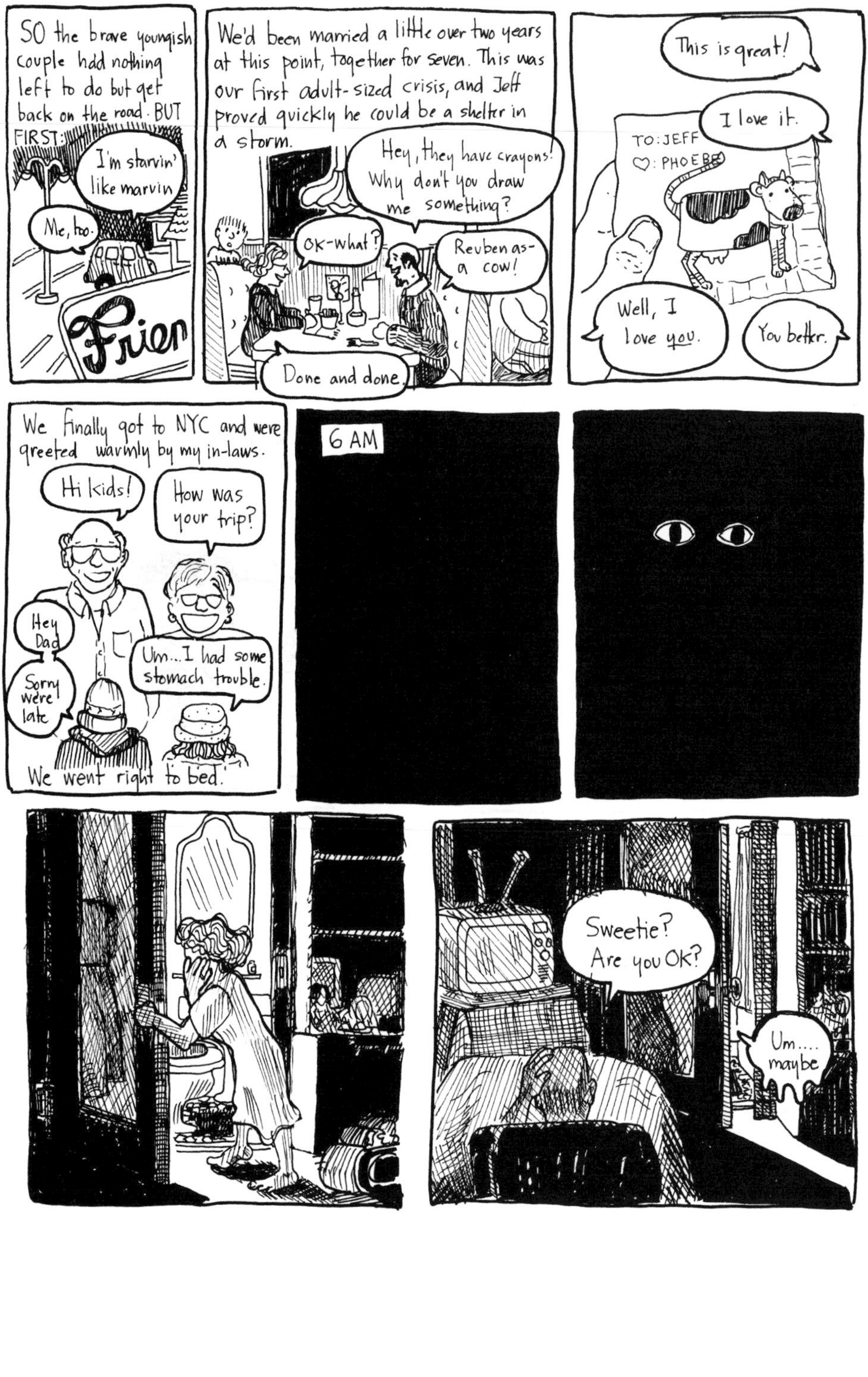
SO the brave youngish couple had nothing left to do but get back on the road. BUT FIRST:
I'm starvin' like marvin
Me, too.
Frien
We'd been married a little over two years at this point, together for seven. This was our first adult-sized crisis, and Jeff proved quickly he could be a shelter in a storm.
Hey, they have crayons! Why don't you draw me something?
OK-what?
Reuben as-a cow!
Done and done.
This is great!
I love it.
TO: JEFF
♡: PHOEBE
Well, I love you.
You better.
We finally got to NYC and were greeted warmly by my in-laws.
Hi kids!
How was your trip?
Hey Dad
Sorry we're late
Um...I had some stomach trouble.
We went right to bed.
6 AM
Sweetie? Are you OK?
Um.... maybe

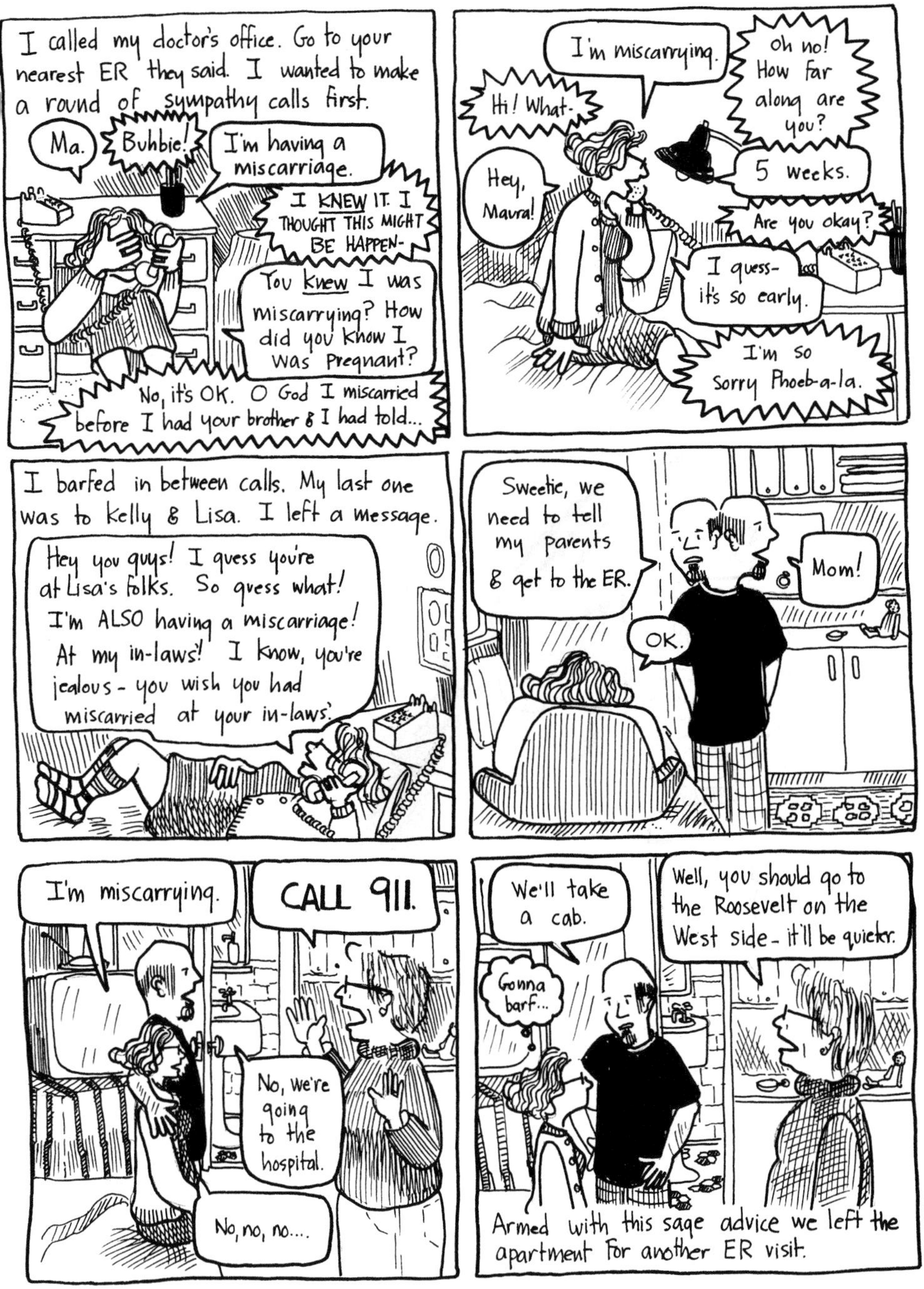
I called my doctor's office. Go to your nearest ER they said. I wanted to make a round of sympathy calls first.
Ma.
Bubbie!
I'm having a miscarriage.
I KNEW IT. I THOUGHT THIS MIGHT BE HAPPEN-
You knew I was miscarrying? How did you know I was pregnant?
No, it's OK. O God I miscarried before I had your brother & I had told...
Hi! What-
Hey, Maura!
I'm miscarrying.
Oh no! How far along are you?
5 weeks.
Are you okay?
I guess- it's so early.
I'm so sorry Phoeb-a-la.
I barfed in between calls. My last one was to Kelly & Lisa. I left a message.
Hey you guys! I guess you're at Lisa's folks. So guess what! I'm ALSO having a miscarriage! At my in-laws'! I know, you're jealous - you wish you had miscarried at your in-laws'.
Sweetie, we need to tell my parents & get to the ER.
Mom!
OK.
I'm miscarrying.
CALL 911.
No, we're going to the hospital.
No, no, no....
We'll take a cab.
Well, you should go to the Roosevelt on the West side - it'll be quicker.
Gonna barf...
Armed with this sage advice we left the apartment for another ER visit.

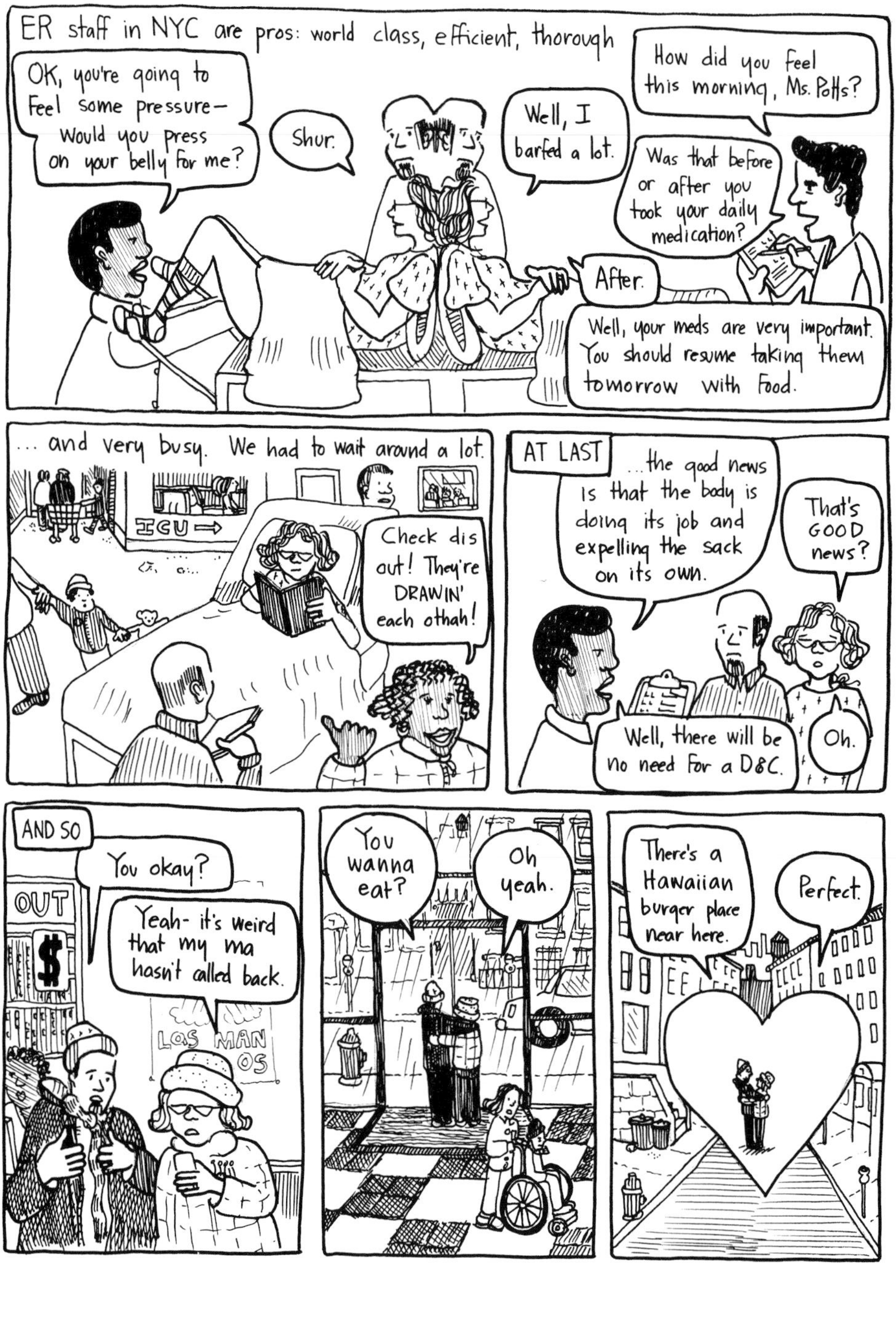
ER staff in NYC are pros: world class, efficient, thorough
OK, you're going to feel some pressure– Would you press on your belly for me?
Shur.
Well, I barfed a lot.
How did you feel this morning, Ms. Potts?
Was that before or after you took your daily medication?
After.
Well, your meds are very important. You should resume taking them tomorrow with food.
... and very busy. We had to wait around a lot.
ICU
Check dis out! They're DRAWIN' each othah!
AT LAST
...the good news is that the body is doing its job and expelling the sack on its own.
That's GOOD news?
Well, there will be no need for a D&C.
Oh.
AND SO
You okay?
Yeah- it's weird that my ma hasn't called back.
OUT
LOS MANOS
You wanna eat?
Oh yeah.
There's a Hawaiian burger place near here.
Perfect.

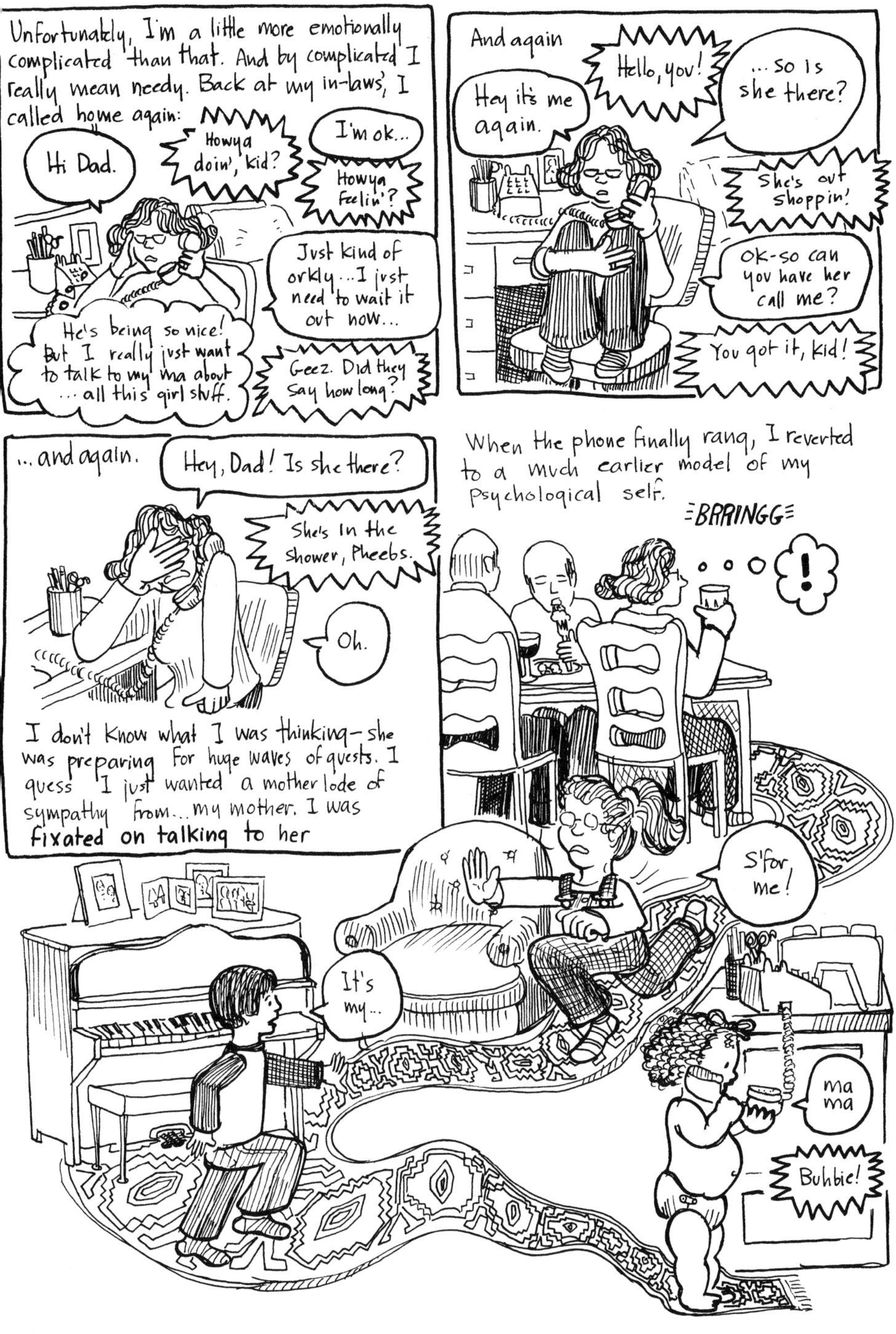
Unfortunately, I'm a little more emotionally complicated than that. And by complicated I really mean needy. Back at my in-laws', I called home again:
Hi Dad.
Howya doin', kid?
I'm ok...
Howya Feelin'?
Just kind of orkly... I just need to wait it out now...
He's being so nice! But I really just want to talk to my ma about ... all this girl stuff.
Geez. Did they say how long?
And again
Hey it's me again.
Hello, you!
... so is she there?
She's out shoppin'.
Ok-so can you have her call me?
You got it, kid!
... and again.
Hey, Dad! Is she there?
She's in the shower, Pheebs.
Oh.
I don't know what I was thinking-she was preparing for huge waves of guests. I guess I just wanted a mother lode of sympathy from... my mother. I was fixated on talking to her
When the phone finally rang, I reverted to a much earlier model of my psychological self.
BRRINGG
!
S'for me!
It's my...
ma ma
Bubbie!

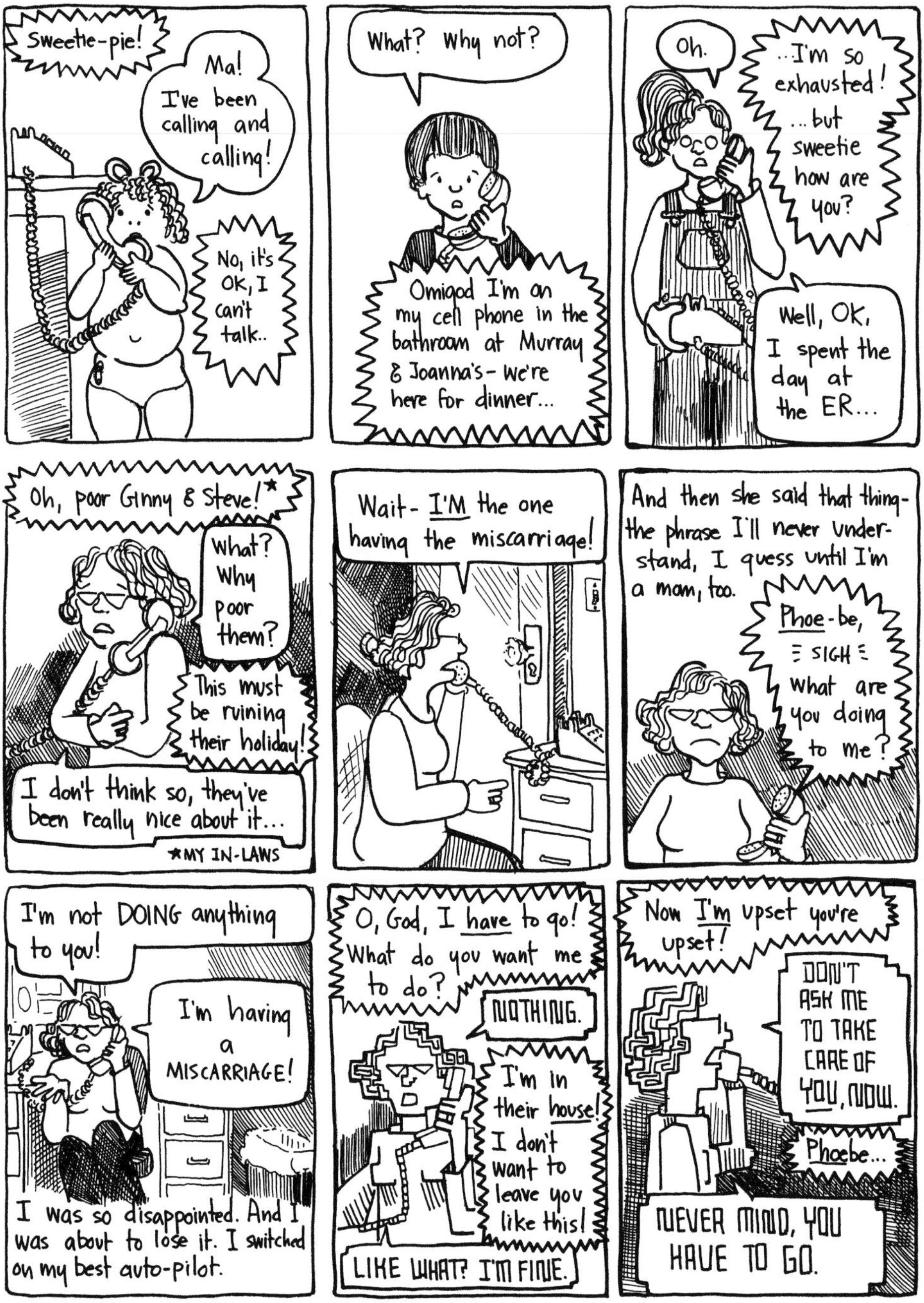
Sweetie-pie!
Ma! I've been calling and calling!
No, it's OK, I can't talk..
What? Why not?
Omigod I'm on my cell phone in the bathroom at Murray & Joanna's - we're here for dinner...
Oh.
...I'm so exhausted! ...but sweetie how are you?
Well, OK, I spent the day at the ER...
Oh, poor Ginny & Steve!*
What? Why poor them?
This must be ruining their holiday!
I don't think so, they've been really nice about it...
*MY IN-LAWS
Wait- I'M the one having the miscarriage!
And then she said that thing- the phrase I'll never understand, I guess until I'm a mom, too.
Phoe-be, SIGH what are you doing to me?
I'm not DOING anything to you!
I'm having a MISCARRIAGE!
I was so disappointed. And I was about to lose it. I switched on my best auto-pilot.
O, God, I have to go! What do you want me to do?
NOTHING.
I'm in their house! I don't want to leave you like this!
LIKE WHAT? I'M FINE.
Now I'm upset you're upset!
DON'T ASK ME TO TAKE CARE OF YOU, NOW.
Phoebe...
NEVER MIND, YOU HAVE TO GO.

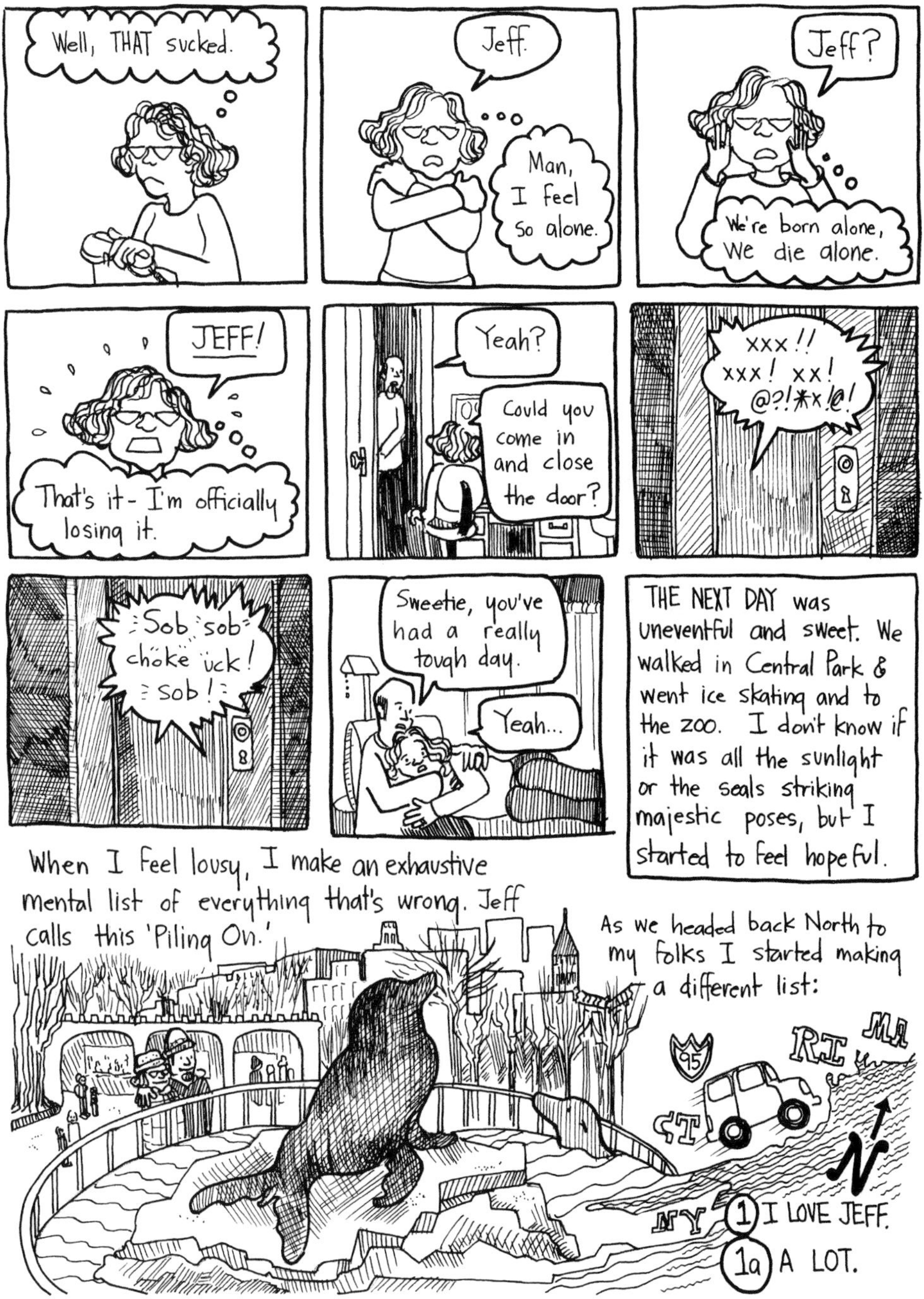
Well, THAT sucked.
Jeff.
Man, I feel so alone.
Jeff?
We're born alone, We die alone.
JEFF!
That's it- I'm officially losing it.
Yeah?
Could you come in and close the door?
xxx!! xxx! xx! @?!*x!@!
Sob sob choke uck! sob!
Sweetie, you've had a really tough day.
Yeah...
THE NEXT DAY was uneventful and sweet. We walked in Central Park & went ice skating and to the zoo. I don't know if it was all the sunlight or the seals striking majestic poses, but I started to feel hopeful.
When I feel lousy, I make an exhaustive mental list of everything that's wrong. Jeff calls this 'Piling On.'
As we headed back North to my folks I started making a different list:
95
RI
MA
CT
N
NY
1 I LOVE JEFF.
1a A LOT.

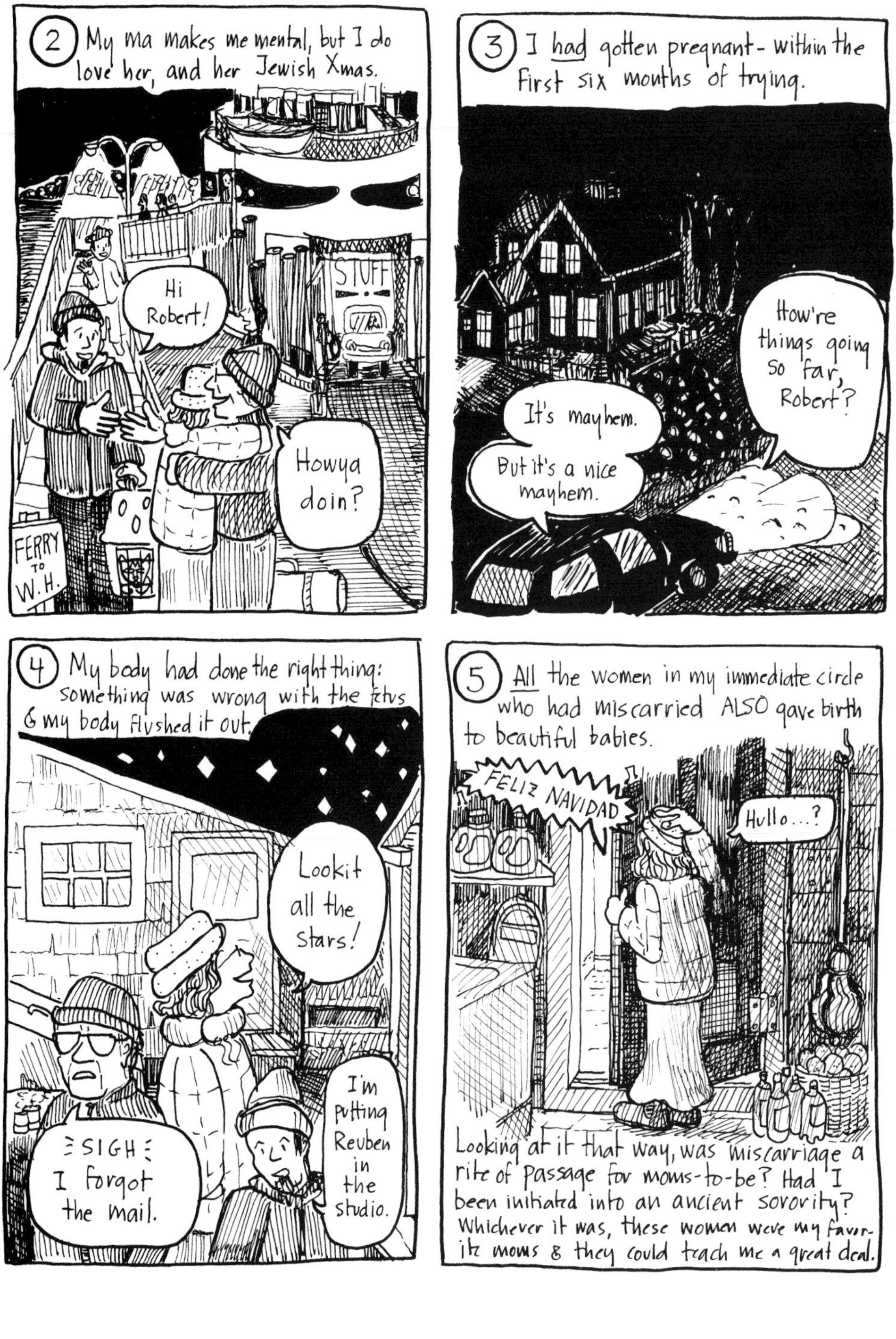
2 My ma makes me mental, but I do love her, and her Jewish Xmas.
Hi Robert!
STUFF
Howya doin?
FERRY TO W.H.
3 I had gotten pregnant- within the first six months of trying.
How're things going so far, Robert?
It's mayhem.
But it's a nice mayhem.
4 My body had done the right thing: something was wrong with the fetus & my body flushed it out.
Lookit all the stars!
SIGH I forgot the mail.
I'm putting Reuben in the studio.
5 All the women in my immediate circle who had miscarried ALSO gave birth to beautiful babies.
FELIZ NAVIDAD
Hullo...?
Looking at it that way, was miscarriage a rite of passage for moms-to-be? Had I been initiated into an ancient sorority? Whichever it was, these women were my favorite moms & they could teach me a great deal.

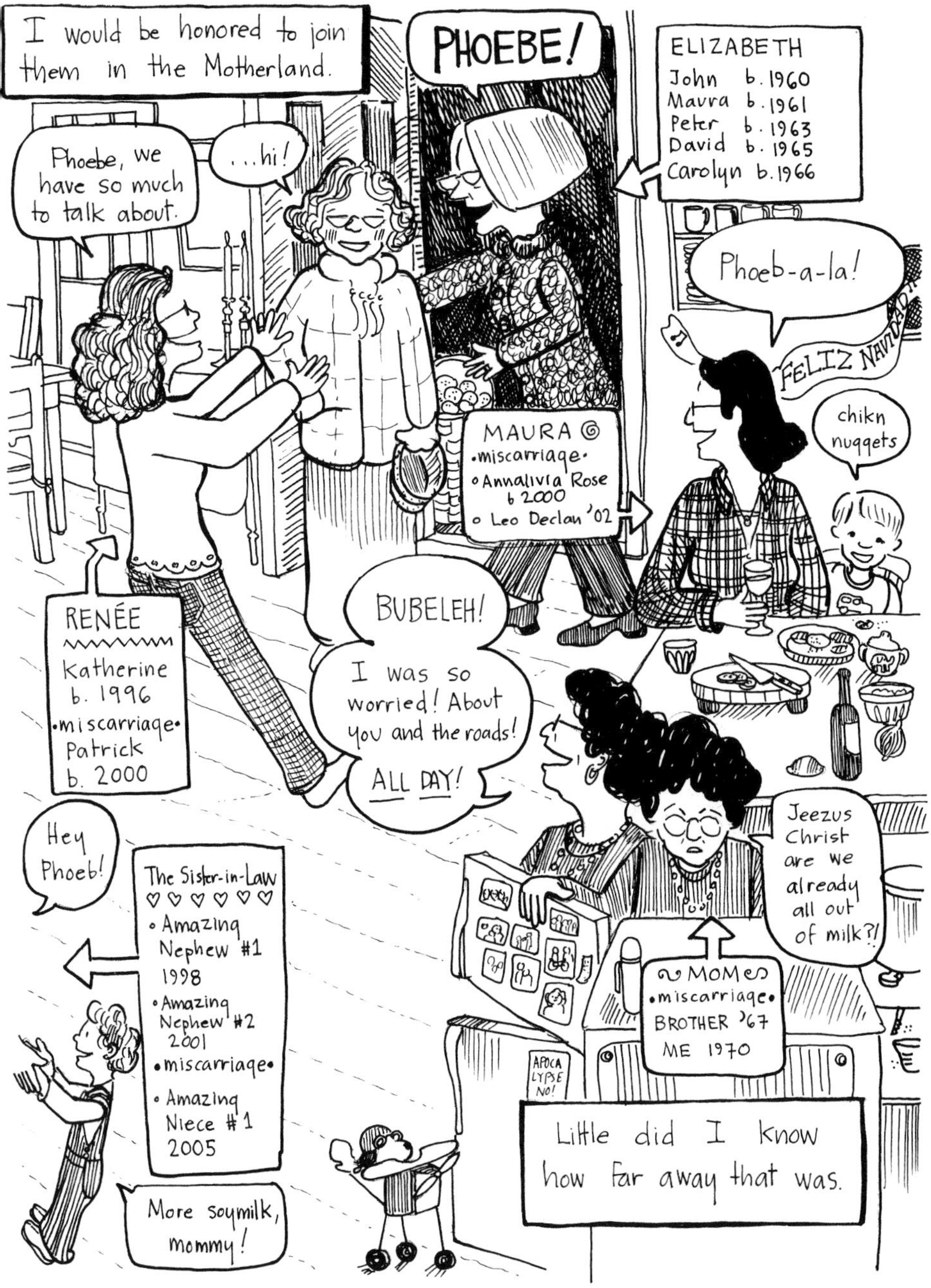
I would be honored to join them in the Motherland.
PHOEBE!
ELIZABETH
John b. 1960
Maura b. 1961
Peter b. 1963
David b. 1965
Carolyn b. 1966
Phoebe, we have so much to talk about.
...hi!
Phoeb-a-la!
FELIZ NAVIDAD
chikn nuggets
MAURA
•miscarriage•
∘Annalivia Rose b 2000
∘ Leo Declan '02
RENÉE
Katherine b. 1996
•miscarriage•
Patrick b. 2000
BUBELEH!
I was so worried! About you and the roads!
ALL DAY!
Hey Phoeb!
The Sister-in-Law
∘ Amazing Nephew #1 1998
∘ Amazing Nephew #2 2001
•miscarriage•
∘ Amazing Niece #1 2005
Jeezus Christ are we already all out of milk?!
MOM
•miscarriage•
BROTHER '67
ME 1970
APOCALYPSE NO!
Little did I know how far away that was.
More soymilk, mommy!

CHAPTER 3

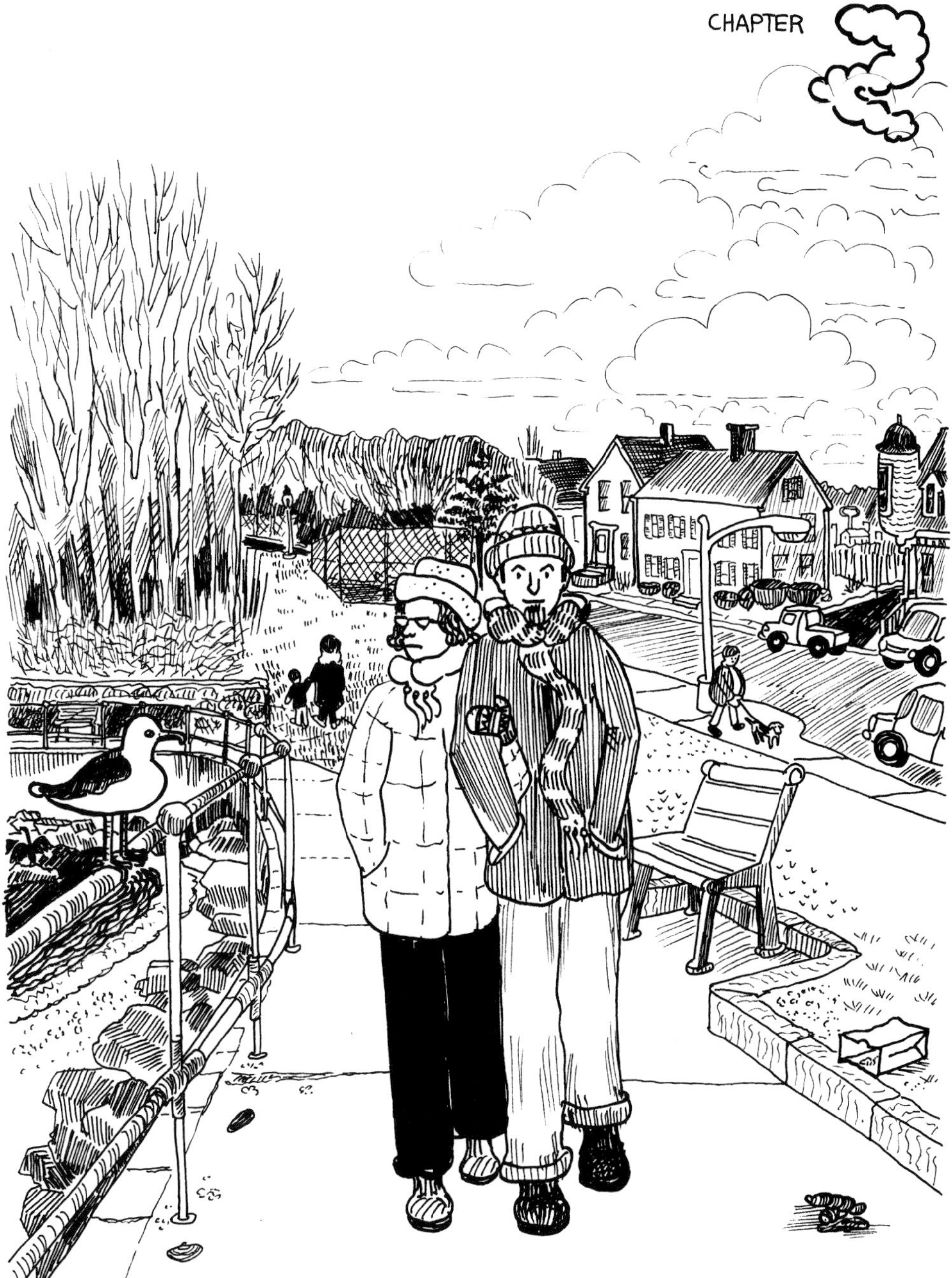

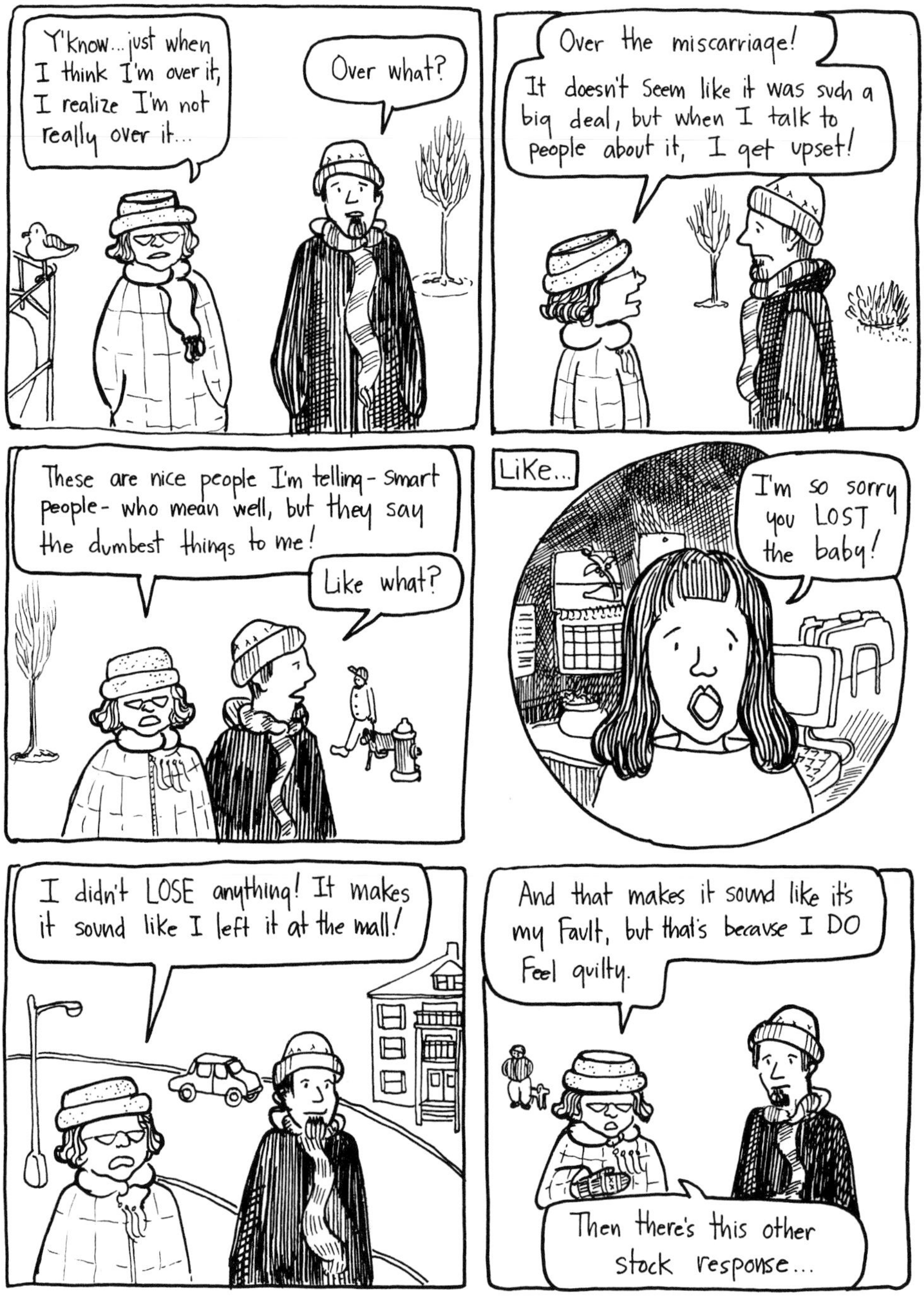
Y'know... just when I think I'm over it, I realize I'm not really over it...
Over what?
Over the miscarriage!
It doesn't seem like it was such a big deal, but when I talk to people about it, I get upset!
These are nice people I'm telling - smart people - who mean well, but they say the dumbest things to me!
Like what?
Like...
I'm so sorry you LOST the baby!
I didn't LOSE anything! It makes it sound like I left it at the mall!
And that makes it sound like it's my fault, but that's because I DO feel guilty.
Then there's this other stock response...

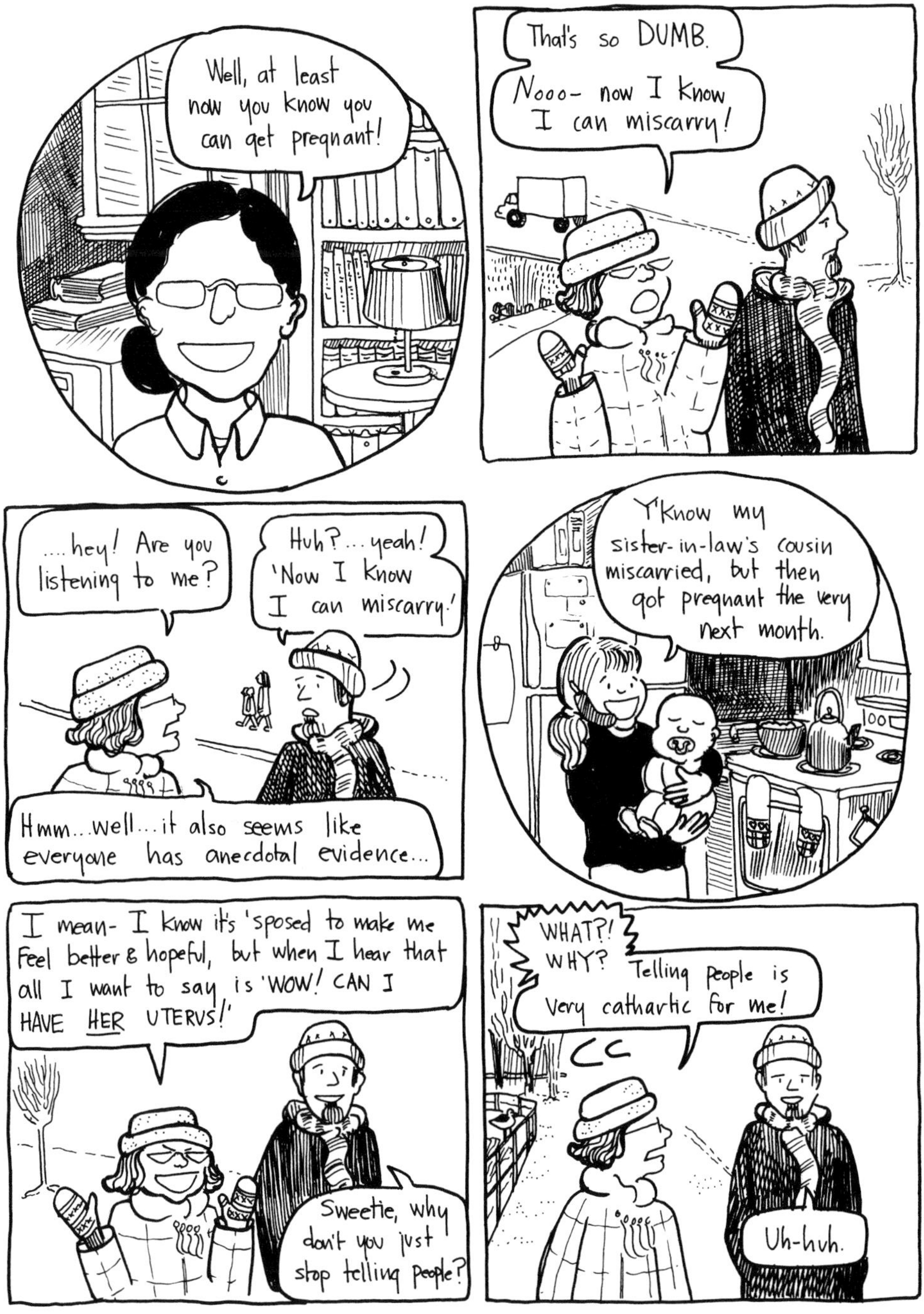
Well, at least now you know you can get pregnant!
That's so DUMB.
Nooo- now I know I can miscarry!
....hey! Are you listening to me?
Huh?...yeah! 'Now I know I can miscarry.'
Hmm...well...it also seems like everyone has anecdotal evidence...
Y'know my sister-in-law's cousin miscarried, but then got pregnant the very next month.
I mean- I know it's 'sposed to make me feel better & hopeful, but when I hear that all I want to say is 'WOW! CAN I HAVE HER UTERUS!'
Sweetie, why don't you just stop telling people?
WHAT?! WHY?
Telling people is very cathartic for me!
Uh-huh.

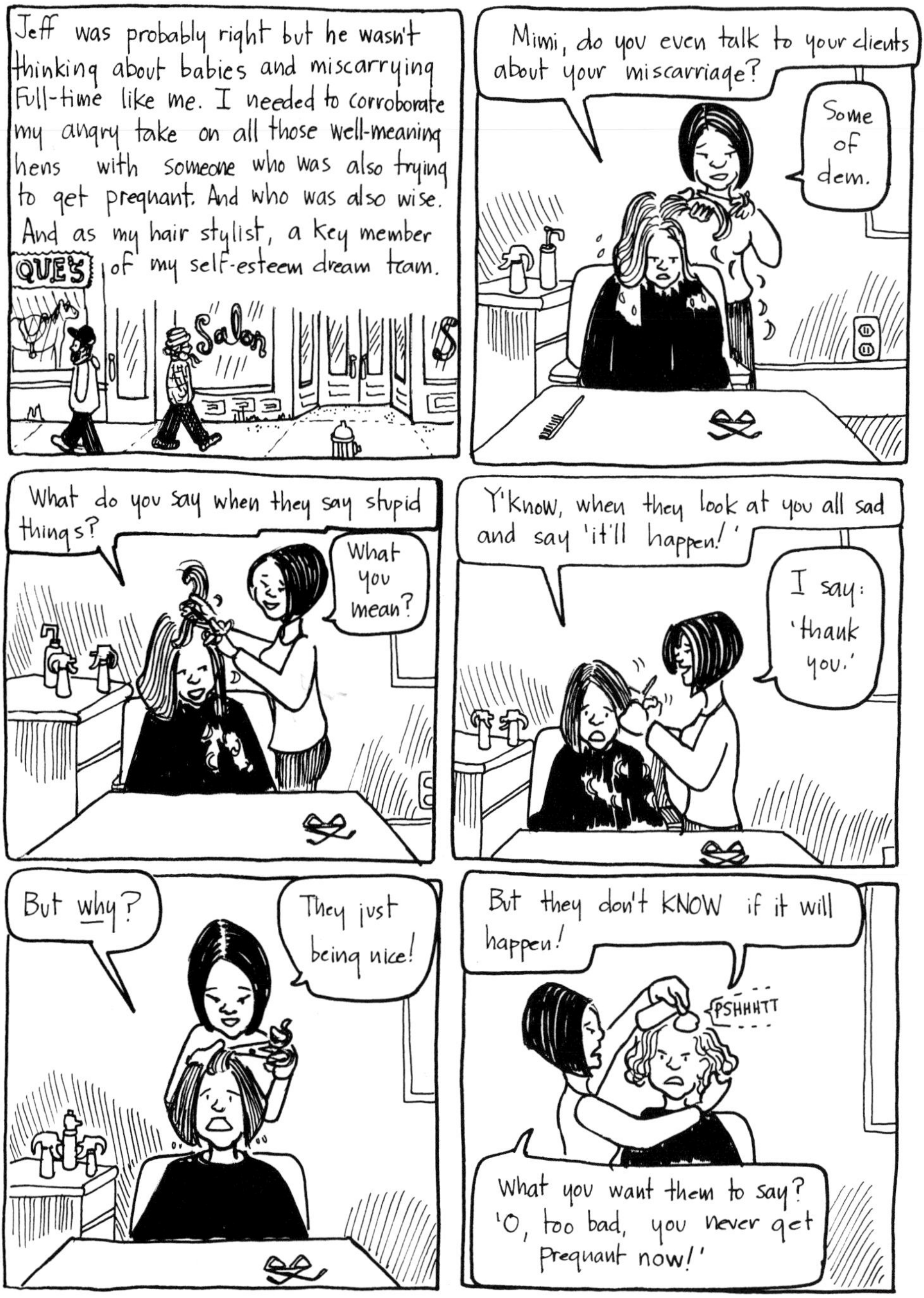
Jeff was probably right but he wasn't thinking about babies and miscarrying full-time like me. I needed to corroborate my angry take on all those well-meaning hens with someone who was also trying to get pregnant. And who was also wise. And as my hair stylist, a key member of my self-esteem dream team.
QUE'S
Salon
Mimi, do you even talk to your clients about your miscarriage?
Some of dem.
What do you say when they say stupid things?
What you mean?
Y'know, when they look at you all sad and say 'it'll happen!'
I say: 'thank you.'
But why?
They just being nice!
But they don't KNOW if it will happen!
PSHHHTT
What you want them to say? 'O, too bad, you never get pregnant now!'

No- I guess not. You're nicer than me.

You nice! Now you cute, too!

CLICK WHIR

OK, so people are nice blah blah I'm probably defensive. And alright, I'm mad I 'lost the baby' and I'll only feel better when I'm working on the next one.

Spleen massage PAMPER YOURSELF!

$45.

DUNG PASTE FACIALS 78⁰⁰

Which is why I was keeping my appointment with Dr. Alvarez, OB.

Train's in 15 minutes

I chose Dr. Alvarez, back when I was pregnant, because she's a she, and because she's from Guatemala.

SHADDAP and eat yer donut!

GLO

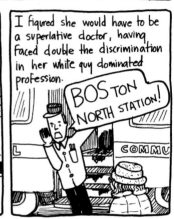

I figured she would have to be a superlative doctor, having faced double the discrimination in her white guy dominated profession.

BOSTON NORTH STATION!

COMMU

And I could increase my Spanish vocabulary with words like 'utero' and 'trimestre sequndo.'

SATANIC VERSES

Plus, I had lived in Guatemala with this family who were so warm & caring... I imagined that she would be impressed with my Spanish and love me & my as-yet-unconceived baby.

CHELSEA!

Thank you.

COMMUTE

Have a good day.

Only one of my deluded liberal stereotypes panned out. Dr. Alvarez was cold, spoke perfect English but was excruciatingly, painstakingly thorough.

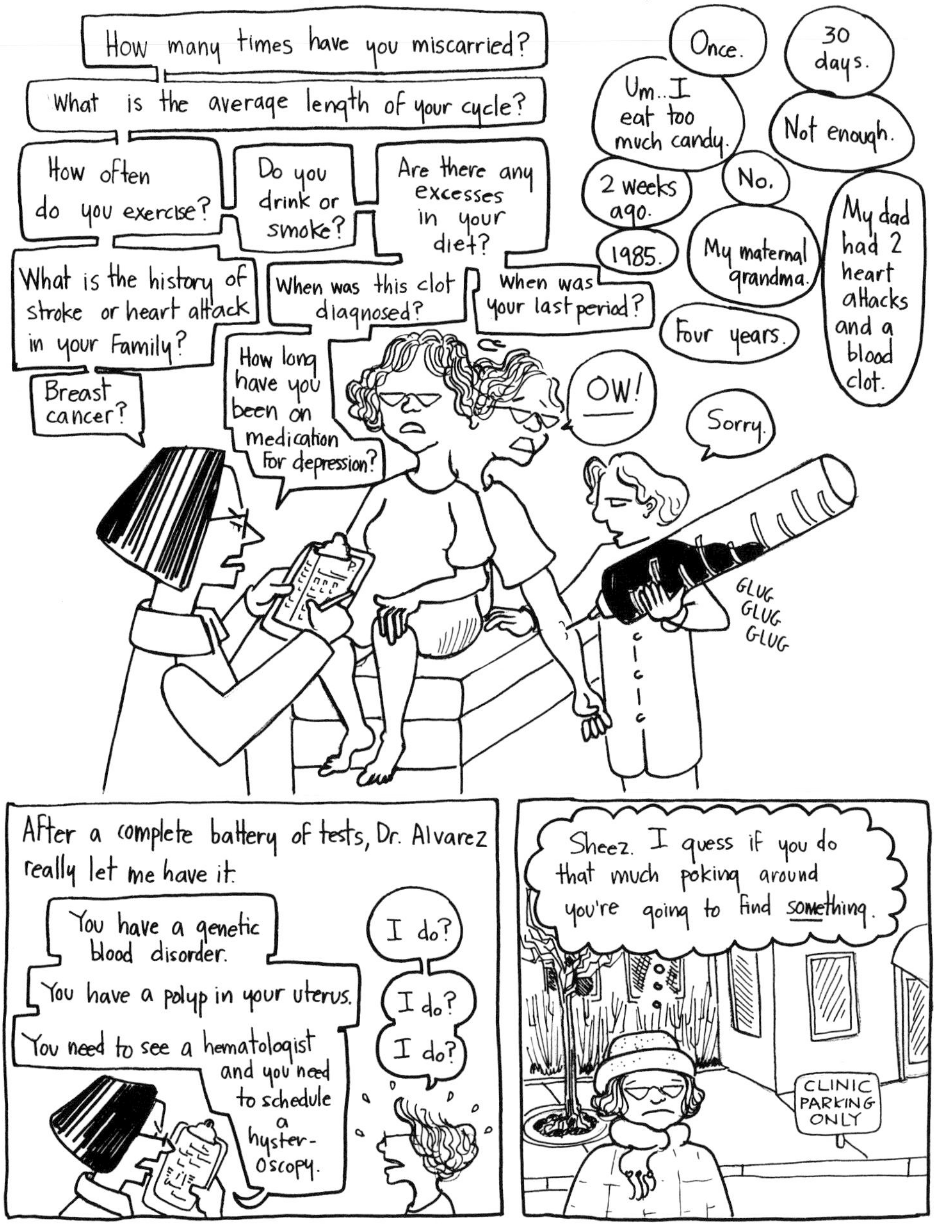
How many times have you miscarried?
What is the average length of your cycle?
How often do you exercise?
Do you drink or smoke?
Are there any excesses in your diet?
What is the history of stroke or heart attack in your family?
When was this clot diagnosed?
When was your last period?
Breast cancer?
How long have you been on medication for depression?
Once.
30 days.
Um...I eat too much candy.
Not enough.
2 weeks ago.
No.
1985.
My maternal grandma.
My dad had 2 heart attacks and a blood clot.
Four years.
OW!
Sorry.
GLUG GLUG GLUG
After a complete battery of tests, Dr. Alvarez really let me have it.
You have a genetic blood disorder.
I do?
You have a polyp in your uterus.
I do?
You need to see a hematologist and you need to schedule a hyster-oscopy.
I do?
Sheez. I guess if you do that much poking around you're going to find something.
CLINIC PARKING ONLY

Jeff came with me after that. It was good to have someone else ask the questions. In theory, anyway.

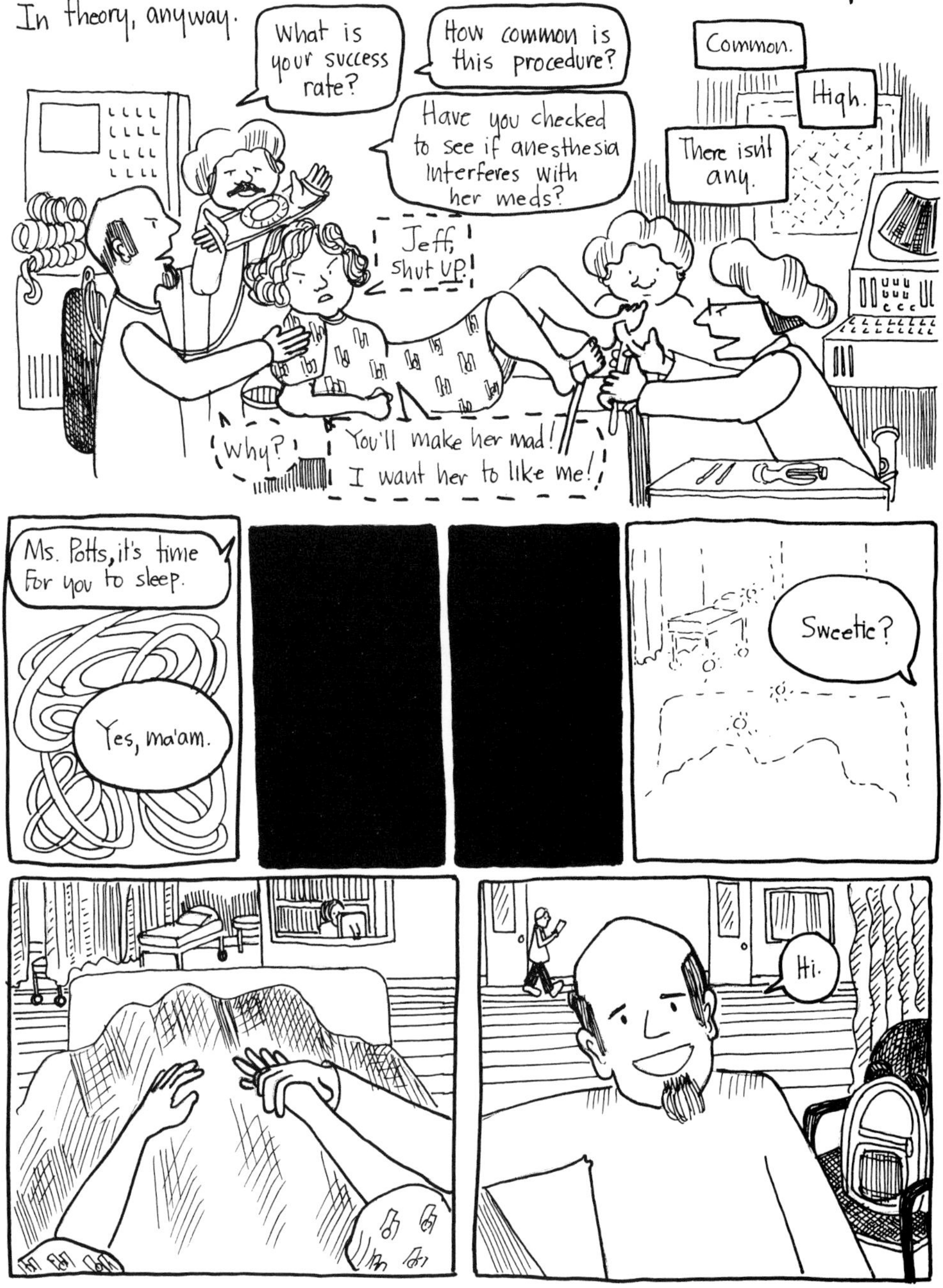

What is your success rate?
How common is this procedure?
Have you checked to see if anesthesia interferes with her meds?
Common.
High.
There isn't any.
Jeff, shut UP!
Why?
You'll make her mad! I want her to like me!
Ms. Potts, it's time for you to sleep.
Yes, ma'am.
Sweetie?
Hi.

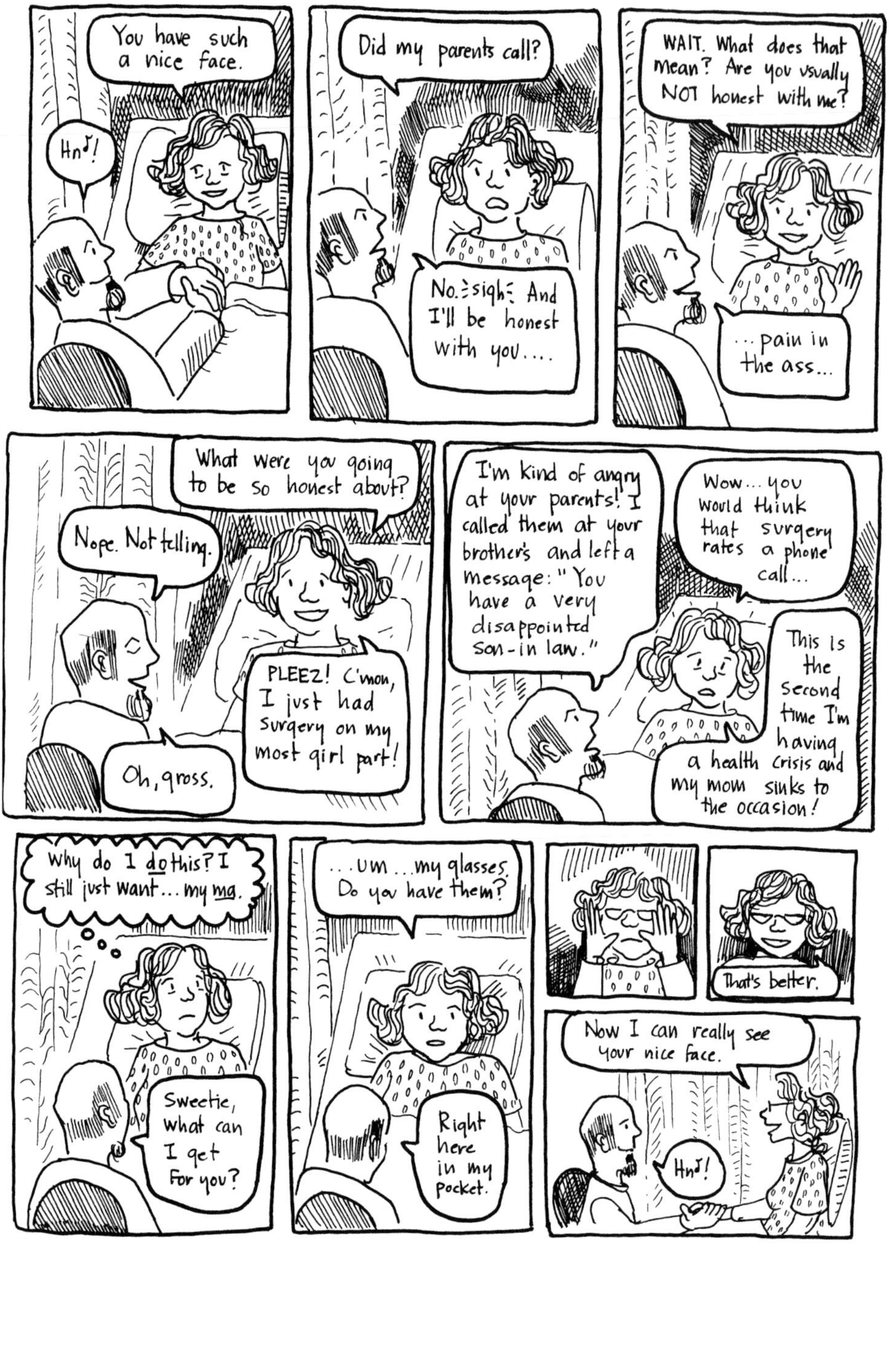
You have such a nice face.
Hnd!
Did my parents call?
No. ≈sigh≈ And I'll be honest with you....
WAIT. What does that mean? Are you usually NOT honest with me?
...pain in the ass...
What were you going to be so honest about?
Nope. Not telling.
PLEEZ! C'mon, I just had surgery on my most girl part!
Oh, gross.
I'm kind of angry at your parents! I called them at your brother's and left a message: "You have a very disappointed son-in law."
Wow... you would think that surgery rates a phone call...
This is the second time I'm having a health crisis and my mom sinks to the occasion!
Why do I do this? I still just want... my ma.
Sweetie, what can I get for you?
...um...my glasses. Do you have them?
Right here in my pocket.
That's better.
Now I can really see your nice face.
Hnd!

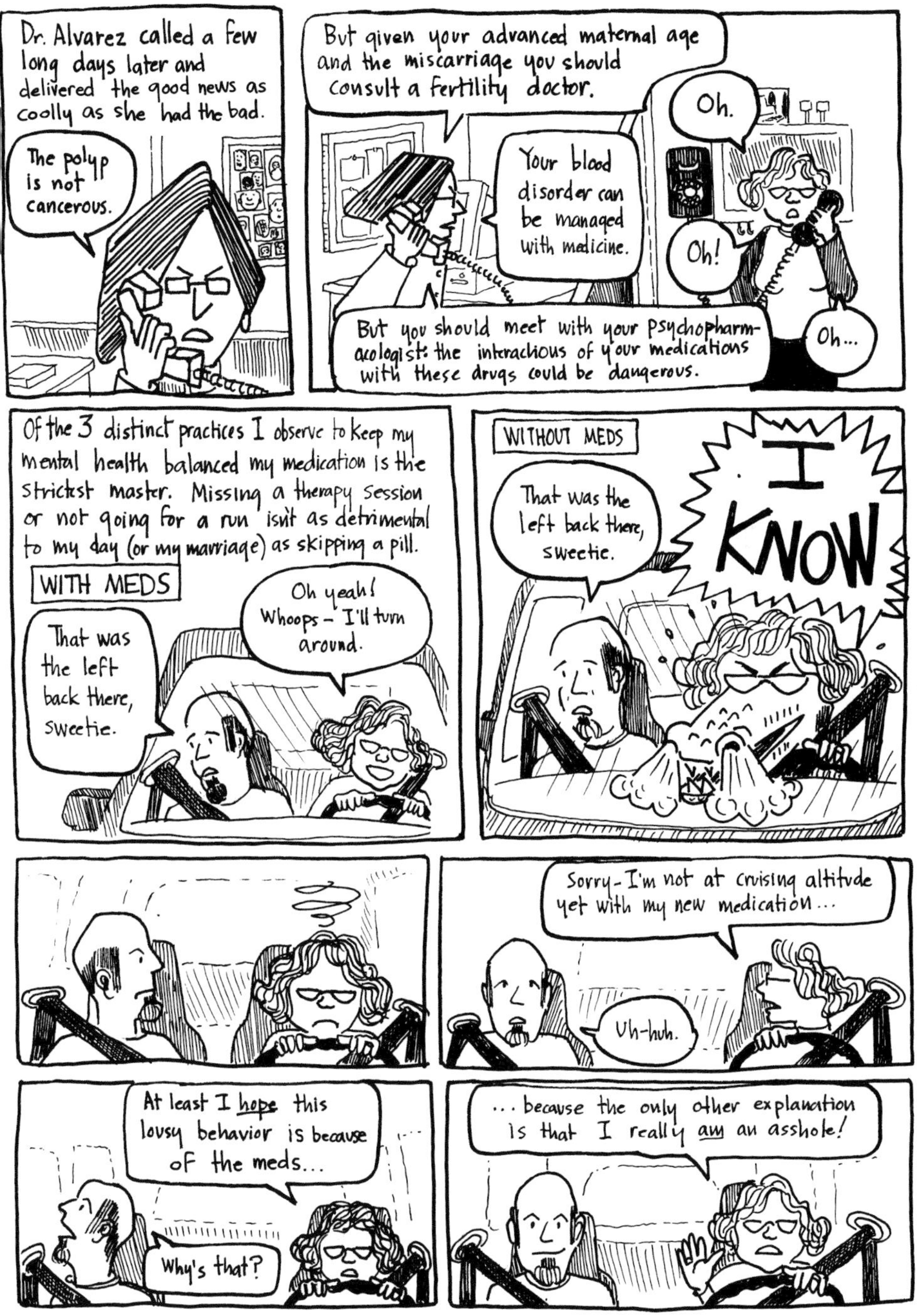
Dr. Alvarez called a few long days later and delivered the good news as coolly as she had the bad.
The polyp is not cancerous.
But given your advanced maternal age and the miscarriage you should consult a fertility doctor.
Oh.
Your blood disorder can be managed with medicine.
Oh!
But you should meet with your psychopharmacologist: the interactions of your medications with these drugs could be dangerous.
Oh...
Of the 3 distinct practices I observe to keep my mental health balanced my medication is the strictest master. Missing a therapy session or not going for a run isn't as detrimental to my day (or my marriage) as skipping a pill.
WITH MEDS
That was the left back there, sweetie.
Oh yeah! Whoops - I'll turn around.
WITHOUT MEDS
That was the left back there, sweetie.
I KNOW
Sorry - I'm not at cruising altitude yet with my new medication...
Uh-huh.
At least I hope this lousy behavior is because of the meds...
Why's that?
...because the only other explanation is that I really am an asshole!

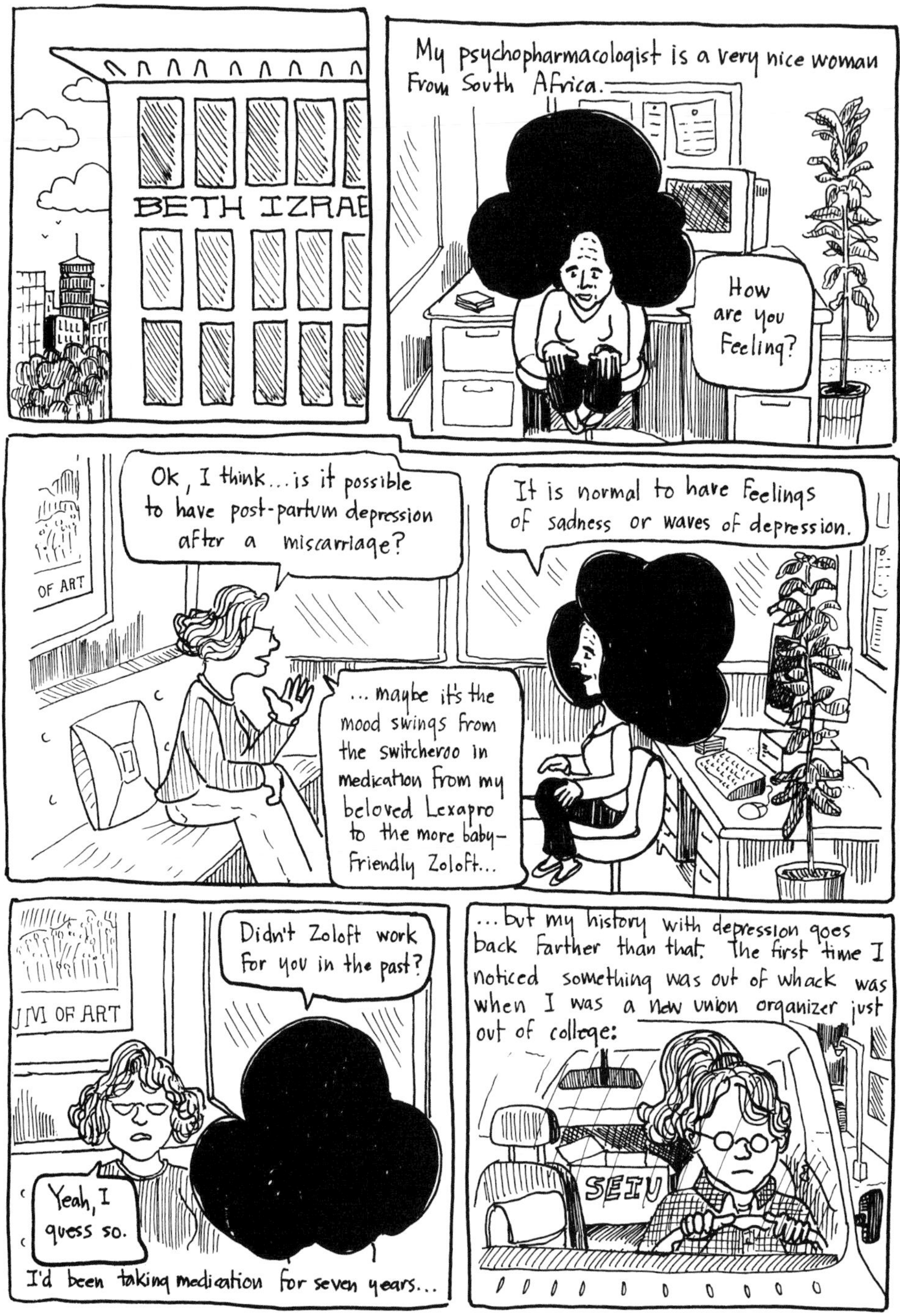
BETH IZRAE
My psychopharmacologist is a very nice woman From South Africa.
How are you Feeling?
OF ART
Ok, I think... is it possible to have post-partum depression after a miscarriage?
...maybe it's the mood swings from the switcheroo in medication from my beloved Lexapro to the more baby-Friendly Zoloft...
It is normal to have Feelings of sadness or waves of depression.
M OF ART
Didn't Zoloft work for you in the past?
Yeah, I guess so.
I'd been taking medication for seven years...
...but my history with depression goes back Farther than that. The first time I noticed something was out of whack was when I was a new union organizer just out of college:
SEIU

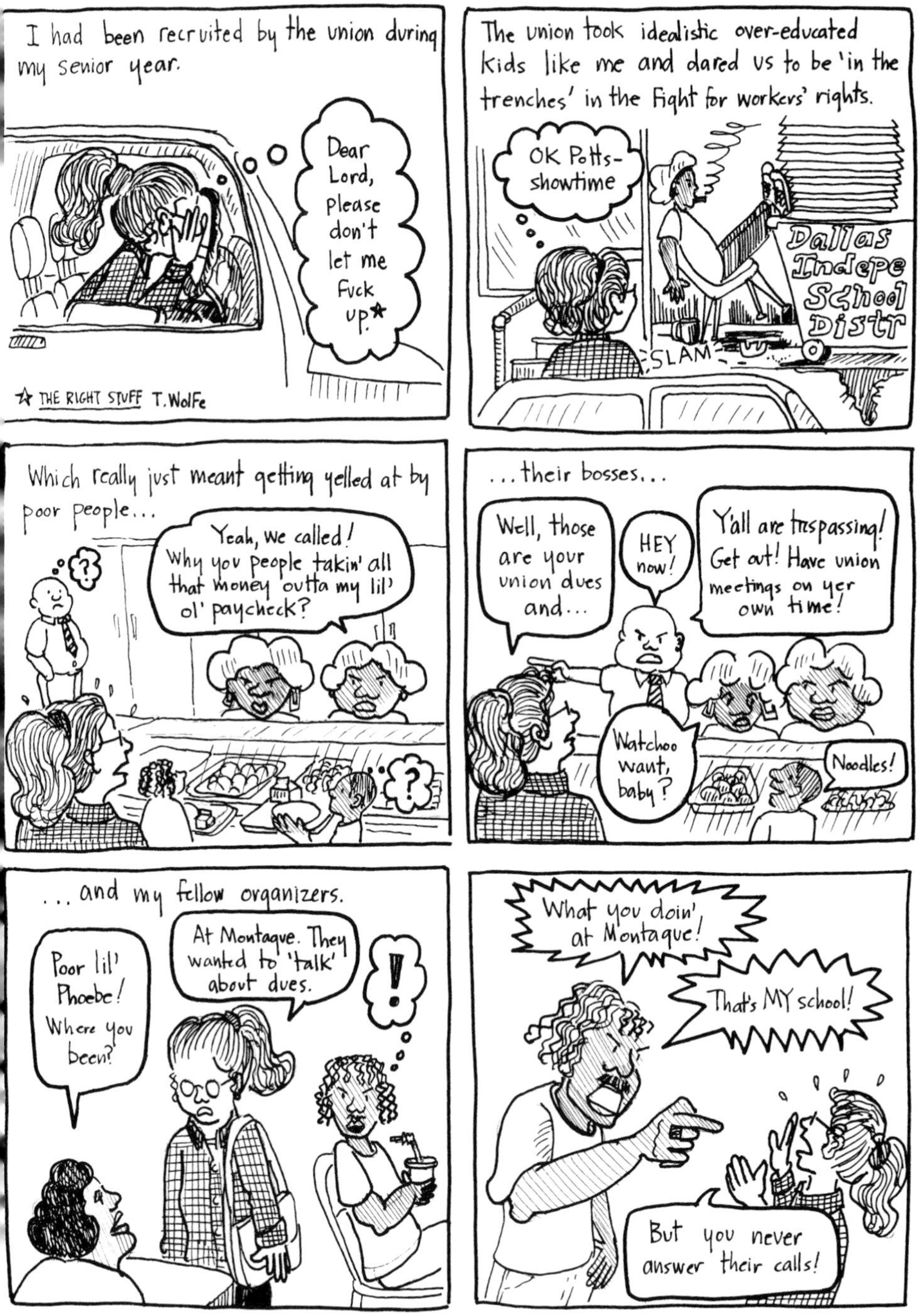
I had been recruited by the union during my senior year.
Dear Lord, please don't let me Fuck up.*
* THE RIGHT STUFF T. WolFe
The union took idealistic over-educated kids like me and dared us to be 'in the trenches' in the fight for workers' rights.
OK Potts-showtime
Dallas Indepe School Distr
SLAM
Which really just meant getting yelled at by poor people...
Yeah, we called! Why you people takin' all that money outta my lil' ol' paycheck?
?
?
...their bosses...
Well, those are your union dues and...
HEY now!
Y'all are trespassing! Get out! Have union meetings on yer own time!
Watchoo want, baby?
Noodles!
...and my fellow organizers.
Poor lil' Phoebe! Where you been?
At Montague. They wanted to 'talk' about dues.
!
What you doin' at Montague!
That's MY school!
But you never answer their calls!

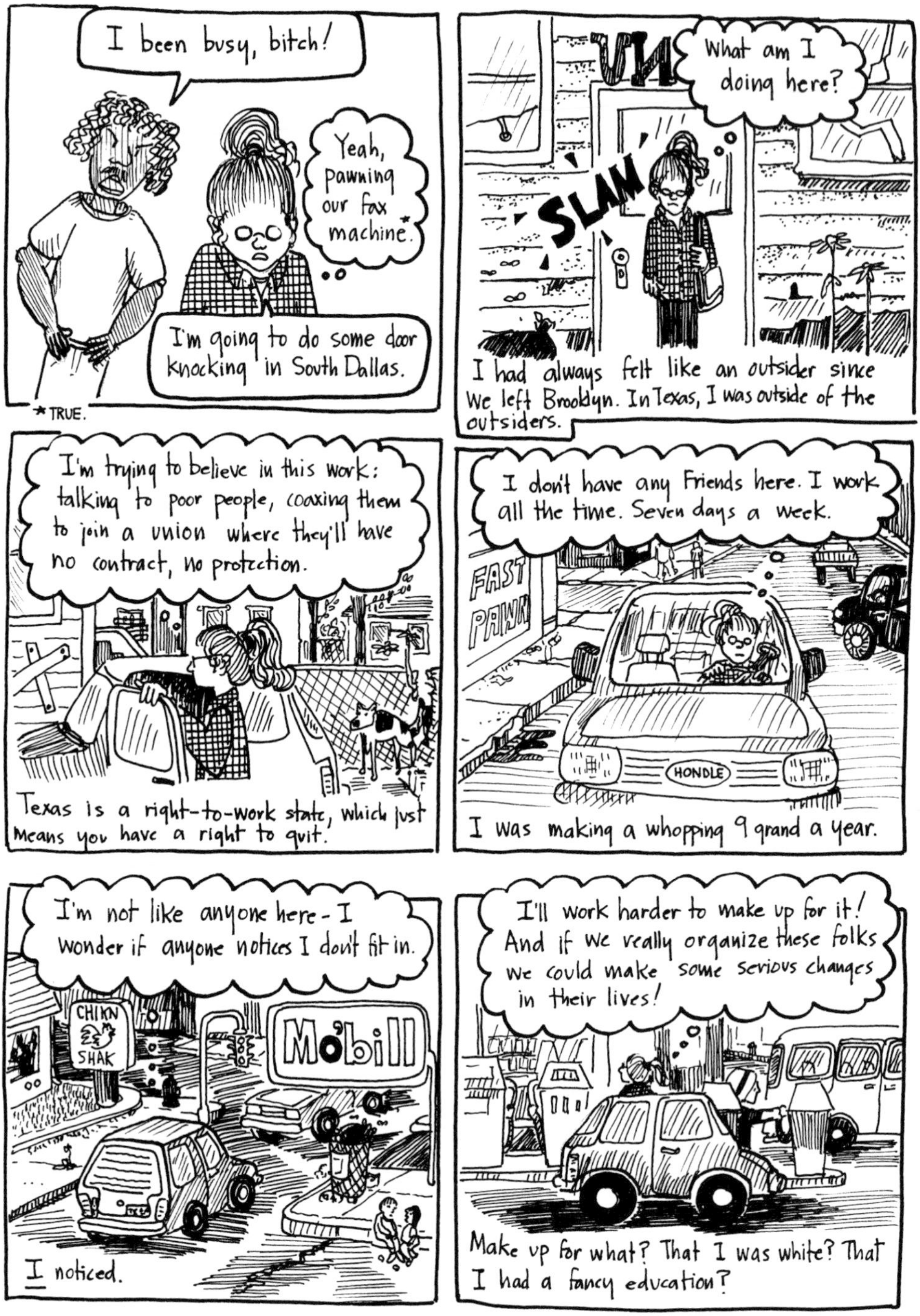
I been busy, bitch!
Yeah, pawning our fax machine.*
I'm going to do some door knocking in South Dallas.
*TRUE.
What am I doing here?
SLAM
I had always felt like an outsider since we left Brooklyn. In Texas, I was outside of the outsiders.
I'm trying to believe in this work: talking to poor people, coaxing them to join a union where they'll have no contract, no protection.
Texas is a right-to-work state, which just means you have a right to quit.
I don't have any friends here. I work all the time. Seven days a week.
FAST PAWN
HONDLE
I was making a whopping 9 grand a year.
I'm not like anyone here - I wonder if anyone notices I don't fit in.
CHIKN SHAK
Mobill
I noticed.
I'll work harder to make up for it! And if we really organize these folks we could make some serious changes in their lives!
Make up for what? That I was white? That I had a fancy education?

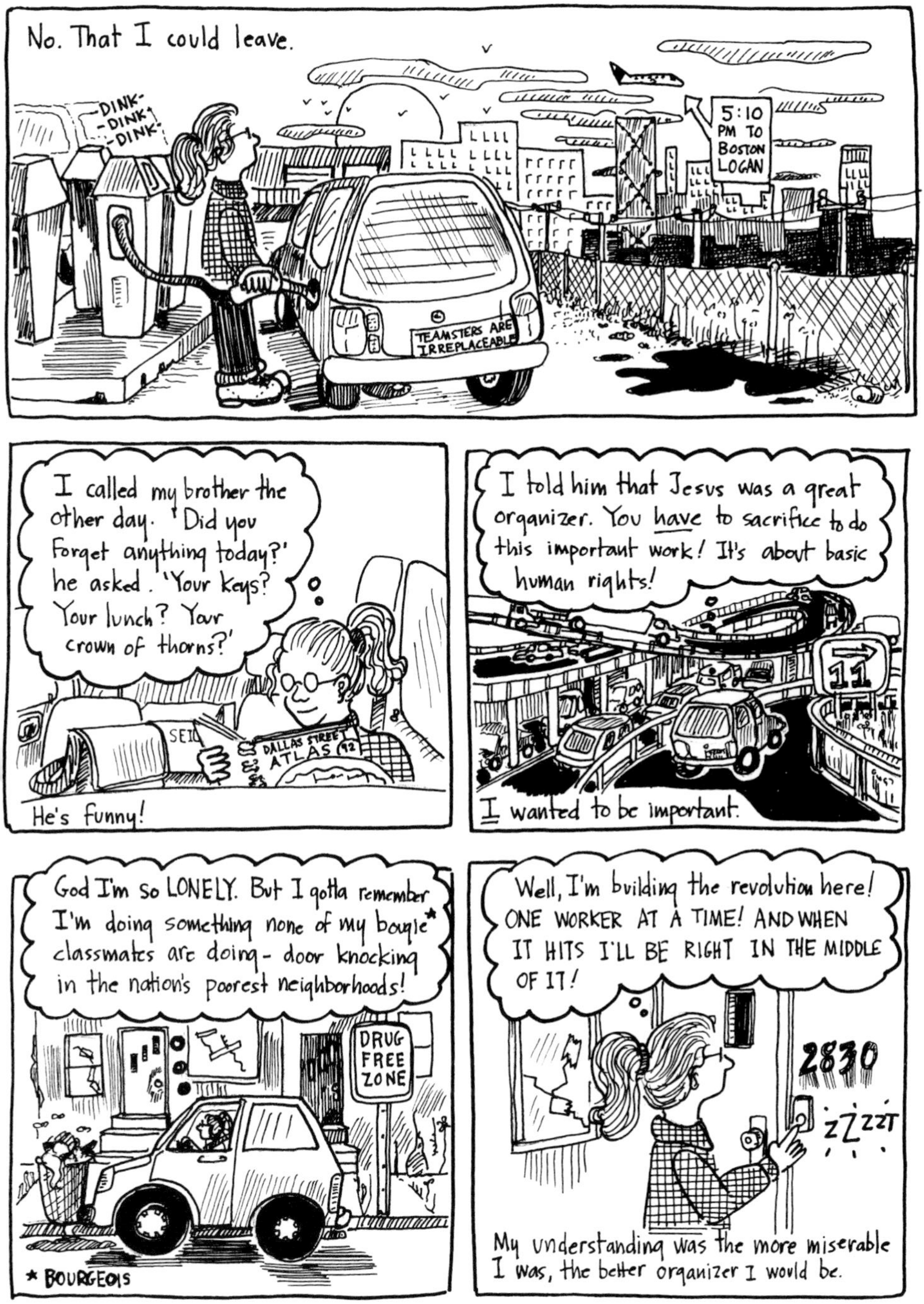

No. That I could leave.
-DINK-
-DINK-
-DINK-
5:10 PM TO BOSTON LOGAN
TEAMSTERS ARE IRREPLACEABLE
I called my brother the other day. 'Did you Forget anything today?' he asked. 'Your keys? Your lunch? Your crown of thorns?'
SEIU
DALLAS STREET ATLAS '92
He's funny!
I told him that Jesus was a great organizer. You have to sacrifice to do this important work! It's about basic human rights!
11
I wanted to be important.
God I'm so LONELY. But I gotta remember I'm doing something none of my bougie* classmates are doing - door knocking in the nation's poorest neighborhoods!
DRUG FREE ZONE
* BOURGEOIS
Well, I'm building the revolution here! ONE WORKER AT A TIME! AND WHEN IT HITS I'LL BE RIGHT IN THE MIDDLE OF IT!
2830
ZZZZT
My understanding was the more miserable I was, the better organizer I would be.

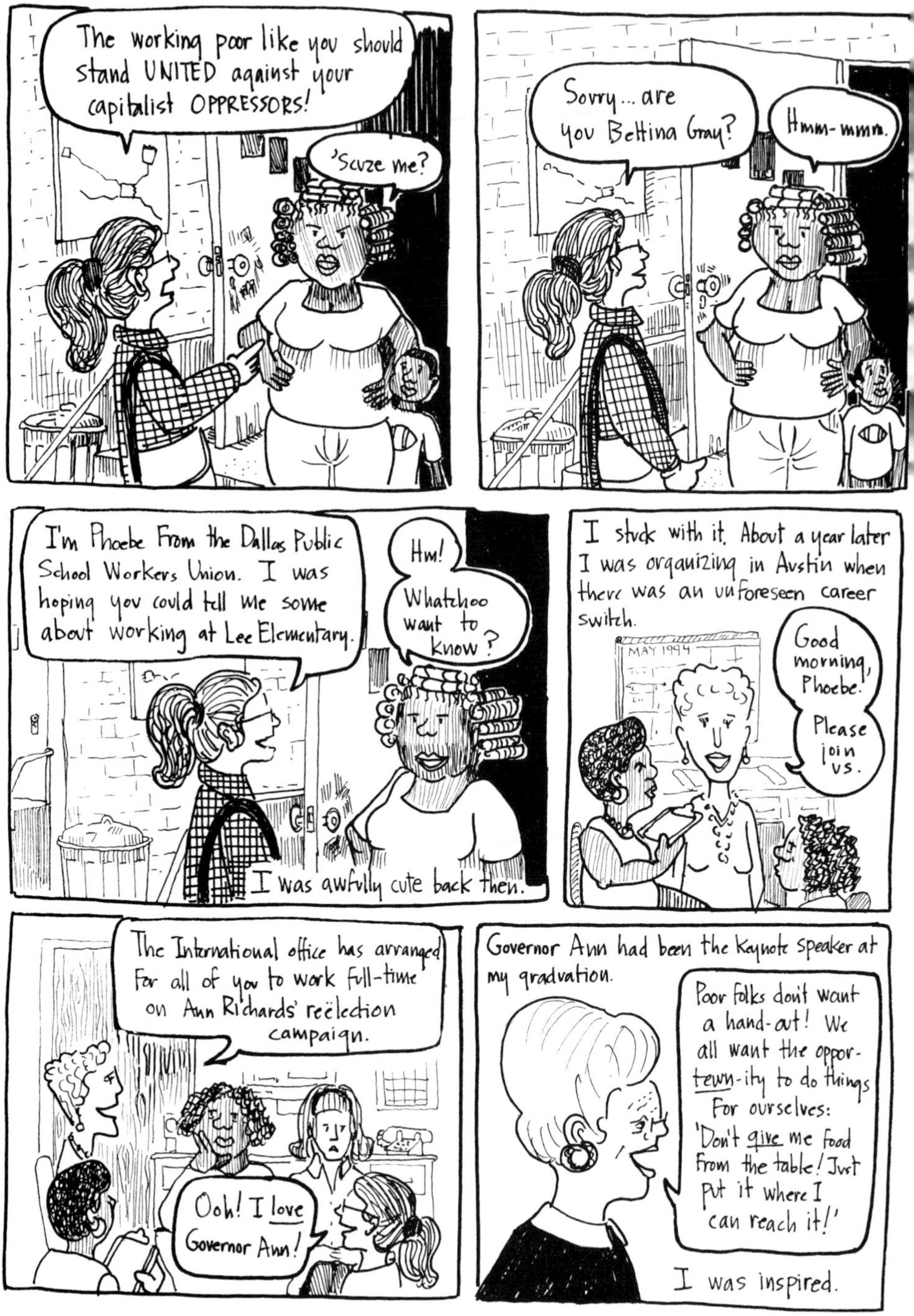
The working poor like you should stand UNITED against your capitalist OPPRESSORS!
'Scuze me?
Sorry... are you Bettina Gray?
Hmm-mmm.
I'm Phoebe from the Dallas Public School Workers Union. I was hoping you could tell me some about working at Lee Elementary.
Hm!
Whatchoo want to know?
I was awfully cute back then.
I stuck with it. About a year later I was organizing in Austin when there was an unforeseen career switch.
MAY 1994
Good morning, Phoebe.
Please join us.
The International office has arranged for all of you to work full-time on Ann Richards' reëlection campaign.
Ooh! I love Governor Ann!
Governor Ann had been the keynote speaker at my graduation.
Poor folks don't want a hand-out! We all want the oppor-tewn-ity to do things for ourselves: 'Don't give me food from the table! Just put it where I can reach it!'
I was inspired.

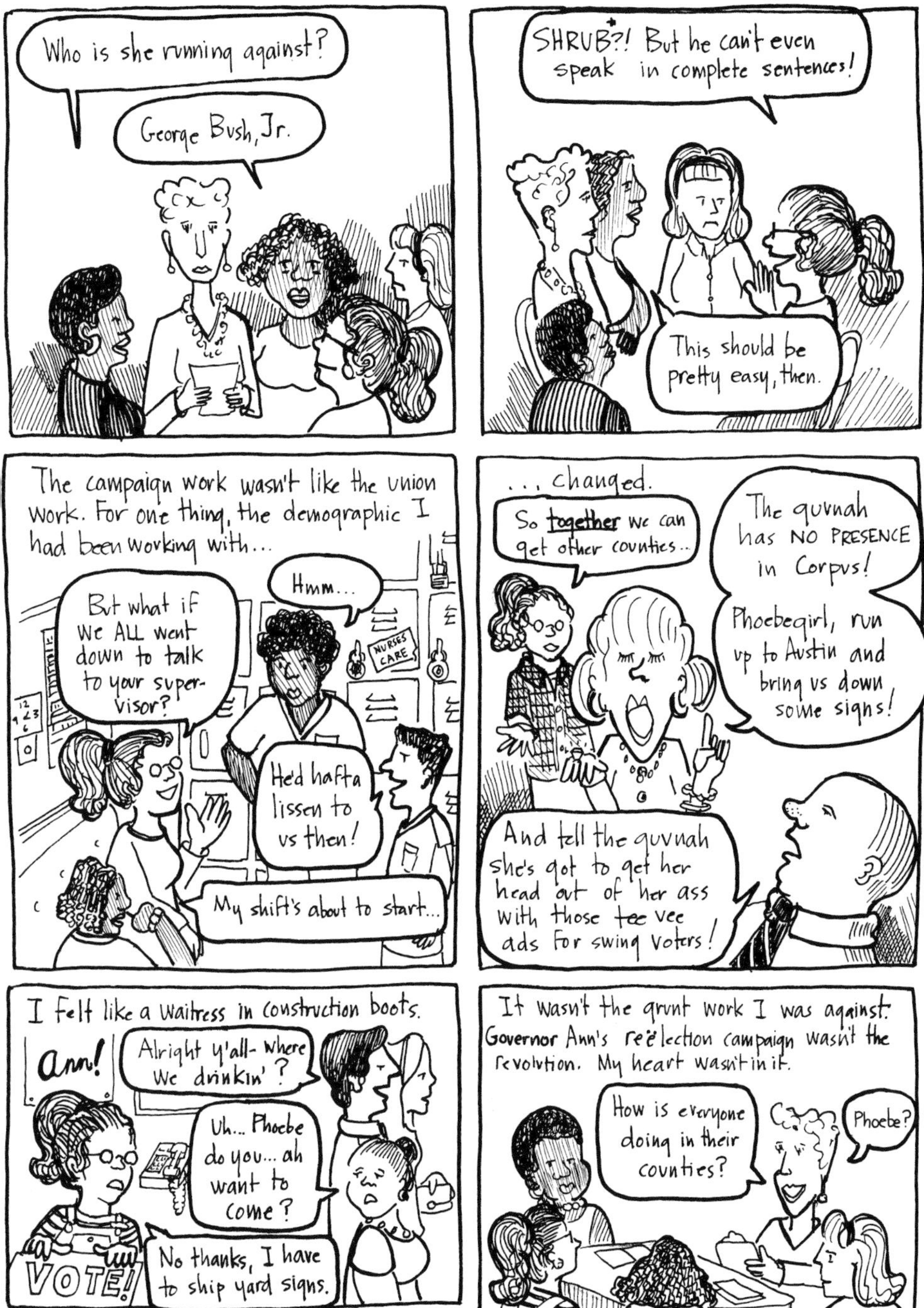
Who is she running against?
George Bush, Jr.
SHRUB?*! But he can't even speak in complete sentences!
This should be pretty easy, then.
The campaign work wasn't like the union work. For one thing, the demographic I had been working with...
But what if we ALL went down to talk to your supervisor?
Hmm...
NURSES CARE
He'd hafta lissen to us then!
My shift's about to start...
...changed.
So together we can get other counties...
The guvnah has NO PRESENCE in Corpus!
Phoebegirl, run up to Austin and bring us down some signs!
And tell the guvnah she's got to get her head out of her ass with those tee vee ads for swing voters!
I felt like a waitress in construction boots.
Ann!
Alright y'all- where we drinkin'?
Uh... Phoebe do you... ah want to come?
VOTE!
No thanks, I have to ship yard signs.
It wasn't the grunt work I was against. Governor Ann's reëlection campaign wasn't the revolution. My heart wasn't in it.
How is everyone doing in their counties?
Phoebe?

*MOLLY IVINS, Dallas Morning News ©1993

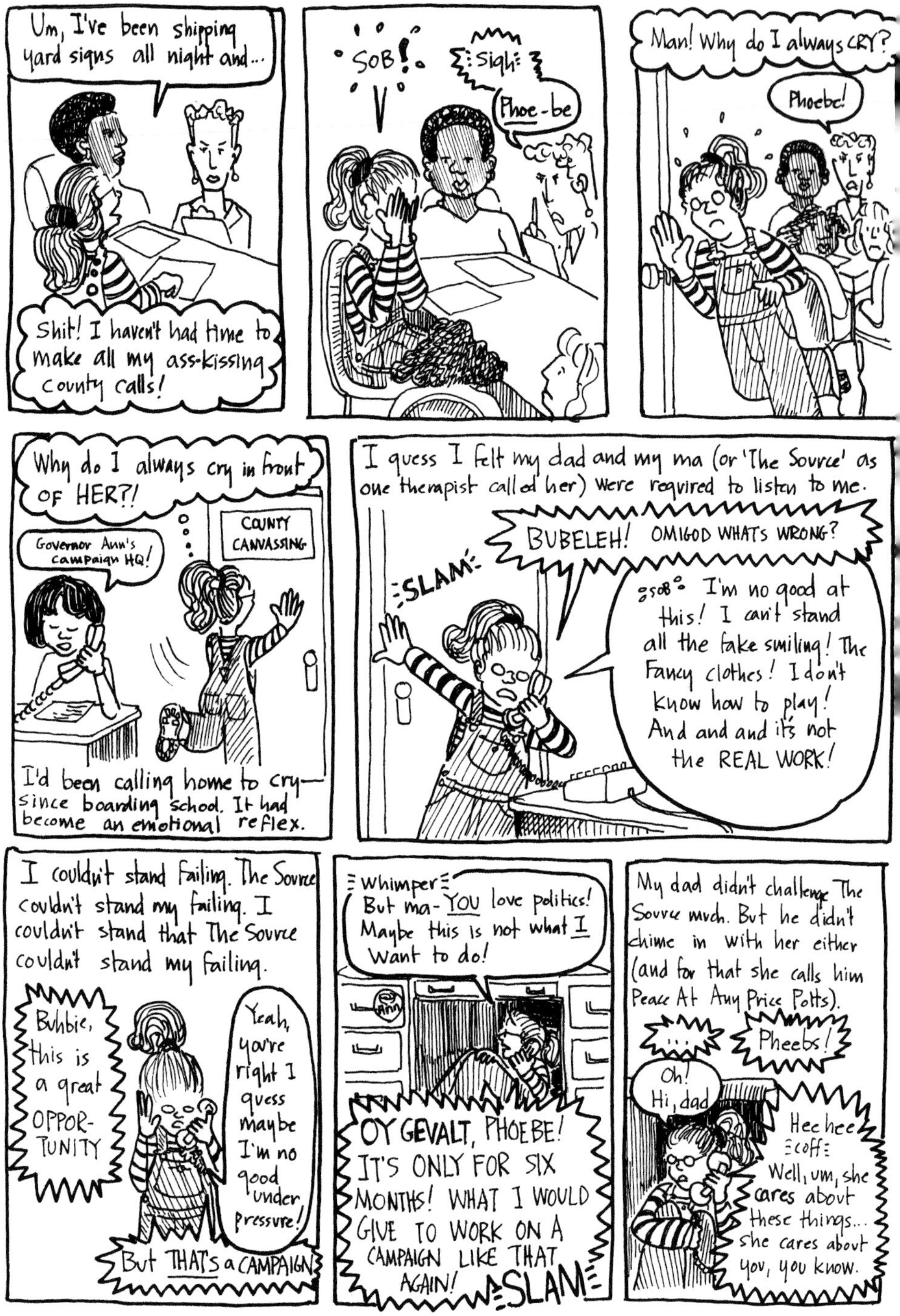
Um, I've been shipping yard signs all night and...
Shit! I haven't had time to make all my ass-kissing county calls!
SOB!
Sigh
Phoe-be
Man! Why do I always CRY?
Phoebe!
Why do I always cry in front OF HER?!
Governor Ann's campaign HQ!
COUNTY CANVASSING
I'd been calling home to cry—since boarding school. It had become an emotional reflex.
I guess I felt my dad and my ma (or 'The Source' as one therapist called her) were required to listen to me.
BUBELEH! OMIGOD WHATS WRONG?
SLAM
SOB I'm no good at this! I can't stand all the fake smiling! The Fancy clothes! I don't know how to play! And and and it's not the REAL WORK!
I couldn't stand failing. The Source couldn't stand my failing. I couldn't stand that The Source couldn't stand my failing.
Bubbie, this is a great OPPORTUNITY
Yeah, you're right I guess maybe I'm no good under pressure!
But THAT'S a CAMPAIGN
Whimper But ma- YOU love politics! Maybe this is not what I want to do!
OY GEVALT, PHOEBE! IT'S ONLY FOR SIX MONTHS! WHAT I WOULD GIVE TO WORK ON A CAMPAIGN LIKE THAT AGAIN!
SLAM
My dad didn't challenge The Source much. But he didn't chime in with her either (and for that she calls him Peace At Any Price Potts).
...
Pheebs!
Oh! Hi, dad
Hee hee coff Well, um, she cares about these things... she cares about you, you know.

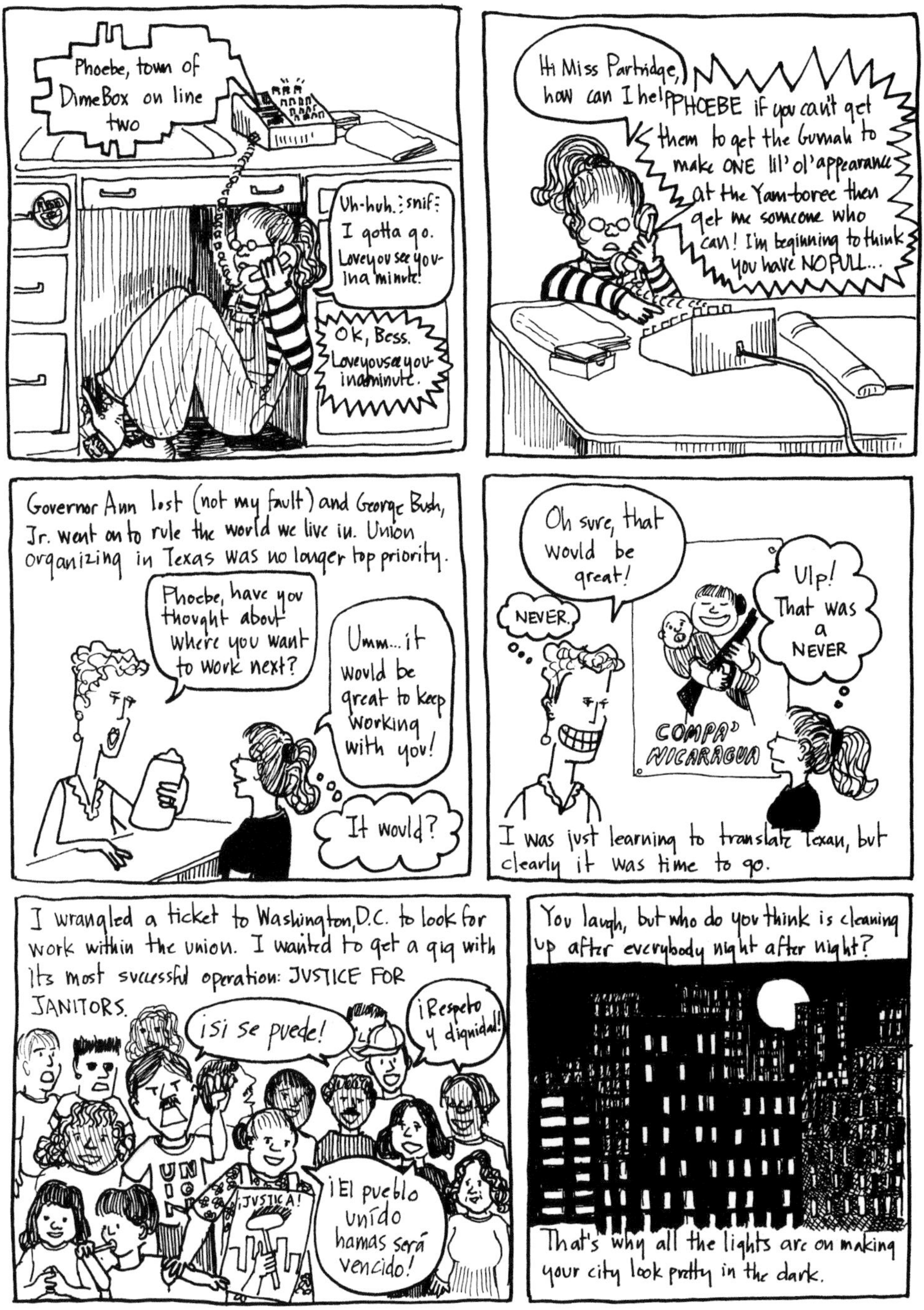
Phoebe, town of DimeBox on line two
Uh-huh. snif I gotta go. Loveyou see you-ina minute.
Ok, Bess. Loveyousee you-inaminute.
Hi Miss Partridge, how can I hel
PHOEBE if you can't get them to get the Guvnah to make ONE lil' ol' appearance at the Yam-boree then get me someone who can! I'm beginning to think you have NO PULL...
Governor Ann lost (not my fault) and George Bush, Jr. went on to rule the world we live in. Union organizing in Texas was no longer top priority.
Phoebe, have you thought about where you want to work next?
Umm... it would be great to keep working with you!
It would?
Oh sure, that would be great!
NEVER.
Ulp! That was a NEVER
NICARAGUA
I was just learning to translate Texan, but clearly it was time to go.
I wrangled a ticket to Washington, D.C. to look for work within the union. I wanted to get a gig with its most successful operation: JUSTICE FOR JANITORS.
¡Si se puede!
¡Respeto y dignidad!
¡JUSTICA!
¡El pueblo unido hamas será vencido!
You laugh, but who do you think is cleaning up after everybody night after night?
That's why all the lights are on making your city look pretty in the dark.

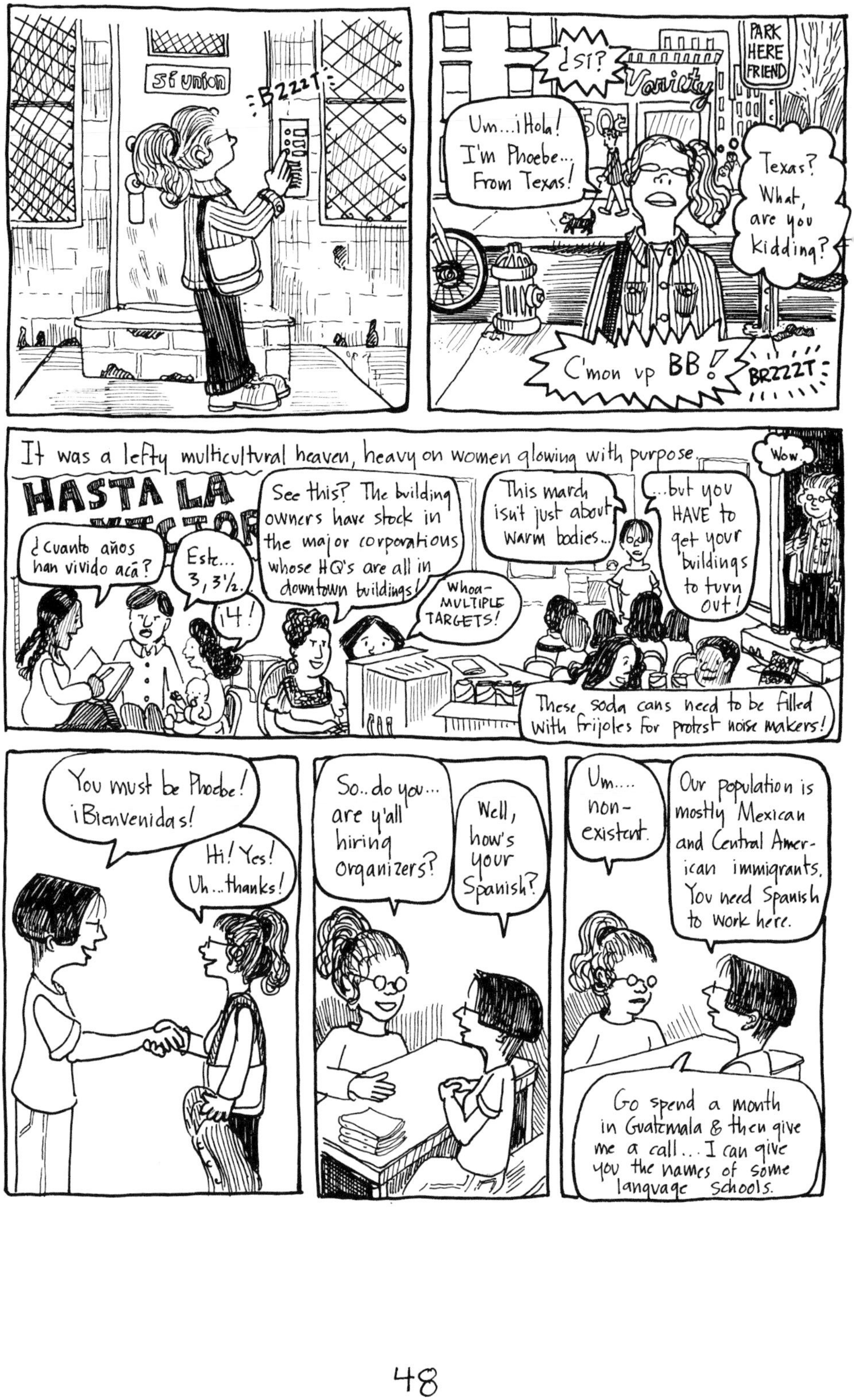

BZZZT
¿SÍ?
PARK HERE FRIEND
Variety
50¢
Um...¡Hola! I'm Phoebe... From Texas!
Texas? What, are you kidding?
C'mon up BB!
BRZZZT
It was a lefty multicultural heaven, heavy on women glowing with purpose.
Wow.
HASTA LA
¿Cuanto años han vivido acá?
Este... 3, 3½.
14!
See this? The building owners have stock in the major corporations whose HQ's are all in downtown buildings!
Whoa- MULTIPLE TARGETS!
This march isn't just about warm bodies...
...but you HAVE to get your buildings to turn out!
These soda cans need to be filled with frijoles for protest noise makers!
You must be Phoebe! ¡Bienvenidas!
Hi! Yes! Uh...thanks!
So..do you... are y'all hiring organizers?
Well, how's your Spanish?
Um.... non-existent.
Our population is mostly Mexican and Central American immigrants. You need Spanish to work here.
Go spend a month in Guatemala & then give me a call... I can give you the names of some language schools.

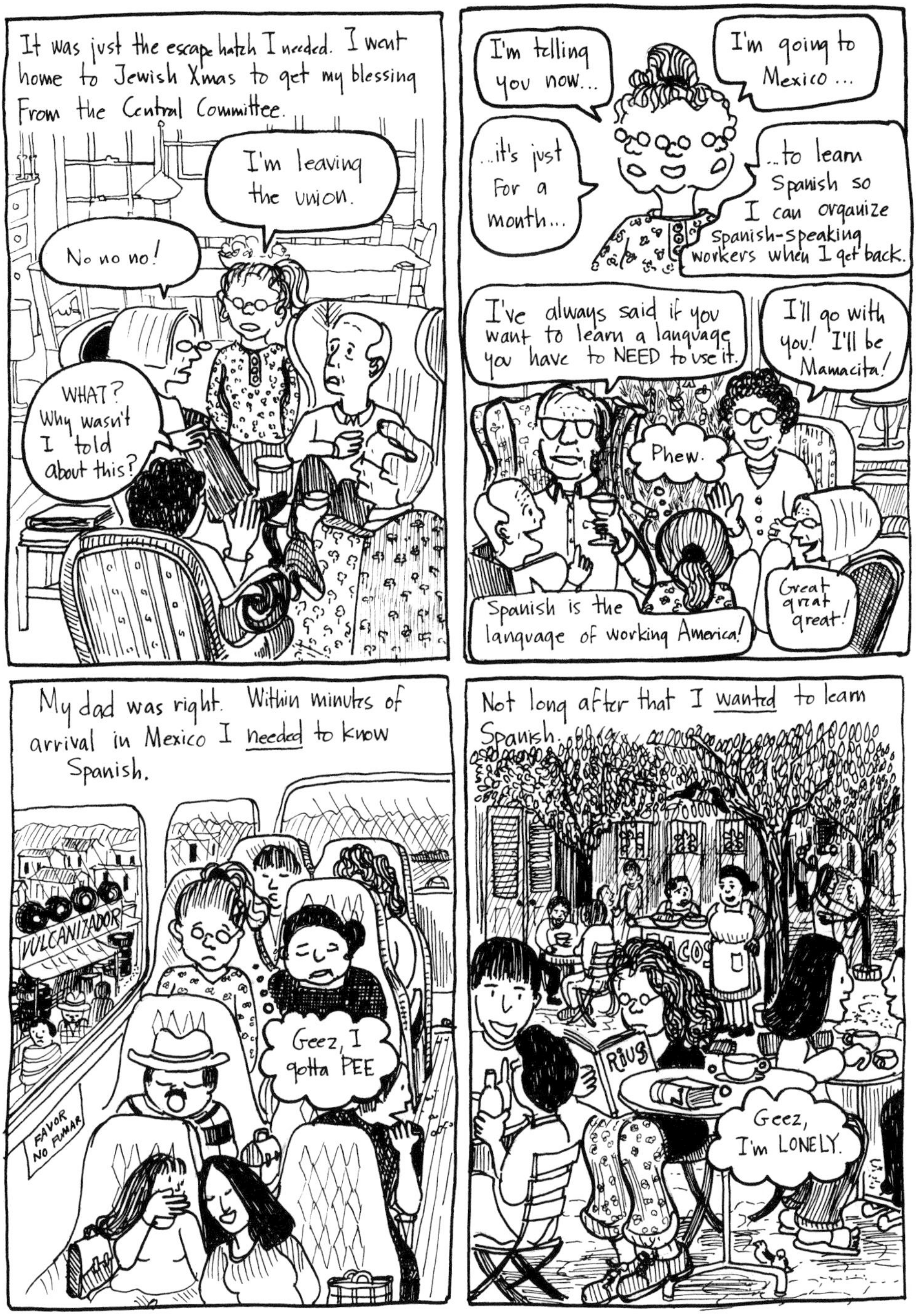
It was just the escape hatch I needed. I went home to Jewish Xmas to get my blessing from the Central Committee.
I'm leaving the union.
No no no!
WHAT? Why wasn't I told about this?
I'm telling you now...
I'm going to Mexico...
...it's just for a month...
...to learn Spanish so I can organize Spanish-speaking workers when I get back.
I've always said if you want to learn a language you have to NEED to use it.
I'll go with you! I'll be Mamacita!
Phew.
Spanish is the language of working America!
Great great great!
My dad was right. Within minutes of arrival in Mexico I needed to know Spanish.
VULCANIZADOR
FAVOR NO FUMAR
Geez, I gotta PEE
Not long after that I wanted to learn Spanish.
RIUS
Geez, I'm LONELY.

I made my own Personal Peace Corps. I studied at a local university.

SABER
FIJAR
CONOCER

Yo sé
Tu sabes
Ella sabe

I lived in a boarding house with Mexican students.

Wow- gringa can EAT!

I 'taught' kids to read in a village school.

...¿y que es esto?

¡Un Pavo!

<How come teacher doesn't know what a duck is?>

I worked on a farm.

¡Vamanos Fee-Vee!

I did make some nice friends.

But mostly I was alone.

Months passed and I stopped calling the union.

I was grateful I could draw. It made me some fast company...

<A fish!>

<A bike!>

<Draw me a dog!>

...and it gave me a reason to be anywhere, looking closely at where I was. It was the only time I didn't feel in limbo.

RECUERDA-ME

VOTA

Just before I arrived in Mexico, there had been a bike-sized uprising in Chiapas state.

el proceso

TOMA
Fanta

SUB-COMANDANTE
MARCOS: intransigente

Phoebe?

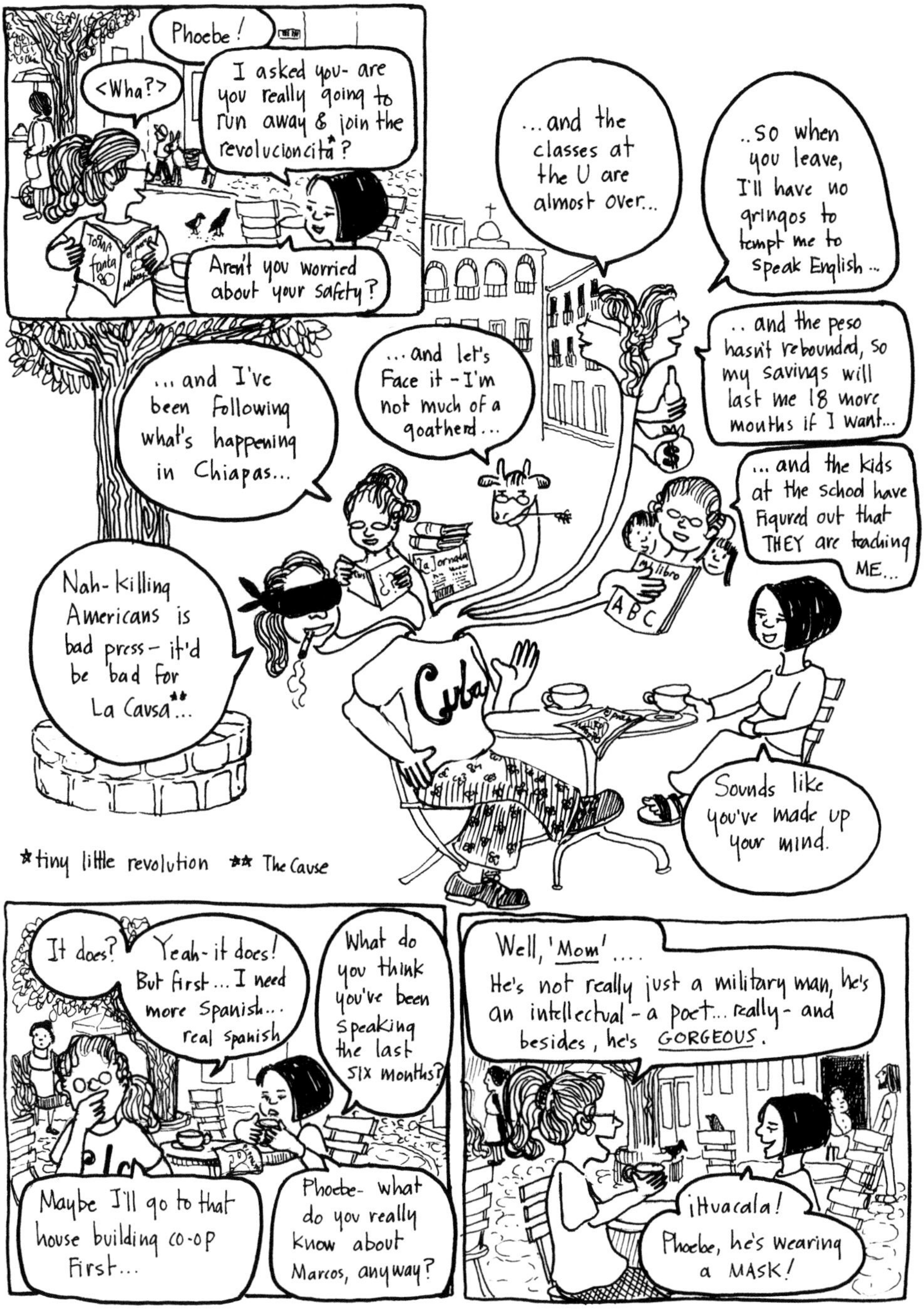
Phoebe!
<Wha?>
I asked you- are you really going to run away & join the revoluciončita*?
Aren't you worried about your safety?
...and the classes at the U are almost over...
..so when you leave, I'll have no gringos to tempt me to speak English...
...and I've been following what's happening in Chiapas...
...and let's face it - I'm not much of a goatherd...
.. and the peso hasn't rebounded, so my savings will last me 18 more months if I want...
...and the kids at the school have figured out that THEY are teaching ME...
Nah-killing Americans is bad press - it'd be bad for La Causa**...
Sounds like you've made up your mind.
*tiny little revolution ** The Cause
It does?
Yeah-it does! But first... I need more Spanish... real Spanish
What do you think you've been speaking the last six months?
Maybe I'll go to that house building co-op first...
Phoebe- what do you really know about Marcos, anyway?
Well, 'Mom'.... He's not really just a military man, he's an intellectual - a poet... really- and besides, he's GORGEOUS.
¡Huacala! Phoebe, he's wearing a MASK!

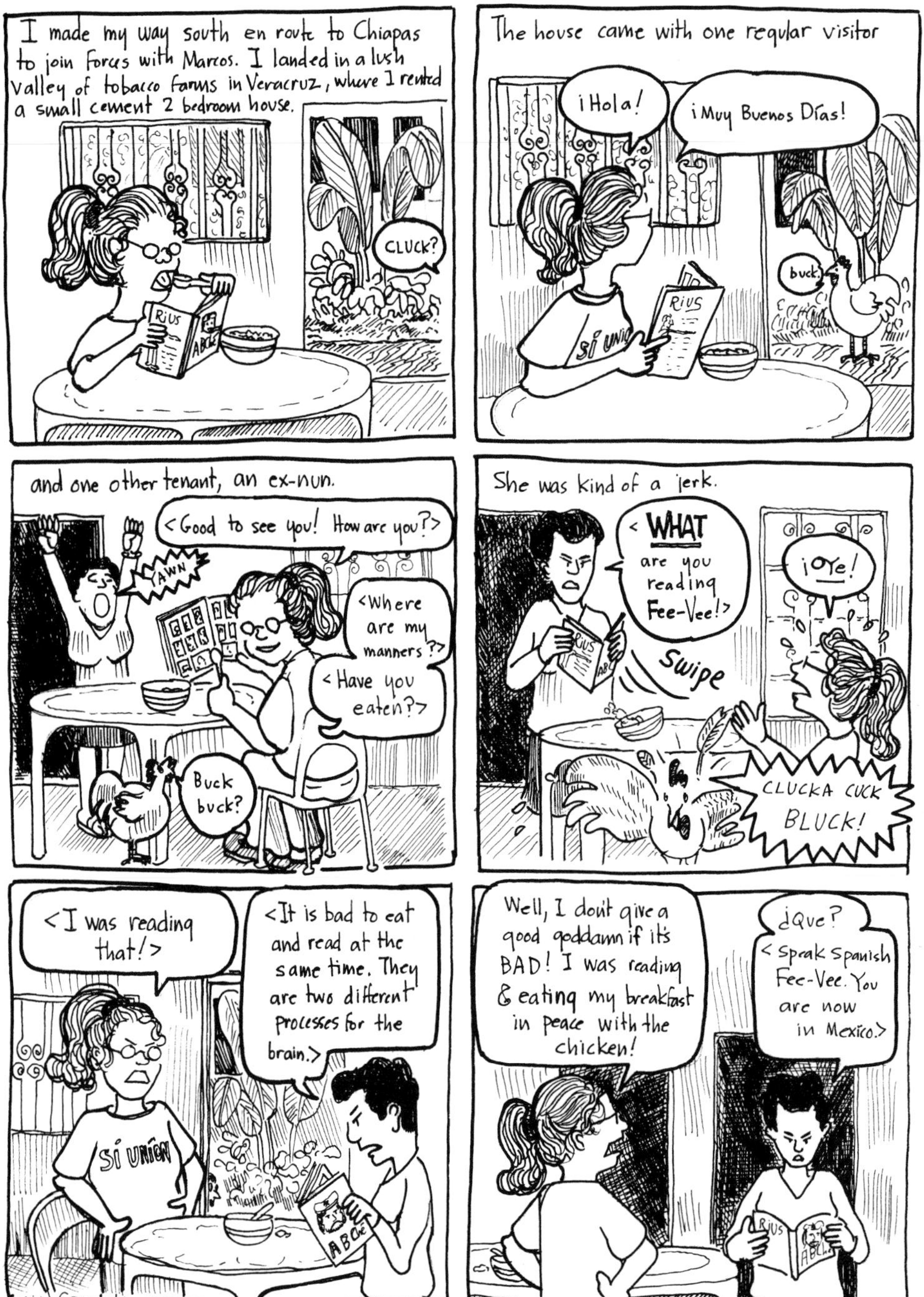
I made my way south en route to Chiapas to join forces with Marcos. I landed in a lush valley of tobacco farms in Veracruz, where I rented a small cement 2 bedroom house.
CLUCK?
RIUS
ABC
The house came with one regular visitor
¡Hola!
¡Muy Buenos Días!
buck.
RIUS
SÍ UNIÓN
and one other tenant, an ex-nun.
<Good to see you! How are you?>
YAWN
<Where are my manners?>
<Have you eaten?>
Buck buck?
She was kind of a jerk.
< WHAT are you reading Fee-Vee!>
¡Oye!
SWIPE
CLUCKA CUCK BLUCK!
<I was reading that!>
<It is bad to eat and read at the same time. They are two different processes for the brain.>
SÍ UNIÓN
ABChe
<in Spanish>
Well, I don't give a good goddamn if it's BAD! I was reading & eating my breakfast in peace with the chicken!
¿Que?
< Speak Spanish Fee-Vee. You are now in Mexico.>
RIUS
ABChe

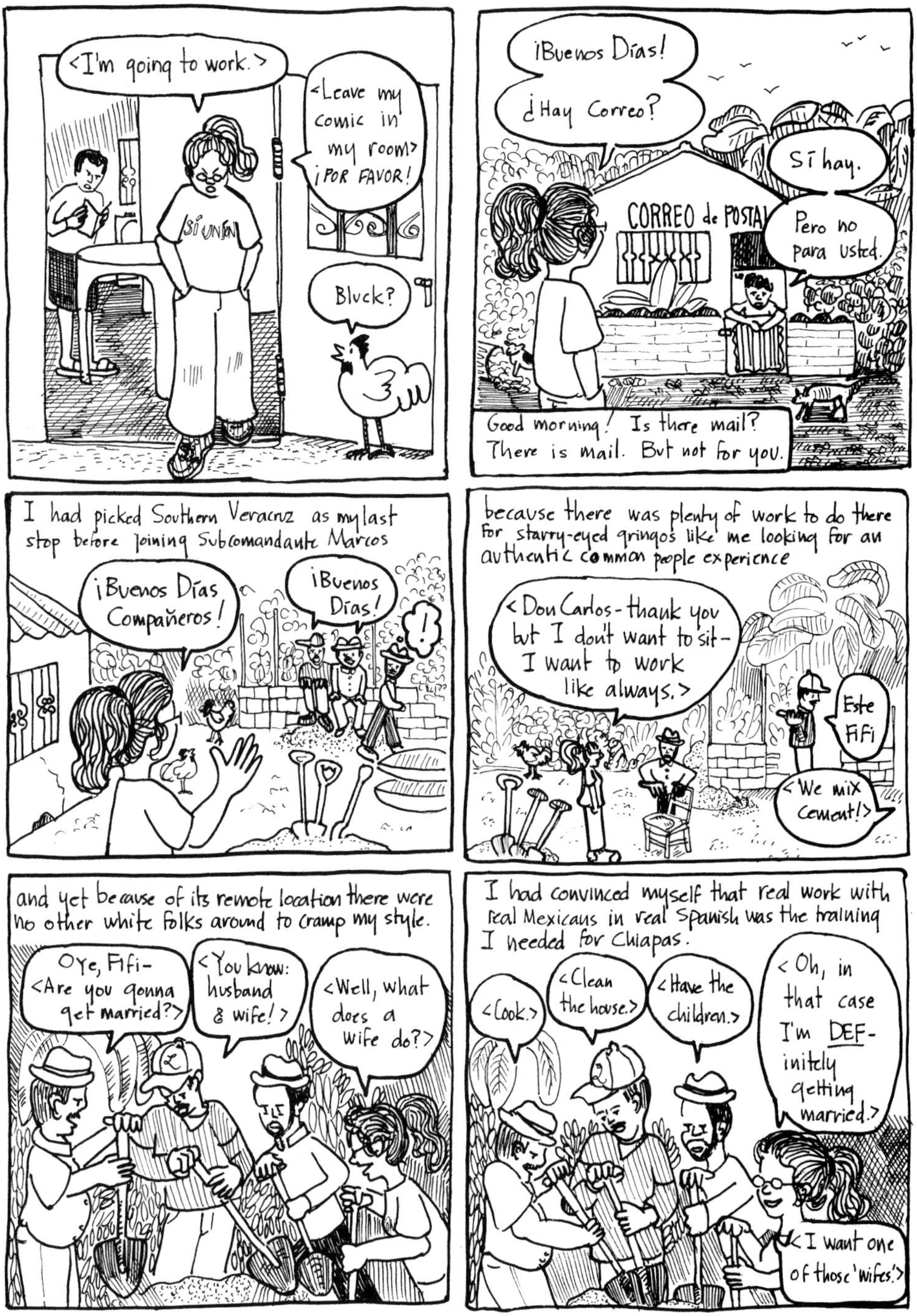

<I'm going to work.>
<Leave my comic in my room> ¡POR FAVOR!
Bluck?
SÍ UNION
¡Buenos Días!
¿Hay Correo?
Sí hay.
Pero no para usted.
CORREO de POSTAL
Good morning! Is there mail? There is mail. But not for you.
I had picked Southern Veracruz as my last stop before joining Subcomandante Marcos
¡Buenos Días Compañeros!
¡Buenos Días!
!
because there was plenty of work to do there for starry-eyed gringos like me looking for an authentic common people experience
<Don Carlos - thank you but I don't want to sit - I want to work like always.>
Este FiFi
<We mix Cement!>
and yet because of its remote location there were no other white folks around to cramp my style.
Oye, Fifi - <Are you gonna get married?>
<You know: husband & wife!>
<Well, what does a wife do?>
I had convinced myself that real work with real Mexicans in real Spanish was the training I needed for Chiapas.
<Cook.>
<Clean the house.>
<Have the children.>
<Oh, in that case I'm DEF-initely getting married.>
<I want one of those 'wifes.'>

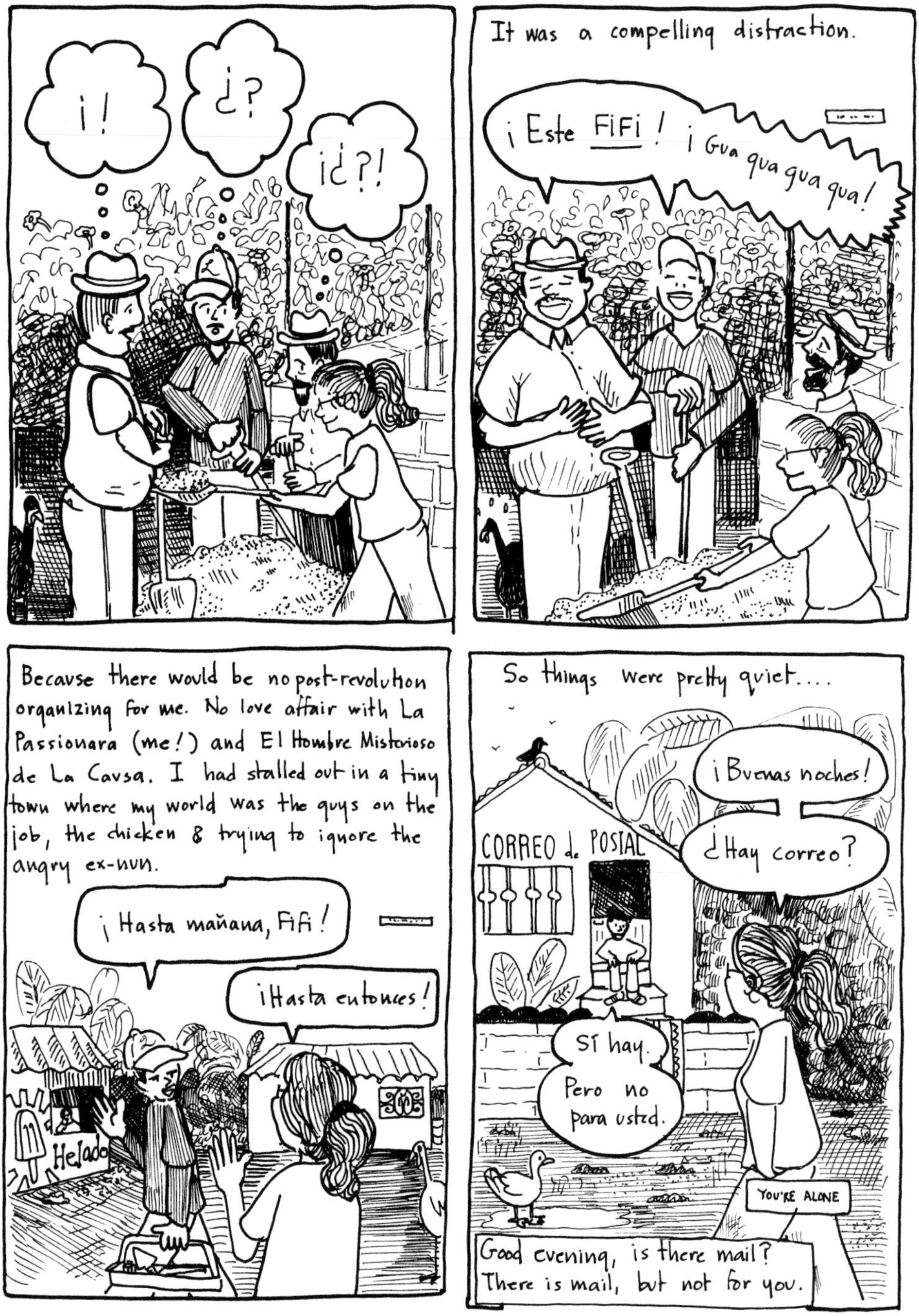
¡!
¿?
¡¿?!
It was a compelling distraction.
¡Este FIFI!
¡Gua qua gua qua!
Because there would be no post-revolution organizing for me. No love affair with La Passionara (me!) and El Hombre Misterioso de La Causa. I had stalled out in a tiny town where my world was the guys on the job, the chicken & trying to ignore the angry ex-nun.
¡Hasta mañana, Fifi!
¡Hasta entonces!
Helado
So things were pretty quiet....
CORREO de POSTAL
¡Buenas noches!
¿Hay correo?
Sí hay.
Pero no para usted.
YOU'RE ALONE
Good evening, is there mail?
There is mail, but not for you.

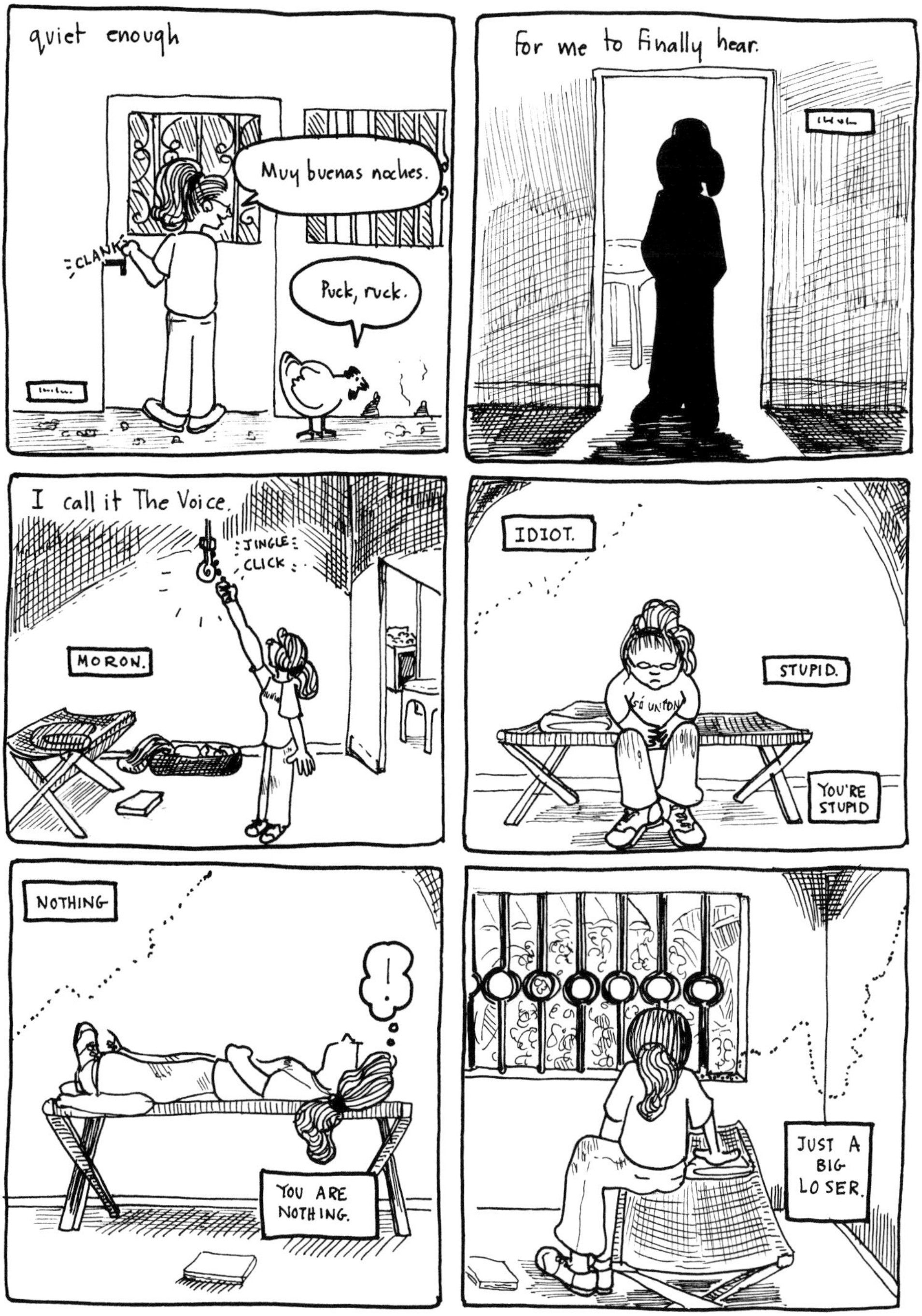
quiet enough
CLANK
Muy buenas noches.
Puck, ruck.
for me to finally hear.
I call it The Voice.
JINGLE
CLICK
MORON.
IDIOT.
STUPID.
YOU'RE STUPID
NOTHING
!
YOU ARE NOTHING.
JUST A BIG LOSER.

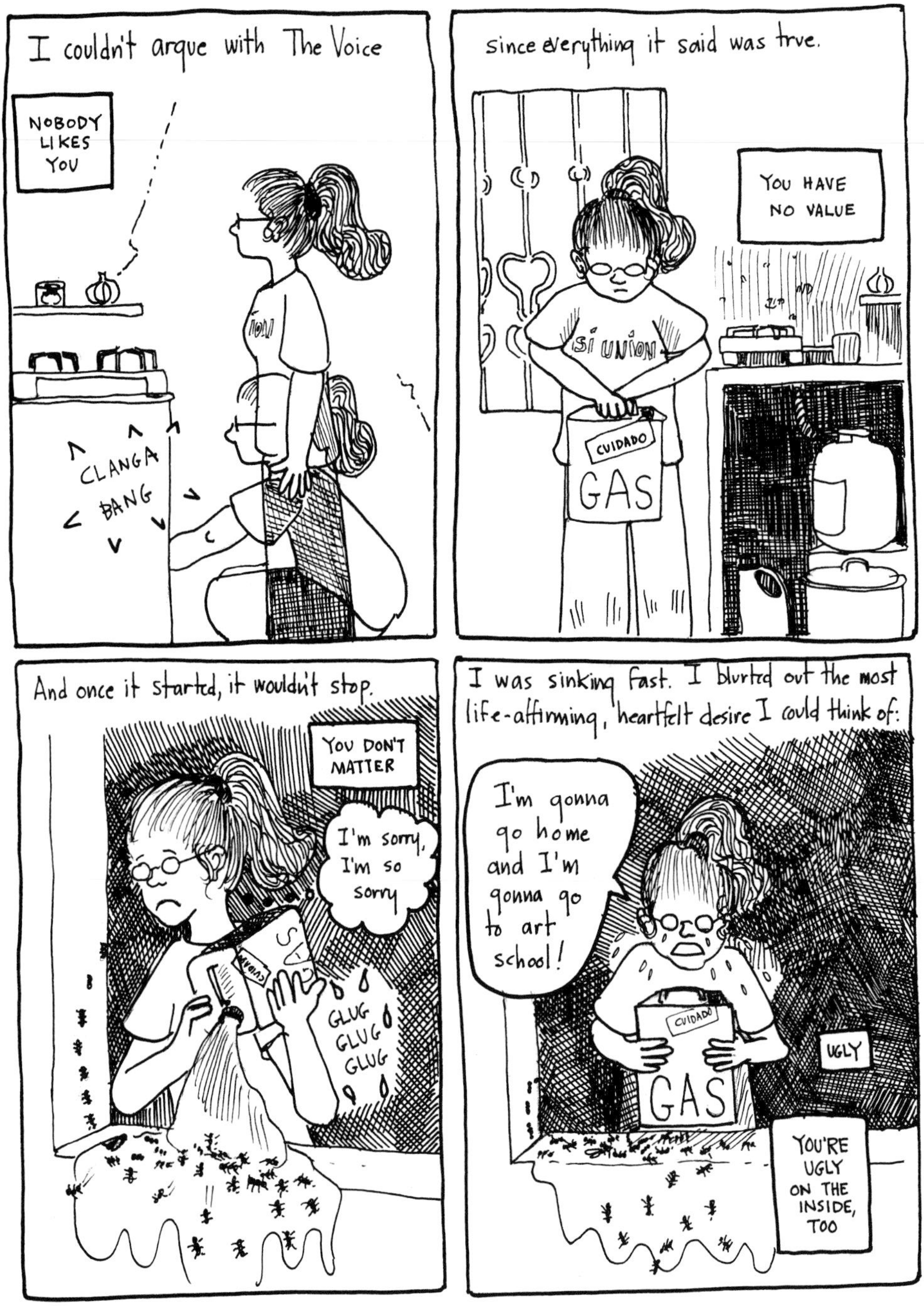
I couldn't argue with The Voice
NOBODY LIKES YOU
CLANGA BANG
since everything it said was true.
YOU HAVE NO VALUE
SÍ UNIÓN
CUIDADO
GAS
And once it started, it wouldn't stop.
YOU DON'T MATTER
I'm sorry, I'm so sorry
GLUG GLUG GLUG
I was sinking fast. I blurted out the most life-affirming, heartfelt desire I could think of:
I'm gonna go home and I'm gonna go to art school!
CUIDADO
GAS
UGLY
YOU'RE UGLY ON THE INSIDE, TOO

I didn't make it to Chiapas. A year after leaving the union, I was heading north to go home, being led into the abyss by The Voice.

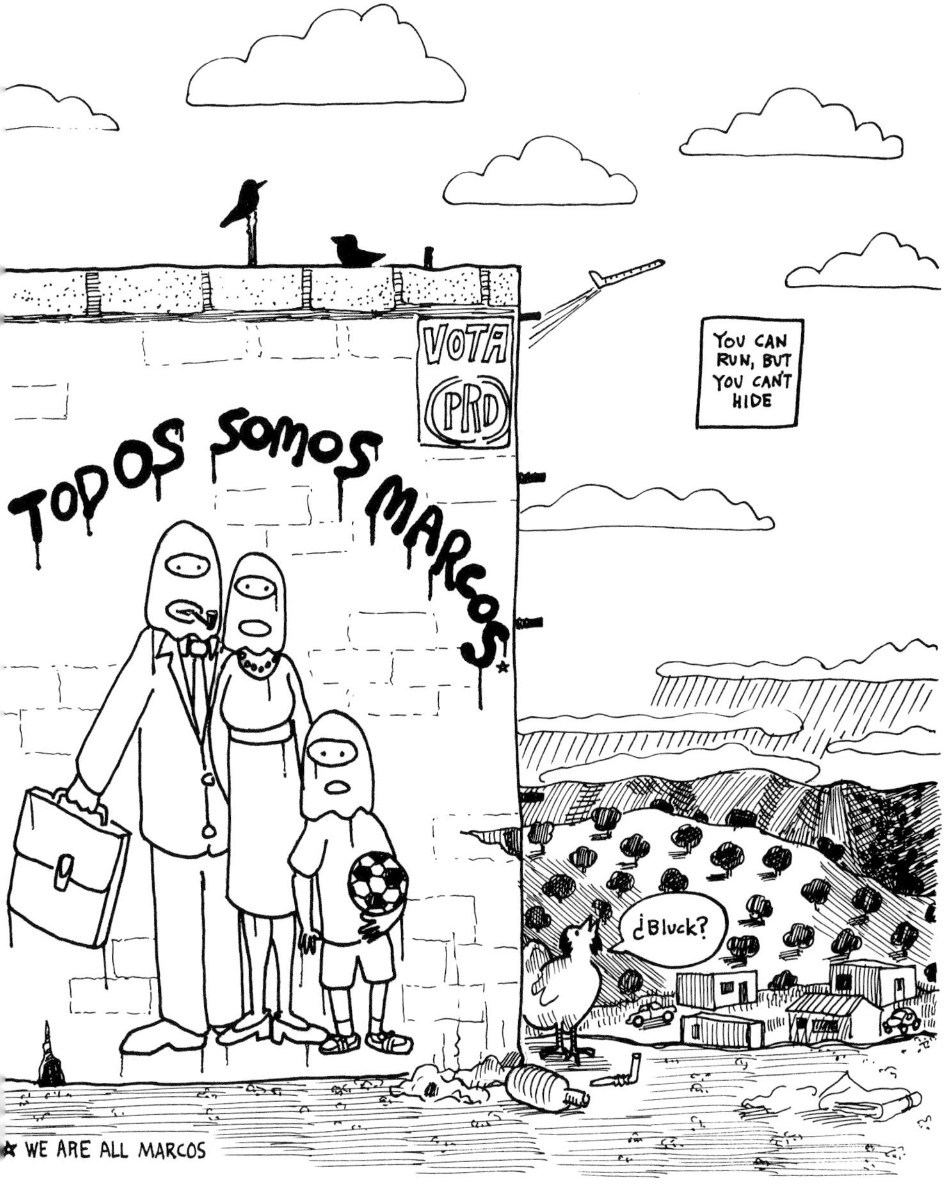
VOTA
PRD
YOU CAN RUN, BUT YOU CAN'T HIDE
TODOS SOMOS MARCOS*
¿Bluck?
* WE ARE ALL MARCOS

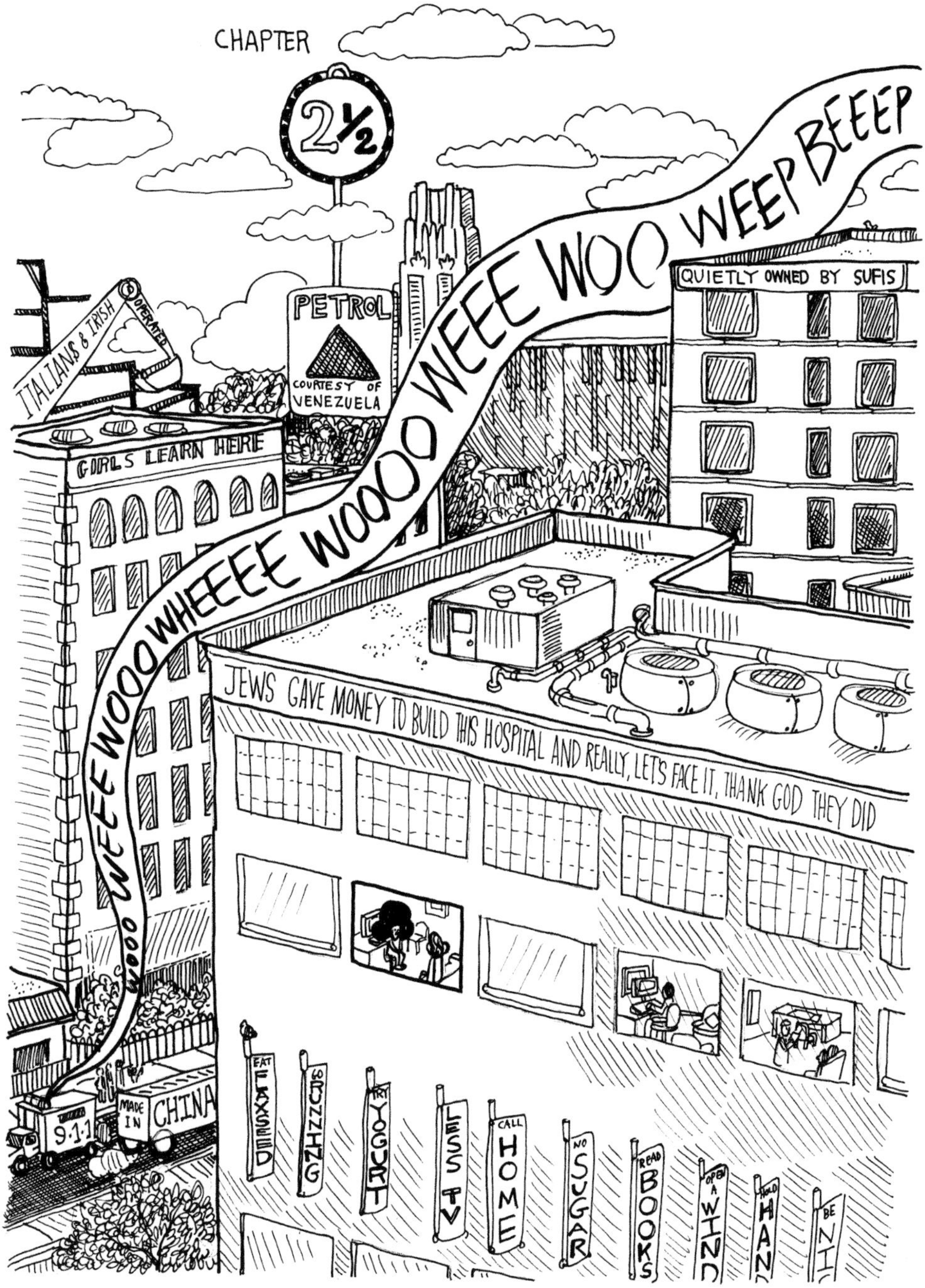
CHAPTER
2½
PETROL
COURTESY OF VENEZUELA
ITALIANS & IRISH OPERATED
GIRLS LEARN HERE
QUIETLY OWNED BY SUFIS
WOOO WEEEWOOOWHEEEE WOOOO WEEE WOO WEEP BEEEP
JEWS GAVE MONEY TO BUILD THIS HOSPITAL AND REALLY, LET'S FACE IT, THANK GOD THEY DID
9·1·1
MADE IN CHINA
EAT FLAXSEED
GO RUNNING
TRY YOGURT
LESS TV
CALL HOME
NO SUGAR
READ BOOKS
OPEN A WIND
HOLD HAN
BE NI

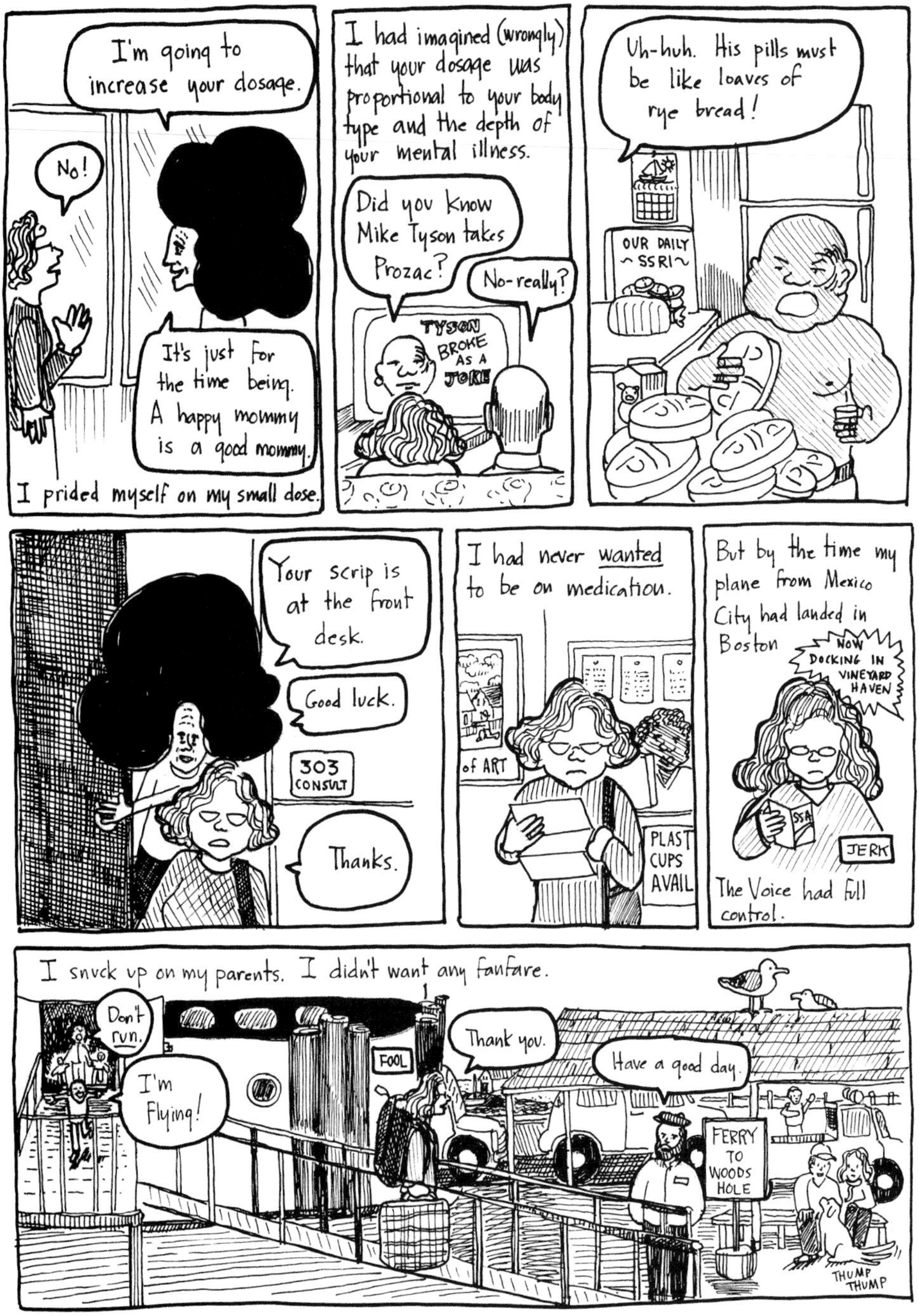
I'm going to increase your dosage.
No!
It's just for the time being. A happy mommy is a good mommy.
I prided myself on my small dose.
I had imagined (wrongly) that your dosage was proportional to your body type and the depth of your mental illness.
Did you know Mike Tyson takes Prozac?
No-really?
TYSON BROKE AS A JOKE
Uh-huh. His pills must be like loaves of rye bread!
OUR DAILY ~SSRI~
Your scrip is at the front desk.
Good luck.
303 CONSULT
Thanks.
I had never wanted to be on medication.
of ART
PLAST CUPS AVAIL
But by the time my plane from Mexico City had landed in Boston
NOW DOCKING IN VINEYARD HAVEN
SSA
JERK
The Voice had full control.
I snuck up on my parents. I didn't want any fanfare.
Don't run.
I'm Flying!
FOOL
Thank you.
Have a good day.
FERRY TO WOODS HOLE
THUMP THUMP

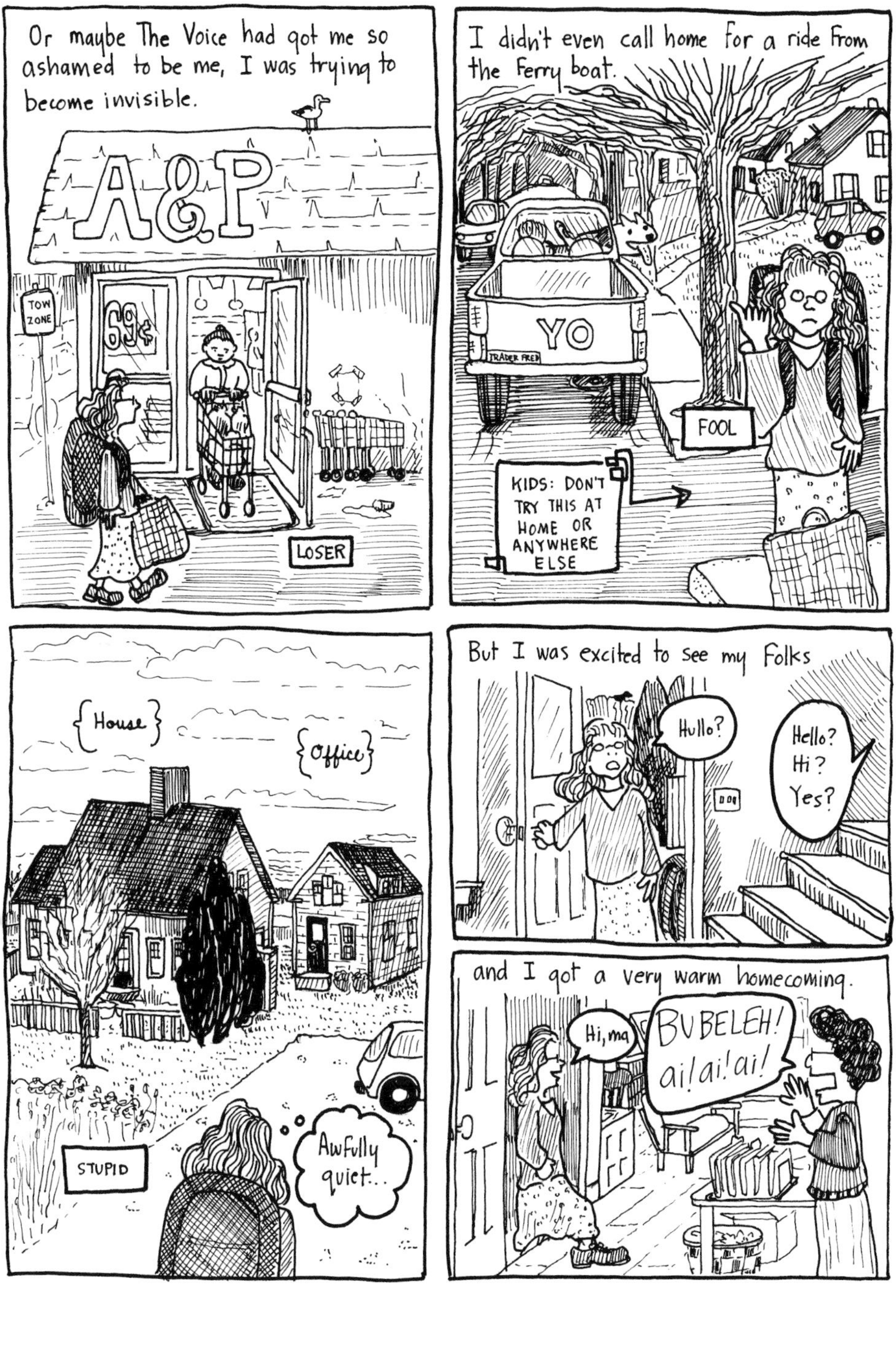
Or maybe The Voice had got me so ashamed to be me, I was trying to become invisible.
A&P
69¢
TOW ZONE
LOSER
I didn't even call home for a ride from the Ferry boat.
YO
TRADER FRED
FOOL
KIDS: DON'T TRY THIS AT HOME OR ANYWHERE ELSE
House
Office
STUPID
Awfully quiet...
But I was excited to see my folks
Hullo?
Hello? Hi? Yes?
and I got a very warm homecoming.
Hi, ma
BUBELEH! ai! ai! ai!

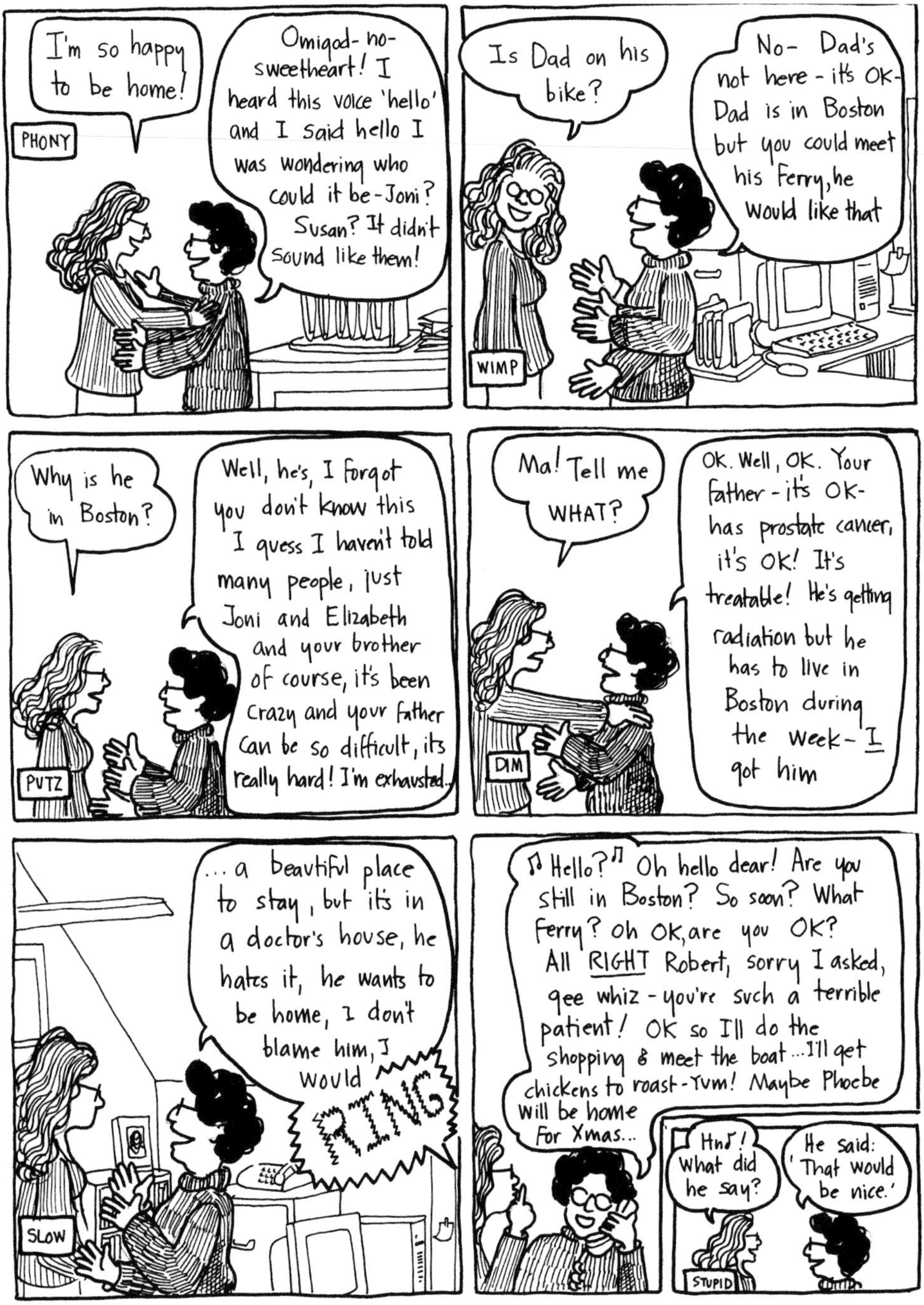
I'm so happy to be home!
PHONY
Omigod- no- sweetheart! I heard this voice 'hello' and I said hello I was wondering who could it be-Joni? Susan? It didn't sound like them!
Is Dad on his bike?
No- Dad's not here - it's OK- Dad is in Boston but you could meet his Ferry, he would like that
WIMP
Why is he in Boston?
Well, he's, I forgot you don't know this I guess I haven't told many people, just Joni and Elizabeth and your brother of course, it's been crazy and your father can be so difficult, its really hard! I'm exhausted...
PUTZ
Ma! Tell me WHAT?
OK. Well, OK. Your father - it's OK- has prostate cancer, it's OK! It's treatable! He's getting radiation but he has to live in Boston during the week - I got him
DIM
... a beautiful place to stay, but it's in a doctor's house, he hates it, he wants to be home, I don't blame him, I would
RING
SLOW
♫ Hello? ♫ Oh hello dear! Are you still in Boston? So soon? What Ferry? oh OK, are you OK? All RIGHT Robert, sorry I asked, gee whiz - you're such a terrible patient! OK so I'll do the shopping & meet the boat ... I'll get chickens to roast - Yum! Maybe Phoebe will be home For Xmas...
Hn♪! What did he say?
He said: 'That would be nice.'
STUPID

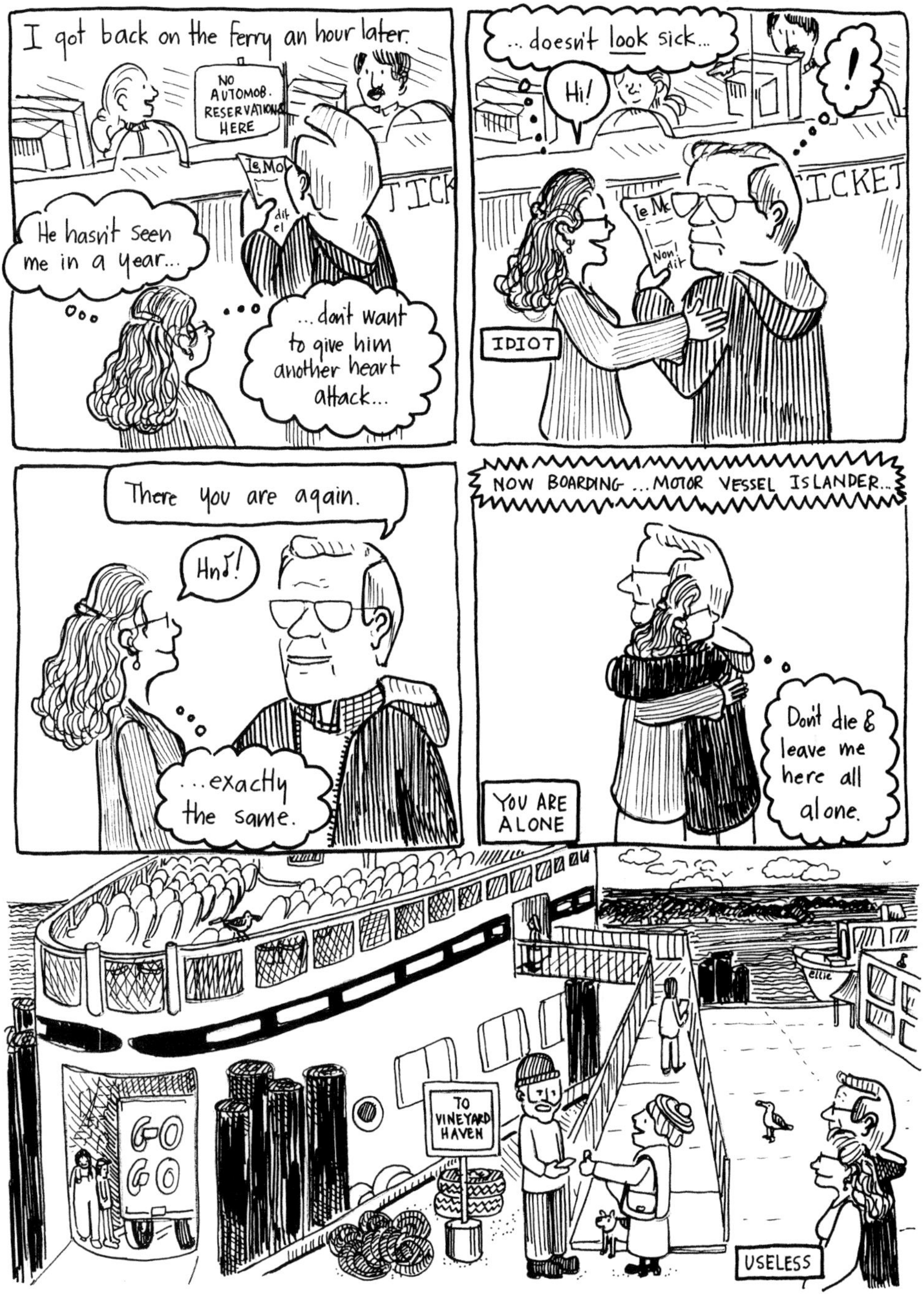
I got back on the ferry an hour later.
NO AUTOMOB. RESERVATIONS HERE
He hasn't seen me in a year...
...don't want to give him another heart attack...
...doesn't look sick...
Hi!
!
IDIOT
There you are again.
Hnd!
...exactly the same.
NOW BOARDING ...MOTOR VESSEL ISLANDER...
YOU ARE ALONE
Don't die & leave me here all alone.
GO GO
TO VINEYARD HAVEN
USELESS

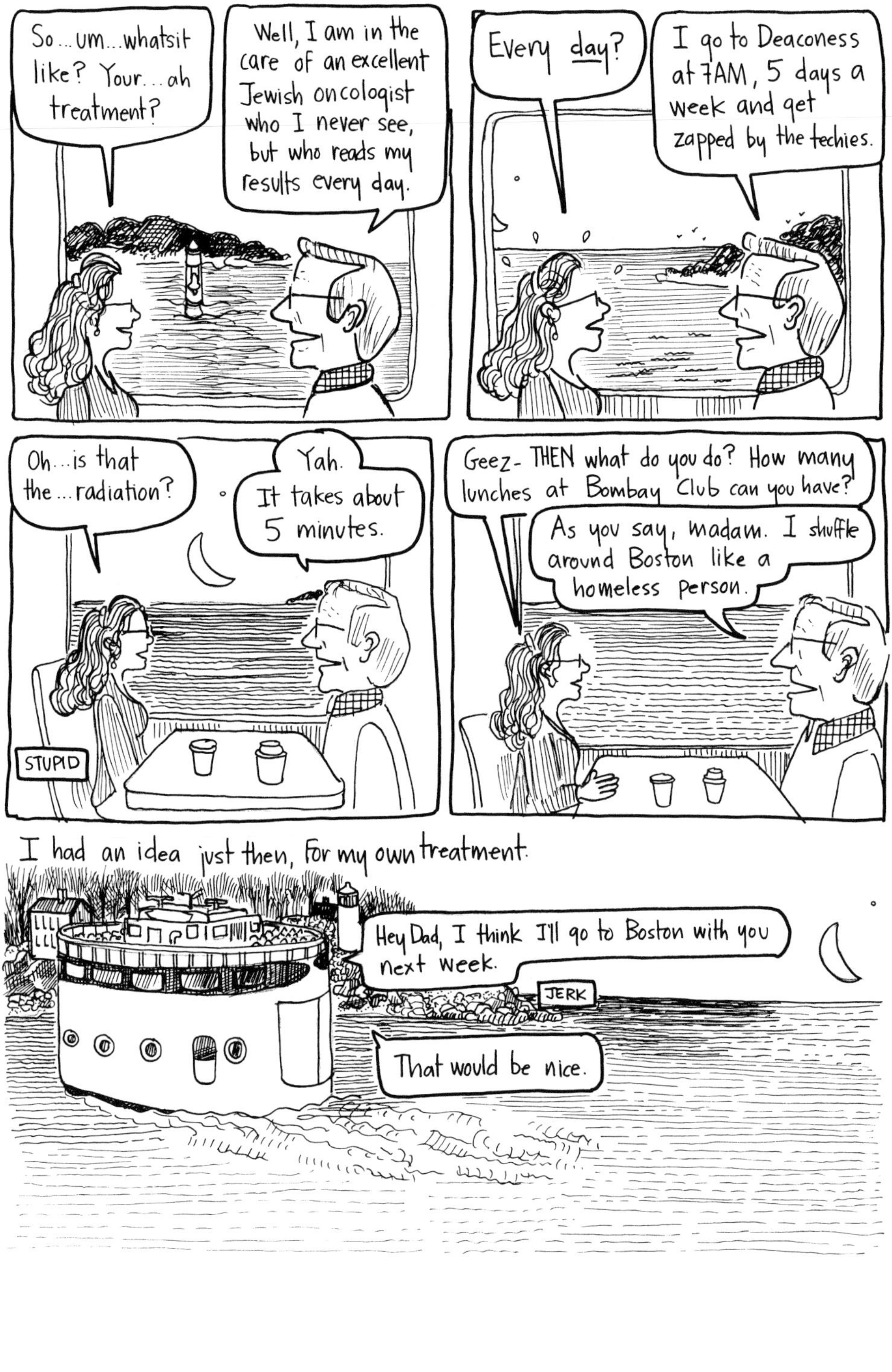
So...um...whatsit like? Your...ah treatment?
Well, I am in the care of an excellent Jewish oncologist who I never see, but who reads my results every day.
Every day?
I go to Deaconess at 7AM, 5 days a week and get zapped by the techies.
Oh...is that the...radiation?
Yah. It takes about 5 minutes.
STUPID
Geez- THEN what do you do? How many lunches at Bombay Club can you have?
As you say, madam. I shuffle around Boston like a homeless person.
I had an idea just then, for my own treatment.
Hey Dad, I think I'll go to Boston with you next week.
JERK
That would be nice.

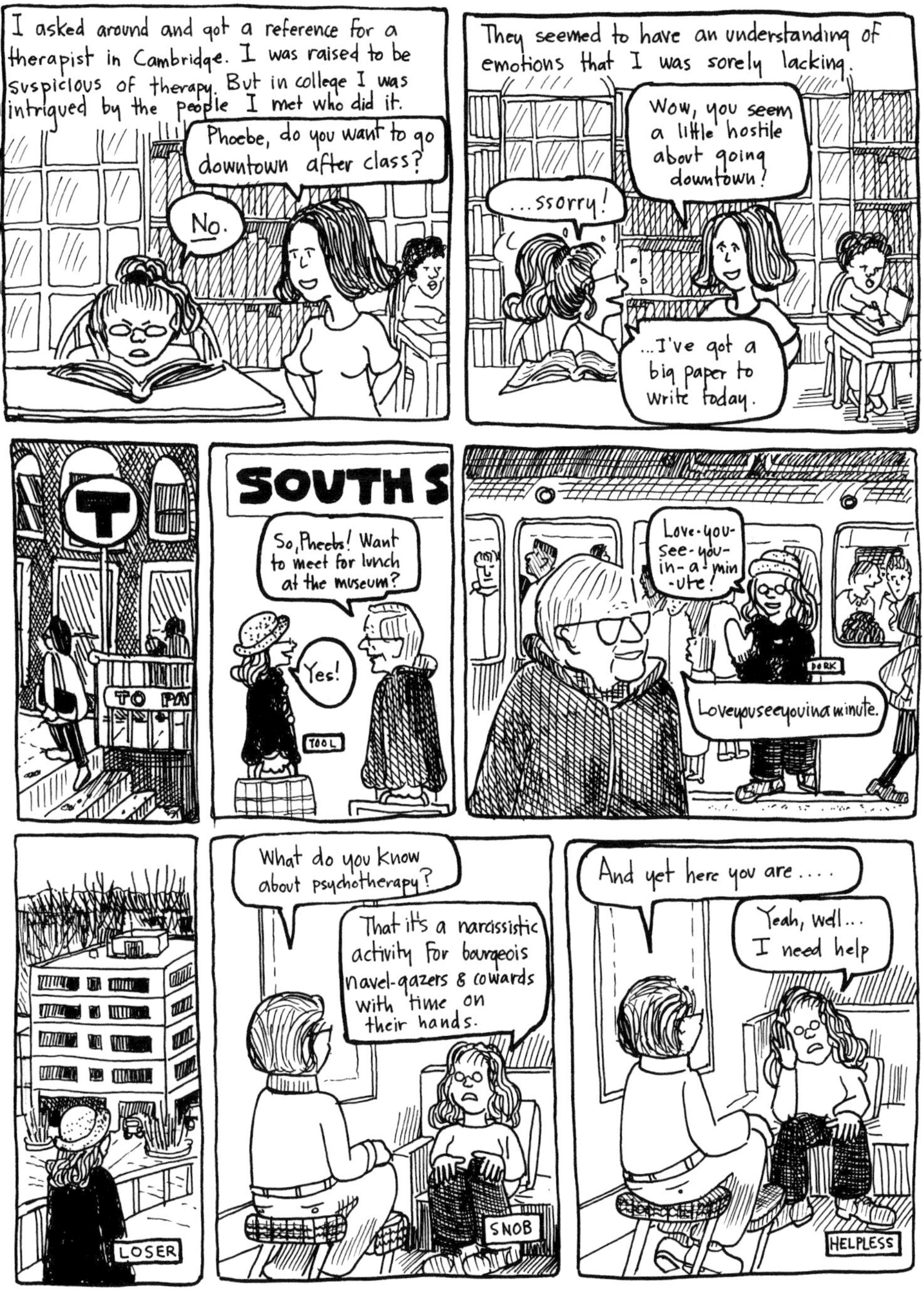
I asked around and got a reference for a therapist in Cambridge. I was raised to be suspicious of therapy. But in college I was intrigued by the people I met who did it.
Phoebe, do you want to go downtown after class?
No.
They seemed to have an understanding of emotions that I was sorely lacking.
Wow, you seem a little hostile about going downtown!
...ssorry!
...I've got a big paper to write today.
T
TO PA
SOUTH S
So, Pheebs! Want to meet for lunch at the museum?
Yes!
TOOL
Love-you-see-you-in-a-min-ute!
DORK
Loveyouseeyouinaminute.
LOSER
What do you know about psychotherapy?
That it's a narcissistic activity for bourgeois navel-gazers & cowards with time on their hands.
SNOB
And yet here you are....
Yeah, well... I need help
HELPLESS

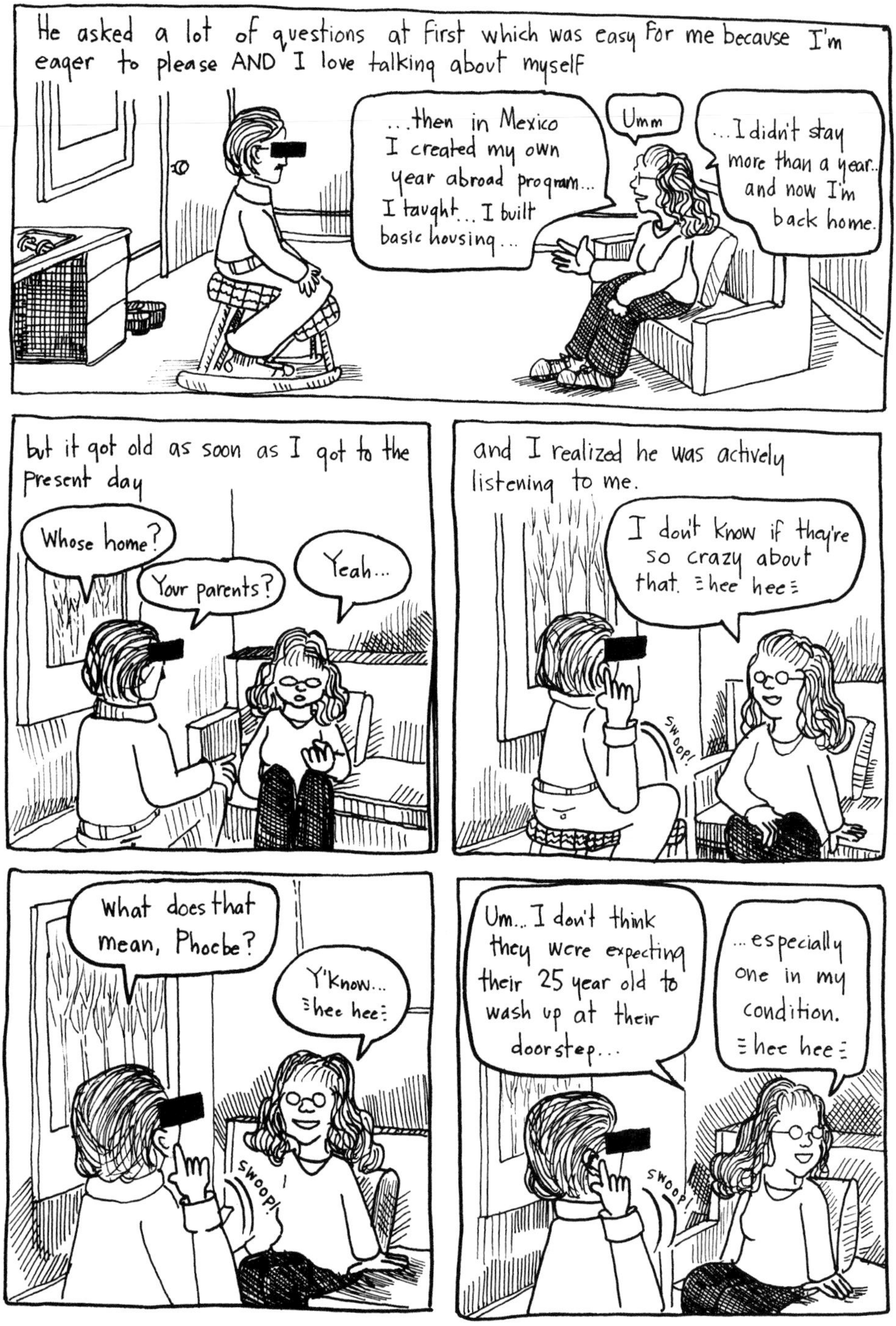
He asked a lot of questions at first which was easy for me because I'm eager to please AND I love talking about myself
...then in Mexico I created my own year abroad program... I taught... I built basic housing...
Umm
...I didn't stay more than a year.. and now I'm back home.
but it got old as soon as I got to the present day
Whose home?
Your parents?
Yeah...
and I realized he was actively listening to me.
I don't know if they're so crazy about that. hee hee
SWOOP!
What does that mean, Phoebe?
Y'know... hee hee
SWOOP!
Um... I don't think they were expecting their 25 year old to wash up at their doorstep...
...especially one in my condition. hee hee
SWOOP!

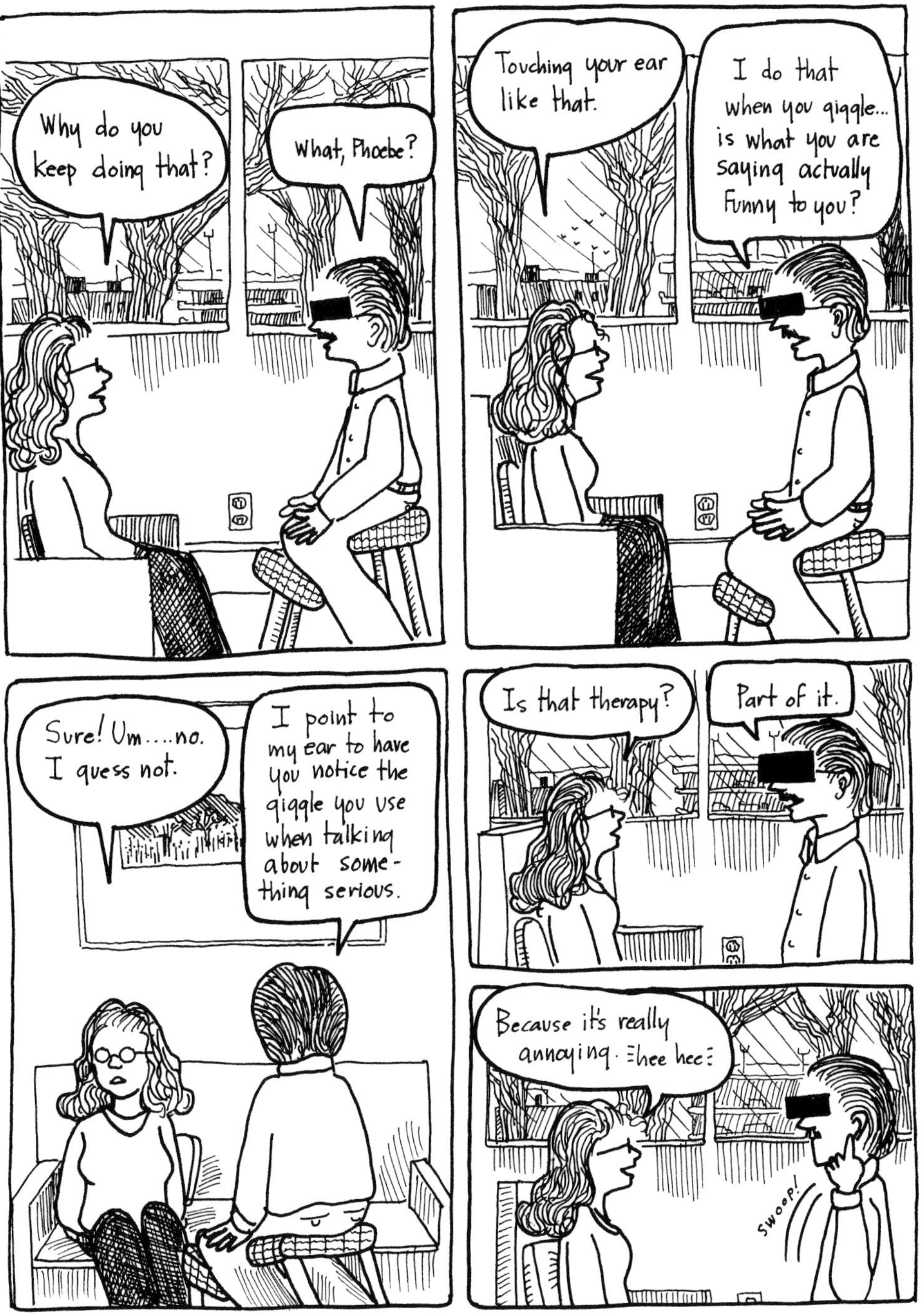
Why do you keep doing that?
What, Phoebe?
Touching your ear like that.
I do that when you giggle... is what you are saying actually funny to you?
Sure! Um....no. I guess not.
I point to my ear to have you notice the giggle you use when talking about something serious.
Is that therapy?
Part of it.
Because it's really annoying. hee hee
SWOOP!

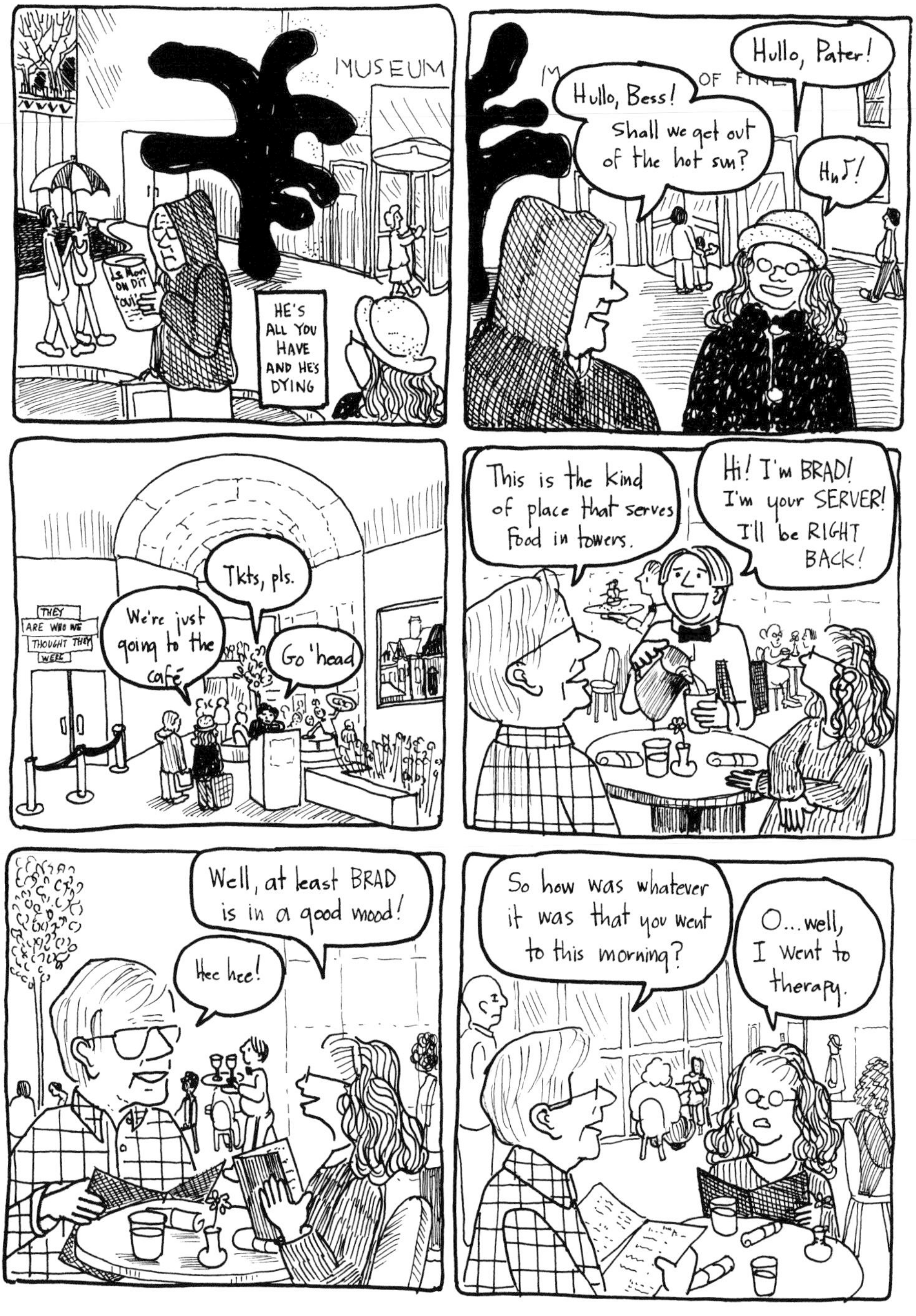
MUSEUM
HE'S ALL YOU HAVE AND HE'S DYING
Hullo, Pater!
Hullo, Bess!
Shall we get out of the hot sun?
THEY ARE WHO WE THOUGHT THEY WERE
Tkts, pls.
We're just going to the café
Go 'head
This is the kind of place that serves food in towers.
Hi! I'm BRAD! I'm your SERVER! I'll be RIGHT BACK!
Well, at least BRAD is in a good mood!
Hee hee!
So how was whatever it was that you went to this morning?
O... well, I went to therapy.

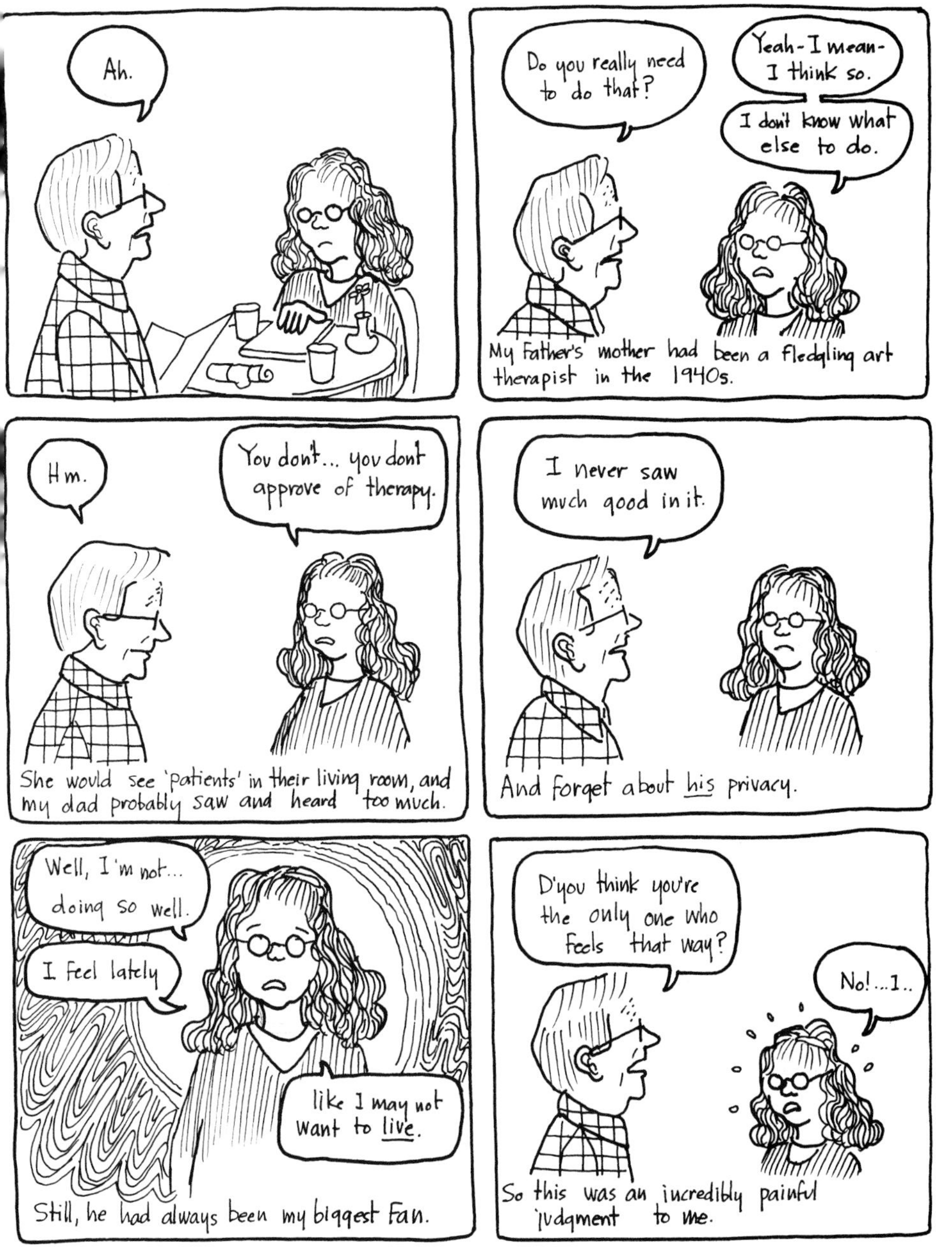
Ah.
Do you really need to do that?
Yeah - I mean - I think so.
I don't know what else to do.
My Father's mother had been a fledgling art therapist in the 1940s.
Hm.
You don't... you don't approve of therapy.
She would see 'patients' in their living room, and my dad probably saw and heard too much.
I never saw much good in it.
And forget about his privacy.
Well, I'm not... doing so well.
I feel lately
like I may not want to live.
Still, he had always been my biggest Fan.
D'you think you're the only one who feels that way?
No!...I..
So this was an incredibly painful judgment to me.

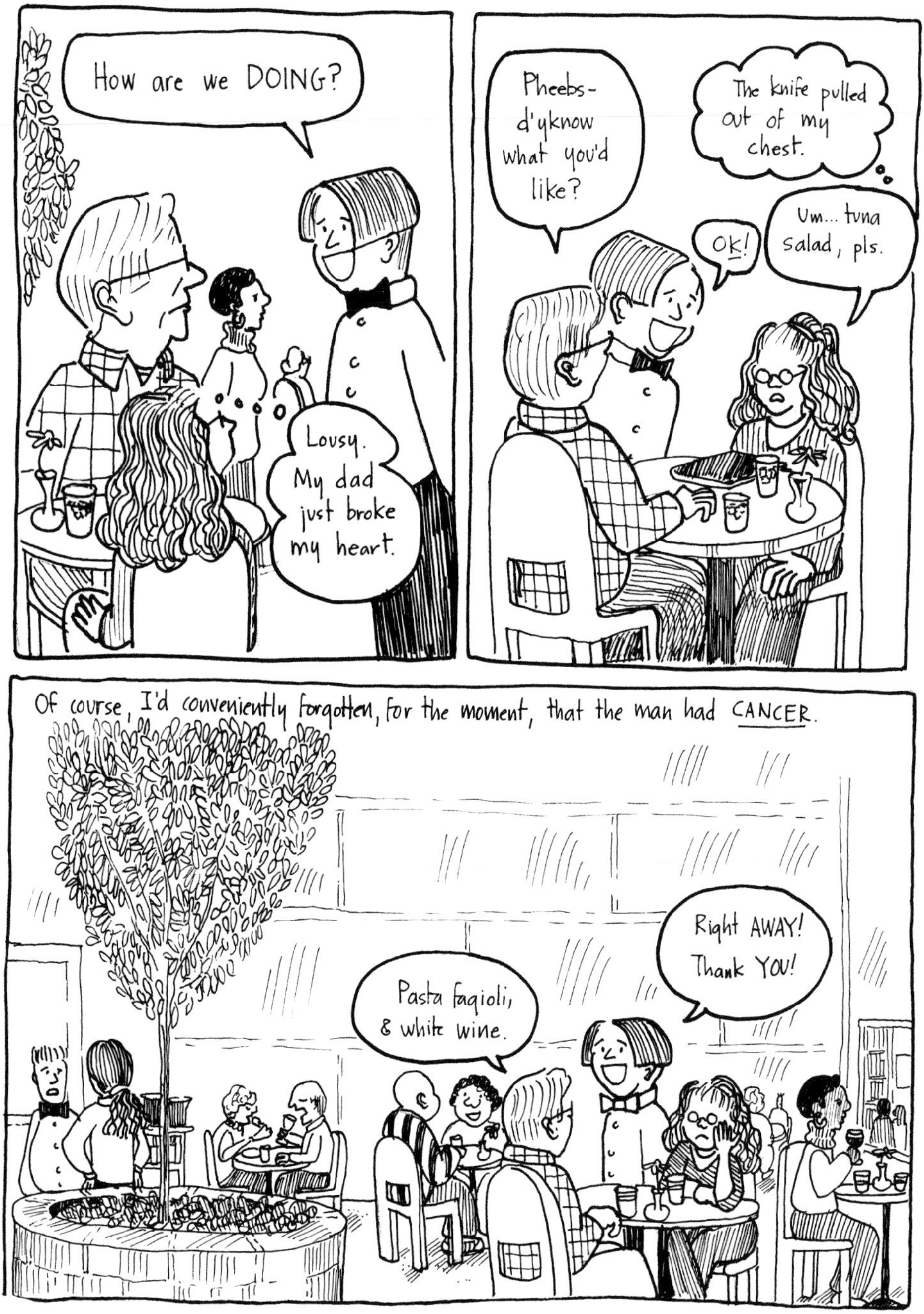
How are we DOING?
Lousy. My dad just broke my heart.
Pheebs- d'yknow what you'd like?
The knife pulled out of my chest.
OK!
Um... tuna salad, pls.
Of course, I'd conveniently forgotten, for the moment, that the man had CANCER.
Pasta fagioli, & white wine.
Right AWAY! Thank YOU!

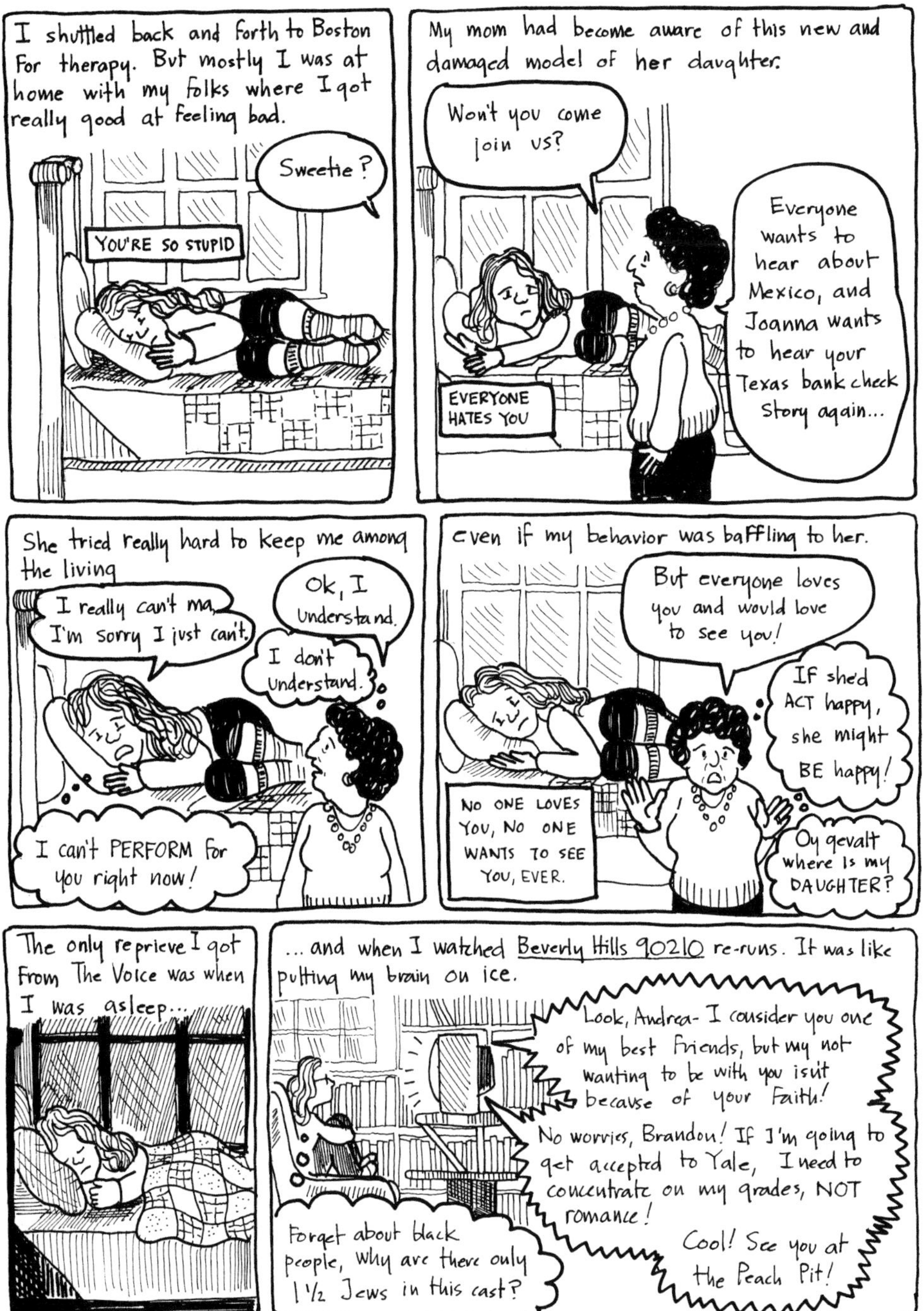
I shuttled back and forth to Boston for therapy. But mostly I was at home with my folks where I got really good at feeling bad.
Sweetie?
YOU'RE SO STUPID
My mom had become aware of this new and damaged model of her daughter.
Won't you come join us?
Everyone wants to hear about Mexico, and Joanna wants to hear your Texas bank check story again...
EVERYONE HATES YOU
She tried really hard to keep me among the living
I really can't ma, I'm sorry I just can't.
Ok, I understand.
I don't understand.
I can't PERFORM for you right now!
even if my behavior was baffling to her.
But everyone loves you and would love to see you!
If she'd ACT happy, she might BE happy!
NO ONE LOVES YOU, NO ONE WANTS TO SEE YOU, EVER.
Oy gevalt where is my DAUGHTER?
The only reprieve I got from The Voice was when I was asleep...
...and when I watched Beverly Hills 90210 re-runs. It was like putting my brain on ice.
Look, Andrea- I consider you one of my best friends, but my not wanting to be with you isn't because of your Faith!
No worries, Brandon! If I'm going to get accepted to Yale, I need to concentrate on my grades, NOT romance!
Cool! See you at the Peach Pit!
Forget about black people, why are there only 1½ Jews in this cast?

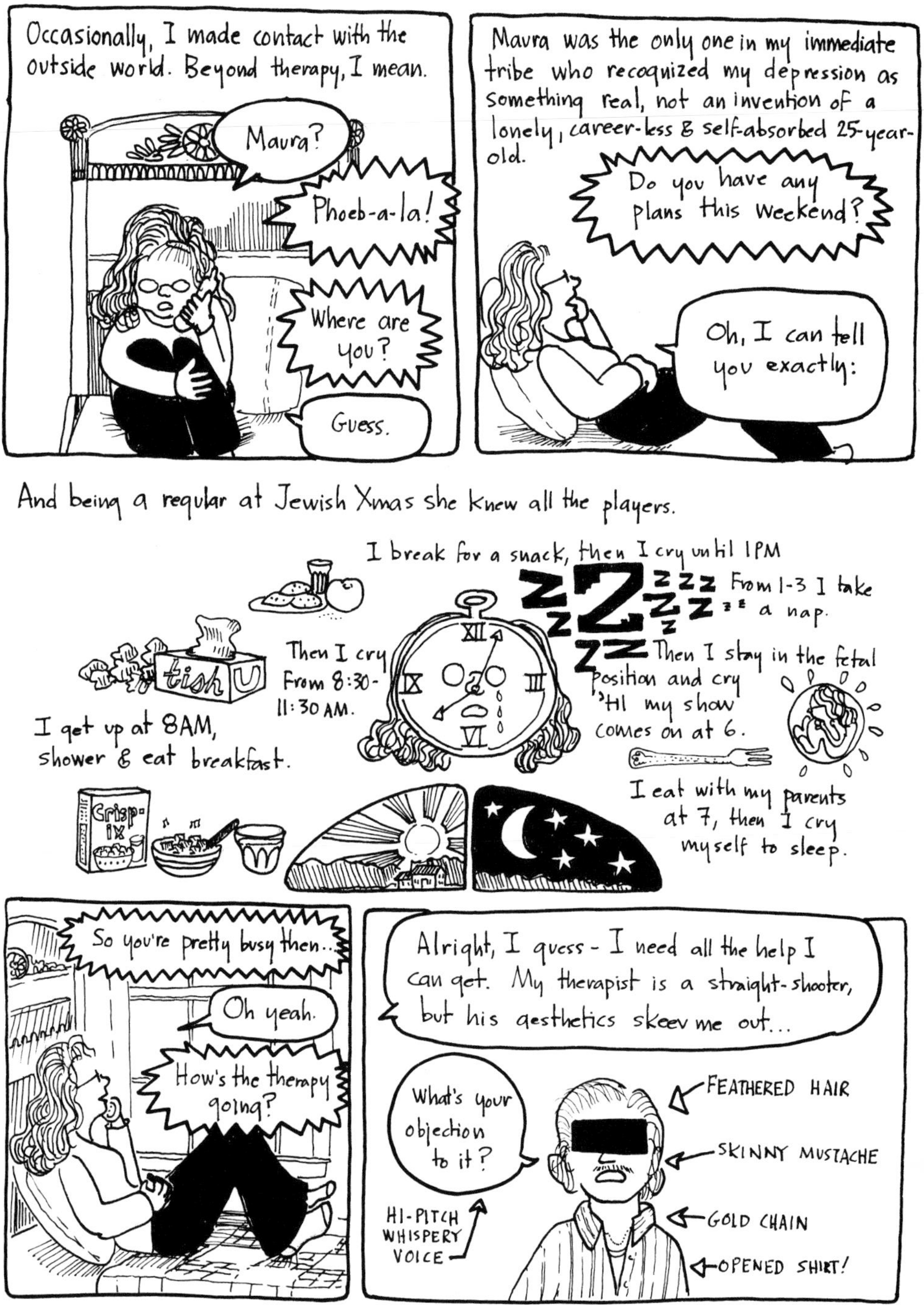
Occasionally, I made contact with the outside world. Beyond therapy, I mean.
Maura?
Phoeb-a-la!
Where are you?
Guess.
Maura was the only one in my immediate tribe who recognized my depression as something real, not an invention of a lonely, career-less & self-absorbed 25-year-old.
Do you have any plans this weekend?
Oh, I can tell you exactly:
And being a regular at Jewish Xmas she knew all the players.
I get up at 8AM, shower & eat breakfast.
Crisp-ix
tishU
Then I cry From 8:30-11:30 AM.
I break for a snack, then I cry until 1PM
XII
IX
III
VI
ZZZZ
From 1-3 I take a nap.
Then I stay in the fetal position and cry 'til my show comes on at 6.
I eat with my parents at 7, then I cry myself to sleep.
So you're pretty busy then...
Oh yeah.
How's the therapy going?
Alright, I guess - I need all the help I can get. My therapist is a straight-shooter, but his aesthetics skeev me out...
What's your objection to it?
FEATHERED HAIR
SKINNY MUSTACHE
GOLD CHAIN
OPENED SHIRT!
HI-PITCH WHISPERY VOICE

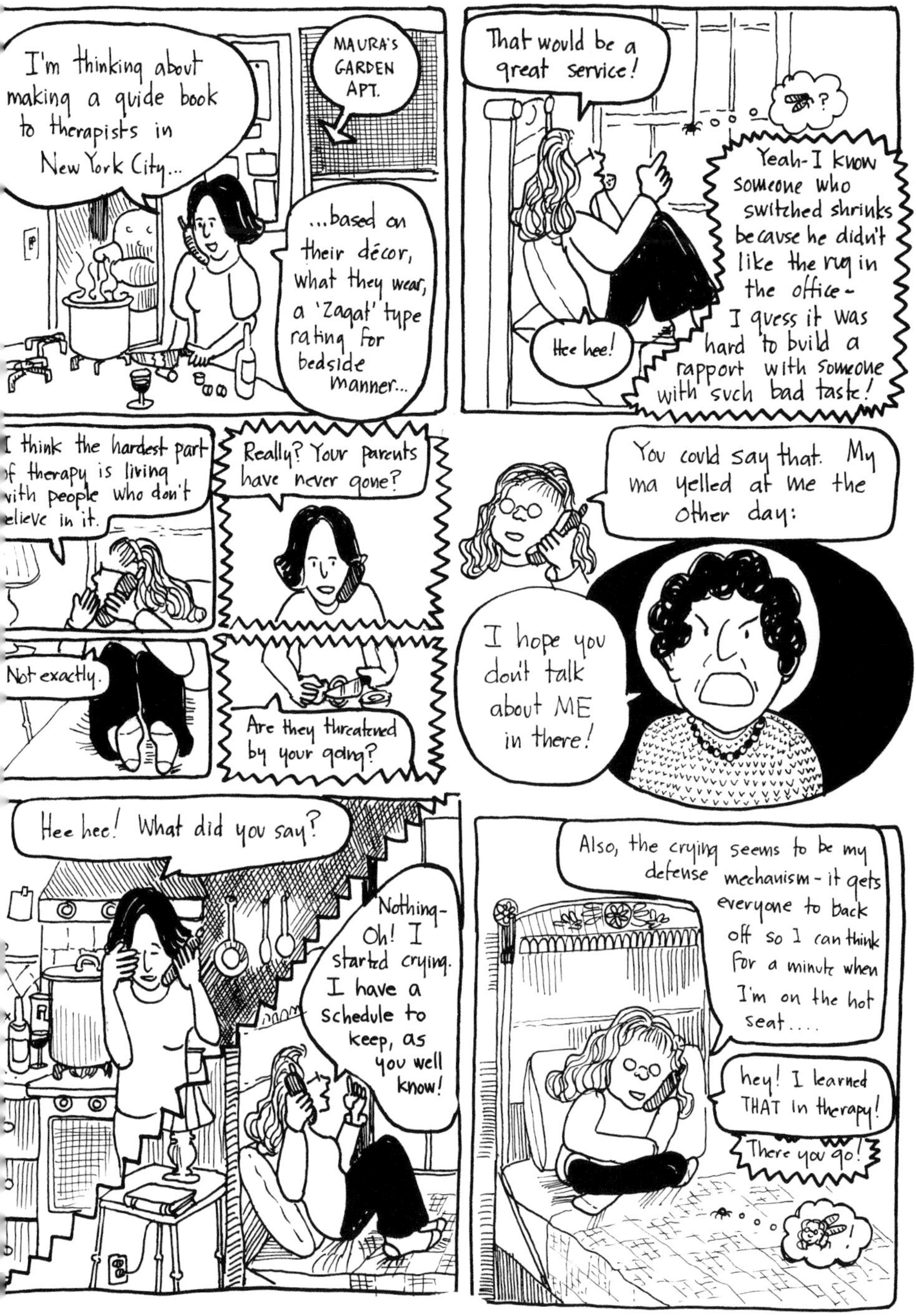
I'm thinking about making a guide book to therapists in New York City...
MAURA'S GARDEN APT.
...based on their décor, what they wear, a 'Zagat' type rating for bedside manner...
That would be a great service!
Hee hee!
Yeah- I know someone who switched shrinks because he didn't like the rug in the office- I guess it was hard to build a rapport with someone with such bad taste!
I think the hardest part of therapy is living with people who don't believe in it.
Really? Your parents have never gone?
You could say that. My ma yelled at me the other day:
I hope you don't talk about ME in there!
Not exactly.
Are they threatened by your going?
Hee hee! What did you say?
Nothing- Oh! I started crying. I have a schedule to keep, as you well know!
Also, the crying seems to be my defense mechanism - it gets everyone to back off so I can think for a minute when I'm on the hot seat....
hey! I learned THAT in therapy!
There you go!

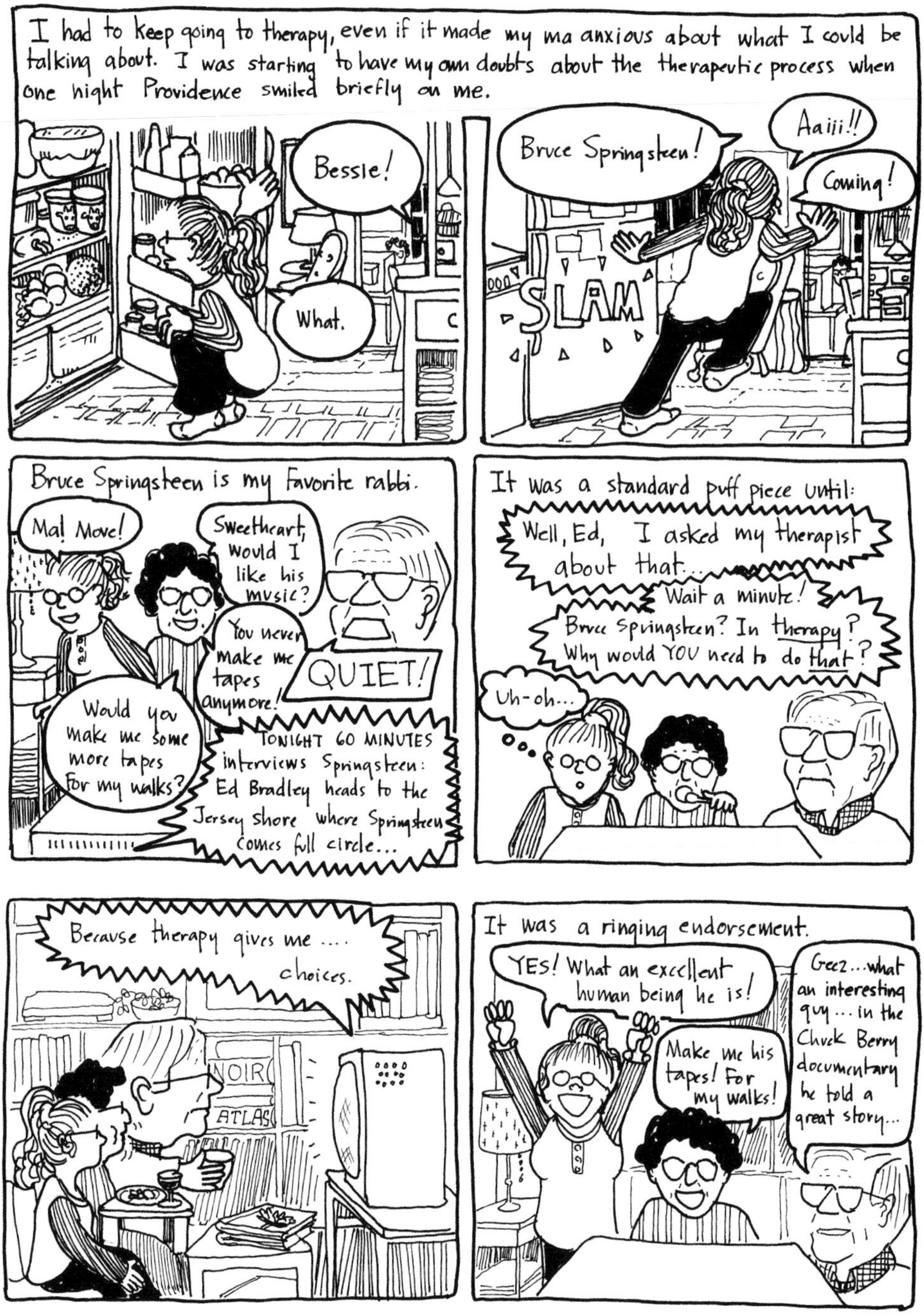
I had to keep going to therapy, even if it made my ma anxious about what I could be talking about. I was starting to have my own doubts about the therapeutic process when one night Providence smiled briefly on me.
Bessie!
What.
Bruce Springsteen!
Aaiii!!
Coming!
SLAM
Bruce Springsteen is my favorite rabbi.
Ma! Move!
Sweetheart, would I like his music?
You never make me tapes anymore!
QUIET!
Would you make me some more tapes for my walks?
TONIGHT 60 MINUTES interviews Springsteen: Ed Bradley heads to the Jersey shore where Springsteen comes full circle...
It was a standard puff piece until:
Well, Ed, I asked my therapist about that...
Wait a minute! Bruce Springsteen? In therapy? Why would YOU need to do that?
Uh-oh...
Because therapy gives me .... choices.
NOIR
ATLAS
It was a ringing endorsement.
YES! What an excellent human being he is!
Make me his tapes! For my walks!
Geez...what an interesting guy... in the Chuck Berry documentary he told a great story...

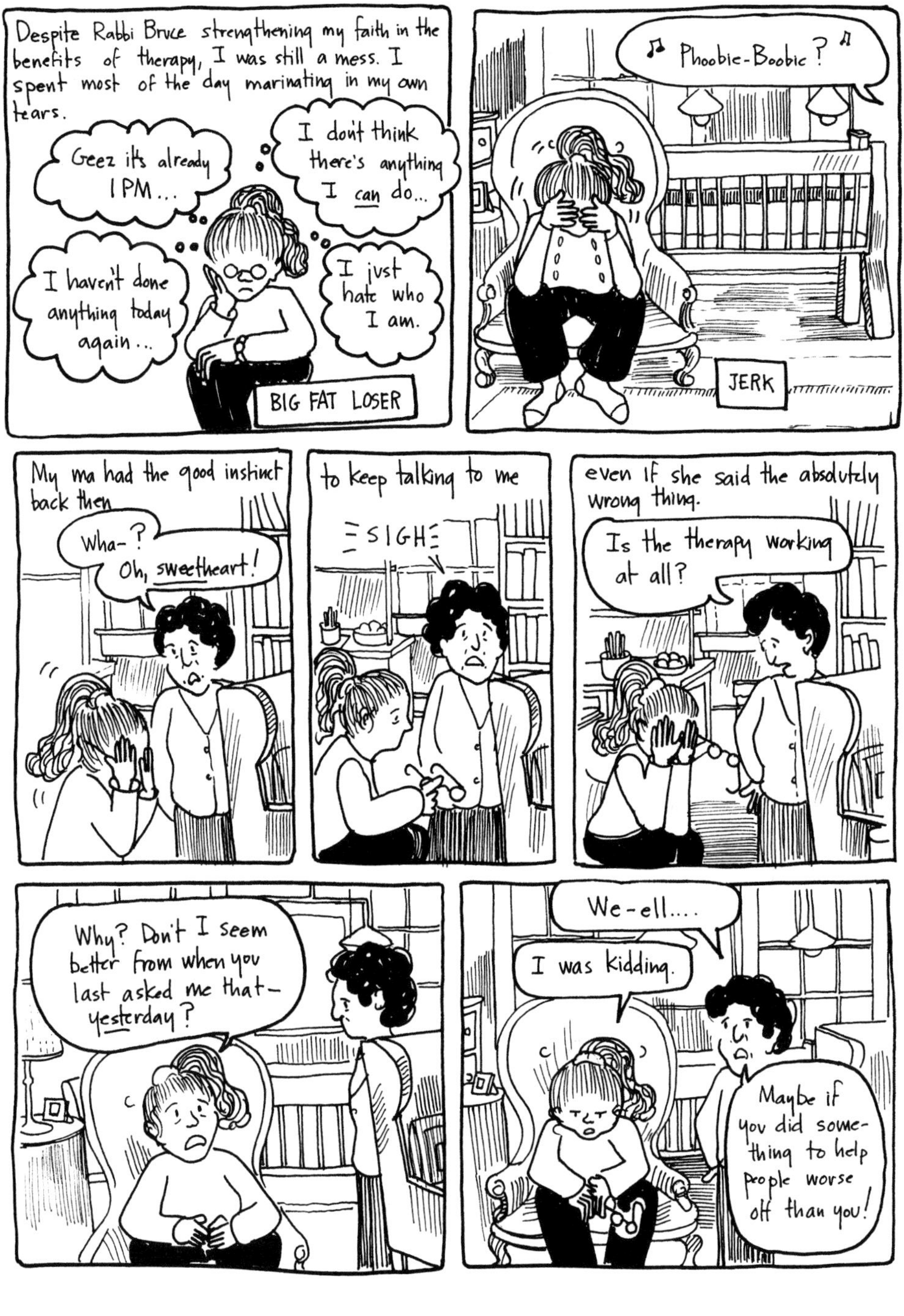
Despite Rabbi Bruce strengthening my faith in the benefits of therapy, I was still a mess. I spent most of the day marinating in my own tears.
Geez it's already 1PM...
I don't think there's anything I can do...
I haven't done anything today again...
I just hate who I am.
BIG FAT LOSER
Phoobie-Boobie?
JERK
My ma had the good instinct back then
Wha-? Oh, sweetheart!
to keep talking to me
SIGH
even if she said the absolutely wrong thing.
Is the therapy working at all?
Why? Don't I seem better from when you last asked me that-yesterday?
We-ell....
I was kidding.
Maybe if you did something to help people worse off than you!

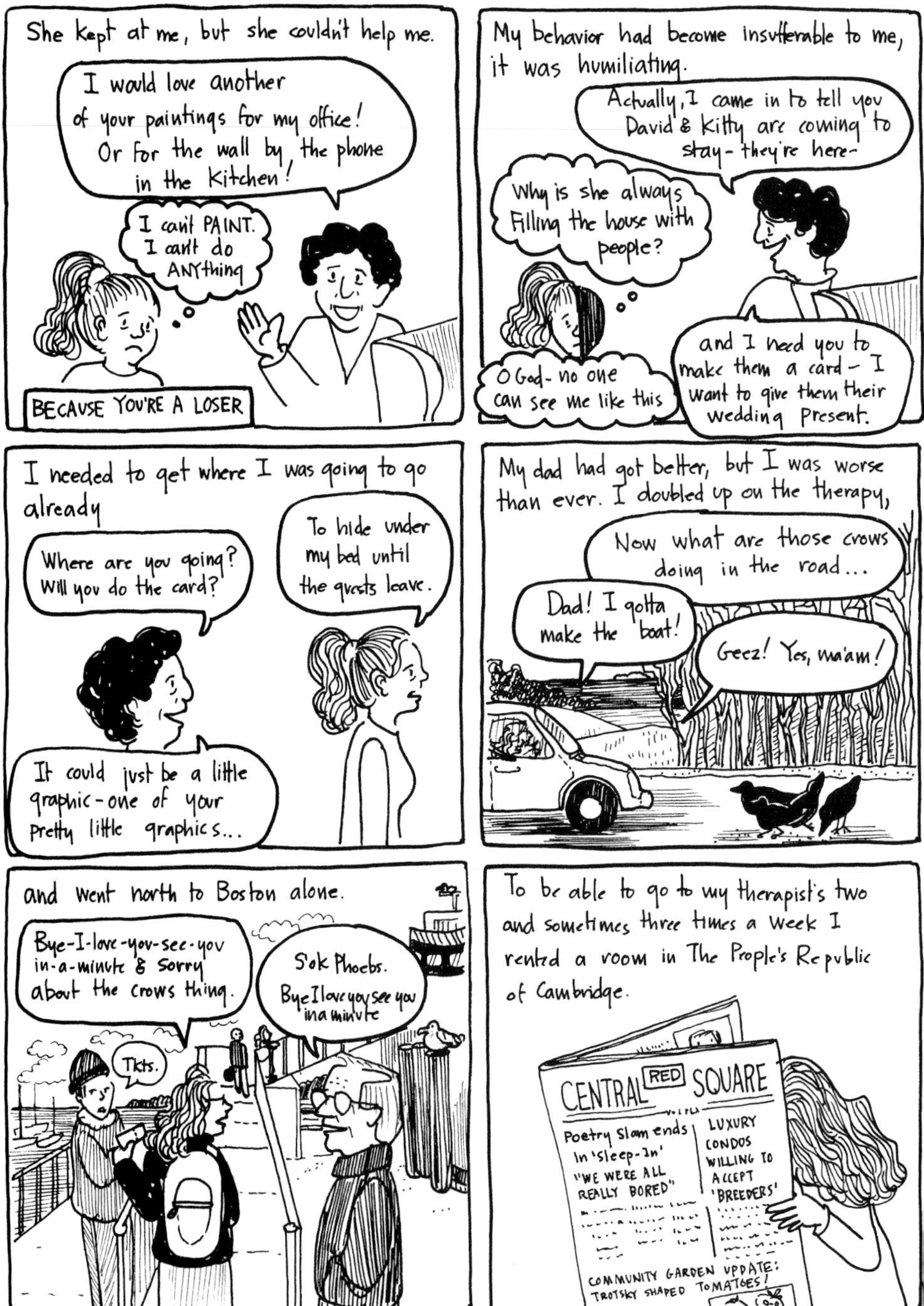
She kept at me, but she couldn't help me.
I would love another of your paintings for my office! Or for the wall by the phone in the kitchen!
I can't PAINT. I can't do ANYthing
BECAUSE YOU'RE A LOSER
My behavior had become insufferable to me, it was humiliating.
Actually, I came in to tell you David & Kitty are coming to stay - they're here -
Why is she always filling the house with people?
and I need you to make them a card - I want to give them their wedding present.
O God - no one can see me like this
I needed to get where I was going to go already
Where are you going? Will you do the card?
To hide under my bed until the guests leave.
It could just be a little graphic - one of your pretty little graphics...
My dad had got better, but I was worse than ever. I doubled up on the therapy,
Now what are those crows doing in the road...
Dad! I gotta make the boat!
Geez! Yes, ma'am!
and went north to Boston alone.
Bye-I-love-you-see-you in-a-minute & sorry about the crows thing.
S'ok Phoebs. Bye I love you see you in a minute
Tkts.
To be able to go to my therapist's two and sometimes three times a week I rented a room in The People's Republic of Cambridge.
CENTRAL RED SQUARE
Poetry Slam ends In 'Sleep-In' "WE WERE ALL REALLY BORED"
LUXURY CONDOS WILLING TO ACCEPT 'BREEDERS'
COMMUNITY GARDEN UPDATE: TROTSKY SHAPED TOMATOES!

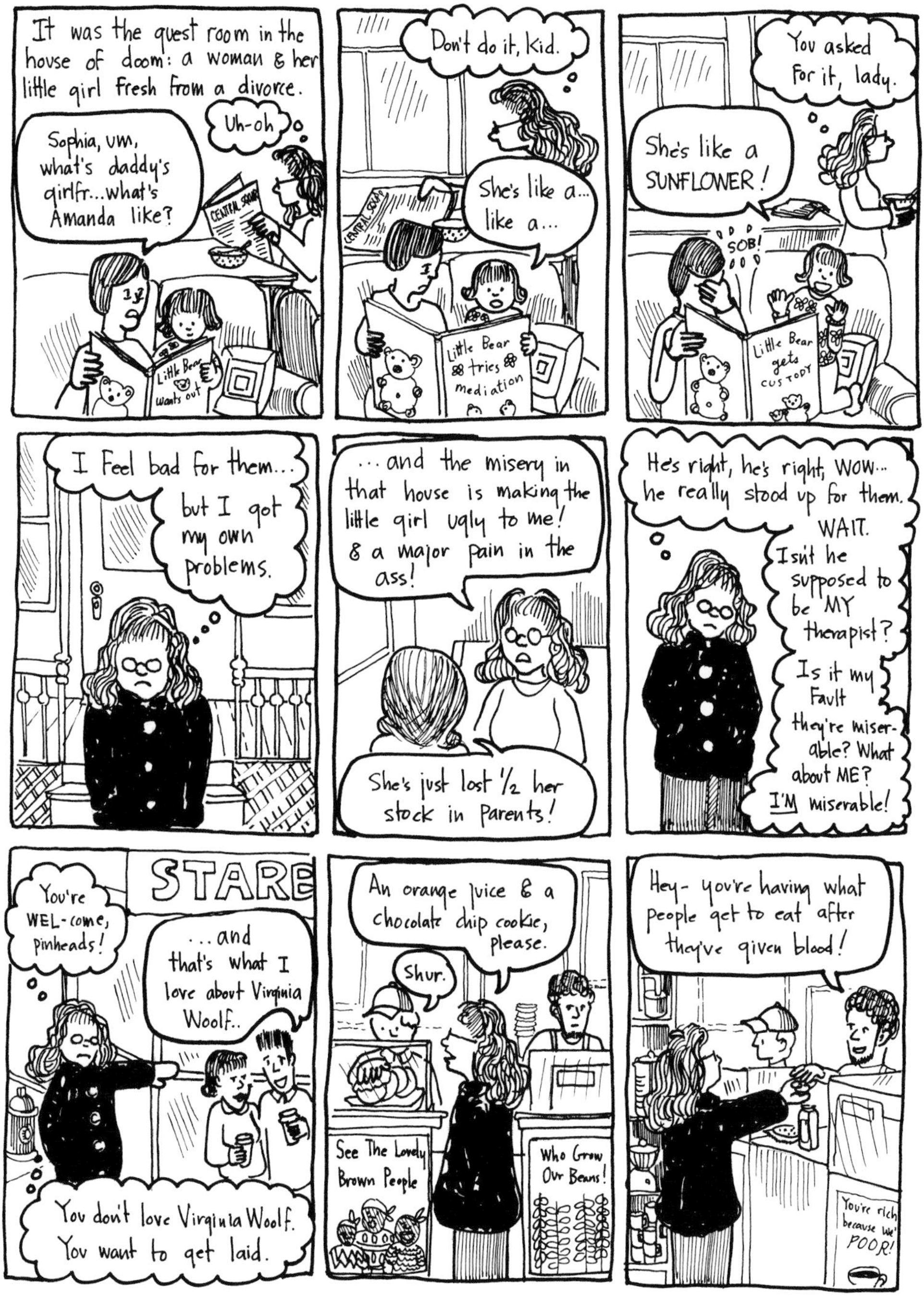
It was the guest room in the house of doom: a woman & her little girl fresh from a divorce.
Sophia, um, what's daddy's girlfr...what's Amanda like?
Uh-oh
CENTRAL SQUARE
Little Bear wants out
Don't do it, Kid.
She's like a... like a...
CENTRAL SQUARE
Little Bear tries mediation
You asked for it, lady.
She's like a SUNFLOWER!
SOB!
Little Bear gets CUSTODY
I feel bad for them...
but I got my own problems.
...and the misery in that house is making the little girl ugly to me! & a major pain in the ass!
She's just lost 1/2 her stock in parents!
He's right, he's right, WOW... he really stood up for them.
WAIT. Isn't he supposed to be MY therapist?
Is it my fault they're miserable? What about ME? I'M miserable!
STARE
You're WEL-come, pinheads!
...and that's what I love about Virginia Woolf..
You don't love Virginia Woolf. You want to get laid.
An orange juice & a chocolate chip cookie, please.
Shur.
See The Lovely Brown People
Who Grow Our Beans!
Hey- you're having what people get to eat after they've given blood!
You're rich because we' POOR!

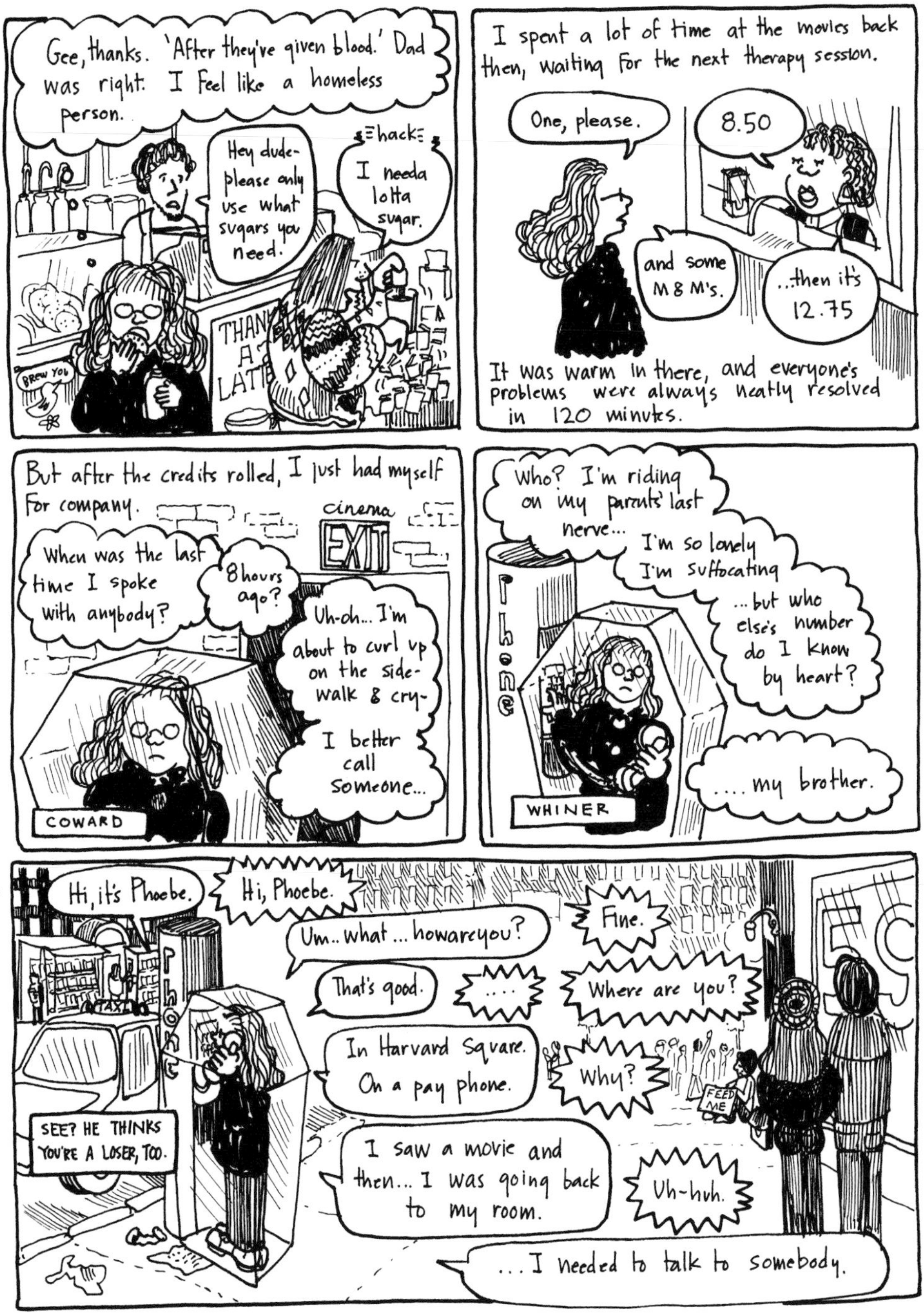
Gee, thanks. 'After they've given blood.' Dad was right. I feel like a homeless person.
Hey dude- please only use what sugars you need.
hack
I needa lotta sugar.
BREW YOU
THANK A LATTE
I spent a lot of time at the movies back then, waiting for the next therapy session.
One, please.
8.50
and some M&M's.
...then it's 12.75
It was warm in there, and everyone's problems were always neatly resolved in 120 minutes.
But after the credits rolled, I just had myself for company.
cinema
EXIT
When was the last time I spoke with anybody?
8 hours ago?
Uh-oh... I'm about to curl up on the side-walk & cry-
I better call someone...
COWARD
Who? I'm riding on my parents' last nerve...
I'm so lonely I'm suffocating
...but who else's number do I know by heart?
phone
WHINER
.... my brother.
Hi, it's Phoebe.
Hi, Phoebe.
Um.. what ... howareyou?
Fine.
That's good.
....
Where are you?
In Harvard Square. On a pay phone.
Why?
TAXI
phone
FEED ME
SEE? HE THINKS YOU'RE A LOSER, TOO.
I saw a movie and then... I was going back to my room.
Uh-huh.
...I needed to talk to somebody.

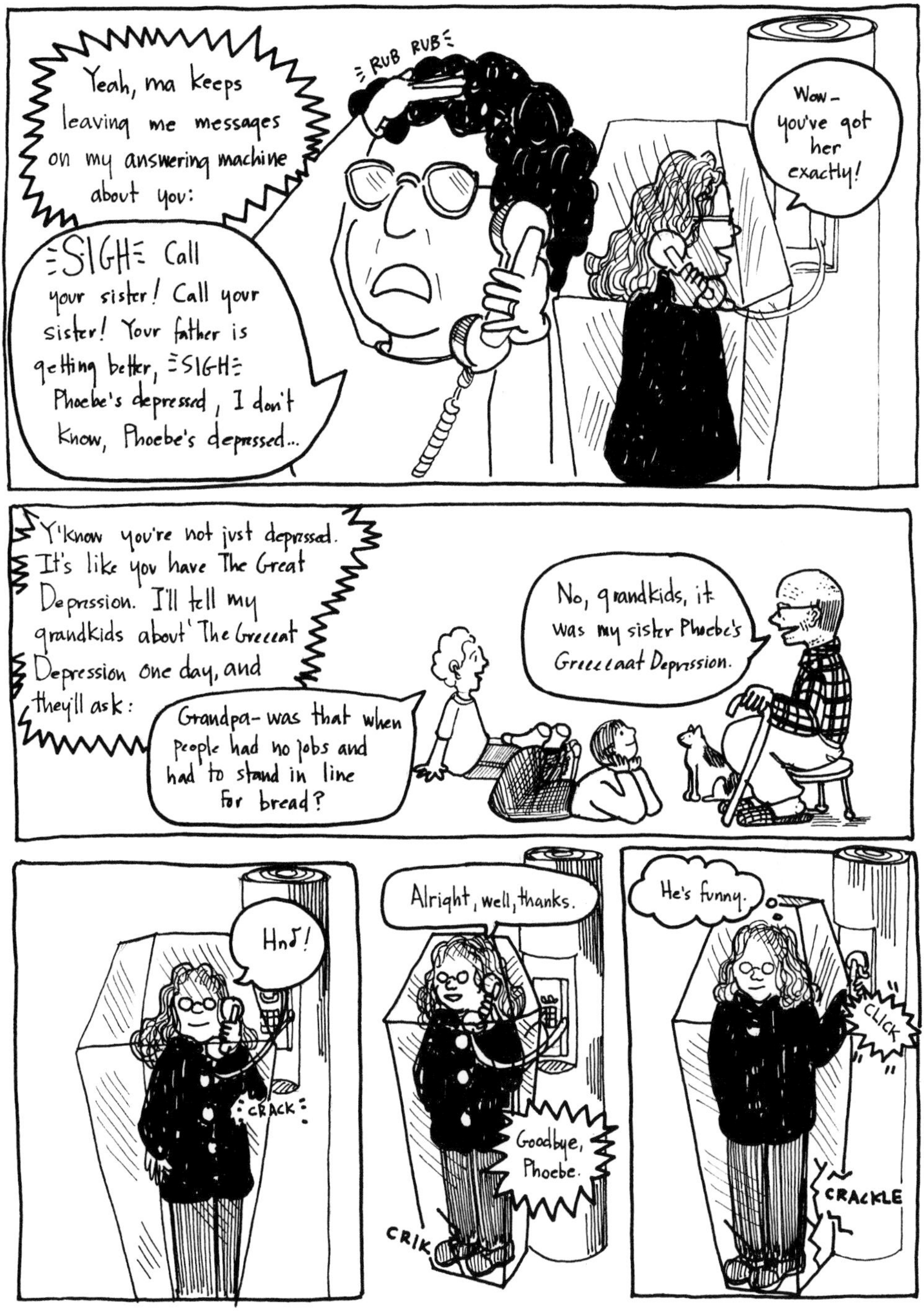
Yeah, ma keeps leaving me messages on my answering machine about you:
RUB RUB
SIGH Call your sister! Call your sister! Your father is getting better, SIGH Phoebe's depressed, I don't know, Phoebe's depressed...
Wow - you've got her exactly!
Y'know you're not just depressed. It's like you have The Great Depression. I'll tell my grandkids about The Greeeat Depression one day, and they'll ask:
Grandpa- was that when people had no jobs and had to stand in line for bread?
No, grandkids, it was my sister Phoebe's Greeeaat Depression.
Hnd!
CRACK
Alright, well, thanks.
Goodbye, Phoebe.
CRIK
He's funny.
CLICK
CRACKLE

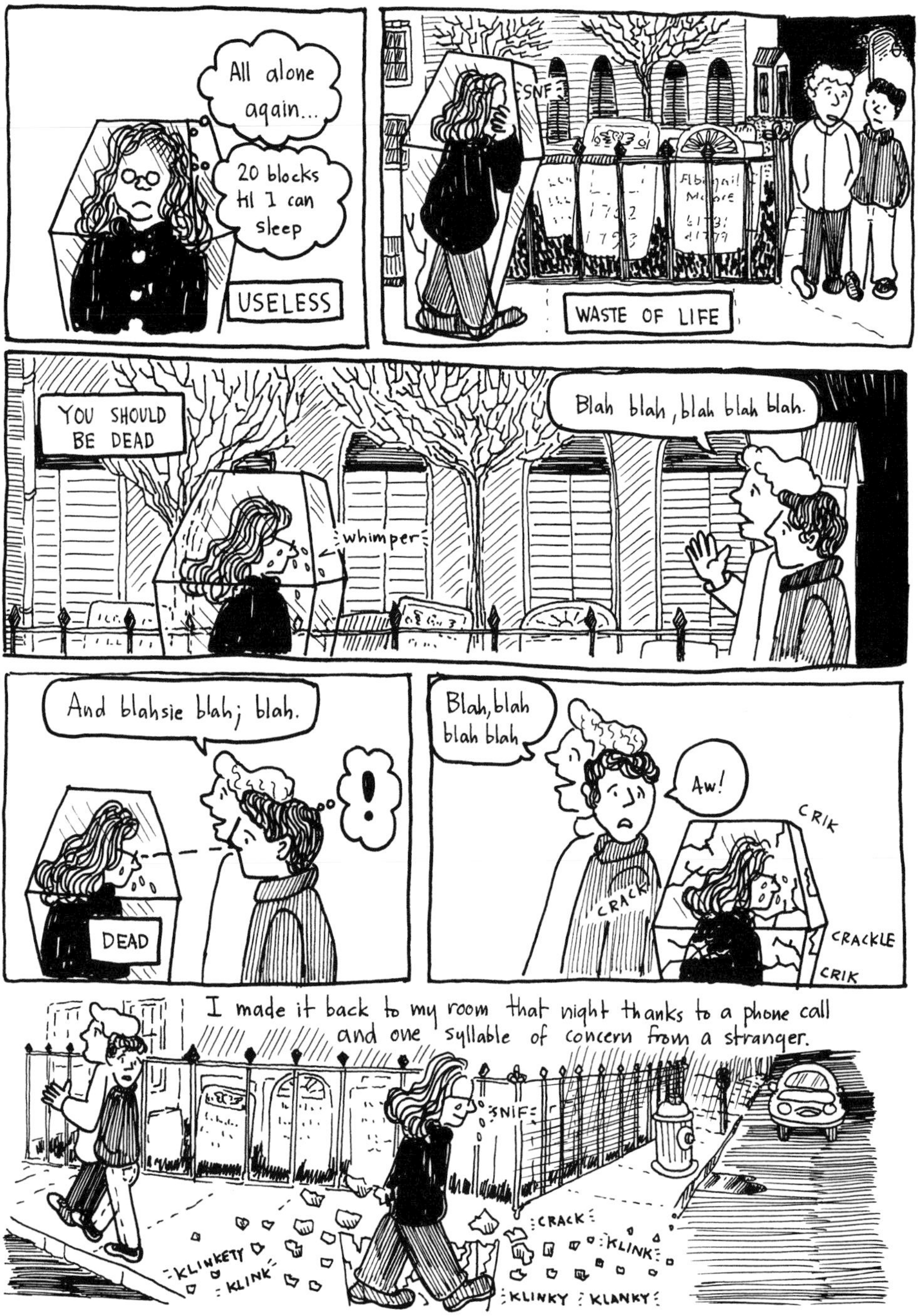
All alone again...
20 blocks til I can sleep
USELESS
SNF
WASTE OF LIFE
YOU SHOULD BE DEAD
Blah blah, blah blah blah.
whimper
And blahsie blah; blah.
!
DEAD
Blah, blah blah blah
Aw!
CRIK
CRACK
CRACKLE
CRIK
I made it back to my room that night thanks to a phone call and one syllable of concern from a stranger.
SNIF
CRACK
KLINK
KLINKETY
KLINK
KLINKY
KLANKY

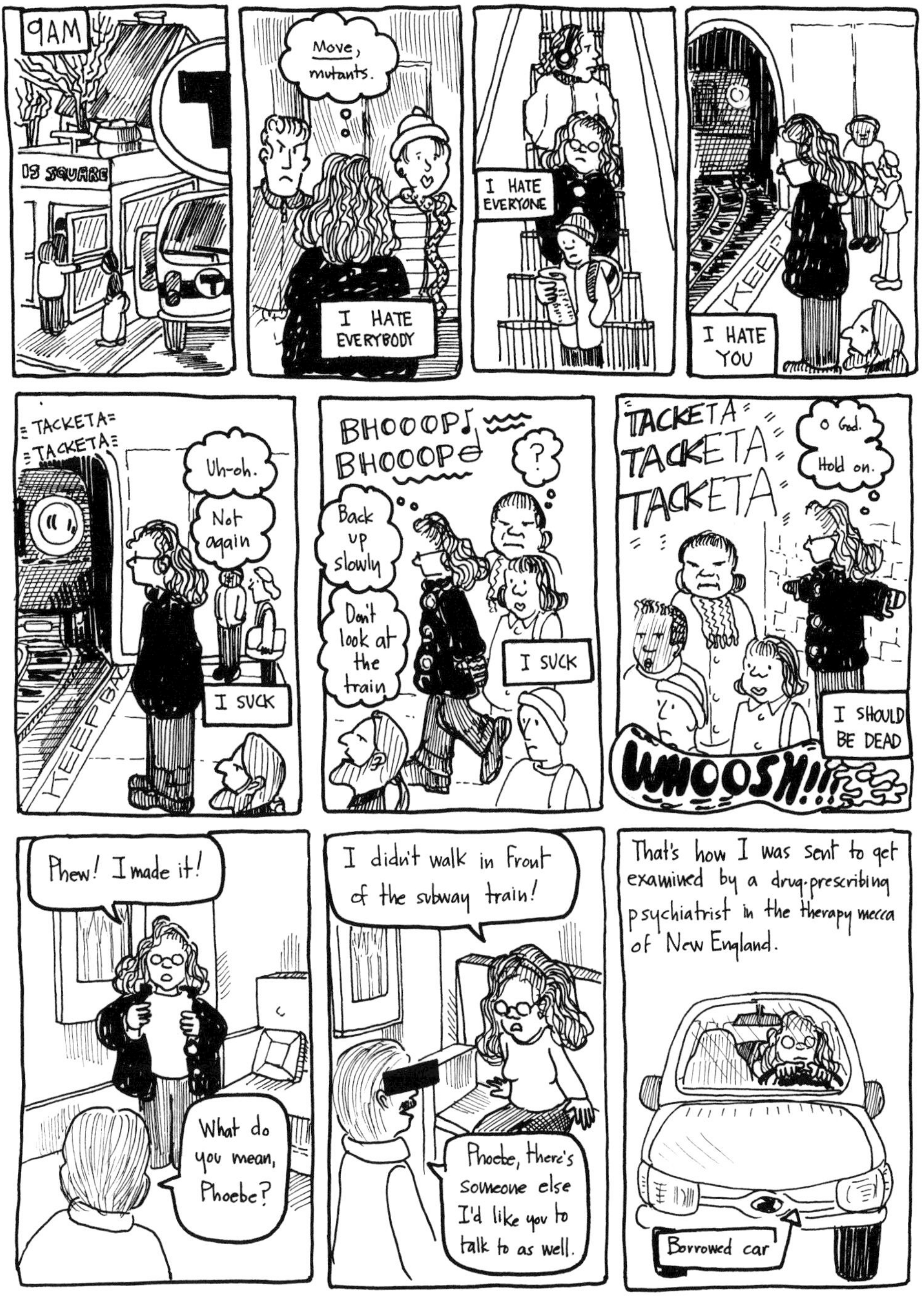
9AM
IS SQUARE
Move, mutants.
I HATE EVERYBODY
I HATE EVERYONE
I HATE YOU
KEEP
TACKETA TACKETA
Uh-oh.
Not again
I SUCK
KEEP BAC
BHOOOP BHOOOP
?
Back up slowly
Don't look at the train
I SUCK
TACKETA TACKETA TACKETA
O God.
Hold on.
I SHOULD BE DEAD
WHOOSH!!!
Phew! I made it!
What do you mean, Phoebe?
I didn't walk in front of the subway train!
Phoebe, there's someone else I'd like you to talk to as well.
That's how I was sent to get examined by a drug-prescribing psychiatrist in the therapy mecca of New England.
Borrowed car

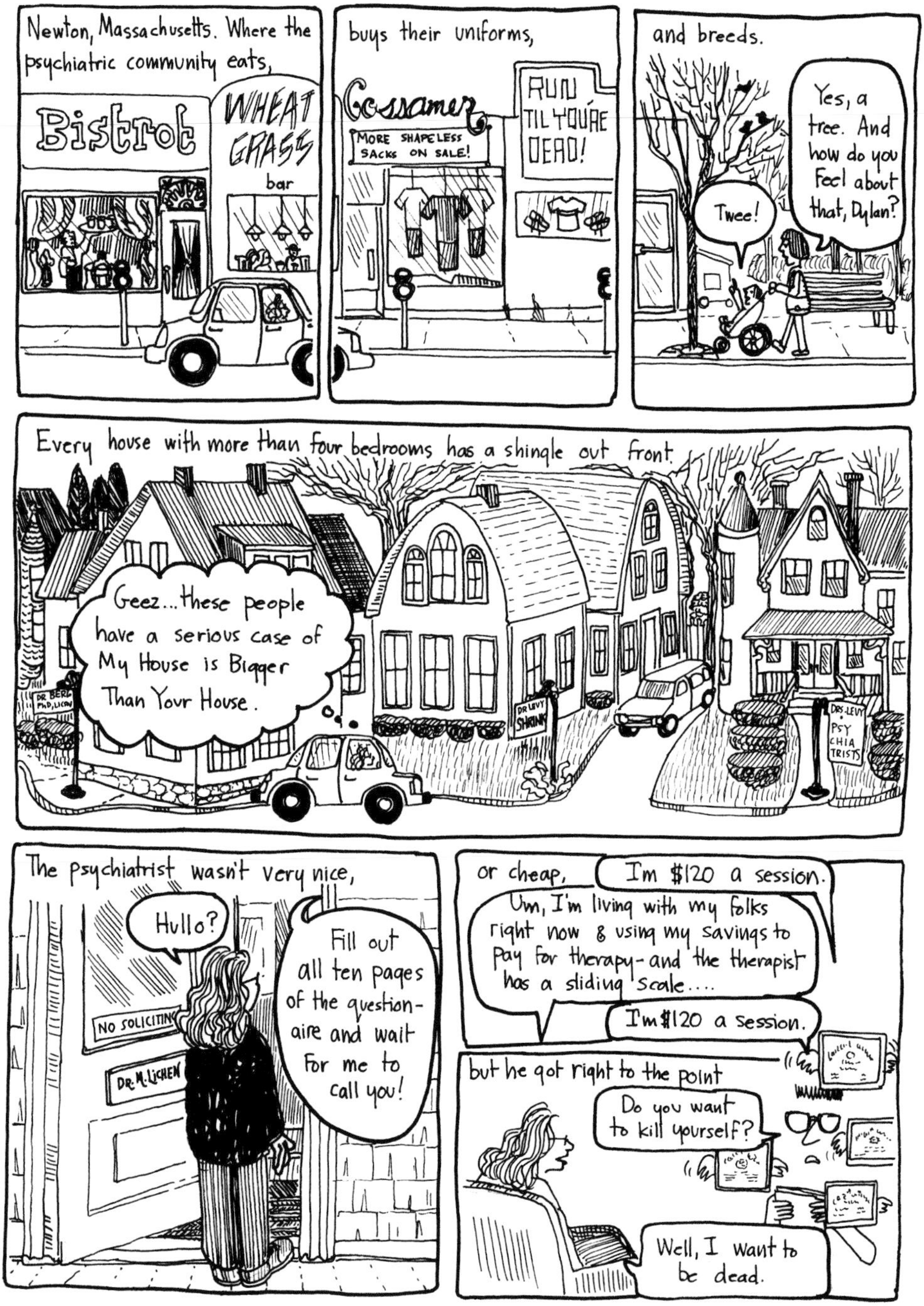
Newton, Massachusetts. Where the psychiatric community eats,
Bistrot
WHEAT GRASS bar
buys their uniforms,
Gossamer
MORE SHAPELESS SACKS ON SALE!
RUN TIL YOU'RE DEAD!
and breeds.
Twee!
Yes, a tree. And how do you feel about that, Dylan?
Every house with more than four bedrooms has a shingle out front.
Geez... these people have a serious case of My House is Bigger Than Your House.
DR BERG PhD, LICSW
DR LEVY SHRINK
DRS. LEVY PSYCHIATRISTS
The psychiatrist wasn't very nice,
Hullo?
NO SOLICITING
DR. M. LICHEN
Fill out all ten pages of the question-aire and wait for me to call you!
or cheap,
I'm $120 a session.
Um, I'm living with my folks right now & using my savings to pay for therapy - and the therapist has a sliding scale....
I'm $120 a session.
but he got right to the point
Do you want to kill yourself?
Well, I want to be dead.

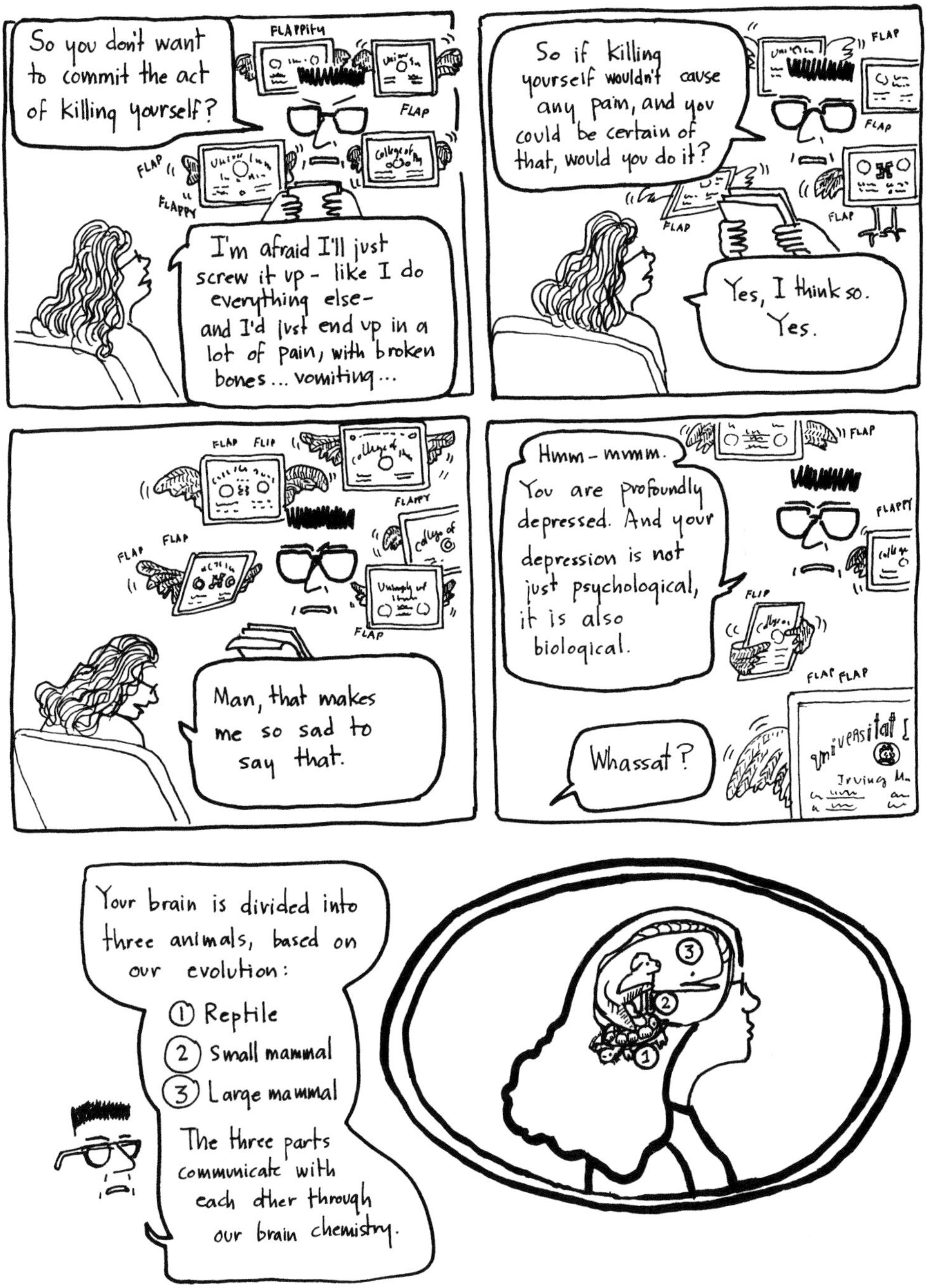
So you don't want to commit the act of killing yourself?
FLAPPity
FLAP
FLAP
FLAPPY
I'm afraid I'll just screw it up - like I do everything else - and I'd just end up in a lot of pain, with broken bones... vomiting...
So if killing yourself wouldn't cause any pain, and you could be certain of that, would you do it?
FLAP
FLAP
FLAP
FLAP
Yes, I think so. Yes.
FLAP FLIP
FLAPPY
FLAP FLAP
FLAP
Man, that makes me so sad to say that.
FLAP
Hmm-mmm.
You are profoundly depressed. And your depression is not just psychological, it is also biological.
FLAPPY
FLIP
FLAP FLAP
Whassat?
Your brain is divided into three animals, based on our evolution:
1 Reptile
2 Small mammal
3 Large mammal
The three parts communicate with each other through our brain chemistry.

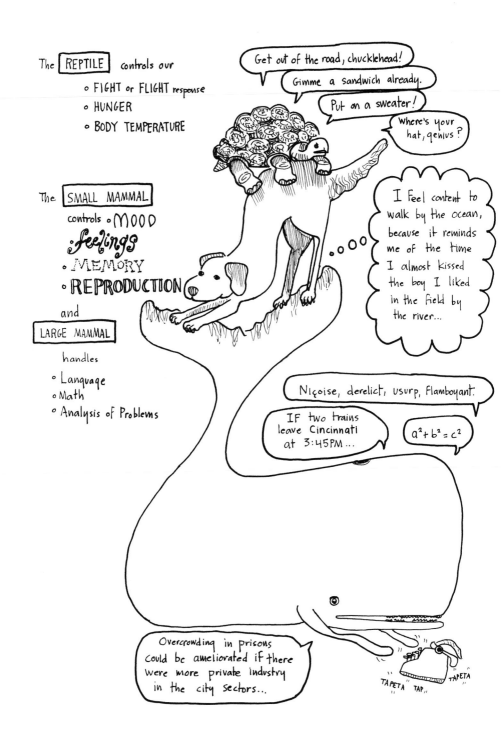

The REPTILE controls our
- FIGHT or FLIGHT response
- HUNGER
- BODY TEMPERATURE

The SMALL MAMMAL controls
- MOOD
- feelings
- MEMORY
- REPRODUCTION

and LARGE MAMMAL handles
- Language
- Math
- Analysis of Problems

Get out of the road, chucklehead!

Gimme a sandwich already.

Put on a sweater!

Where's your hat, genius?

I feel content to walk by the ocean, because it reminds me of the time I almost kissed the boy I liked in the field by the river...

Niçoise, derelict, usurp, flamboyant.

IF two trains leave Cincinnati at 3:45PM...

$a^2 + b^2 = c^2$

Overcrowding in prisons could be ameliorated if there were more private industry in the city sectors...

TAPETA TAP,, TAPETA

84

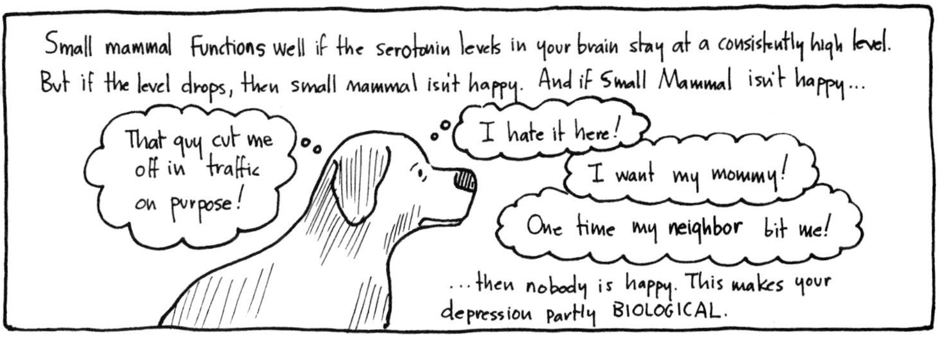
Small mammal functions well if the serotonin levels in your brain stay at a consistently high level. But if the level drops, then small mammal isn't happy. And if Small Mammal isn't happy...
That guy cut me off in traffic on purpose!
I hate it here!
I want my mommy!
One time my neighbor bit me!
...then nobody is happy. This makes your depression partly BIOLOGICAL.

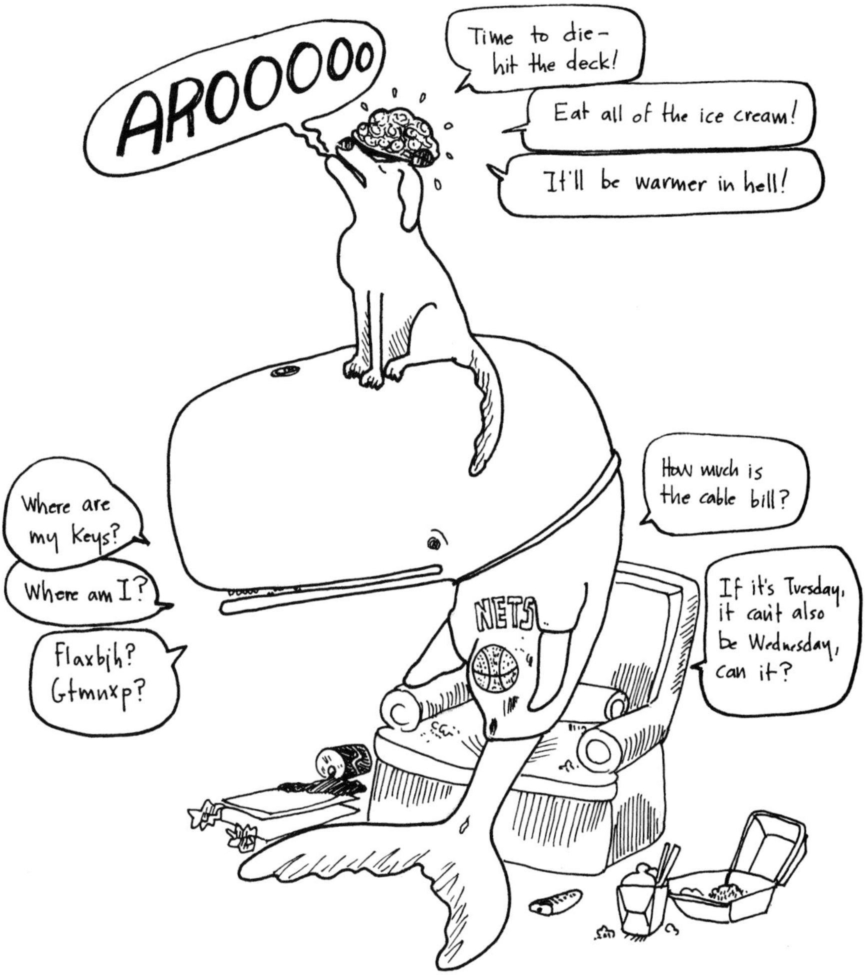
AROOOOO
Time to die- hit the deck!
Eat all of the ice cream!
It'll be warmer in hell!
Where are my keys?
Where am I?
Flaxbjh? Gtmnxp?
How much is the cable bill?
If it's Tuesday, it can't also be Wednesday, can it?
NETS

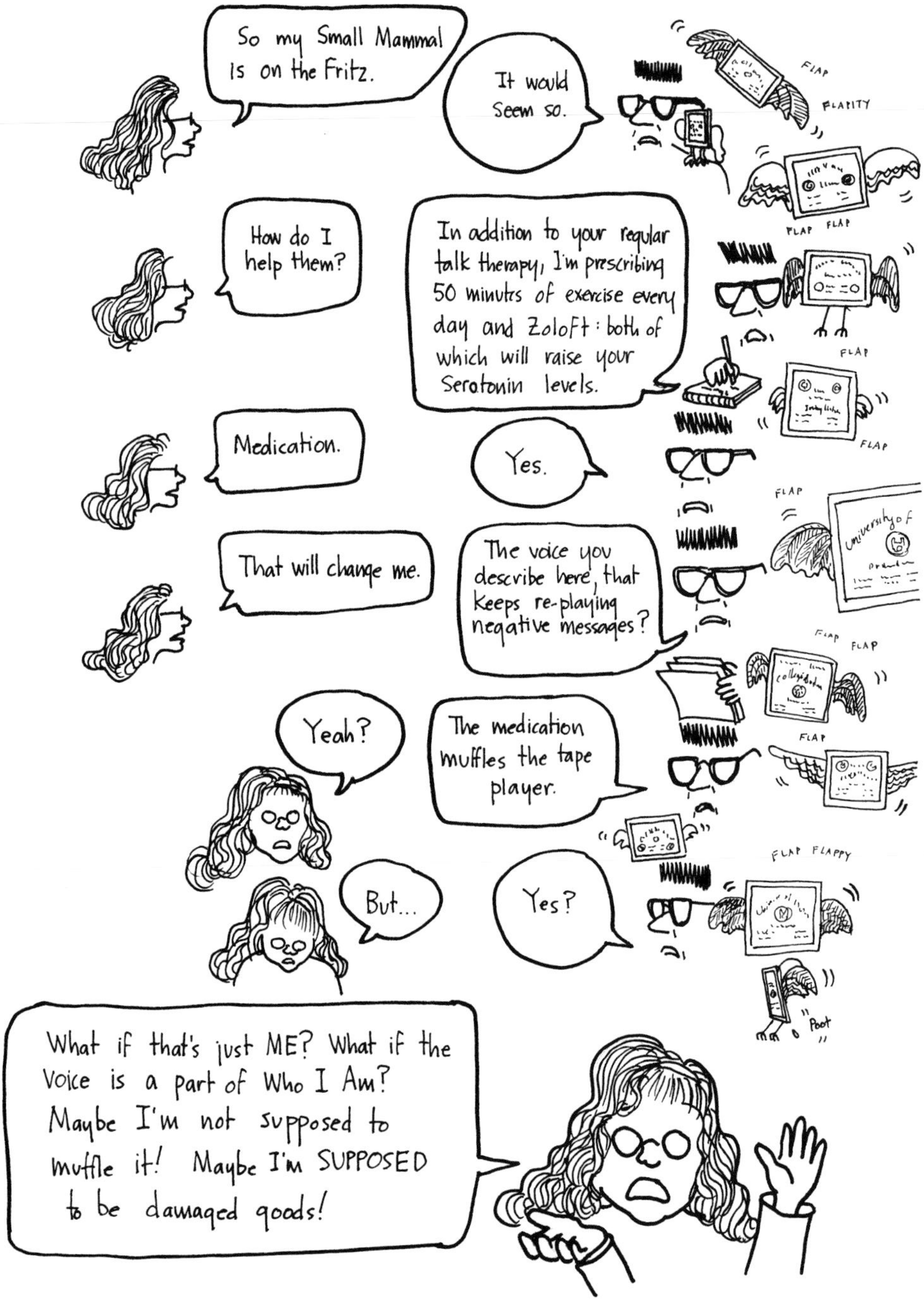
So my Small Mammal is on the Fritz.
It would seem so.
FLAP
FLAPITY
How do I help them?
In addition to your regular talk therapy, I'm prescribing 50 minutes of exercise every day and Zoloft: both of which will raise your Serotonin levels.
FLAP FLAP
FLAP
Medication.
Yes.
FLAP
FLAP
That will change me.
The voice you describe here, that keeps re-playing negative messages?
FLAP FLAP
Yeah?
The medication muffles the tape player.
FLAP
But...
Yes?
FLAP FLAPPY
Poot
What if that's just ME? What if the Voice is a part of Who I Am? Maybe I'm not supposed to muffle it! Maybe I'm SUPPOSED to be damaged goods!

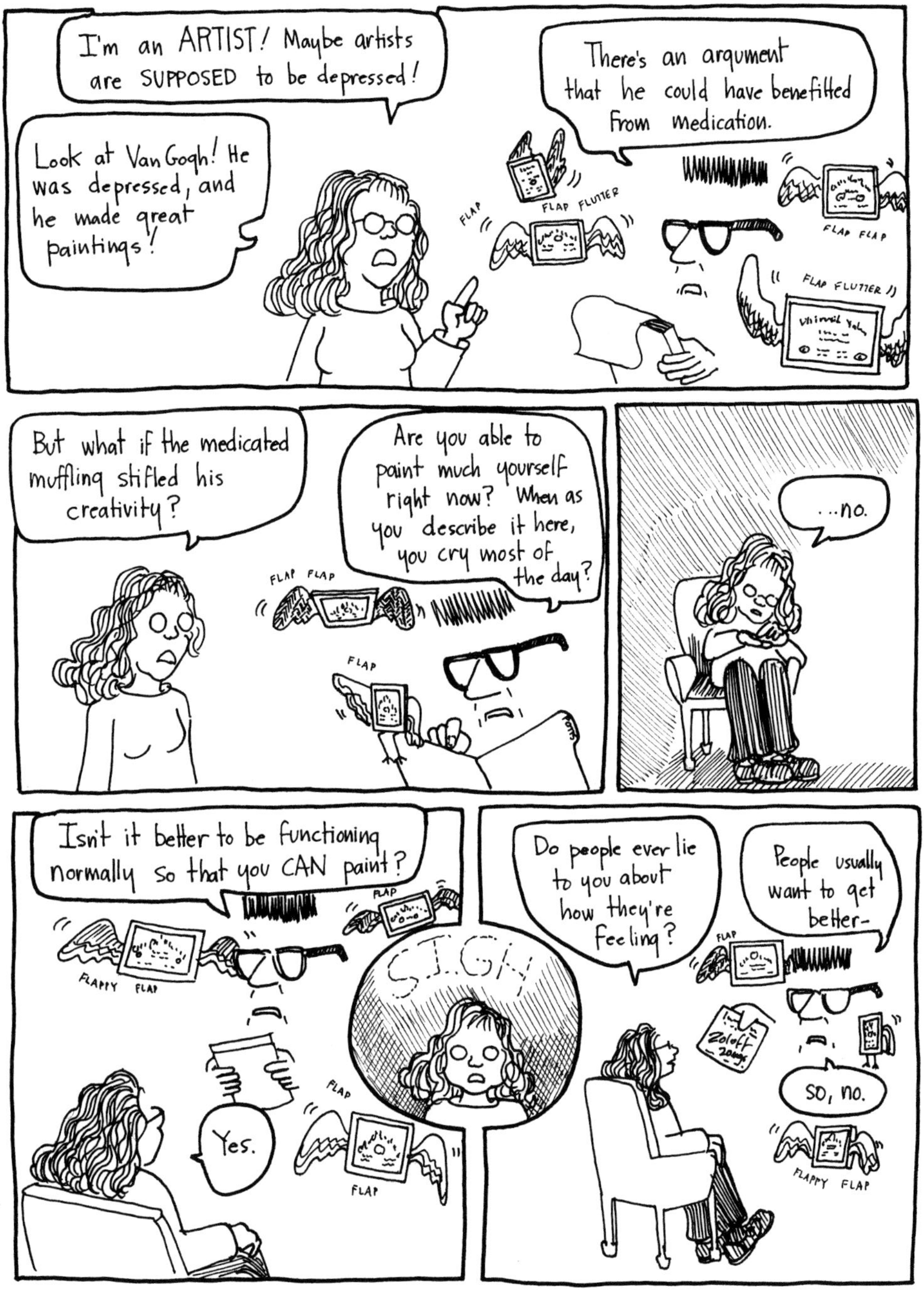
I'm an ARTIST! Maybe artists are SUPPOSED to be depressed!
Look at Van Gogh! He was depressed, and he made great paintings!
There's an argument that he could have benefitted from medication.
FLAP
FLAP FLUTTER
FLAP FLAP
FLAP FLUTTER
But what if the medicated muffling stifled his creativity?
Are you able to paint much yourself right now? When as you describe it here, you cry most of the day?
FLAP FLAP
FLAP
...no.
Isn't it better to be functioning normally so that you CAN paint?
FLAP
FLAPPY FLAP
SIGH
Yes.
FLAP
FLAP
Do people ever lie to you about how they're feeling?
People usually want to get better-
FLAP
Zoloft
So, no.
FLAPPY FLAP

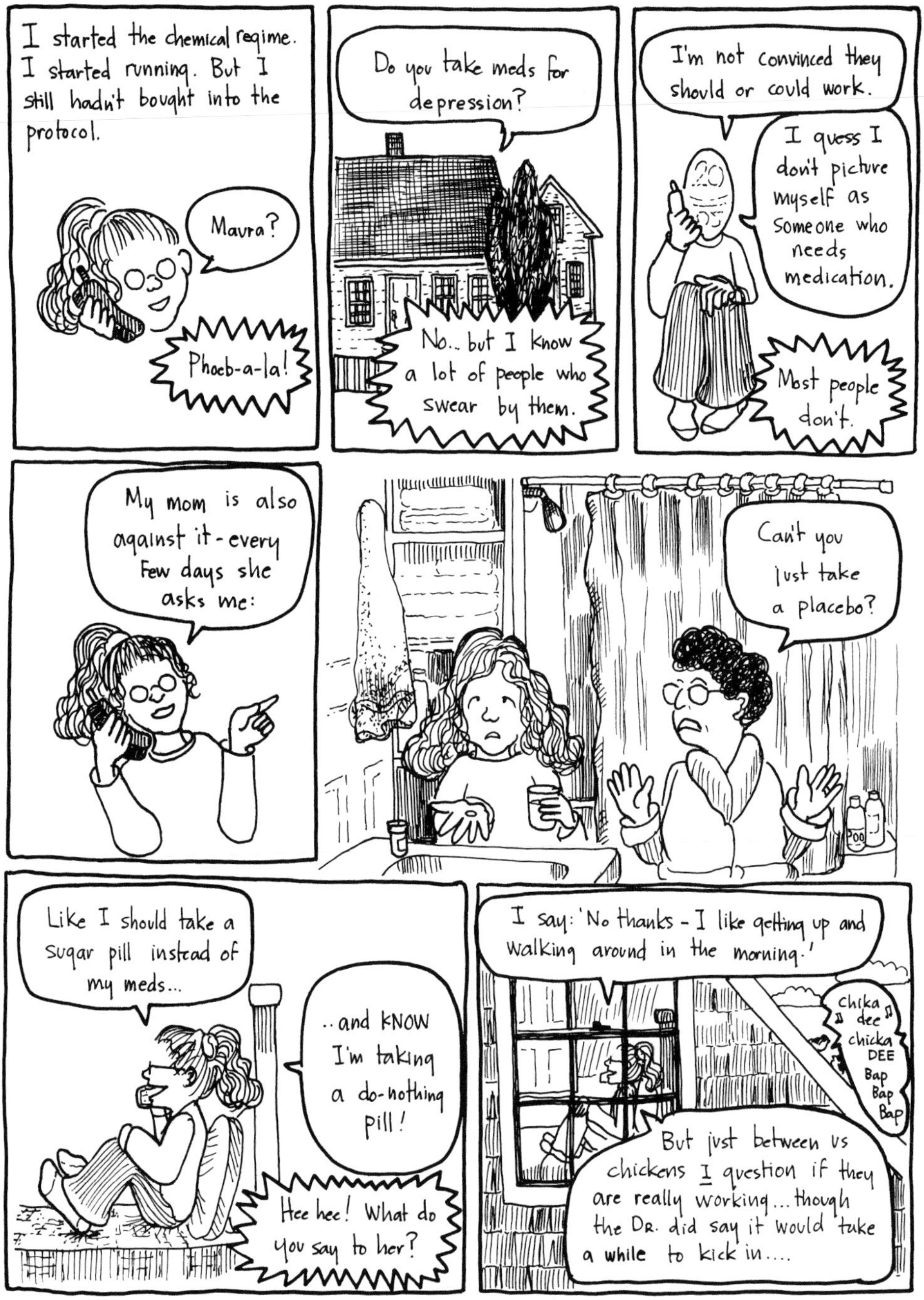
I started the chemical regime. I started running. But I still hadn't bought into the protocol.
Maura?
Phoeb-a-la!
Do you take meds for depression?
No.. but I know a lot of people who swear by them.
I'm not convinced they should or could work.
I guess I don't picture myself as someone who needs medication.
Most people don't.
My mom is also against it - every few days she asks me:
Can't you just take a placebo?
Like I should take a sugar pill instead of my meds...
..and KNOW I'm taking a do-nothing pill!
Hee hee! What do you say to her?
I say: 'No thanks - I like getting up and walking around in the morning.'
Chika dee chicka DEE Bap Bap Bap
But just between us chickens I question if they are really working... though the Dr. did say it would take a while to kick in....

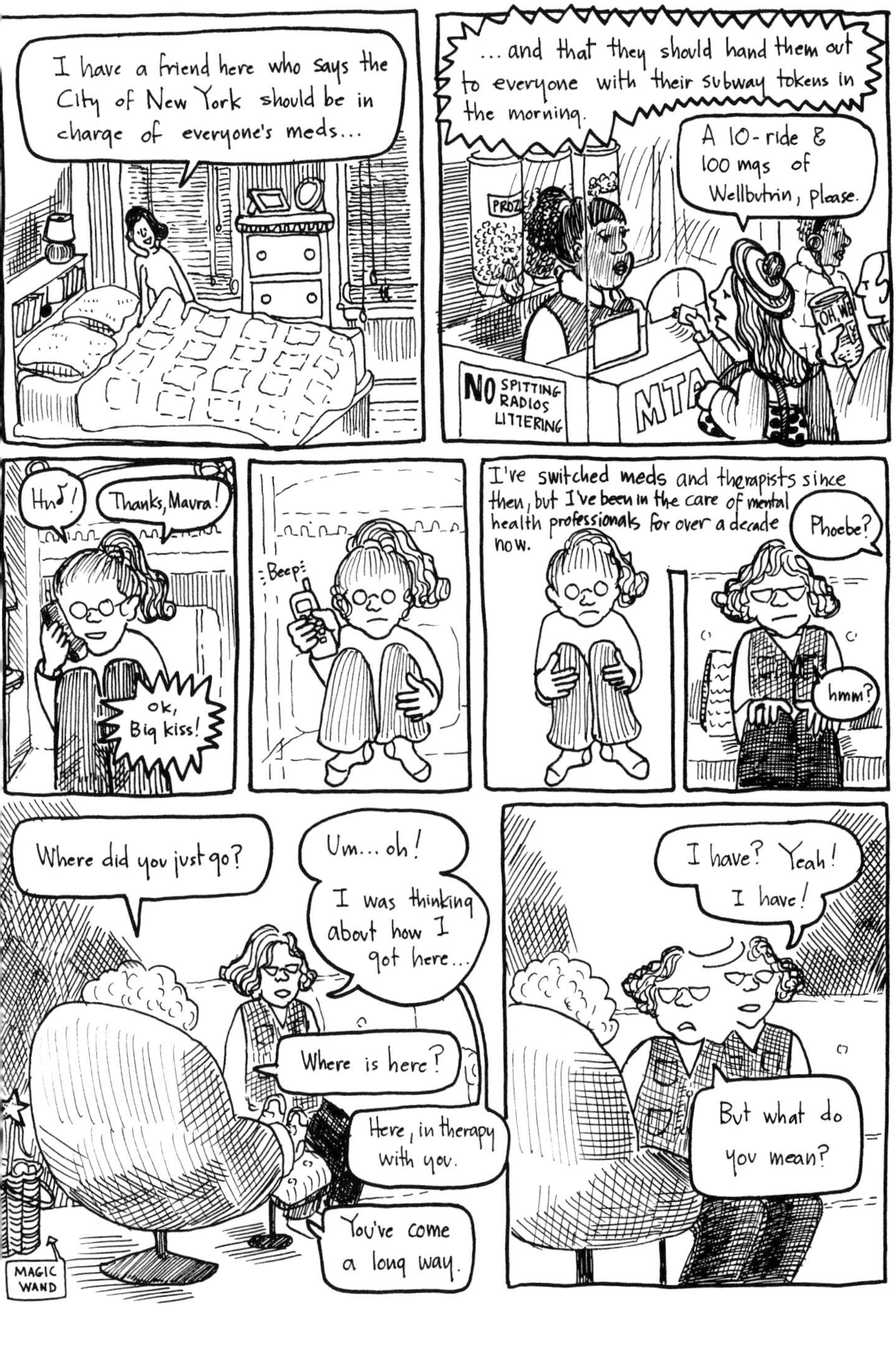
I have a friend here who says the City of New York should be in charge of everyone's meds...
...and that they should hand them out to everyone with their subway tokens in the morning.
A 10-ride & 100 mgs of Wellbutrin, please.
PROZ
NO SPITTING RADIOS LITTERING
MTA
Hn♪!
Thanks, Mavra!
ok, Big kiss!
Beep
I've switched meds and therapists since then, but I've been in the care of mental health professionals for over a decade now.
Phoebe?
hmm?
Where did you just go?
Um... oh!
I was thinking about how I got here...
Where is here?
Here, in therapy with you.
You've come a long way.
MAGIC WAND
I have? Yeah! I have!
But what do you mean?

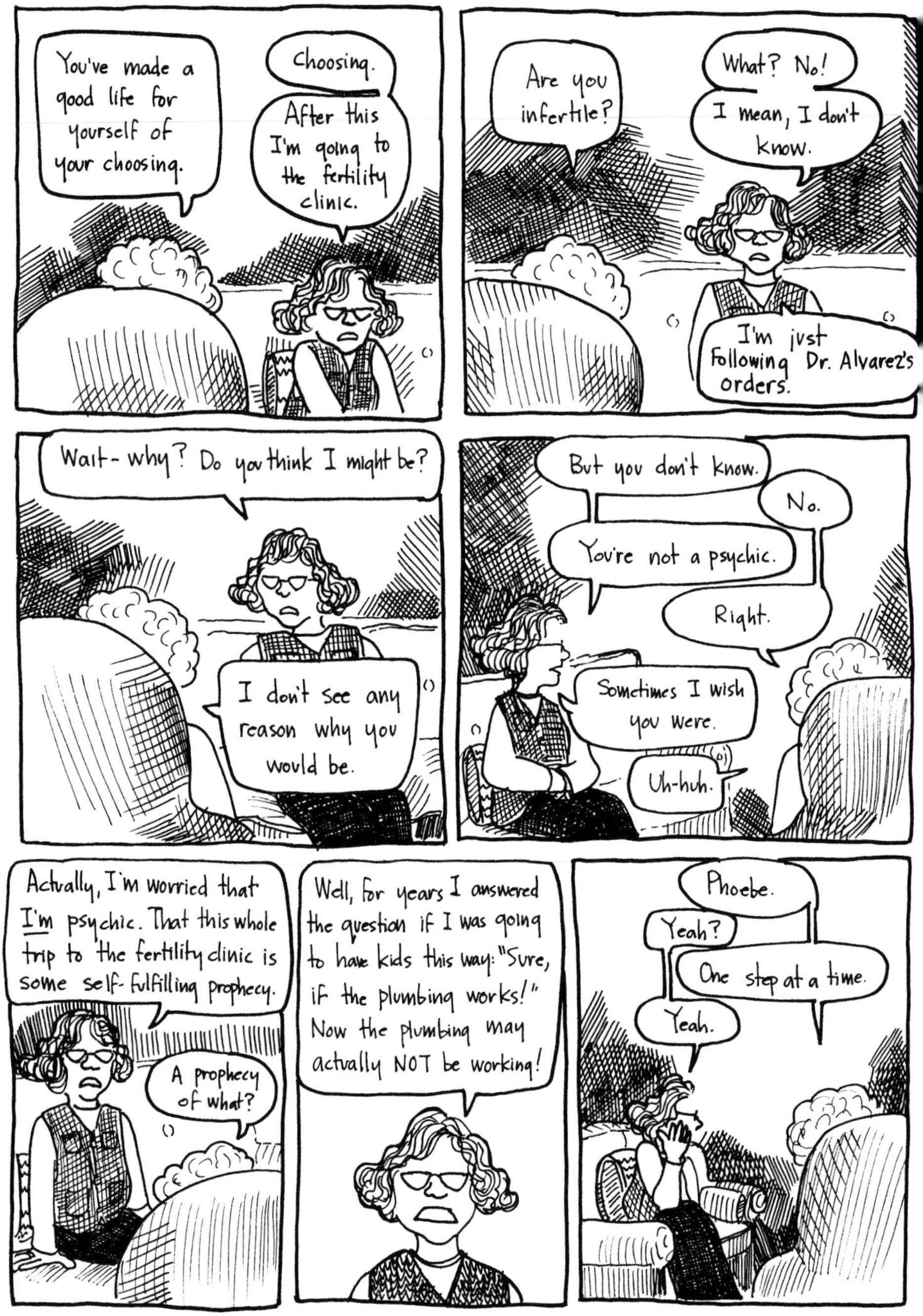

You've made a good life for yourself of your choosing.
Choosing.
After this I'm going to the fertility clinic.
Are you infertile?
What? No!
I mean, I don't know.
I'm just following Dr. Alvarez's orders.
Wait- why? Do you think I might be?
I don't see any reason why you would be.
But you don't know.
No.
You're not a psychic.
Right.
Sometimes I wish you were.
Uh-huh.
Actually, I'm worried that I'm psychic. That this whole trip to the fertility clinic is some self-fulfilling prophecy.
A prophecy of what?
Well, for years I answered the question if I was going to have kids this way: "Sure, if the plumbing works!" Now the plumbing may actually NOT be working!
Phoebe.
Yeah?
One step at a time.
Yeah.

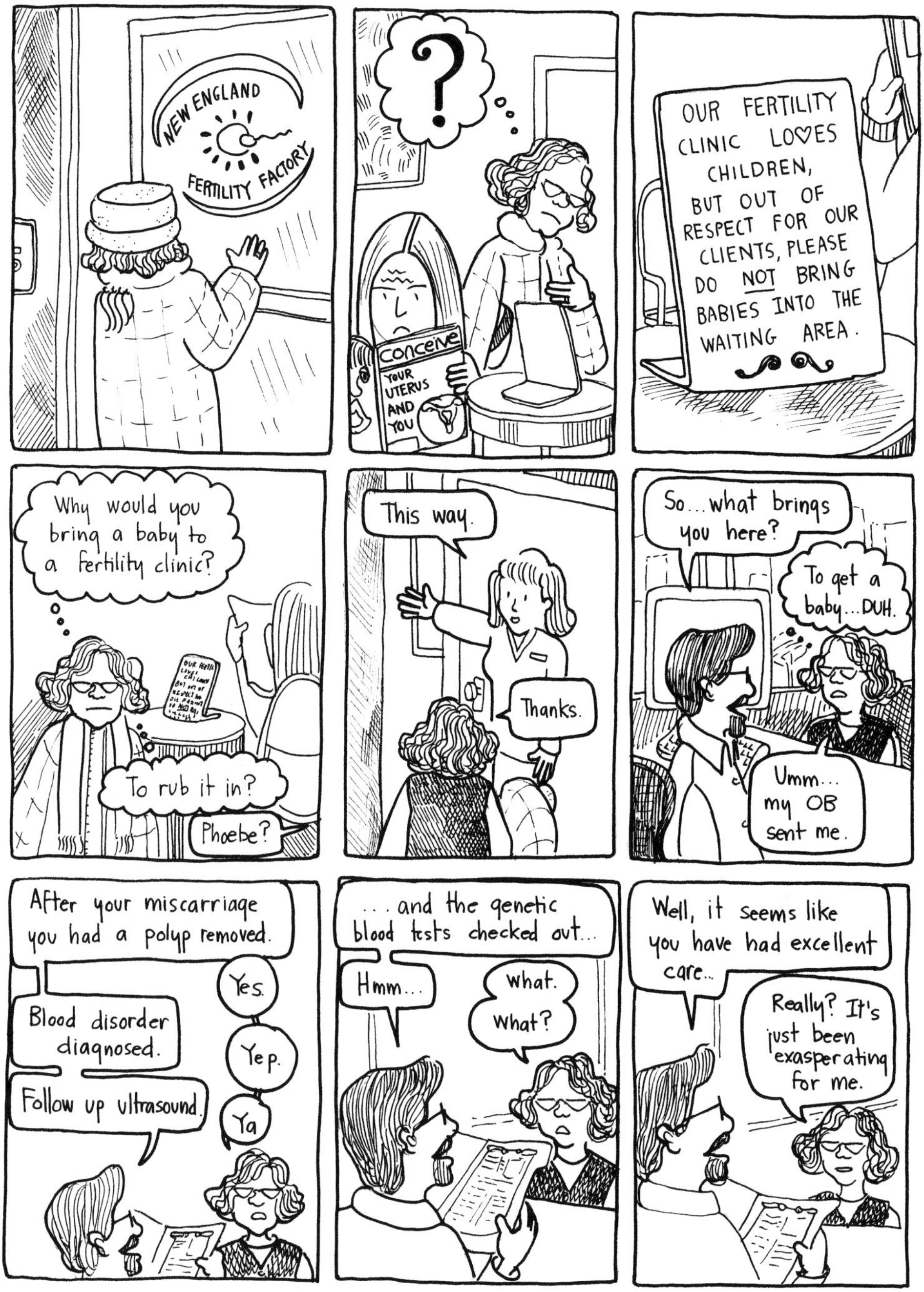

NEW ENGLAND FERTILITY FACTORY
?
Conceive
YOUR UTERUS AND YOU
OUR FERTILITY CLINIC LOVES CHILDREN, BUT OUT OF RESPECT FOR OUR CLIENTS, PLEASE DO NOT BRING BABIES INTO THE WAITING AREA.
Why would you bring a baby to a fertility clinic?
To rub it in?
Phoebe?
This way.
Thanks.
So...what brings you here?
To get a baby...DUH.
Umm... my OB sent me.
After your miscarriage you had a polyp removed.
Yes.
Blood disorder diagnosed.
Yep.
Follow up ultrasound.
Ya
...and the genetic blood tests checked out...
Hmm...
what.
What?
Well, it seems like you have had excellent care...
Really? It's just been exasperating for me.

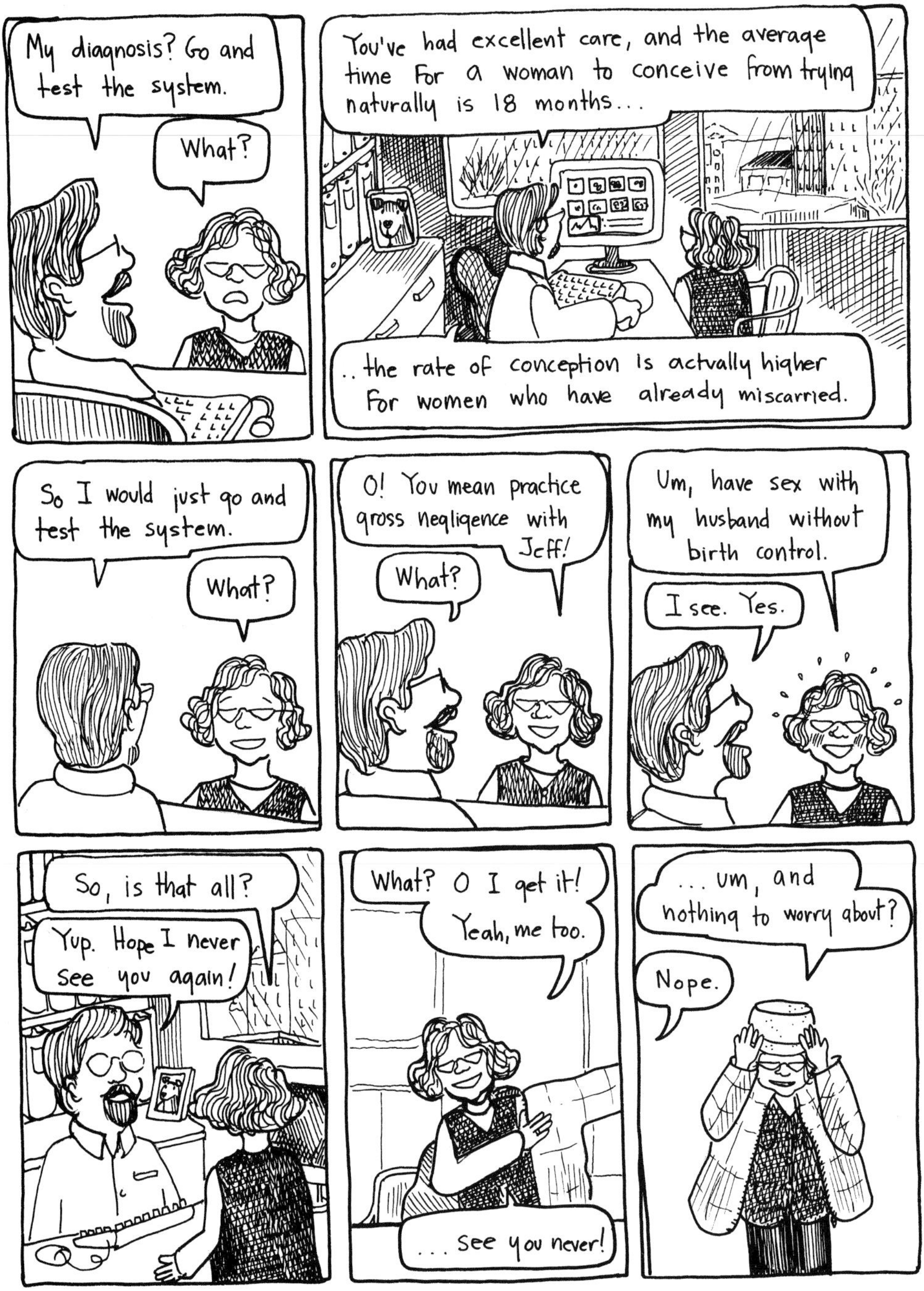
My diagnosis? Go and test the system.
What?
You've had excellent care, and the average time for a woman to conceive from trying naturally is 18 months...
...the rate of conception is actually higher for women who have already miscarried.
So I would just go and test the system.
What?
O! You mean practice gross negligence with Jeff!
What?
Um, have sex with my husband without birth control.
I see. Yes.
So, is that all?
Yup. Hope I never see you again!
What? O I get it! Yeah, me too.
...see you never!
...um, and nothing to worry about?
Nope.

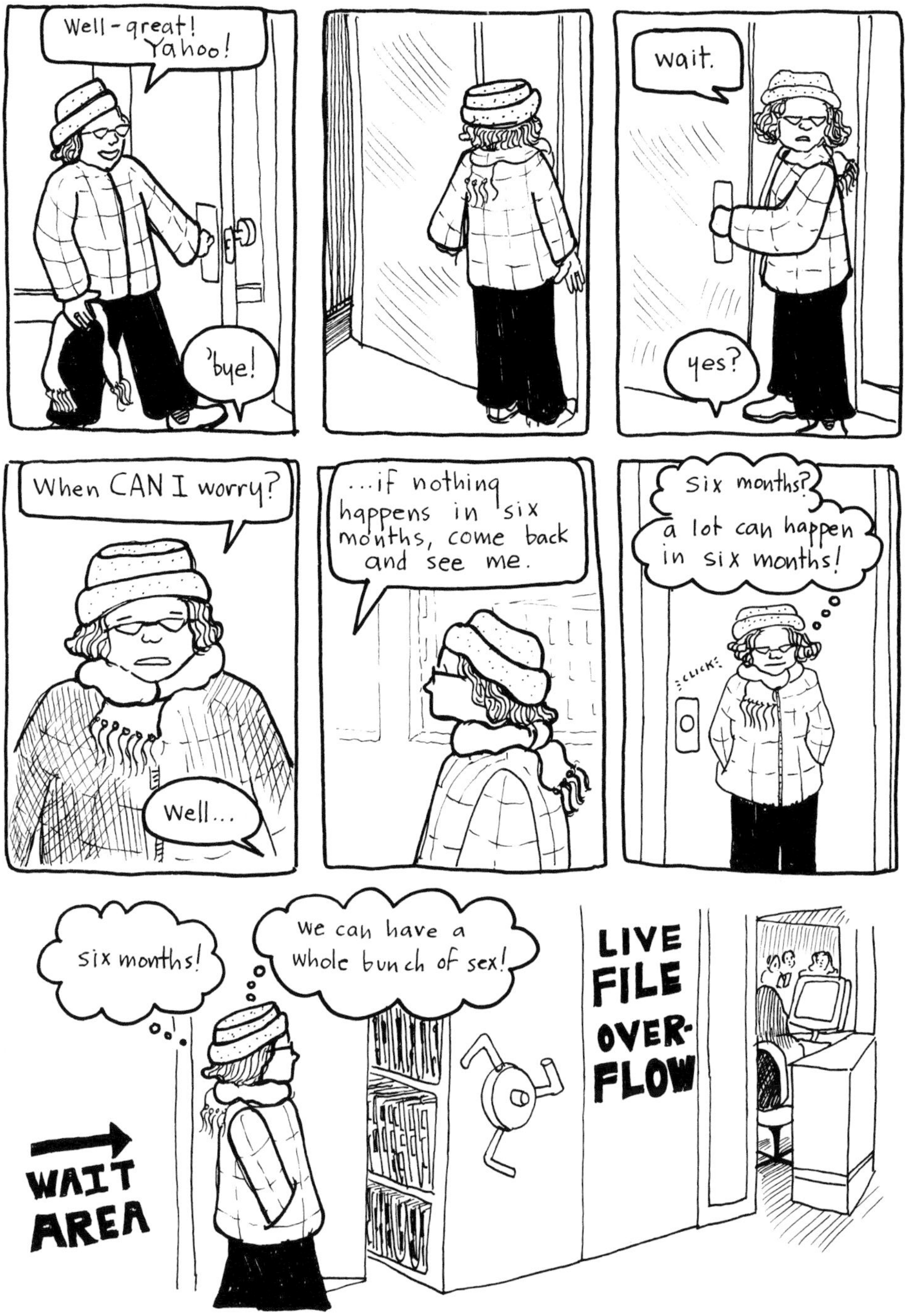
Well-great! Yahoo!
'bye!
wait.
yes?
When CAN I worry?
Well...
...if nothing happens in six months, come back and see me.
six months?
a lot can happen in six months!
CLICK
six months!
We can have a whole bunch of sex!
LIVE FILE OVER-FLOW
WAIT AREA

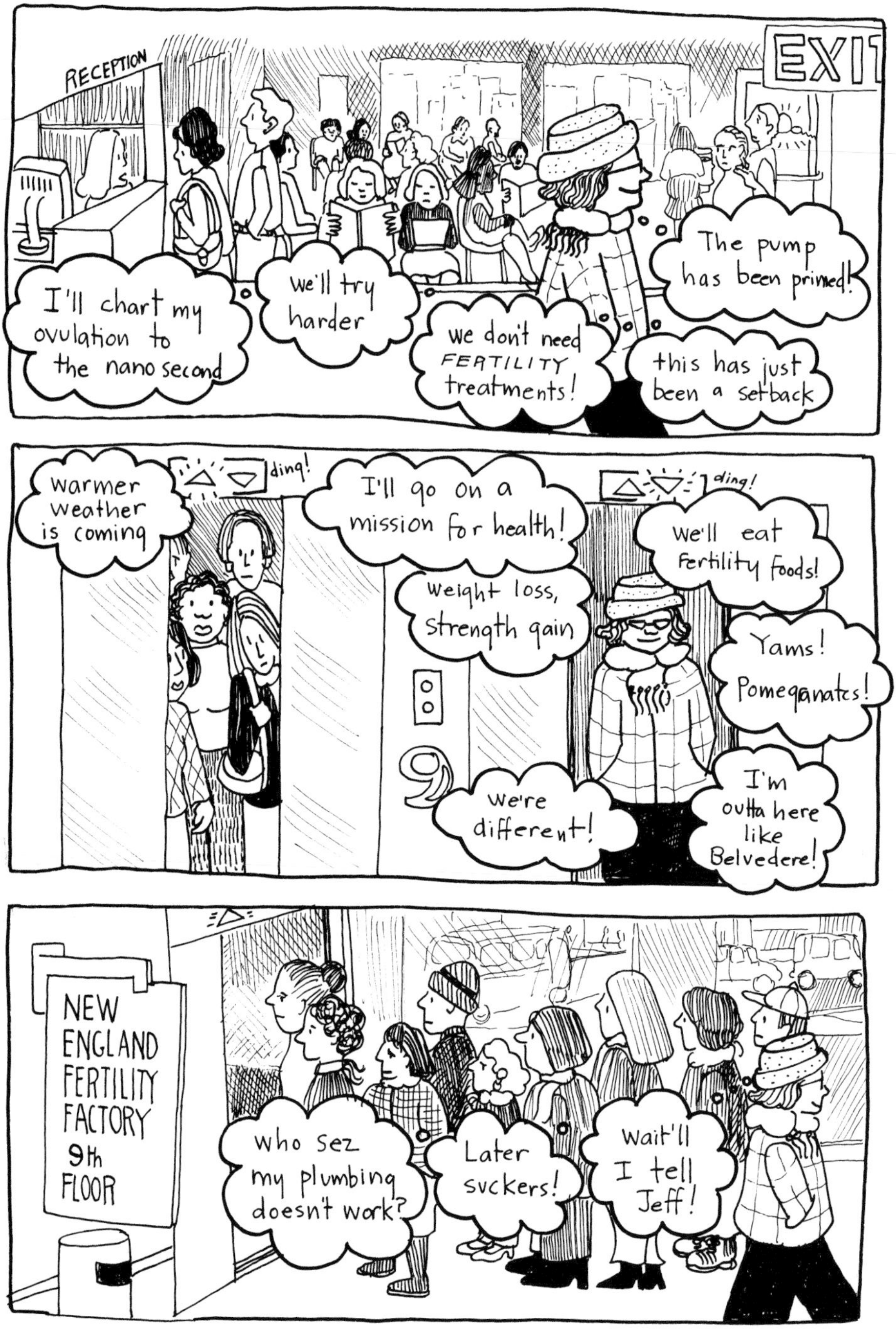
RECEPTION
EXIT
I'll chart my ovulation to the nano second
we'll try harder
we don't need FERTILITY treatments!
The pump has been primed!
this has just been a setback
warmer weather is coming
ding!
I'll go on a mission for health!
Weight loss, Strength gain
ding!
We'll eat Fertility Foods!
Yams!
Pomegranates!
9
we're different!
I'm outta here like Belvedere!
NEW ENGLAND FERTILITY FACTORY 9th FLOOR
Who sez my plumbing doesn't work?
Later suckers!
Wait'll I tell Jeff!

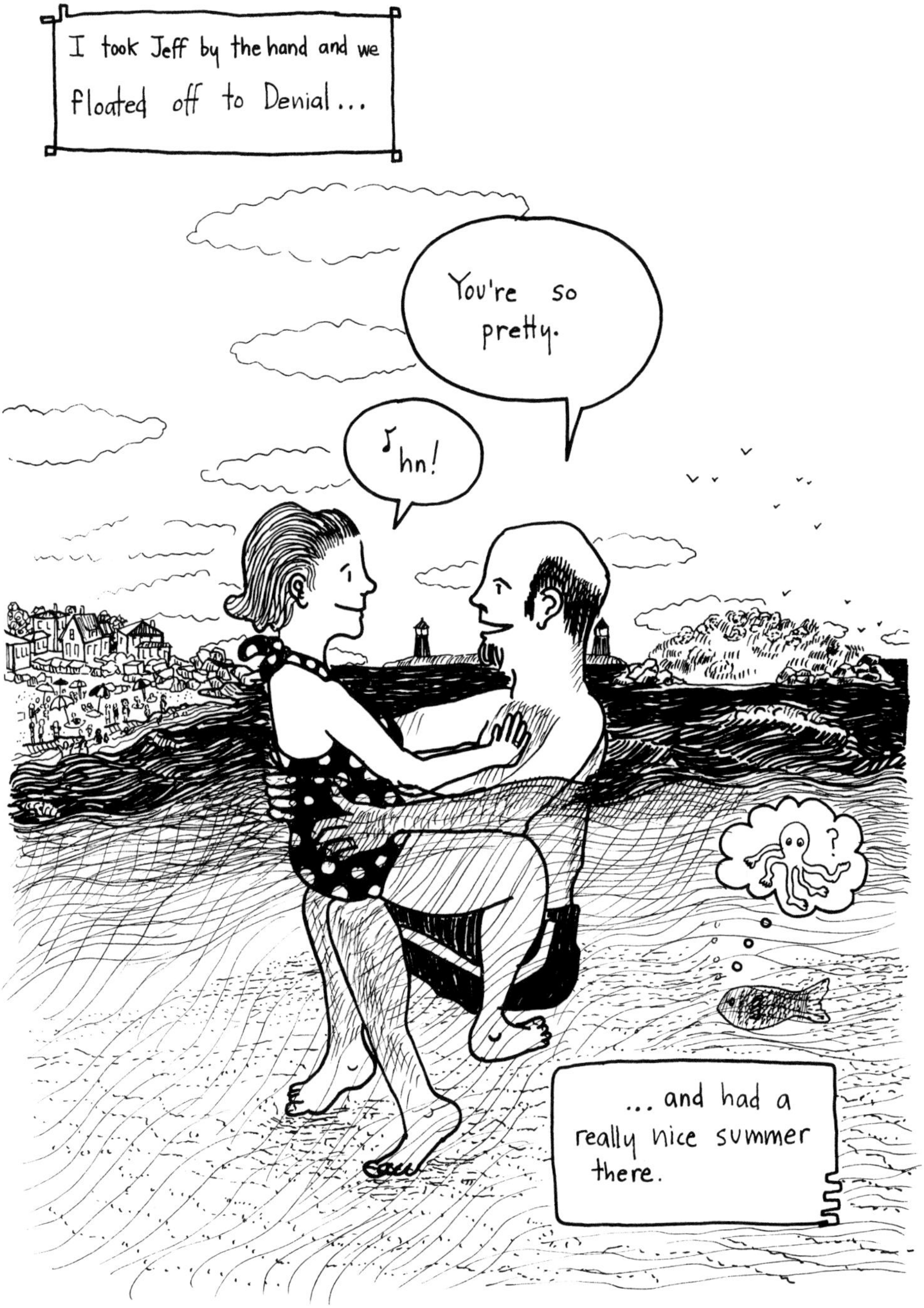
I took Jeff by the hand and we floated off to Denial...
You're so pretty.
♪hn!
...and had a really nice summer there.

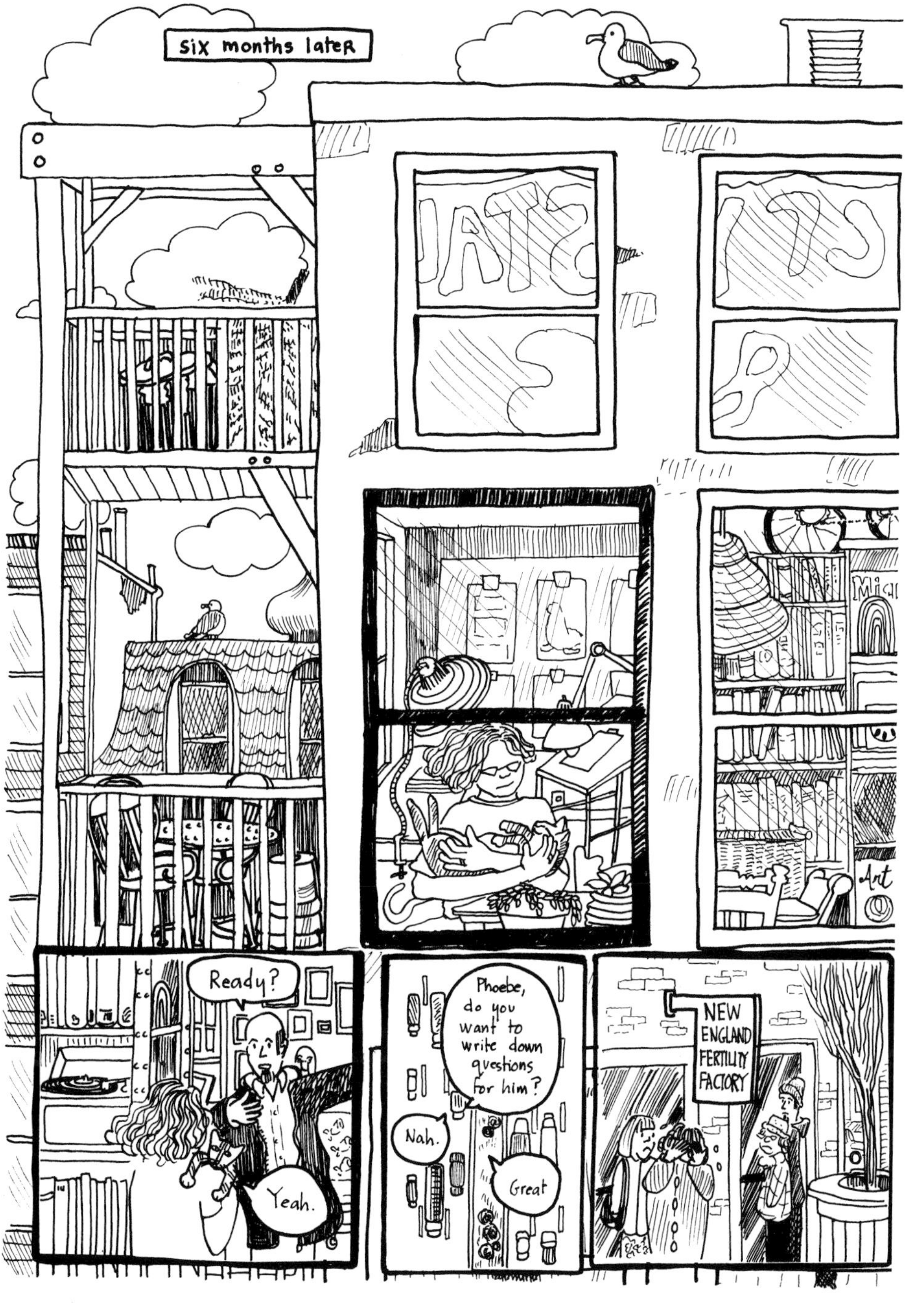
six months later
Ready?
Yeah.
Phoebe, do you want to write down questions for him?
Nah.
Great
NEW ENGLAND FERTILITY FACTORY

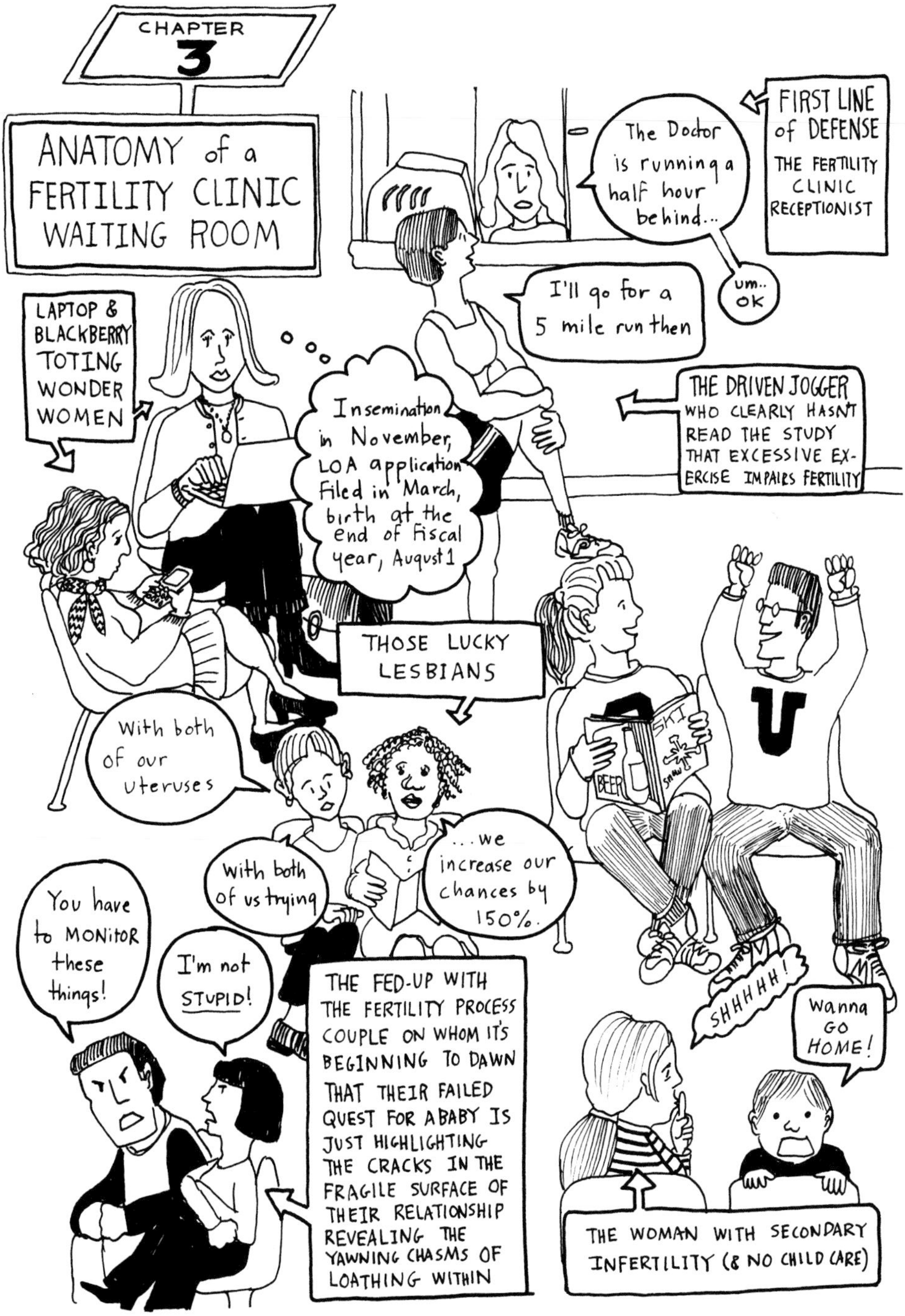
CHAPTER 3
ANATOMY of a FERTILITY CLINIC WAITING ROOM
FIRST LINE of DEFENSE THE FERTILITY CLINIC RECEPTIONIST
The Doctor is running a half hour behind...
um.. ok
I'll go for a 5 mile run then
THE DRIVEN JOGGER WHO CLEARLY HASN'T READ THE STUDY THAT EXCESSIVE EXERCISE IMPAIRS FERTILITY
LAPTOP & BLACKBERRY TOTING WONDER WOMEN
Insemination in November, LOA application filed in March, birth at the end of fiscal year, August 1
THOSE LUCKY LESBIANS
With both of our uteruses
With both of us trying
...we increase our chances by 150%.
BEER
SKI
U
SHHHHH!
You have to MONITOR these things!
I'm not STUPID!
THE FED-UP WITH THE FERTILITY PROCESS COUPLE ON WHOM IT'S BEGINNING TO DAWN THAT THEIR FAILED QUEST FOR A BABY IS JUST HIGHLIGHTING THE CRACKS IN THE FRAGILE SURFACE OF THEIR RELATIONSHIP REVEALING THE YAWNING CHASMS OF LOATHING WITHIN
Wanna GO HOME!
THE WOMAN WITH SECONDARY INFERTILITY (& NO CHILD CARE)

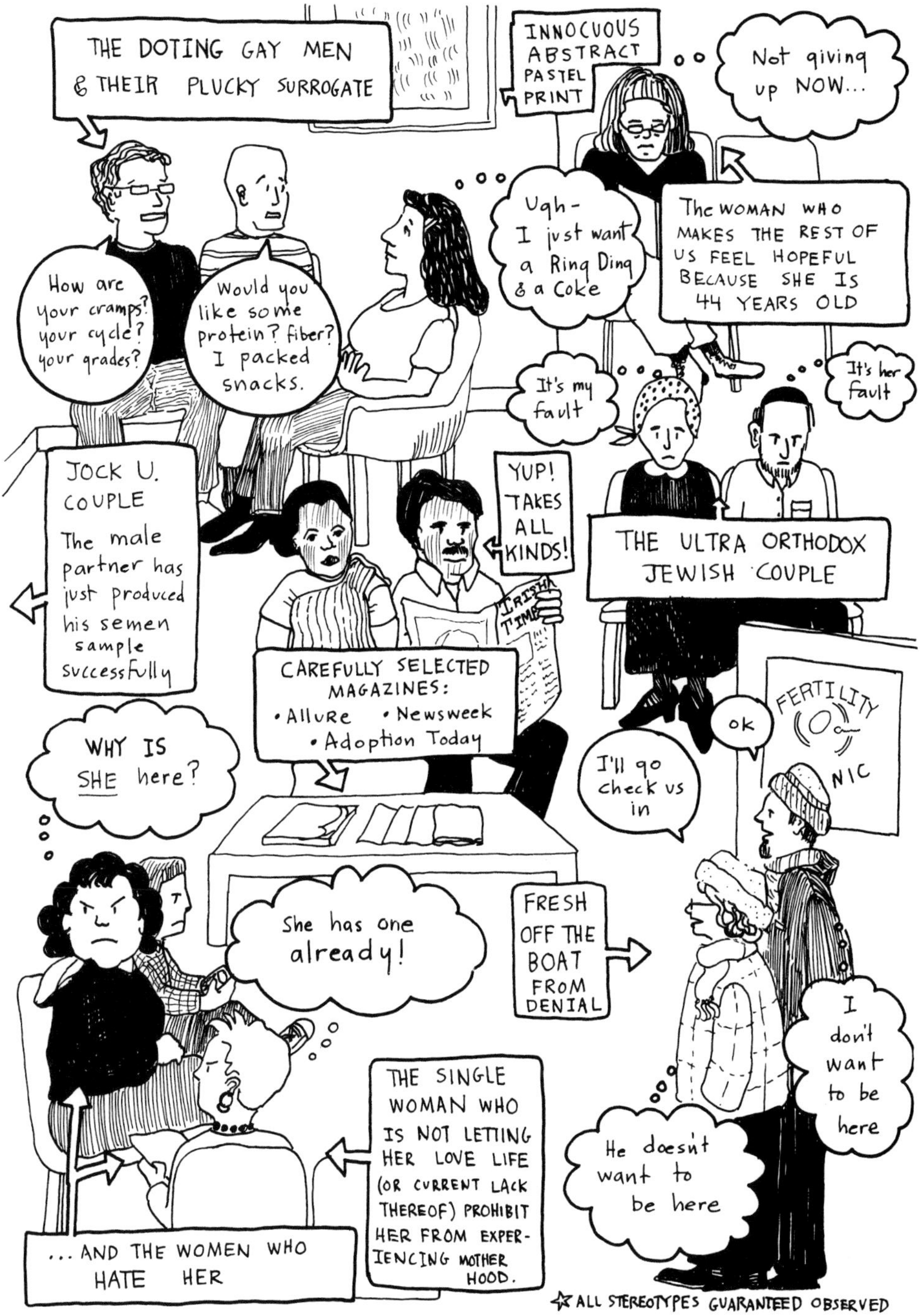
THE DOTING GAY MEN & THEIR PLUCKY SURROGATE
INNOCUOUS ABSTRACT PASTEL PRINT
Not giving up NOW...
How are your cramps? your cycle? your grades?
Would you like some protein? fiber? I packed snacks.
Ugh- I just want a Ring Ding & a Coke
The WOMAN WHO MAKES THE REST OF US FEEL HOPEFUL BECAUSE SHE IS 44 YEARS OLD
It's my fault
It's her fault
JOCK U. COUPLE The male partner has just produced his semen sample successfully
YUP! TAKES ALL KINDS!
IRISH TIMES
THE ULTRA ORTHODOX JEWISH COUPLE
CAREFULLY SELECTED MAGAZINES: • Allure • Newsweek • Adoption Today
FERTILITY CLINIC
ok
I'll go check us in
WHY IS SHE here?
She has one already!
FRESH OFF THE BOAT FROM DENIAL
I don't want to be here
He doesn't want to be here
THE SINGLE WOMAN WHO IS NOT LETTING HER LOVE LIFE (OR CURRENT LACK THEREOF) PROHIBIT HER FROM EXPERIENCING MOTHERHOOD.
... AND THE WOMEN WHO HATE HER
☆ ALL STEREOTYPES GUARANTEED OBSERVED

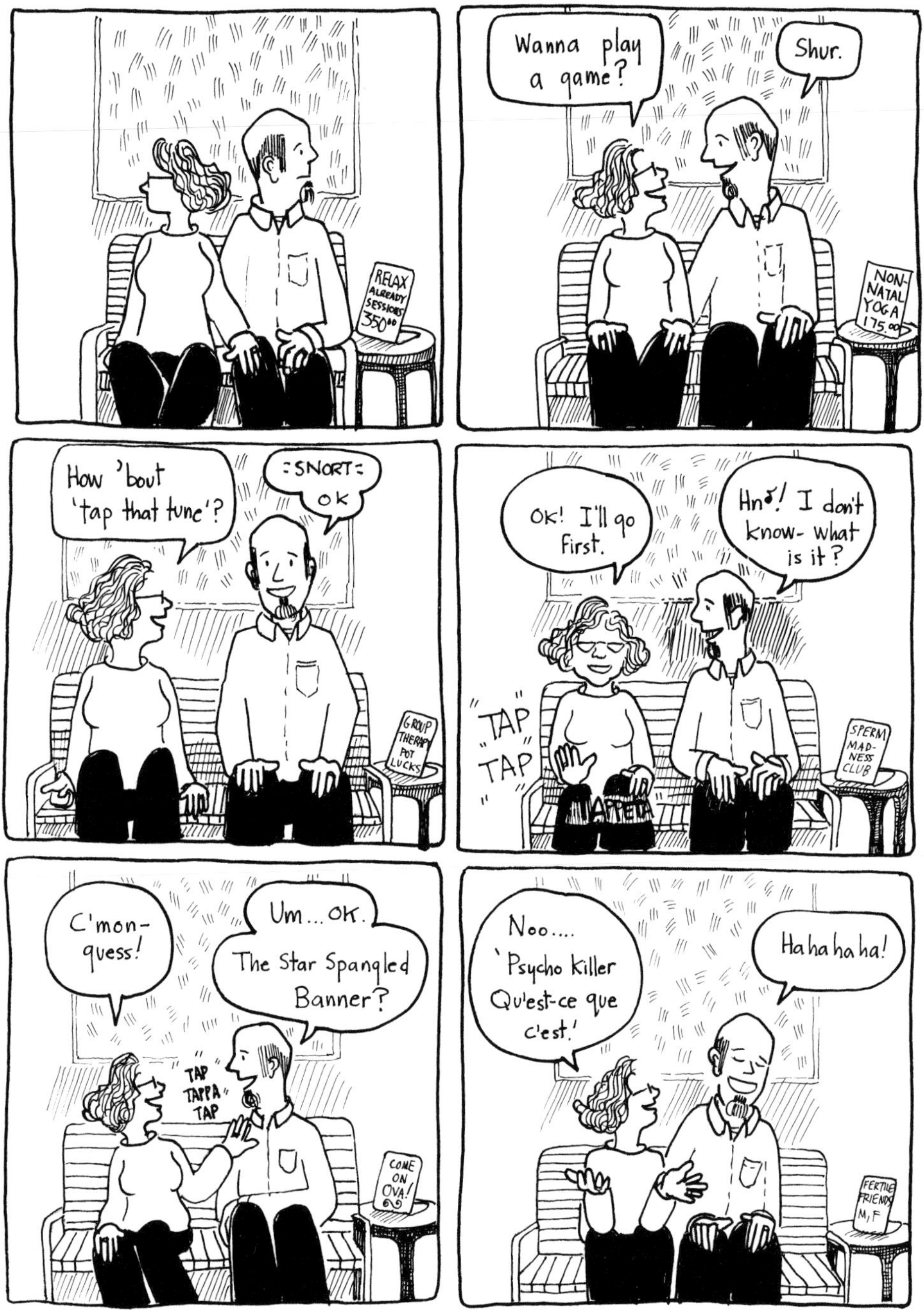
RELAX ALREADY SESSIONS 350.00
Wanna play a game?
Shur.
NON-NATAL YOGA 175.00
How 'bout 'tap that tune'?
:SNORT: OK
GROUP THERAPY POT LUCKS
OK! I'll go first.
Hn♪! I don't know- what is it?
"TAP" "TAP"
TAPPETA
SPERM MADNESS CLUB
C'mon- guess!
Um... OK. The Star Spangled Banner?
TAP TAPPA TAP
COME ON OVA!
Noo.... 'Psycho Killer Qu'est-ce que c'est.'
Hahahaha!
FERTILE FRIENDS M, F

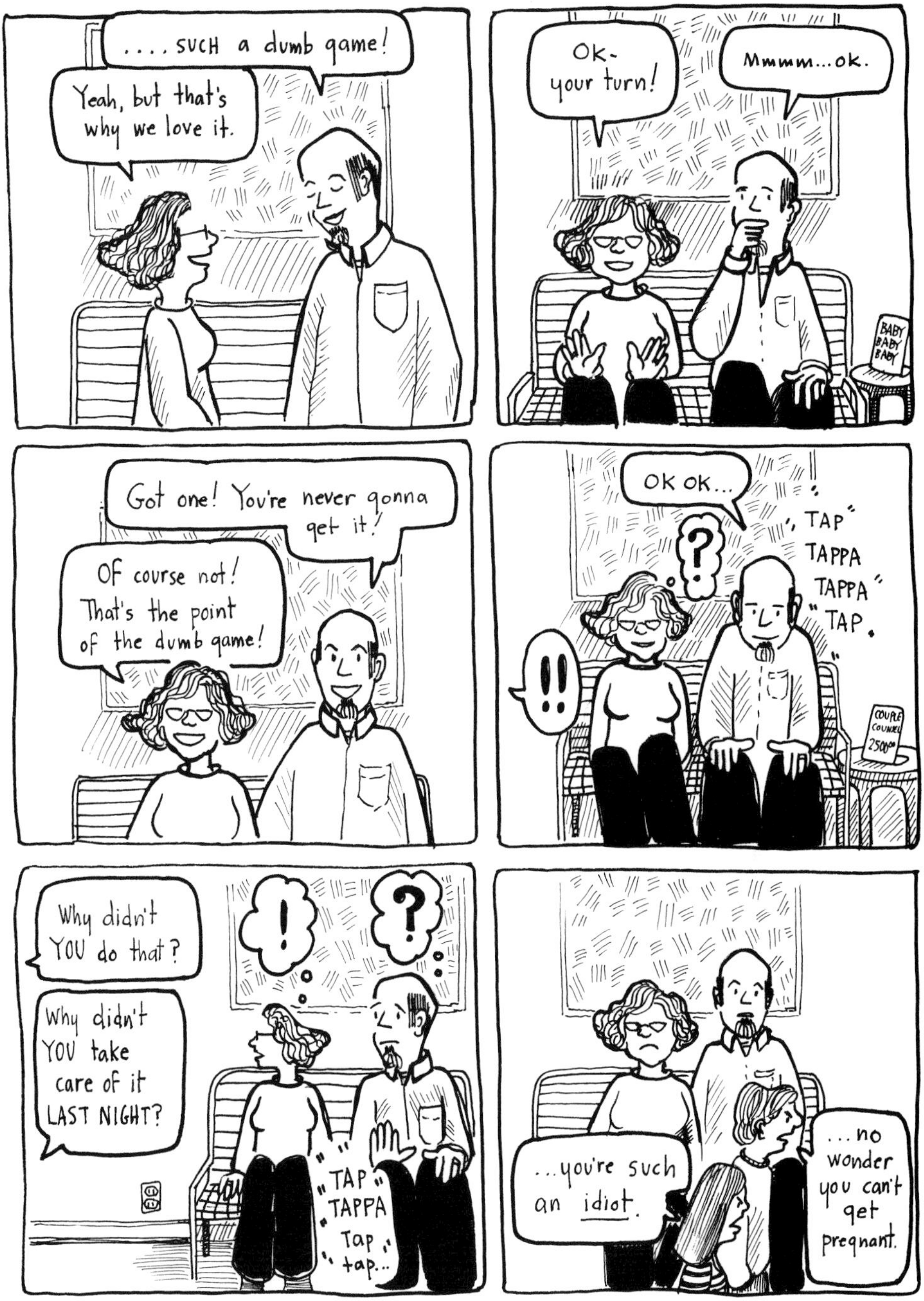

....SUCH a dumb game!
Yeah, but that's why we love it.
Ok- your turn!
Mmmm...ok.
BABY BABY BABY
Got one! You're never gonna get it!
Of course not! That's the point of the dumb game!
OK OK...
?
TAP TAPPA TAPPA TAP.
!!
COUPLE COUNSEL
Why didn't YOU do that?
Why didn't YOU take care of it LAST NIGHT?
!
?
TAP TAPPA Tap tap...
...you're such an idiot.
...no wonder you can't get pregnant.

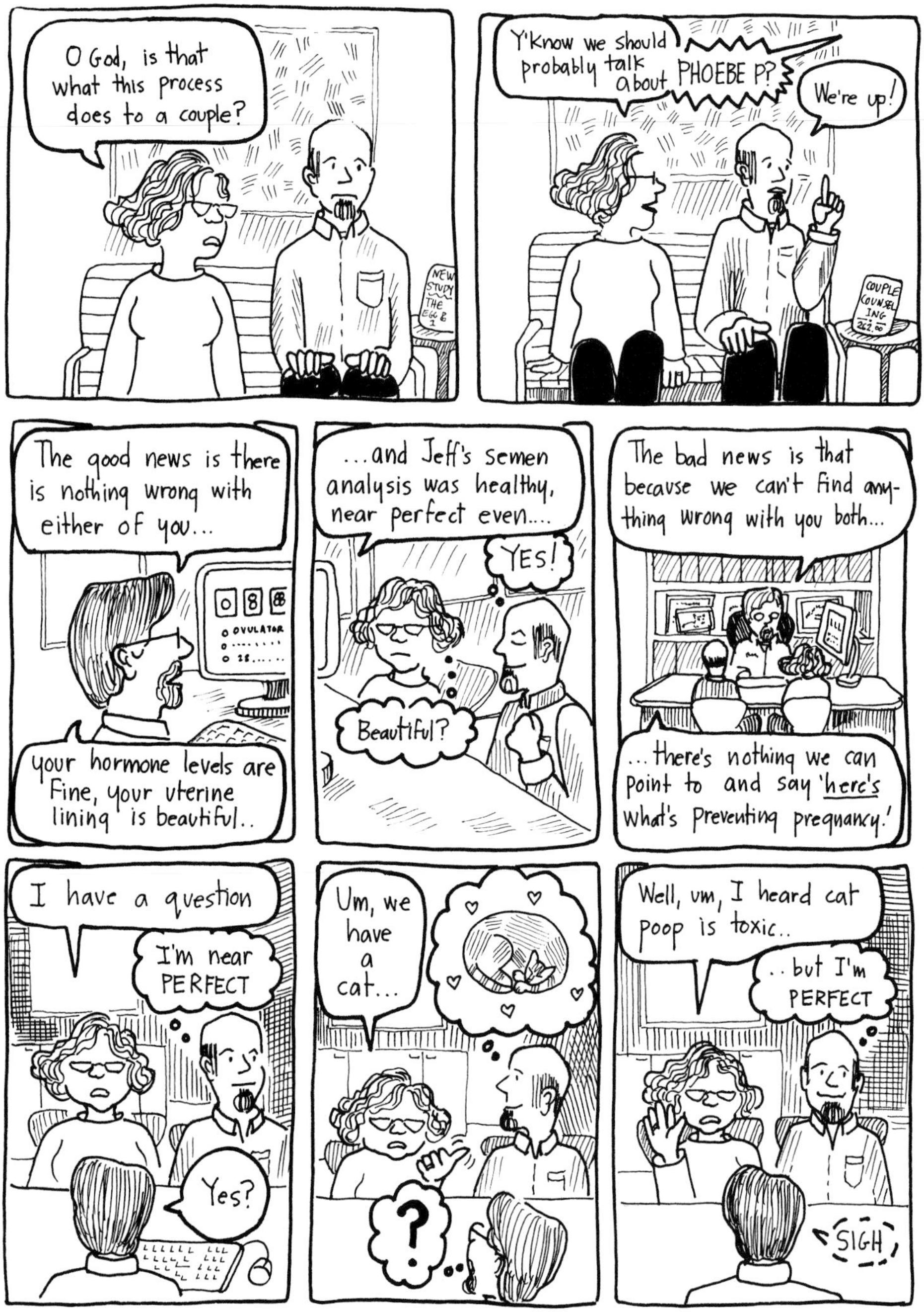
O God, is that what this process does to a couple?
Y'know we should probably talk about
PHOEBE P?
We're up!
COUPLE COUNSELING
The good news is there is nothing wrong with either of you...
OVULATOR
your hormone levels are fine, your uterine lining is beautiful..
...and Jeff's semen analysis was healthy, near perfect even....
YES!
Beautiful?
The bad news is that because we can't find anything wrong with you both...
...there's nothing we can point to and say 'here's what's preventing pregnancy.'
I have a question
I'm near PERFECT
Yes?
Um, we have a cat...
?
Well, um, I heard cat poop is toxic..
..but I'm PERFECT
SIGH

You can use gloves to change the litter, but having a cat does not impair your fertility.

PURRR-fect

Ok, well, I stay in the kitchen when the microwave is on, and I've read that there's all kinds of the bad soy in half of what I eat, and I have a desk job I hate in a biolab so not only am I stressed but the air I'm breathing has who knows what in it, I commute to said hated job 3 hours a day, our city's water is full of who knows what

Look, all our parents got drunk and conceived us on New Year's Eve...

What I'm saying is if all those things hurt our fertility, none of us would be here.

Oh.

OK.

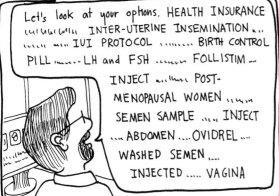

Let's look at your options. HEALTH INSURANCE .... INTER-UTERINE INSEMINATION .... IUI PROTOCOL .... BIRTH CONTROL PILL .... LH and FSH .... FOLLISTIM ... INJECT .... POST- MENOPAUSAL WOMEN .... SEMEN SAMPLE ...... INJECT .... ABDOMEN .... OVIDREL .... WASHED SEMEN .... INJECTED ..... VAGINA

Huh?

Um...

Right now your ovaries release one egg a month, if that

POP

♪ START SPREADIN' THE NEWS! ♪

SHOW OFF

but if the hormones in the pre-ovulatory phase are stimulated enough, the amount of eggs released from the follicles can be increased.

:CLICKA: :CLICK:

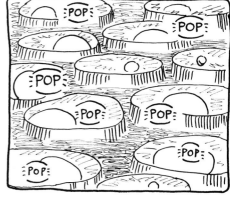

POP
POP
POP
POP
POP
POP

Fxlpht!

—YAWN— is it 2010 already?

are we really ALL going?

how exciting!

c'mon! race you to the uterus!

UNACCEPT-ABLE! I work ALONE!

but....but... I'm not on the schedule until just before menopause!

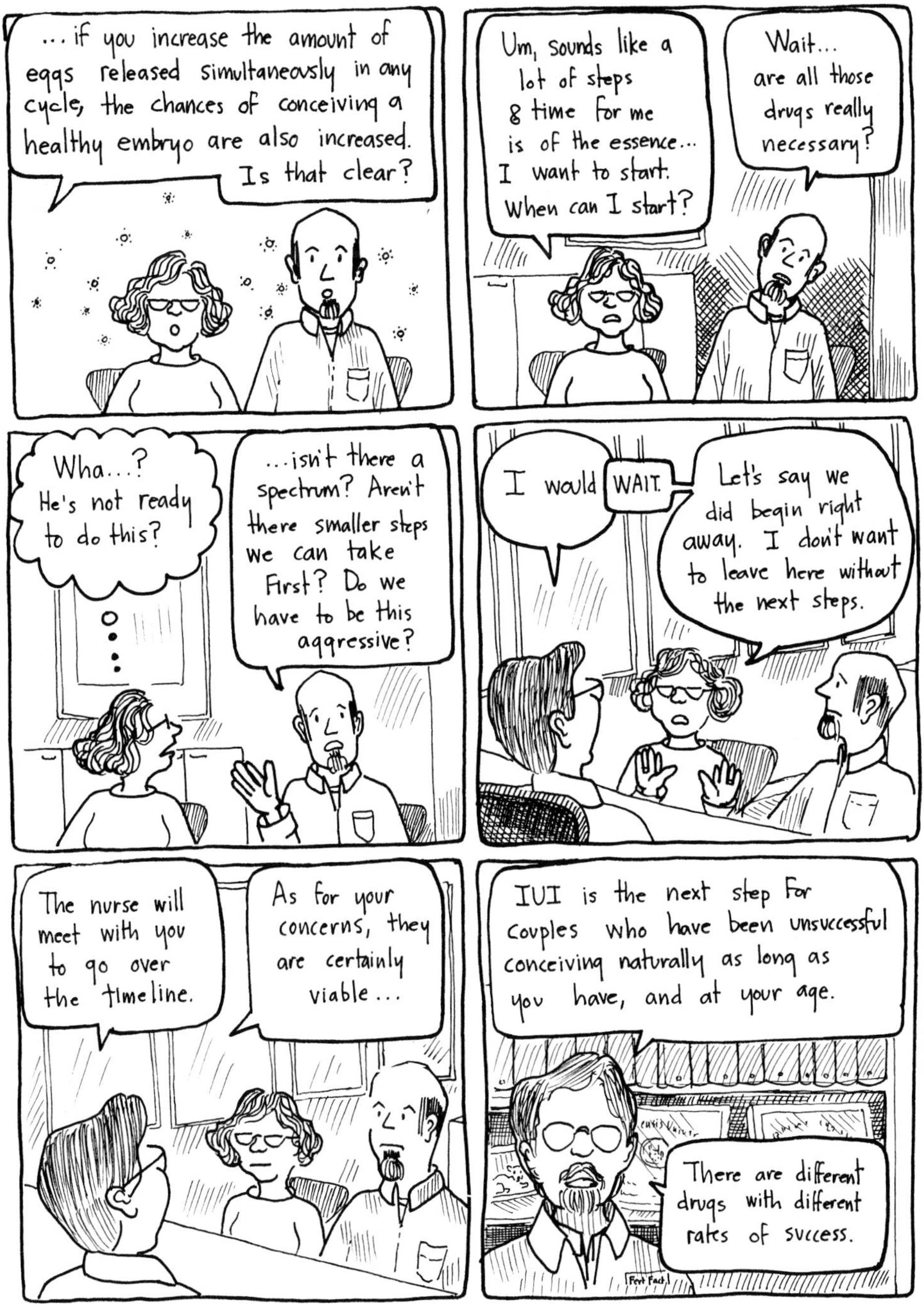
...if you increase the amount of eggs released simultaneously in any cycle, the chances of conceiving a healthy embryo are also increased. Is that clear?
Um, sounds like a lot of steps & time for me is of the essence... I want to start. When can I start?
Wait... are all those drugs really necessary?
Wha...? He's not ready to do this?
...isn't there a spectrum? Aren't there smaller steps we can take first? Do we have to be this aggressive?
I would
WAIT.
Let's say we did begin right away. I don't want to leave here without the next steps.
The nurse will meet with you to go over the timeline.
As for your concerns, they are certainly viable...
IUI is the next step for couples who have been unsuccessful conceiving naturally as long as you have, and at your age.
There are different drugs with different rates of success.

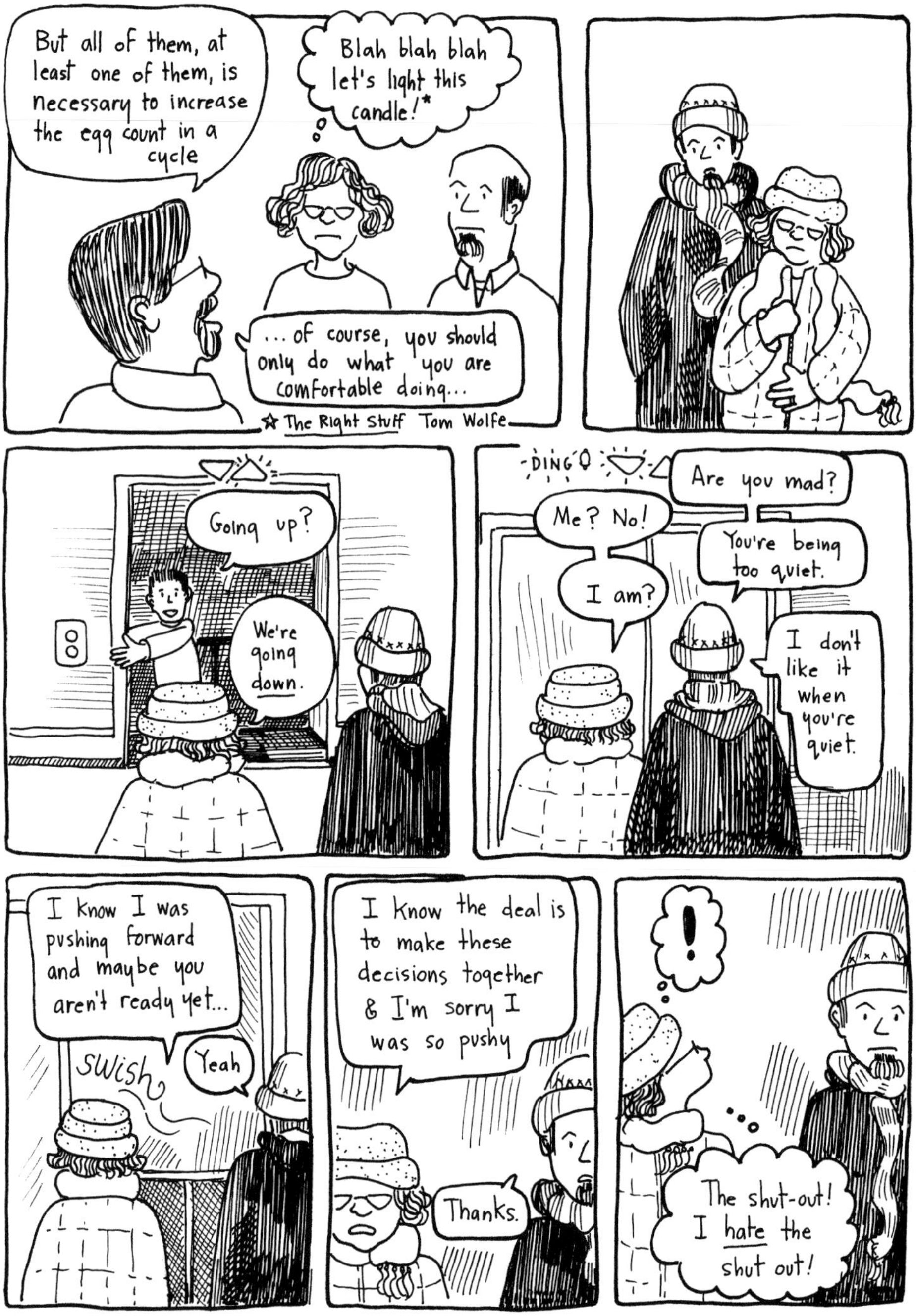
But all of them, at least one of them, is necessary to increase the egg count in a cycle
Blah blah blah let's light this candle!*
...of course, you should only do what you are comfortable doing...
☆ The Right Stuff Tom Wolfe
Going up?
We're going down.
-DING-
Are you mad?
Me? No!
You're being too quiet.
I am?
I don't like it when you're quiet.
I know I was pushing forward and maybe you aren't ready yet...
SWISH
Yeah
I know the deal is to make these decisions together & I'm sorry I was so pushy
Thanks.
!
...
The shut-out! I hate the shut out!

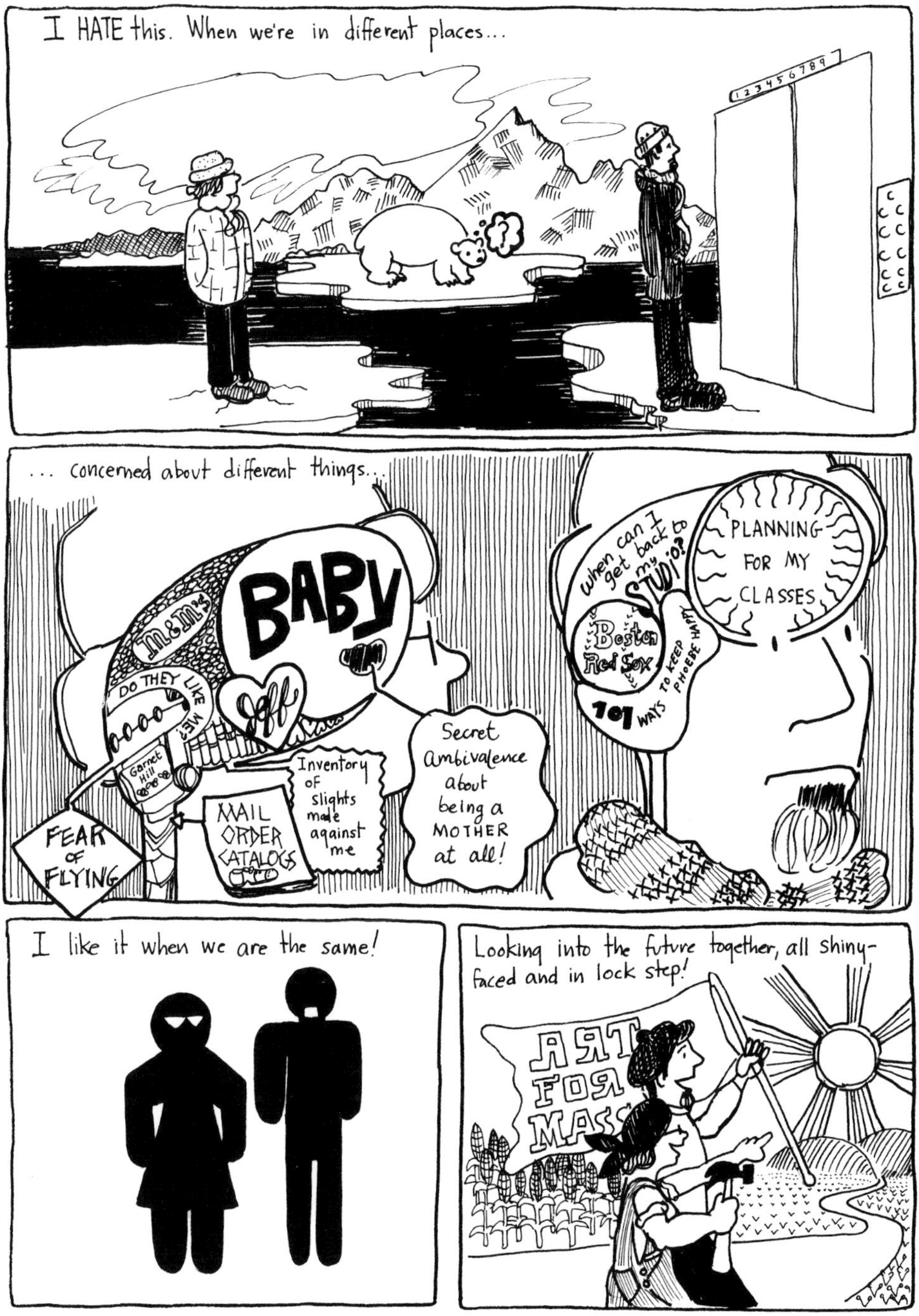

I HATE this. When we're in different places...
... concerned about different things...
BABY
m&m's
DO THEY LIKE ME?
Jeff
Garnet Hill
FEAR OF FLYING
MAIL ORDER CATALOGS
Inventory of slights made against me
Secret ambivalence about being a MOTHER at all!
when can I get back to my STUDIO?
PLANNING FOR MY CLASSES
Boston Red Sox
101 WAYS TO KEEP PHOEBE HAPPY
I like it when we are the same!
Looking into the future together, all shiny-faced and in lock step!
ART
FOR

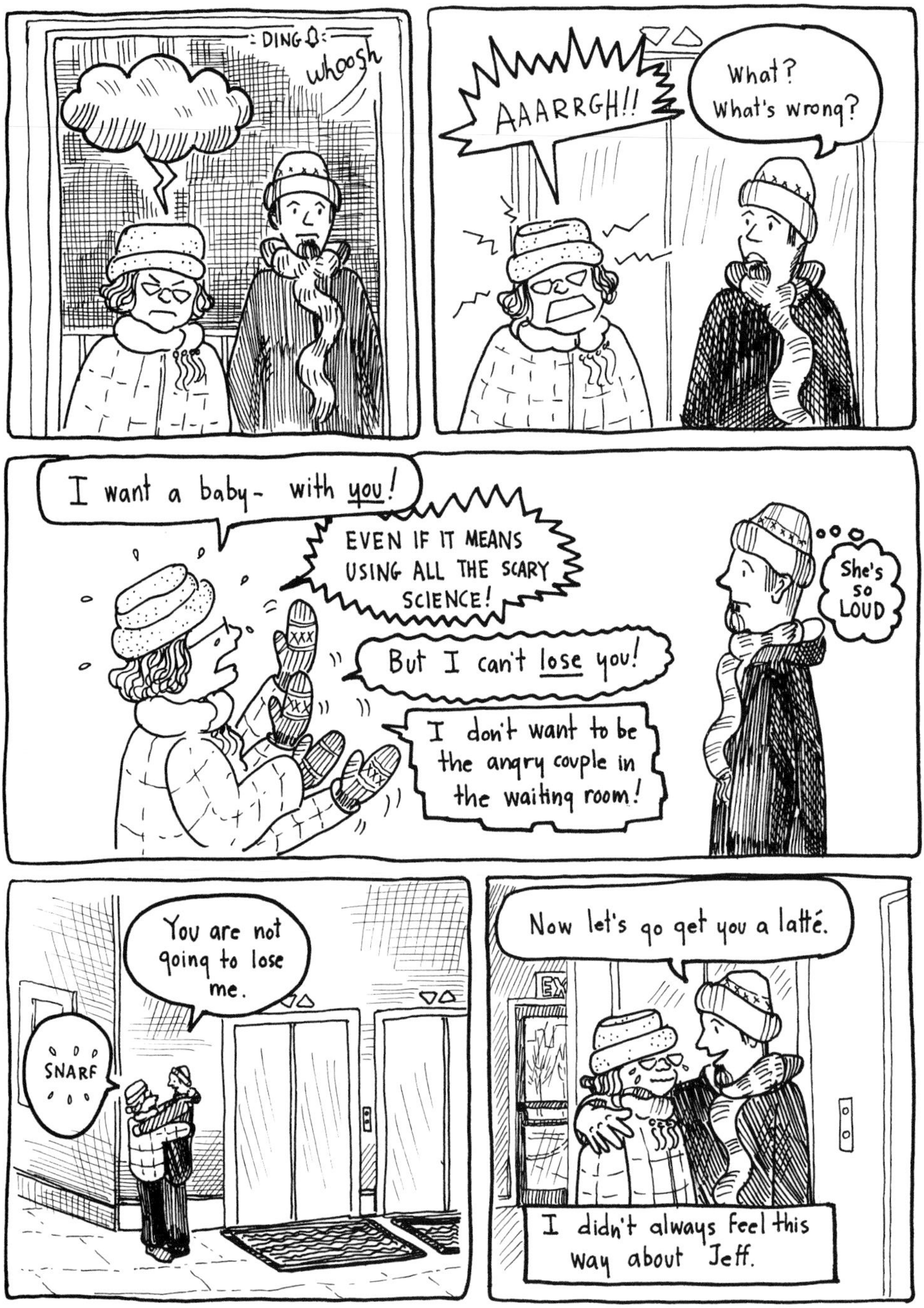
DING
whoosh
AAARRGH!!
What? What's wrong?
I want a baby- with you!
EVEN IF IT MEANS USING ALL THE SCARY SCIENCE!
But I can't lose you!
I don't want to be the angry couple in the waiting room!
She's so LOUD
You are not going to lose me.
SNARF
Now let's go get you a latté.
I didn't always feel this way about Jeff.

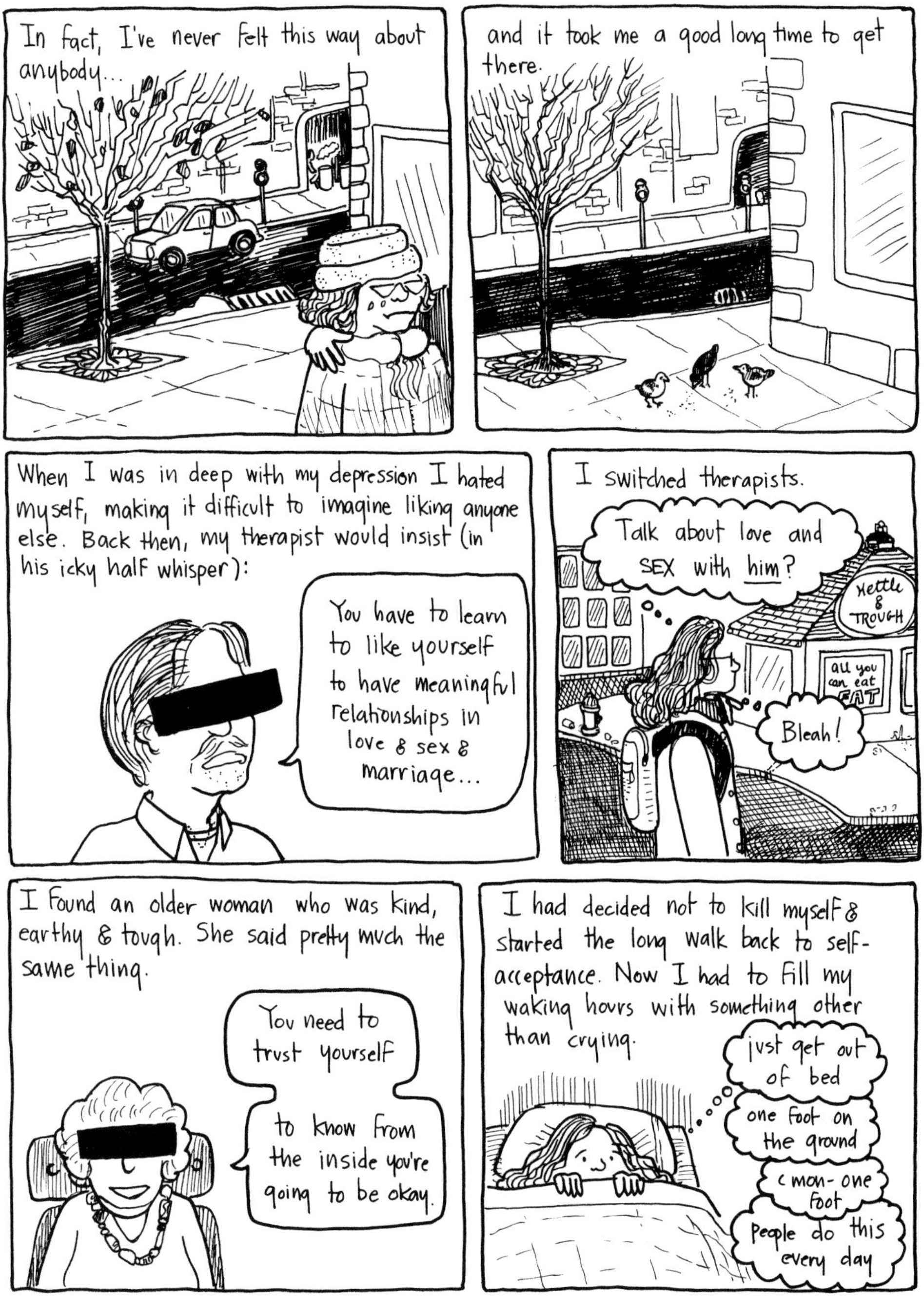
In fact, I've never felt this way about anybody...
and it took me a good long time to get there.
When I was in deep with my depression I hated myself, making it difficult to imagine liking anyone else. Back then, my therapist would insist (in his icky half whisper):
You have to learn to like yourself to have meaningful relationships in love & sex & marriage...
I switched therapists.
Talk about love and SEX with him?
Kettle & Trough
all you can eat FAT
Bleah!
I found an older woman who was kind, earthy & tough. She said pretty much the same thing.
You need to trust yourself
to know from the inside you're going to be okay.
I had decided not to kill myself & started the long walk back to self-acceptance. Now I had to fill my waking hours with something other than crying.
just get out of bed
one foot on the ground
c'mon- one foot
People do this every day

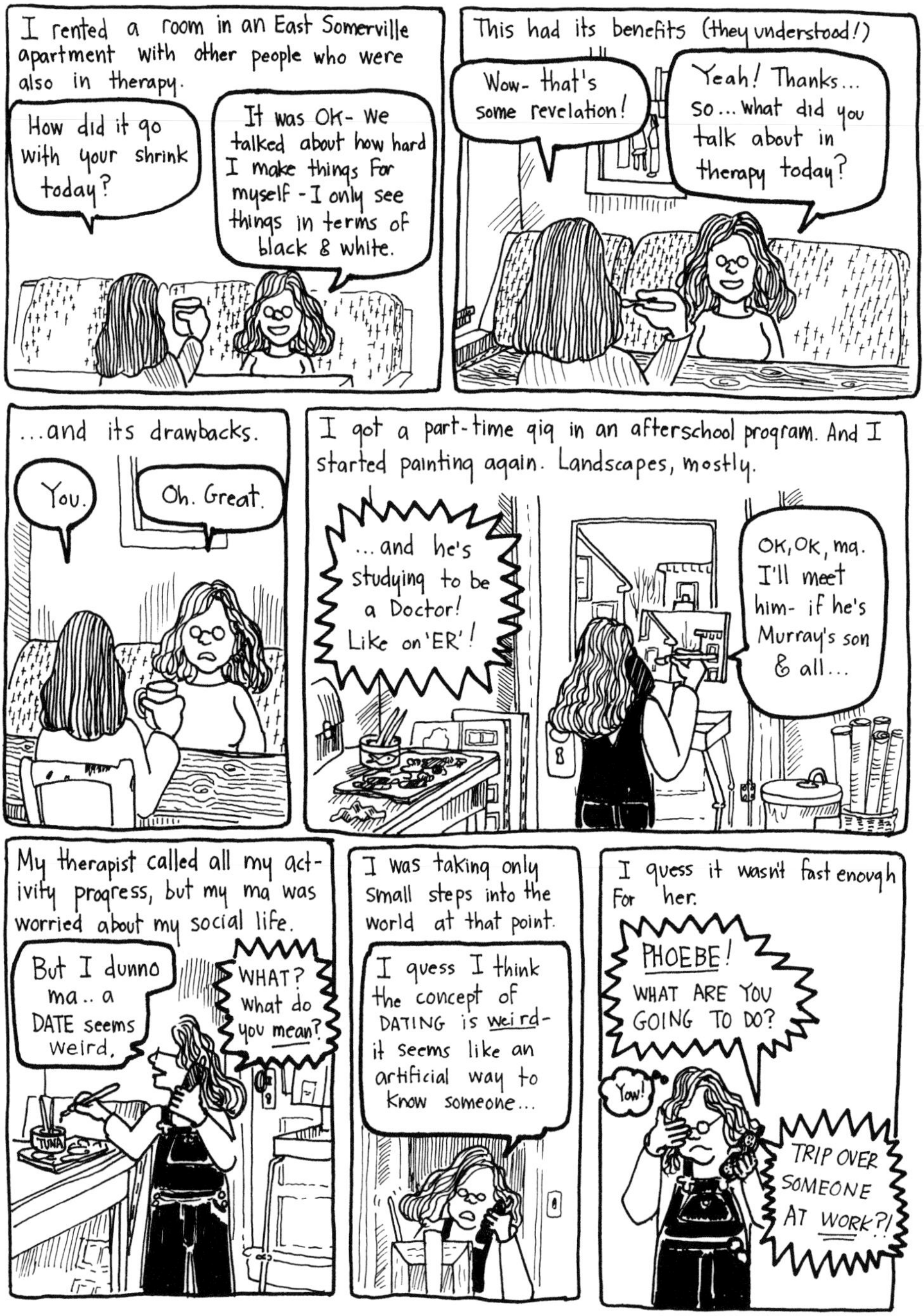
I rented a room in an East Somerville apartment with other people who were also in therapy.
How did it go with your shrink today?
It was OK- we talked about how hard I make things for myself - I only see things in terms of black & white.
This had its benefits (they understood!)
Wow- that's some revelation!
Yeah! Thanks... so... what did you talk about in therapy today?
...and its drawbacks.
You.
Oh. Great.
I got a part-time gig in an afterschool program. And I started painting again. Landscapes, mostly.
...and he's studying to be a Doctor! Like on 'ER'!
OK, OK, ma. I'll meet him- if he's Murray's son & all...
My therapist called all my activity progress, but my ma was worried about my social life.
But I dunno ma.. a DATE seems weird.
WHAT? What do you mean?
TUNA
I was taking only small steps into the world at that point.
I guess I think the concept of DATING is weird- it seems like an artificial way to know someone...
I guess it wasn't fast enough for her.
PHOEBE! WHAT ARE YOU GOING TO DO?
Yow!
TRIP OVER SOMEONE AT WORK?!

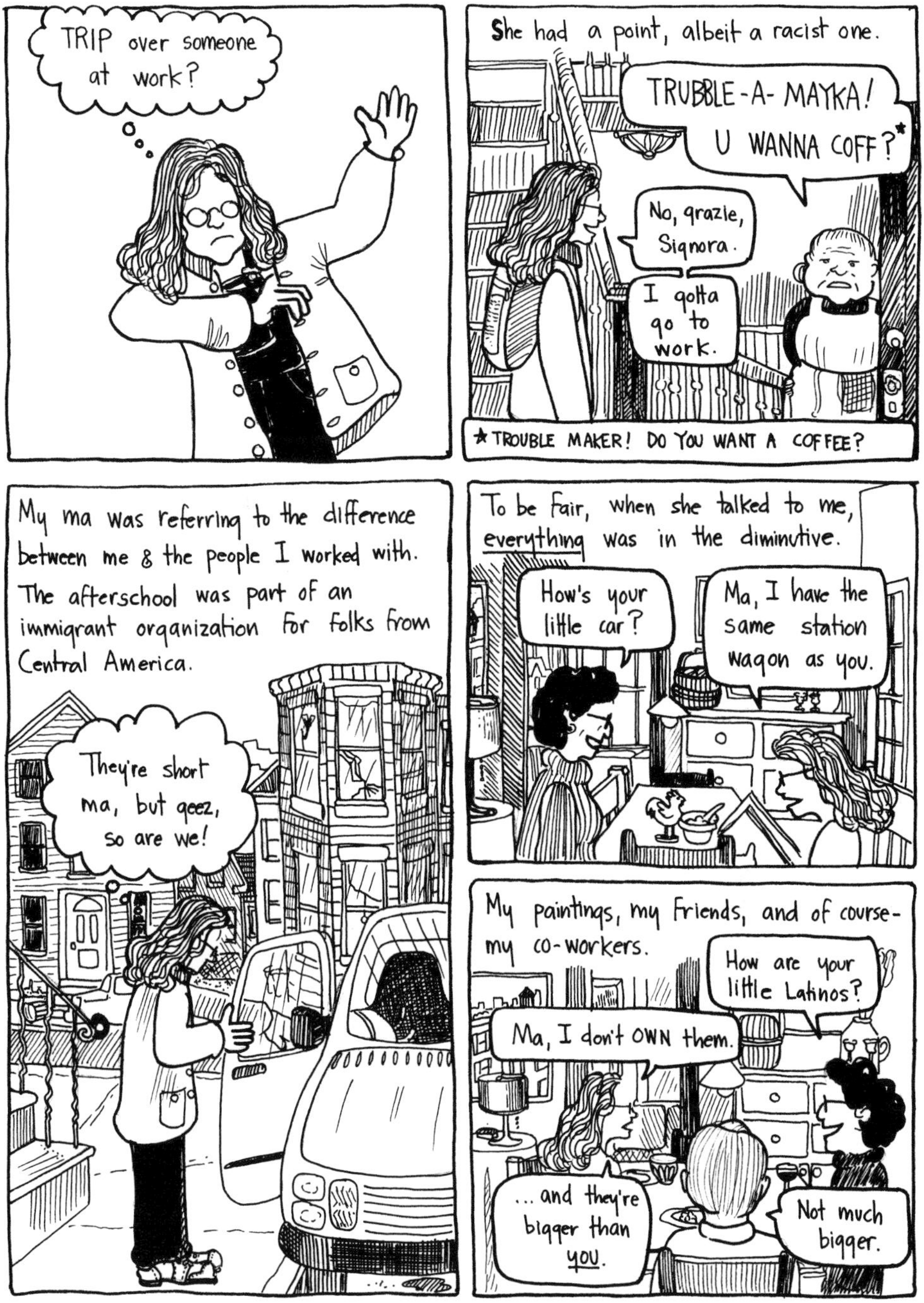
TRIP over someone at work?
She had a point, albeit a racist one.
TRUBBLE-A-MAYKA! U WANNA COFF?*
No, grazie, Signora.
I gotta go to work.
* TROUBLE MAKER! DO YOU WANT A COFFEE?
My ma was referring to the difference between me & the people I worked with. The afterschool was part of an immigrant organization for folks from Central America.
They're short ma, but geez, so are we!
To be fair, when she talked to me, everything was in the diminutive.
How's your little car?
Ma, I have the same station wagon as you.
My paintings, my friends, and of course-my co-workers.
How are your little Latinos?
Ma, I don't OWN them.
...and they're bigger than you.
Not much bigger.

But finding something in common, let alone romance, with a man where I worked would be challenging. My ma was right about that.

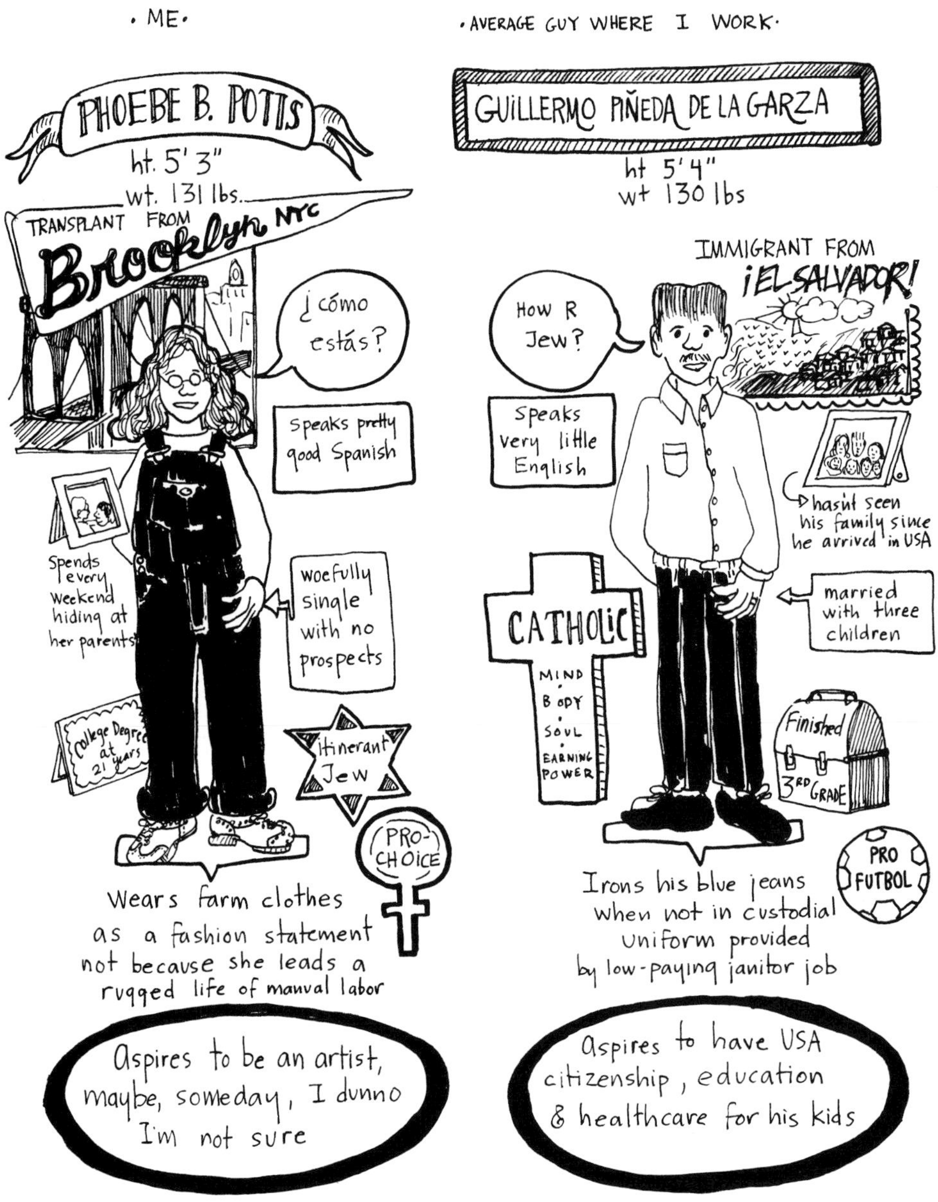

• ME •
PHOEBE B. POTTS
ht. 5' 3"
wt. 131 lbs.
TRANSPLANT FROM Brooklyn NYC
¿cómo estás?
speaks pretty good Spanish
Spends every weekend hiding at her parents'
woefully single with no prospects
College Degree at 21 years
itinerant Jew
PRO-CHOICE
Wears farm clothes as a fashion statement not because she leads a rugged life of manual labor
Aspires to be an artist, maybe, someday, I dunno I'm not sure
• AVERAGE GUY WHERE I WORK •
GUILLERMO PIÑEDA DE LA GARZA
ht 5' 4"
wt 130 lbs
IMMIGRANT FROM ¡EL SALVADOR!
How R Jew?
Speaks very little English
hasn't seen his family since he arrived in USA
CATHOLIC
MIND • BODY • SOUL • EARNING POWER
married with three children
Finished 3RD GRADE
PRO FUTBOL
Irons his blue jeans when not in custodial uniform provided by low-paying janitor job
Aspires to have USA citizenship, education & healthcare for his kids

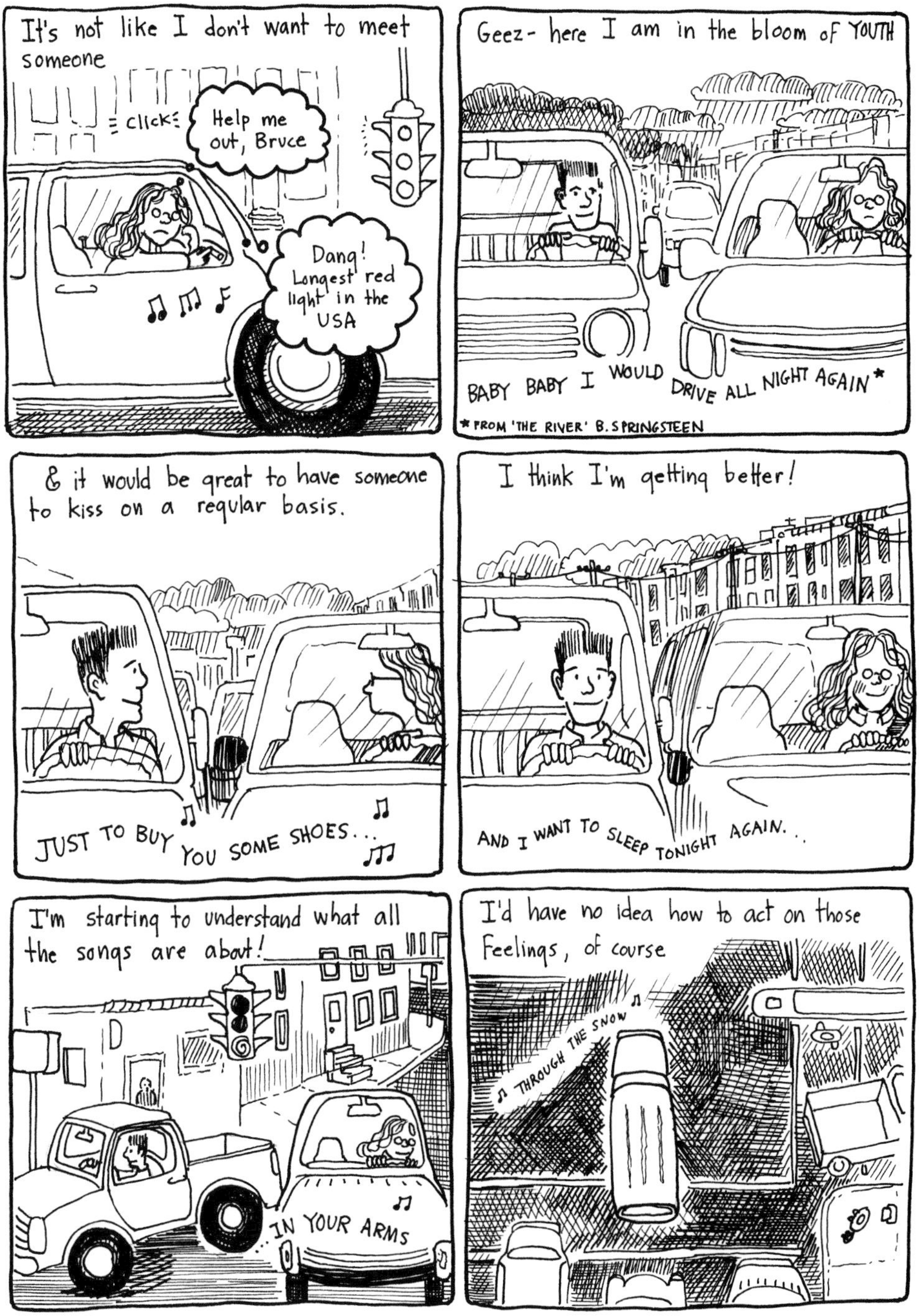
It's not like I don't want to meet someone
click
Help me out, Bruce
Dang! Longest red light in the USA
Geez- here I am in the bloom of YOUTH
BABY BABY I WOULD DRIVE ALL NIGHT AGAIN*
* FROM 'THE RIVER' B. SPRINGSTEEN
& it would be great to have someone to kiss on a regular basis.
JUST TO BUY YOU SOME SHOES...
I think I'm getting better!
AND I WANT TO SLEEP TONIGHT AGAIN...
I'm starting to understand what all the songs are about!
IN YOUR ARMS
I'd have no idea how to act on those Feelings, of course
THROUGH THE SNOW

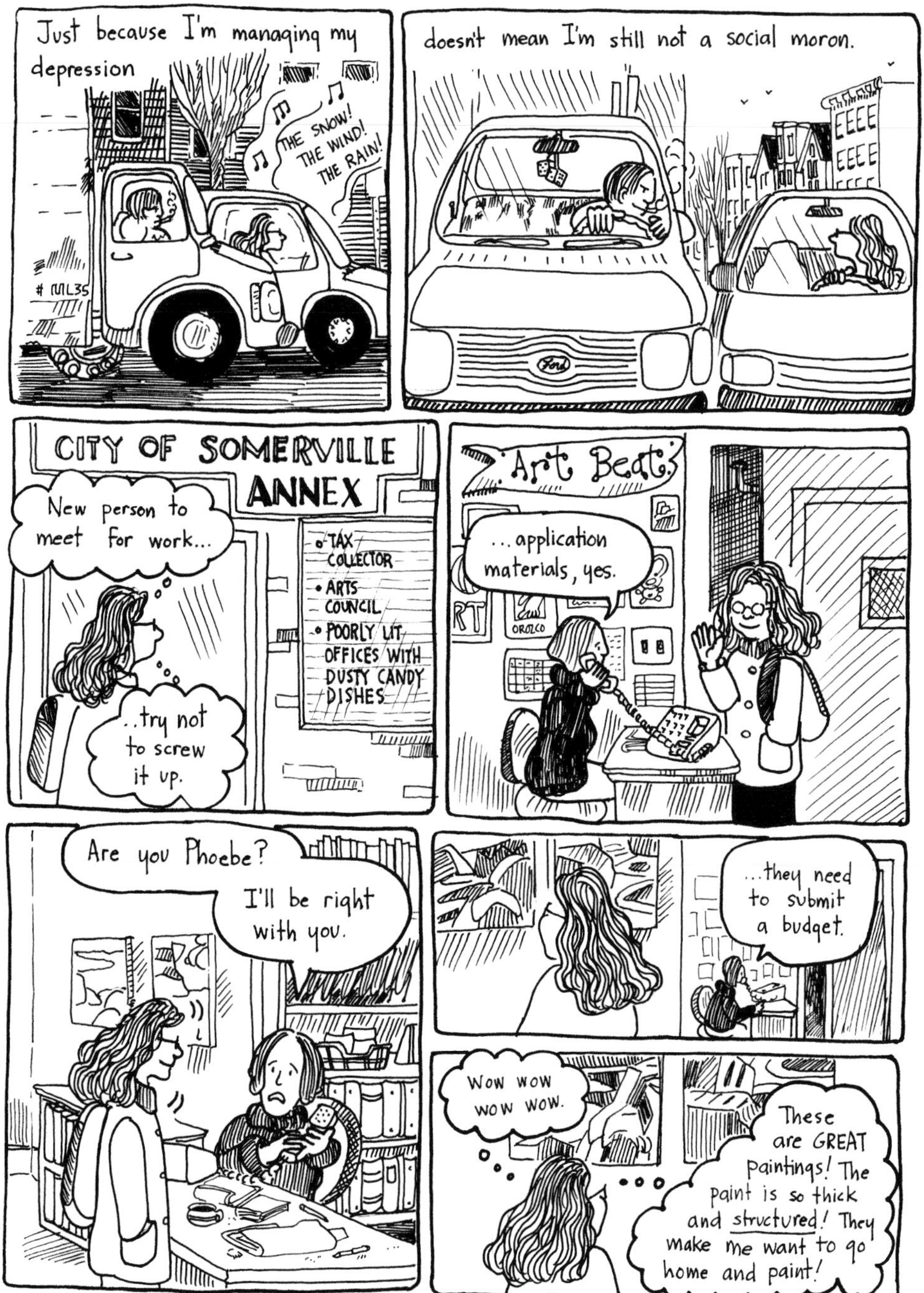

Just because I'm managing my depression
THE SNOW! THE WIND! THE RAIN!
ML35
doesn't mean I'm still not a social moron.
CITY OF SOMERVILLE ANNEX
New person to meet for work...
..try not to screw it up.
• TAX COLLECTOR
• ARTS COUNCIL
• POORLY LIT OFFICES WITH DUSTY CANDY DISHES
Art Beat
...application materials, yes.
OROZCO
Are you Phoebe?
I'll be right with you.
...they need to submit a budget.
Wow wow wow wow.
These are GREAT paintings! The paint is so thick and structured! They make me want to go home and paint!

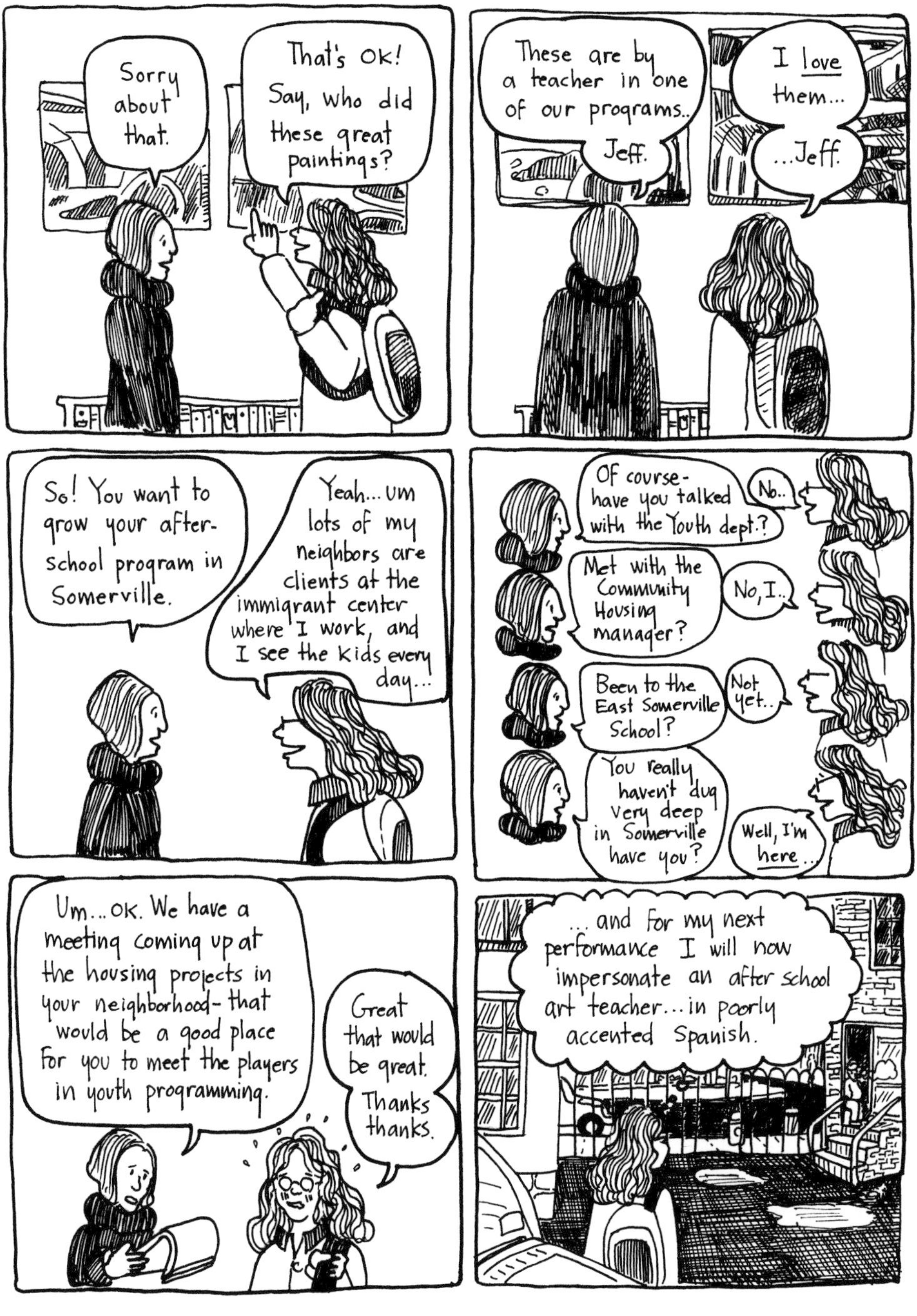
Sorry about that.
That's OK! Say, who did these great paintings?
These are by a teacher in one of our programs..
Jeff.
I love them...
...Jeff.
So! You want to grow your after-school program in Somerville.
Yeah... um lots of my neighbors are clients at the immigrant center where I work, and I see the kids every day...
Of course- have you talked with the Youth dept.?
No..
Met with the Community Housing manager?
No, I..
Been to the East Somerville School?
Not yet..
You really haven't dug very deep in Somerville have you?
Well, I'm here..
Um... OK. We have a meeting coming up at the housing projects in your neighborhood- that would be a good place for you to meet the players in youth programming.
Great that would be great. Thanks thanks.
...and for my next performance I will now impersonate an after school art teacher... in poorly accented Spanish.

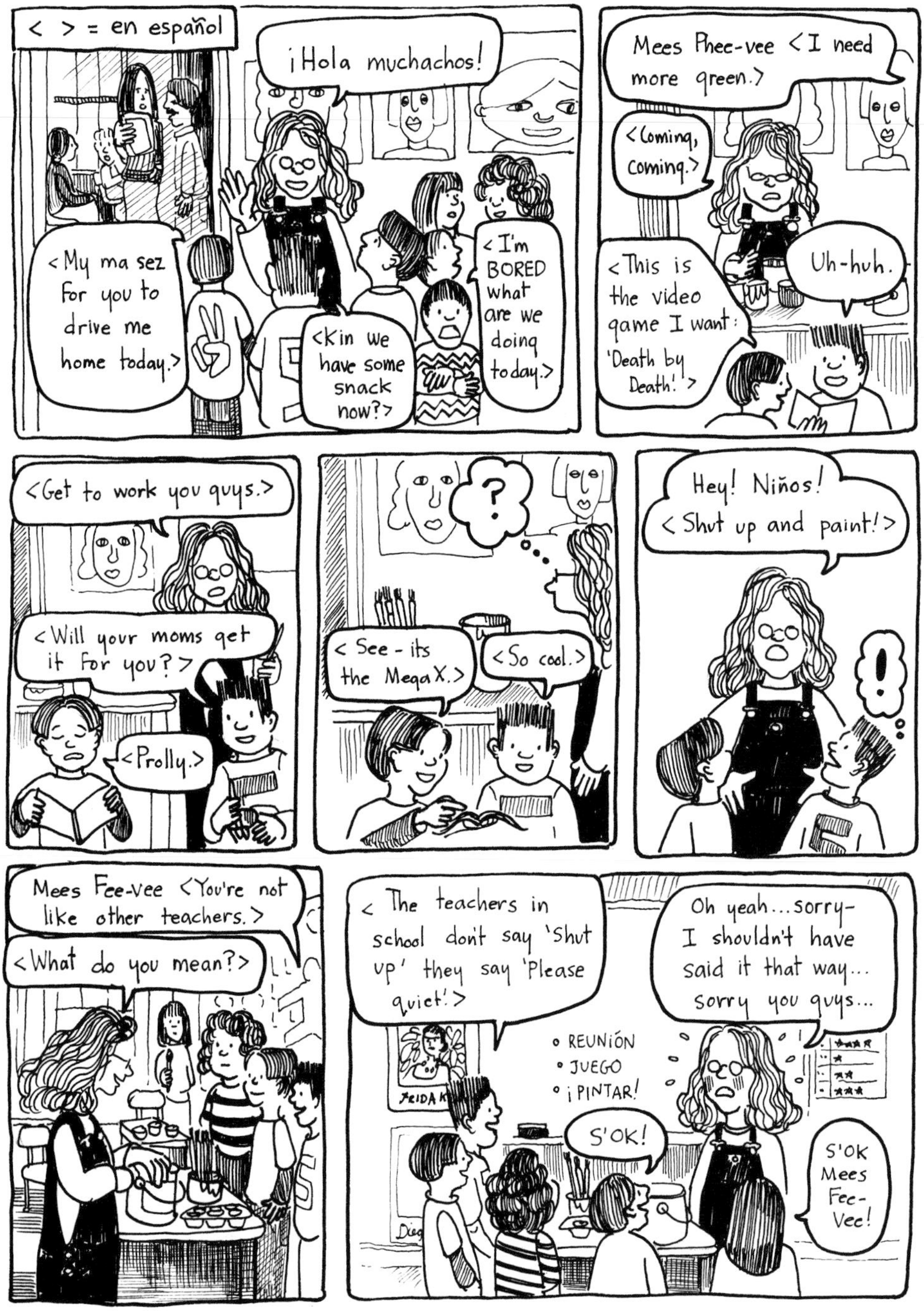
< > = en español
¡Hola muchachos!
<My ma sez for you to drive me home today.>
<Kin we have some snack now?>
<I'm BORED what are we doing today.>
Mees Phee-vee <I need more green.>
<Coming, coming.>
<This is the video game I want: 'Death by Death.'>
Uh-huh.
<Get to work you guys.>
<Will your moms get it for you?>
<Prolly.>
?
<See - its the Mega X.>
<So cool.>
Hey! Niños! <Shut up and paint!>
!
Mees Fee-vee <You're not like other teachers.>
<What do you mean?>
< The teachers in school don't say 'Shut up' they say 'Please quiet.'>
Oh yeah... sorry- I shouldn't have said it that way... sorry you guys...
REUNIÓN
JUEGO
¡PINTAR!
S'OK!
S'OK Mees Fee-Vee!

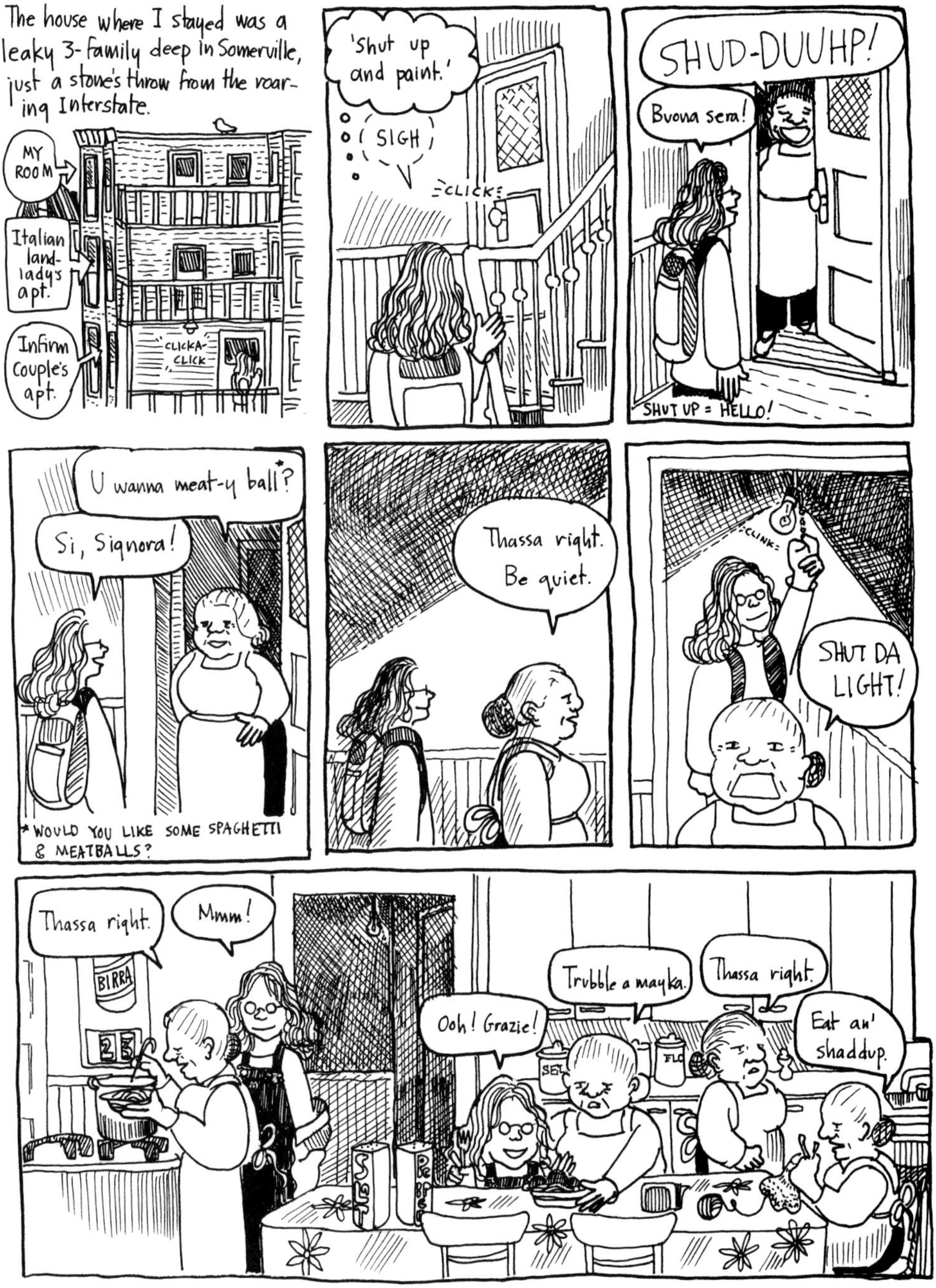

The house where I stayed was a leaky 3-family deep in Somerville, just a stone's throw from the roaring Interstate.
MY ROOM
Italian land-lady's apt.
Infirm couple's apt.
CLICKA-CLICK
'Shut up and paint.'
SIGH
CLICK
SHUD-DUUHP!
Buona sera!
SHUT UP = HELLO!
U wanna meat-y ball*?
Si, Signora!
* WOULD YOU LIKE SOME SPAGHETTI & MEATBALLS?
Thassa right. Be quiet.
CLINK
SHUT DA LIGHT!
Thassa right.
Mmm!
BIRRA
Ooh! Grazie!
Trubble a mayka.
Thassa right.
Eat an' shaddup.

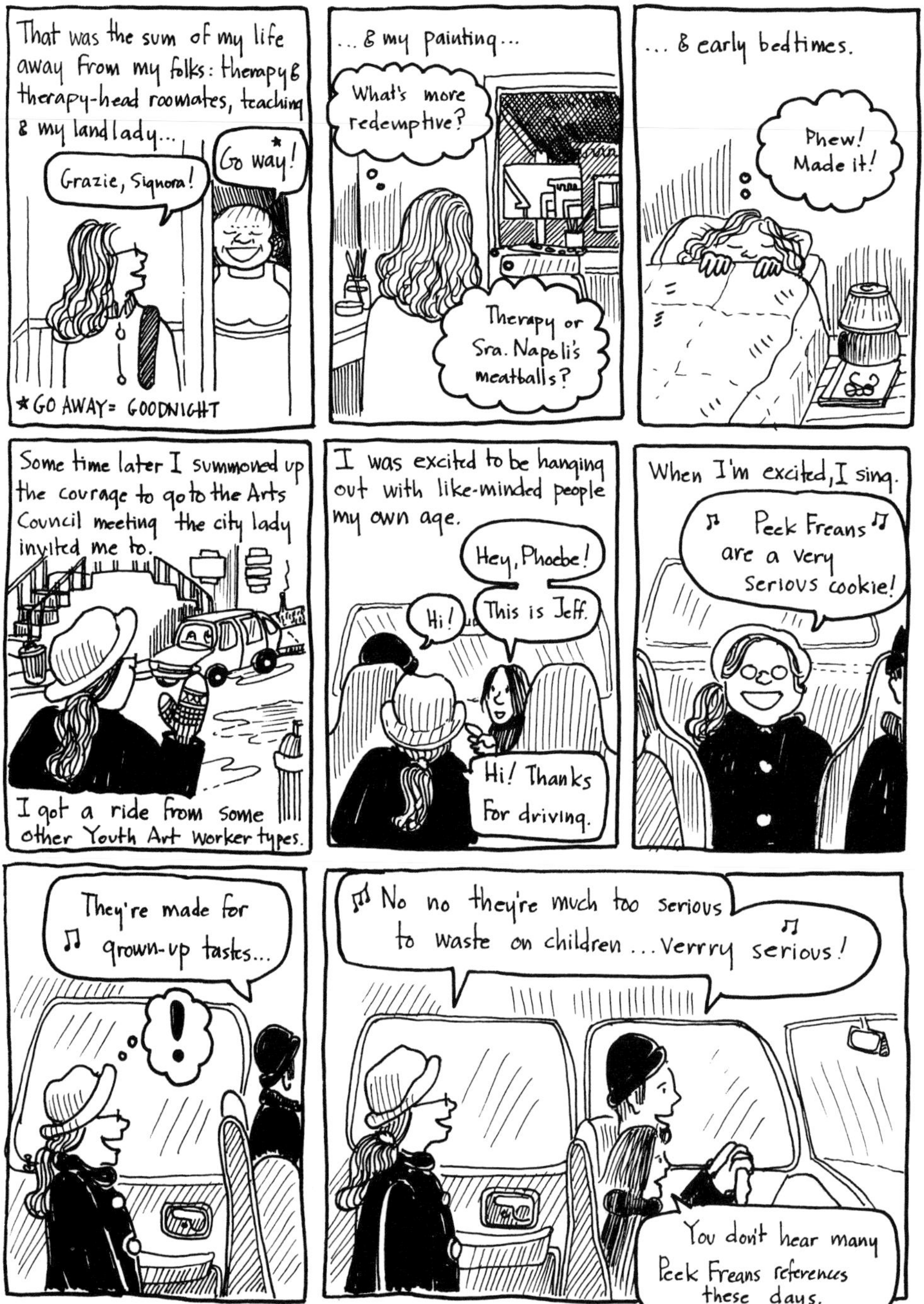
That was the sum of my life away from my folks: therapy & therapy-head roomates, teaching & my landlady...
Grazie, Signora!
Go way!*
*GO AWAY= GOODNIGHT
...& my painting...
What's more redemptive?
Therapy or Sra. Napoli's meatballs?
...& early bedtimes.
Phew! Made it!
Some time later I summoned up the courage to go to the Arts Council meeting the city lady invited me to.
I got a ride from some other Youth Art Worker types.
I was excited to be hanging out with like-minded people my own age.
Hey, Phoebe!
This is Jeff.
Hi!
Hi! Thanks for driving.
When I'm excited, I sing.
♫ Peek Freans ♫ are a very serious cookie!
They're made for ♫ grown-up tastes...
!
♫ No no they're much too serious to waste on children ... verrry ♫ serious!
You don't hear many Peek Freans references these days.

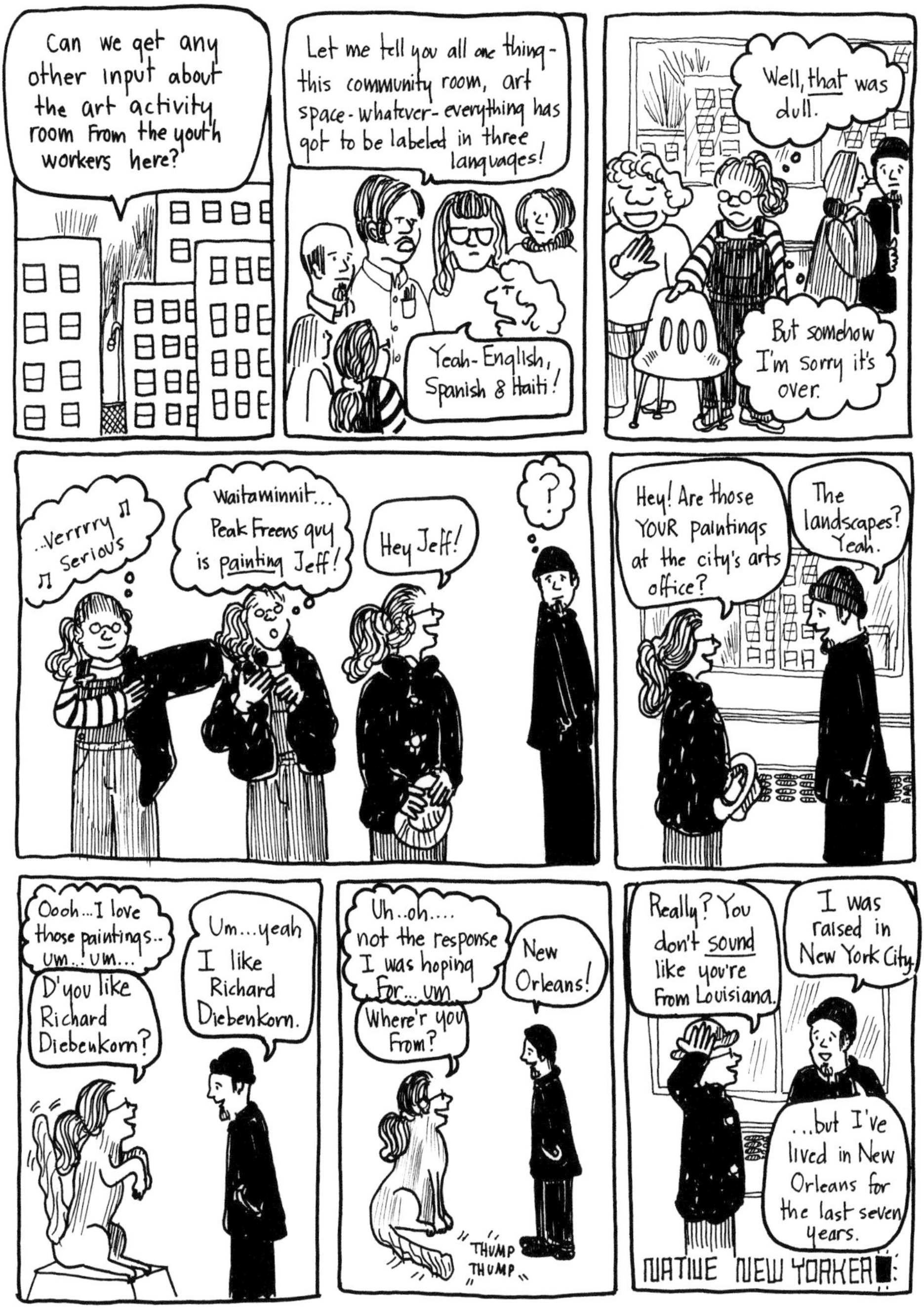
Can we get any other input about the art activity room from the youth workers here?
Let me tell you all one thing- this community room, art space-whatever-everything has got to be labeled in three languages!
Yeah-English, Spanish & Haiti!
Well, that was dull.
But somehow I'm sorry it's over.
...Verrrry ♫ Serious ♫
Waitaminnit... Peak Freens guy is painting Jeff!
Hey Jeff!
?
Hey! Are those YOUR paintings at the city's arts office?
The landscapes? Yeah.
Oooh...I love those paintings.. um..! um...
D'you like Richard Diebenkorn?
Um...yeah I like Richard Diebenkorn.
Uh..oh.... not the response I was hoping for... um
Where'r you from?
New Orleans!
THUMP THUMP
Really? You don't sound like you're from Louisiana.
I was raised in New York City.
...but I've lived in New Orleans for the last seven years.
NATIVE NEW YORKER

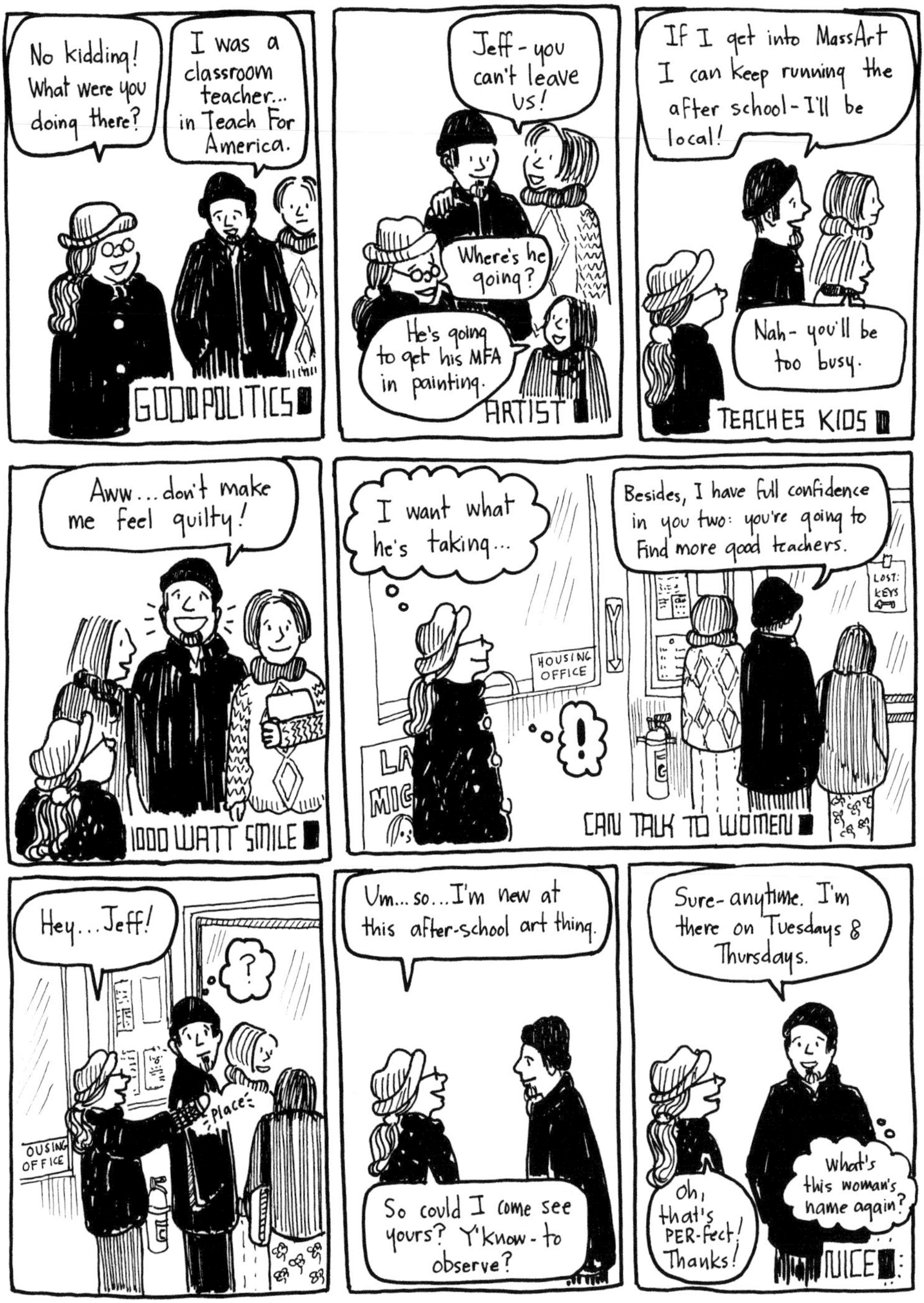
No kidding! What were you doing there?
I was a classroom teacher... in Teach For America.
GOOD POLITICS
Jeff - you can't leave us!
Where's he going?
He's going to get his MFA in painting.
ARTIST
If I get into MassArt I can keep running the after school - I'll be local!
Nah - you'll be too busy.
TEACHES KIDS
Aww... don't make me feel guilty!
1000 WATT SMILE
I want what he's taking...
Besides, I have full confidence in you two: you're going to find more good teachers.
HOUSING OFFICE
LOST: KEYS
!
CAN TALK TO WOMEN
Hey... Jeff!
?
Place
OUSING OFFICE
Um... so... I'm new at this after-school art thing.
So could I come see yours? Y'know - to observe?
Sure - anytime. I'm there on Tuesdays & Thursdays.
Oh, that's PER-fect! Thanks!
What's this woman's name again?
NICE

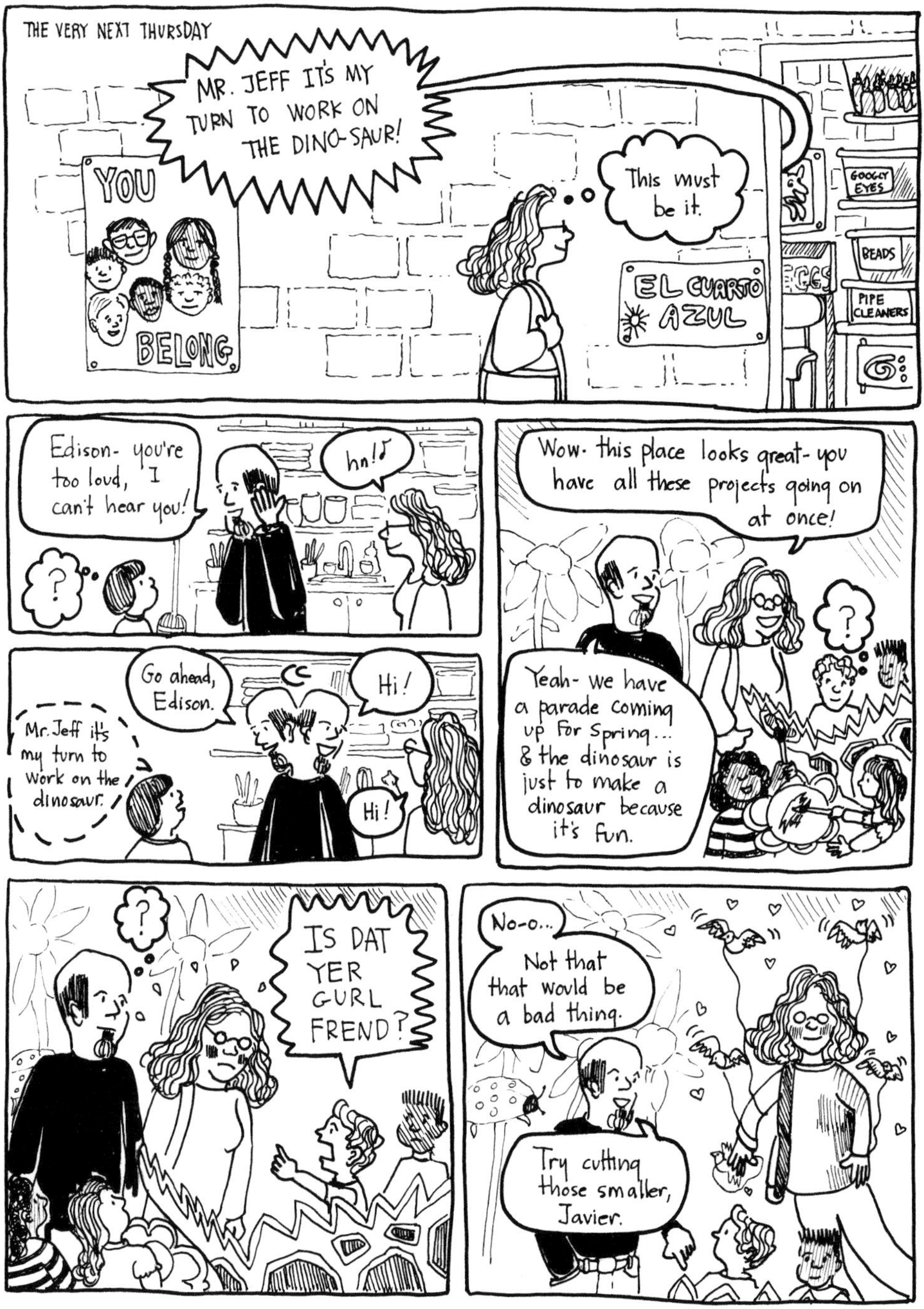
THE VERY NEXT THURSDAY
MR. JEFF IT'S MY TURN TO WORK ON THE DINO-SAUR!
YOU BELONG
This must be it.
EL CUARTO AZUL
GOOGLY EYES
BEADS
PIPE CLEANERS
Edison- you're too loud, I can't hear you!
?
hn!
Wow. this place looks great- you have all these projects going on at once!
Go ahead, Edison.
Hi!
Hi!
Mr. Jeff it's my turn to work on the dinosaur.
Yeah- we have a parade coming up for Spring... & the dinosaur is just to make a dinosaur because it's fun.
?
?
IS DAT YER GURL FREND?
No-o...
Not that that would be a bad thing.
Try cutting those smaller, Javier.

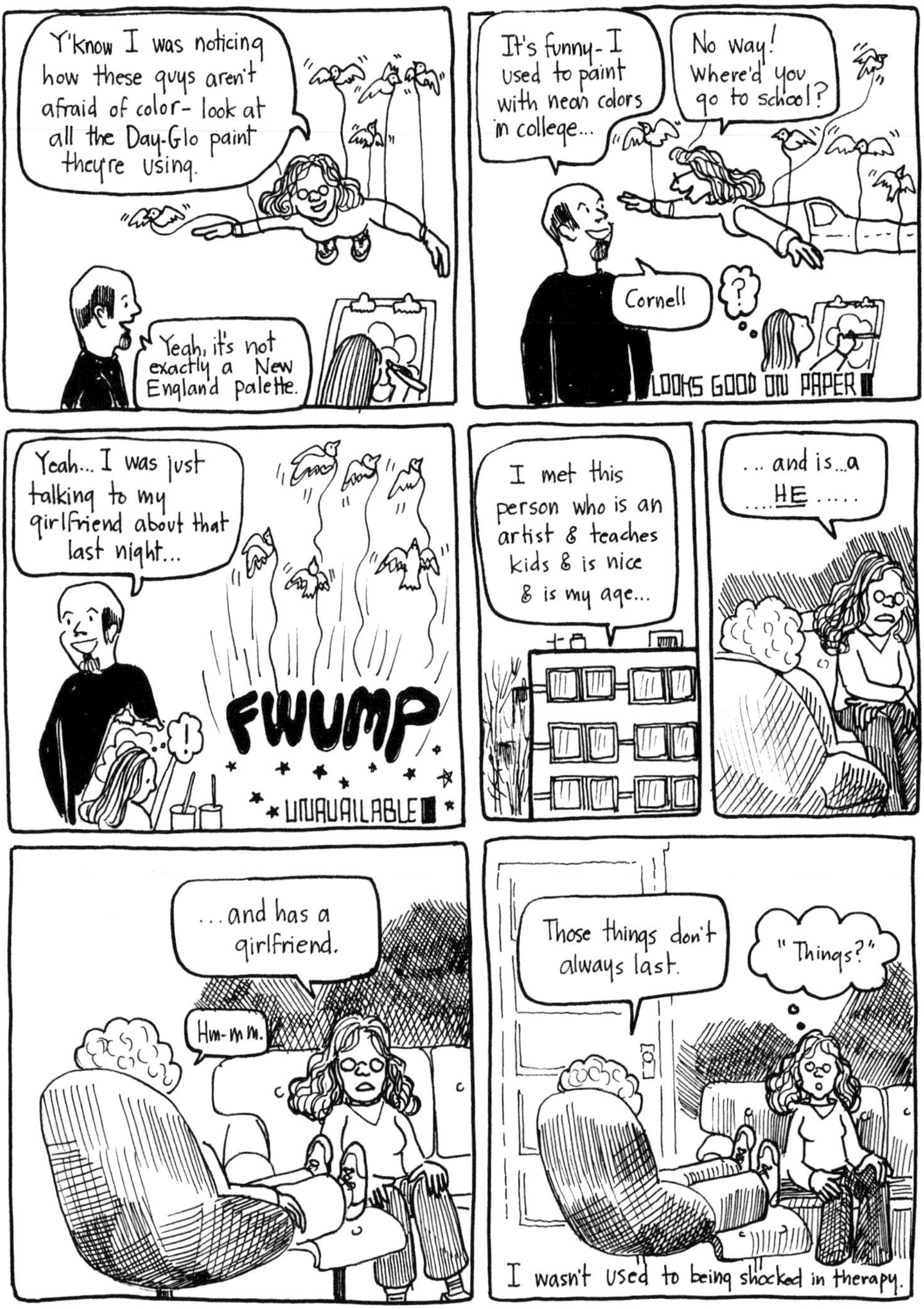
Y'know I was noticing how these guys aren't afraid of color- look at all the Day-Glo paint they're using.
Yeah, it's not exactly a New England palette.
It's funny- I used to paint with neon colors in college...
No way! Where'd you go to school?
Cornell
?
LOOKS GOOD ON PAPER
Yeah... I was just talking to my girlfriend about that last night...
!
FWUMP
UNAVAILABLE
I met this person who is an artist & teaches kids & is nice & is my age...
... and is...a ....HE.....
...and has a girlfriend.
Hm-mm.
Those things don't always last.
"Things?"
I wasn't used to being shocked in therapy.

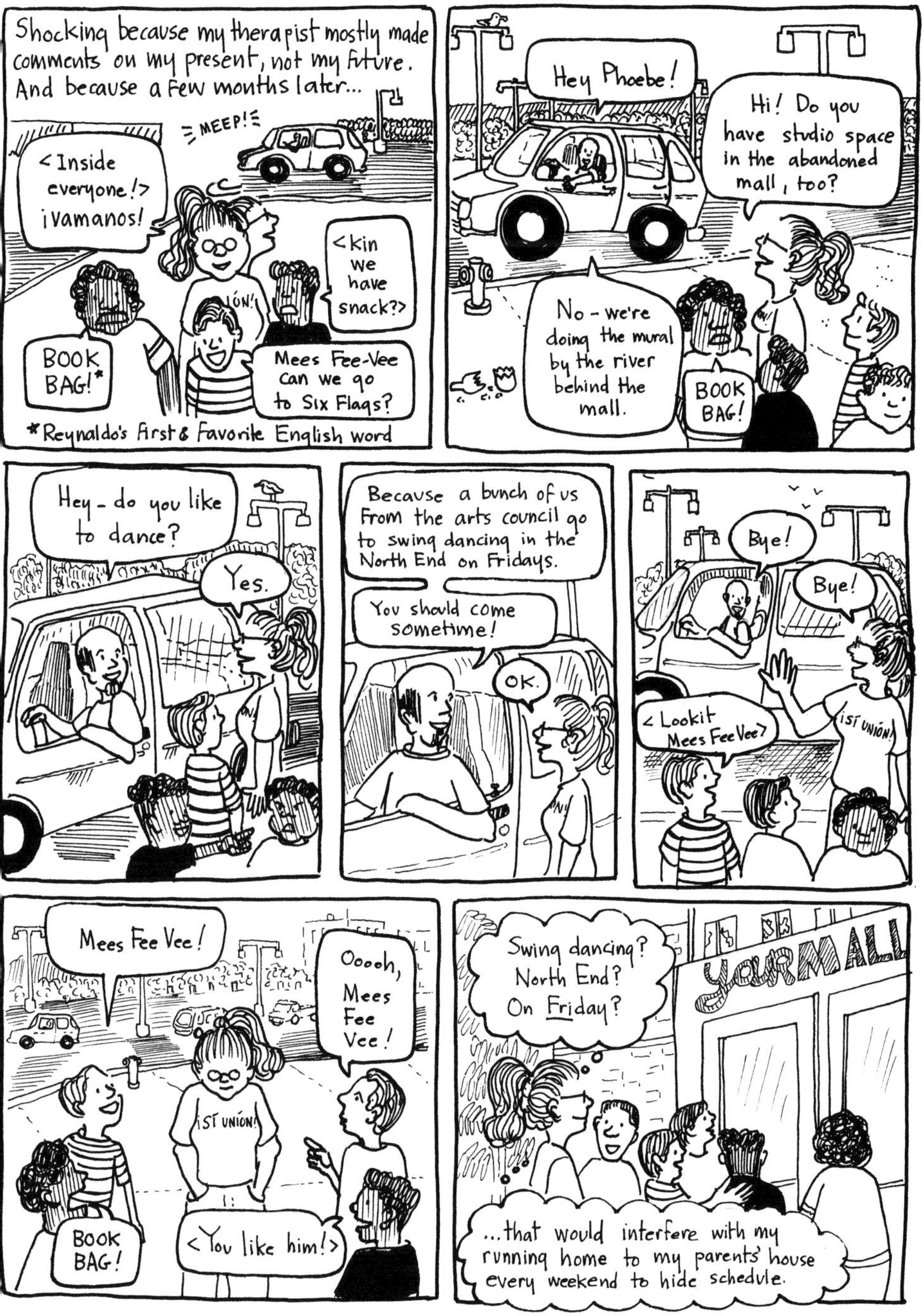
Shocking because my therapist mostly made comments on my present, not my future. And because a few months later...
MEEP!
<Inside everyone!> ¡Vamanos!
<Kin we have snack?>
BOOK BAG!*
Mees Fee-Vee can we go to Six Flags?
*Reynaldo's first & favorite English word
Hey Phoebe!
Hi! Do you have studio space in the abandoned mall, too?
No - we're doing the mural by the river behind the mall.
BOOK BAG!
Hey - do you like to dance?
Yes.
Because a bunch of us from the arts council go to swing dancing in the North End on Fridays.
You should come sometime!
OK.
Bye!
Bye!
<Lookit Mees Fee Vee>
¡ST UNIÓN!
Mees Fee Vee!
Ooooh, Mees Fee Vee!
¡ST UNIÓN!
BOOK BAG!
<You like him!>
Swing dancing? North End? On Friday?
YOUR MALL
...that would interfere with my running home to my parents' house every weekend to hide schedule.

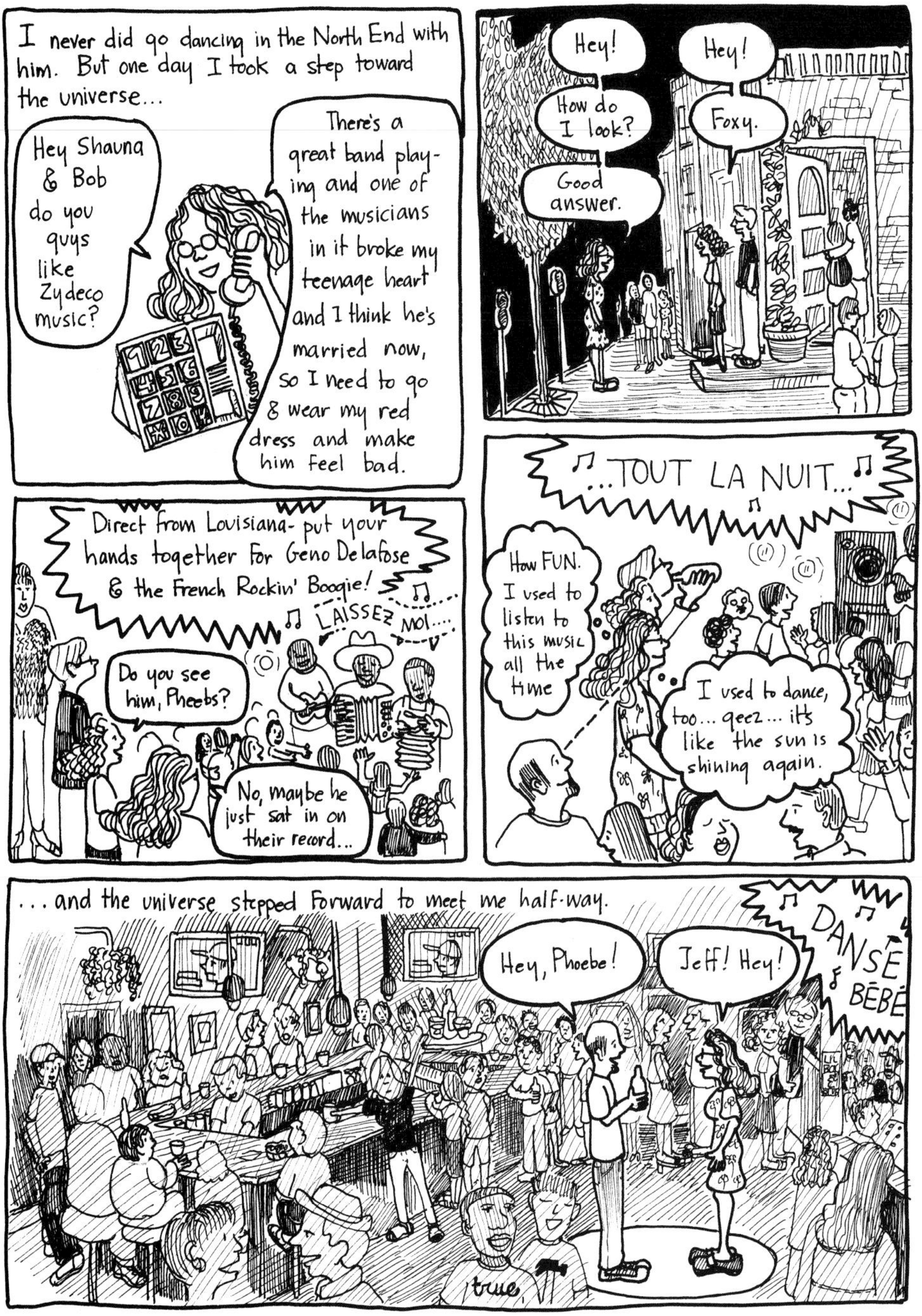

I never did go dancing in the North End with him. But one day I took a step toward the universe...
Hey Shauna & Bob do you guys like Zydeco music?
There's a great band playing and one of the musicians in it broke my teenage heart and I think he's married now, so I need to go & wear my red dress and make him feel bad.
Hey!
How do I look?
Good answer.
Hey!
Foxy.
Direct from Lovisiana- put your hands together for Geno Delafose & the French Rockin' Boogie!
LAISSEZ MOI....
Do you see him, Pheebs?
No, maybe he just sat in on their record...
...TOUT LA NUIT...
How FUN. I used to listen to this music all the time
I used to dance, too... geez... it's like the sun is shining again.
...and the universe stepped forward to meet me half-way.
DANSE BÉBÉ
Hey, Phoebe!
Jeff! Hey!
true

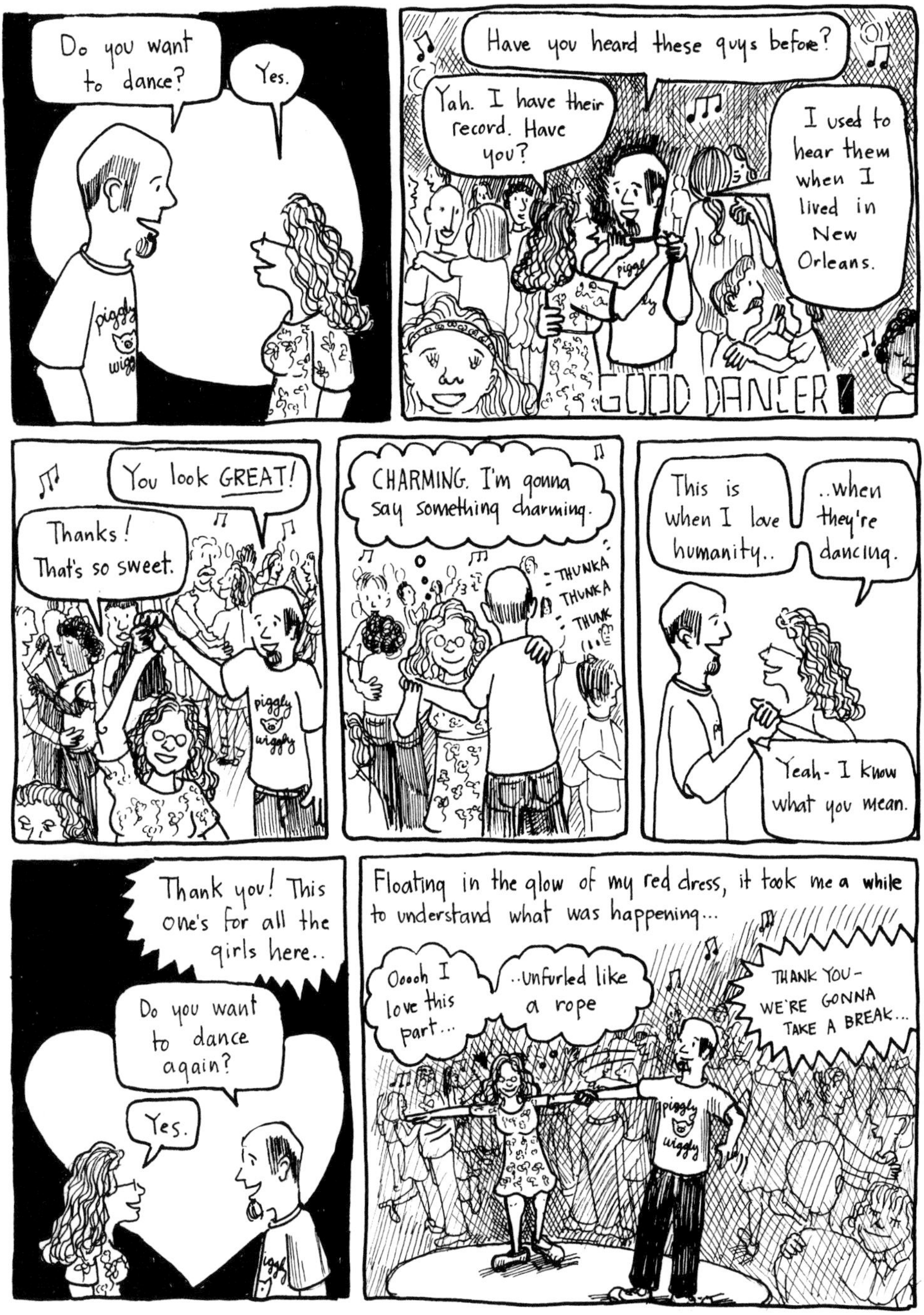

Do you want to dance?
Yes.
Have you heard these guys before?
Yah. I have their record. Have you?
I used to hear them when I lived in New Orleans.
GOOD DANCER
You look GREAT!
Thanks! That's so sweet.
CHARMING. I'm gonna say something charming.
THUNKA
THUNKA
THUNK
This is when I love humanity..
..when they're dancing.
Yeah- I know what you mean.
Thank you! This one's for all the girls here..
Do you want to dance again?
Yes.
Floating in the glow of my red dress, it took me a while to understand what was happening...
Ooooh I love this part...
..unfurled like a rope
THANK YOU- WE'RE GONNA TAKE A BREAK...

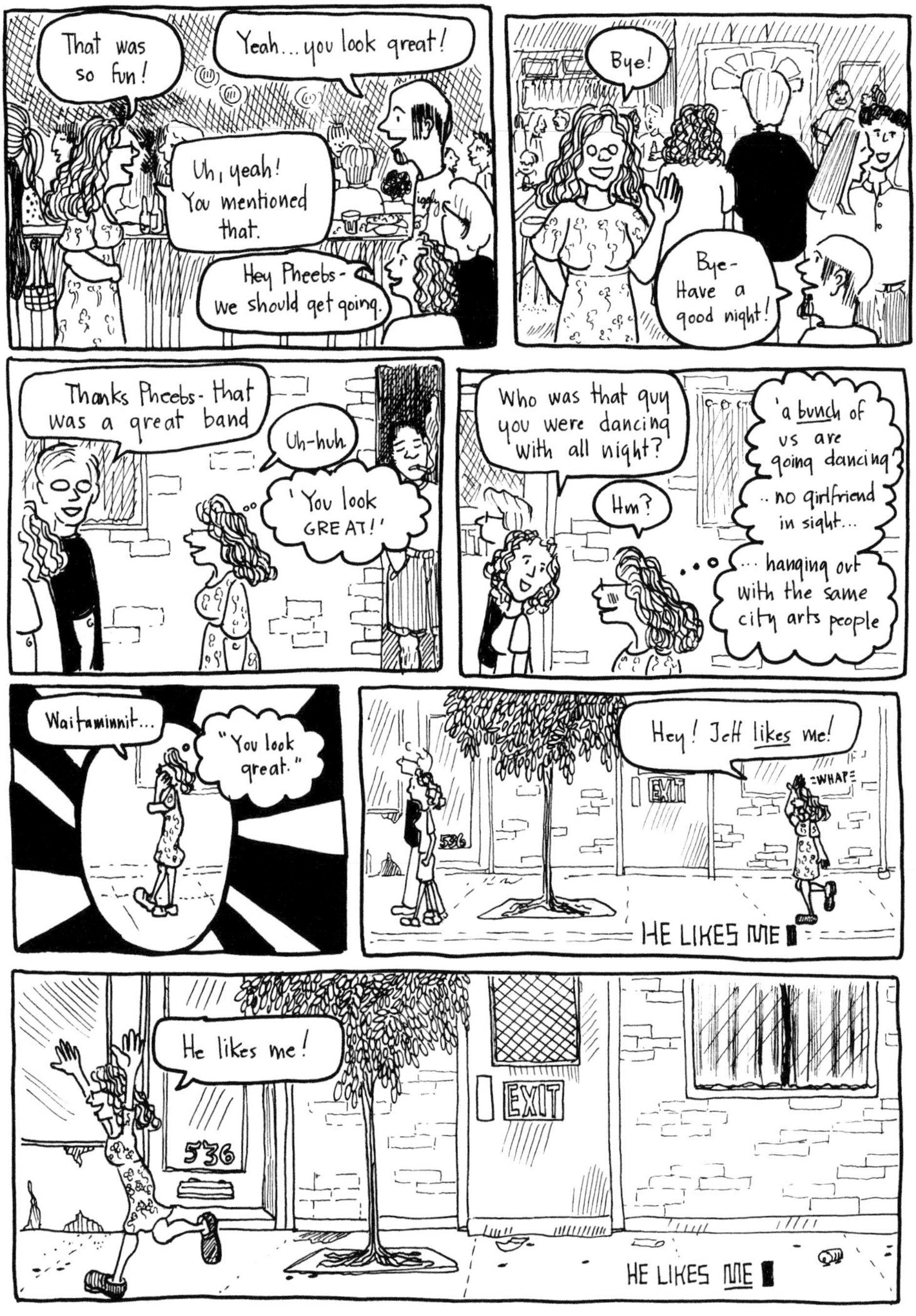
That was so fun!
Yeah... you look great!
Uh, yeah! You mentioned that.
Hey Pheebs- we should get going.
Bye!
Bye- Have a good night!
Thanks Pheebs- that was a great band
Uh-huh.
'You look GREAT!'
Who was that guy you were dancing with all night?
Hm?
'a bunch of us are going dancing'
..no girlfriend in sight...
... hanging out with the same city arts people
Waitaminnit...
"You look great."
Hey! Jeff likes me!
WHAP
HE LIKES ME
He likes me!
536
EXIT
HE LIKES ME

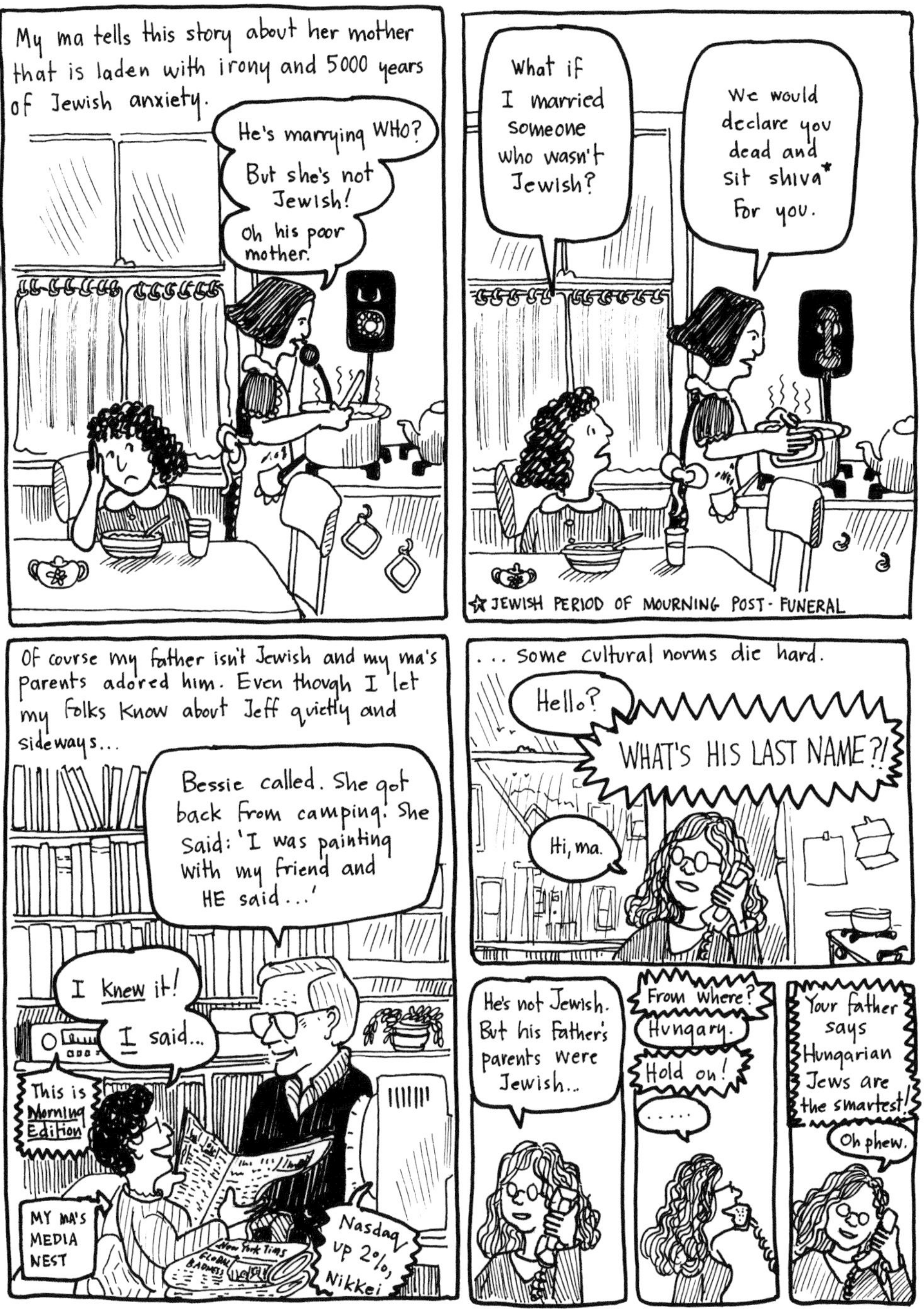
My ma tells this story about her mother that is laden with irony and 5000 years of Jewish anxiety.
He's marrying WHO?
But she's not Jewish!
Oh his poor mother.
What if I married someone who wasn't Jewish?
We would declare you dead and sit shiva* for you.
* JEWISH PERIOD OF MOURNING POST-FUNERAL
Of course my father isn't Jewish and my ma's parents adored him. Even though I let my folks know about Jeff quietly and sideways...
Bessie called. She got back from camping. She said: 'I was painting with my friend and HE said...'
I knew it!
I said...
This is Morning Edition
MY MA'S MEDIA NEST
Nasdaq up 2%, Nikkei
... some cultural norms die hard.
Hello?
WHAT'S HIS LAST NAME?!
Hi, ma.
He's not Jewish. But his father's parents were Jewish...
From where?
Hungary.
Hold on!
.....
Your father says Hungarian Jews are the smartest!
Oh phew.

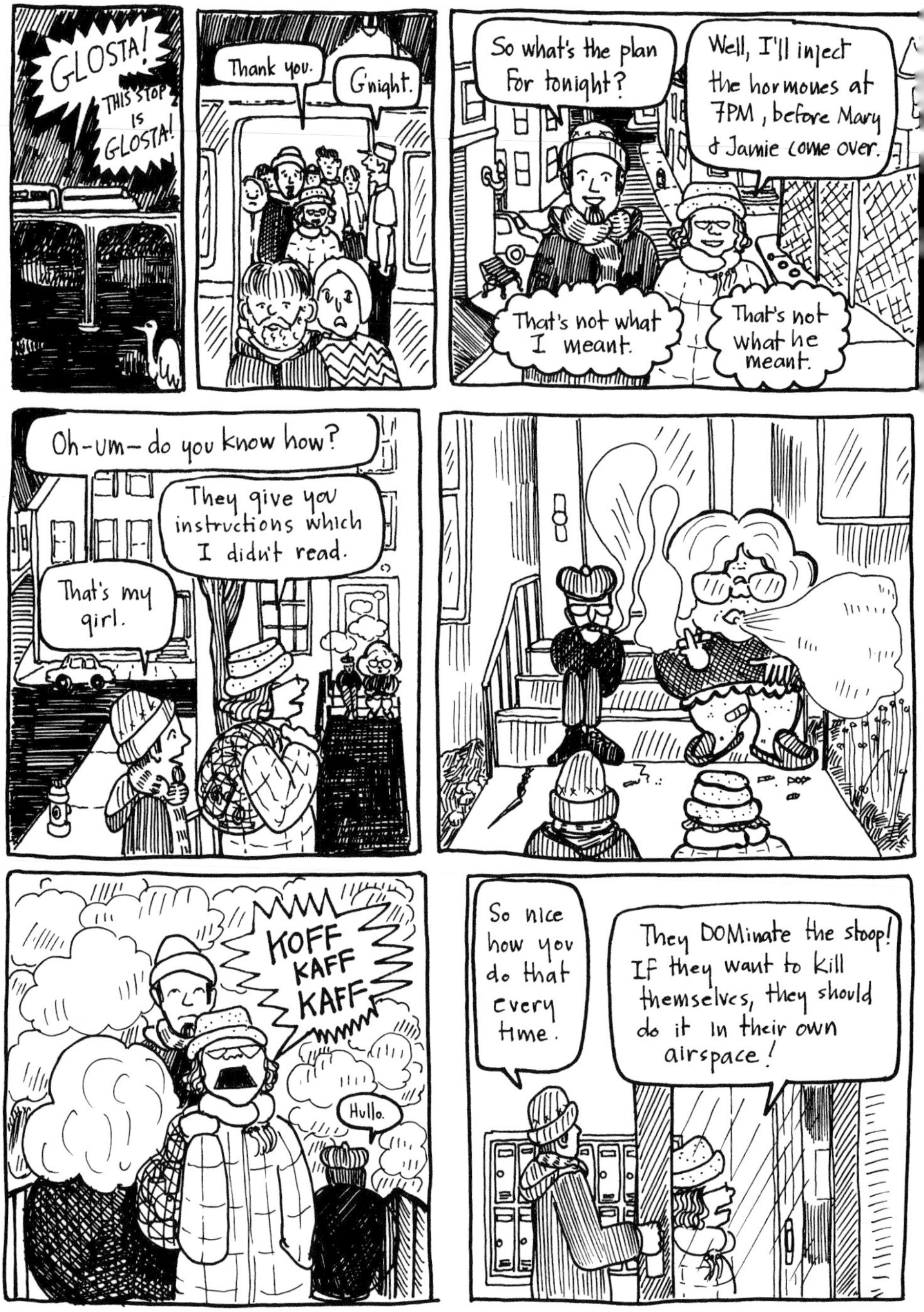
GLOSTA!
THIS STOP IS GLOSTA!
Thank you.
G'night.
So what's the plan for tonight?
Well, I'll inject the hormones at 7PM, before Mary & Jamie come over.
That's not what I meant.
That's not what he meant.
Oh-um- do you know how?
They give you instructions which I didn't read.
That's my girl.
KOFF KAFF KAFF
Hullo.
So nice how you do that every time.
They DOMinate the stoop! If they want to kill themselves, they should do it in their own airspace!

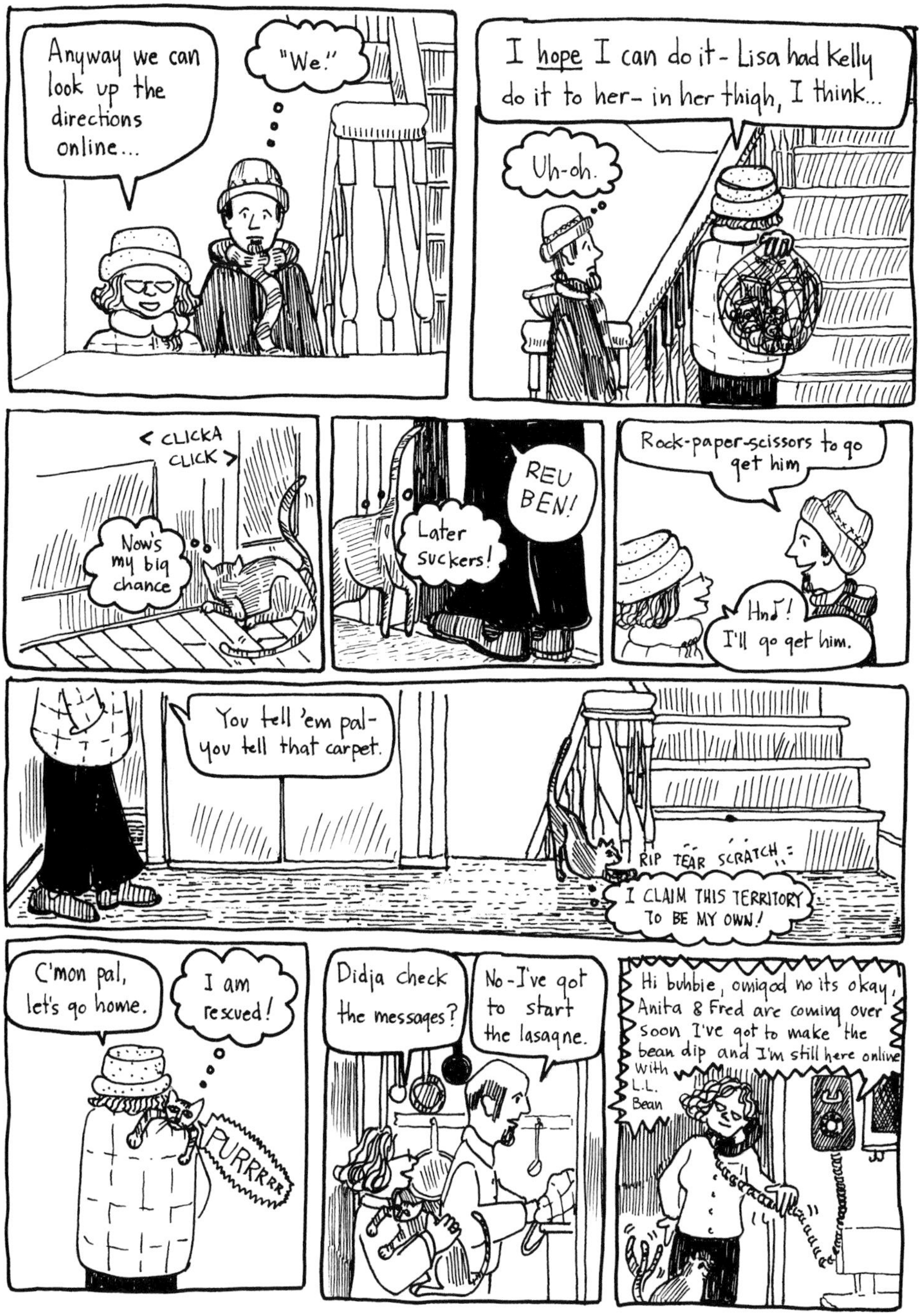

Anyway we can look up the directions online...
"We."
I hope I can do it - Lisa had Kelly do it to her - in her thigh, I think...
Uh-oh.
< CLICKA CLICK >
Now's my big chance
REU BEN!
Later suckers!
Rock-paper-scissors to go get him
Hnd! I'll go get him.
You tell 'em pal - you tell that carpet.
RIP TEAR SCRATCH
I CLAIM THIS TERRITORY TO BE MY OWN!
C'mon pal, let's go home.
I am rescued!
PURRRRR
Didja check the messages?
No - I've got to start the lasagne.
Hi bubbie, omigod no its okay, Anita & Fred are coming over soon I've got to make the bean dip and I'm still here online with L.L. Bean

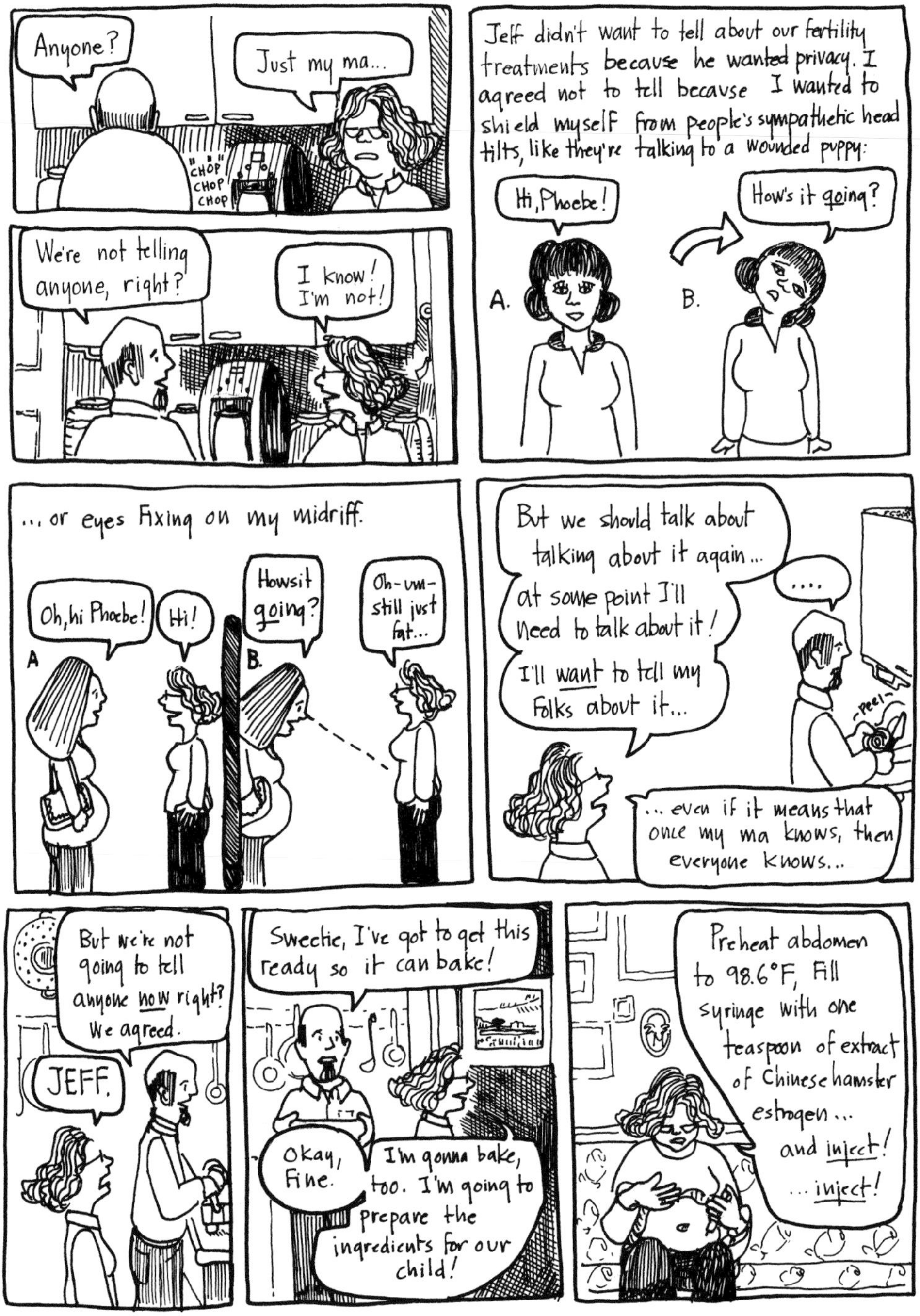
Anyone?
Just my ma...
"CHOP" CHOP CHOP
Jeff didn't want to tell about our fertility treatments because he wanted privacy. I agreed not to tell because I wanted to shield myself from people's sympathetic head tilts, like they're talking to a wounded puppy:
Hi, Phoebe!
A.
How's it going?
B.
We're not telling anyone, right?
I know! I'm not!
... or eyes fixing on my midriff.
A
Oh, hi Phoebe!
Hi!
B.
Howsit going?
Oh-um- still just fat...
But we should talk about talking about it again...
at some point I'll need to talk about it!
I'll want to tell my folks about it...
....
-peel-
... even if it means that once my ma knows, then everyone knows...
But we're not going to tell anyone now right? We agreed.
JEFF.
Sweetie, I've got to get this ready so it can bake!
Okay, Fine.
I'm gonna bake, too. I'm going to prepare the ingredients for our child!
Preheat abdomen to 98.6°F, Fill syringe with one teaspoon of extract of Chinese hamster estrogen...
and inject!
...inject!

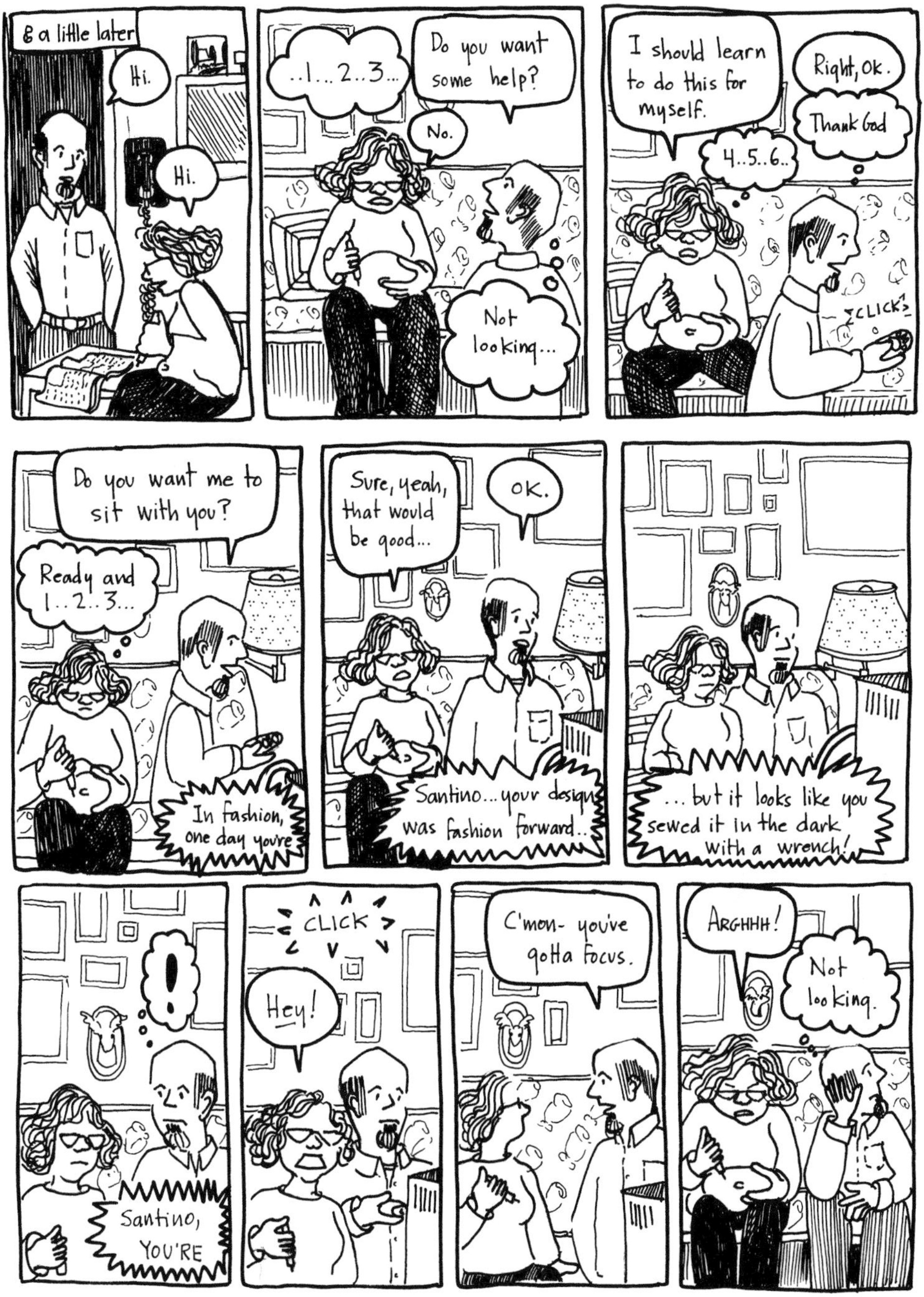
& a little later
Hi.
Hi.
..1...2..3...
Do you want some help?
No.
Not looking...
I should learn to do this for myself.
4..5..6..
Right, OK.
Thank God
CLICK
Do you want me to sit with you?
Ready and 1..2..3...
In fashion, one day you're
Sure, yeah, that would be good...
OK.
Santino...your design was fashion forward...
...but it looks like you sewed it in the dark with a wrench!
!
Santino, YOU'RE
CLICK
Hey!
C'mon- you've gotta focus.
ARGHHH!
Not looking.

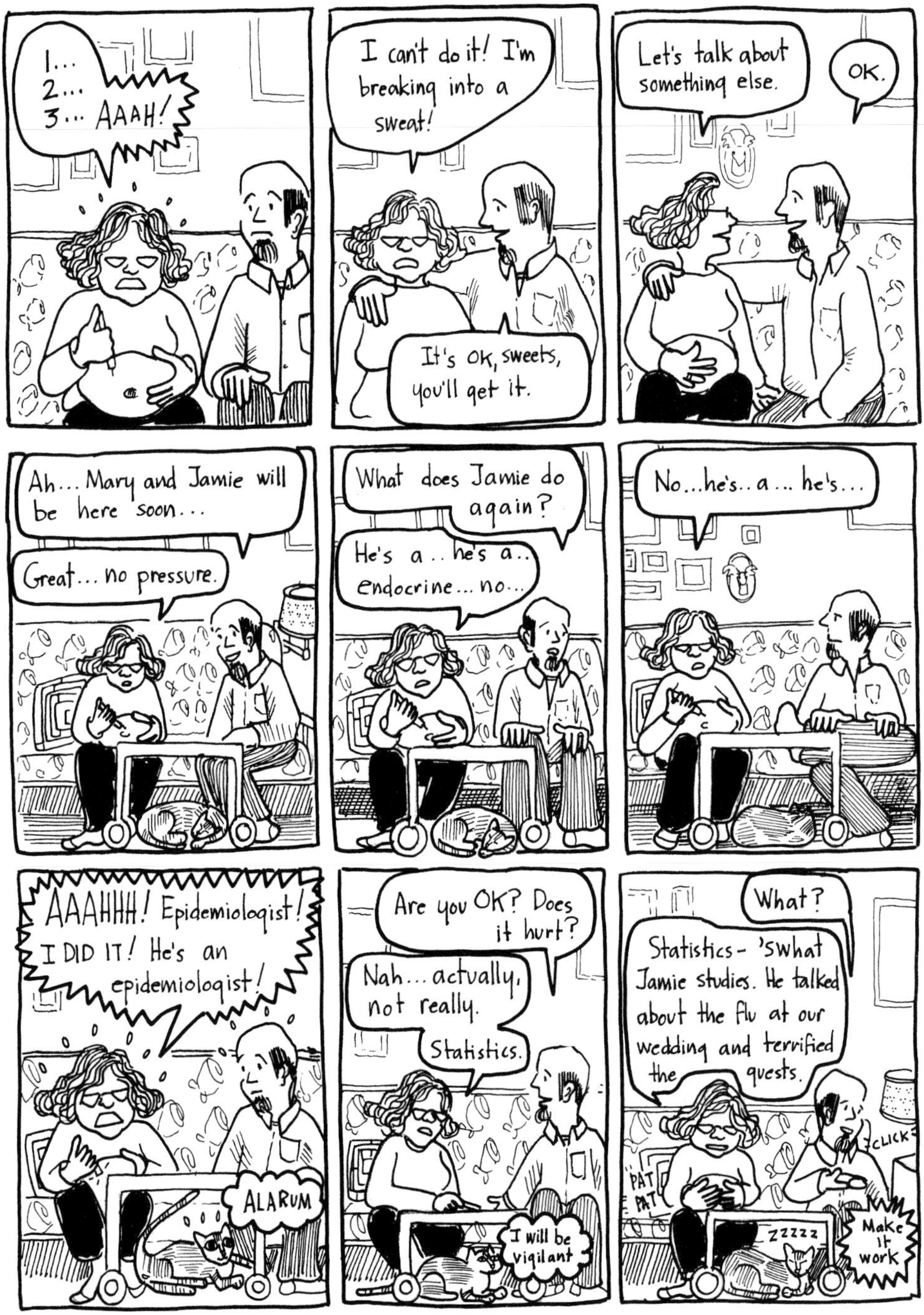
1...
2...
3... AAAH!
I can't do it! I'm breaking into a sweat!
It's OK, sweets, you'll get it.
Let's talk about something else.
OK.
Ah... Mary and Jamie will be here soon...
Great... no pressure.
What does Jamie do again?
He's a.. he's a.. endocrine... no...
No...he's.. a... he's...
AAAHHH! Epidemiologist! I DID IT! He's an epidemiologist!
ALARUM
Are you OK? Does it hurt?
Nah... actually, not really.
Statistics.
I will be vigilant
What?
Statistics- 'swhat Jamie studies. He talked about the flu at our wedding and terrified the guests.
PAT PAT
CLICK
ZZZZZ
Make it work

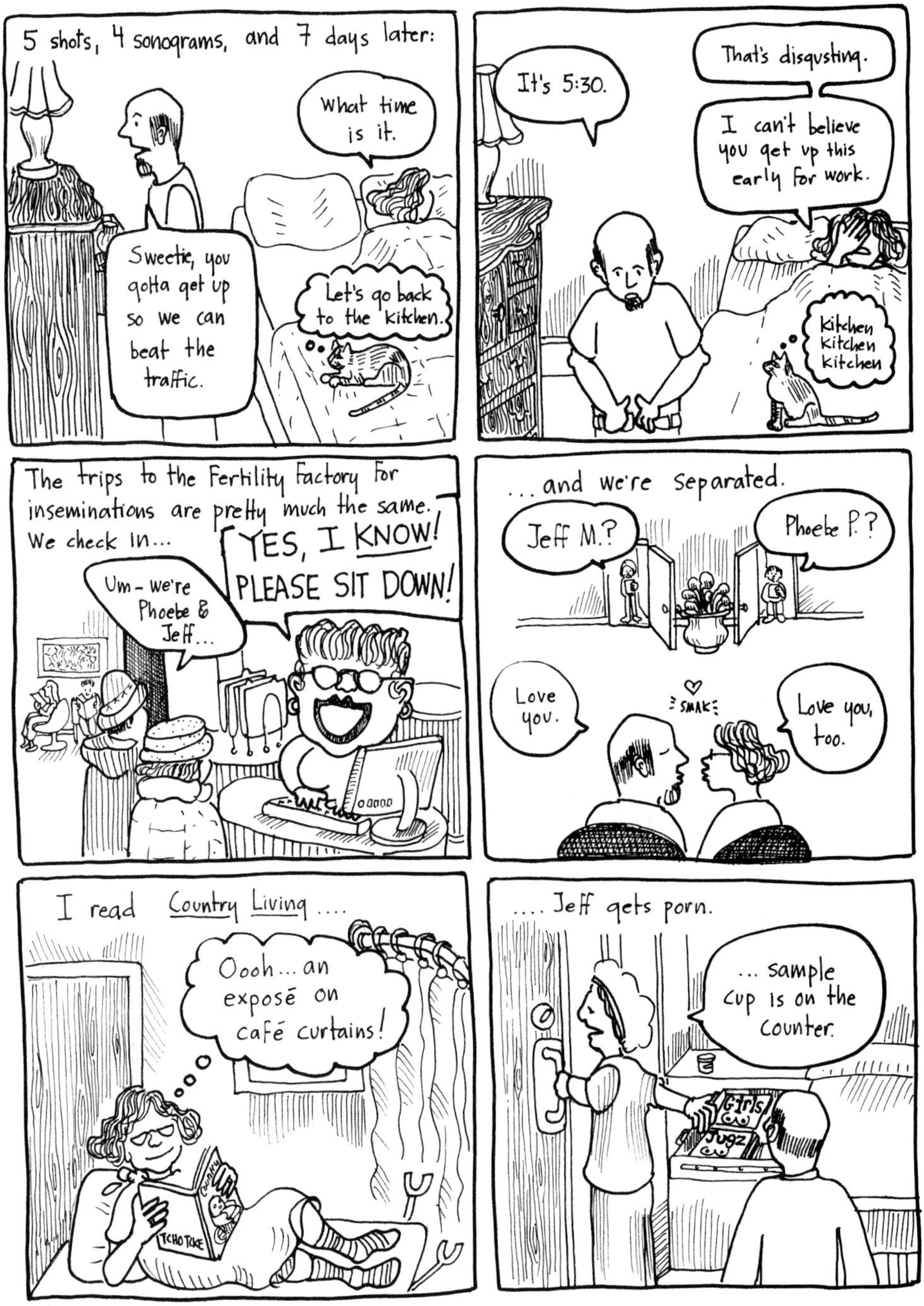
5 shots, 4 sonograms, and 7 days later:
What time is it.
Sweetie, you gotta get up so we can beat the traffic.
Let's go back to the kitchen.
It's 5:30.
That's disgusting.
I can't believe you get up this early for work.
kitchen kitchen kitchen
The trips to the Fertility Factory for inseminations are pretty much the same. We check in...
Um- we're Phoebe & Jeff...
YES, I KNOW! PLEASE SIT DOWN!
...and we're separated.
Jeff M.?
Phoebe P.?
Love you.
SMAK
Love you, too.
I read Country Living....
Oooh... an exposé on café curtains!
....Jeff gets porn.
... sample cup is on the counter.
Girls
Jugz

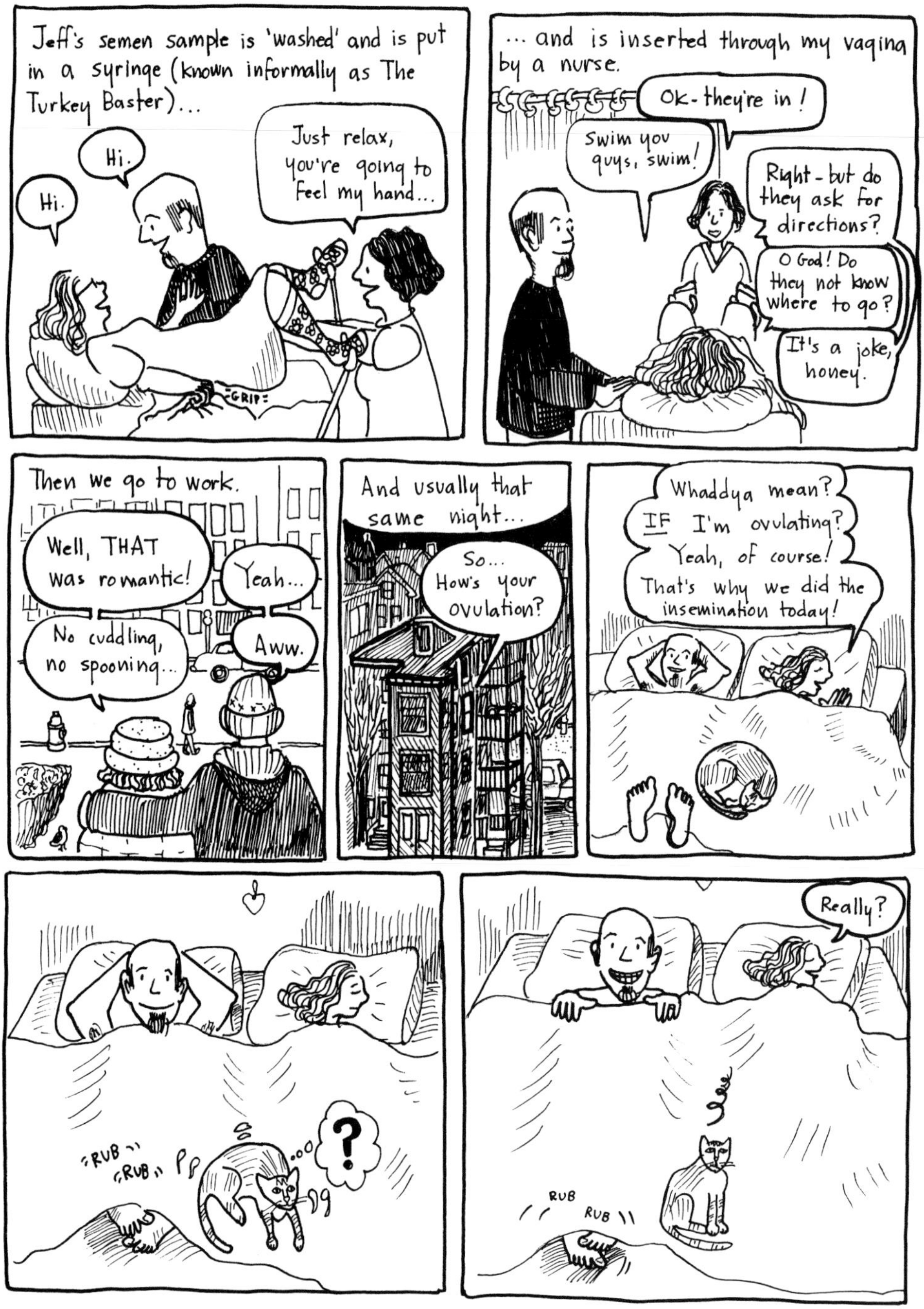
Jeff's semen sample is 'washed' and is put in a syringe (known informally as The Turkey Baster)...
Hi.
Hi.
Just relax, you're going to feel my hand...
GRIP
... and is inserted through my vagina by a nurse.
Ok - they're in!
Swim you guys, swim!
Right - but do they ask for directions?
O God! Do they not know where to go?
It's a joke, honey.
Then we go to work.
Well, THAT was romantic!
Yeah...
No cuddling, no spooning...
Aww.
And usually that same night...
So... How's your ovulation?
Whaddya mean? IF I'm ovulating? Yeah, of course! That's why we did the insemination today!
RUB
RUB
?
Really?
RUB
RUB

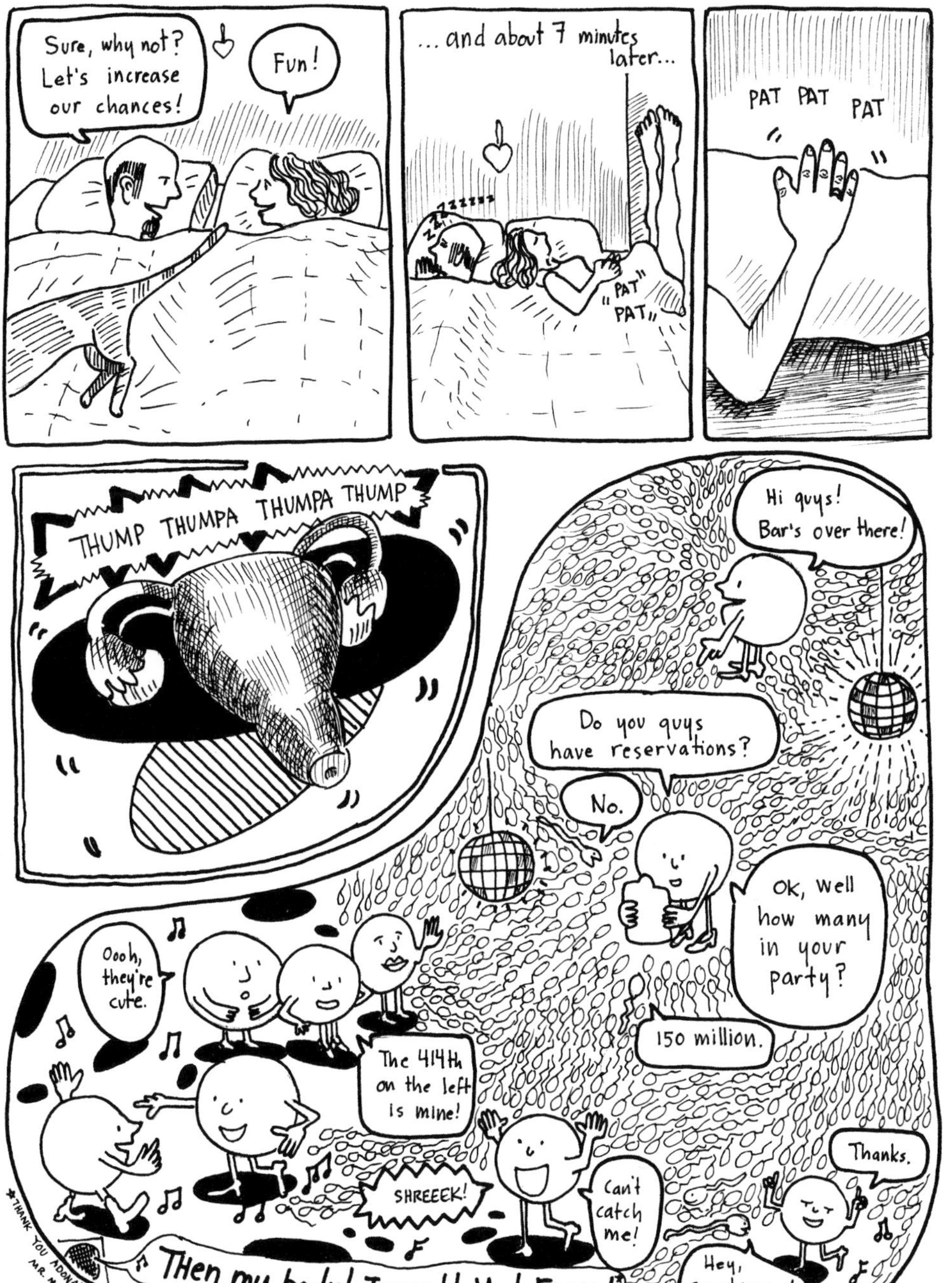

Sure, why not? Let's increase our chances!
Fun!
...and about 7 minutes later...
PAT PAT
PAT PAT PAT
THUMP THUMPA THUMPA THUMP
Hi guys! Bar's over there!
Do you guys have reservations?
No.
Ok, well how many in your party?
150 million.
Oooh, they're cute.
The 414th on the left is mine!
SHREEEK!
Can't catch me!
Thanks.
Hey, great moves!
Then my body! Turned! Me! FREE!*
*THANK YOU ADONAI FOR MR. MARVIN GAYE

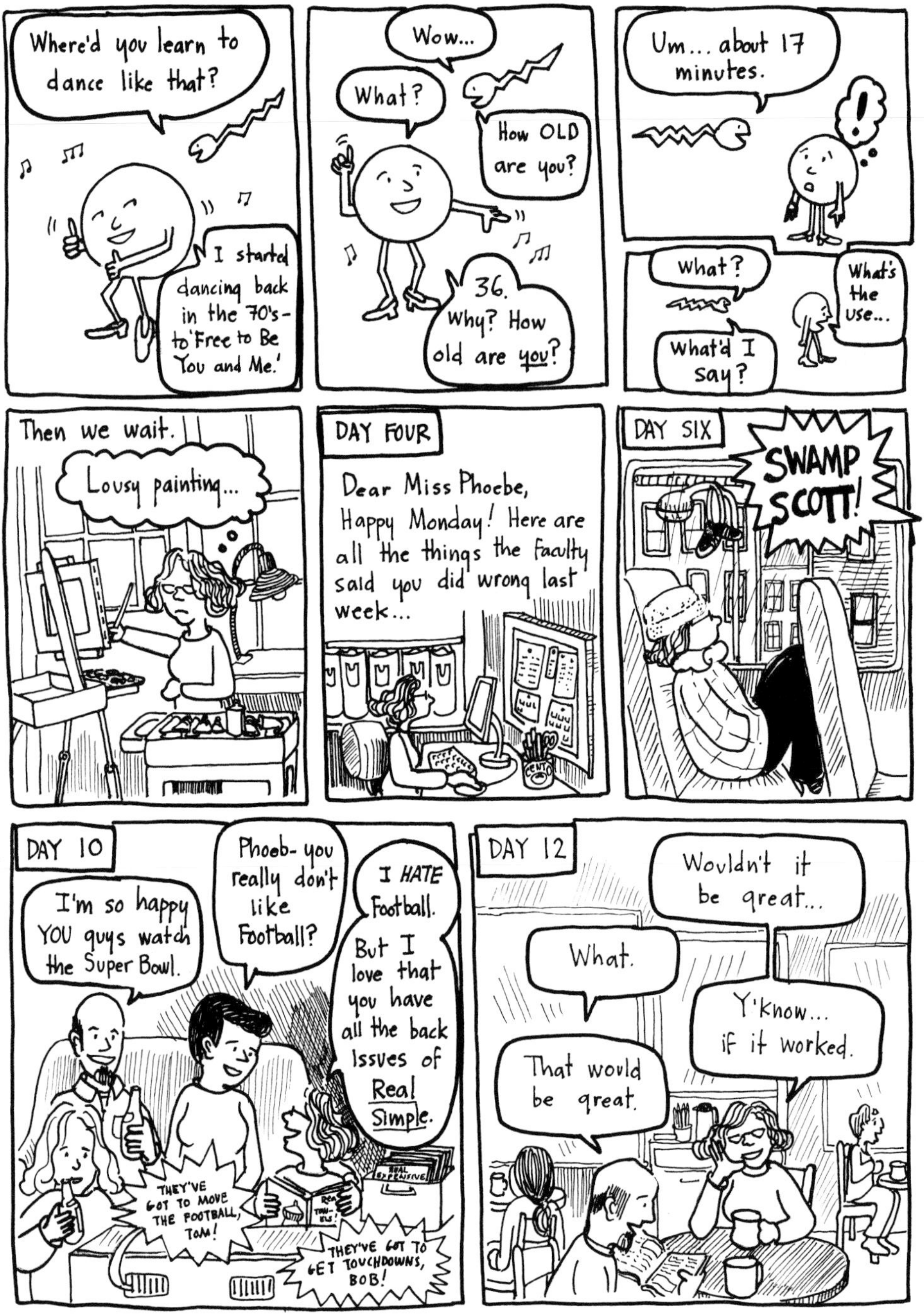
Where'd you learn to dance like that?
I started dancing back in the 70's - to 'Free to Be You and Me.'
Wow...
What?
How OLD are you?
36. Why? How old are you?
Um... about 17 minutes.
!
What?
What'd I say?
What's the use...
Then we wait.
Lousy painting...
DAY FOUR
Dear Miss Phoebe, Happy Monday! Here are all the things the faculty said you did wrong last week...
DAY SIX
SWAMP SCOTT!
DAY 10
I'm so happy YOU guys watch the Super Bowl.
Phoob- you really don't like Football?
I HATE Football.
But I love that you have all the back Issues of Real Simple.
THEY'VE GOT TO MOVE THE FOOTBALL, TOM!
REAL EXPENSIVE
THEY'VE GOT TO GET TOUCHDOWNS, BOB!
DAY 12
Wouldn't it be great...
What.
Y'know... if it worked.
That would be great.

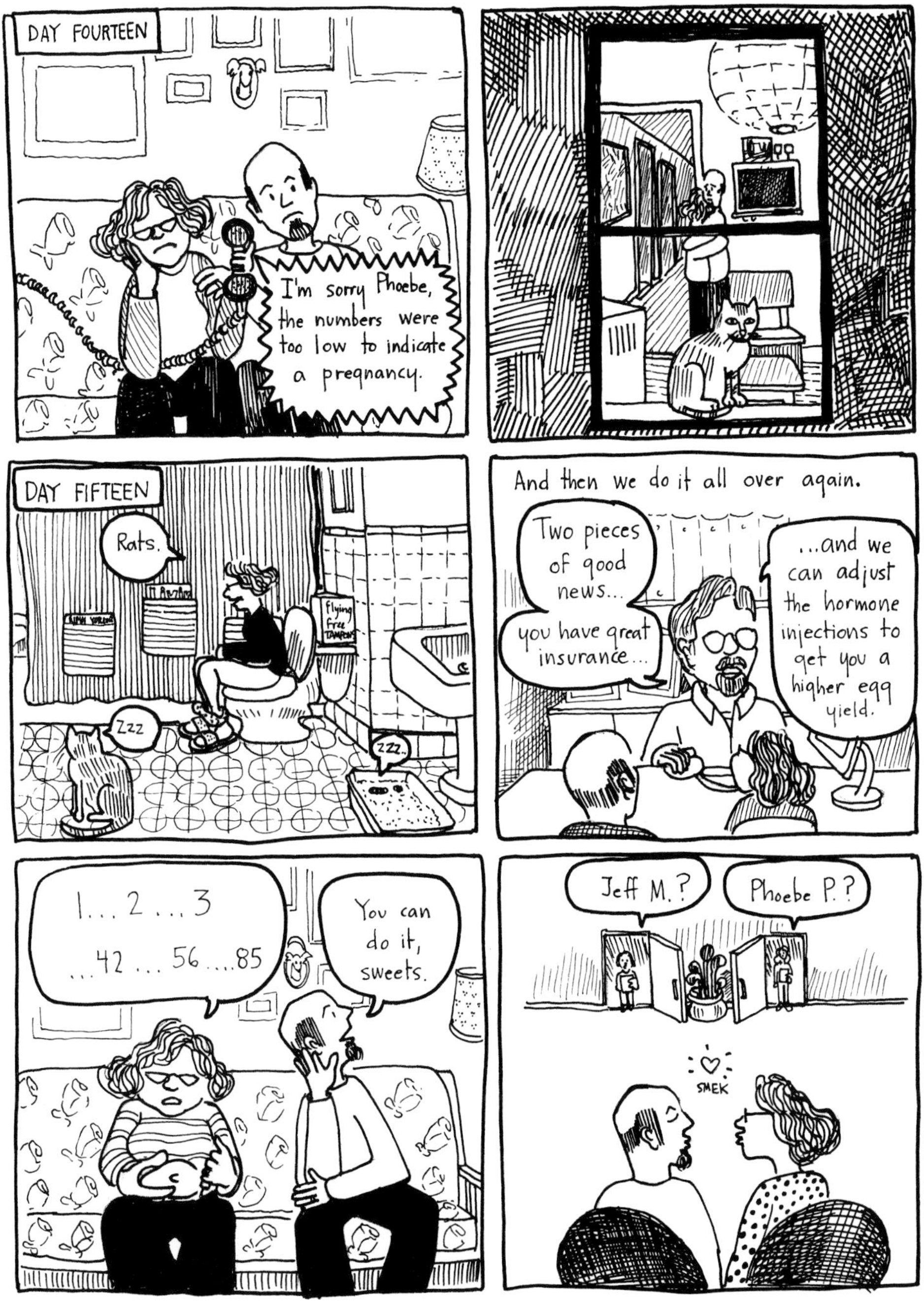
DAY FOURTEEN
I'm sorry Phoebe, the numbers were too low to indicate a pregnancy.
DAY FIFTEEN
Rats.
Zzz
zzz..
Flying free TAMPONS
And then we do it all over again.
Two pieces of good news...
you have great insurance...
...and we can adjust the hormone injections to get you a higher egg yield.
1... 2 ... 3
...42 ... 56 85
You can do it, sweets.
Jeff M.?
Phoebe P.?
SMEK

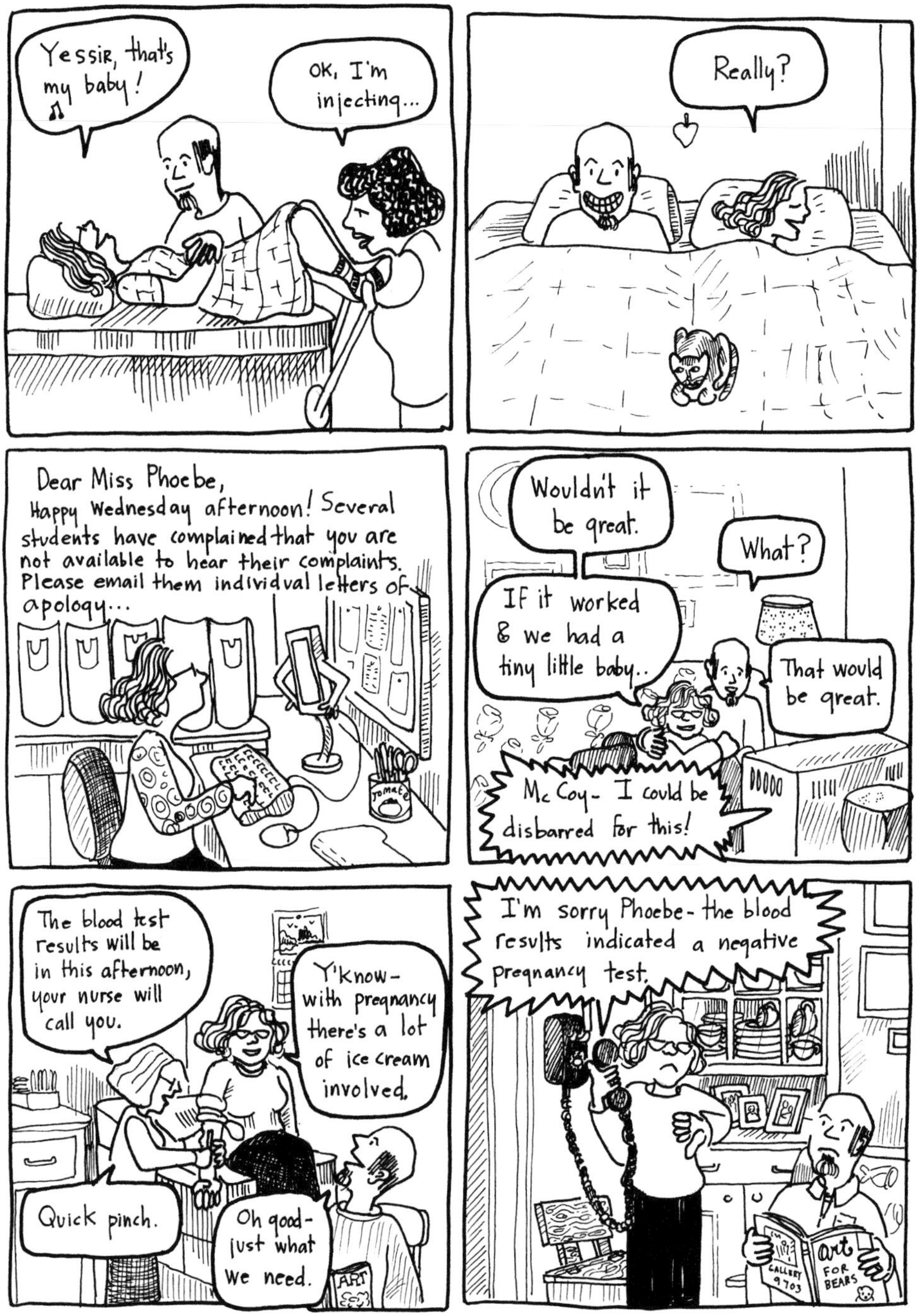
Yessir, that's my baby!
OK, I'm injecting...
Really?
Dear Miss Phoebe, Happy Wednesday afternoon! Several students have complained that you are not available to hear their complaints. Please email them individual letters of apology...
TOMATO
Wouldn't it be great.
What?
If it worked & we had a tiny little baby..
That would be great.
McCoy- I could be disbarred for this!
The blood test results will be in this afternoon, your nurse will call you.
Y'know- with pregnancy there's a lot of ice cream involved.
Quick pinch.
Oh good- just what we need.
ART
I'm sorry Phoebe- the blood results indicated a negative pregnancy test.
art FOR BEARS
GALLERY 9703

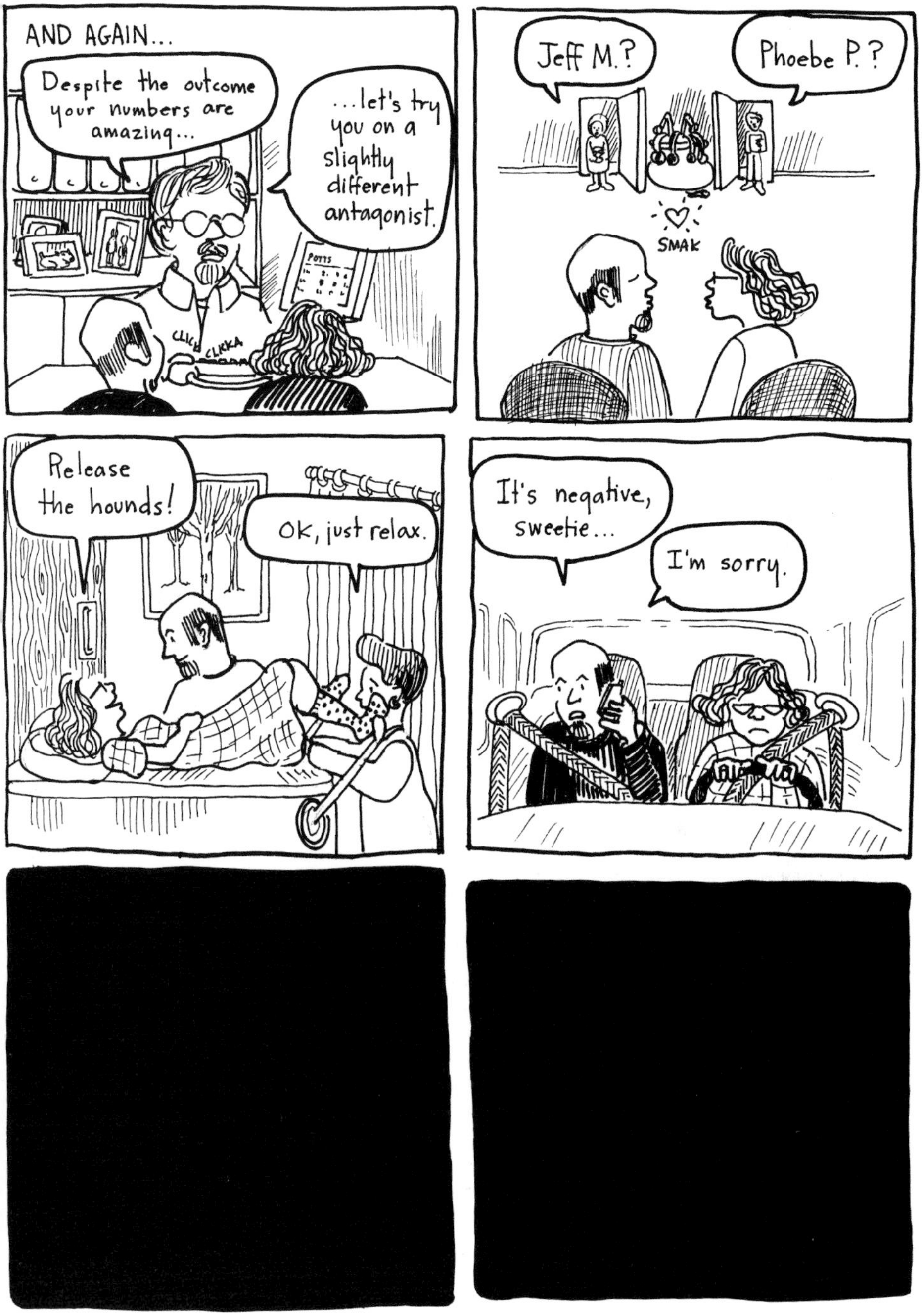
AND AGAIN...
Despite the outcome your numbers are amazing...
...let's try you on a slightly different antagonist.
Jeff M.?
Phoebe P.?
SMAK
Release the hounds!
Ok, just relax.
It's negative, sweetie...
I'm sorry.

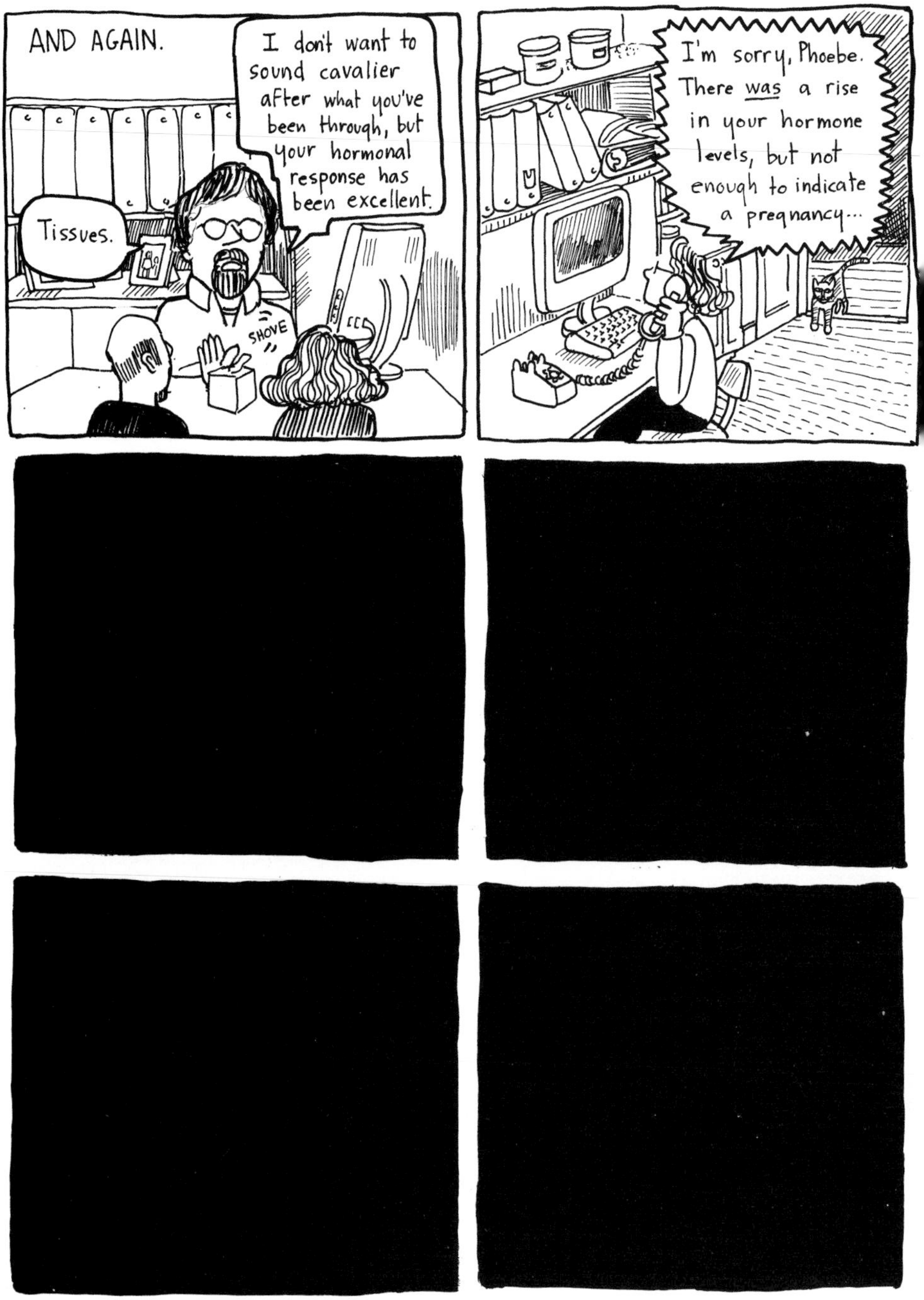
AND AGAIN.
I don't want to sound cavalier after what you've been through, but your hormonal response has been excellent.
Tissues.
SHOVE
I'm sorry, Phoebe. There was a rise in your hormone levels, but not enough to indicate a pregnancy...

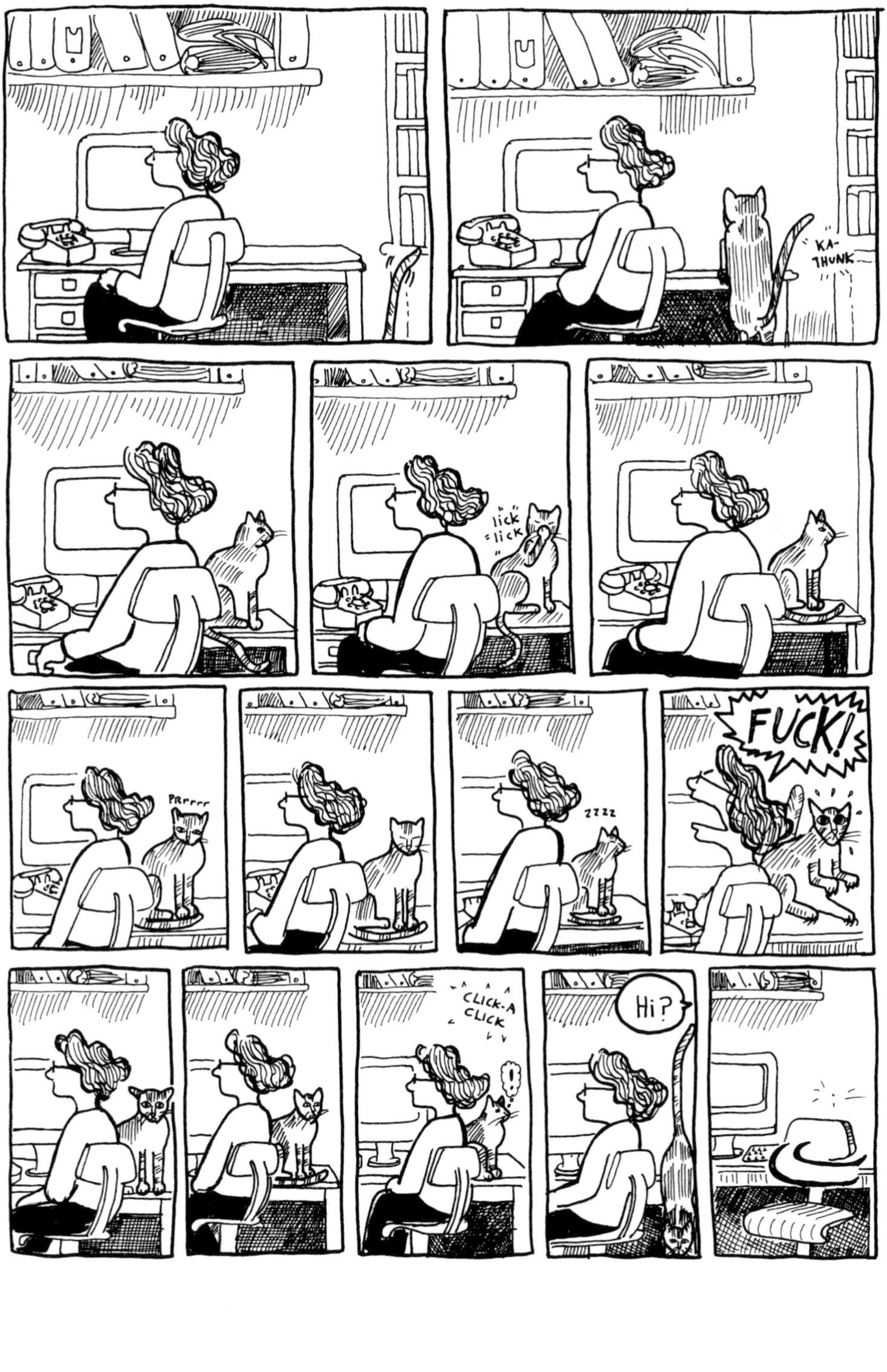
KA-
THUNK
lick
lick
PRrrrr
zzzz
FUCK!
CLICK-A
CLICK
!
Hi?

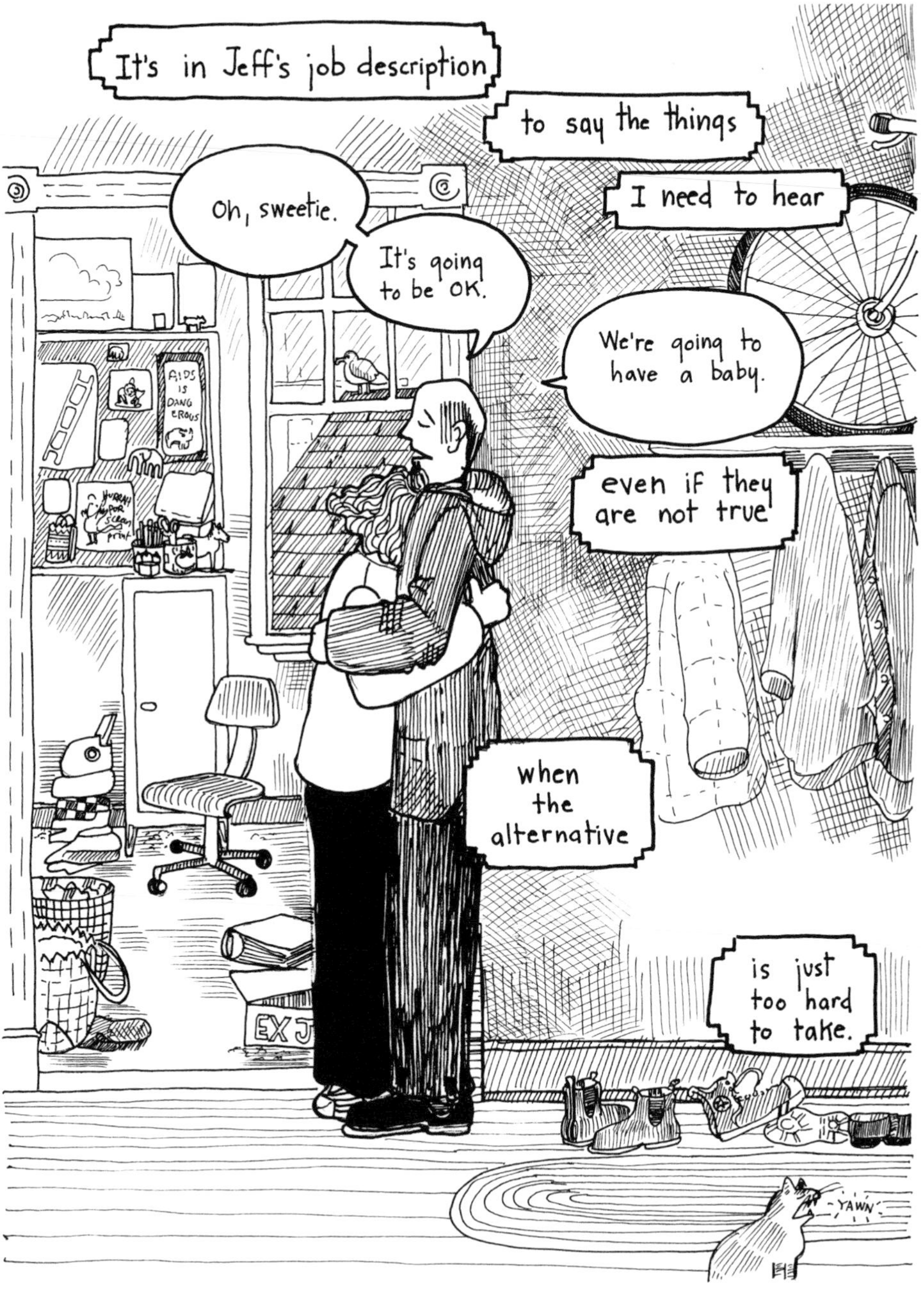
It's in Jeff's job description
to say the things
I need to hear
Oh, sweetie.
It's going to be OK.
We're going to have a baby.
even if they are not true
when the alternative
is just too hard to take.
YAWN

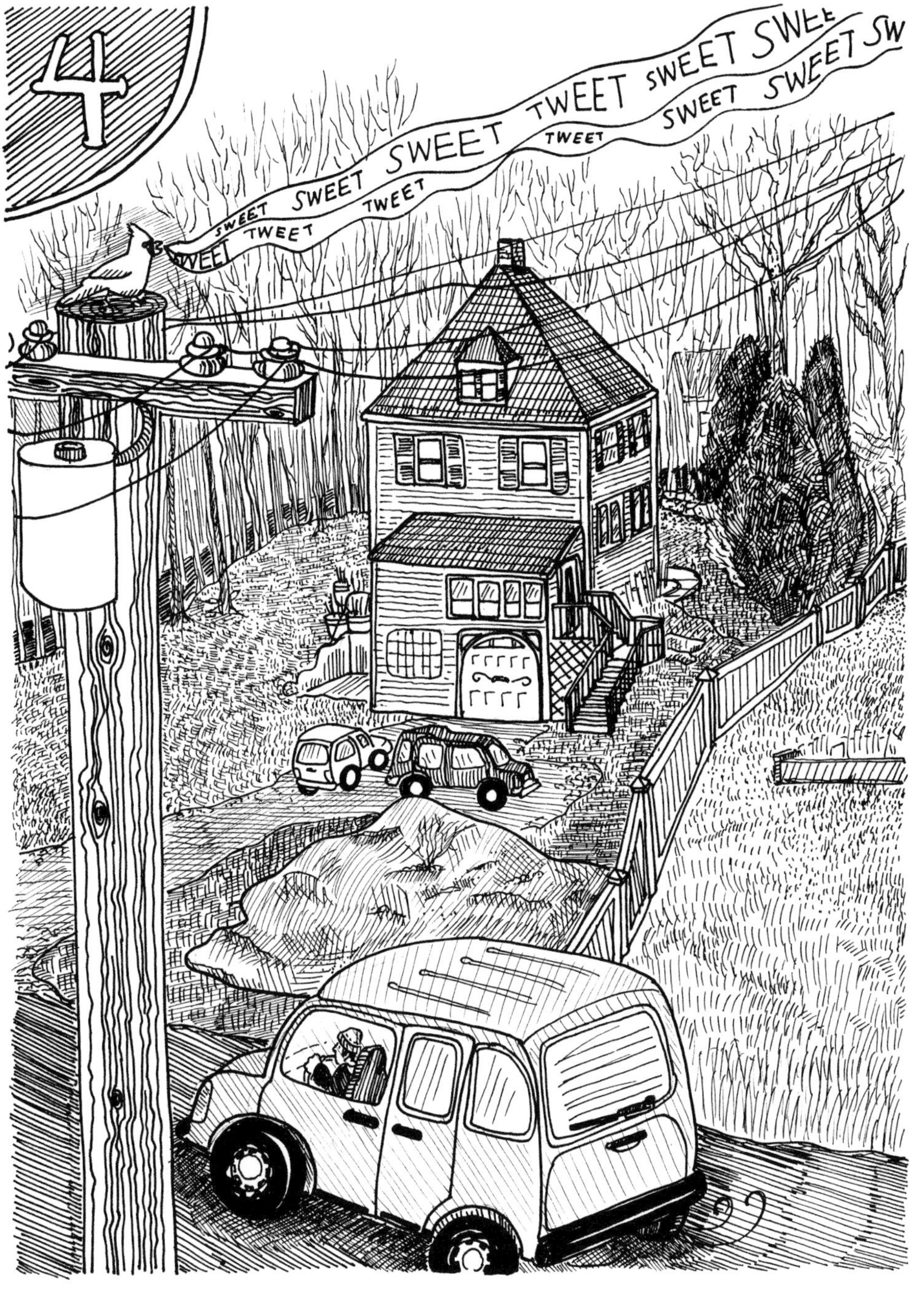
4
SWEET TWEET
SWEET
SWEET TWEET
SWEET
TWEET
TWEET SWEET SWEE
TWEET
SWEET SWEET SW

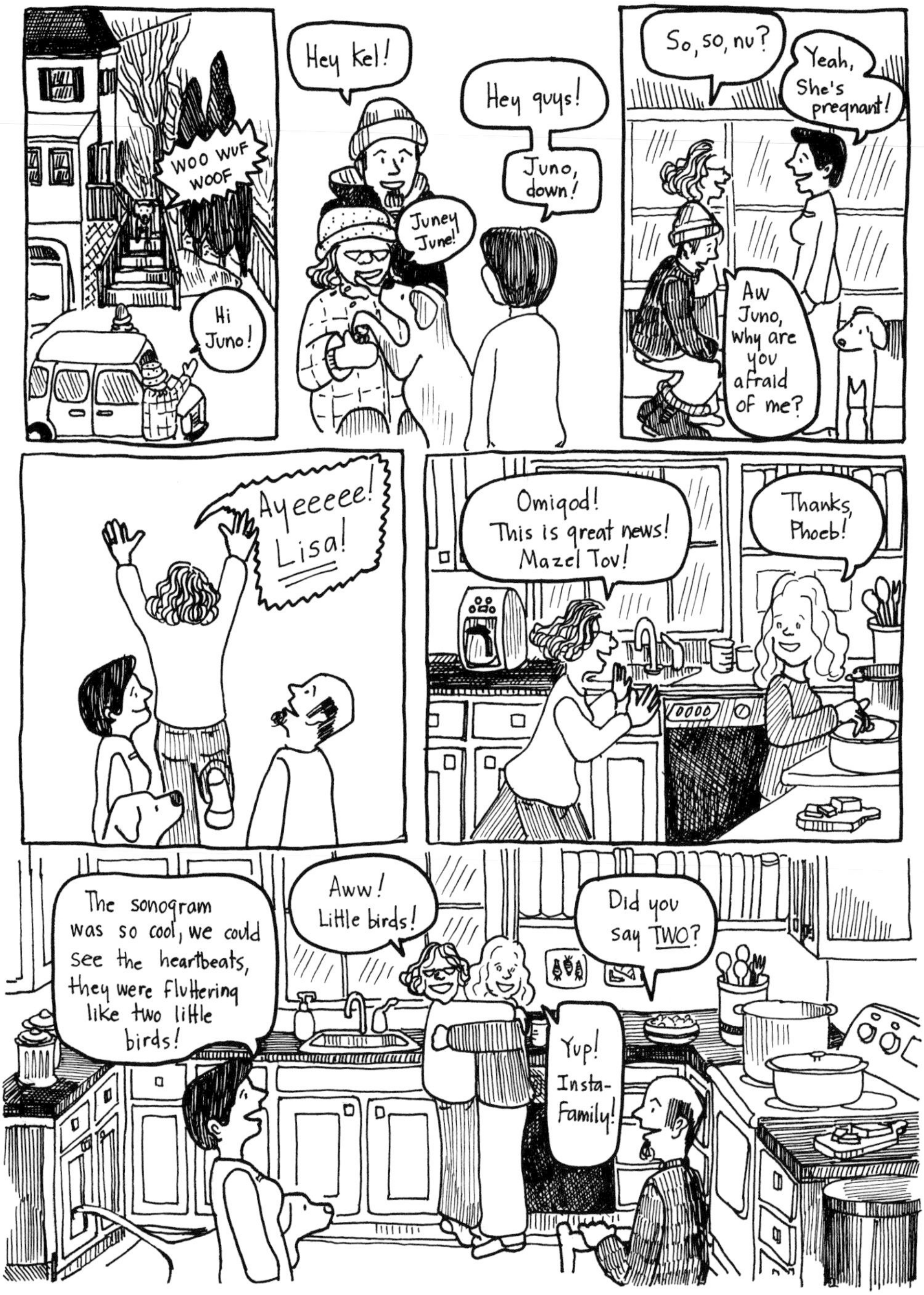
WOO WUF WOOF
Hi Juno!
Hey Kel!
Juney June!
Hey guys!
Juno, down!
So, so, nu?
Yeah, She's pregnant!
Aw Juno, why are you afraid of me?
Ayeeeee! Lisa!
Omigod! This is great news! Mazel Tov!
Thanks, Phoeb!
The sonogram was so cool, we could see the heartbeats, they were fluttering like two little birds!
Aww! Little birds!
Did you say TWO?
Yup! Insta-Family!

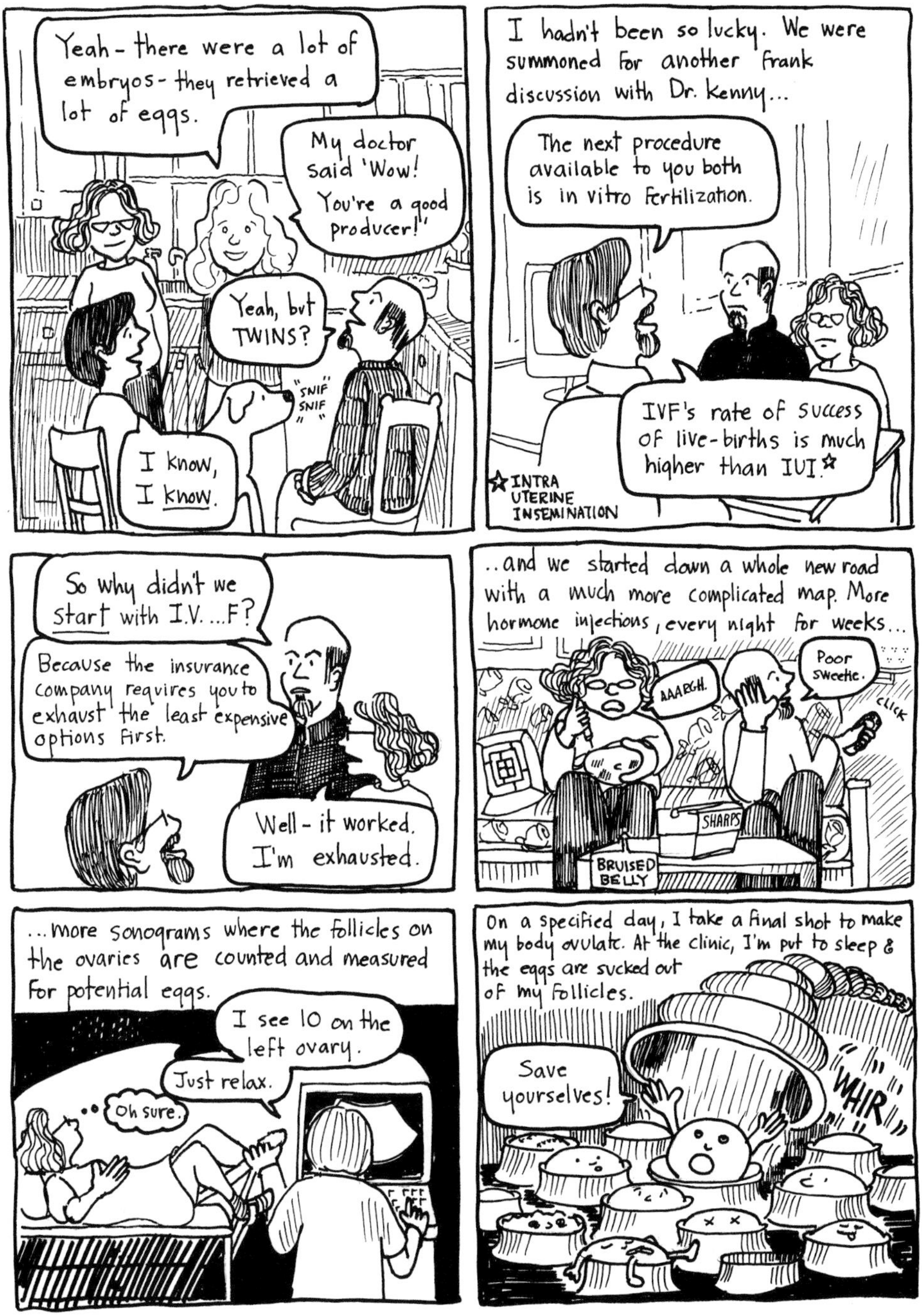
Yeah - there were a lot of embryos - they retrieved a lot of eggs.
My doctor said 'Wow! You're a good producer!'
Yeah, but TWINS?
"SNIF SNIF"
I know, I know.
I hadn't been so lucky. We were summoned for another frank discussion with Dr. Kenny...
The next procedure available to you both is in vitro fertilization.
IVF's rate of success of live-births is much higher than IUI.☆
☆ INTRA UTERINE INSEMINATION
So why didn't we start with I.V. ...F?
Because the insurance company requires you to exhaust the least expensive options first.
Well - it worked. I'm exhausted.
..and we started down a whole new road with a much more complicated map. More hormone injections, every night for weeks...
AAAEGH.
Poor sweetie.
CLICK
SHARPS
BRUISED BELLY
...more sonograms where the follicles on the ovaries are counted and measured for potential eggs.
I see 10 on the left ovary.
Just relax.
Oh sure.
On a specified day, I take a final shot to make my body ovulate. At the clinic, I'm put to sleep & the eggs are sucked out of my follicles.
Save yourselves!
WHIR

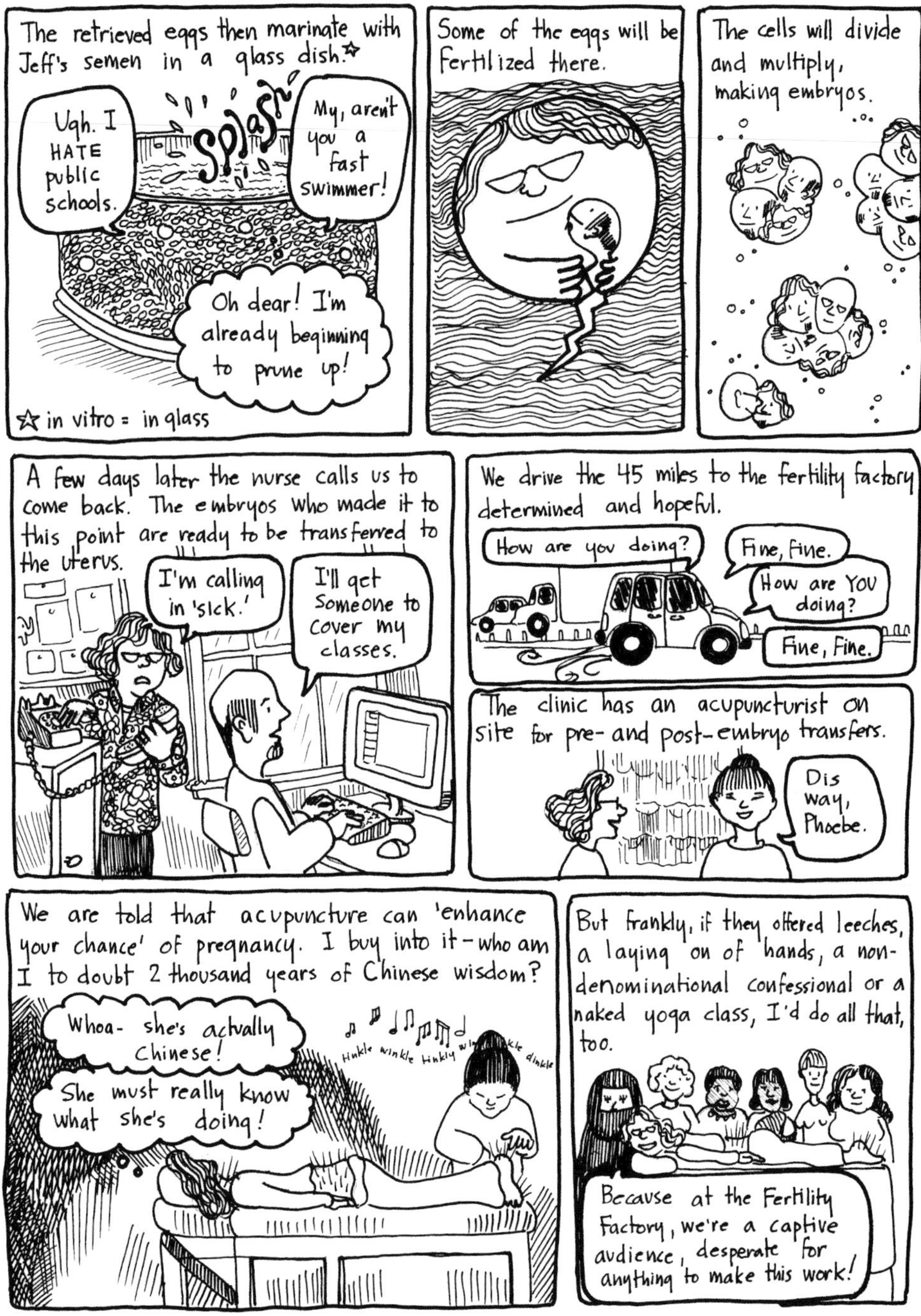
The retrieved eggs then marinate with Jeff's semen in a glass dish.☆
Ugh. I HATE public schools.
SPLASH
My, aren't you a fast swimmer!
Oh dear! I'm already beginning to prune up!
☆ in vitro = in glass
Some of the eggs will be fertilized there.
The cells will divide and multiply, making embryos.
A few days later the nurse calls us to come back. The embryos who made it to this point are ready to be transferred to the uterus.
I'm calling in 'sick.'
I'll get someone to cover my classes.
We drive the 45 miles to the fertility factory determined and hopeful.
How are you doing?
Fine, fine.
How are YOU doing?
Fine, Fine.
The clinic has an acupuncturist on site for pre- and post-embryo transfers.
Dis way, Phoebe.
We are told that acupuncture can 'enhance your chance' of pregnancy. I buy into it – who am I to doubt 2 thousand years of Chinese wisdom?
Whoa- she's actually Chinese!
She must really know what she's doing!
But frankly, if they offered leeches, a laying on of hands, a non-denominational confessional or a naked yoga class, I'd do all that, too.
Because at the Fertility Factory, we're a captive audience, desperate for anything to make this work!

After the first round of acupuncture Jeff & I get suited up for the embryo transfer.

You look like you're having a sleepover in a microchip factory.

Nice, sweetie. Thanks.

In order for the doctor to guide the embryos into the uterus he needs to see what he's doing on the sonogram. To see the uterus on the sonogram though, the bladder has to be full.

But I drank on my way here!

No, honey. More.

Yes, ma'am.

The uterus lurks behind the bladder. A full bladder acts like a window for the sonogram. This was <u>not</u> what it was designed for, even though it's convenient for this procedure.

Can't find me.

CAN'T. HOLD. ON. MUCH. LONGER!

The embryos go into a syringe in a catheter which is threaded through the cervix into the uterus...

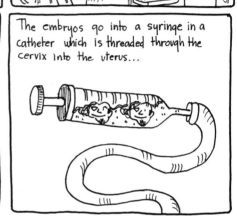

...where they are injected & hopefully will implant. This is a ten minute procedure for most women.

WHEEEeee!!

Except for me, of course.

NNNNGHHHH!!!!

Hmm... I can't get in. Her uterus is severely tipped.

Please get me a straightener.

Yes, doctor.

147

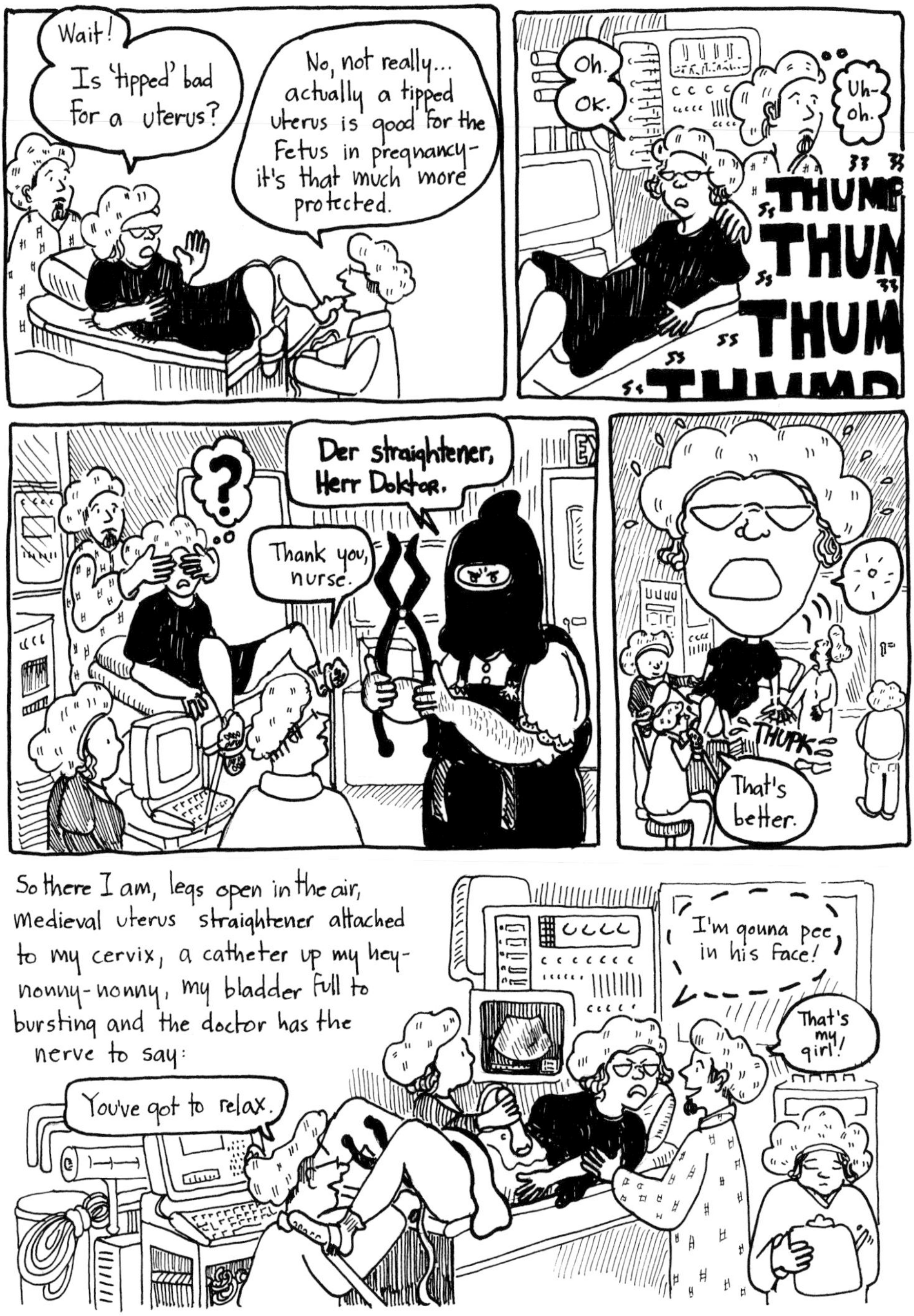
Wait!
Is 'tipped' bad for a uterus?
No, not really... actually a tipped uterus is good for the fetus in pregnancy- it's that much more protected.
Oh. Ok.
Uh-oh.
THUMP
THUMP
THUMP
THUMP
Der straightener, Herr Doktor.
Thank you, nurse.
?
THUPK
That's better.
So there I am, legs open in the air, medieval uterus straightener attached to my cervix, a catheter up my hey-nonny-nonny, my bladder full to bursting and the doctor has the nerve to say:
You've got to relax.
I'm gonna pee in his face!
That's my girl!

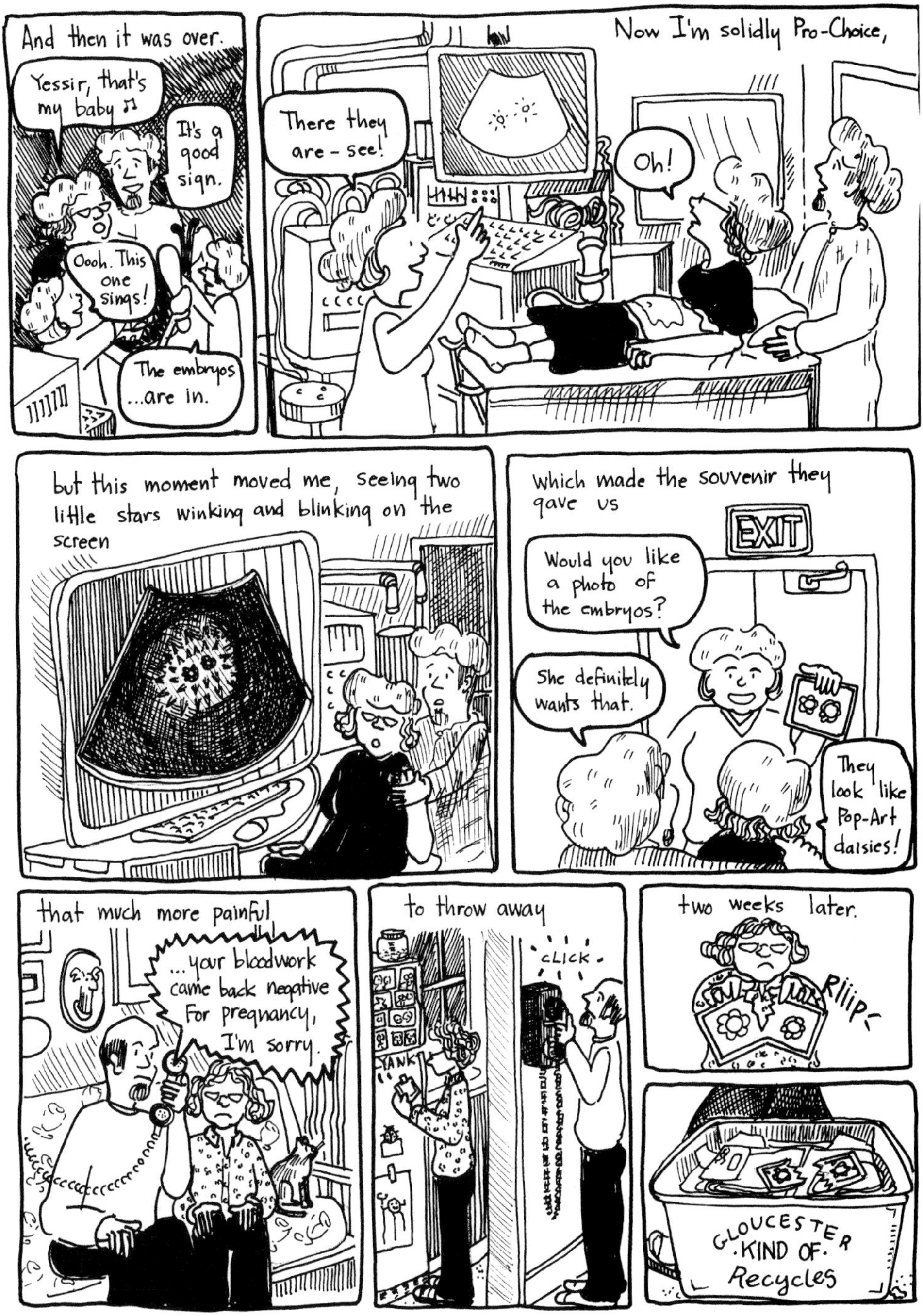
And then it was over.
Yessir, that's my baby ♫
It's a good sign.
Oooh. This one sings!
The embryos ...are in.
Now I'm solidly Pro-Choice,
There they are - see!
Oh!
but this moment moved me, seeing two little stars winking and blinking on the screen
which made the souvenir they gave us
EXIT
Would you like a photo of the embryos?
She definitely wants that.
They look like Pop-Art daisies!
that much more painful
...your bloodwork came back negative for pregnancy, I'm sorry.
to throw away
CLICK
YANK
two weeks later.
Rlip!
GLOUCESTER
KIND OF
Recycles

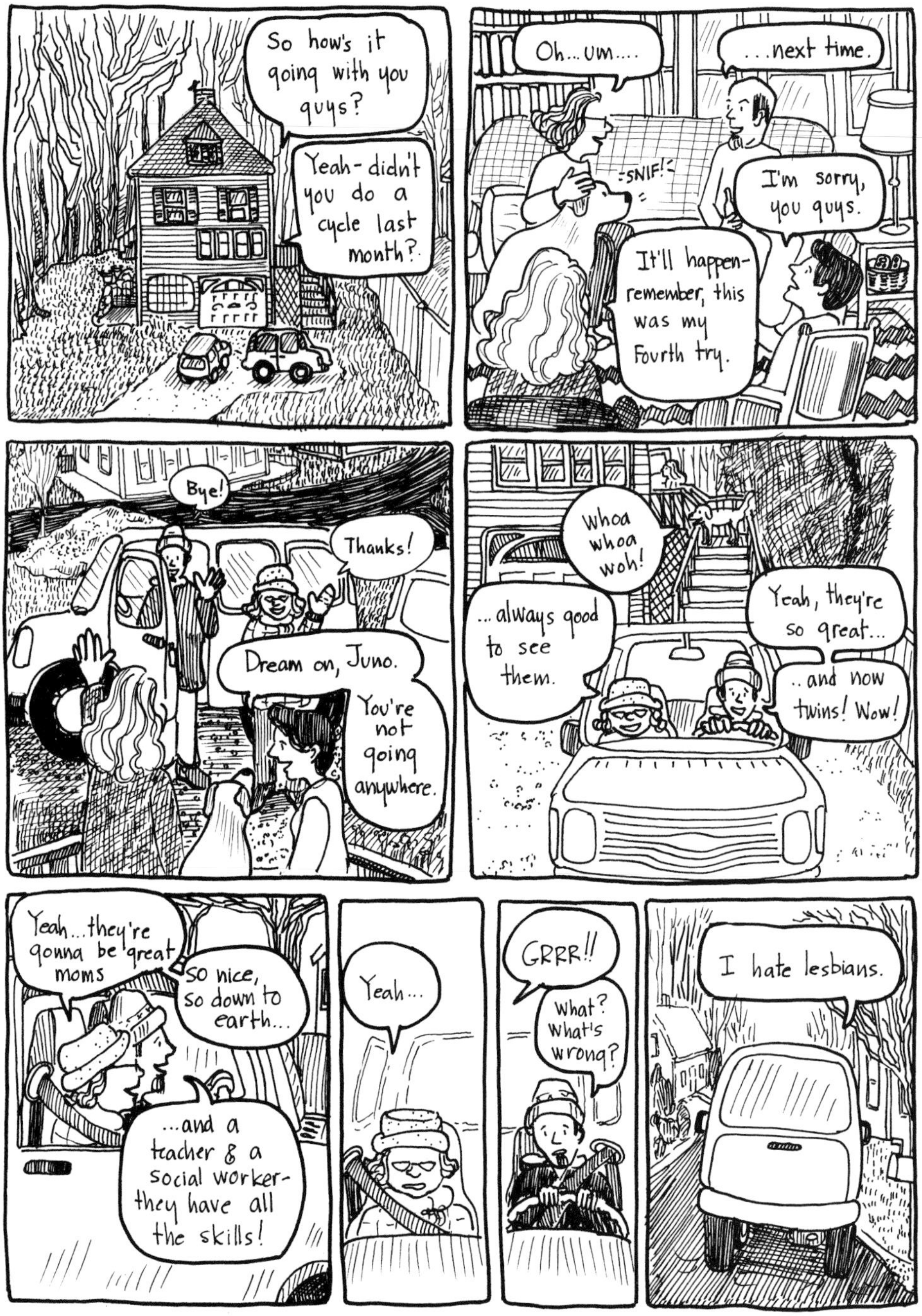
So how's it going with you guys?
Yeah- didn't you do a cycle last month?
Oh...um....
...next time.
SNIF!
I'm sorry, you guys.
It'll happen- remember, this was my fourth try.
Bye!
Thanks!
Dream on, Juno.
You're not going anywhere.
whoa whoa woh!
...always good to see them.
Yeah, they're so great...
..and now twins! Wow!
Yeah...they're gonna be great moms
so nice, so down to earth...
...and a teacher & a social worker- they have all the skills!
Yeah...
GRRR!!
What? What's wrong?
I hate lesbians.

OK, so I don't HATE lesbians. I hate how I see fertility treatments so differently than they do. For lesbians, IVF & IUI are wonderful options, new beginnings, inconceivable just thirty years ago. But for lil' ol' heterosexual me, IVF means I've come to the end of the road. It means I've failed to do what I'm supposed to do naturally.

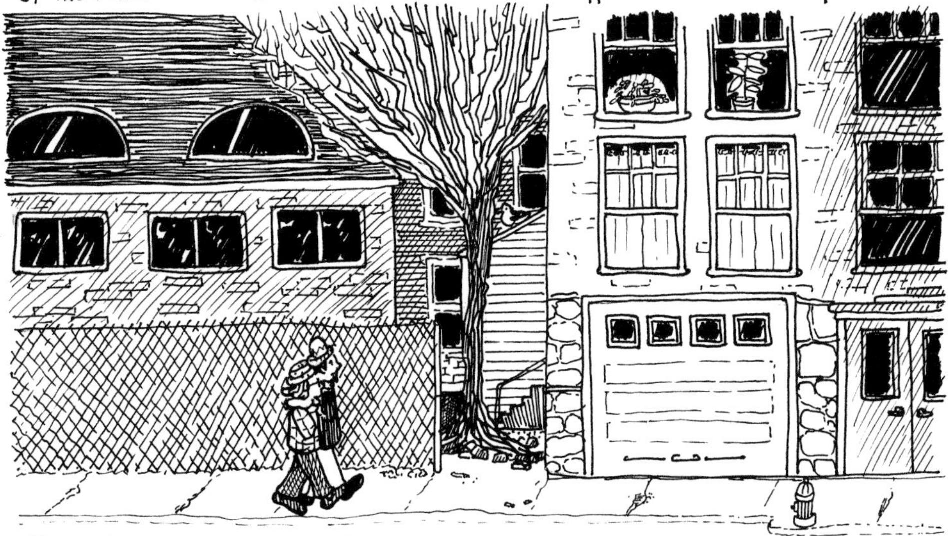

I've got a nice warm sperm bank on the premises, low cost, unlimited access...

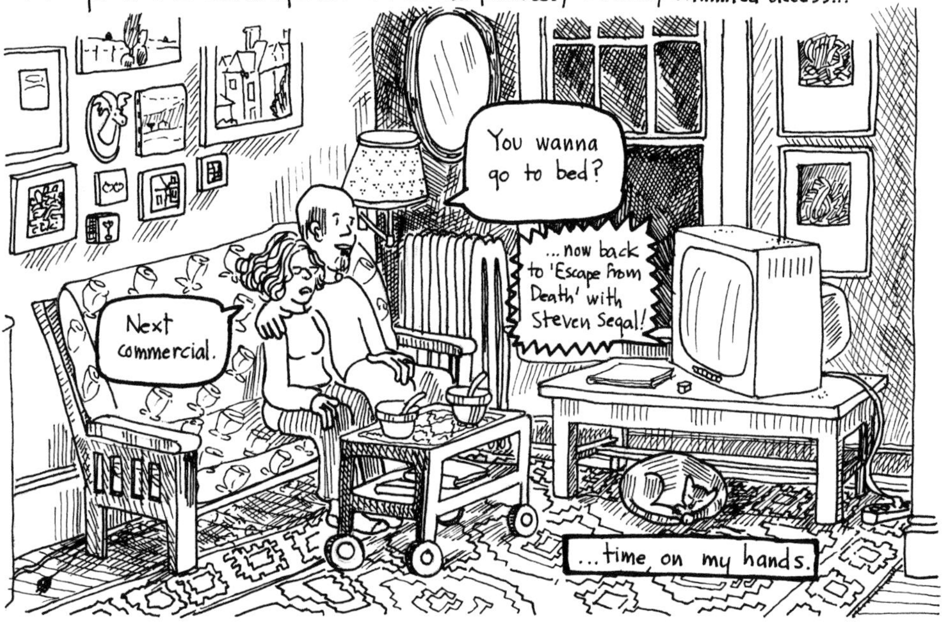
You wanna go to bed?
...now back to 'Escape from Death' with Steven Segal!
Next commercial.
...time on my hands.

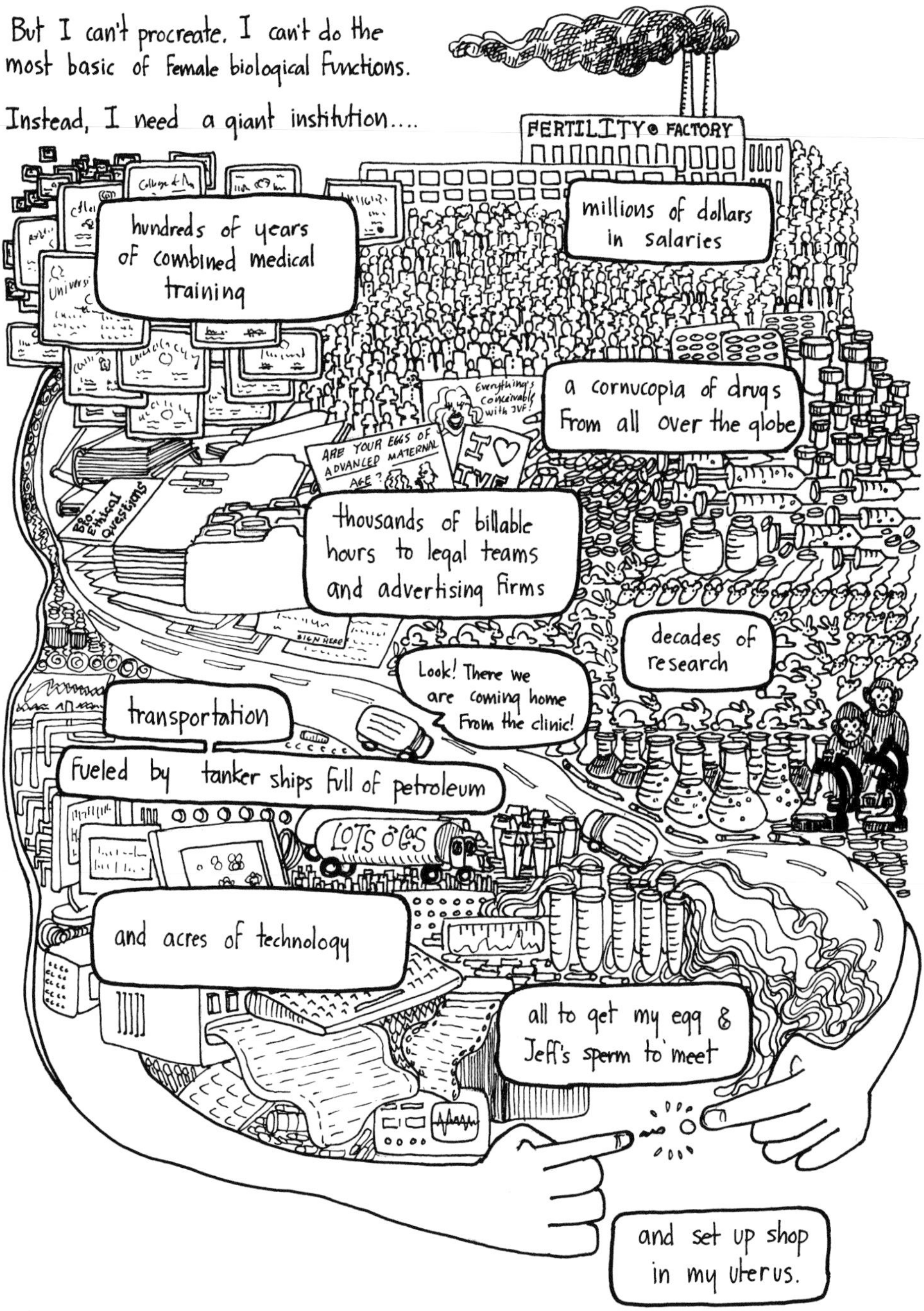
But I can't procreate. I can't do the most basic of female biological functions.
Instead, I need a giant institution....
FERTILITY FACTORY
hundreds of years of combined medical training
millions of dollars in salaries
Everything's Conceivable with IVF!
a cornucopia of drugs from all over the globe
ARE YOUR EGGS OF ADVANCED MATERNAL AGE?
Bio-Ethical Questions
thousands of billable hours to legal teams and advertising firms
SIGN HERE
decades of research
Look! There we are coming home from the clinic!
transportation
fueled by tanker ships full of petroleum
LOTS O' GAS
and acres of technology
all to get my egg & Jeff's sperm to meet
and set up shop in my uterus.

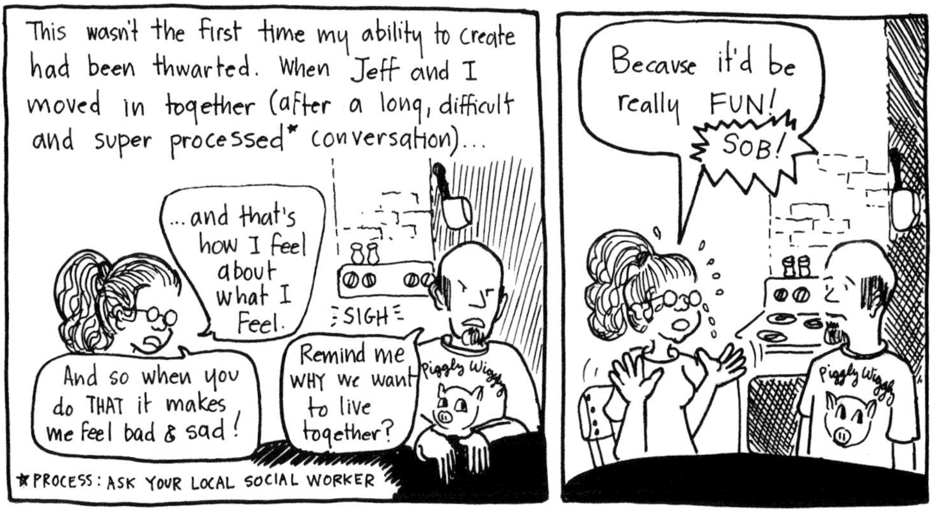
This wasn't the first time my ability to create had been thwarted. When Jeff and I moved in together (after a long, difficult and super processed* conversation)...
...and that's how I feel about what I Feel.
And so when you do THAT it makes me feel bad & sad!
SIGH
Remind me WHY we want to live together?
Piggly Wiggly
*PROCESS: ASK YOUR LOCAL SOCIAL WORKER
Because it'd be really FUN!
SOB!
Piggly Wiggly

...the planets seemed to be finally in alignment & I fulfilled my promise to myself: I went to art school.

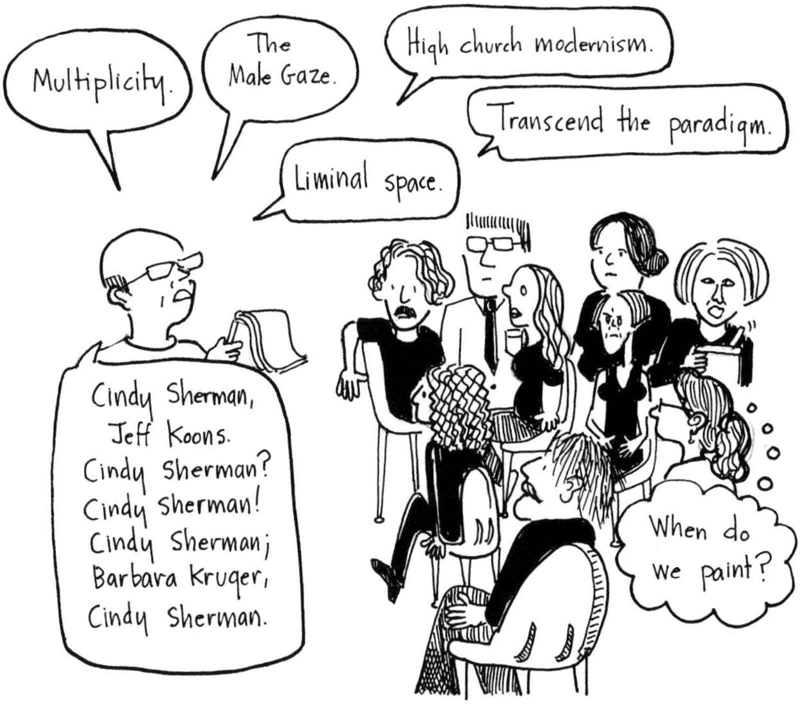
Multiplicity.
The Male Gaze.
High church modernism.
Transcend the paradigm.
Liminal space.
Cindy Sherman, Jeff Koons. Cindy Sherman? Cindy Sherman! Cindy Sherman; Barbara Kruger, Cindy Sherman.
When do we paint?

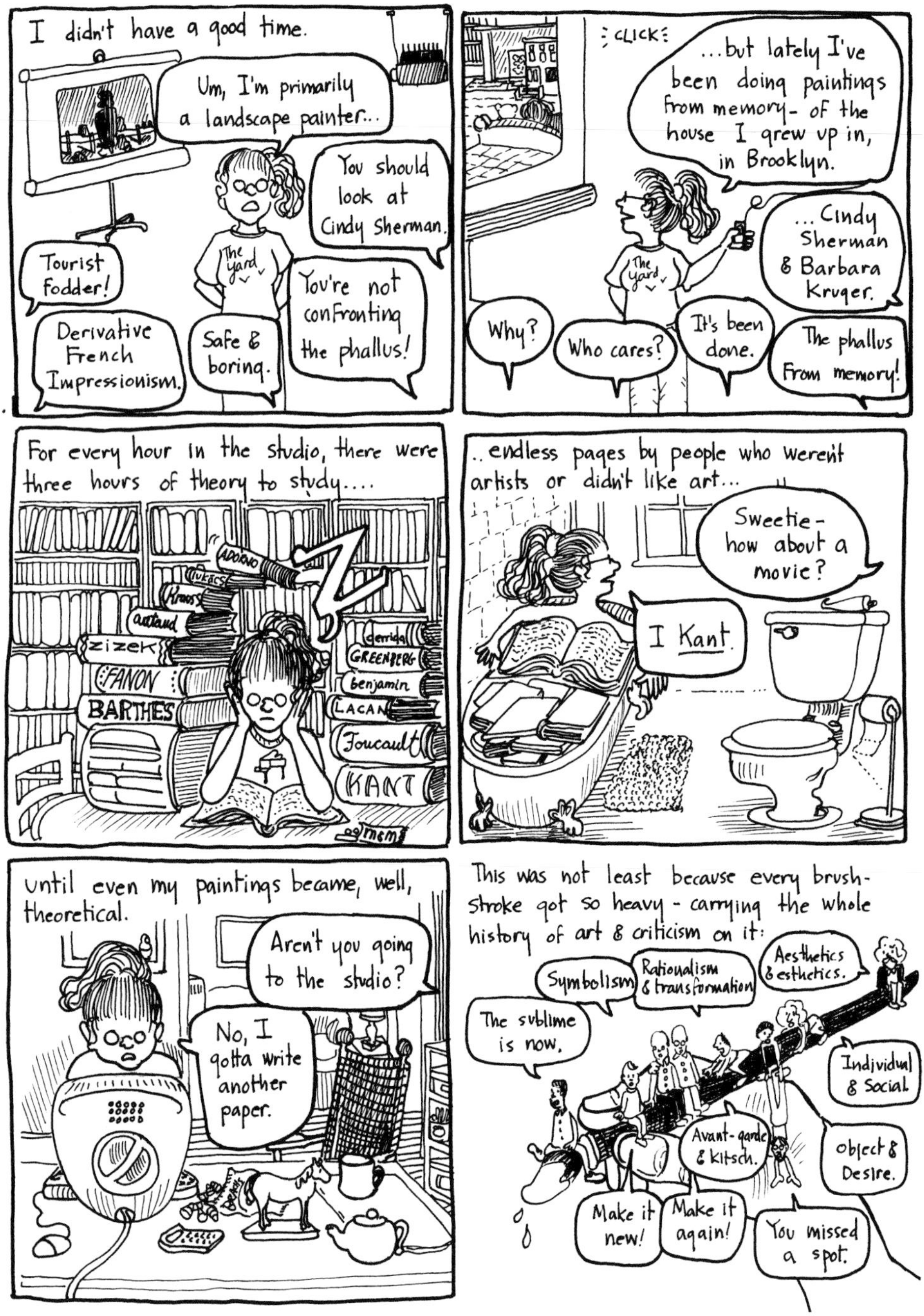
I didn't have a good time.
Um, I'm primarily a landscape painter...
You should look at Cindy Sherman.
Tourist fodder!
Derivative French Impressionism.
Safe & boring.
You're not confronting the phallus!
CLICK
...but lately I've been doing paintings from memory- of the house I grew up in, in Brooklyn.
...Cindy Sherman & Barbara Kruger.
Why?
Who cares?
It's been done.
The phallus from memory!
For every hour in the studio, there were three hours of theory to study....
ADORNO
LUKÁCS
Krauss
artaud
ZIZEK
FANON
BARTHES
derrida
GREENBERG
benjamin
LACAN
Foucault
KANT
..endless pages by people who weren't artists or didn't like art...
Sweetie- how about a movie?
I Kant.
until even my paintings became, well, theoretical.
Aren't you going to the studio?
No, I gotta write another paper.
This was not least because every brush-stroke got so heavy - carrying the whole history of art & criticism on it:
Symbolism
Rationalism & transformation
Aesthetics & esthetics.
The sublime is now.
Individual & Social.
Avant-garde & kitsch.
object & Desire.
Make it new!
Make it again!
You missed a spot.

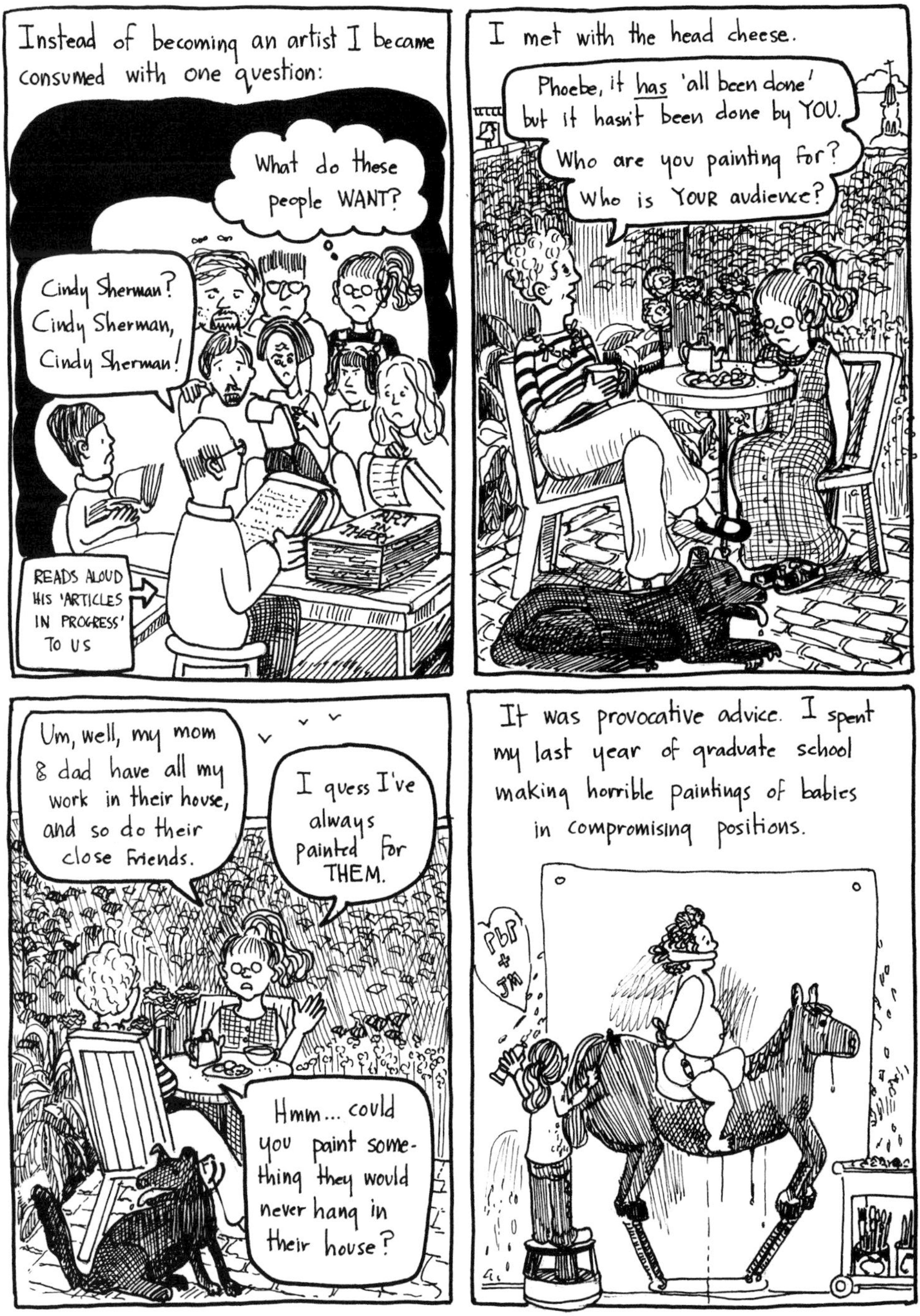
Instead of becoming an artist I became consumed with one question:
What do these people WANT?
Cindy Sherman? Cindy Sherman, Cindy Sherman!
READS ALOUD HIS 'ARTICLES IN PROGRESS' TO US
I met with the head cheese.
Phoebe, it has 'all been done' but it hasn't been done by YOU.
Who are you painting for? Who is YOUR audience?
Um, well, my mom & dad have all my work in their house, and so do their close friends.
I guess I've always painted for THEM.
Hmm... could you paint something they would never hang in their house?
It was provocative advice. I spent my last year of graduate school making horrible paintings of babies in compromising positions.
PbP + JM

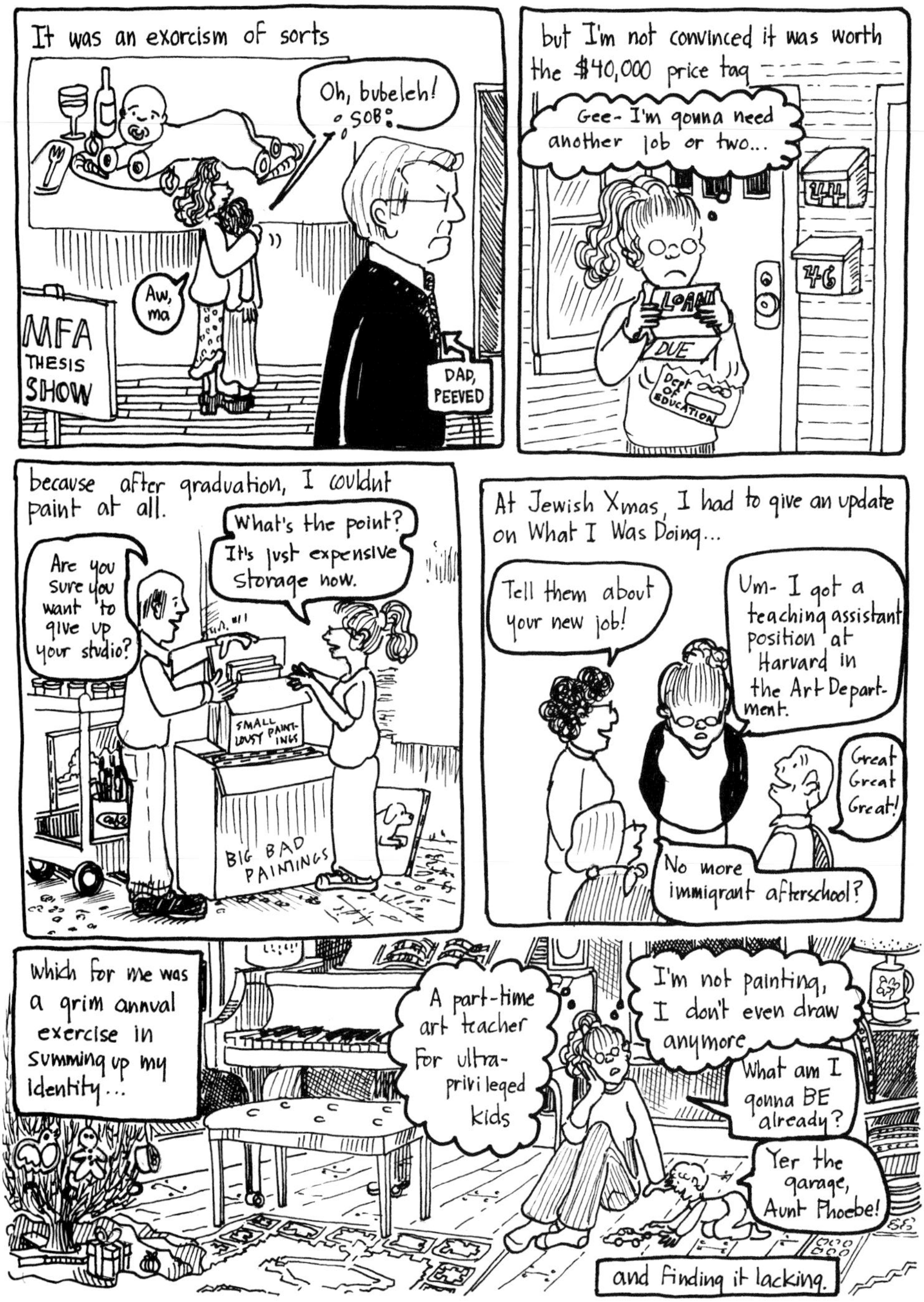
It was an exorcism of sorts
Oh, bubeleh! SOB
Aw, ma
MFA THESIS SHOW
DAD, PEEVED
but I'm not convinced it was worth the $40,000 price tag
Gee- I'm gonna need another job or two...
44
46
LOAN DUE
Dept OF EDUCATION
because after graduation, I couldnt paint at all.
Are you sure you want to give up your studio?
What's the point? It's just expensive storage now.
SMALL LOUSY PAINTINGS
BIG BAD PAINTINGS
At Jewish Xmas, I had to give an update on What I Was Doing...
Tell them about your new job!
Um- I got a teaching assistant position at Harvard in the Art Department.
Great Great Great!
No more immigrant afterschool?
which for me was a grim annual exercise in summing up my identity...
A part-time art teacher for ultra-privileged kids
I'm not painting, I don't even draw anymore
What am I gonna BE already?
Yer the garage, Aunt Phoebe!
and finding it lacking.

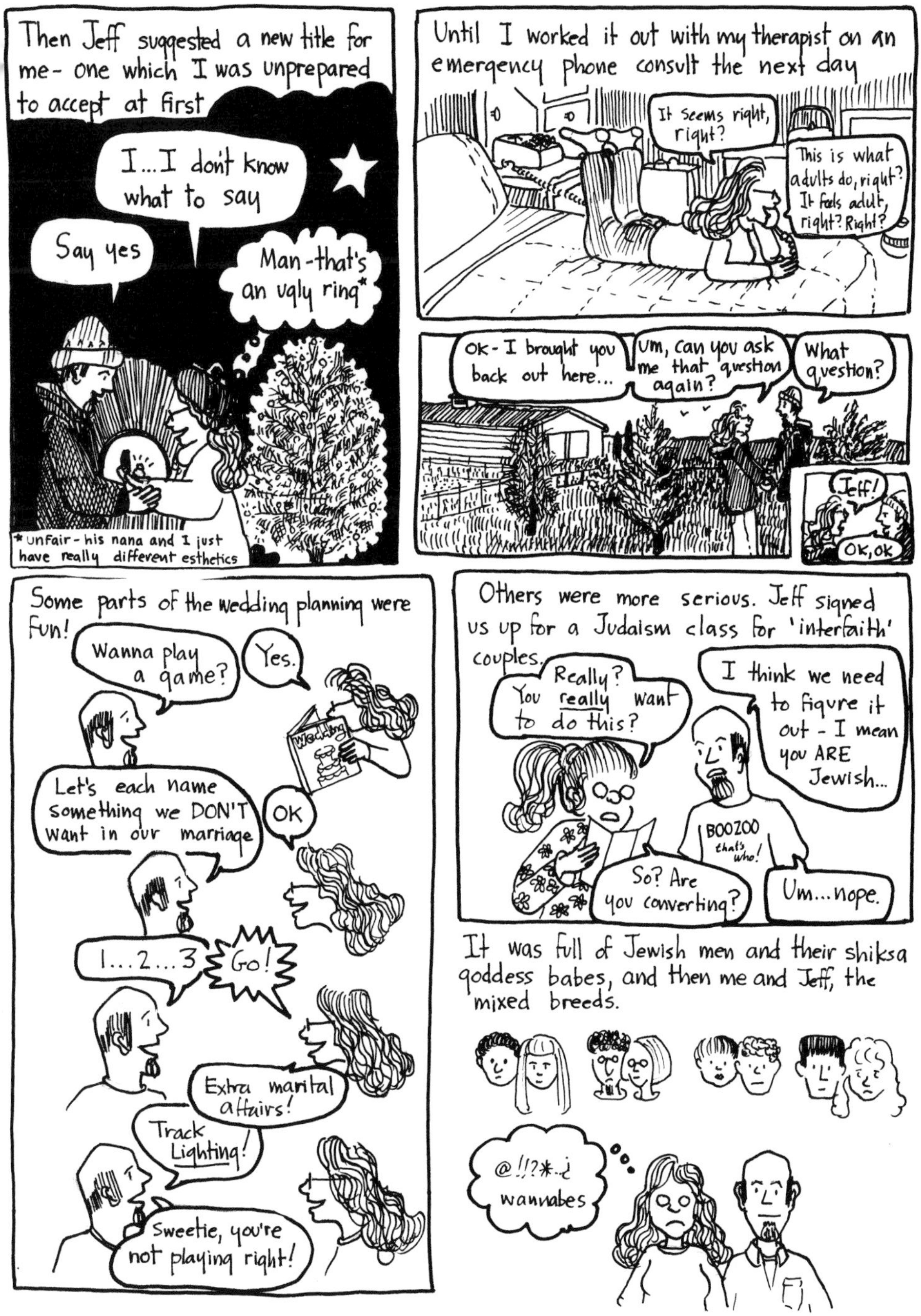

Then Jeff suggested a new title for me- one which I was unprepared to accept at first
I...I don't know what to say
Say yes
Man-that's an ugly ring*
*unfair-his nana and I just have really different esthetics
Until I worked it out with my therapist on an emergency phone consult the next day
It seems right, right?
This is what adults do, right? It feels adult, right? Right?
Ok-I brought you back out here...
Um, can you ask me that question again?
What question?
Jeff!
Ok, ok
Some parts of the wedding planning were fun!
Wanna play a game?
Yes.
Wedding
Let's each name something we DON'T want in our marriage
OK
1...2...3
Go!
Extra marital affairs!
Track Lighting!
Sweetie, you're not playing right!
Others were more serious. Jeff signed us up for a Judaism class for 'interfaith' couples.
Really? You really want to do this?
I think we need to figure it out - I mean you ARE Jewish...
BOOZOO that's who!
So? Are you converting?
Um...nope.
It was full of Jewish men and their shiksa goddess babes, and then me and Jeff, the mixed breeds.
@!!?*..¿ wannabes

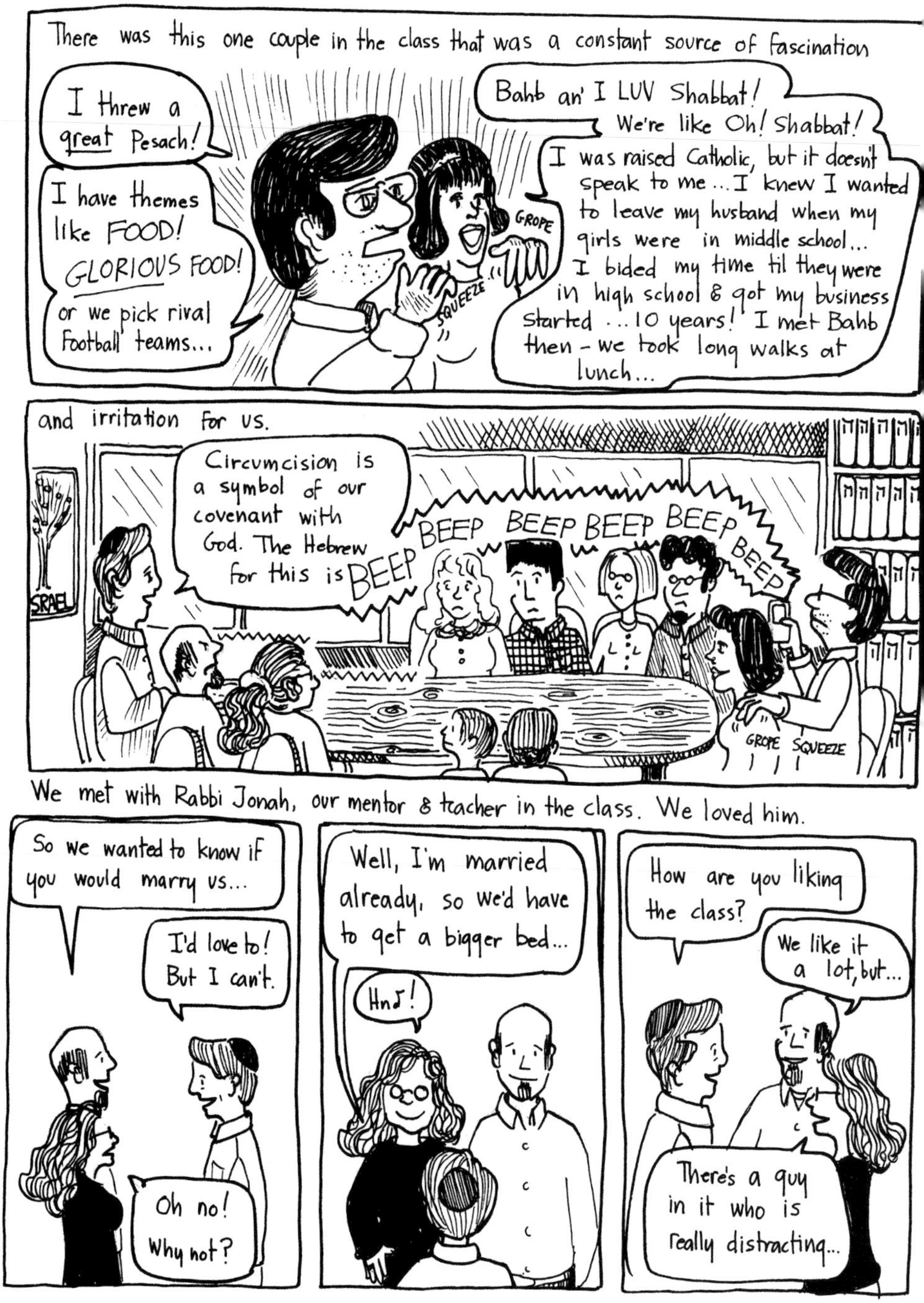
There was this one couple in the class that was a constant source of fascination
I threw a great Pesach!
I have themes like FOOD! GLORIOUS FOOD! or we pick rival Football teams...
Bahb an' I LUV Shabbat!
We're like Oh! Shabbat!
I was raised Catholic, but it doesn't speak to me... I knew I wanted to leave my husband when my girls were in middle school... I bided my time til they were in high school & got my business started ...10 years! I met Bahb then - we took long walks at lunch...
GROPE
SQUEEZE
and irritation for us.
Circumcision is a symbol of our covenant with God. The Hebrew for this is BEEP
BEEP BEEP BEEP BEEP BEEP BEEP
SRAEL
GROPE SQUEEZE
We met with Rabbi Jonah, our mentor & teacher in the class. We loved him.
So we wanted to know if you would marry us...
I'd love to! But I can't.
Oh no! Why not?
Well, I'm married already, so we'd have to get a bigger bed...
Hnd!
How are you liking the class?
We like it a lot, but...
There's a guy in it who is really distracting...

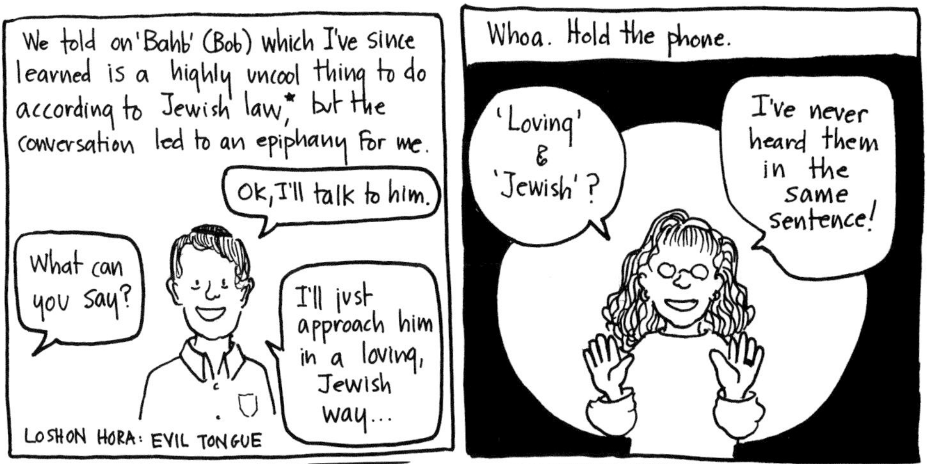
We told on 'Bahb' (Bob) which I've since learned is a highly uncool thing to do according to Jewish law,* but the conversation led to an epiphany for me.
Ok, I'll talk to him.
What can you say?
I'll just approach him in a loving, Jewish way...
LOSHON HORA: EVIL TONGUE
Whoa. Hold the phone.
'Loving' & 'Jewish'?
I've never heard them in the same sentence!

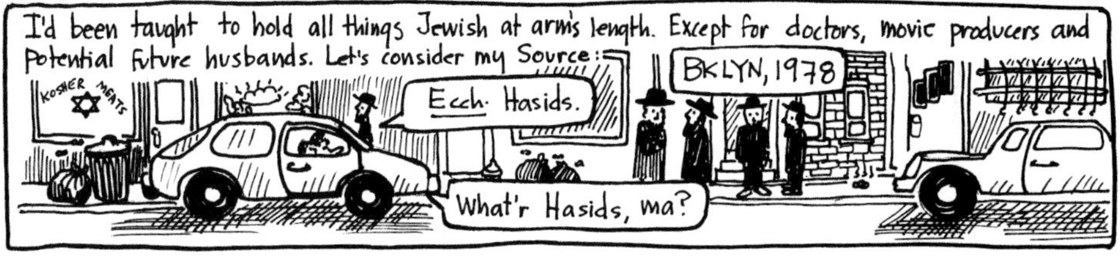
I'd been taught to hold all things Jewish at arm's length. Except for doctors, movie producers and potential future husbands. Let's consider my Source:
KOSHER MEATS
BKLYN, 1978
Ecch. Hasids.
What'r Hasids, ma?

Well, let's consider The Source's source. Remember, my ma grew up in the only Jewish family in town. Her father made her lunch every day for school.

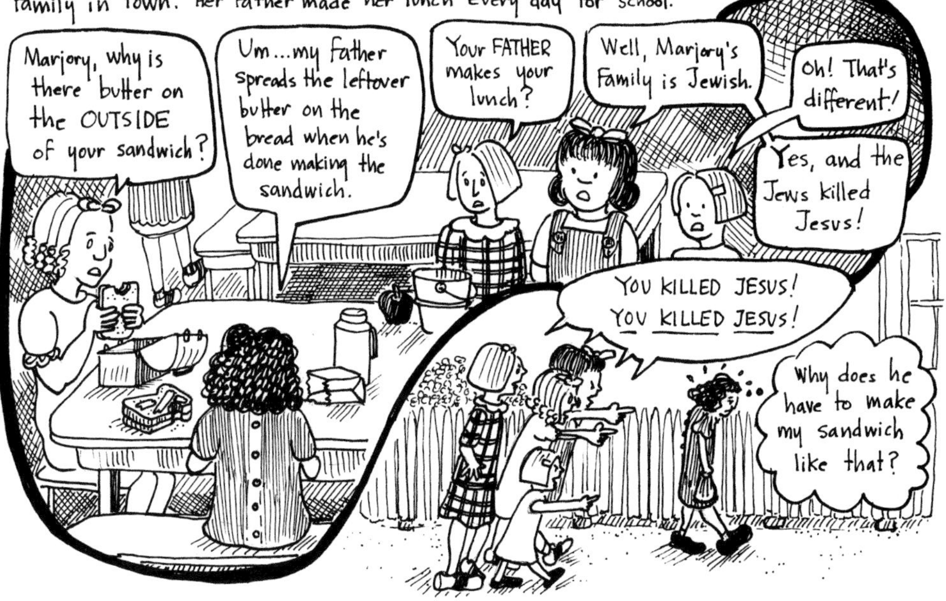
Marjory, why is there butter on the OUTSIDE of your sandwich?
Um...my father spreads the leftover butter on the bread when he's done making the sandwich.
Your FATHER makes your lunch?
Well, Marjory's family is Jewish.
Oh! That's different!
Yes, and the Jews killed Jesus!
YOU KILLED JESUS! YOU KILLED JESUS!
Why does he have to make my sandwich like that?

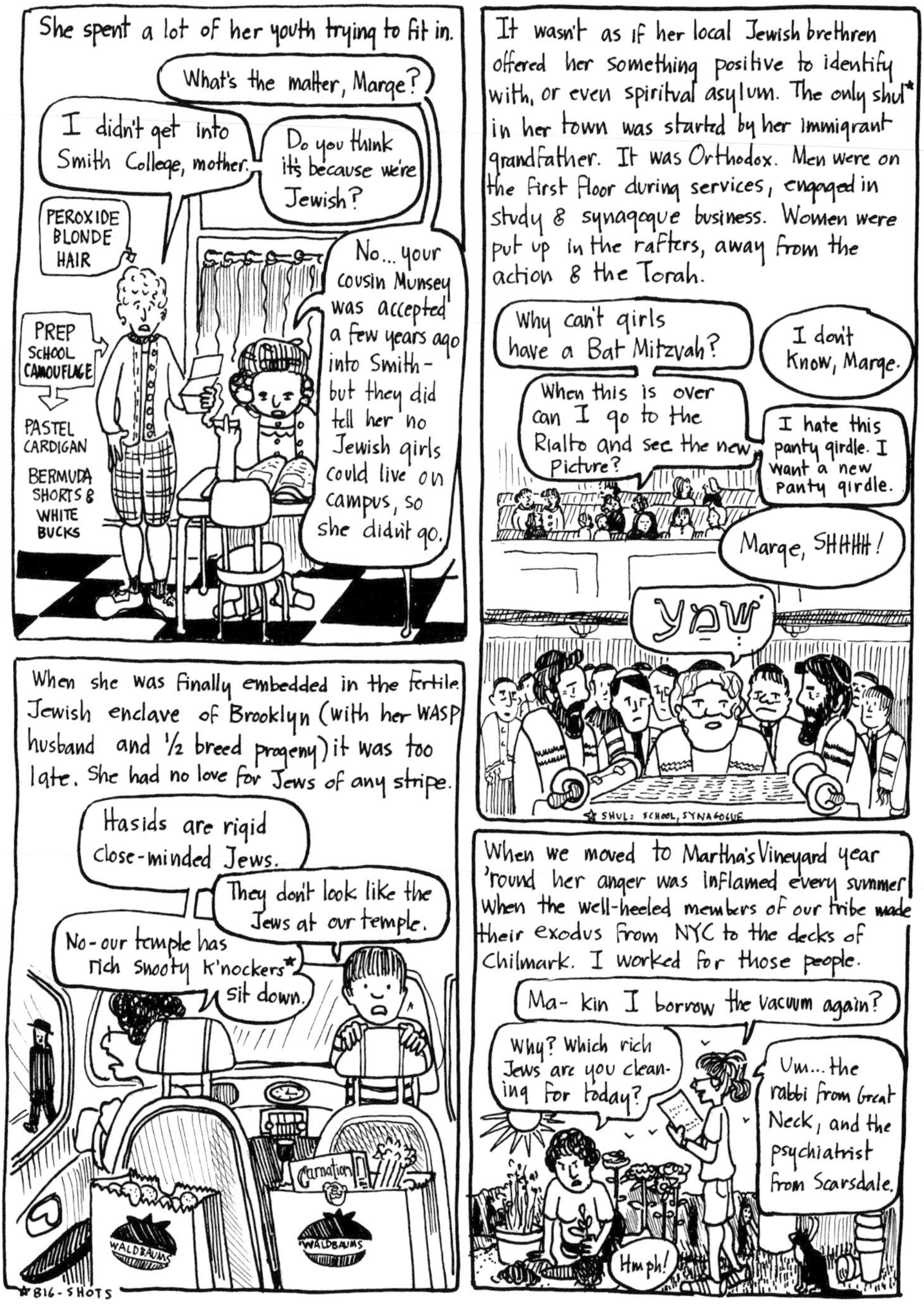
She spent a lot of her youth trying to fit in.
What's the matter, Marge?
I didn't get into Smith College, mother.
Do you think it's because we're Jewish?
PEROXIDE BLONDE HAIR
PREP SCHOOL CAMOUFLAGE
PASTEL CARDIGAN
BERMUDA SHORTS & WHITE BUCKS
No... your cousin Munsey was accepted a few years ago into Smith - but they did tell her no Jewish girls could live on campus, so she didn't go.
It wasn't as if her local Jewish brethren offered her something positive to identify with, or even spiritual asylum. The only shul* in her town was started by her immigrant grandfather. It was Orthodox. Men were on the first floor during services, engaged in study & synagogue business. Women were put up in the rafters, away from the action & the Torah.
Why can't girls have a Bat Mitzvah?
I don't know, Marge.
When this is over can I go to the Rialto and see the new picture?
I hate this panty girdle. I want a new panty girdle.
Marge, SHHHH!
שְׁמַע
☆ SHUL: SCHOOL, SYNAGOGUE
When she was finally embedded in the fertile Jewish enclave of Brooklyn (with her WASP husband and ½ breed progeny) it was too late. She had no love for Jews of any stripe.
Hasids are rigid close-minded Jews.
They don't look like the Jews at our temple.
No - our temple has rich snooty k'nockers* sit down.
Carnation
WALDBAUMS
WALDBAUMS
☆ BIG-SHOTS
When we moved to Martha's Vineyard year 'round her anger was inflamed every summer when the well-heeled members of our tribe made their exodus from NYC to the decks of Chilmark. I worked for those people.
Ma- kin I borrow the vacuum again?
Why? Which rich Jews are you cleaning for today?
Um... the rabbi from Great Neck, and the psychiatrist from Scarsdale.
Hmph!

When I went out in the world, far from home and the middle class, my contact with Jews and Judaism was pretty limited. Except to confirm some of my ma's experiences.

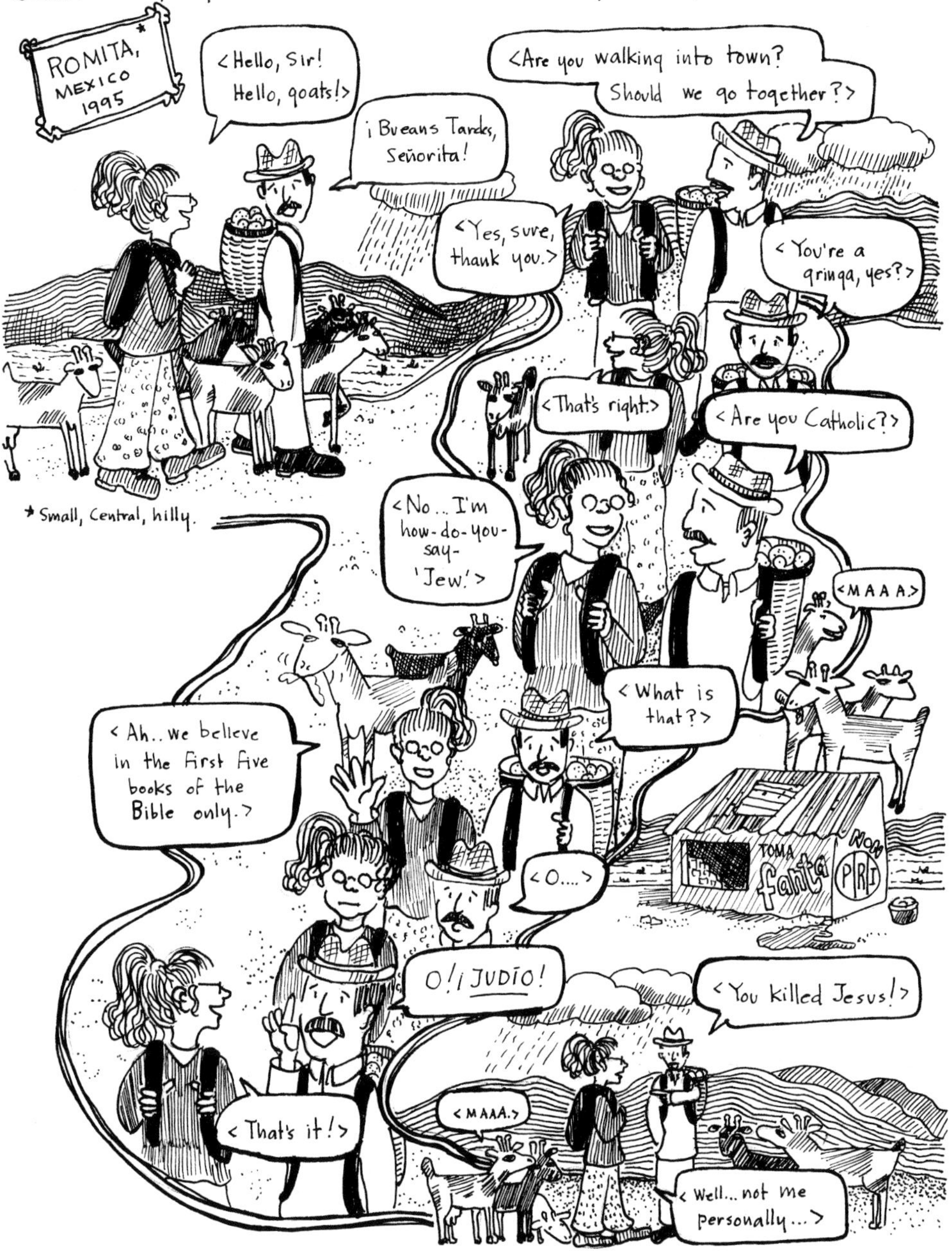
ROMITA,* MEXICO 1995
<Hello, Sir! Hello, goats!>
¡Bueans Tardes, Señorita!
<Are you walking into town? Should we go together?>
<Yes, sure, thank you.>
<You're a gringa, yes?>
<That's right.>
<Are you Catholic?>
<No... I'm how-do-you-say- 'Jew.'>
<MAAA.>
<What is that?>
<Ah.. we believe in the first five books of the Bible only.>
TOMA fanta
PRI
<O....>
O! ¡JUDIO!
<You killed Jesus!>
<That's it!>
<MAAA.>
<Well... not me personally...>

* Small, central, hilly.

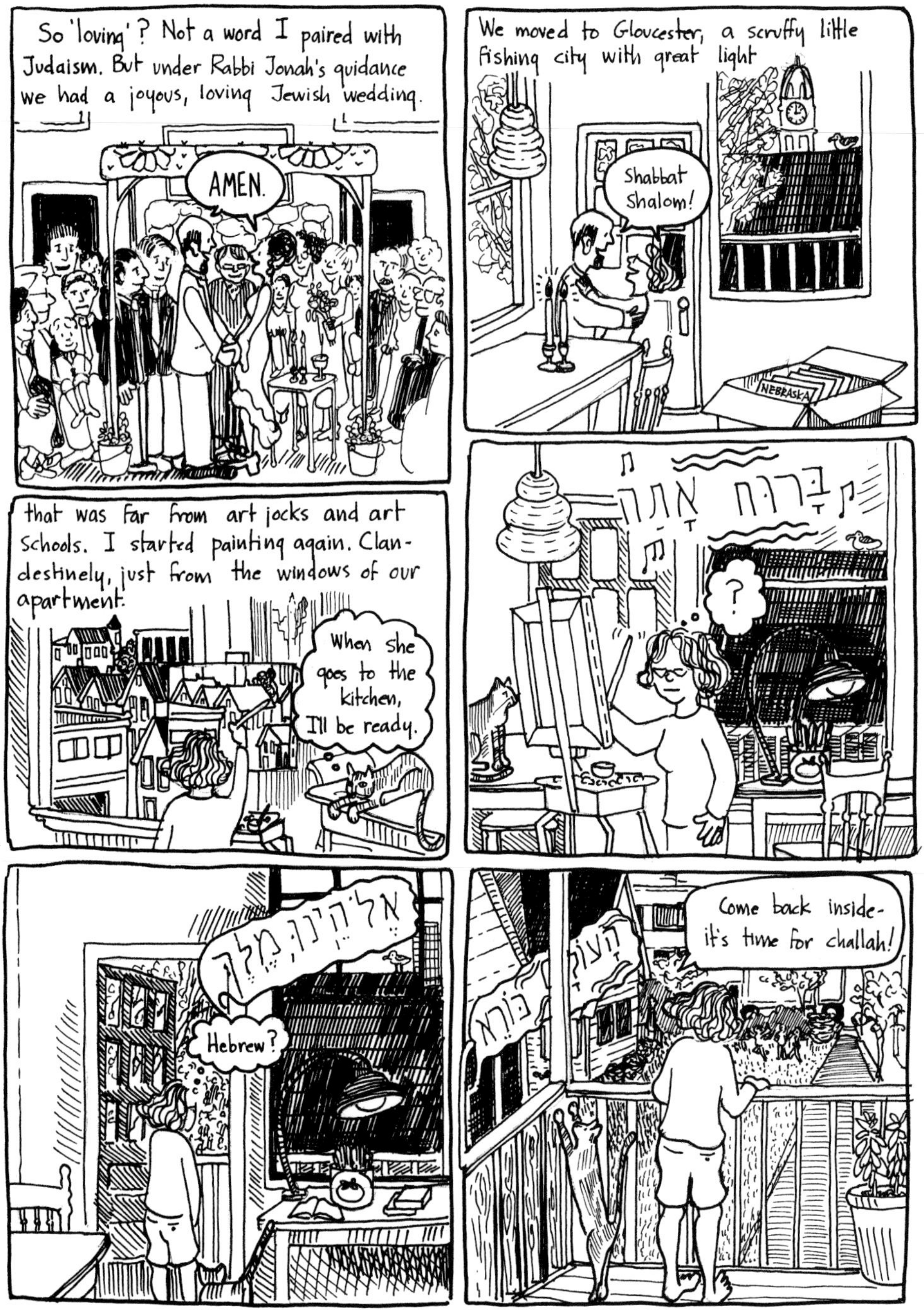

So 'loving'? Not a word I paired with Judaism. But under Rabbi Jonah's guidance we had a joyous, loving Jewish wedding.
AMEN.
We moved to Gloucester, a scruffy little fishing city with great light
Shabbat Shalom!
NEBRASKA
that was far from art jocks and art schools. I started painting again. Clandestinely, just from the windows of our apartment.
When she goes to the kitchen, I'll be ready.
ברוך אתה
?
אלהינו מלך
Hebrew?
Come back inside - it's time for challah!

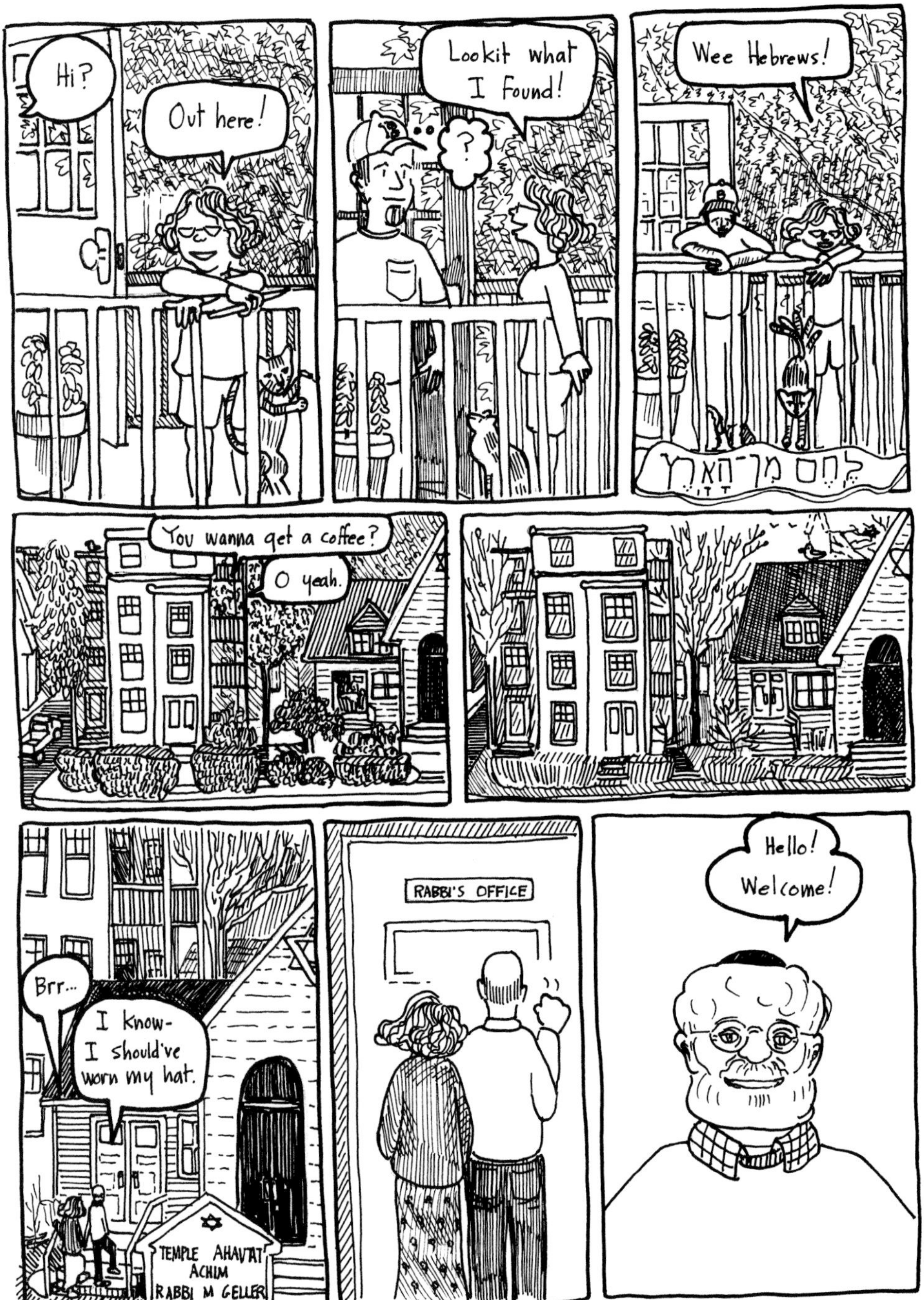
Hi?
Out here!
Lookit what I found!
?
Wee Hebrews!
לחם מן הארץ
You wanna get a coffee?
O yeah.
Brr...
I know- I should've worn my hat.
TEMPLE AHAVAT ACHIM RABBI M GELLER
RABBI'S OFFICE
Hello! Welcome!

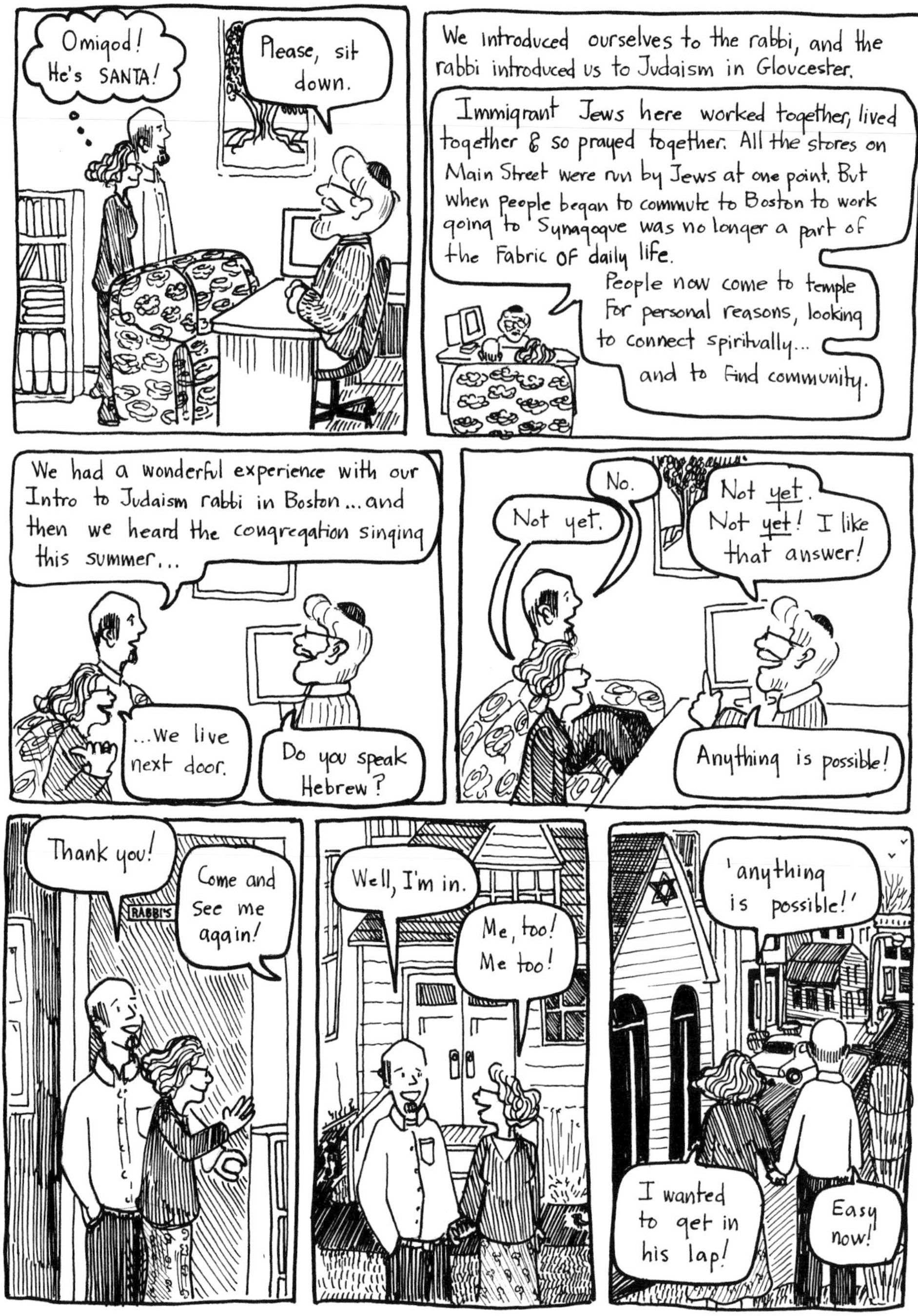
Omigod! He's SANTA!
Please, sit down.
We introduced ourselves to the rabbi, and the rabbi introduced us to Judaism in Gloucester.
Immigrant Jews here worked together, lived together & so prayed together. All the stores on Main Street were run by Jews at one point. But when people began to commute to Boston to work going to Synagogue was no longer a part of the fabric of daily life.
People now come to temple for personal reasons, looking to connect spiritually...
and to find community.
We had a wonderful experience with our Intro to Judaism rabbi in Boston... and then we heard the congregation singing this summer...
...we live next door.
Do you speak Hebrew?
Not yet.
No.
Not yet. Not yet! I like that answer!
Anything is possible!
Thank you!
RABBI'S
Come and see me again!
Well, I'm in.
Me, too! Me too!
'anything is possible!'
I wanted to get in his lap!
Easy now!

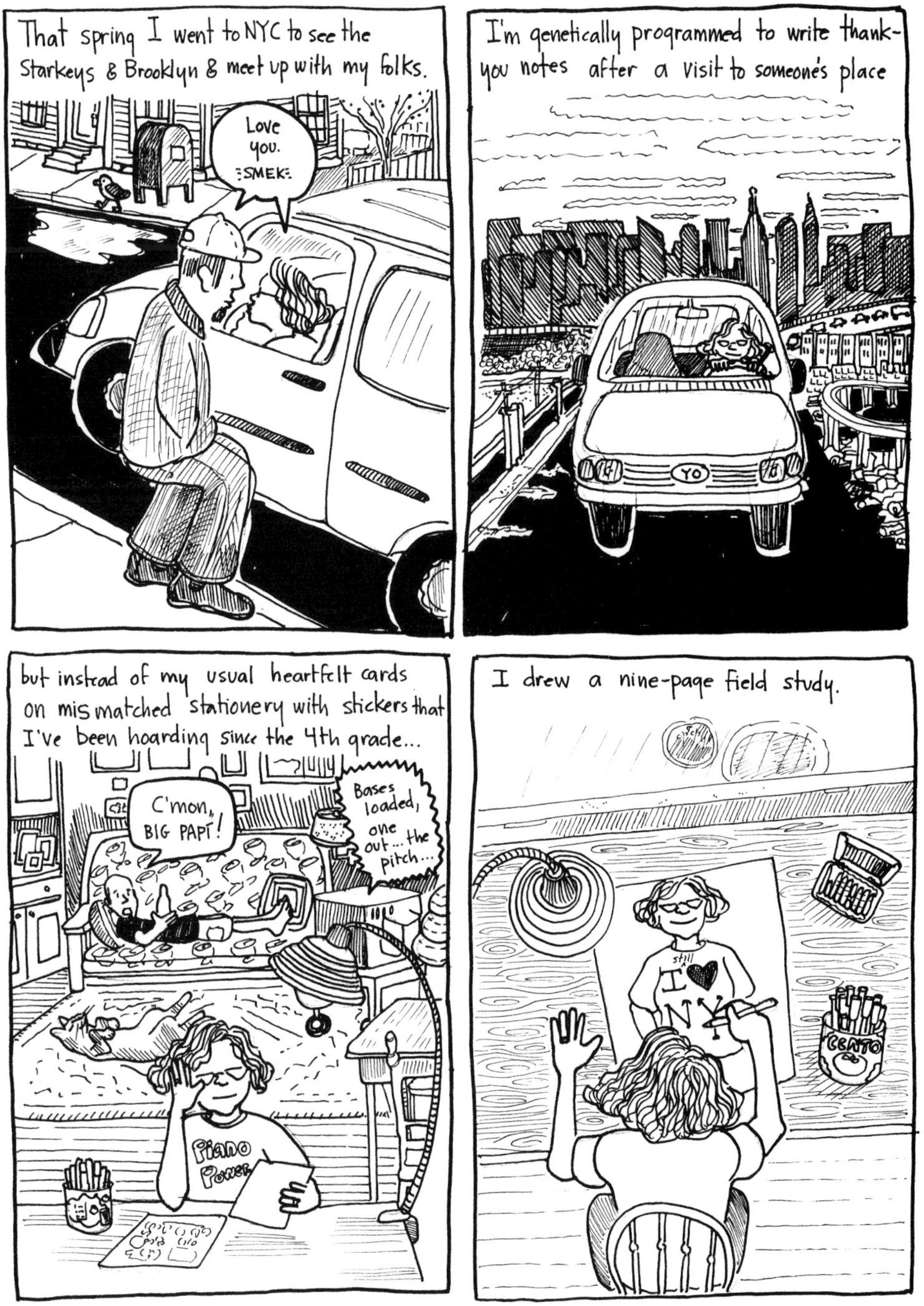
That spring I went to NYC to see the Starkeys & Brooklyn & meet up with my folks.
Love you. SMEK
I'm genetically programmed to write thank-you notes after a visit to someone's place
YO
but instead of my usual heartfelt cards on mismatched stationery with stickers that I've been hoarding since the 4th grade...
C'mon, BIG PAPI!
Bases loaded, one out... the pitch...
Piano Power
I drew a nine-page field study.
CENTO

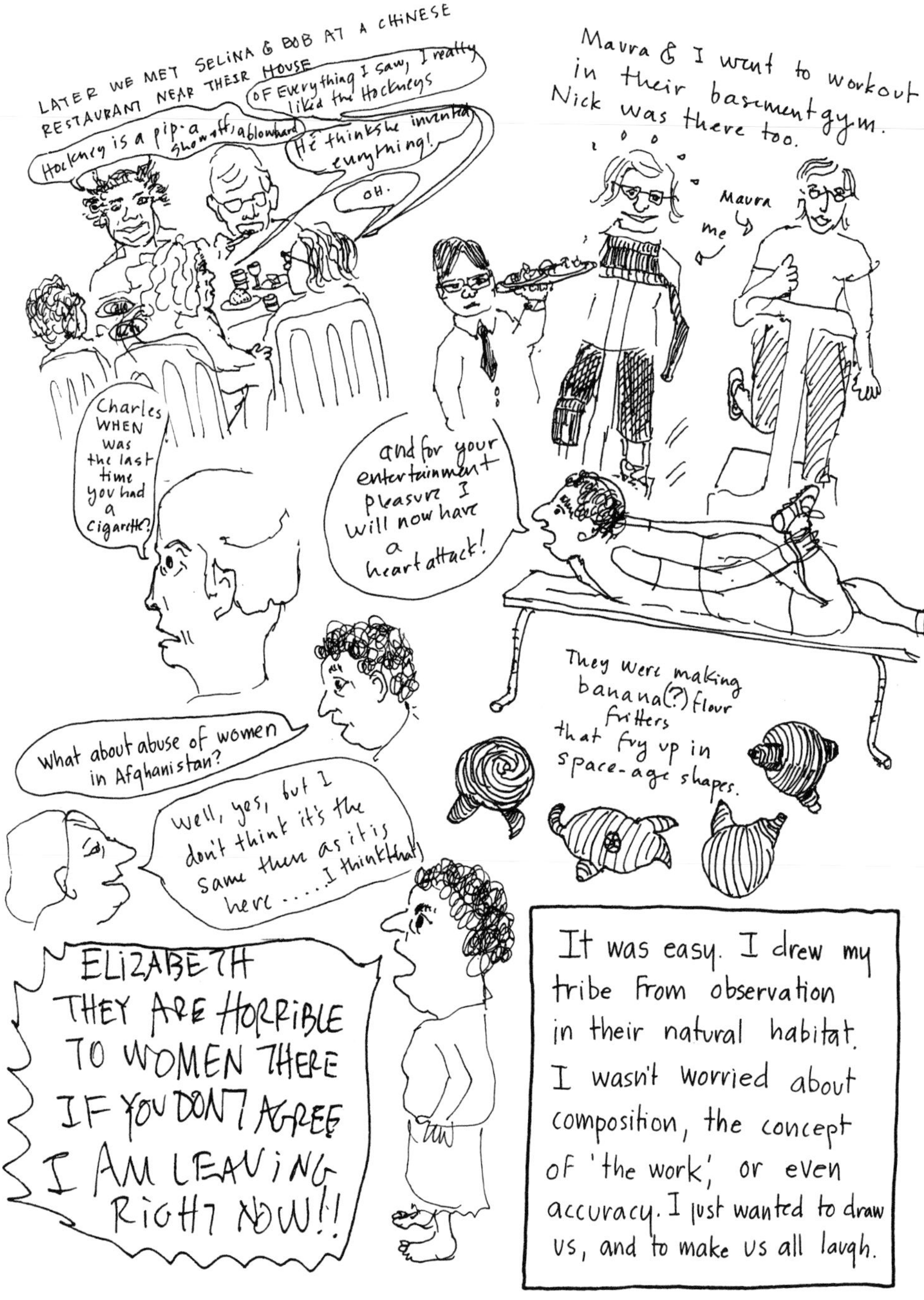

LATER WE MET SELINA & BOB AT A CHINESE RESTAURANT NEAR THEIR HOUSE
Hockney is a pip·a showoff, a blowhard
Of Everything I saw, I really liked the Hockneys
He thinks he invented everything!
OH.
Maura & I went to workout in their basement gym. Nick was there too.
Maura
me
Charles WHEN was the last time you had a cigarette?
and for your entertainment + pleasure I will now have a heart attack!
They were making banana(?) flour fritters that fry up in space-age shapes.
What about abuse of women in Afghanistan?
Well, yes, but I don't think it's the same there as it is here ..... I think that
ELIZABETH THEY ARE HORRIBLE TO WOMEN THERE IF YOU DON'T AGREE I AM LEAVING RIGHT NOW!!
It was easy. I drew my tribe from observation in their natural habitat. I wasn't worried about composition, the concept of 'the work,' or even accuracy. I just wanted to draw us, and to make us all laugh.

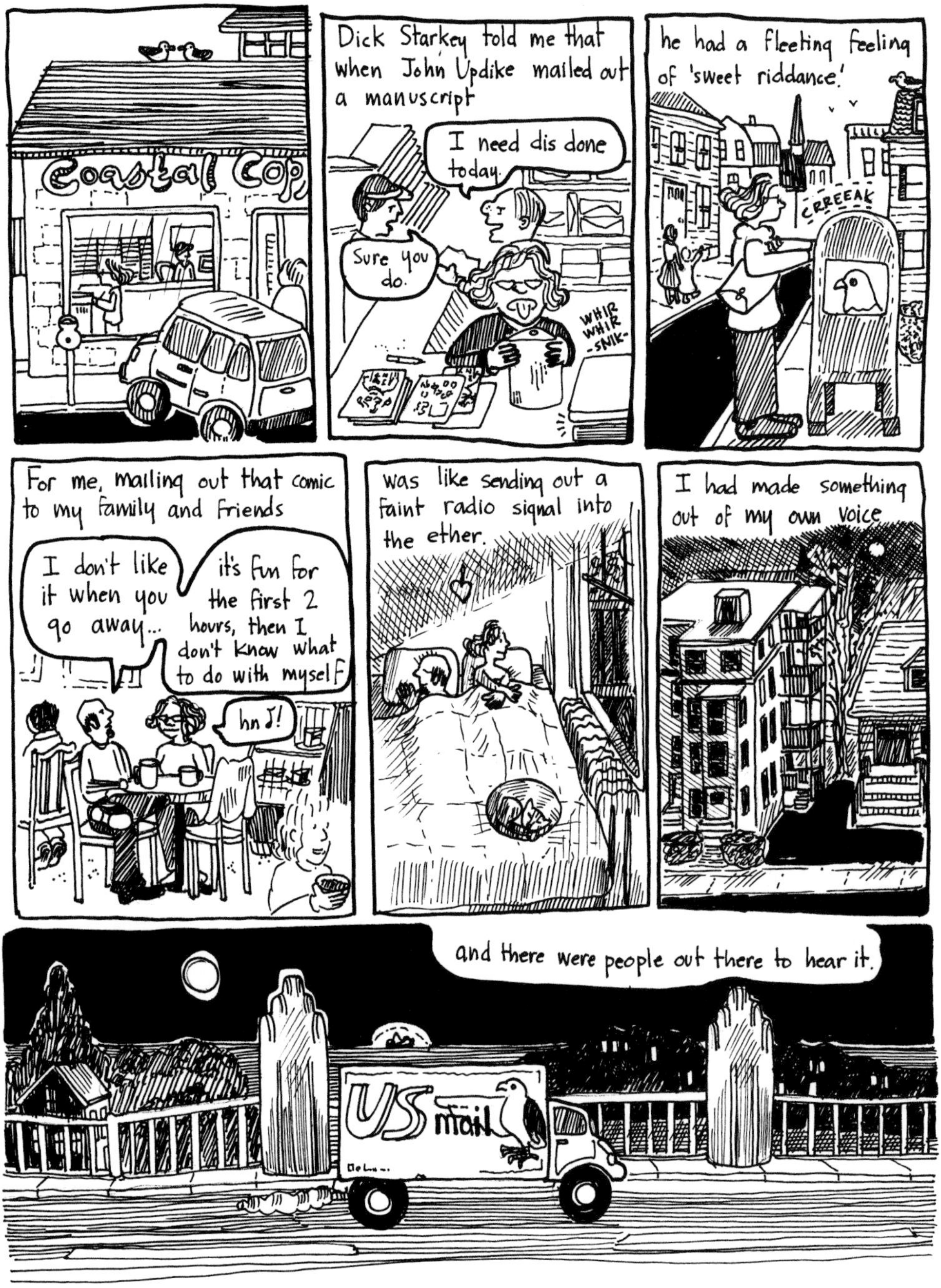
Coastal Cop
Dick Starkey told me that when John Updike mailed out a manuscript
I need dis done today.
Sure you do.
WHIR WHIR -SNIK-
he had a fleeting feeling of 'sweet riddance.'
CRREEAK
For me, mailing out that comic to my family and friends
I don't like it when you go away...
it's fun for the first 2 hours, then I don't know what to do with myself
hn♪!
was like sending out a faint radio signal into the ether.
I had made something out of my own voice
and there were people out there to hear it.
US mail

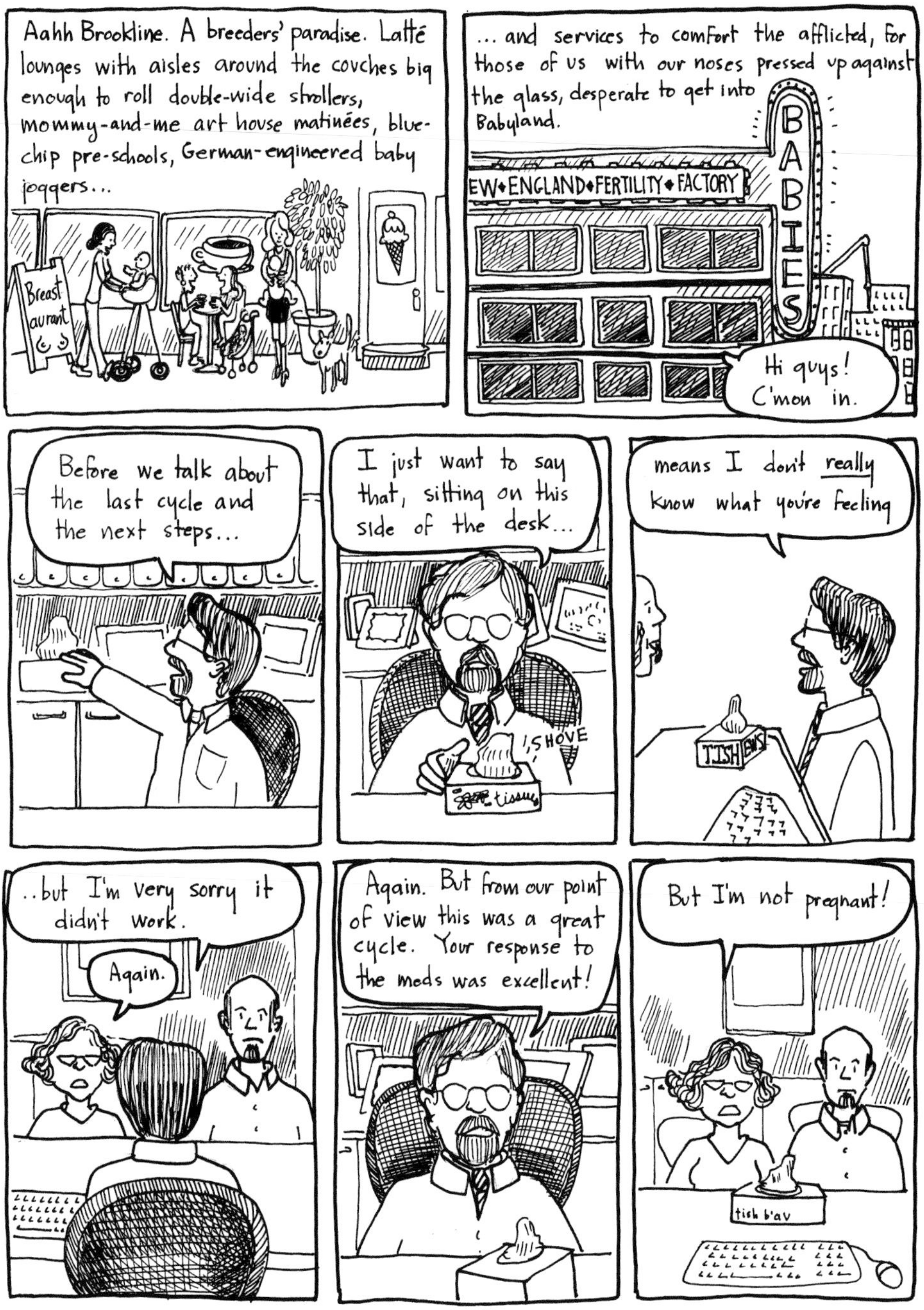
Aahh Brookline. A breeders' paradise. Latté lounges with aisles around the couches big enough to roll double-wide strollers, mommy-and-me art house matinées, blue-chip pre-schools, German-engineered baby joggers...
Breast aurant
... and services to comfort the afflicted, for those of us with our noses pressed up against the glass, desperate to get into Babyland.
EW♦ENGLAND♦FERTILITY♦FACTORY
BABIES
Hi guys! C'mon in.
Before we talk about the last cycle and the next steps...
I just want to say that, sitting on this side of the desk...
SHOVE
means I don't really know what you're feeling
TISHEWS
..but I'm very sorry it didn't work.
Again.
Again. But from our point of view this was a great cycle. Your response to the meds was excellent!
But I'm not pregnant!
tish b'av

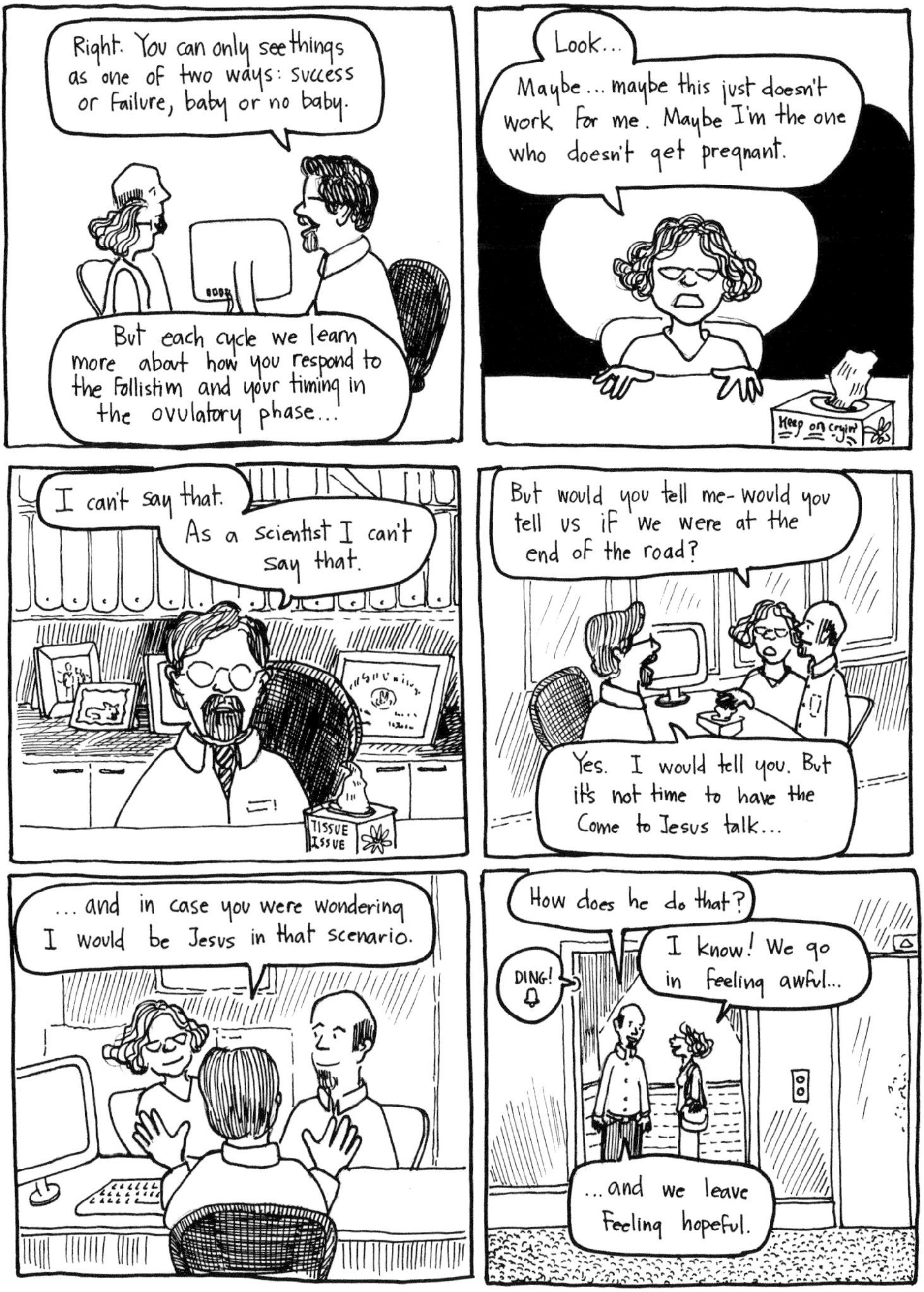
Right. You can only see things as one of two ways: success or failure, baby or no baby.
But each cycle we learn more about how you respond to the Follistim and your timing in the ovulatory phase...
Look...
Maybe... maybe this just doesn't work for me. Maybe I'm the one who doesn't get pregnant.
Keep on cryin'
I can't say that.
As a scientist I can't say that.
TISSUE ISSUE
But would you tell me- would you tell us if we were at the end of the road?
Yes. I would tell you. But it's not time to have the Come to Jesus talk...
...and in case you were wondering I would be Jesus in that scenario.
How does he do that?
DING!
I know! We go in feeling awful...
...and we leave feeling hopeful.

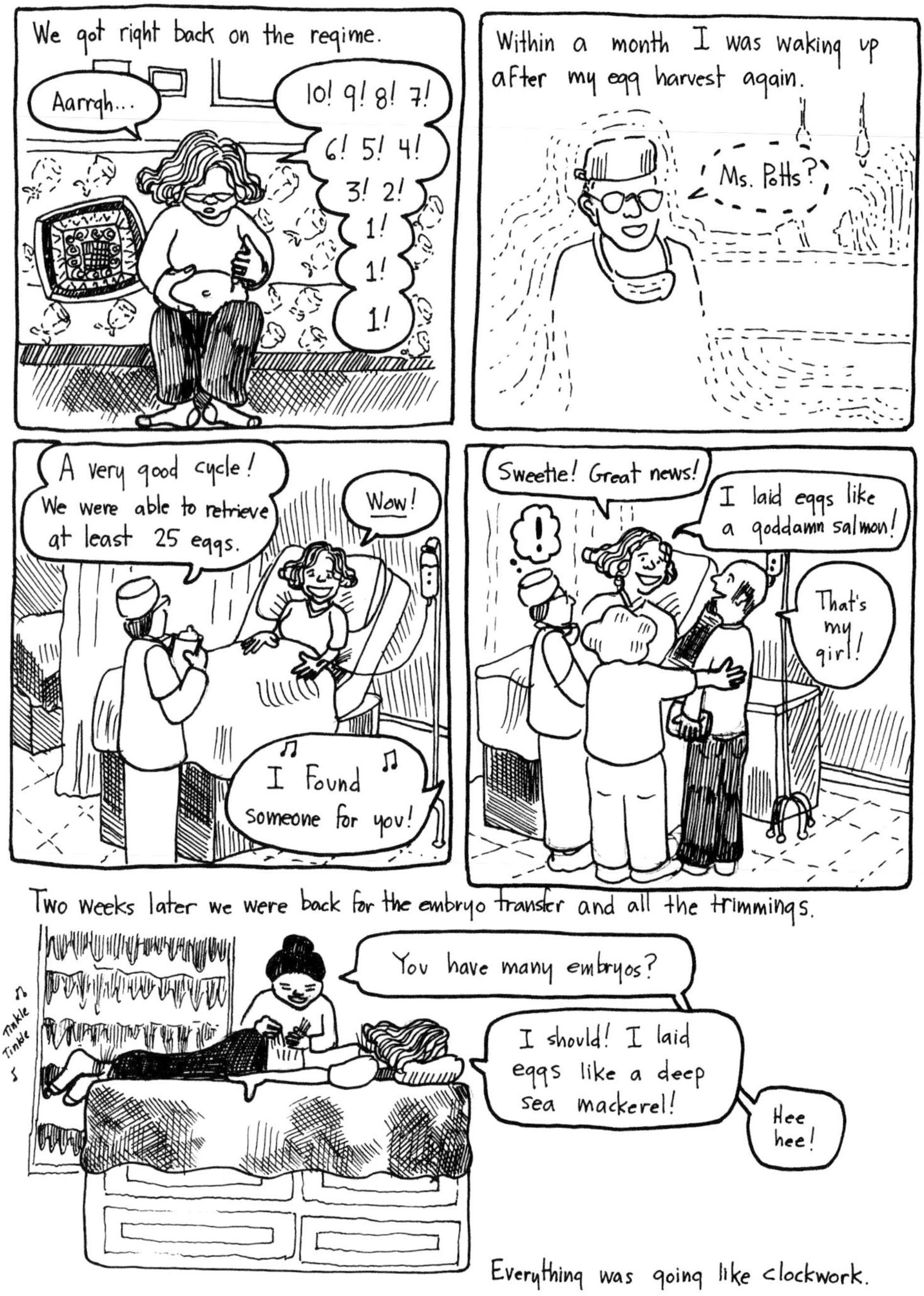
We got right back on the regime.
Aarrgh...
10! 9! 8! 7! 6! 5! 4! 3! 2! 1! 1! 1!
Within a month I was waking up after my egg harvest again.
Ms. Potts?
A very good cycle! We were able to retrieve at least 25 eggs.
Wow!
I Found someone for you!
Sweetie! Great news!
I laid eggs like a goddamn salmon!
That's my girl!
Two weeks later we were back for the embryo transfer and all the trimmings.
Tinkle Tinkle
You have many embryos?
I should! I laid eggs like a deep sea mackerel!
Hee hee!
Everything was going like clockwork.

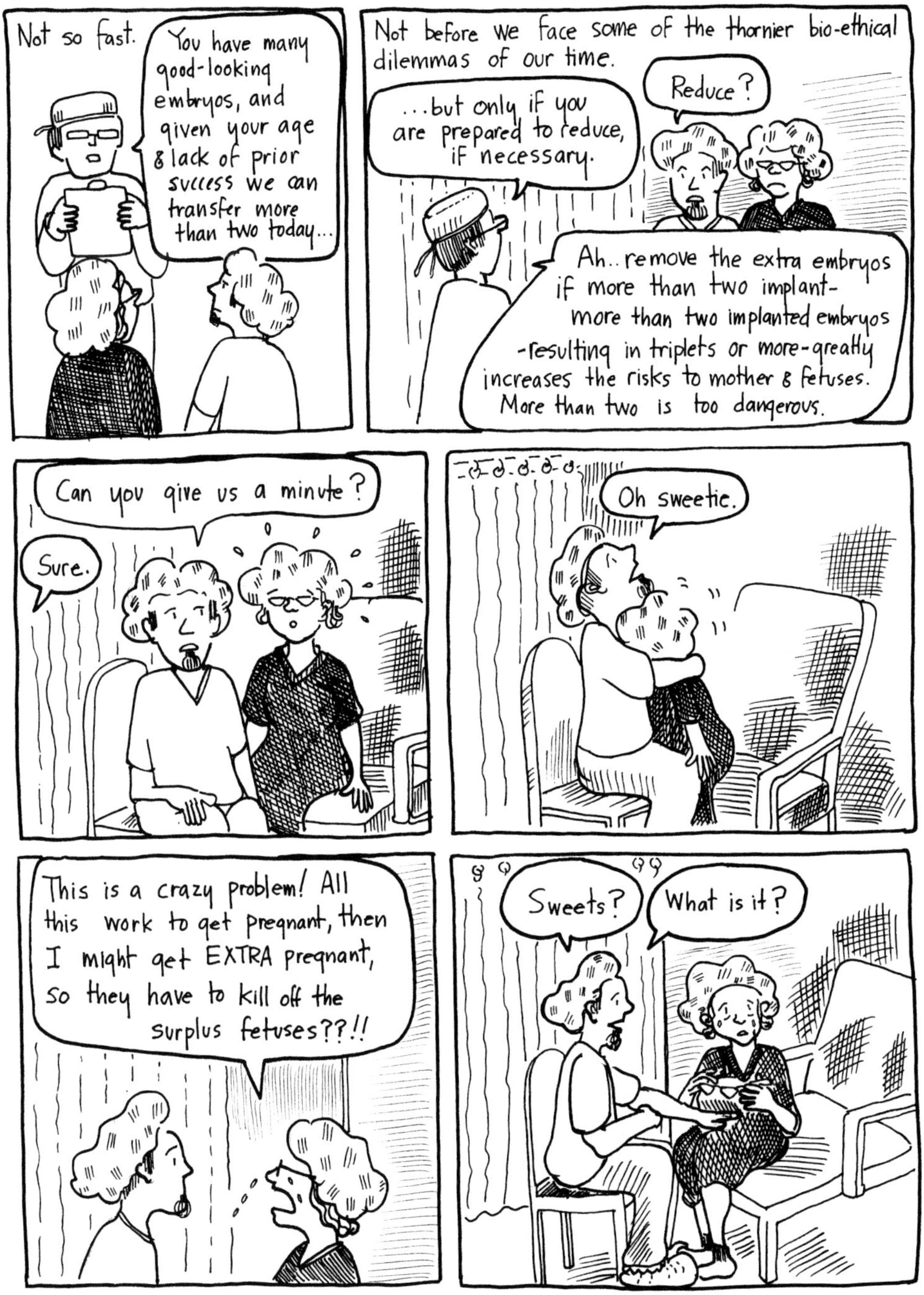
Not so fast.
You have many good-looking embryos, and given your age & lack of prior success we can transfer more than two today...
Not before we face some of the thornier bio-ethical dilemmas of our time.
...but only if you are prepared to reduce, if necessary.
Reduce?
Ah.. remove the extra embryos if more than two implant- more than two implanted embryos -resulting in triplets or more-greatly increases the risks to mother & fetuses. More than two is too dangerous.
Can you give us a minute?
Sure.
Oh sweetie.
This is a crazy problem! All this work to get pregnant, then I might get EXTRA pregnant, so they have to kill off the surplus fetuses??!!
Sweets?
What is it?

Will God hate me?

I think the question is - will you hate you.
But I won't.

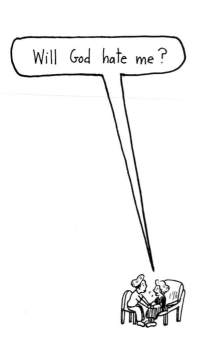

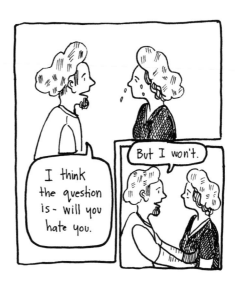

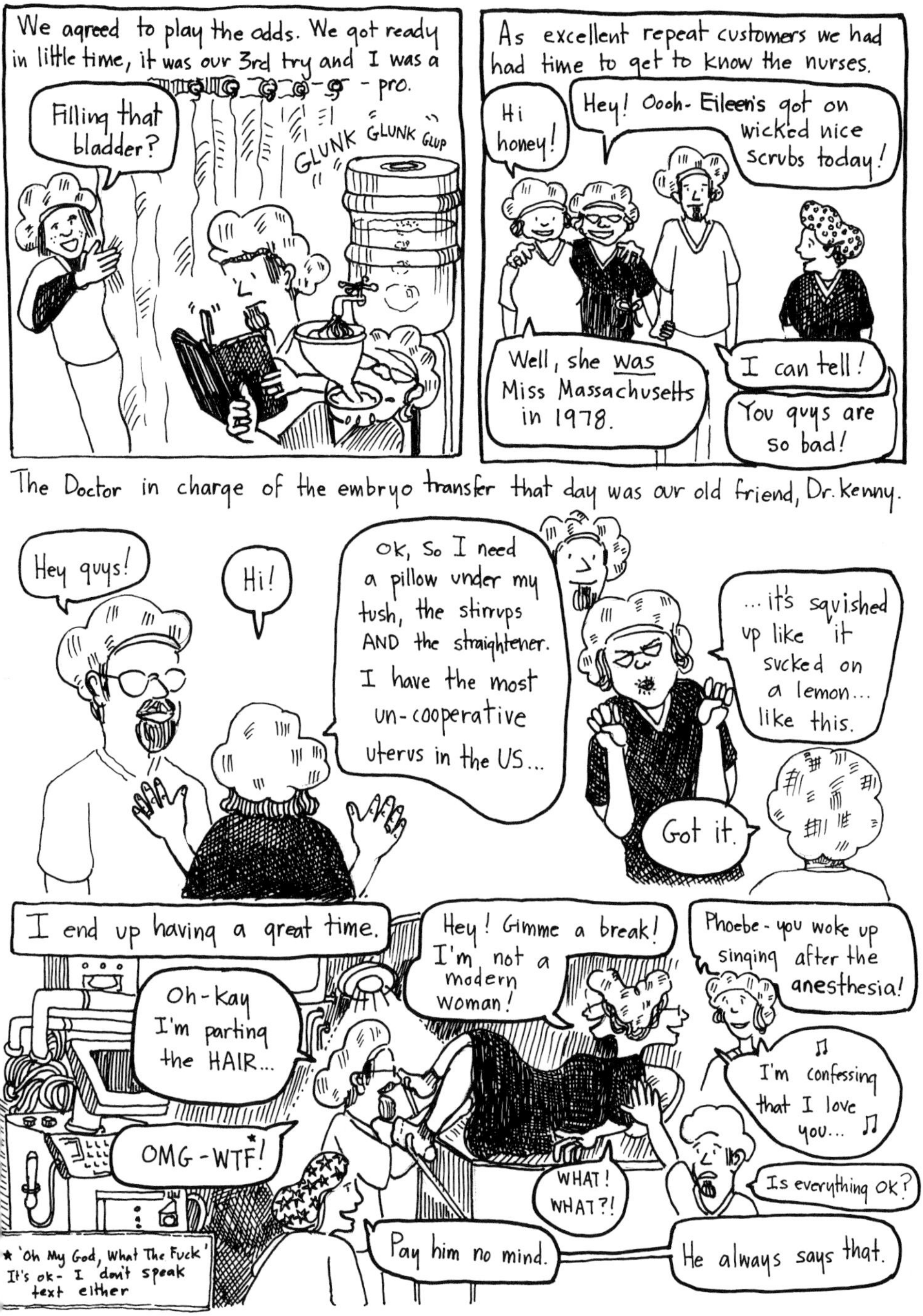
We agreed to play the odds. We got ready in little time, it was our 3rd try and I was a pro.
Filling that bladder?
GLUNK GLUNK GLUP
As excellent repeat customers we had had time to get to know the nurses.
Hi honey!
Hey! Oooh- Eileen's got on wicked nice scrubs today!
Well, she was Miss Massachusetts in 1978.
I can tell!
You guys are so bad!
The Doctor in charge of the embryo transfer that day was our old friend, Dr. Kenny.
Hey guys!
Hi!
Ok, So I need a pillow under my tush, the stirrups AND the straightener. I have the most un-cooperative uterus in the US...
...it's squished up like it sucked on a lemon... like this.
Got it.
I end up having a great time.
Oh-kay I'm parting the HAIR...
OMG-WTF!*
Hey! Gimme a break! I'm not a modern woman!
Phoebe- you woke up singing after the anesthesia!
I'm confessing that I love you...
WHAT! WHAT?!
Is everything ok?
Pay him no mind.
He always says that.
* 'Oh My God, What The Fuck' It's ok- I don't speak text either

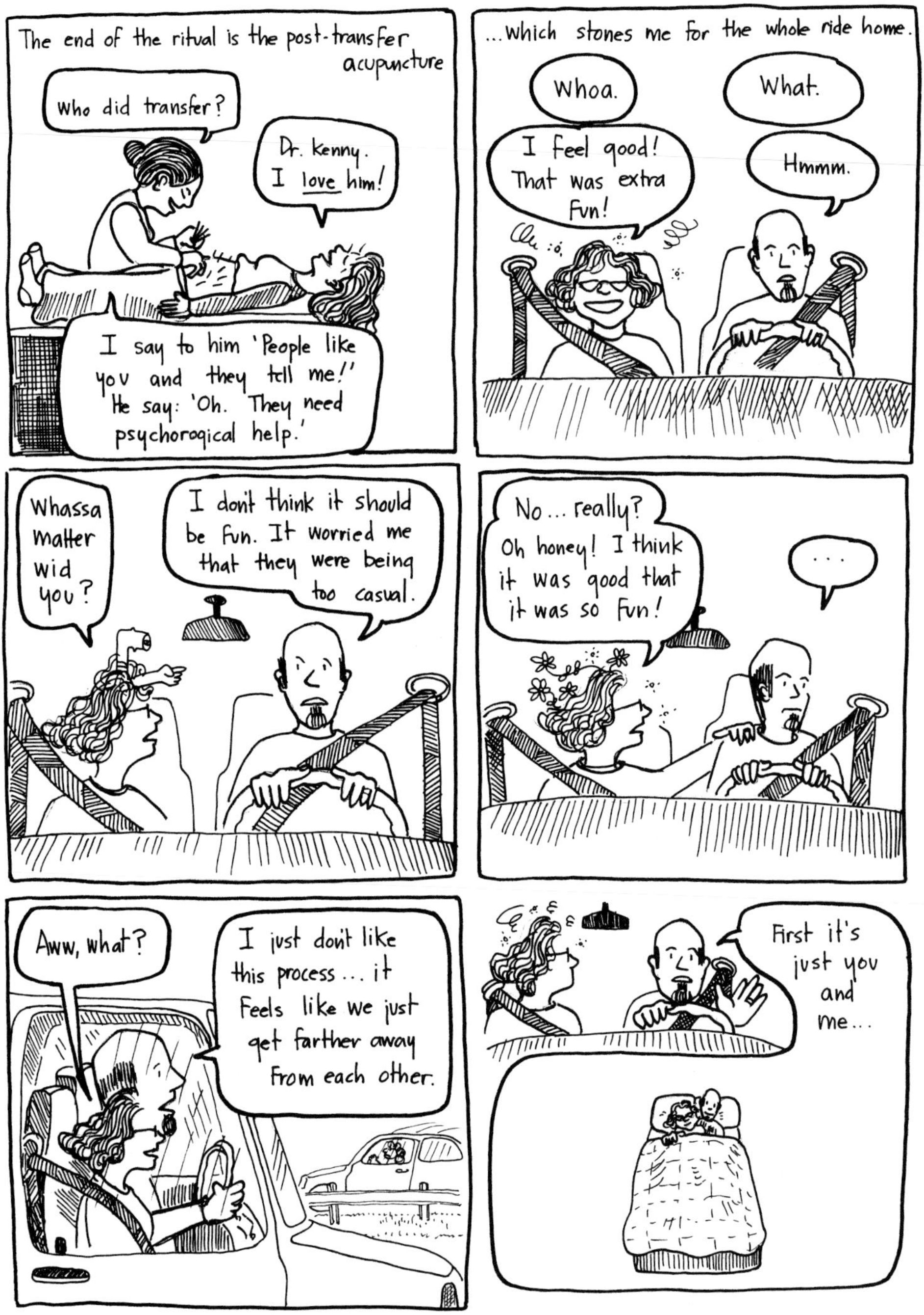
The end of the ritual is the post-transfer acupuncture
Who did transfer?
Dr. Kenny. I love him!
I say to him 'People like you and they tell me!' He say: 'Oh. They need psychorogical help.'
...which stones me for the whole ride home.
Whoa.
What.
I feel good! That was extra fun!
Hmmm.
Whassa matter wid you?
I don't think it should be fun. It worried me that they were being too casual.
No... really? Oh honey! I think it was good that it was so fun!
...
Aww, what?
I just don't like this process... it feels like we just get farther away from each other.
First it's just you and me...

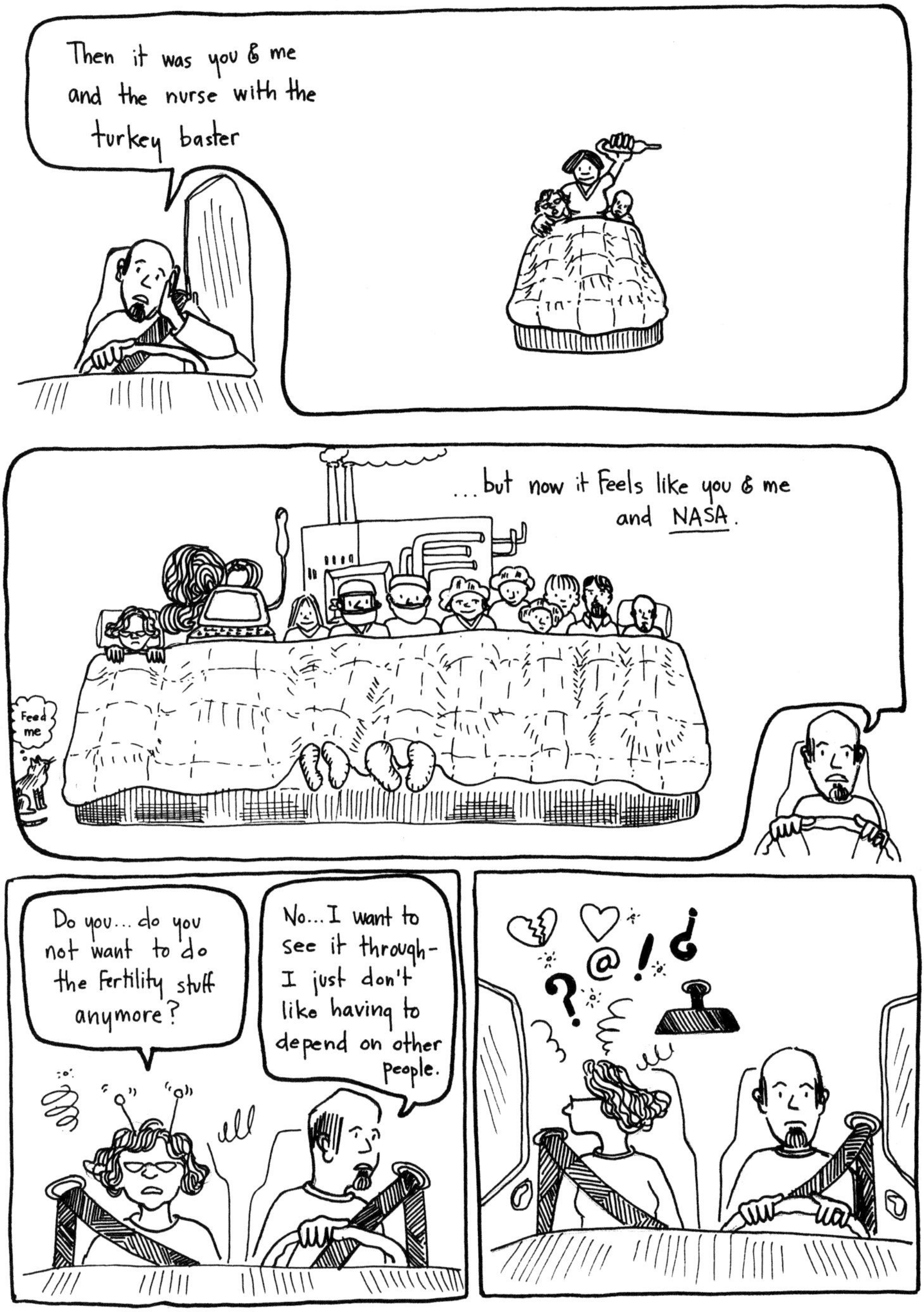
Then it was you & me and the nurse with the turkey baster
...but now it Feels like you & me and NASA.
Feed me
Do you... do you not want to do the Fertility stuff anymore?
No... I want to see it through- I just don't like having to depend on other people.

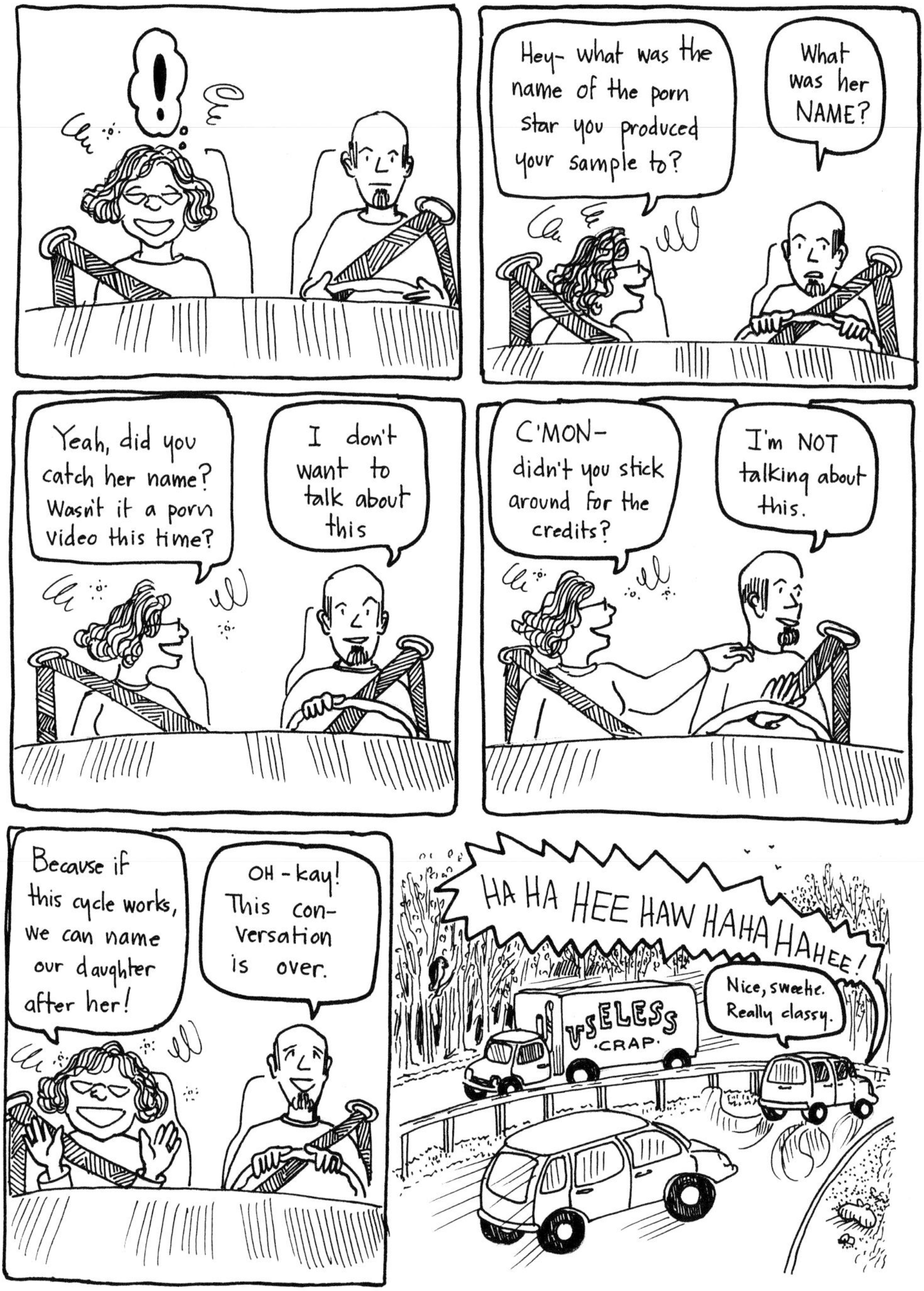
!
Hey- what was the name of the porn star you produced your sample to?
What was her NAME?
Yeah, did you catch her name? Wasn't it a porn video this time?
I don't want to talk about this
C'MON- didn't you stick around for the credits?
I'm NOT talking about this.
Because if this cycle works, we can name our daughter after her!
OH-kay! This con-versation is over.
HA HA HEE HAW HAHA HAHEE!
USELESS CRAP
Nice, sweetie. Really classy.

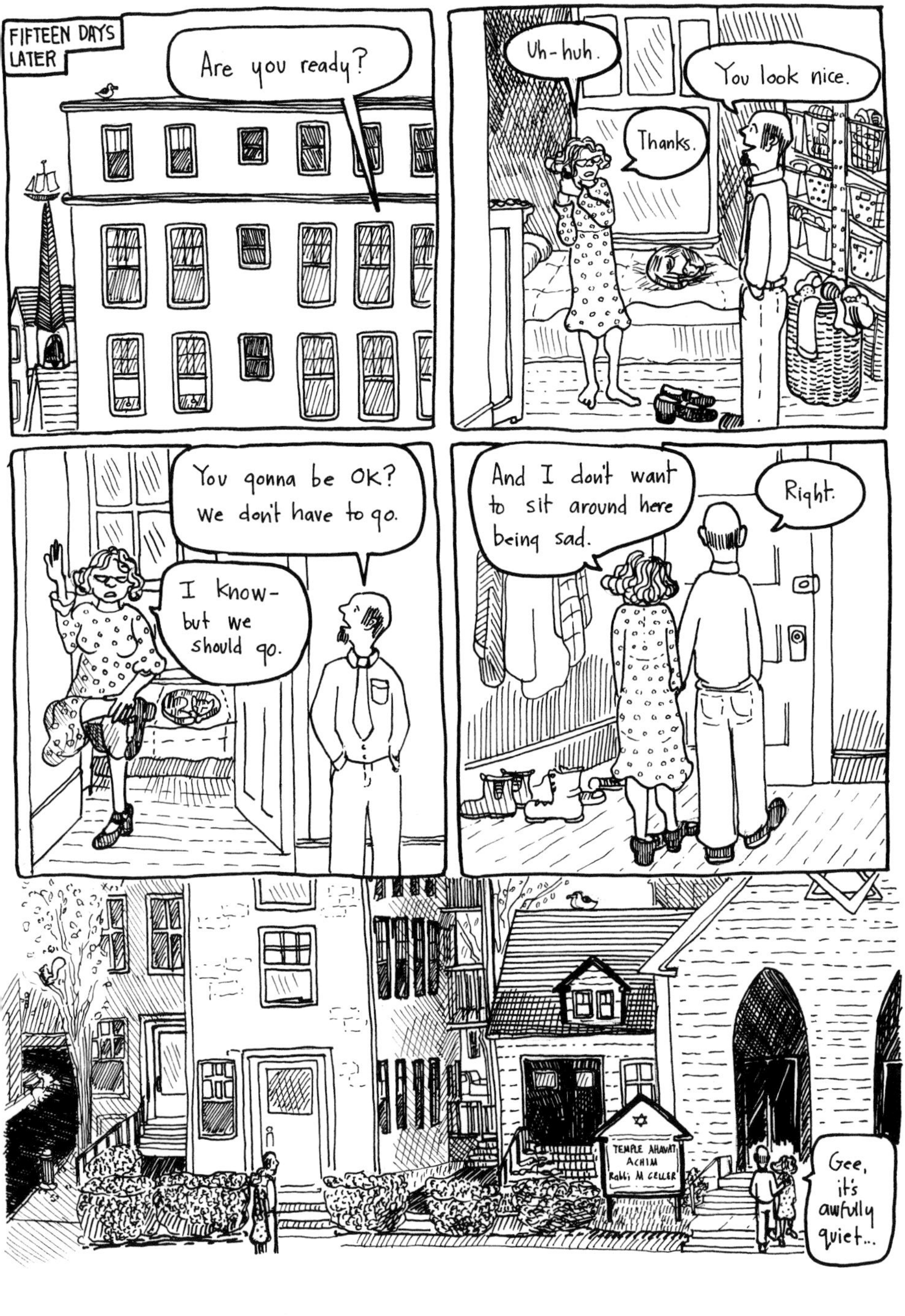
FIFTEEN DAYS LATER
Are you ready?
Uh-huh.
You look nice.
Thanks.
You gonna be OK? We don't have to go.
I know- but we should go.
And I don't want to sit around here being sad.
Right.
TEMPLE AHAVAT ACHIM Rabbi M GELLER
Gee, it's awfully quiet...

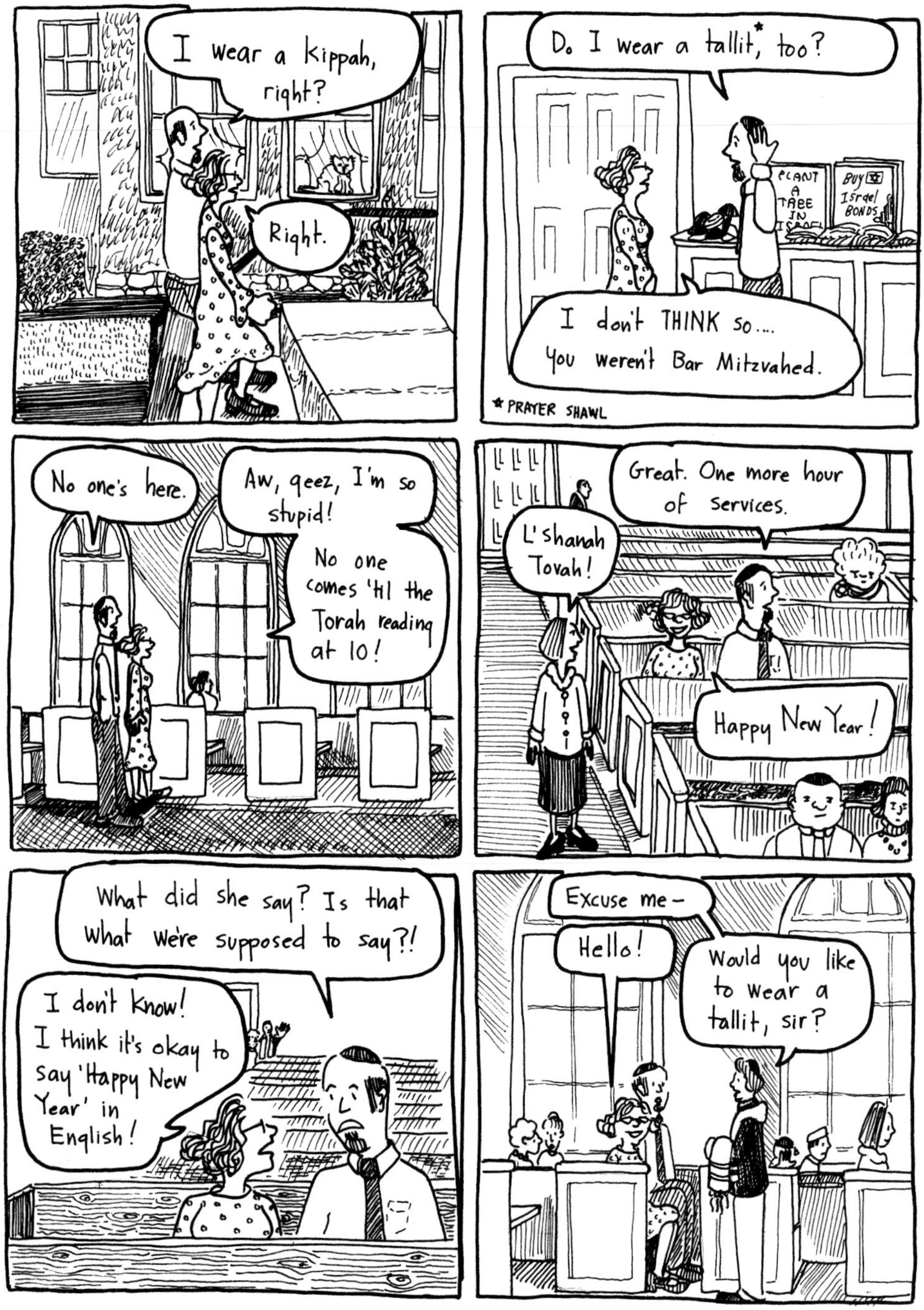
I wear a kippah, right?
Right.
D. I wear a tallit,* too?
PLANT A TREE IN ISRAEL
BUY ISRAEL BONDS
I don't THINK so.... You weren't Bar Mitzvahed.
* PRAYER SHAWL
No one's here.
Aw, geez, I'm so stupid!
No one comes 'til the Torah reading at 10!
Great. One more hour of services.
L'shanah Tovah!
Happy New Year!
What did she say? Is that what we're supposed to say?!
I don't know! I think it's okay to say 'Happy New Year' in English!
Excuse me-
Hello!
Would you like to wear a tallit, sir?

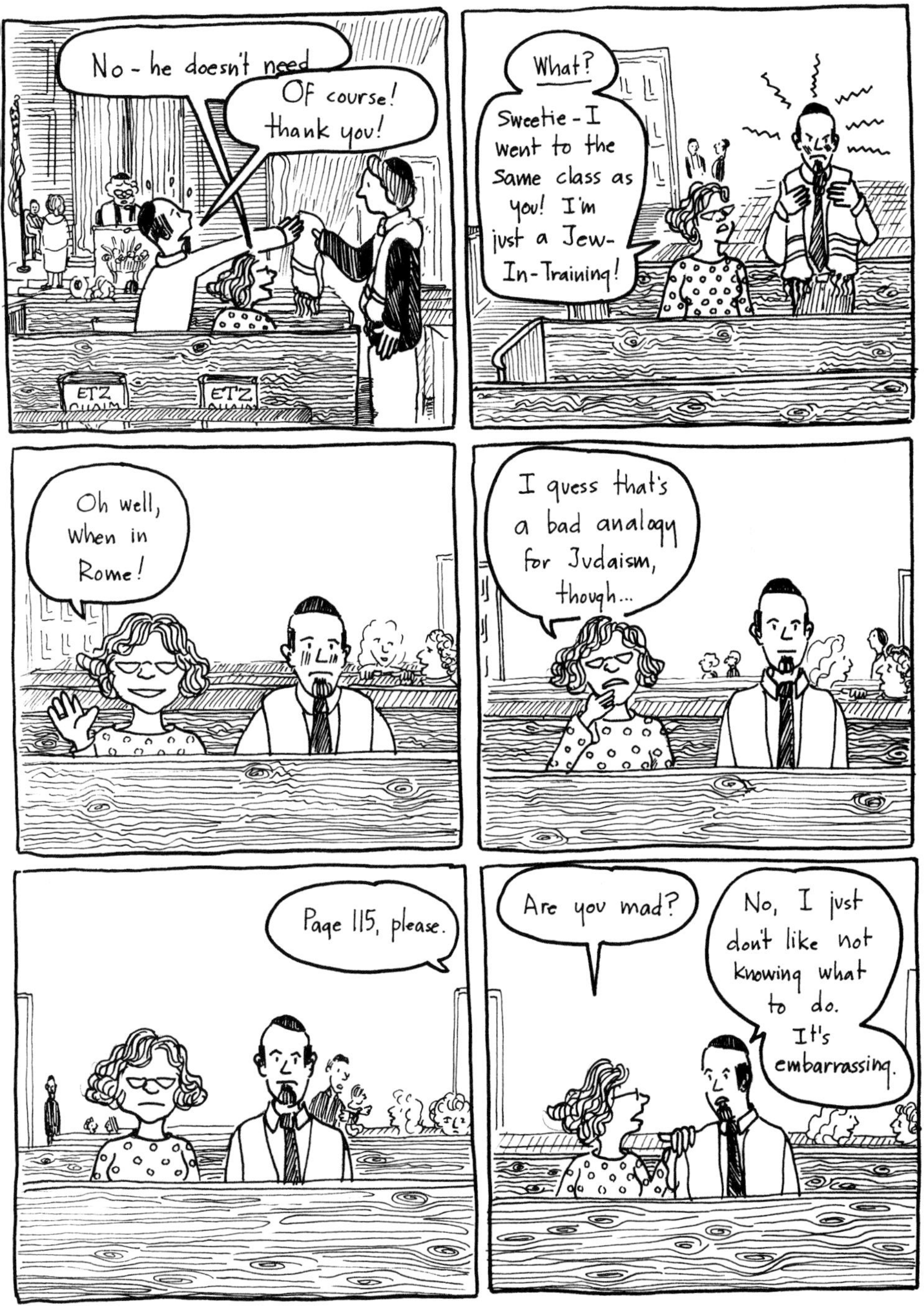
No - he doesn't need
Of course! thank you!
What?
Sweetie - I went to the same class as you! I'm just a Jew-In-Training!
Oh well, when in Rome!
I guess that's a bad analogy for Judaism, though...
Page 115, please.
Are you mad?
No, I just don't like not knowing what to do. It's embarrassing.

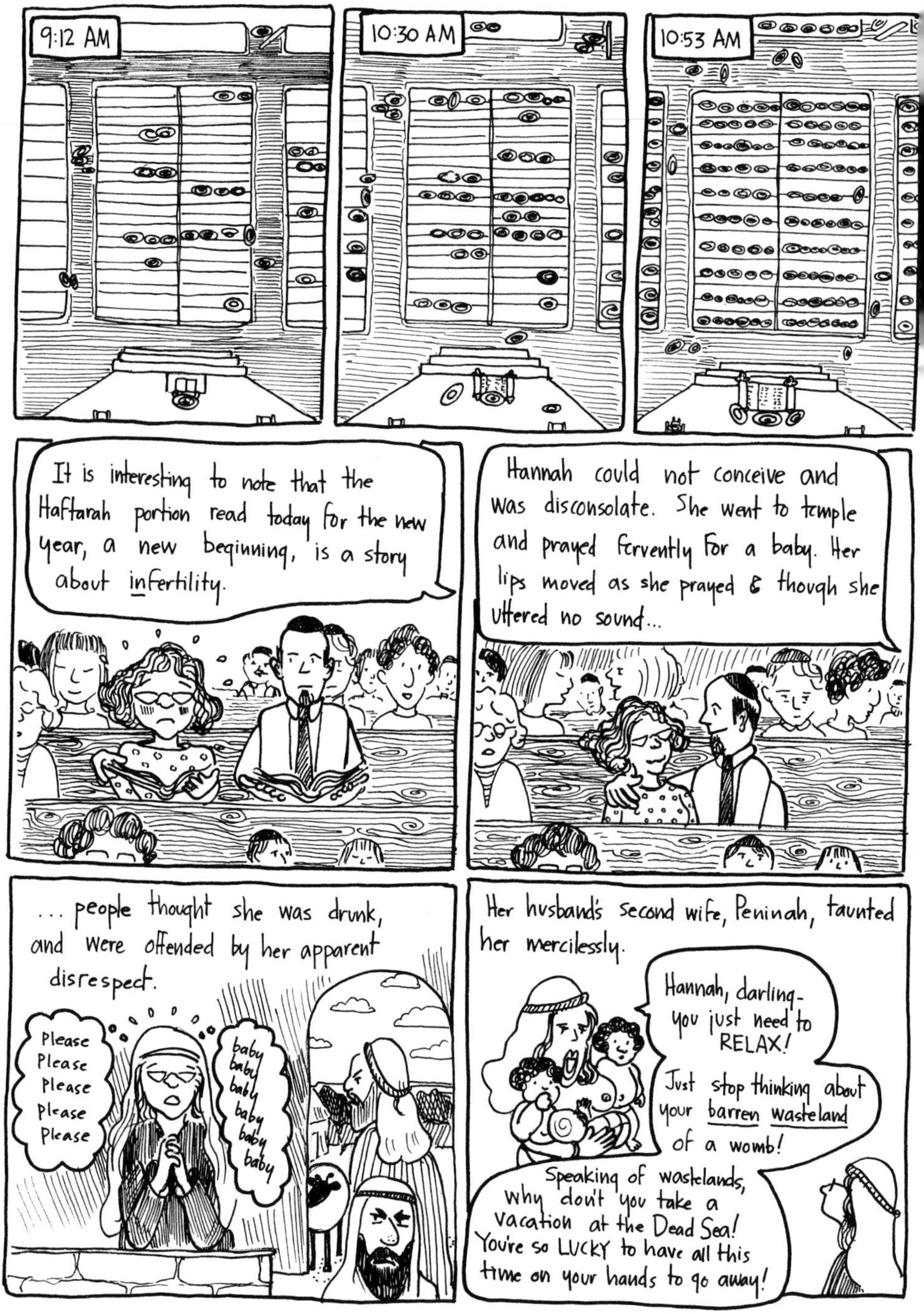
9:12 AM
10:30 AM
10:53 AM
It is interesting to note that the Haftarah portion read today for the new year, a new beginning, is a story about infertility.
Hannah could not conceive and was disconsolate. She went to temple and prayed fervently for a baby. Her lips moved as she prayed & though she uttered no sound...
... people thought she was drunk, and were offended by her apparent disrespect.
Please Please Please Please Please
baby baby baby baby baby baby
Her husband's second wife, Peninah, taunted her mercilessly.
Hannah, darling- you just need to RELAX!
Just stop thinking about your barren wasteland of a womb!
Speaking of wastelands, why don't you take a vacation at the Dead Sea! You're so LUCKY to have all this time on your hands to go away!

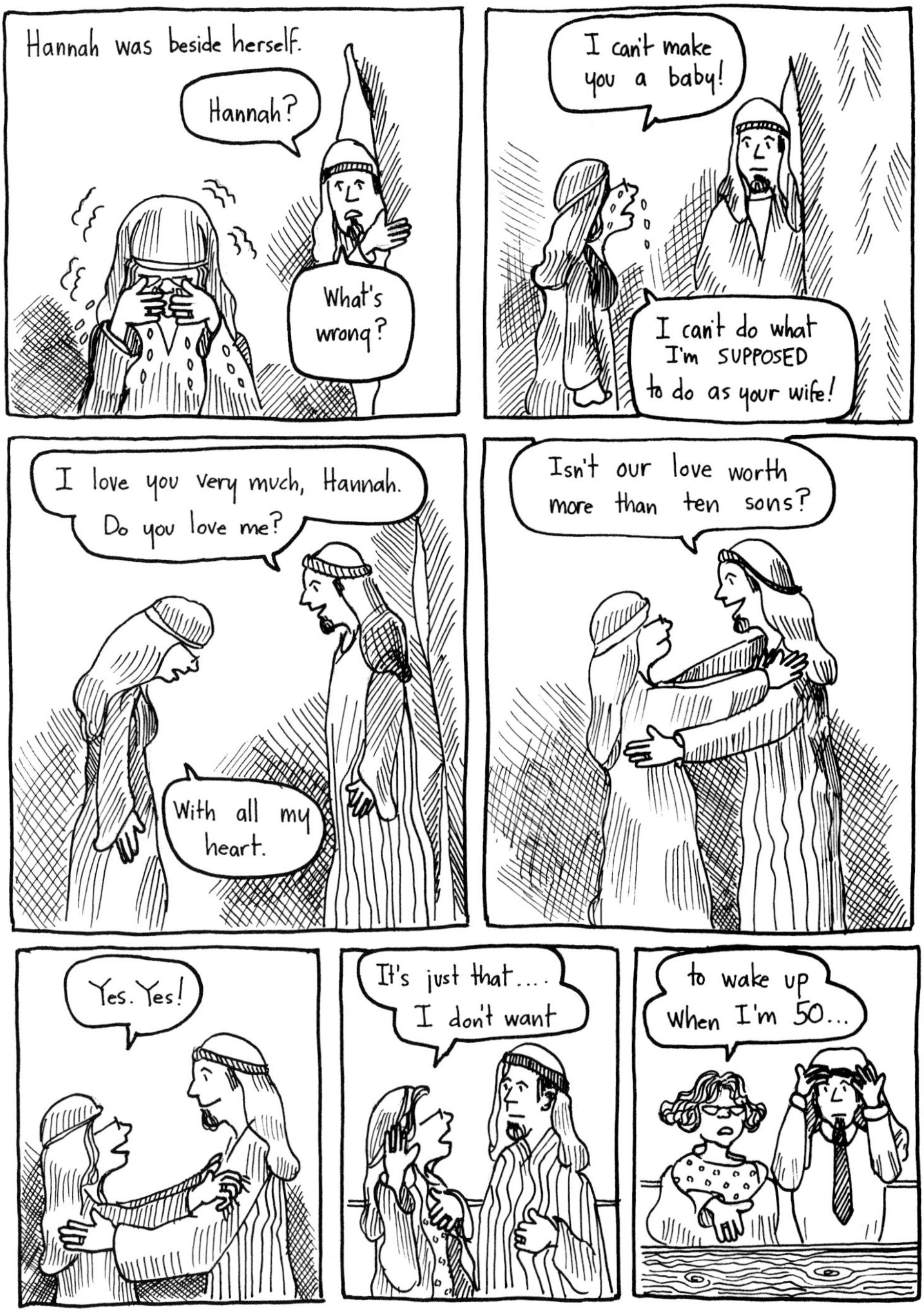
Hannah was beside herself.
Hannah?
What's wrong?
I can't make you a baby!
I can't do what I'm SUPPOSED to do as your wife!
I love you very much, Hannah. Do you love me?
With all my heart.
Isn't our love worth more than ten sons?
Yes. Yes!
It's just that.... I don't want
to wake up when I'm 50...

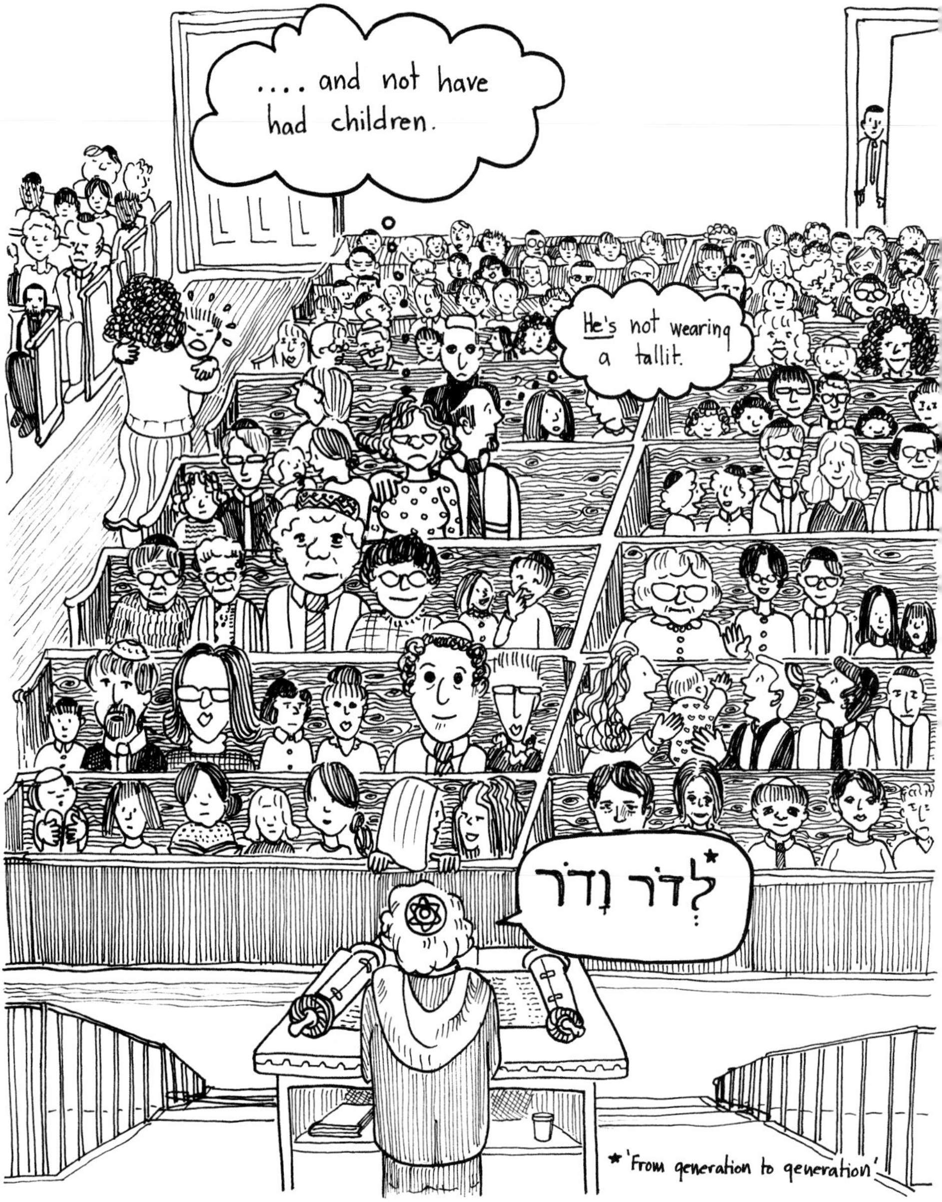
.... and not have had children.
He's not wearing a tallit.
לְדֹר וָדֹר*
*'From generation to generation'

CHAPTER 5

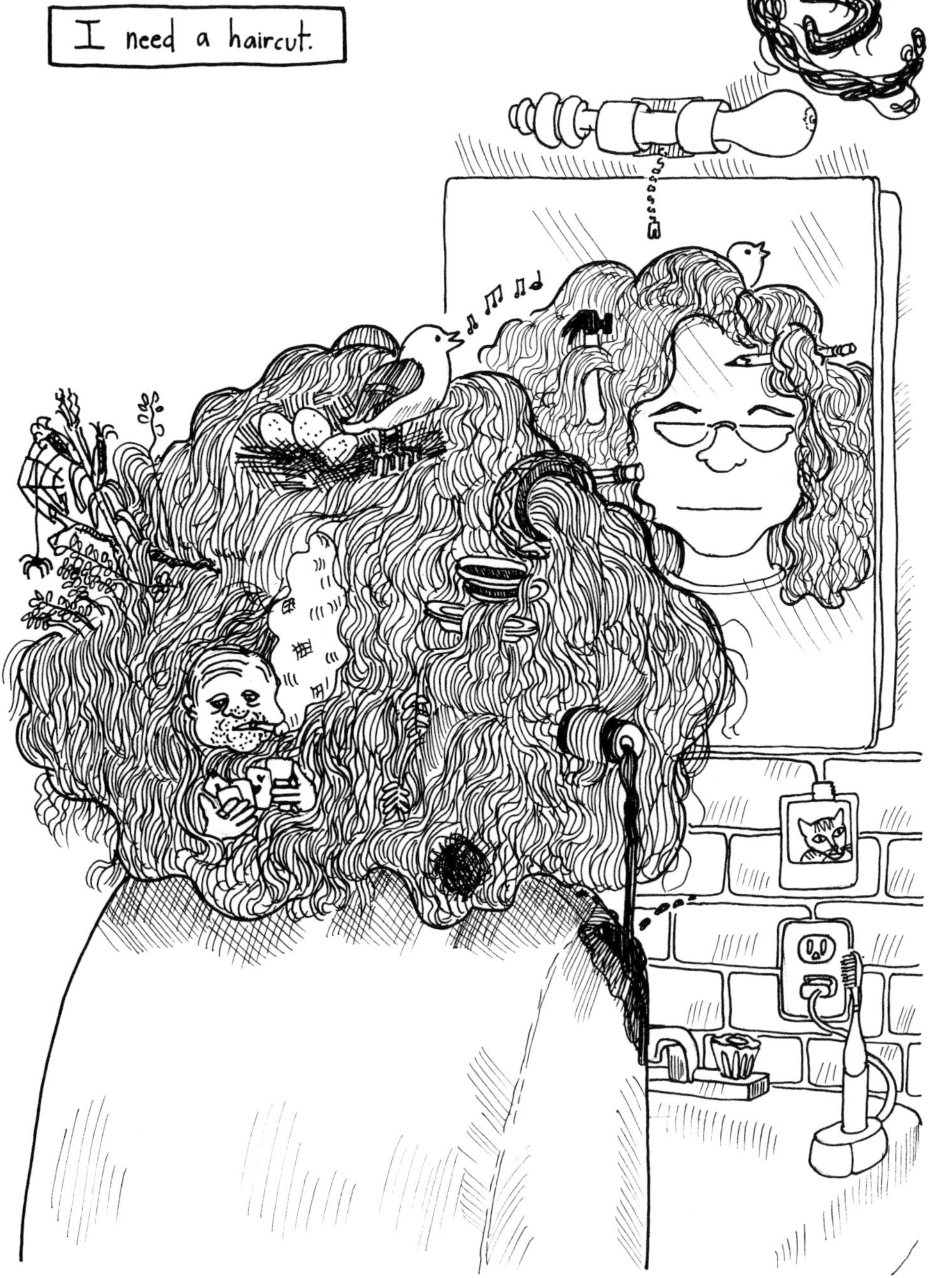
I need a haircut.

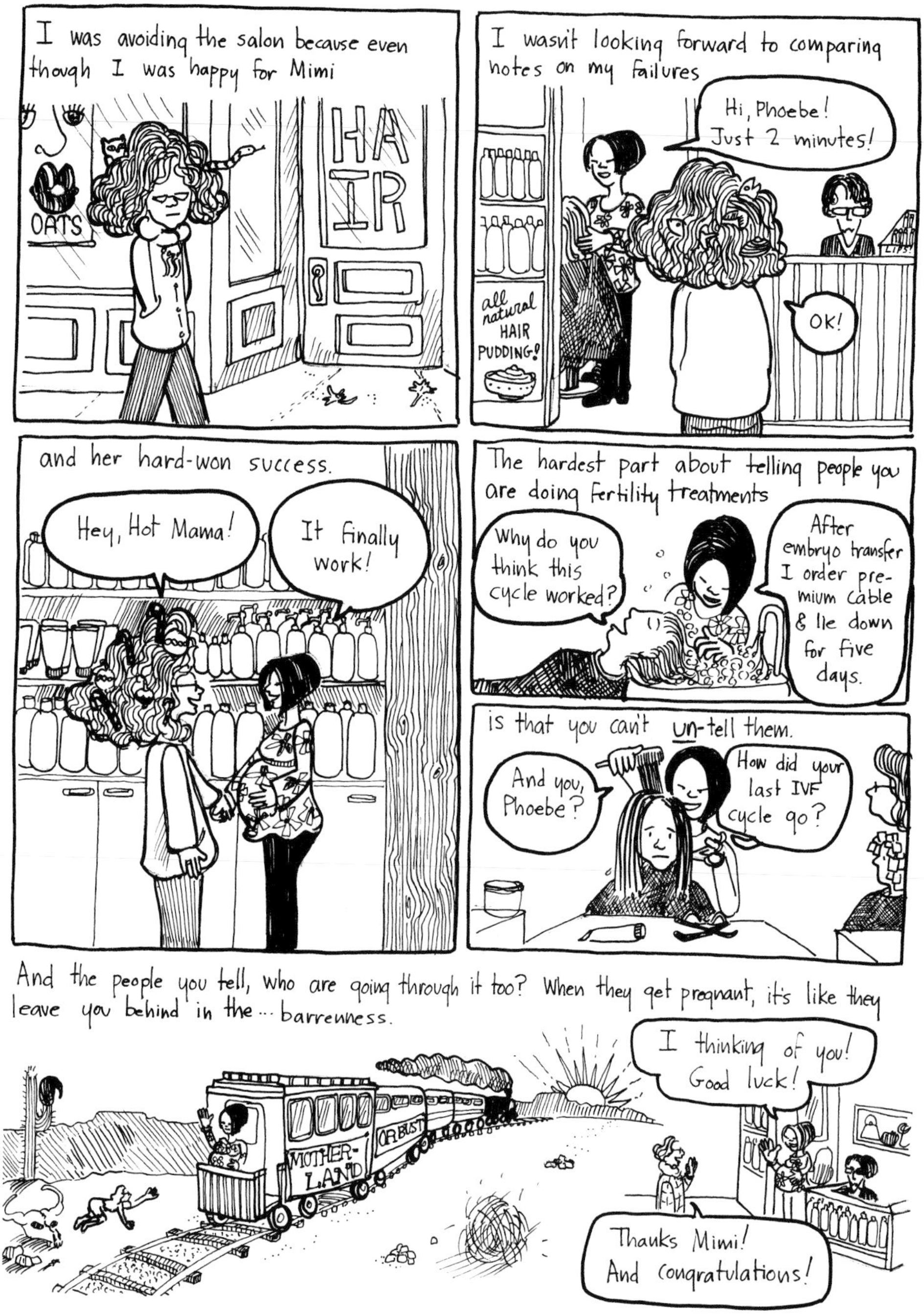
I was avoiding the salon because even though I was happy for Mimi
OATS
HA IR
I wasn't looking forward to comparing notes on my failures
Hi, Phoebe! Just 2 minutes!
all natural HAIR PUDDING!
LIPS!
OK!
and her hard-won success.
Hey, Hot Mama!
It finally work!
The hardest part about telling people you are doing fertility treatments
Why do you think this cycle worked?
After embryo transfer I order premium cable & lie down for five days.
is that you can't un-tell them.
And you, Phoebe?
How did your last IVF cycle go?
And the people you tell, who are going through it too? When they get pregnant, it's like they leave you behind in the... barrenness.
MOTHER-LAND
OR BUST
I thinking of you! Good luck!
Thanks Mimi! And congratulations!

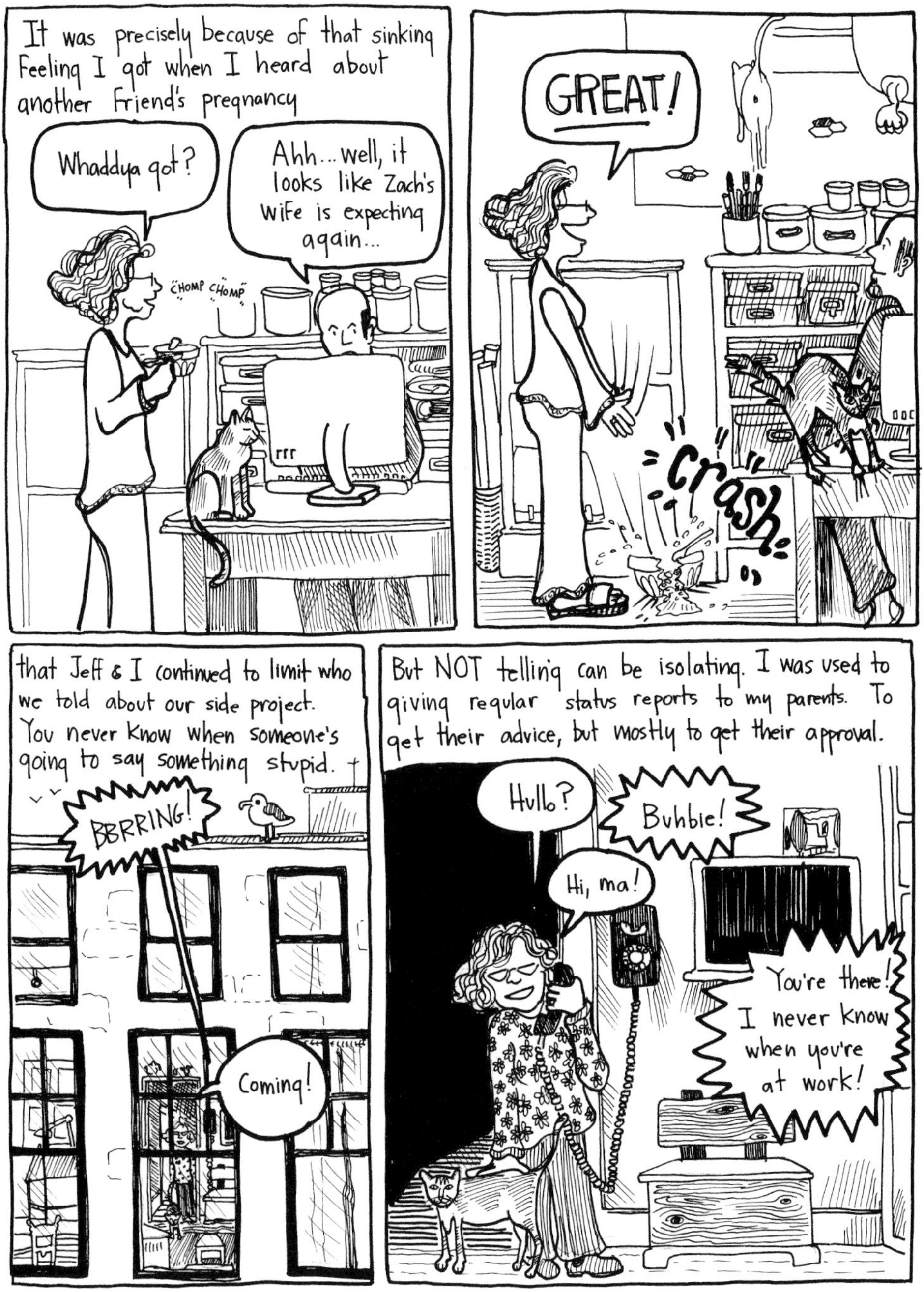
It was precisely because of that sinking feeling I got when I heard about another friend's pregnancy
Whaddya got?
Ahh... well, it looks like Zach's wife is expecting again...
CHOMP CHOMP
rrr
GREAT!
crash
that Jeff & I continued to limit who we told about our side project. You never know when someone's going to say something stupid.
BBRRING!
Coming!
But NOT telling can be isolating. I was used to giving regular status reports to my parents. To get their advice, but mostly to get their approval.
Hullo?
Bubbie!
Hi, ma!
You're there! I never know when you're at work!

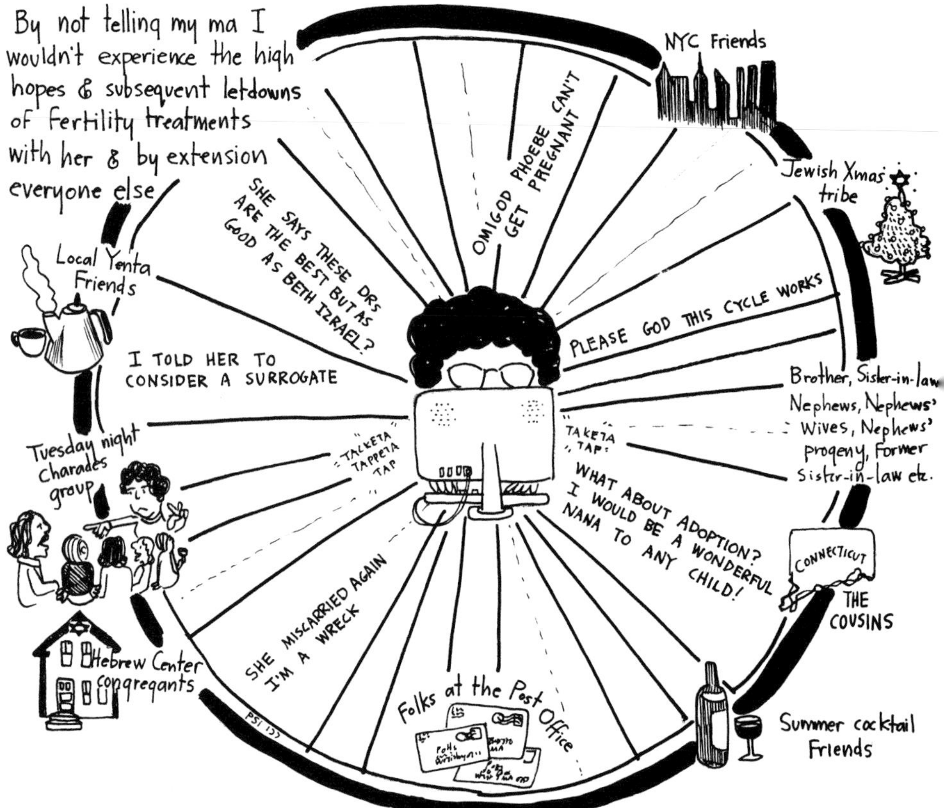

By not telling my ma I wouldn't experience the high hopes & subsequent letdowns of fertility treatments with her & by extension everyone else
NYC Friends
Jewish Xmas tribe
Brother, Sister-in-law Nephews, Nephews' Wives, Nephews' progeny, Former Sister-in-law etc.
CONNECTICUT
THE COUSINS
Summer cocktail Friends
Folks at the Post Office
Hebrew Center congregants
Tuesday night Charades group
Local Yenta Friends
OMIGOD PHOEBE CAN'T GET PREGNANT
SHE SAYS THESE DRS ARE THE BEST BUT AS GOOD AS BETH IZRAEL?
PLEASE GOD THIS CYCLE WORKS
I TOLD HER TO CONSIDER A SURROGATE
"TACKETA TAPPETA TAP"
"TAKETA TAP"
WHAT ABOUT ADOPTION? I WOULD BE A WONDERFUL NANA TO ANY CHILD!
SHE MISCARRIED AGAIN I'M A WRECK

My therapist once gave me permission to not tell Everybody Everything. Not telling my ma was a complicated, if mature, strategy. So every time I felt compelled to spill it, I played a script in my head, a dialogue for a parallel universe, where she only said supportive & empathetic things.

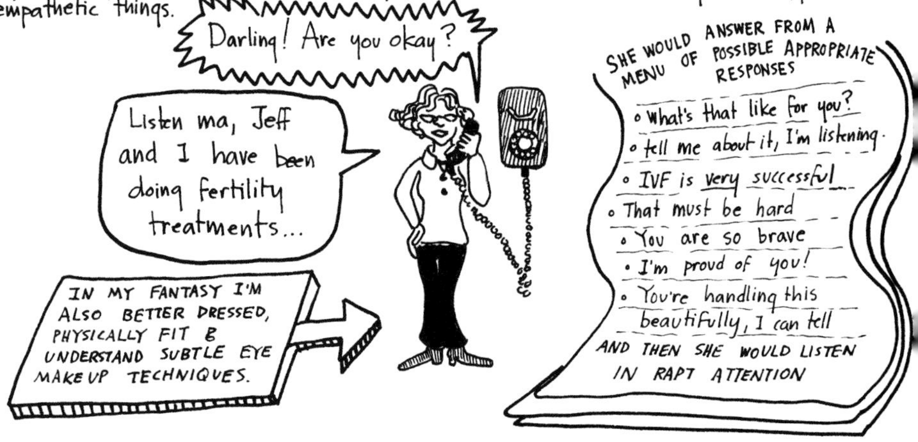

Listen ma, Jeff and I have been doing fertility treatments...
Darling! Are you okay?
SHE WOULD ANSWER FROM A MENU OF POSSIBLE APPROPRIATE RESPONSES
• What's that like for you?
• tell me about it, I'm listening.
• IVF is very successful
• That must be hard
• You are so brave
• I'm proud of you!
• You're handling this beautifully, I can tell
AND THEN SHE WOULD LISTEN IN RAPT ATTENTION
IN MY FANTASY I'M ALSO BETTER DRESSED, PHYSICALLY FIT & UNDERSTAND SUBTLE EYE MAKE UP TECHNIQUES.

The best practice was to keep the conversations short.

Ma— I gotta catch my train. Can I call you back?

...and WHEN will I see you? YOU'RE NEVER HOME WHEN CAN WE TALK I MISS YOU! WE'RE COMING TO BOSTON IN OCTOBER FOR MY BONE DENSITY SCAN YOUR FATHER...

This is no small task.

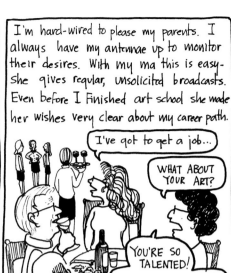

I'm hard-wired to please my parents. I always have my antennae up to monitor their desires. With my ma this is easy— she gives regular, unsolicited broadcasts. Even before I finished art school she made her wishes very clear about my career path.

I've got to get a job...

WHAT ABOUT YOUR ART?

YOU'RE SO TALENTED!

EVERYONE THINKS SO!

WHAT ABOUT YOUR ROOF-TOP PAINTINGS? I LOVE YOUR ROOFTOPS!

The thing is, nobody's hiring artists in America, yet art schools keep churning them out. In my grad school we were offered two possible models of how to be working artists. #1 was the ART STAR

'BALLOON DOG' J. KOONS

Jeff Koons should be imprinted in your mind's eye. He is in control of his image & all the marketing of his work. Jeff Koons runs Jeff Koons. He knows that 97% of museum go-ers never make it past the gift shop. All his large work is for sale in mass-manufactured miniature. Learn from him.

Getting recognition as an Art Star isn't a lock. Securing one of the few slots in the art world would be like making the NBA and becoming the next Michael Jordan.

And #2, the less preferred option, was to teach. Recycle yourself back into art school. Or at least on the college level. But really only if you'd really truly exhausted all possibility of being recognized as the next Jeff Koons. Or at least Cindy Sherman.

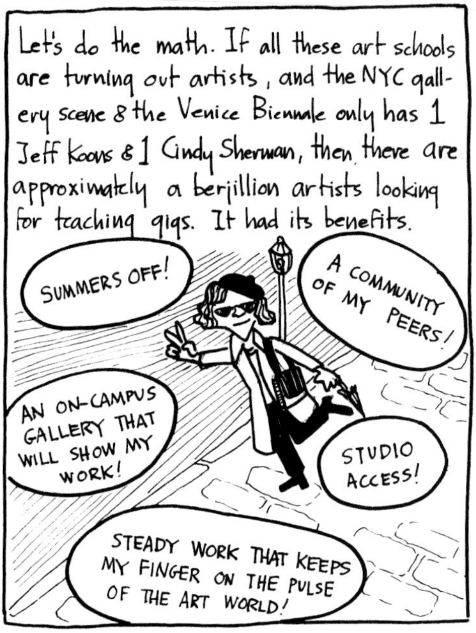
Let's do the math. If all these art schools are turning out artists, and the NYC gallery scene & the Venice Biennale only has 1 Jeff Koons & 1 Cindy Sherman, then there are approximately a berjillion artists looking for teaching gigs. It had its benefits.
SUMMERS OFF!
A COMMUNITY OF MY PEERS!
AN ON-CAMPUS GALLERY THAT WILL SHOW MY WORK!
STUDIO ACCESS!
STEADY WORK THAT KEEPS MY FINGER ON THE PULSE OF THE ART WORLD!

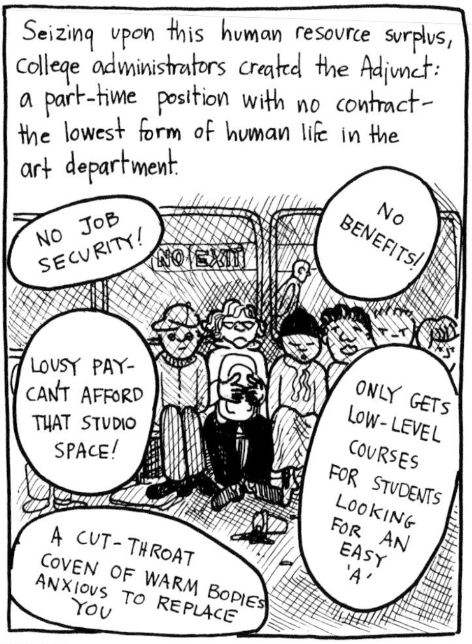
Seizing upon this human resource surplus, college administrators created the Adjunct: a part-time position with no contract- the lowest form of human life in the art department.
NO JOB SECURITY!
NO BENEFITS!
NO EXIT
LOUSY PAY- CAN'T AFFORD THAT STUDIO SPACE!
ONLY GETS LOW-LEVEL COURSES FOR STUDENTS LOOKING FOR AN EASY 'A'
A CUT-THROAT COVEN OF WARM BODIES ANXIOUS TO REPLACE YOU

I secured a variety of these adjunct jobs at local colleges. I liked the kids and even though they were majoring in Criminology or Sports Management I tried to inspire them with my passion.

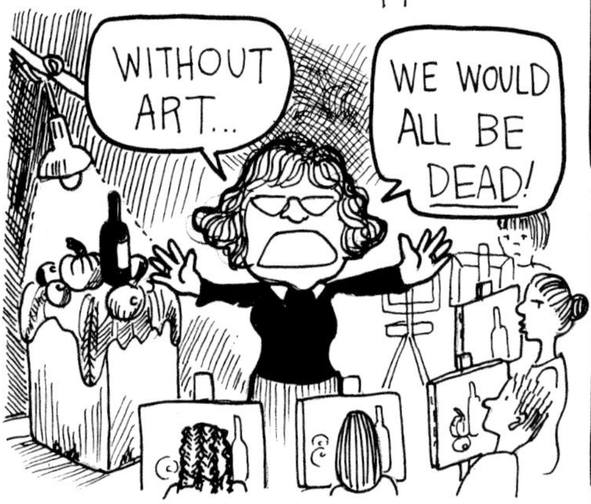
WITHOUT ART...
WE WOULD ALL BE DEAD!

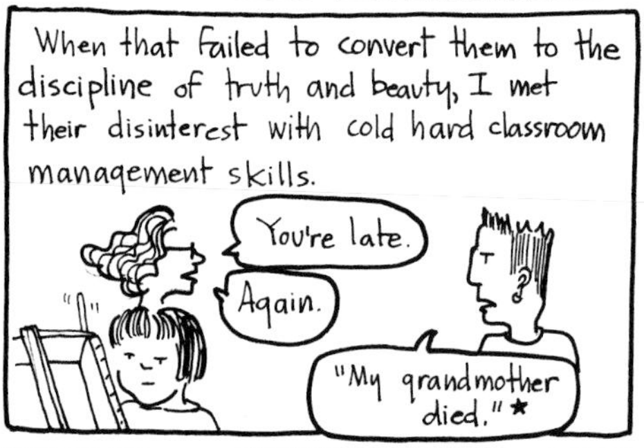
When that failed to convert them to the discipline of truth and beauty, I met their disinterest with cold hard classroom management skills.
You're late.
Again.
"My grandmother died."*

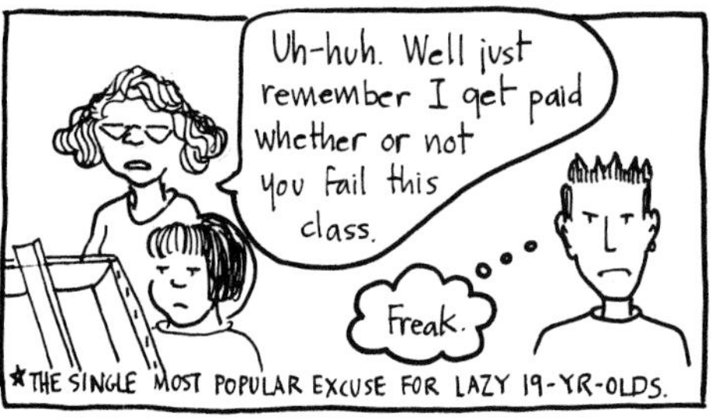
Uh-huh. Well just remember I get paid whether or not you fail this class.
Freak.
*THE SINGLE MOST POPULAR EXCUSE FOR LAZY 19-YR-OLDS.

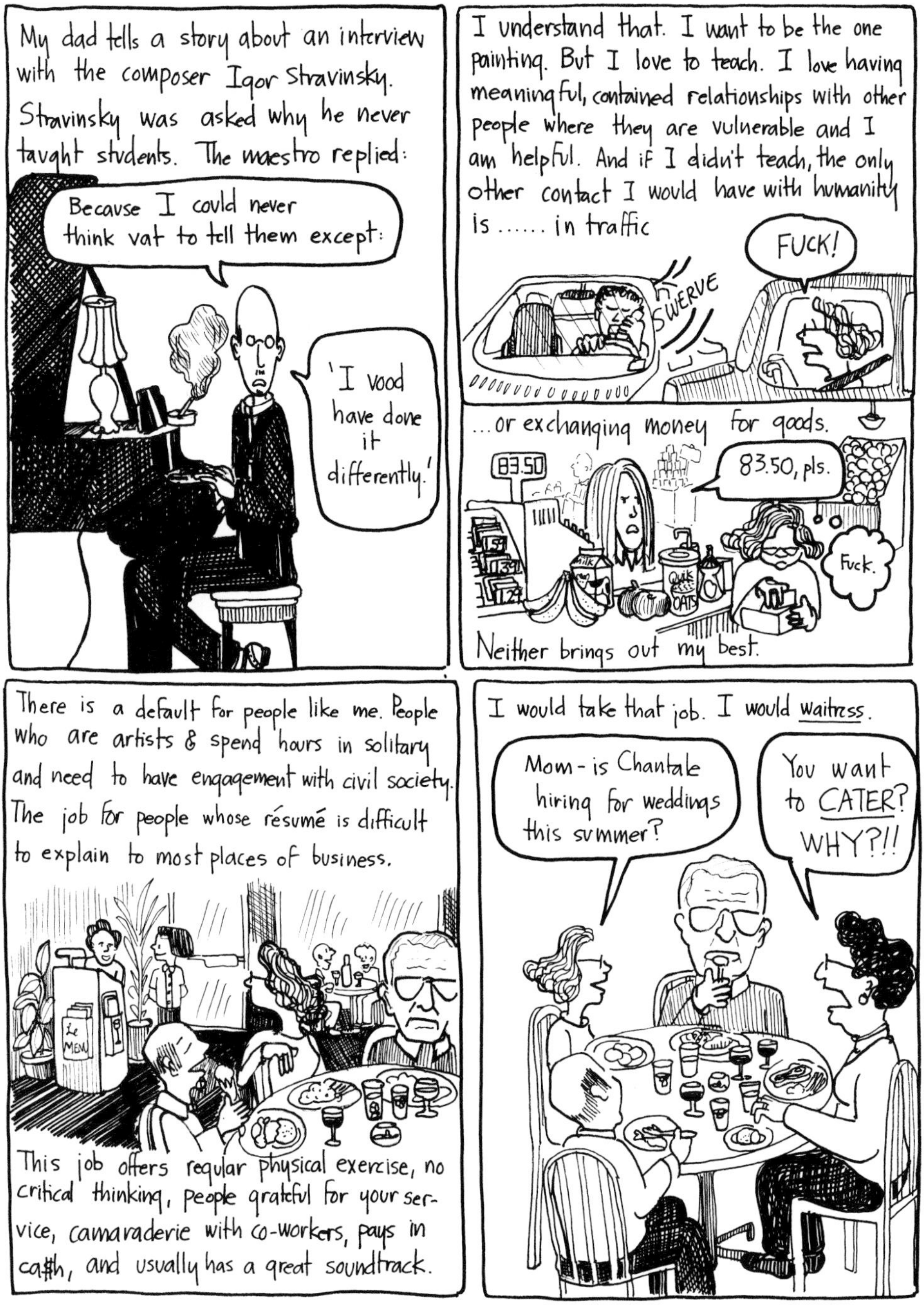
My dad tells a story about an interview with the composer Igor Stravinsky. Stravinsky was asked why he never taught students. The maestro replied:
Because I could never think vat to tell them except:
'I vood have done it differently.'
I understand that. I want to be the one painting. But I love to teach. I love having meaningful, contained relationships with other people where they are vulnerable and I am helpful. And if I didn't teach, the only other contact I would have with humanity is ...... in traffic
SWERVE
FUCK!
...or exchanging money for goods.
83.50
83.50, pls.
MILK
QUIK OATS
Fuck.
Neither brings out my best.
There is a default for people like me. People who are artists & spend hours in solitary and need to have engagement with civil society. The job for people whose résumé is difficult to explain to most places of business.
Le MENU
This job offers regular physical exercise, no critical thinking, people grateful for your service, camaraderie with co-workers, pays in ca$h, and usually has a great soundtrack.
I would take that job. I would waitress.
Mom - is Chantale hiring for weddings this summer?
You want to CATER? WHY?!!

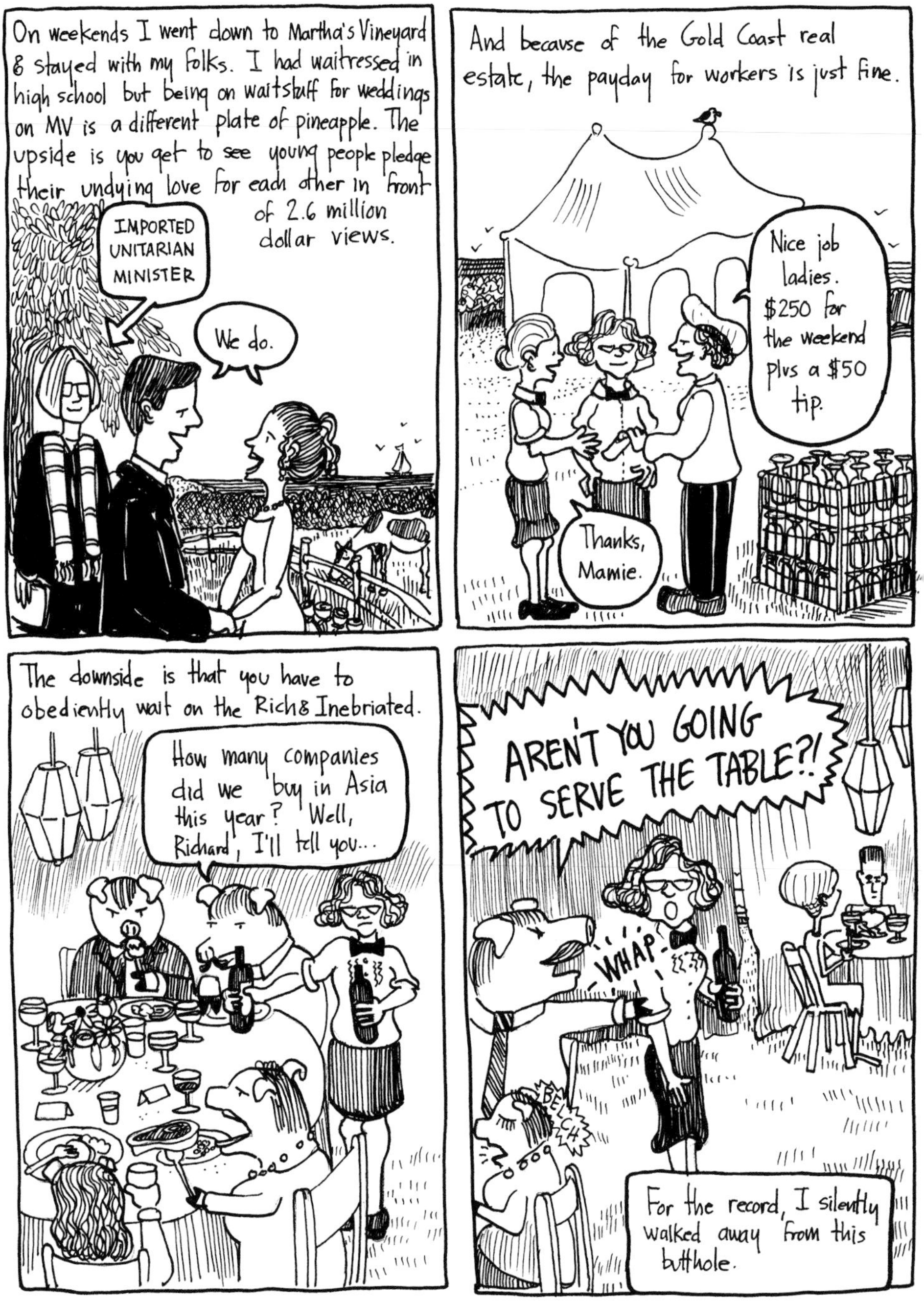
On weekends I went down to Martha's Vineyard & stayed with my folks. I had waitressed in high school but being on waitstaff for weddings on MV is a different plate of pineapple. The upside is you get to see young people pledge their undying love for each other in front of 2.6 million dollar views.
IMPORTED UNITARIAN MINISTER
We do.
And because of the Gold Coast real estate, the payday for workers is just fine.
Nice job ladies. $250 for the weekend plus a $50 tip.
Thanks, Mamie.
The downside is that you have to obediently wait on the Rich & Inebriated.
How many companies did we buy in Asia this year? Well, Richard, I'll tell you...
AREN'T YOU GOING TO SERVE THE TABLE?!
WHAP
BELCH
For the record, I silently walked away from this butthole.

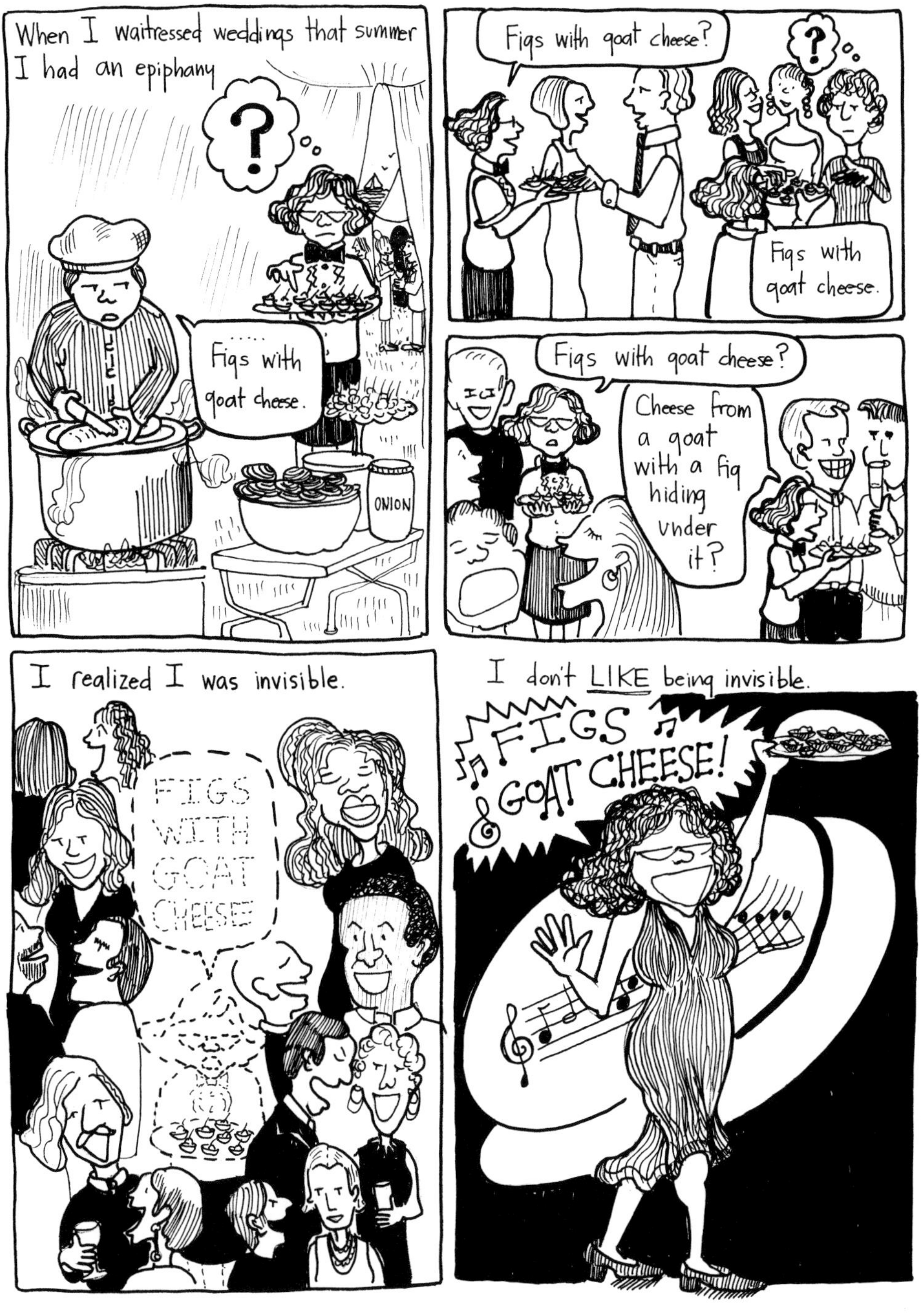
When I waitressed weddings that summer I had an epiphany
?
..... Figs with goat cheese.
ONION
Figs with goat cheese?
?
Figs with goat cheese.
Figs with goat cheese?
Cheese from a goat with a fig hiding under it?
I realized I was invisible.
FIGS WITH GOAT CHEESE
I don't LIKE being invisible.
FIGS & GOAT CHEESE!

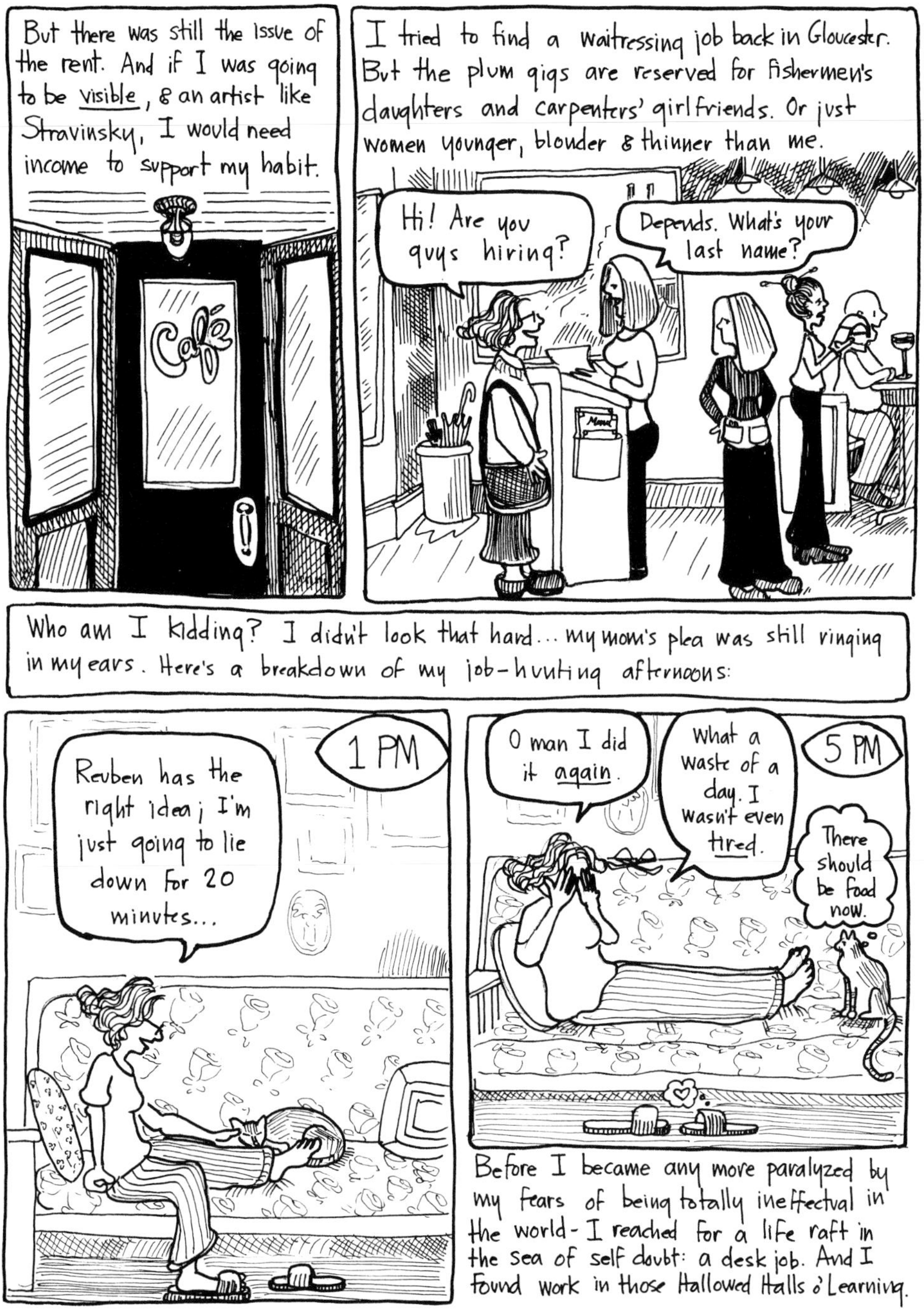
But there was still the issue of the rent. And if I was going to be visible, & an artist like Stravinsky, I would need income to support my habit.
Café
I tried to find a waitressing job back in Gloucester. But the plum gigs are reserved for fishermen's daughters and carpenters' girlfriends. Or just women younger, blonder & thinner than me.
Hi! Are you guys hiring?
Depends. What's your last name?
Who am I kidding? I didn't look that hard... my mom's plea was still ringing in my ears. Here's a breakdown of my job-hunting afternoons:
1 PM
Reuben has the right idea; I'm just going to lie down for 20 minutes...
5 PM
O man I did it again.
What a waste of a day. I wasn't even tired.
There should be food now.
Before I became any more paralyzed by my fears of being totally ineffectual in the world - I reached for a life raft in the sea of self doubt: a desk job. And I found work in those Hallowed Halls o' Learning.

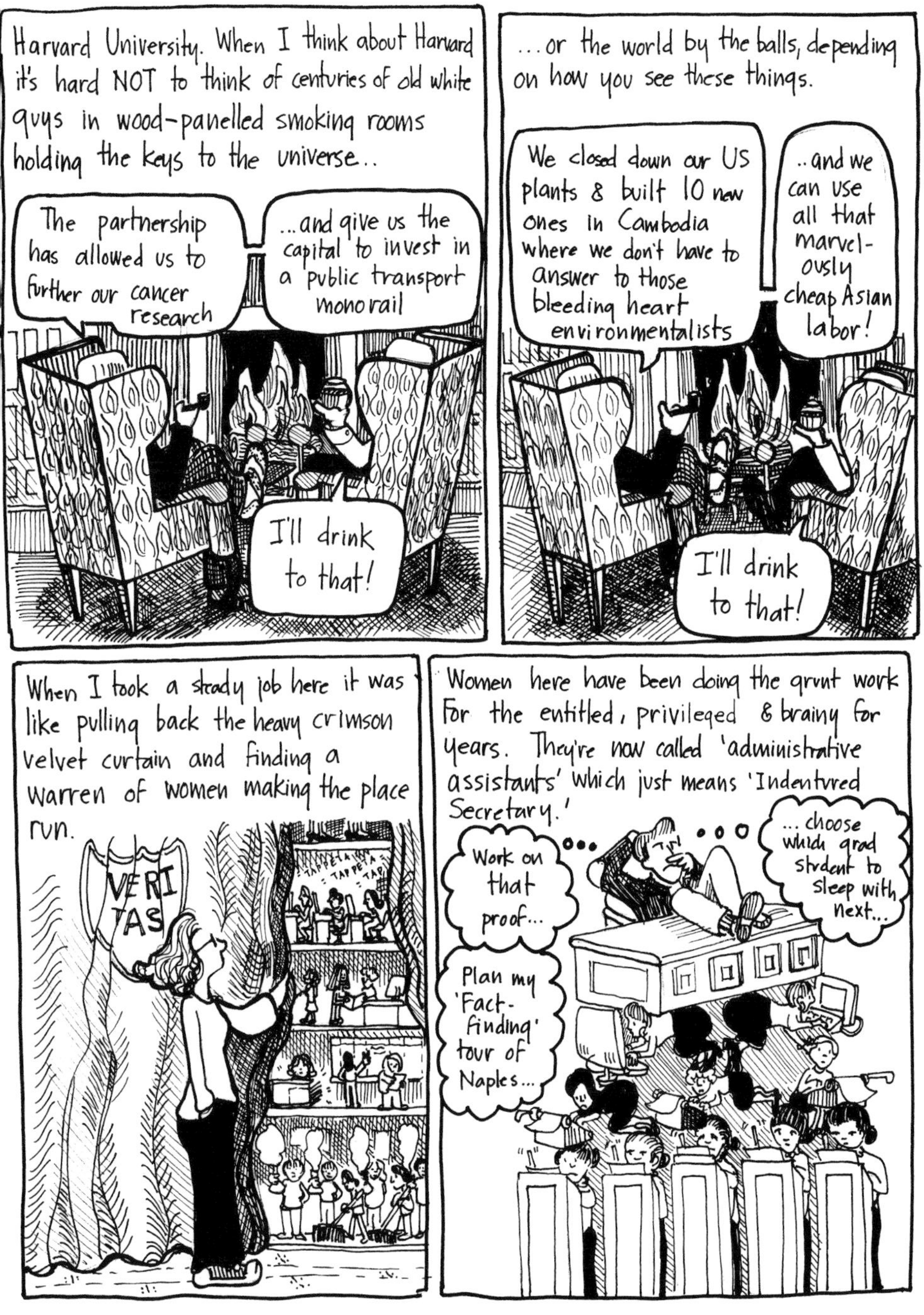
Harvard University. When I think about Harvard it's hard NOT to think of centuries of old white guys in wood-panelled smoking rooms holding the keys to the universe..
The partnership has allowed us to further our cancer research
...and give us the capital to invest in a public transport monorail
I'll drink to that!
...or the world by the balls, depending on how you see these things.
We closed down our US plants & built 10 new ones in Cambodia where we don't have to answer to those bleeding heart environmentalists
..and we can use all that marvel-ously cheap Asian labor!
I'll drink to that!
When I took a steady job here it was like pulling back the heavy crimson velvet curtain and finding a warren of women making the place run.
VERITAS
TAPPETA TAPPETA TAP
Women here have been doing the grunt work for the entitled, privileged & brainy for years. They're now called 'administrative assistants' which just means 'Indentured Secretary.'
Work on that proof...
Plan my 'Fact-finding' tour of Naples...
... choose which grad student to sleep with next...

In some ways, things have changed for secretaries at Harvard over the years:

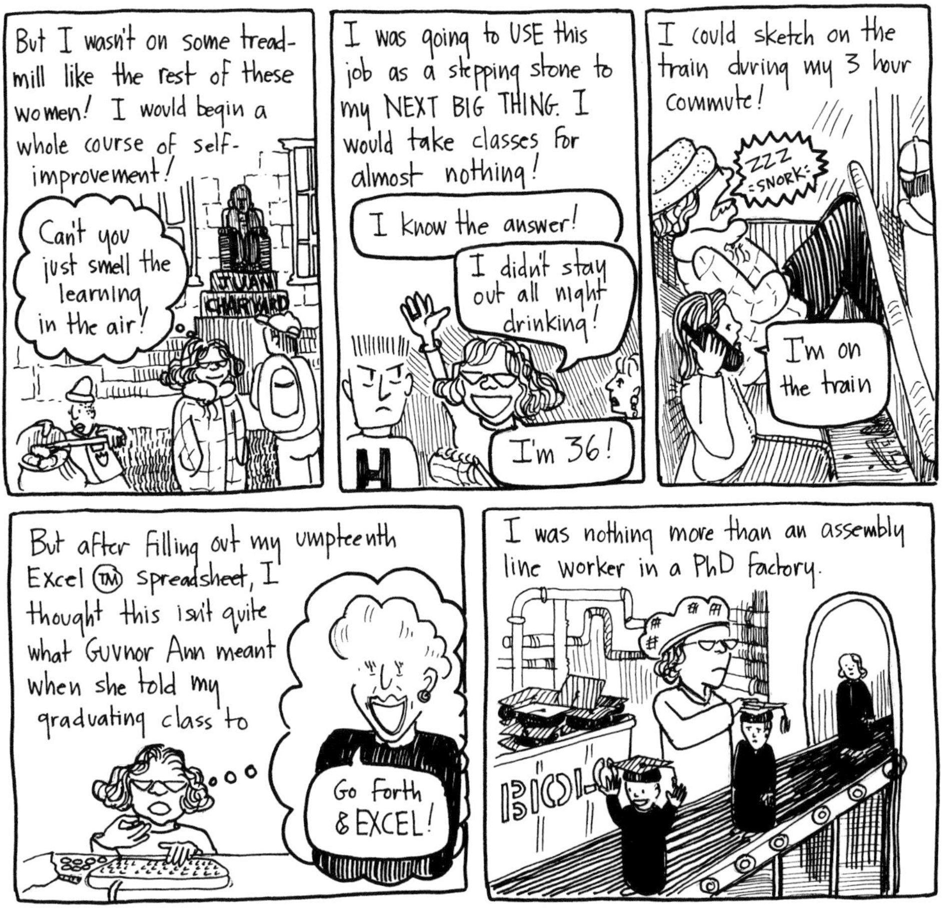
But I wasn't on some treadmill like the rest of these women! I would begin a whole course of self-improvement!
Can't you just smell the learning in the air!
HARVARD
I was going to USE this job as a stepping stone to my NEXT BIG THING. I would take classes for almost nothing!
I know the answer!
I didn't stay out all night drinking!
I'm 36!
I could sketch on the train during my 3 hour commute!
ZZZ SNORK
I'm on the train
But after filling out my umpteenth Excel (TM) spreadsheet, I thought this isn't quite what Guvnor Ann meant when she told my graduating class to
Go Forth & EXCEL!
I was nothing more than an assembly line worker in a PhD factory.

This was soul desiccating work. And it was drying up my sense of self-worth, too.

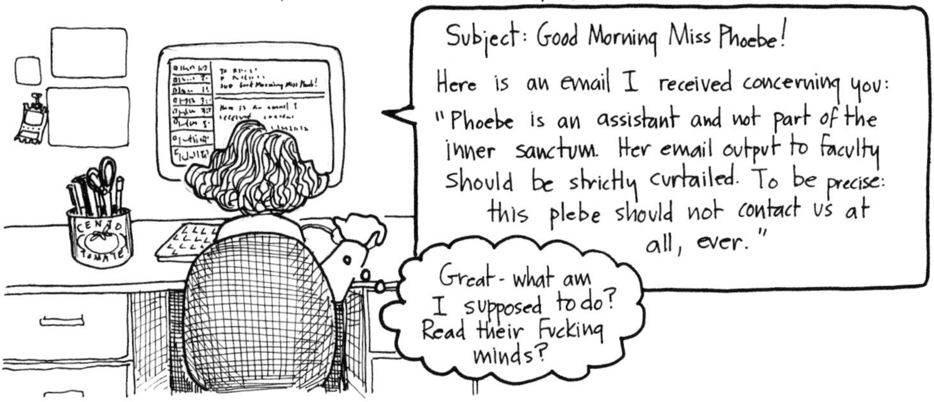
Subject: Good Morning Miss Phoebe!
Here is an email I received concerning you: "Phoebe is an assistant and not part of the inner sanctum. Her email output to faculty should be strictly curtailed. To be precise: this plebe should not contact us at all, ever."
Great- what am I supposed to do? Read their Fucking minds?
CENTO TOMATE

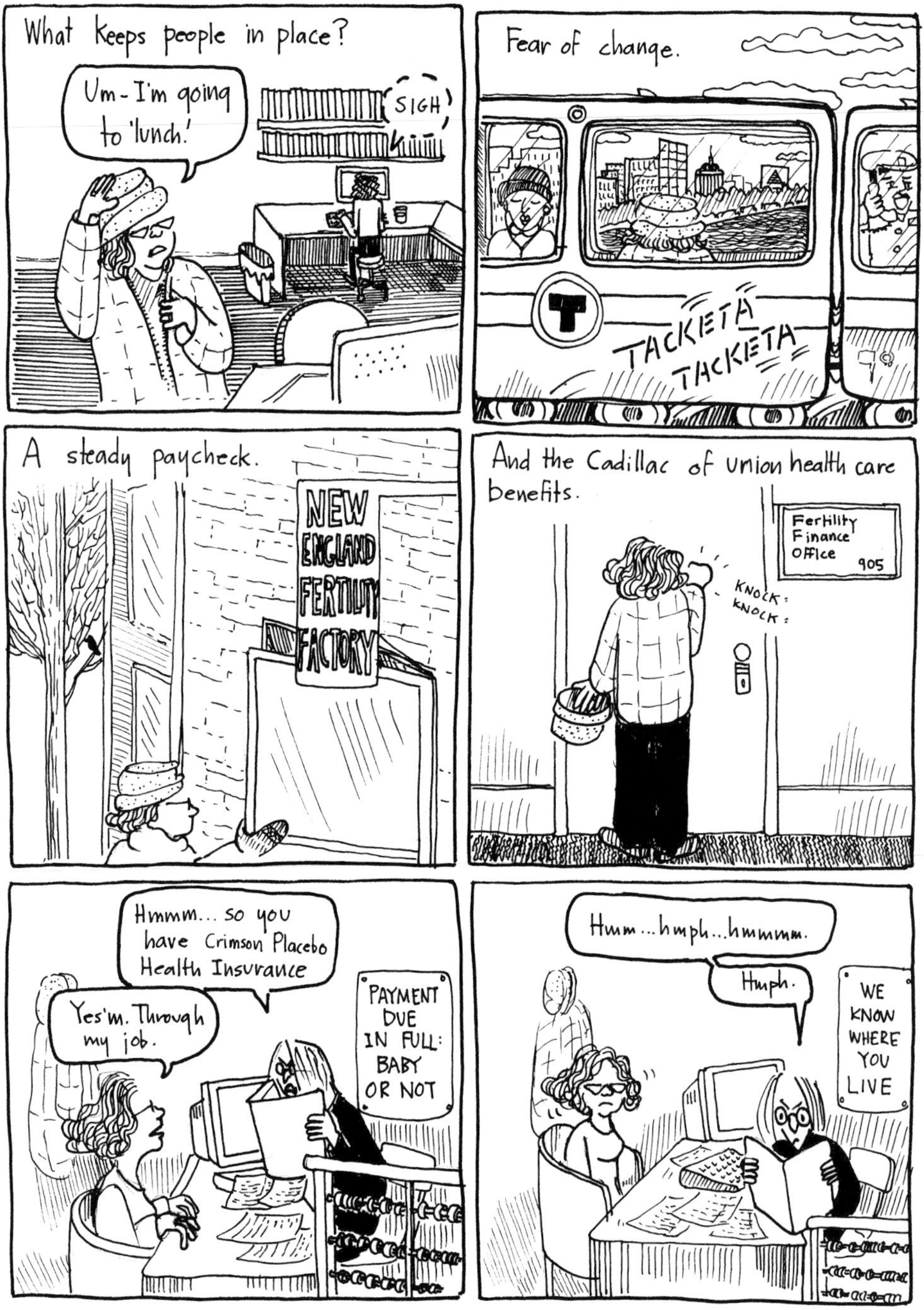
What keeps people in place?
Um-I'm going to 'lunch.'
SIGH
Fear of change.
TACKETA TACKETA
A steady paycheck.
NEW ENGLAND FERTILITY FACTORY
And the Cadillac of union health care benefits.
Fertility Finance Office 905
KNOCK: KNOCK:
Hmmm... so you have Crimson Placebo Health Insurance
Yes'm. Through my job.
PAYMENT DUE IN FULL: BABY OR NOT
Hmm...hmph...hmmmm.
Hmph.
WE KNOW WHERE YOU LIVE

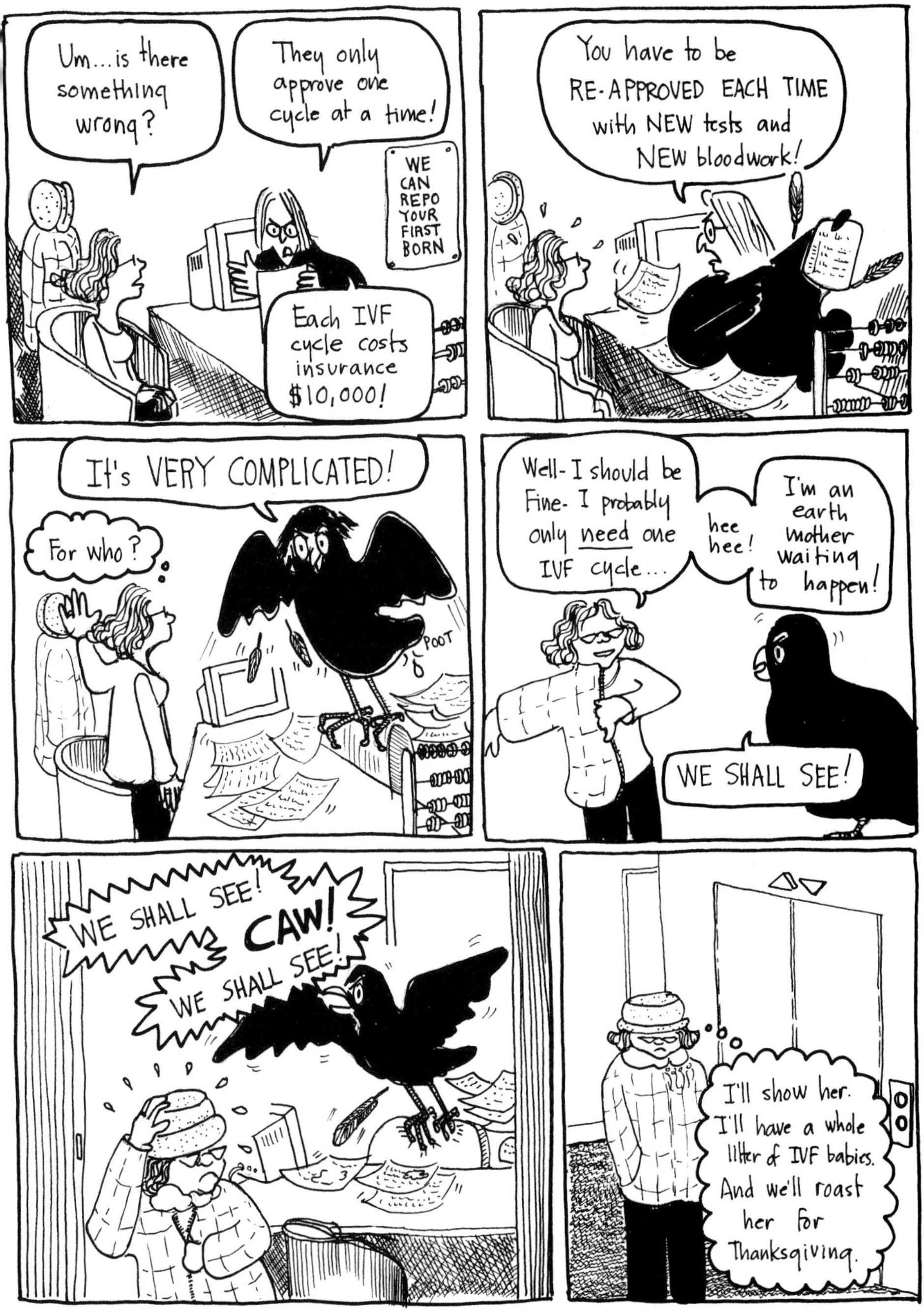

Um... is there something wrong?
They only approve one cycle at a time!
WE CAN REPO YOUR FIRST BORN
Each IVF cycle costs insurance $10,000!
You have to be RE-APPROVED EACH TIME with NEW tests and NEW bloodwork!
It's VERY COMPLICATED!
For who?
POOT
Well- I should be Fine- I probably only need one IVF cycle...
hee hee!
I'm an earth mother waiting to happen!
WE SHALL SEE!
WE SHALL SEE!
CAW!
WE SHALL SEE!
I'll show her. I'll have a whole litter of IVF babies. And we'll roast her for Thanksgiving.

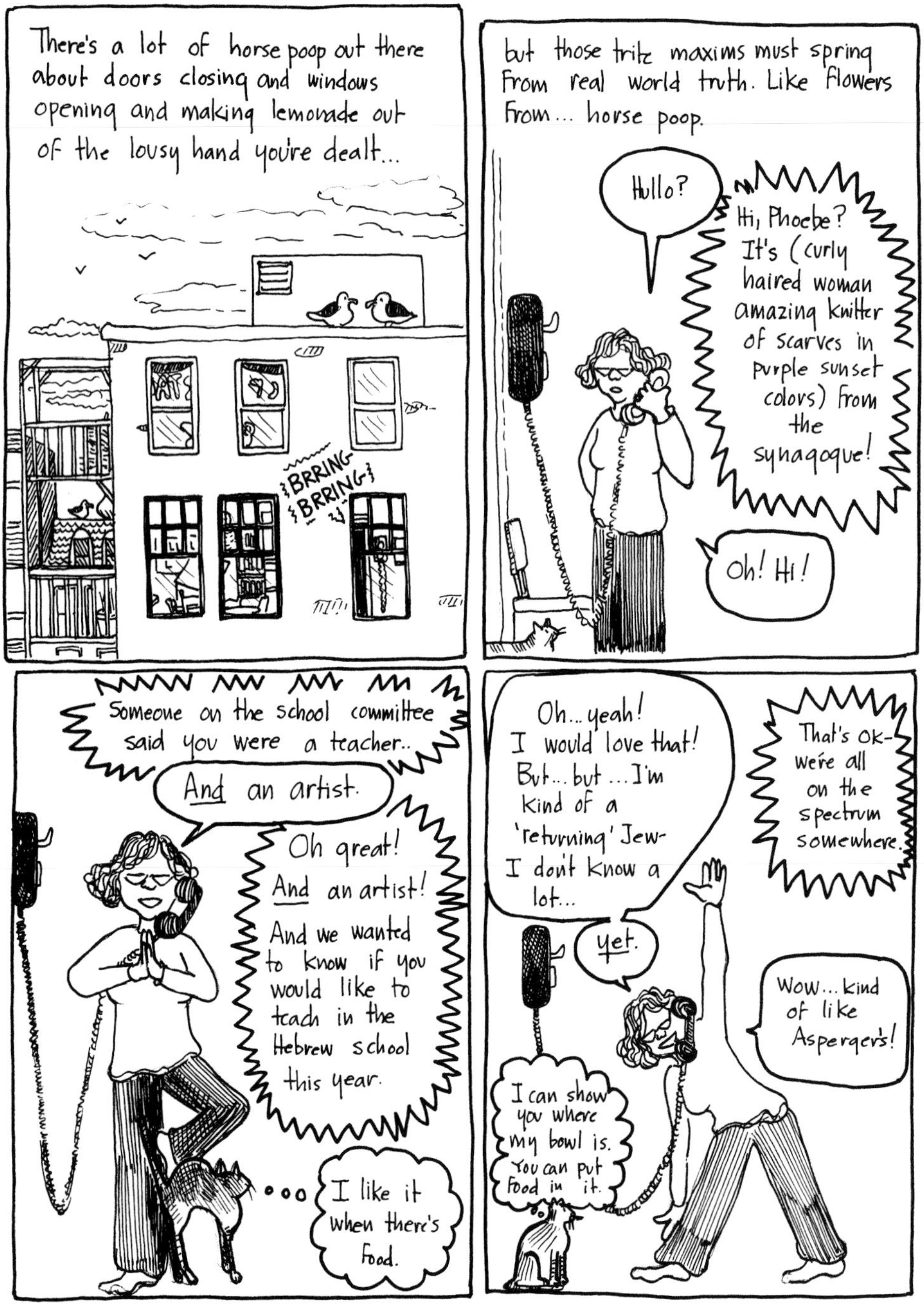
There's a lot of horse poop out there about doors closing and windows opening and making lemonade out of the lousy hand you're dealt...
BRRING BRRING
but those trite maxims must spring from real world truth. Like flowers from... horse poop.
Hullo?
Hi, Phoebe? It's (curly haired woman amazing knitter of scarves in purple sunset colors) from the synagogue!
Oh! Hi!
Someone on the school committee said you were a teacher..
And an artist.
Oh great! And an artist! And we wanted to know if you would like to teach in the Hebrew school this year.
I like it when there's food.
Oh... yeah! I would love that! But... but ... I'm kind of a 'returning' Jew- I don't know a lot...
Yet.
That's OK- we're all on the spectrum somewhere.
Wow... kind of like Aspergers!
I can show you where my bowl is. You can put food in it.

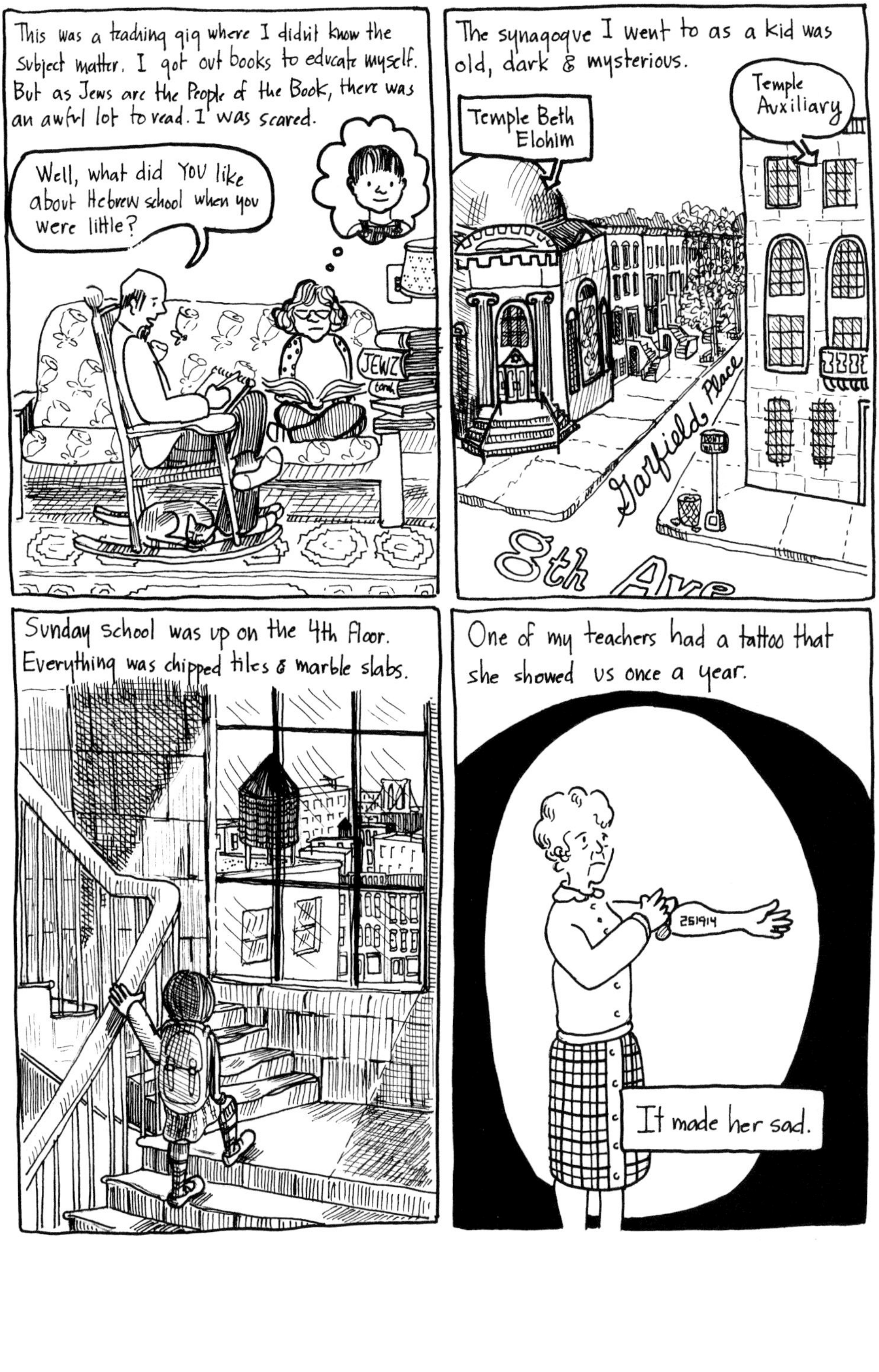
This was a teaching gig where I didn't know the subject matter. I got out books to educate myself. But as Jews are the People of the Book, there was an awful lot to read. I was scared.
Well, what did YOU like about Hebrew school when you were little?
JEWZ
The synagogue I went to as a kid was old, dark & mysterious.
Temple Beth Elohim
Temple Auxiliary
Garfield Place
8th Ave
Sunday school was up on the 4th floor. Everything was chipped tiles & marble slabs.
One of my teachers had a tattoo that she showed us once a year.
251914
It made her sad.

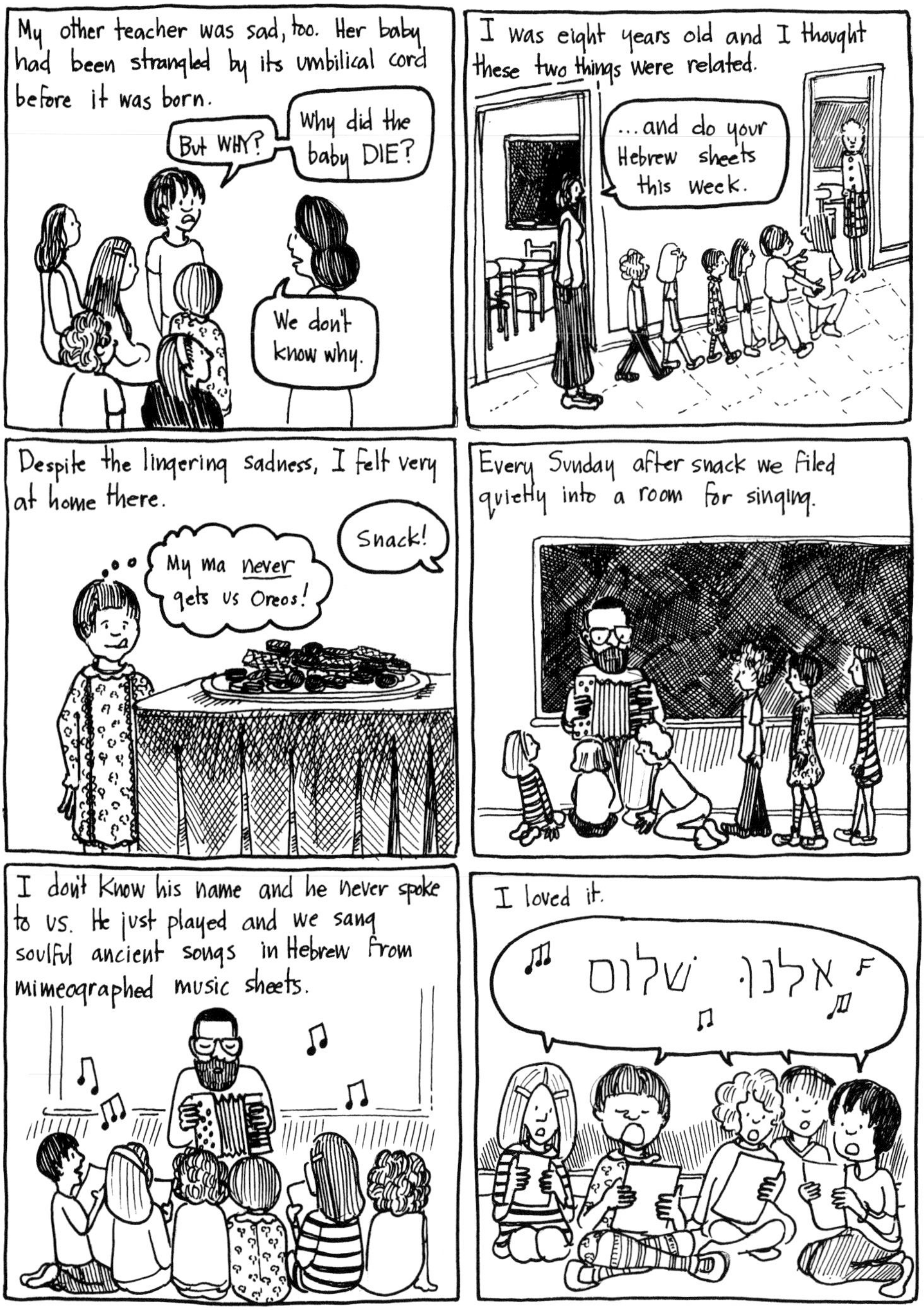
My other teacher was sad, too. Her baby had been strangled by its umbilical cord before it was born.
But WHY?
Why did the baby DIE?
We don't know why.
I was eight years old and I thought these two things were related.
...and do your Hebrew sheets this week.
Despite the lingering sadness, I felt very at home there.
My ma never gets us Oreos!
Snack!
Every Sunday after snack we filed quietly into a room for singing.
I don't know his name and he never spoke to us. He just played and we sang soulful ancient songs in Hebrew from mimeographed music sheets.
I loved it.
אלנו· שלום

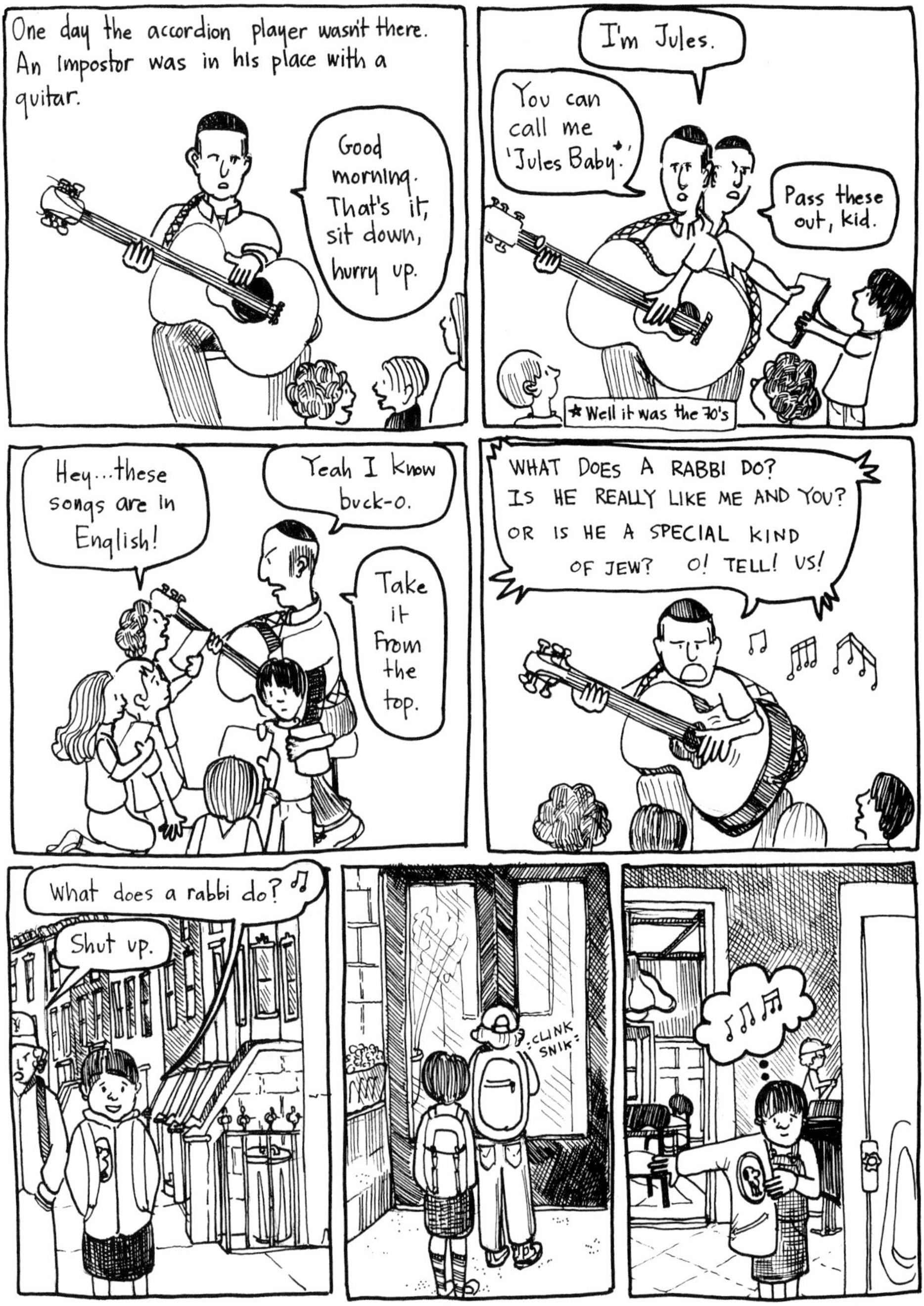
One day the accordion player wasn't there. An impostor was in his place with a quitar.
Good morning. That's it, sit down, hurry up.
I'm Jules.
You can call me 'Jules Baby*.'
Pass these out, kid.
* Well it was the 70's
Hey...these songs are in English!
Yeah I know buck-o.
Take it from the top.
WHAT DOES A RABBI DO? IS HE REALLY LIKE ME AND YOU? OR IS HE A SPECIAL KIND OF JEW? O! TELL! US!
What does a rabbi do?
Shut up.
CLINK SNIK

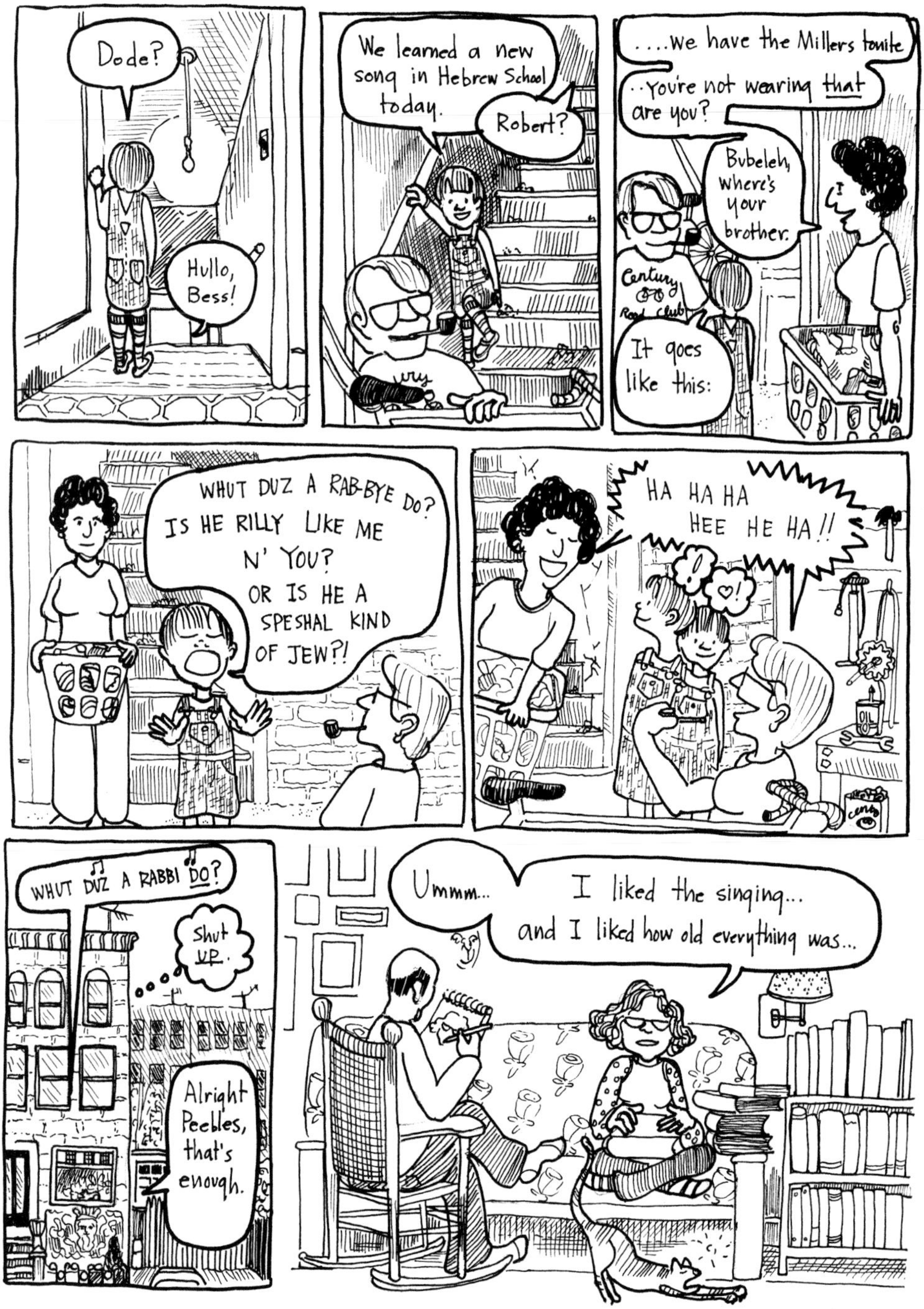
Dode?
Hullo, Bess!
We learned a new song in Hebrew School today.
Robert?
....we have the Millers tonite
..You're not wearing that are you?
Bubeleh, where's your brother.
Century Road Club
It goes like this:
WHUT DUZ A RAB-BYE DO? IS HE RILLY LIKE ME N' YOU? OR IS HE A SPESHAL KIND OF JEW?!
HA HA HA HEE HE HA!!
!
♡!
OIL
WHUT DUZ A RABBI DO?
Shut UP.
Alright Peebles, that's enough.
Ummm...
I liked the singing... and I liked how old everything was...

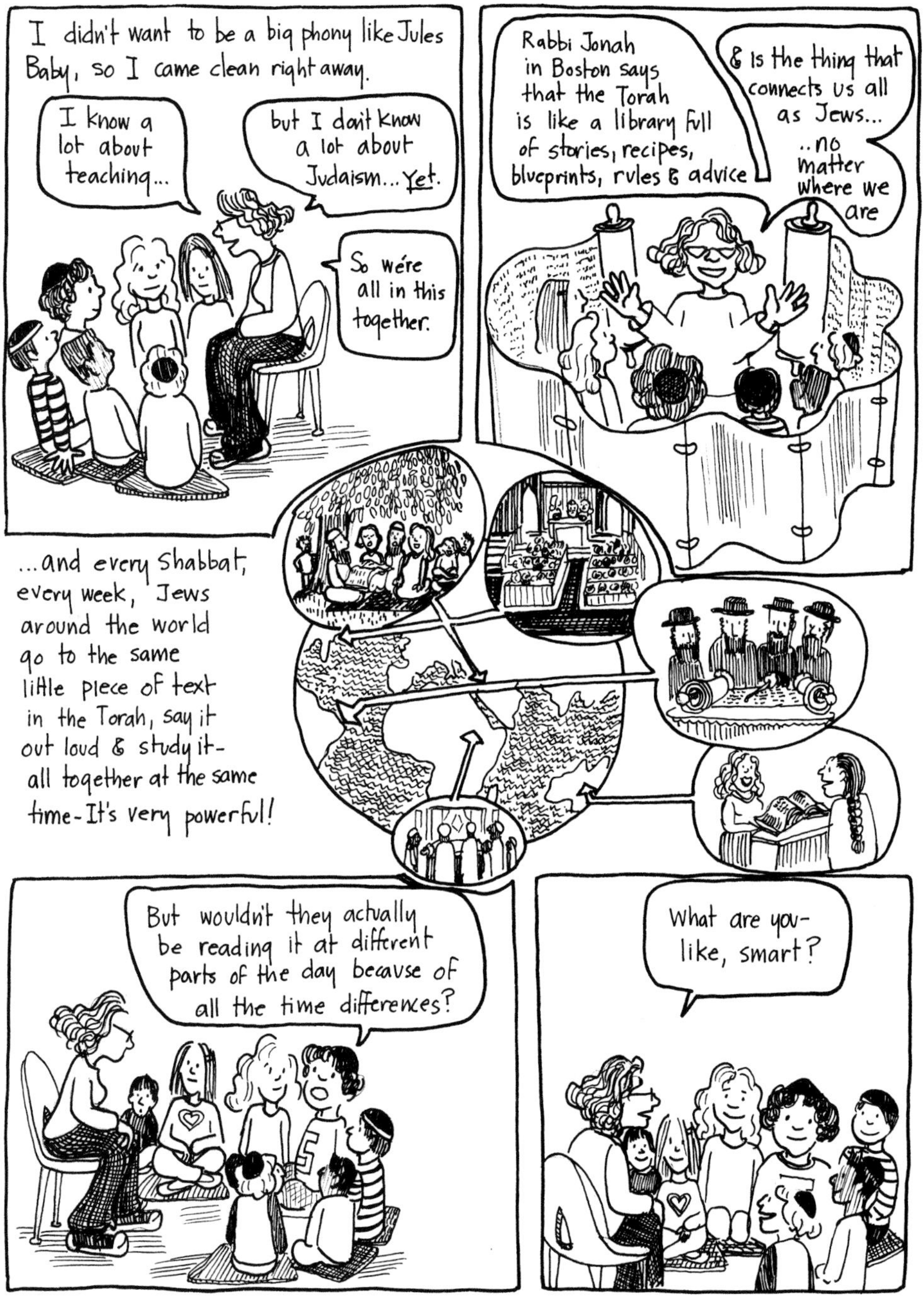
I didn't want to be a big phony like Jules Baby, so I came clean right away.
I know a lot about teaching...
but I don't know a lot about Judaism... Yet.
So we're all in this together.
Rabbi Jonah in Boston says that the Torah is like a library full of stories, recipes, blueprints, rules & advice
& is the thing that connects us all as Jews...
..no matter where we are
...and every Shabbat, every week, Jews around the world go to the same little piece of text in the Torah, say it out loud & study it- all together at the same time- It's very powerful!
But wouldn't they actually be reading it at different parts of the day because of all the time differences?
What are you- like, smart?

As a returning Jew I found I had a lot of questions of my own. This stuff was easy to get excited about. And who better to discuss the spiritual & ethical concerns of what it means to be a Jew in the 21st century than a bunch of 10 year olds?

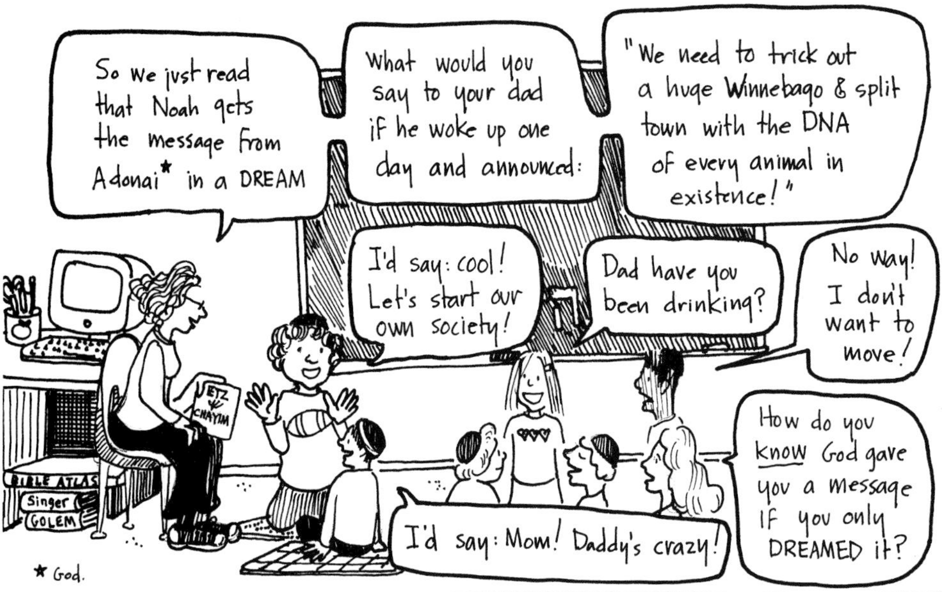
So we just read that Noah gets the message from Adonai* in a DREAM
What would you say to your dad if he woke up one day and announced:
"We need to trick out a huge Winnebago & split town with the DNA of every animal in existence!"
I'd say: cool! Let's start our own society!
Dad have you been drinking?
No way! I don't want to move!
How do you know God gave you a message if you only DREAMED it?
I'd say: Mom! Daddy's crazy!
ETZ CHAYIM
BIBLE ATLAS
Singer
GOLEM

* God.

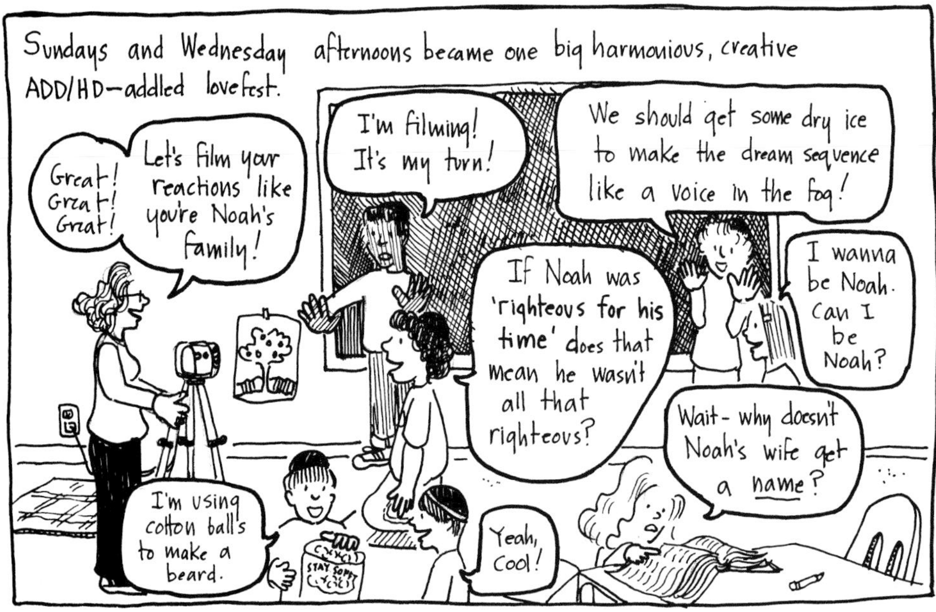
Sundays and Wednesday afternoons became one big harmonious, creative ADD/HD-addled lovefest.
Great! Great! Great!
Let's film your reactions like you're Noah's family!
I'm filming! It's my turn!
We should get some dry ice to make the dream sequence like a voice in the fog!
If Noah was 'righteous for his time' does that mean he wasn't all that righteous?
I wanna be Noah. Can I be Noah?
Wait- why doesn't Noah's wife get a name?
I'm using cotton balls to make a beard.
Yeah, cool!
STAY SOFT

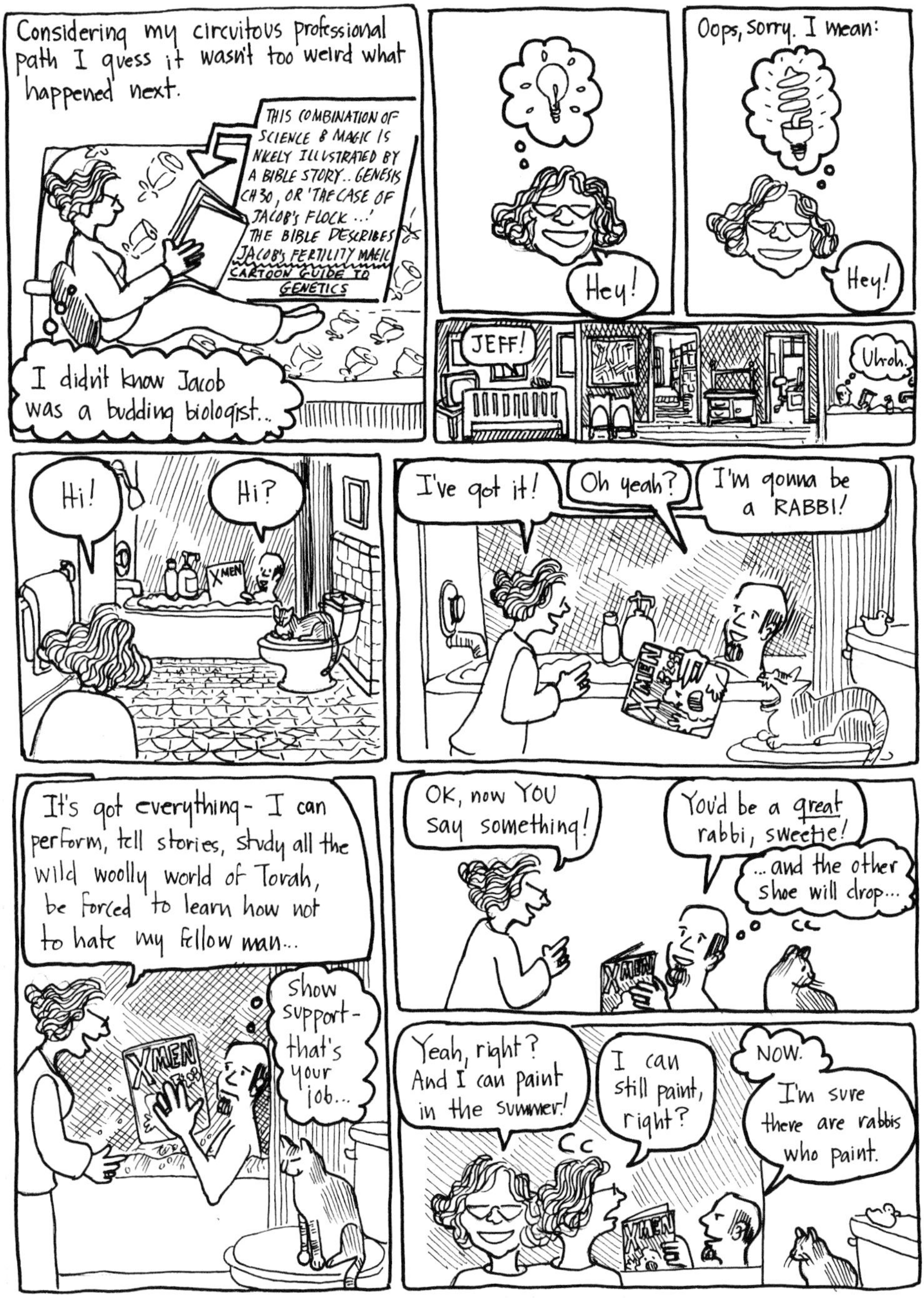

Considering my circuitous professional path I guess it wasn't too weird what happened next.
THIS COMBINATION OF SCIENCE & MAGIC IS NICELY ILLUSTRATED BY A BIBLE STORY.. GENESIS CH 30, OR 'THE CASE OF JACOB'S FLOCK...' THE BIBLE DESCRIBES JACOB'S FERTILITY MAGIC
CARTOON GUIDE TO GENETICS
I didn't know Jacob was a budding biologist...
Hey!
Oops, sorry. I mean:
Hey!
JEFF!
Uh oh.
Hi!
Hi?
X MEN
I've got it!
Oh yeah?
I'm gonna be a RABBI!
It's got everything - I can perform, tell stories, study all the wild woolly world of Torah, be forced to learn how not to hate my fellow man...
Show support - that's your job...
X MEN
OK, now YOU say something!
You'd be a great rabbi, sweetie!
...and the other shoe will drop...
Yeah, right? And I can paint in the summer!
I can still paint, right?
NOW. I'm sure there are rabbis who paint.

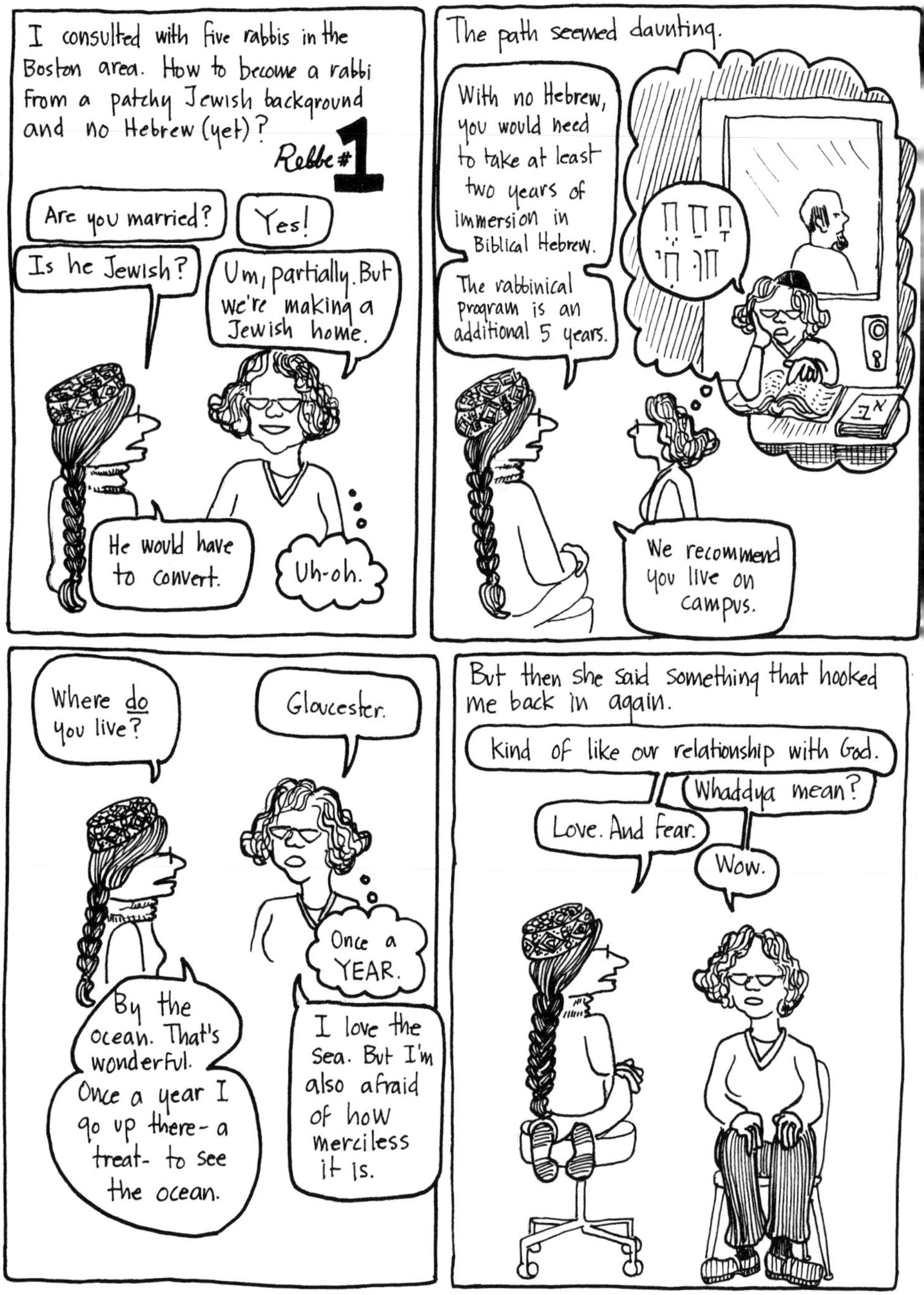

I consulted with five rabbis in the Boston area. How to become a rabbi from a patchy Jewish background and no Hebrew (yet)?
Rebbe #1
Are you married?
Yes!
Is he Jewish?
Um, partially. But we're making a Jewish home.
He would have to convert.
Uh-oh.
The path seemed daunting.
With no Hebrew, you would need to take at least two years of immersion in Biblical Hebrew.
The rabbinical program is an additional 5 years.
We recommend you live on campus.
Where do you live?
Gloucester.
Once a YEAR.
By the ocean. That's wonderful.
Once a year I go up there - a treat - to see the ocean.
I love the sea. But I'm also afraid of how merciless it is.
But then she said something that hooked me back in again.
Kind of like our relationship with God.
Whaddya mean?
Love. And fear.
Wow.

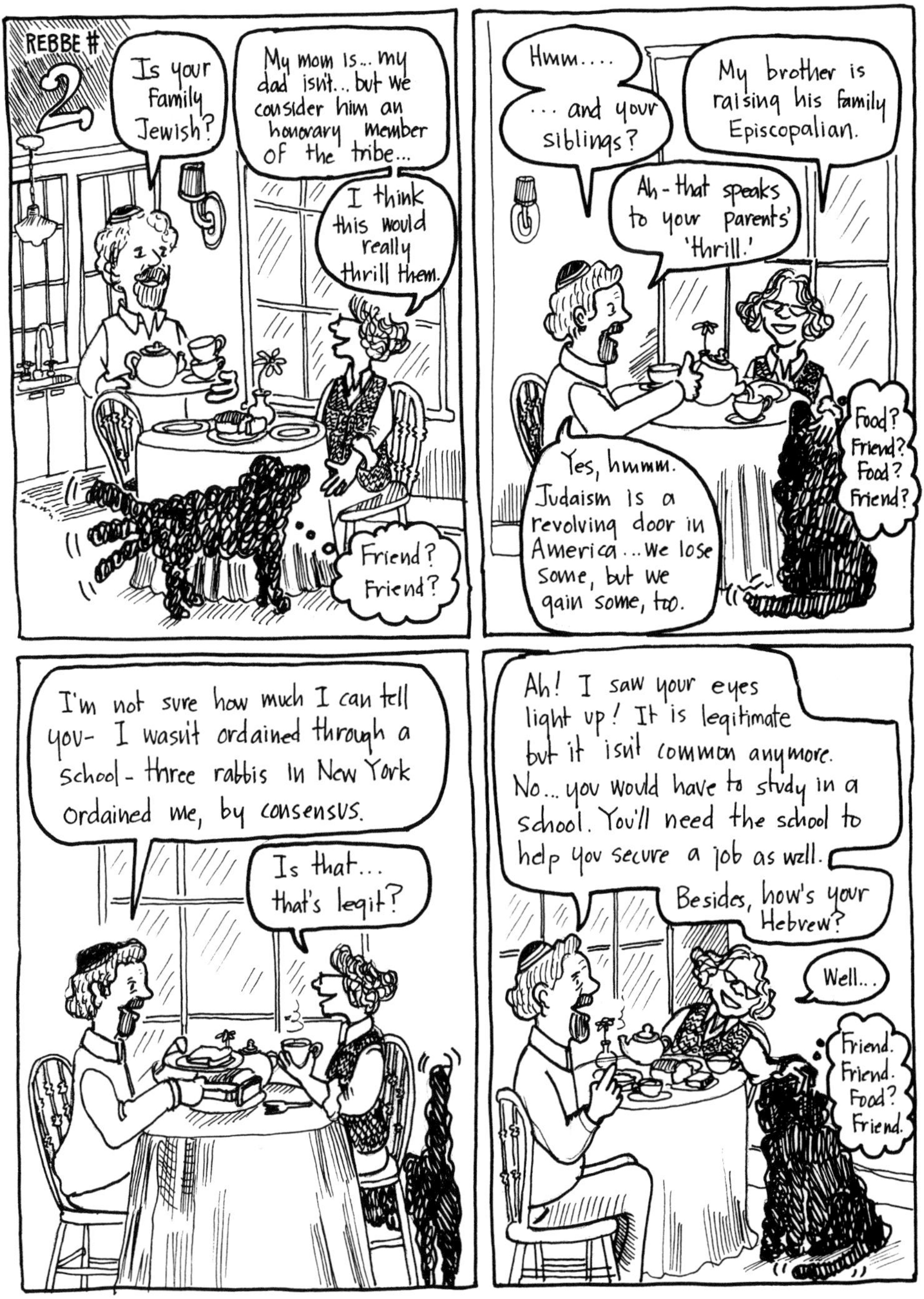
REBBE # 2
Is your family Jewish?
My mom is... my dad isn't... but we consider him an honorary member of the tribe...
I think this would really thrill them.
Friend? Friend?
Hmm....
... and your siblings?
My brother is raising his family Episcopalian.
Ah - that speaks to your parents' 'thrill.'
Yes, hmmm. Judaism is a revolving door in America... we lose some, but we gain some, too.
Food? Friend? Food? Friend?
I'm not sure how much I can tell you- I wasn't ordained through a school - three rabbis in New York ordained me, by consensus.
Is that... that's legit?
Ah! I saw your eyes light up! It is legitimate but it isn't common anymore. No... you would have to study in a school. You'll need the school to help you secure a job as well.
Besides, how's your Hebrew?
Well...
Friend. Friend. Food? Friend.

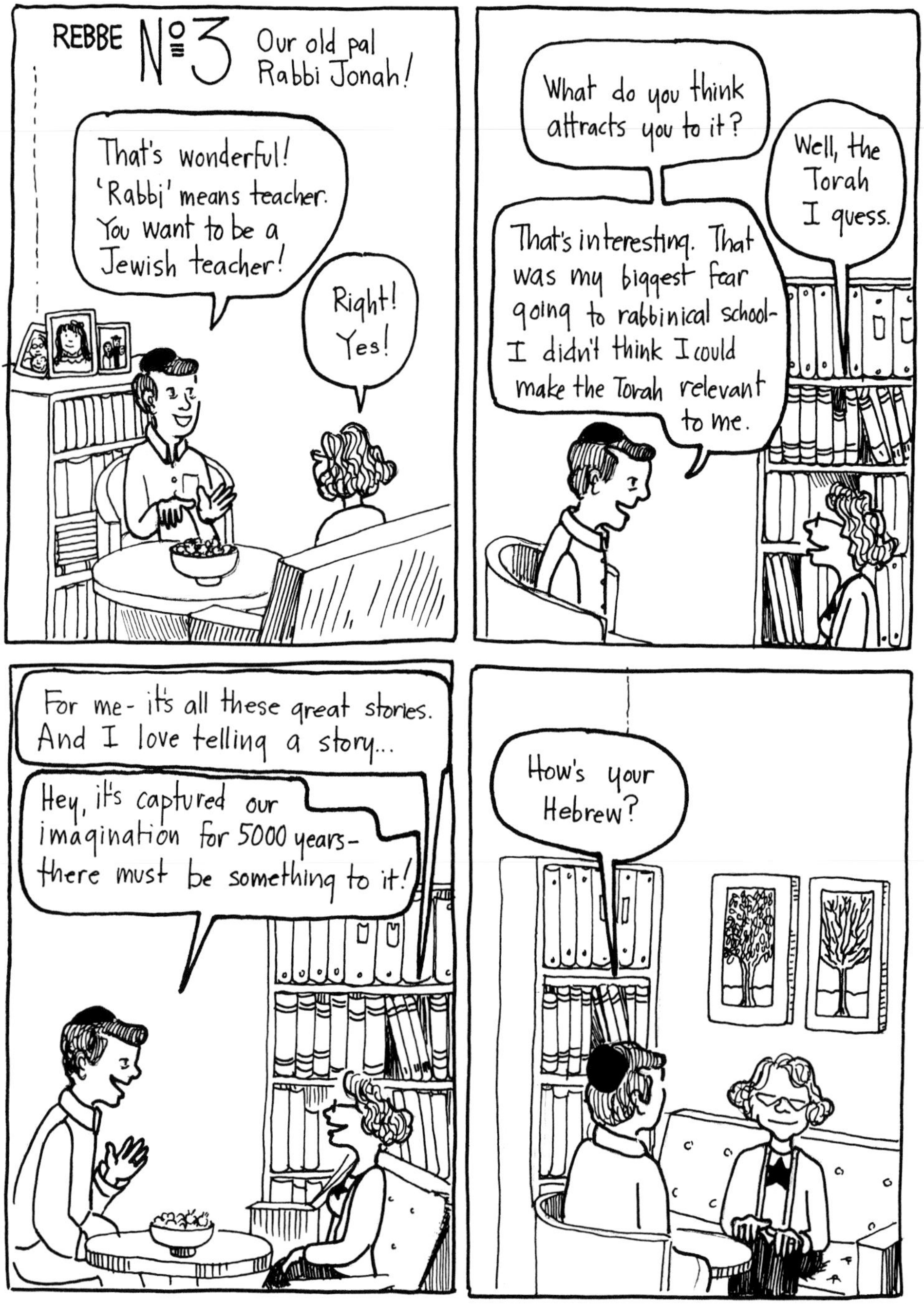
REBBE No 3
Our old pal Rabbi Jonah!
That's wonderful! 'Rabbi' means teacher. You want to be a Jewish teacher!
Right! Yes!
What do you think attracts you to it?
Well, the Torah I guess.
That's interesting. That was my biggest fear going to rabbinical school- I didn't think I could make the Torah relevant to me.
For me- it's all these great stories. And I love telling a story...
Hey, it's captured our imagination for 5000 years- there must be something to it!
How's your Hebrew?

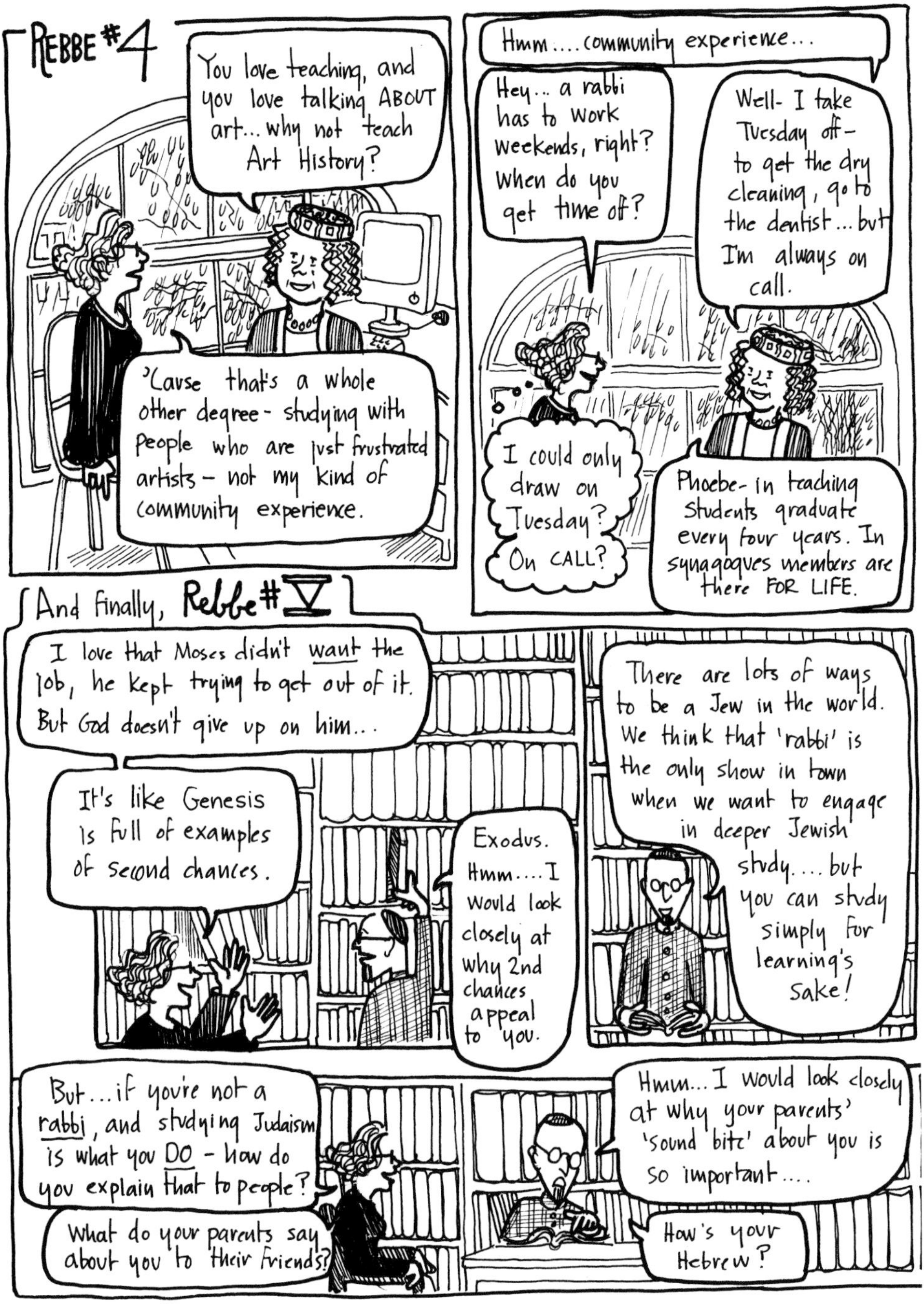
REBBE #4
You love teaching, and you love talking ABOUT art... why not teach Art History?
'Cause that's a whole other degree - studying with people who are just frustrated artists - not my kind of community experience.
Hmm.... community experience...
Hey... a rabbi has to work weekends, right? When do you get time off?
Well- I take Tuesday off - to get the dry cleaning, go to the dentist... but I'm always on call.
I could only draw on Tuesday? On CALL?
Phoebe- in teaching students graduate every four years. In synagogues members are there FOR LIFE.
And finally, Rebbe #V
I love that Moses didn't want the job, he kept trying to get out of it. But God doesn't give up on him...
It's like Genesis is full of examples of second chances.
Exodus. Hmm.... I would look closely at why 2nd chances appeal to you.
There are lots of ways to be a Jew in the world. We think that 'rabbi' is the only show in town when we want to engage in deeper Jewish study.... but you can study simply for learning's sake!
But... if you're not a rabbi, and studying Judaism is what you DO - how do you explain that to people?
What do your parents say about you to their friends?
Hmm... I would look closely at why your parents' 'sound bite' about you is so important....
How's your Hebrew?

I signed up for Biblical Hebrew at the Harvard Divinity School (one of those juicy union perks). The first class was mercilessly straightforward.

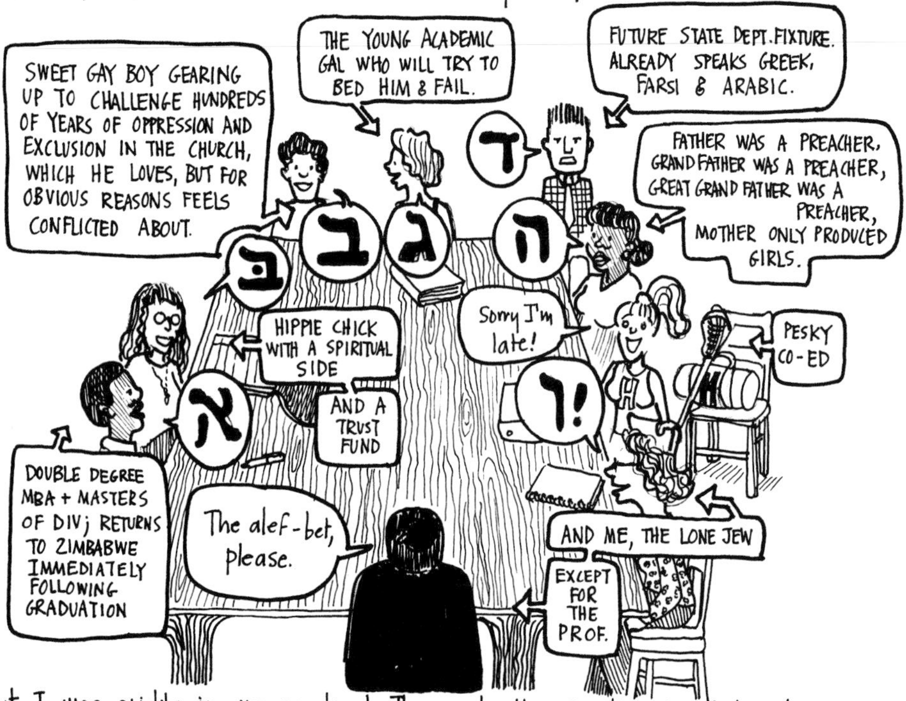
SWEET GAY BOY GEARING UP TO CHALLENGE HUNDREDS OF YEARS OF OPPRESSION AND EXCLUSION IN THE CHURCH, WHICH HE LOVES, BUT FOR OBVIOUS REASONS FEELS CONFLICTED ABOUT.
THE YOUNG ACADEMIC GAL WHO WILL TRY TO BED HIM & FAIL.
FUTURE STATE DEPT. FIXTURE. ALREADY SPEAKS GREEK, FARSI & ARABIC.
FATHER WAS A PREACHER, GRANDFATHER WAS A PREACHER, GREAT GRANDFATHER WAS A PREACHER, MOTHER ONLY PRODUCED GIRLS.
א
בּ
ב
ג
ד
ה
HIPPIE CHICK WITH A SPIRITUAL SIDE
AND A TRUST FUND
Sorry I'm late!
ר!
PESKY CO-ED
DOUBLE DEGREE MBA + MASTERS OF DIV; RETURNS TO ZIMBABWE IMMEDIATELY FOLLOWING GRADUATION
The alef-bet, please.
AND ME, THE LONE JEW
EXCEPT FOR THE PROF.

But I was quickly in over my head. The vowels, the rules, the antiquated syntax. It was all memorization for me because I had no reference for it. I couldn't make it stick.

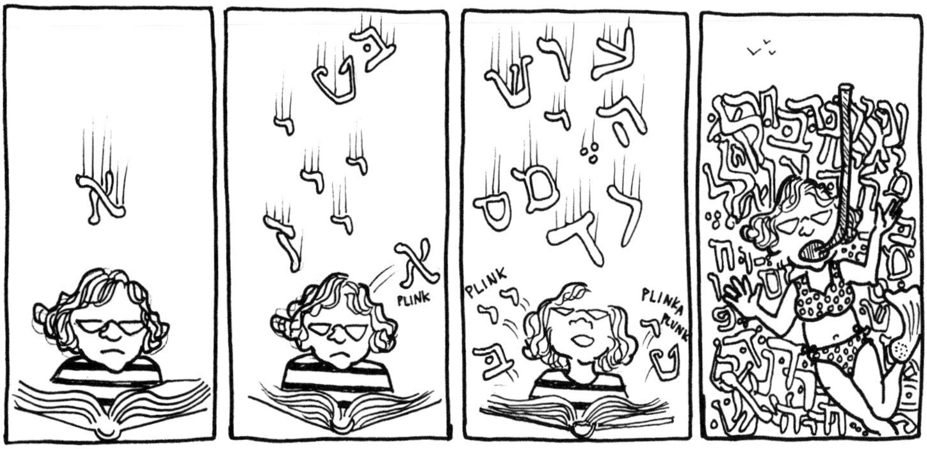
PLINK
PLINK
PLINKA
PLUNK

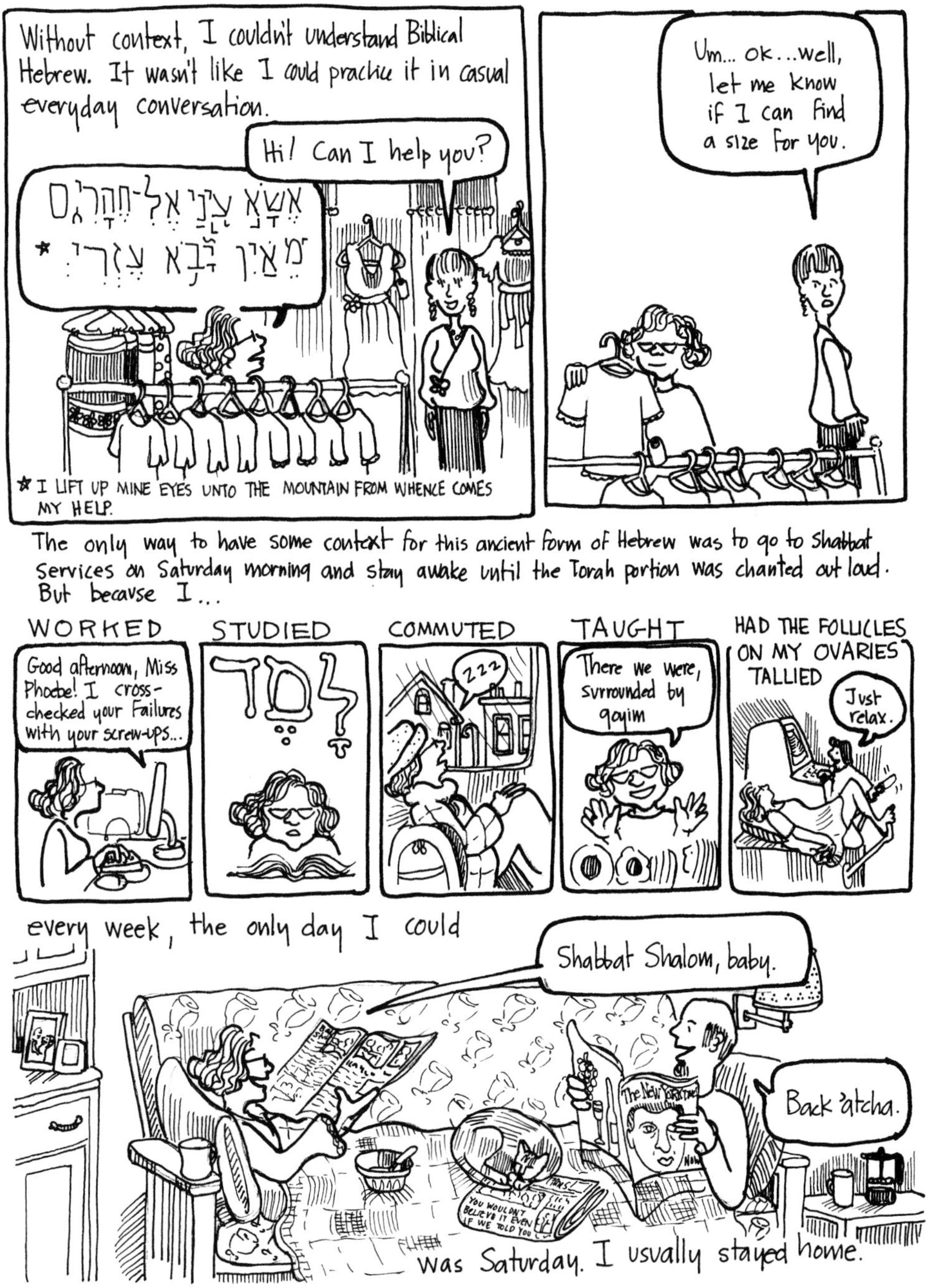
Without context, I couldn't understand Biblical Hebrew. It wasn't like I could practice it in casual everyday conversation.
Hi! Can I help you?
אֶשָּׂא עֵינַי אֶל-הֶהָרִים מֵאַיִן יָבֹא עֶזְרִי *
* I LIFT UP MINE EYES UNTO THE MOUNTAIN FROM WHENCE COMES MY HELP.
Um... ok...well, let me know if I can find a size for you.
The only way to have some context for this ancient form of Hebrew was to go to Shabbat services on Saturday morning and stay awake until the Torah portion was chanted out loud. But because I...
WORKED
Good afternoon, Miss Phoebe! I cross-checked your failures with your screw-ups...
STUDIED
COMMUTED
ZZZ
TAUGHT
There we were, surrounded by goyim
HAD THE FOLLICLES ON MY OVARIES TALLIED
Just relax.
every week, the only day I could
Shabbat Shalom, baby.
Back 'atcha.
YOU WOULDN'T BELIEVE IT EVEN IF WE TOLD YOU
was Saturday. I usually stayed home.

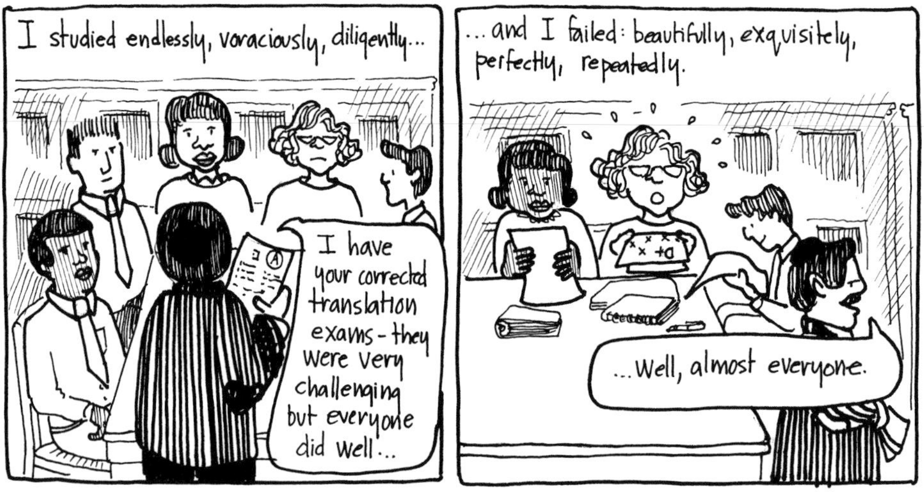
I studied endlessly, voraciously, diligently...
I have your corrected translation exams - they were very challenging but everyone did well...
...and I failed: beautifully, exquisitely, perfectly, repeatedly.
...Well, almost everyone.

Jeff stepped carefully, giving me enough rope to hang myself.

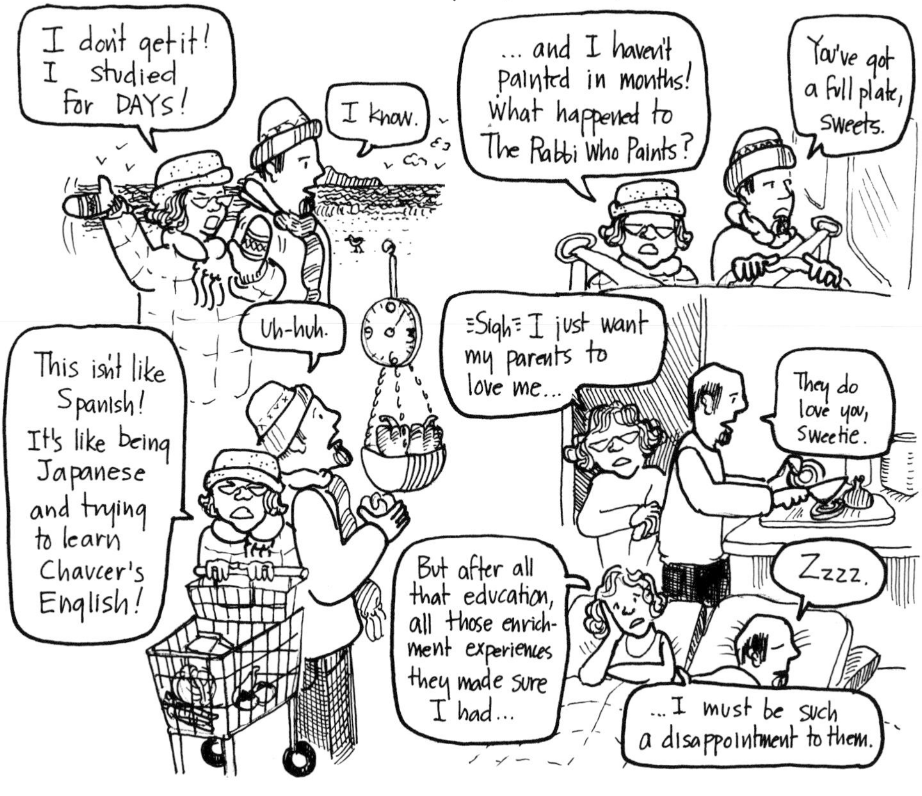
I don't get it! I studied for DAYS!
I know.
... and I haven't painted in months! What happened to The Rabbi Who Paints?
You've got a full plate, sweets.
Uh-huh.
This isn't like Spanish! It's like being Japanese and trying to learn Chaucer's English!
=Sigh= I just want my parents to love me...
They do love you, sweetie.
But after all that education, all those enrichment experiences they made sure I had...
Zzzz.
...I must be such a disappointment to them.

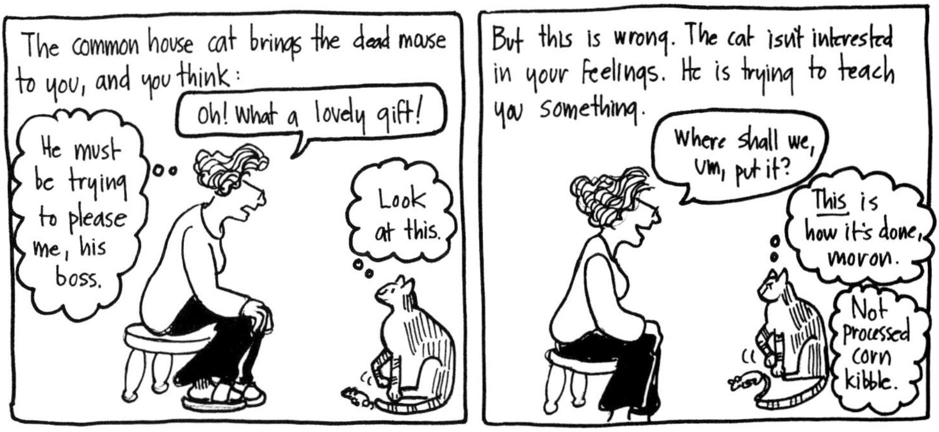
The common house cat brings the dead mouse to you, and you think:
Oh! What a lovely gift!
He must be trying to please me, his boss.
Look at this.
But this is wrong. The cat isn't interested in your feelings. He is trying to teach you something.
Where shall we, um, put it?
This is how it's done, moron.
Not processed corn kibble.

Unlike the cat, my gifts are meant to solicit a specific reaction: 'Phoebe, I love you. You're amazing.' When my parents came to town (to eat Indian food and see the folks at the Beth Israel brain trust for their various ailments) I had a special gift for them, though my ma beat me to it.

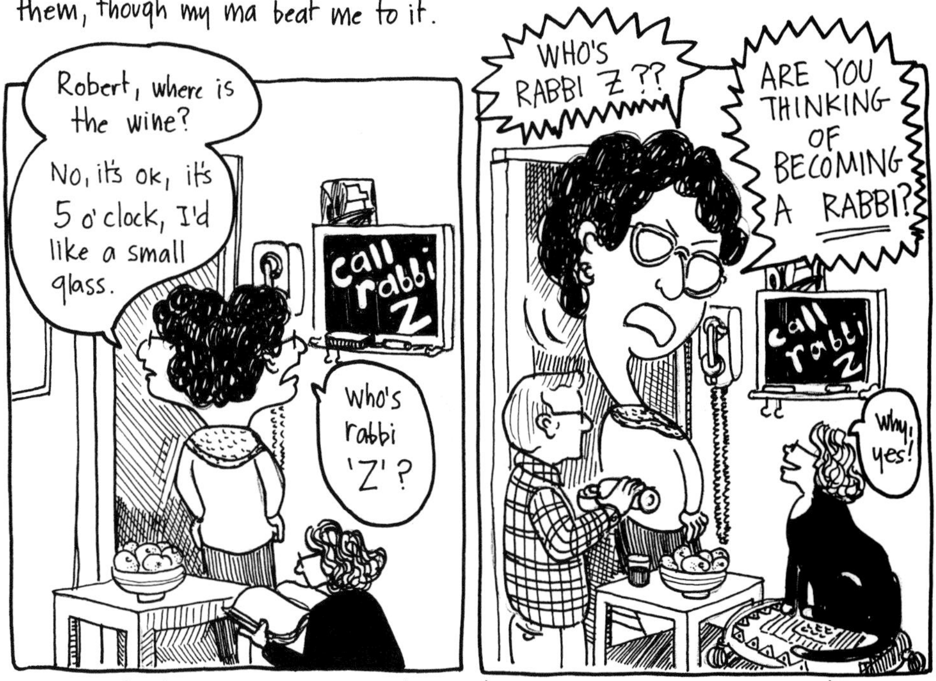
Robert, where is the wine?
No, it's ok, it's 5 o'clock, I'd like a small glass.
call rabbi Z
Who's rabbi 'Z'?
WHO'S RABBI Z??
ARE YOU THINKING OF BECOMING A RABBI?
call rabbi Z
Why, yes!

I thought it was an offering to my teachers, my masters, to show them I understood their wishes of what they wanted me to be.

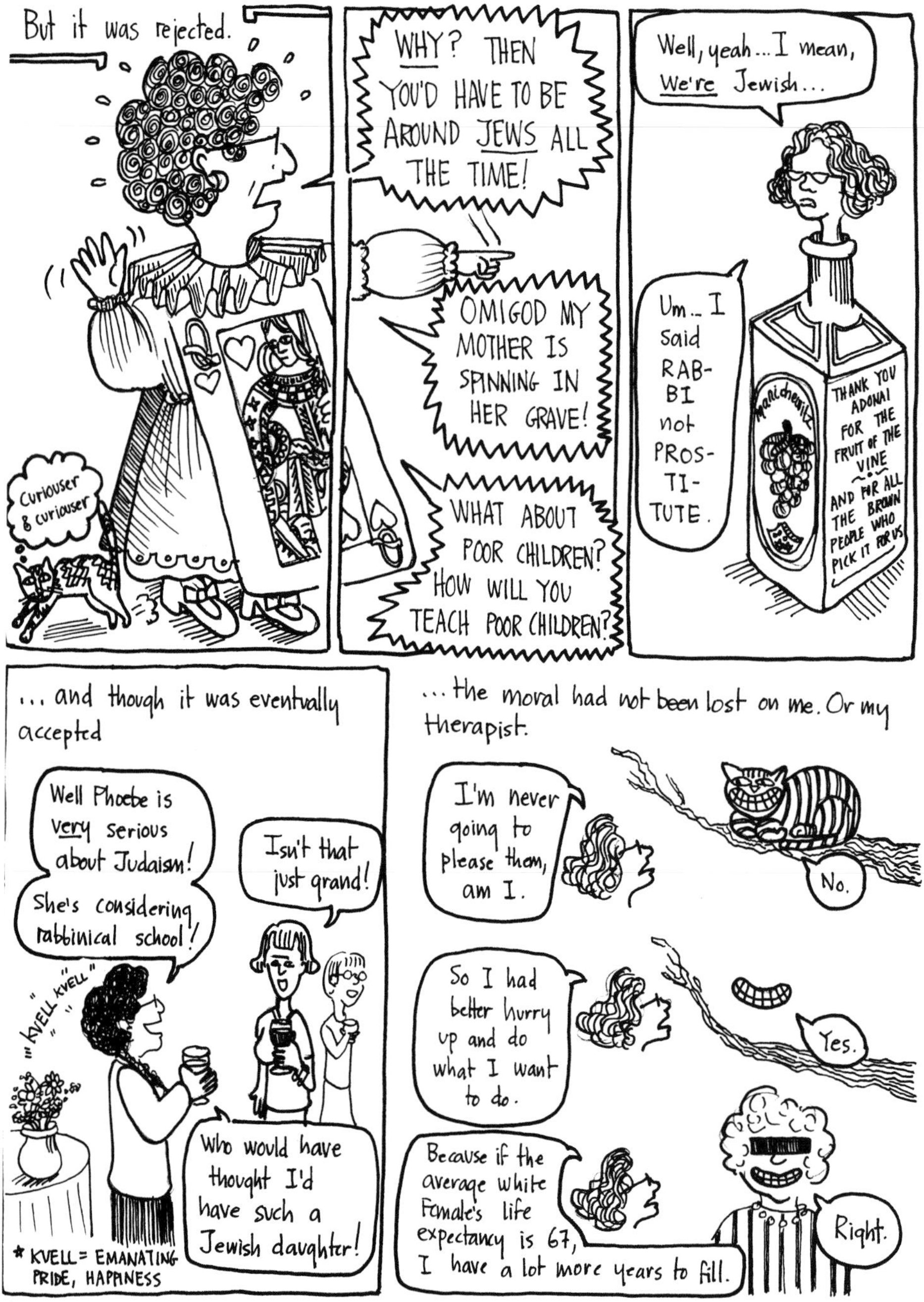
But it was rejected.
WHY? THEN YOU'D HAVE TO BE AROUND JEWS ALL THE TIME!
OMIGOD MY MOTHER IS SPINNING IN HER GRAVE!
WHAT ABOUT POOR CHILDREN? HOW WILL YOU TEACH POOR CHILDREN?
Curiouser & curiouser
Well, yeah... I mean, We're Jewish...
Um... I said RAB-BI not PROS-TI-TUTE.
THANK YOU ADONAI FOR THE FRUIT OF THE VINE AND FOR ALL THE BROWN PEOPLE WHO PICK IT FOR US
... and though it was eventually accepted
Well Phoebe is very serious about Judaism!
She's considering rabbinical school!
Isn't that just grand!
"KVELL KVELL"
Who would have thought I'd have such a Jewish daughter!
* KVELL = EMANATING PRIDE, HAPPINESS
... the moral had not been lost on me. Or my therapist.
I'm never going to please them, am I.
No.
So I had better hurry up and do what I want to do.
Yes.
Because if the average white Female's life expectancy is 67, I have a lot more years to fill.
Right.

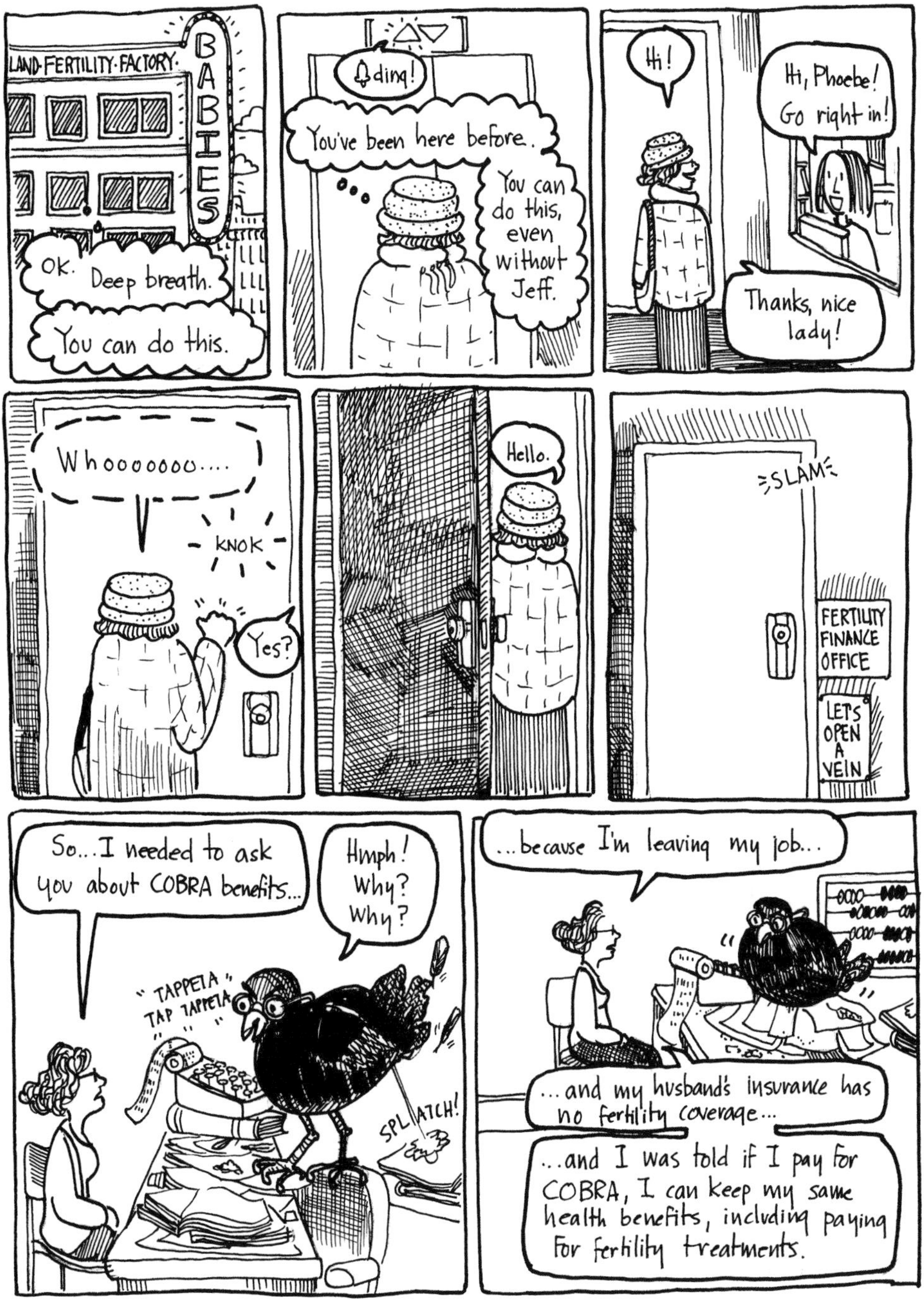
LAND·FERTILITY·FACTORY·
BABIES
OK. Deep breath.
You can do this.
ding!
You've been here before.
You can do this, even without Jeff.
Hi!
Hi, Phoebe! Go right in!
Thanks, nice lady!
Whooooooo....
KNOK
Yes?
Hello.
SLAM
FERTILITY FINANCE OFFICE
LET'S OPEN A VEIN
So... I needed to ask you about COBRA benefits...
TAPPETA TAP TAPPETA
Hmph! Why? Why?
SPLATCH!
...because I'm leaving my job...
...and my husband's insurance has no fertility coverage...
...and I was told if I pay for COBRA, I can keep my same health benefits, including paying for fertility treatments.

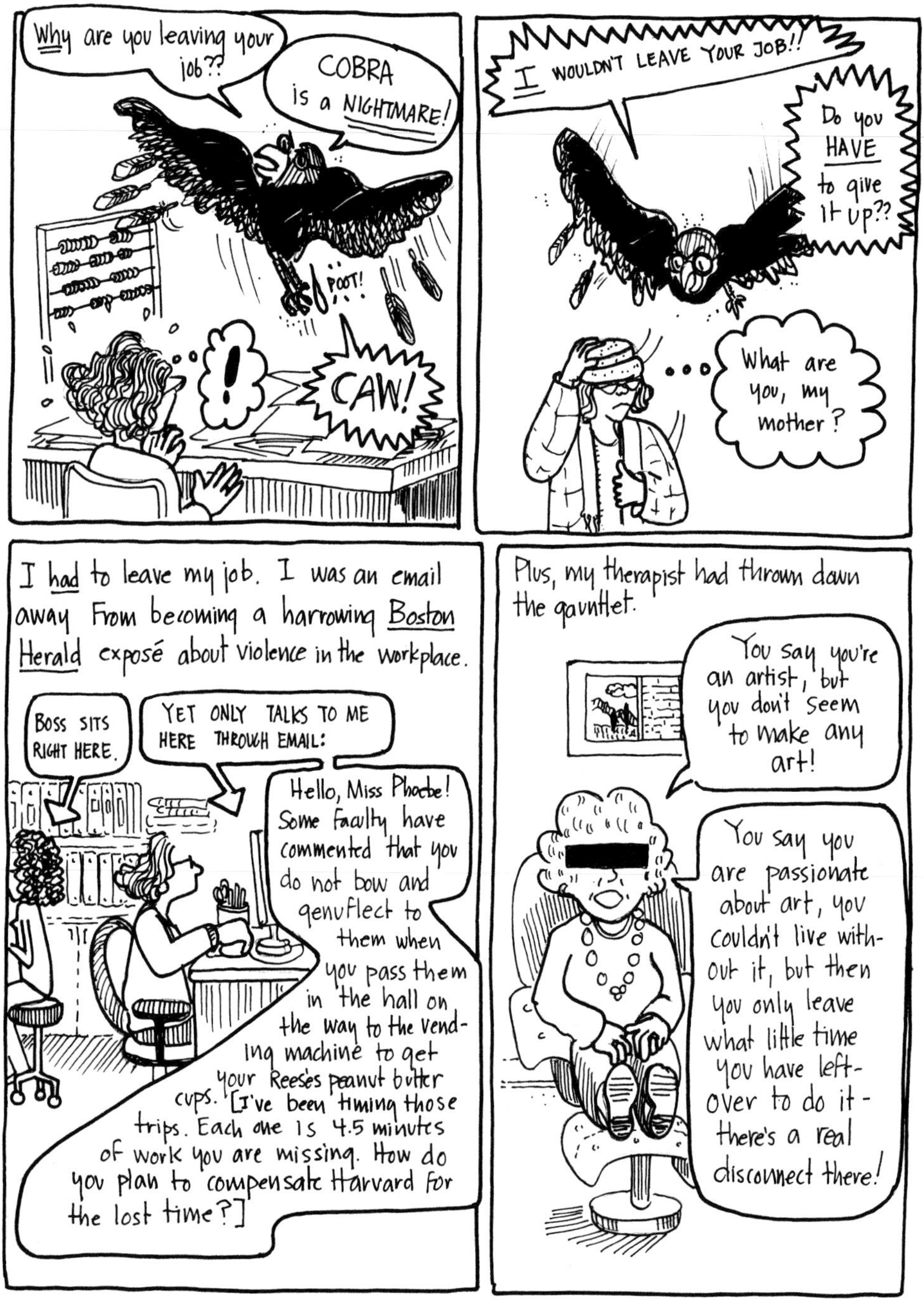
Why are you leaving your job??
COBRA is a NIGHTMARE!
POOT!
!
CAW!
I WOULDN'T LEAVE YOUR JOB!!
Do you HAVE to give it up??
What are you, my mother?
I had to leave my job. I was an email away from becoming a harrowing Boston Herald exposé about violence in the workplace.
BOSS SITS RIGHT HERE.
YET ONLY TALKS TO ME HERE THROUGH EMAIL:
Hello, Miss Phoebe! Some faculty have commented that you do not bow and genuflect to them when you pass them in the hall on the way to the vending machine to get your Reese's peanut butter cups. [I've been timing those trips. Each one is 4.5 minutes of work you are missing. How do you plan to compensate Harvard for the lost time?]
Plus, my therapist had thrown down the gauntlet.
You say you're an artist, but you don't seem to make any art!
You say you are passionate about art, you couldn't live without it, but then you only leave what little time you have leftover to do it - there's a real disconnect there!

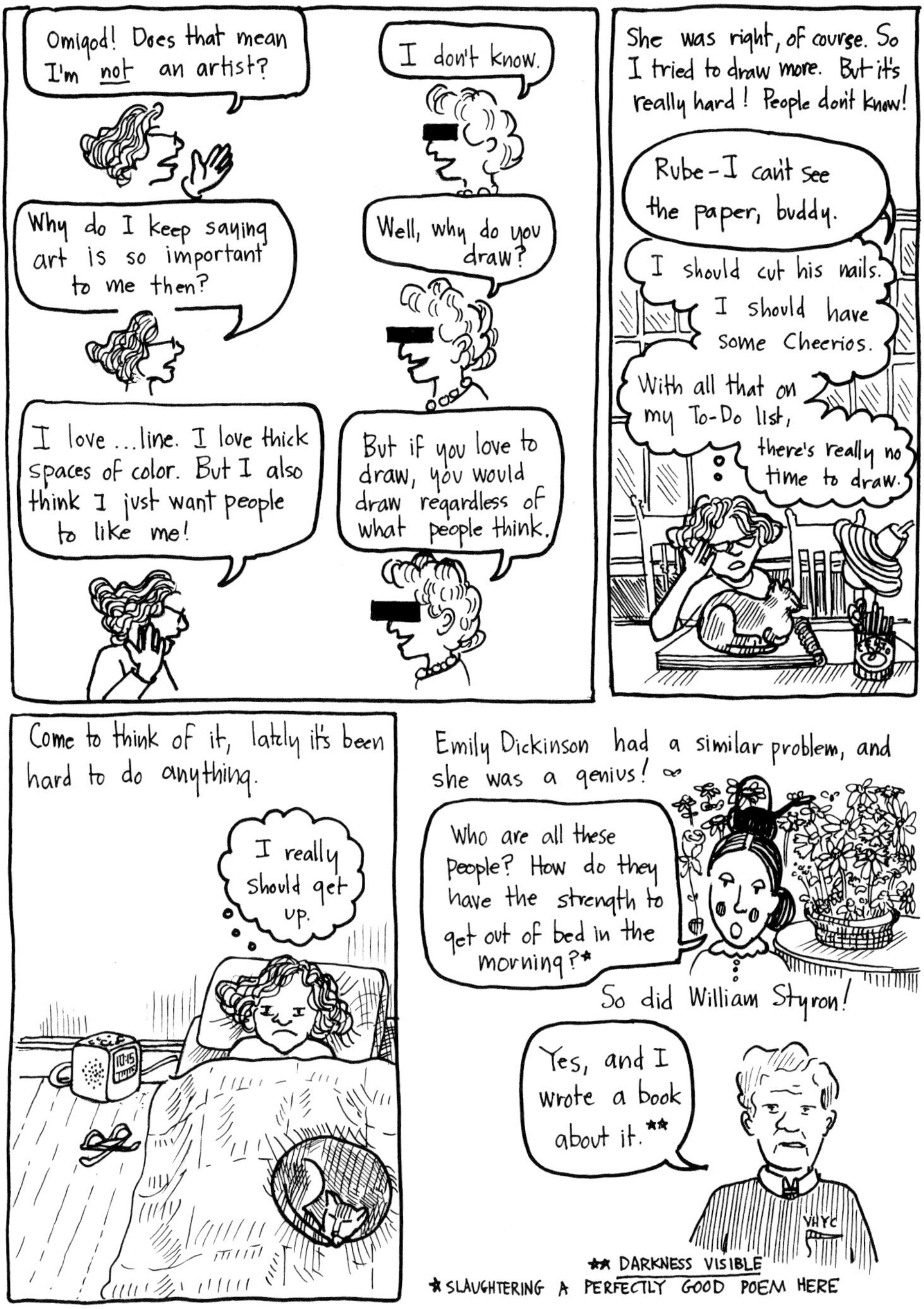
Omigod! Does that mean I'm not an artist?
I don't know.
Why do I keep saying art is so important to me then?
Well, why do you draw?
I love ...line. I love thick spaces of color. But I also think I just want people to like me!
But if you love to draw, you would draw regardless of what people think.
She was right, of course. So I tried to draw more. But it's really hard! People don't know!
Rube - I can't see the paper, buddy.
I should cut his nails.
I should have some Cheerios.
With all that on my To-Do list,
there's really no time to draw.
Come to think of it, lately it's been hard to do anything.
I really should get up.
10:15
Emily Dickinson had a similar problem, and she was a genius!
Who are all these people? How do they have the strength to get out of bed in the morning?*
So did William Styron!
Yes, and I wrote a book about it.**
YHYC
** DARKNESS VISIBLE
* SLAUGHTERING A PERFECTLY GOOD POEM HERE

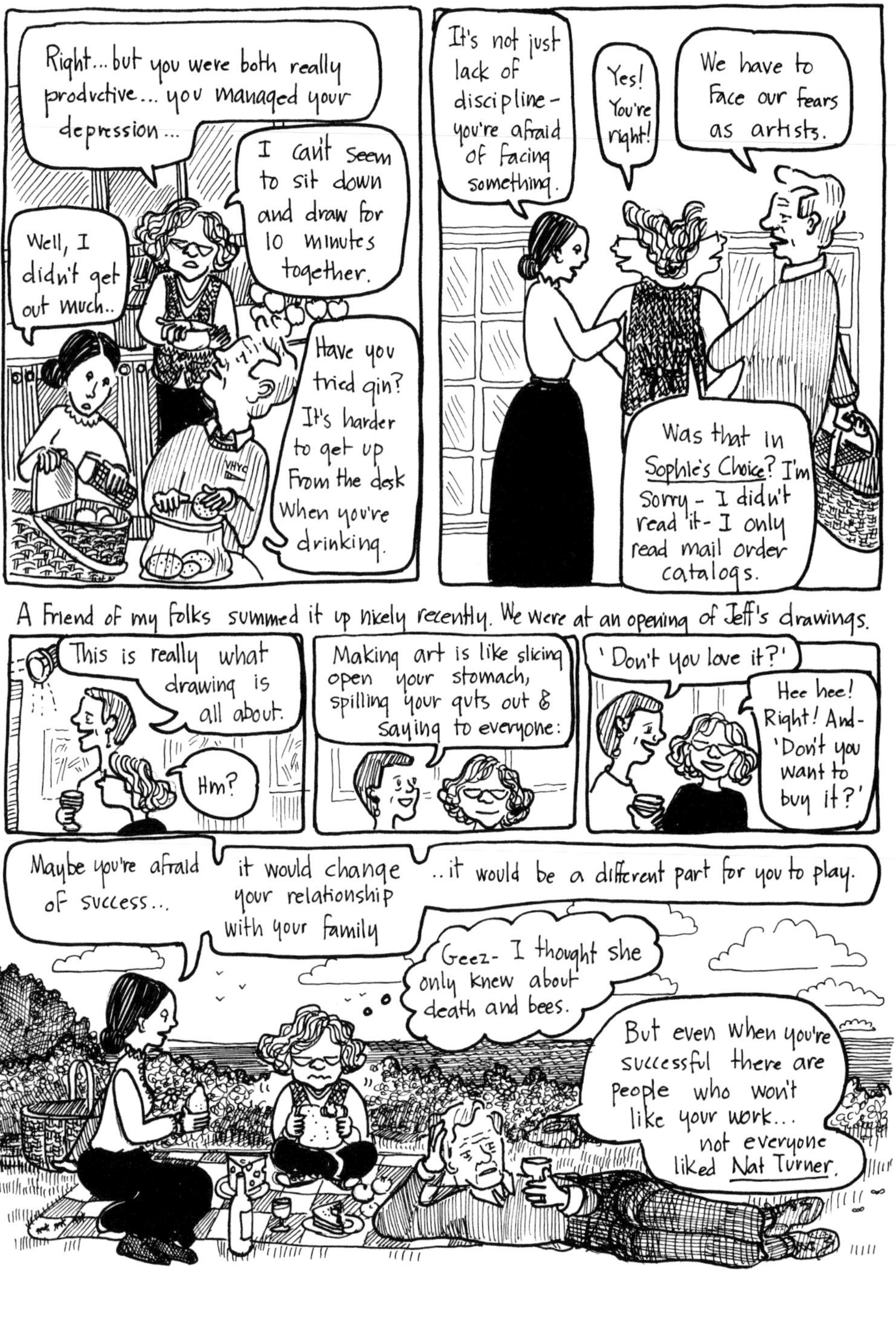
Right... but you were both really productive... you managed your depression...
Well, I didn't get out much..
I can't seem to sit down and draw for 10 minutes together.
Have you tried gin? It's harder to get up from the desk when you're drinking.
VHYC
It's not just lack of discipline - you're afraid of facing something.
Yes! You're right!
We have to face our fears as artists.
Was that in Sophie's Choice? I'm sorry - I didn't read it - I only read mail order catalogs.
A Friend of my folks summed it up nicely recently. We were at an opening of Jeff's drawings.
This is really what drawing is all about.
Hm?
Making art is like slicing open your stomach, spilling your guts out & saying to everyone:
'Don't you love it?'
Hee hee! Right! And- 'Don't you want to buy it?'
Maybe you're afraid of success...
it would change your relationship with your family
..it would be a different part for you to play.
Geez- I thought she only knew about death and bees.
But even when you're successful there are people who won't like your work... not everyone liked Nat Turner.

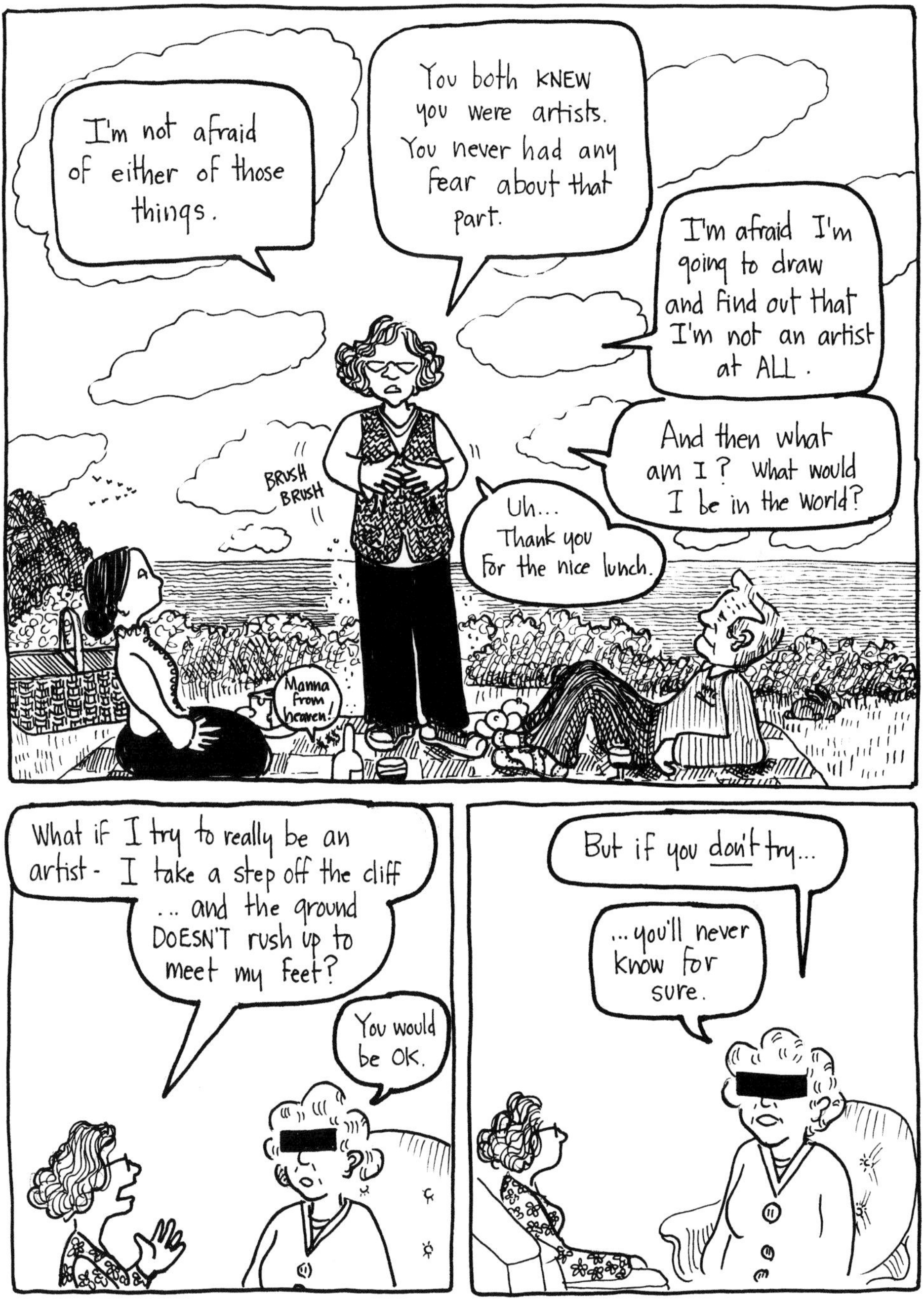
I'm not afraid of either of those things.
You both KNEW you were artists. You never had any fear about that part.
I'm afraid I'm going to draw and find out that I'm not an artist at ALL.
And then what am I? What would I be in the world?
BRUSH BRUSH
Uh... Thank you for the nice lunch.
Manna from heaven!
What if I try to really be an artist - I take a step off the cliff ... and the ground DOESN'T rush up to meet my feet?
You would be OK.
But if you don't try...
...you'll never know for sure.

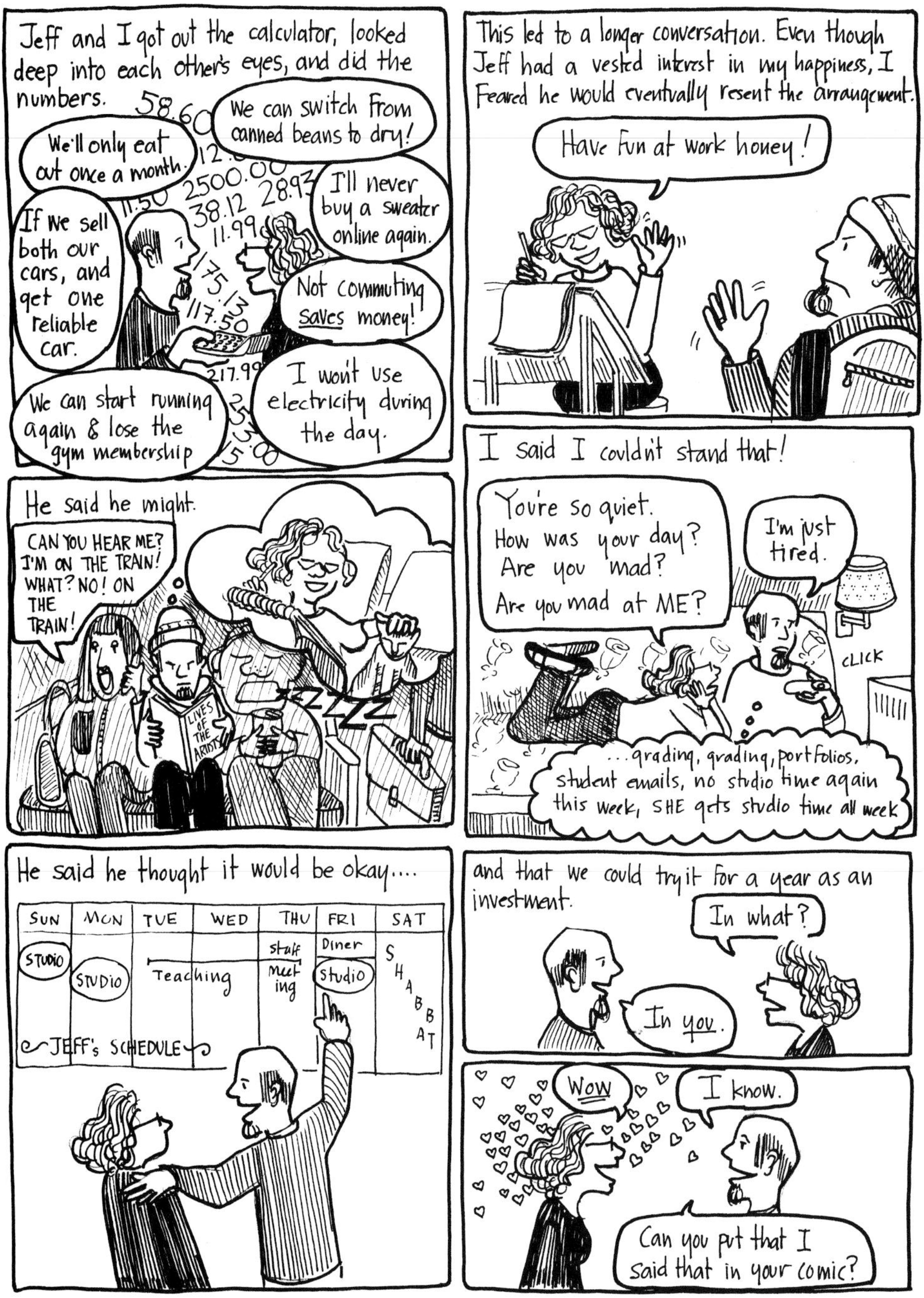
Jeff and I got out the calculator, looked deep into each other's eyes, and did the numbers.
We'll only eat out once a month.
We can switch from canned beans to dry!
I'll never buy a sweater online again.
If we sell both our cars, and get one reliable car.
Not commuting saves money!
We can start running again & lose the gym membership
I won't use electricity during the day.
This led to a longer conversation. Even though Jeff had a vested interest in my happiness, I feared he would eventually resent the arrangement.
Have fun at work honey!
He said he might.
CAN YOU HEAR ME? I'M ON THE TRAIN! WHAT? NO! ON THE TRAIN!
LIVES OF THE ARTISTS
ZZZZ
I said I couldn't stand that!
You're so quiet. How was your day? Are you mad? Are you mad at ME?
I'm just tired.
CLICK
...grading, grading, portfolios, student emails, no studio time again this week, SHE gets studio time all week
He said he thought it would be okay....
SUN MON TUE WED THU FRI SAT
STUDIO STUDIO Teaching Staff Meeting Diner Studio SHABBAT
JEFF's SCHEDULE
and that we could try it for a year as an investment.
In what?
In you.
Wow
I know.
Can you put that I said that in your comic?

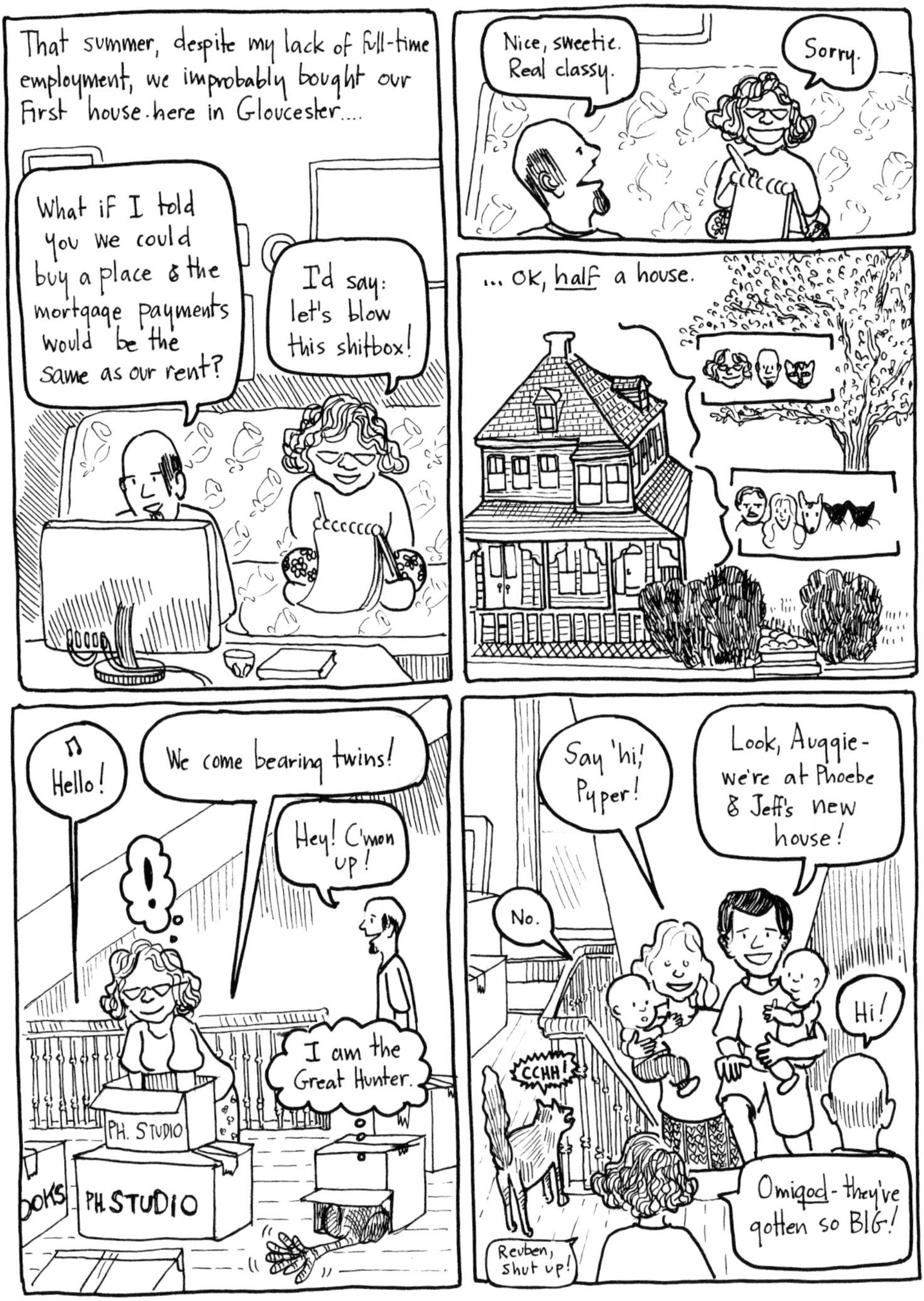
That summer, despite my lack of full-time employment, we improbably bought our First house here in Gloucester....
What if I told you we could buy a place & the mortgage payments would be the same as our rent?
I'd say: let's blow this shitbox!
Nice, sweetie. Real classy.
Sorry.
... OK, half a house.
♫ Hello!
We come bearing twins!
Hey! C'mon up!
!
I am the Great Hunter.
PH. STUDIO
BOOKS
PH. STUDIO
Say 'hi,' Pyper!
Look, Auggie- we're at Phoebe & Jeff's new house!
No.
Hi!
CCHH!
Omigod- they've gotten so BIG!
Reuben, shut up!

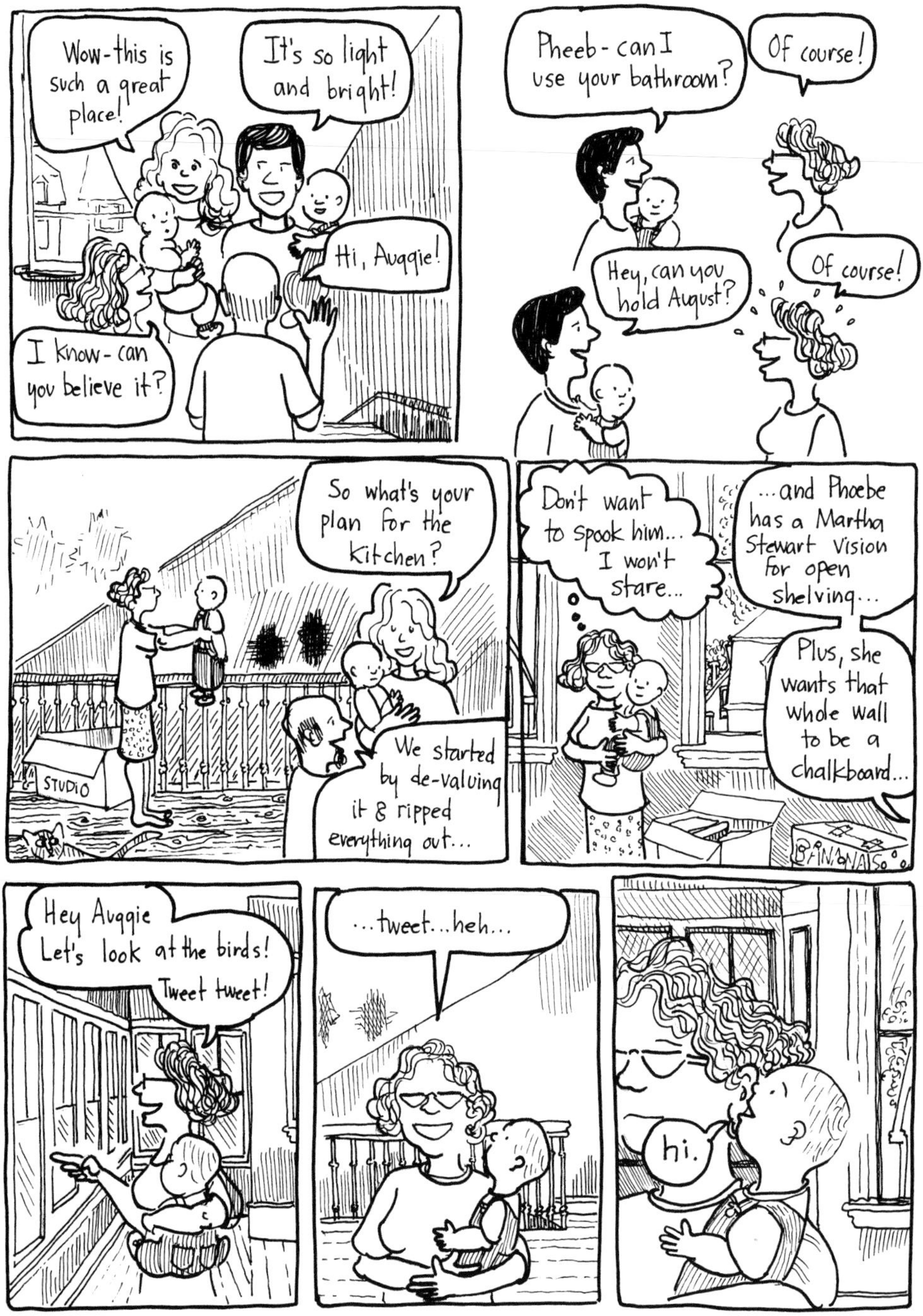
Wow-this is such a great place!
It's so light and bright!
Hi, Auggie!
I know-can you believe it?
Pheeb-can I use your bathroom?
Of course!
Hey, can you hold August?
Of course!
So what's your plan for the kitchen?
We started by de-valuing it & ripped everything out...
STUDIO
Don't want to spook him... I won't stare...
...and Phoebe has a Martha Stewart vision for open shelving...
Plus, she wants that whole wall to be a chalkboard...
Hey Auggie Let's look at the birds! Tweet tweet!
...tweet...heh...
hi.

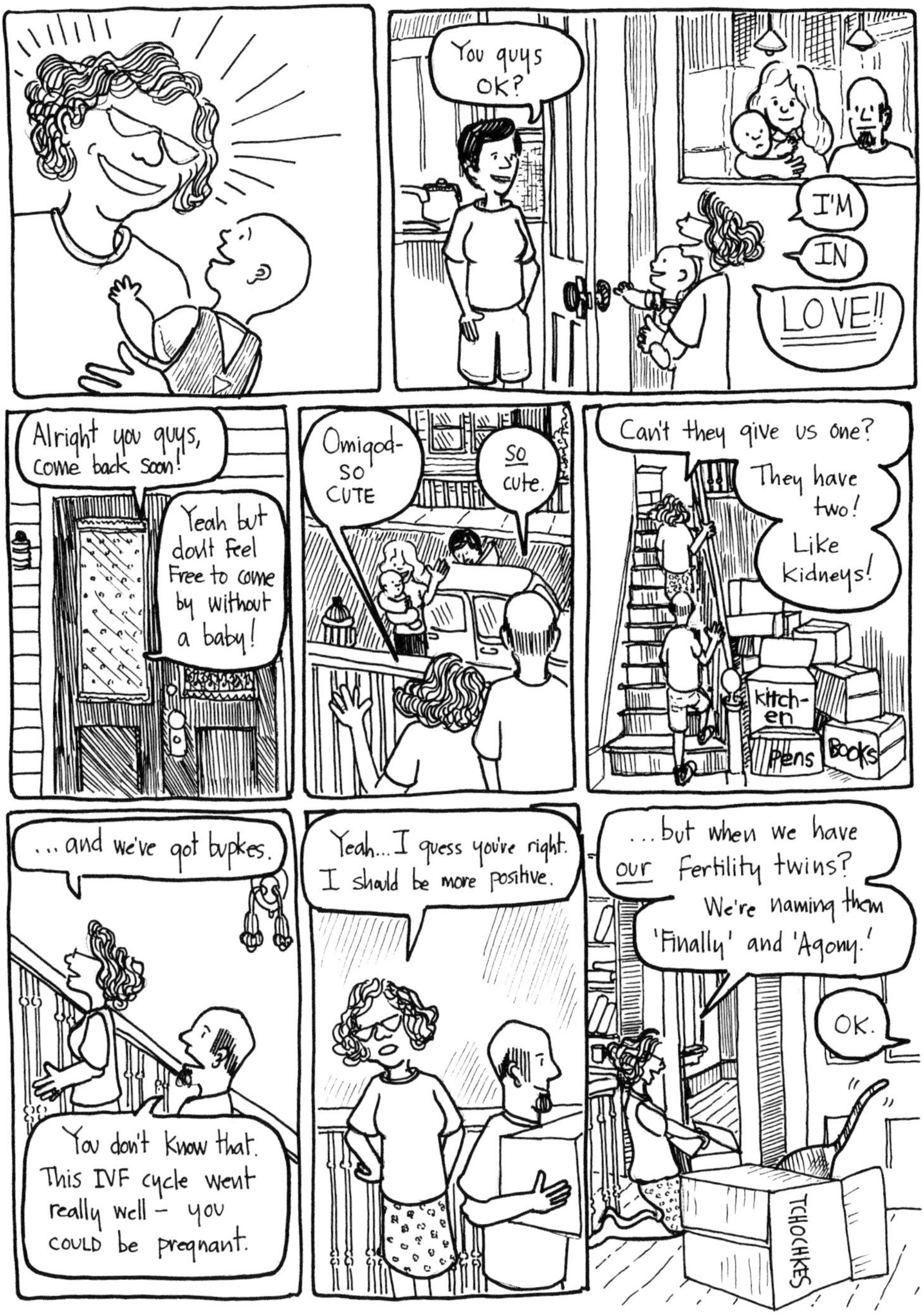
You guys OK?
I'M
IN
LOVE!!
Alright you guys, come back soon!
Yeah but don't feel free to come by without a baby!
Omigod- SO CUTE
SO cute.
Can't they give us one?
They have two! Like kidneys!
kitchen
Pens
Books
... and we've got bupkes.
You don't know that. This IVF cycle went really well - you COULD be pregnant.
Yeah... I guess you're right. I should be more positive.
...but when we have our fertility twins?
We're naming them 'Finally' and 'Agony.'
OK.
TCHOCHKES

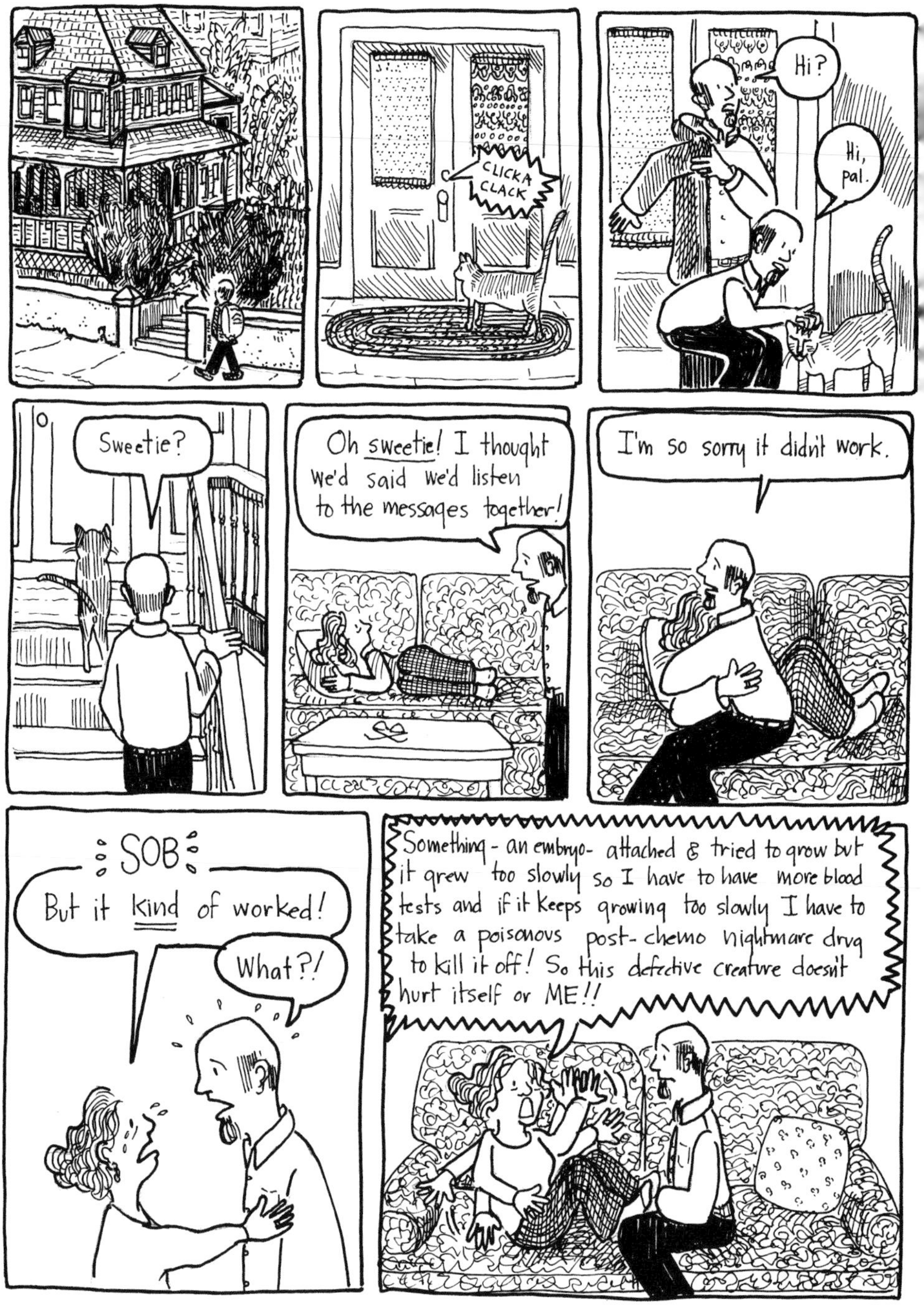
CLICKA CLACK
Hi?
Hi, pal.
Sweetie?
Oh sweetie! I thought we'd said we'd listen to the messages together!
I'm so sorry it didn't work.
SOB
But it kind of worked!
What?!
Something - an embryo- attached & tried to grow but it grew too slowly so I have to have more blood tests and if it keeps growing too slowly I have to take a poisonous post-chemo nightmare drug to kill it off! So this defective creature doesn't hurt itself or ME!!

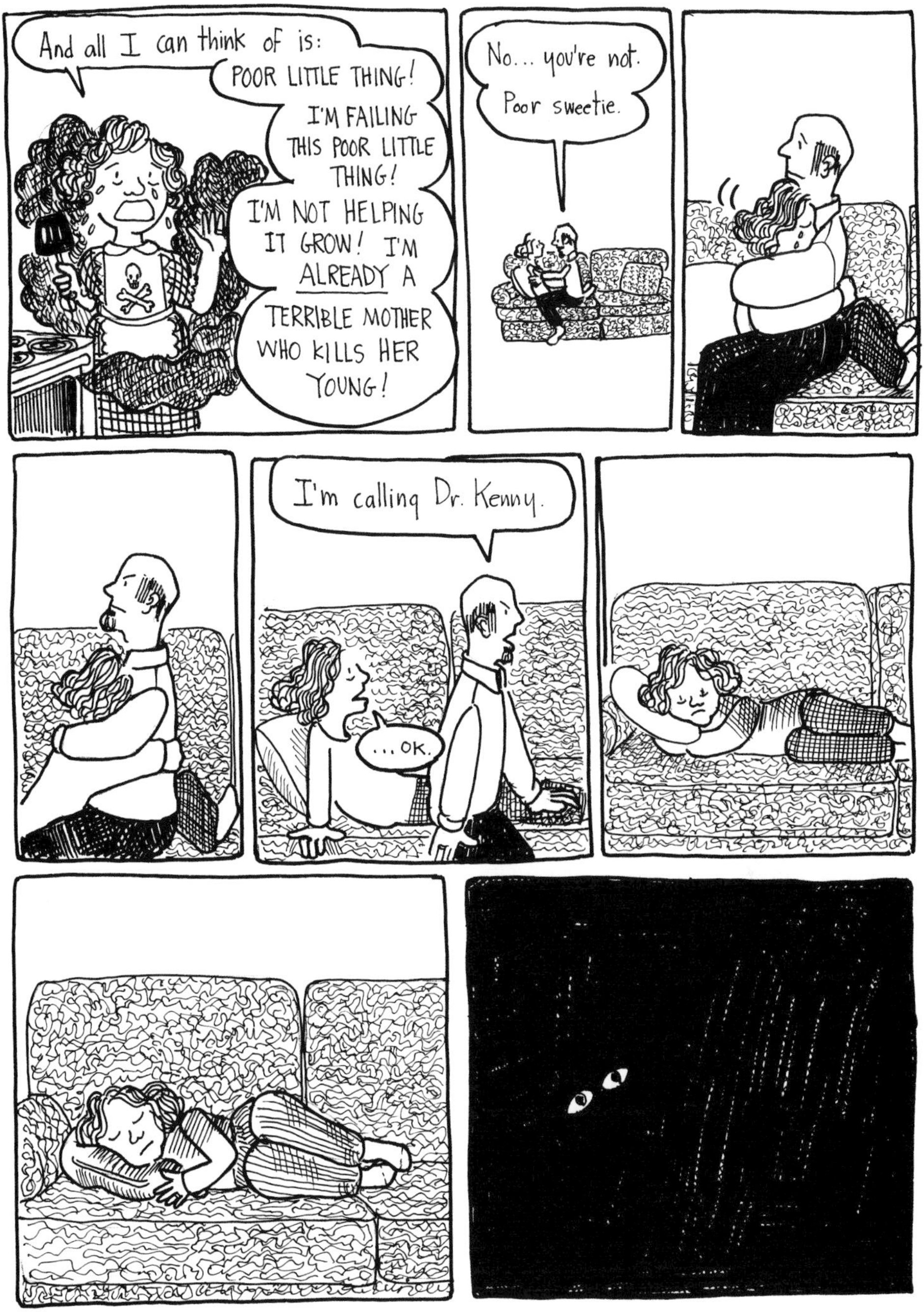
And all I can think of is:
POOR LITTLE THING! I'M FAILING THIS POOR LITTLE THING! I'M NOT HELPING IT GROW! I'M ALREADY A TERRIBLE MOTHER WHO KILLS HER YOUNG!
No... you're not. Poor sweetie.
I'm calling Dr. Kenny.
...OK.

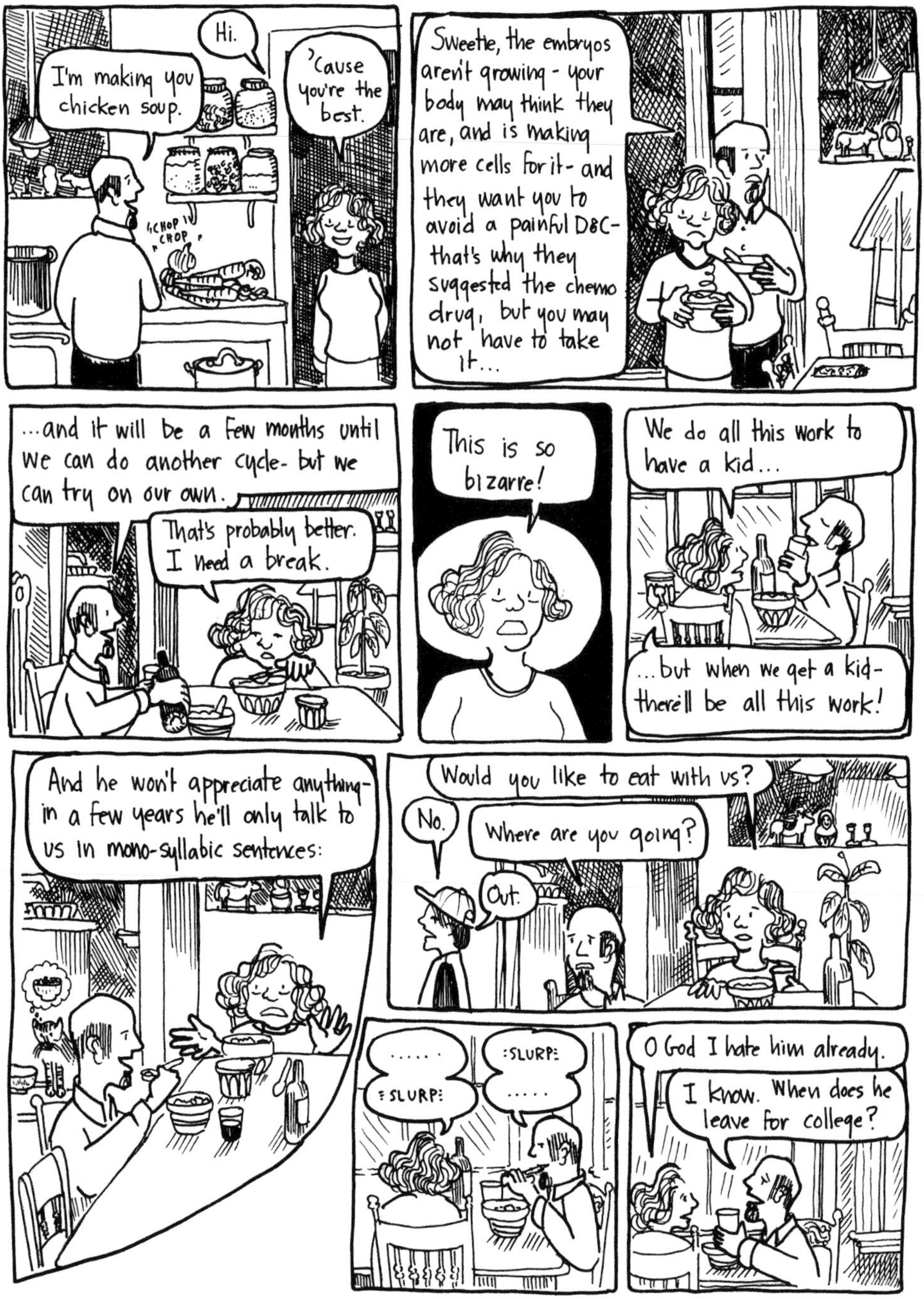
I'm making you chicken soup.
Hi.
'Cause you're the best.
CHOP CHOP
Sweetie, the embryos aren't growing - your body may think they are, and is making more cells for it - and they want you to avoid a painful D&C - that's why they suggested the chemo drug, but you may not have to take it...
...and it will be a few months until we can do another cycle - but we can try on our own.
That's probably better. I need a break.
This is so bizarre!
We do all this work to have a kid...
...but when we get a kid - there'll be all this work!
And he won't appreciate anything - in a few years he'll only talk to us in mono-syllabic sentences:
Would you like to eat with us?
No.
Where are you going?
Out.
......
SLURP
SLURP
......
O God I hate him already.
I know. When does he leave for college?

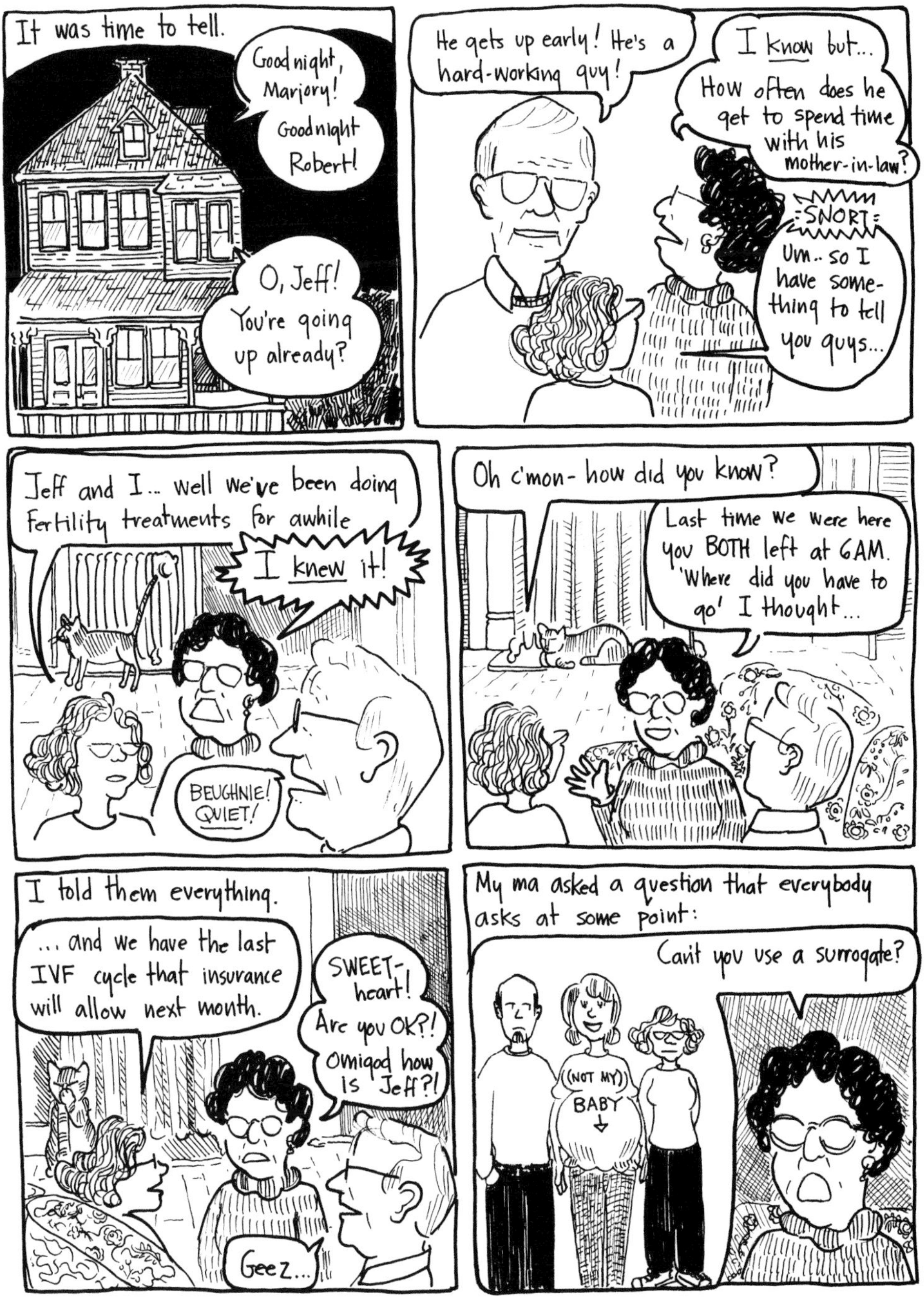
It was time to tell.
Goodnight, Marjory!
Goodnight Robert!
O, Jeff! You're going up already?
He gets up early! He's a hard-working guy!
I know but...
How often does he get to spend time with his mother-in-law?
SNORT
Um.. so I have something to tell you guys...
Jeff and I... well we've been doing fertility treatments for awhile
I knew it!
BEUGHNIE! QUIET!
Oh c'mon- how did you know?
Last time we were here you BOTH left at 6AM. 'Where did you have to go' I thought...
I told them everything.
... and we have the last IVF cycle that insurance will allow next month.
SWEET-heart! Are you OK?! Omigod how is Jeff?!
Geez...
My ma asked a question that everybody asks at some point:
Can't you use a surrogate?
(NOT MY) BABY

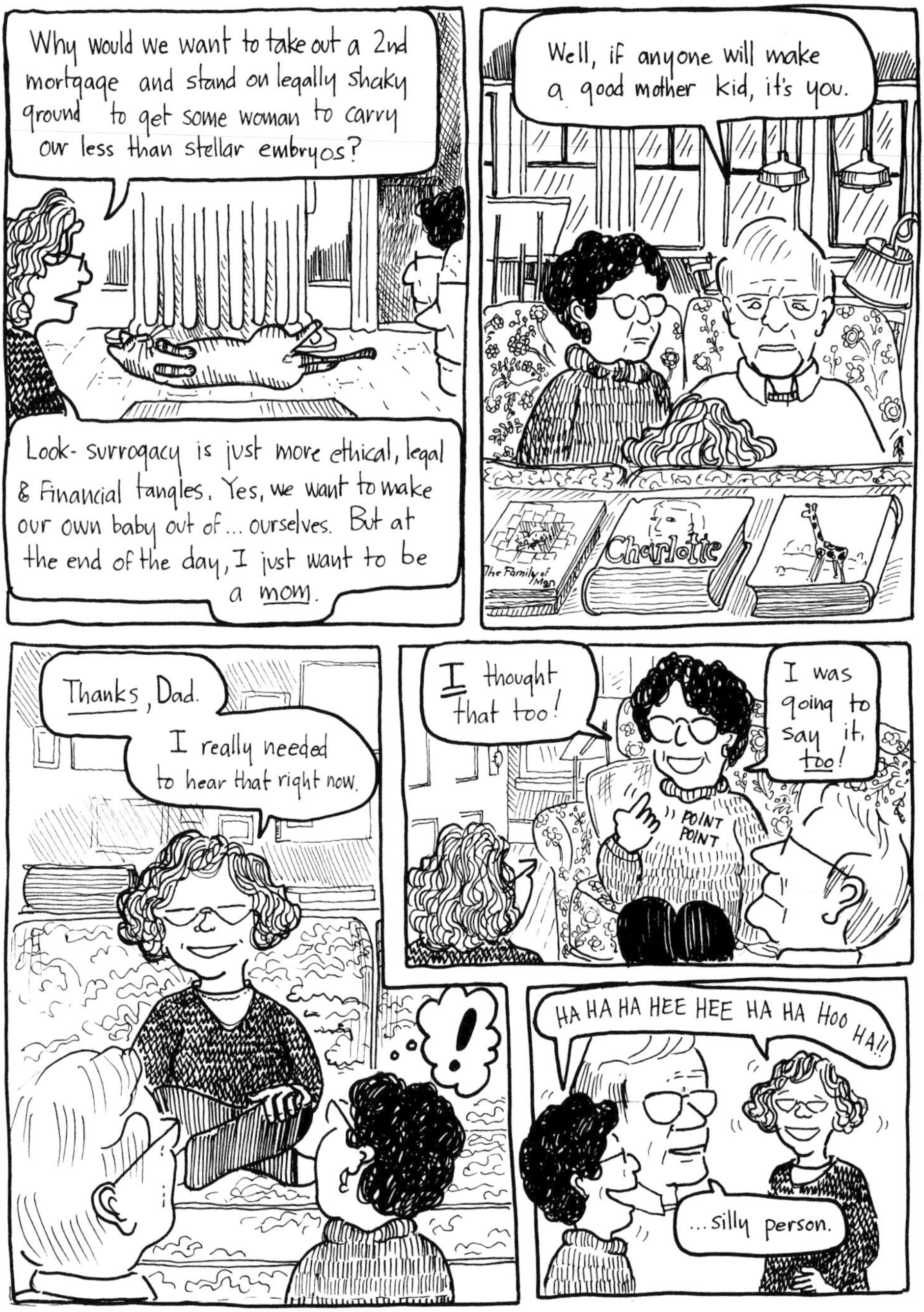
Why would we want to take out a 2nd mortgage and stand on legally shaky ground to get some woman to carry our less than stellar embryos?
Look- surrogacy is just more ethical, legal & financial tangles. Yes, we want to make our own baby out of... ourselves. But at the end of the day, I just want to be a mom.
Well, if anyone will make a good mother kid, it's you.
The Family of Man
Charlotte
Thanks, Dad.
I really needed to hear that right now.
I thought that too!
I was going to say it, too!
POINT POINT
!
HA HA HA HEE HEE HA HA HOO HA!!
...silly person.

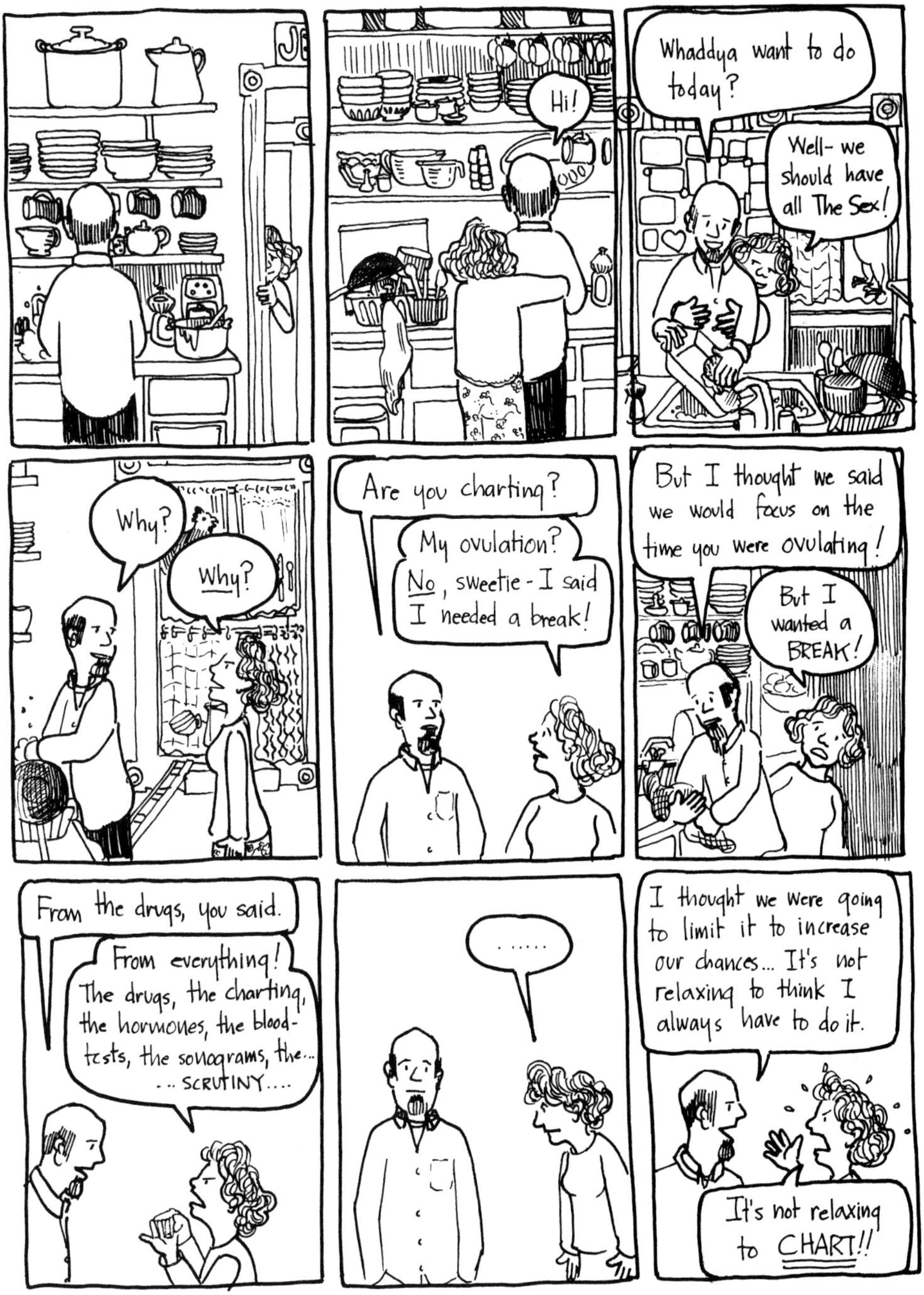
Hi!
Whaddya want to do today?
Well- we should have all The Sex!
Why?
Why?
Are you charting?
My ovulation? No, sweetie - I said I needed a break!
But I thought we said we would focus on the time you were ovulating!
But I wanted a BREAK!
From the drugs, you said.
From everything! The drugs, the charting, the hormones, the blood-tests, the sonograms, the... ...SCRUTINY....
......
I thought we were going to limit it to increase our chances... It's not relaxing to think I always have to do it.
It's not relaxing to CHART!!

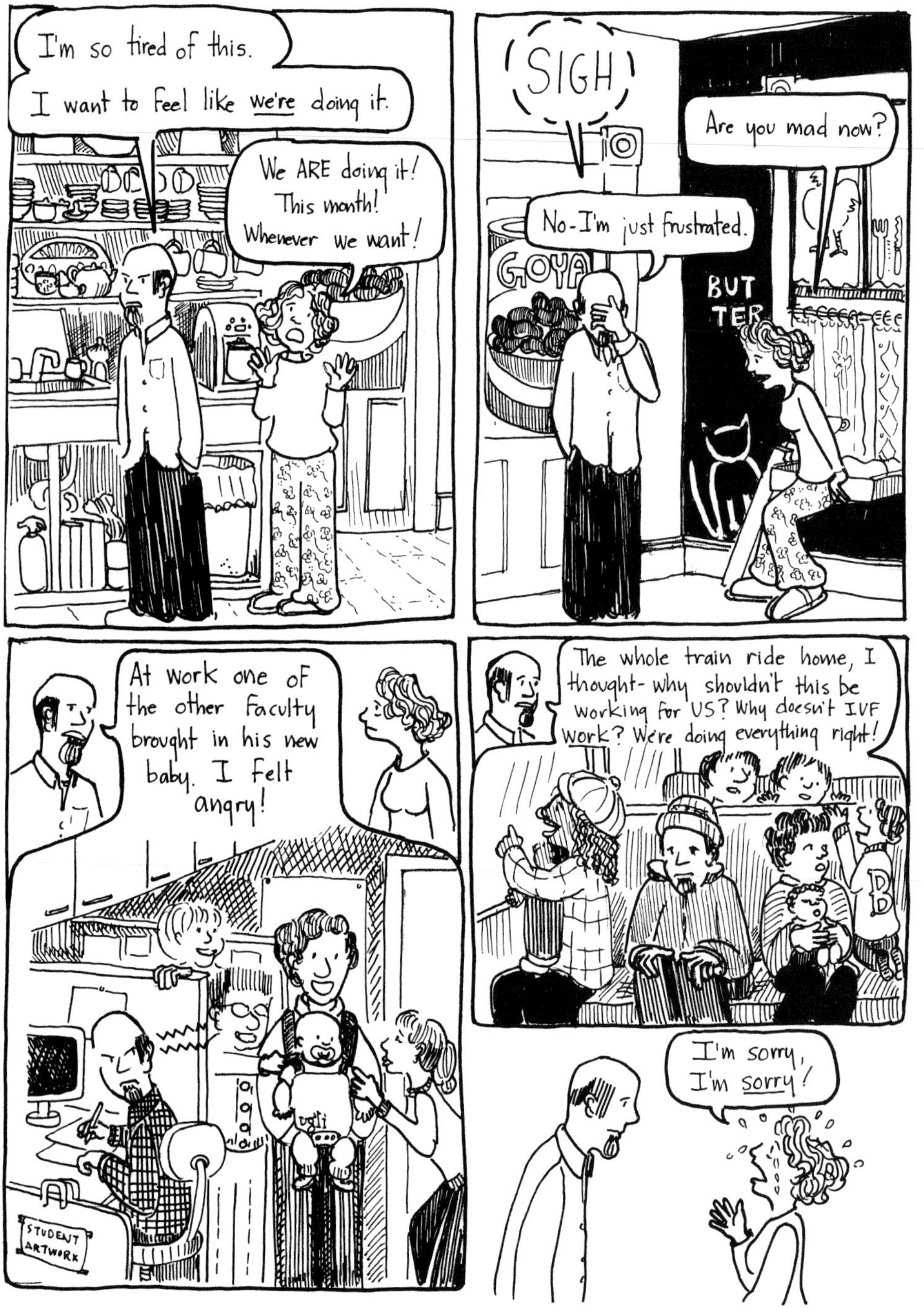

I'm so tired of this.
I want to feel like we're doing it.
We ARE doing it! This month! Whenever we want!
SIGH
Are you mad now?
No-I'm just frustrated.
GOYA
BUT TER
At work one of the other faculty brought in his new baby. I felt angry!
STUDENT ARTWORK
The whole train ride home, I thought- why shouldn't this be working for US? Why doesn't IVF work? We're doing everything right!
B
I'm sorry, I'm sorry!

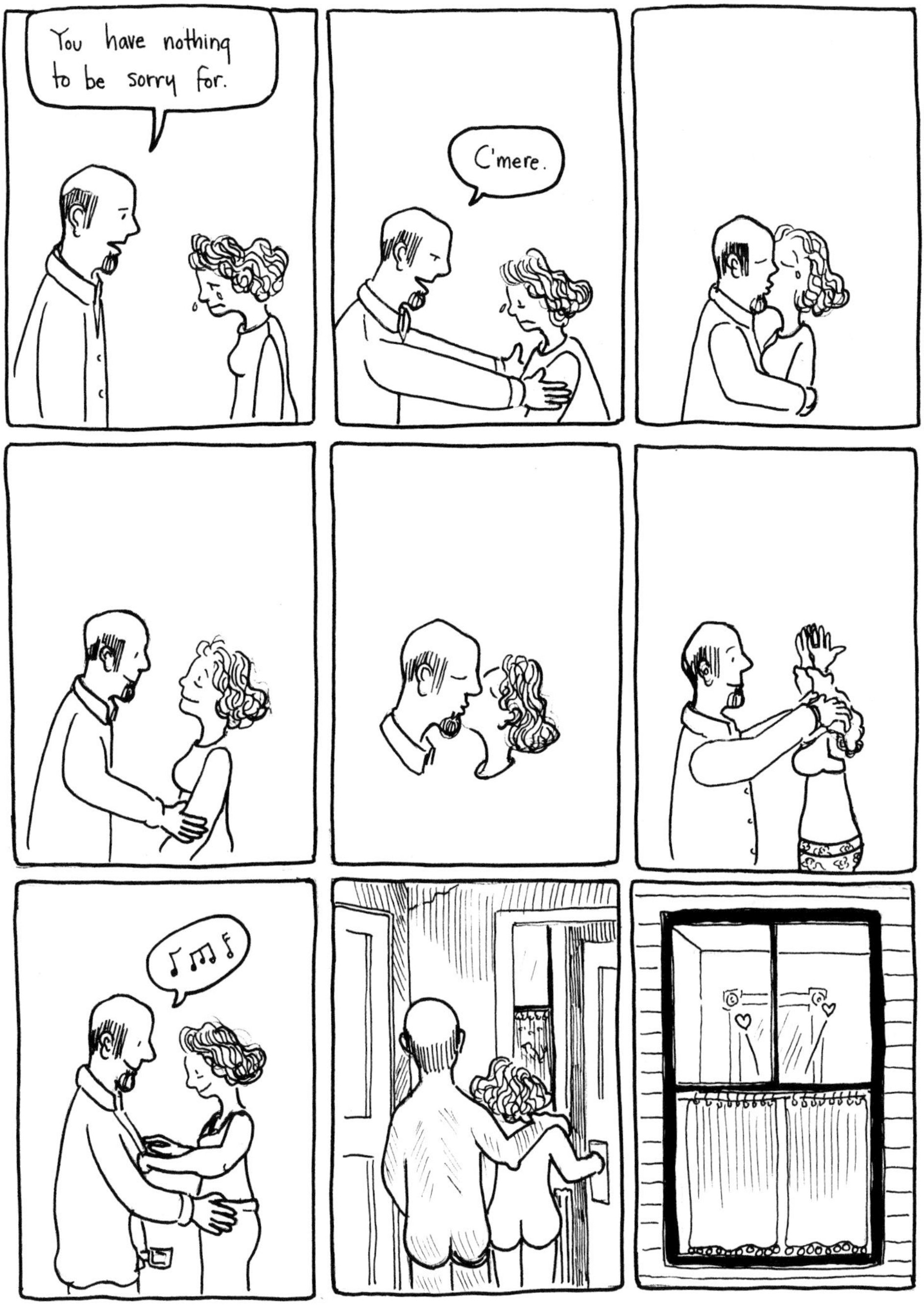
You have nothing to be sorry for.
C'mere.

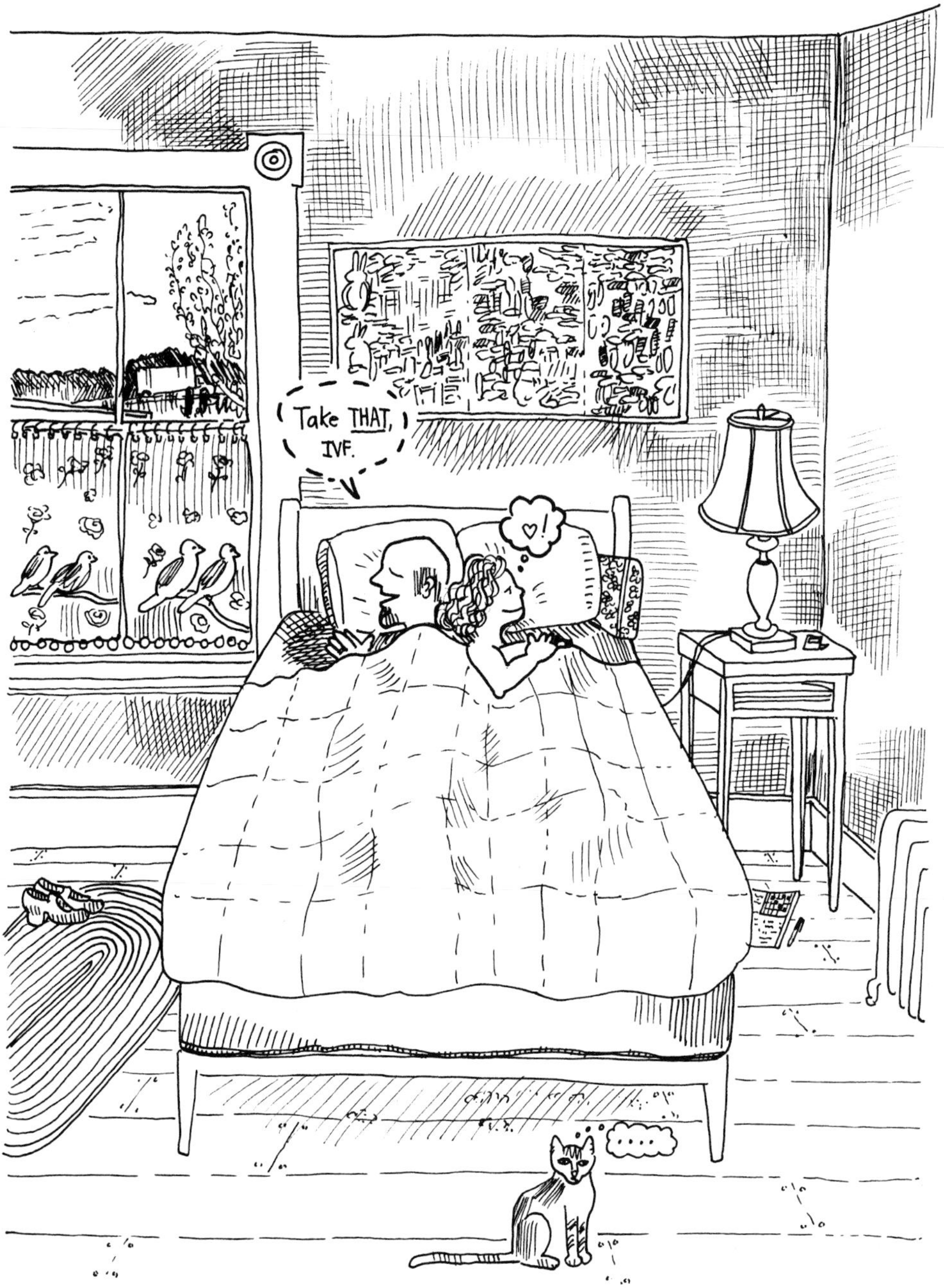
Take THAT, IVF.
♡!
....

Hey, Phoebe!
BABIES
Alexandra! How DARE you go on vacation!
My whole Fertility world crumbles without you!
Aww... I missed you, too, Phoeb! Here's Dr. Kenny...
BABIES

Hey, kiddo!
Hey, Dr. Kenny
We...ah... we didn't on our own...um I mean- we're still not pregnant so-what's next?
Alright- have you heard of PGD? No? Ok- we take one cell from each of your 4 cell embryos & send it to the lab to be screened for abnormalities.
PLUCK!
Normal embryos have a higher rate of implementation Screening out the abnormal ones tells us which ones to transfer.
Yes
NO

I signed on to hand-pick the best-looking embryos. We cast our last lot with biotech baby engineering.

And I laid **20** eggs!

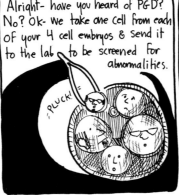

of which **18** became embryos!

After the genetic testing **10** came back from the lab normal!

☑☑☑☑☑☑☑
☑☑☑

A grand total of **4** were transferred to my long-suffering uterus. Resulting in...

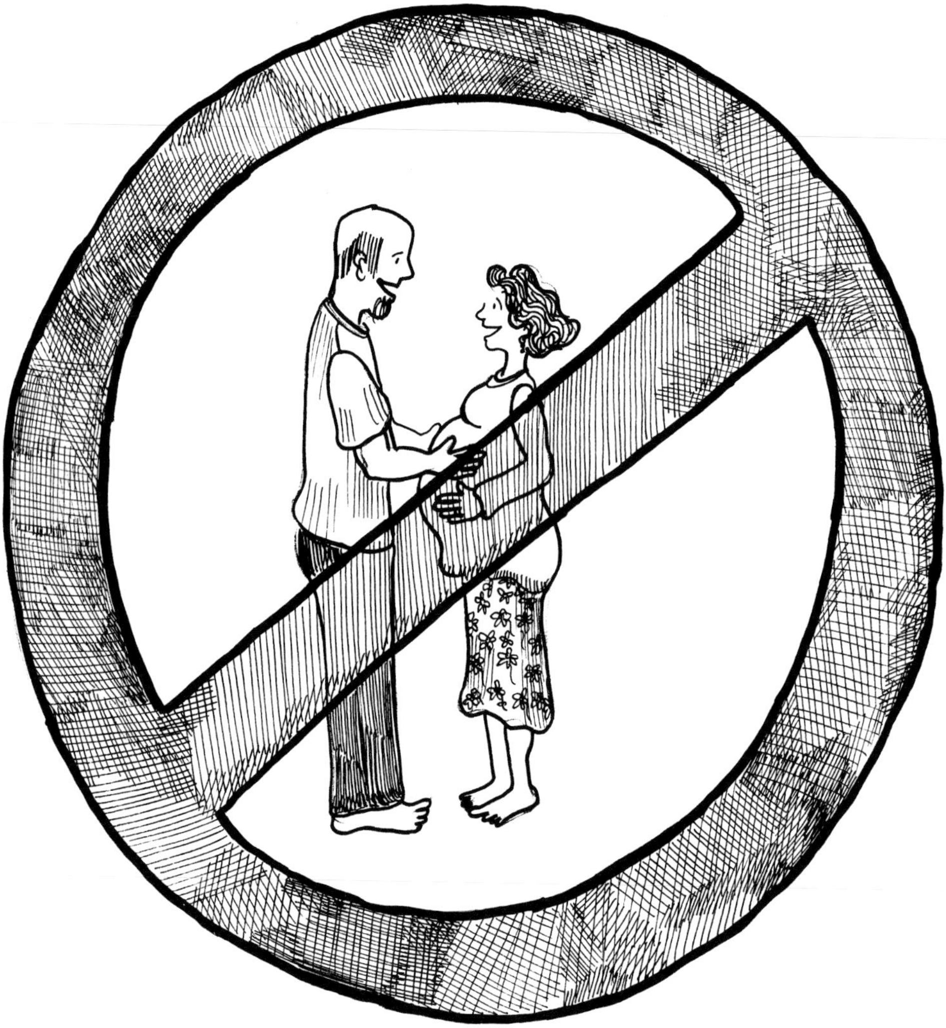

Zero. Zip. Zilch. Nada. Nothing. None. Nil. Not.

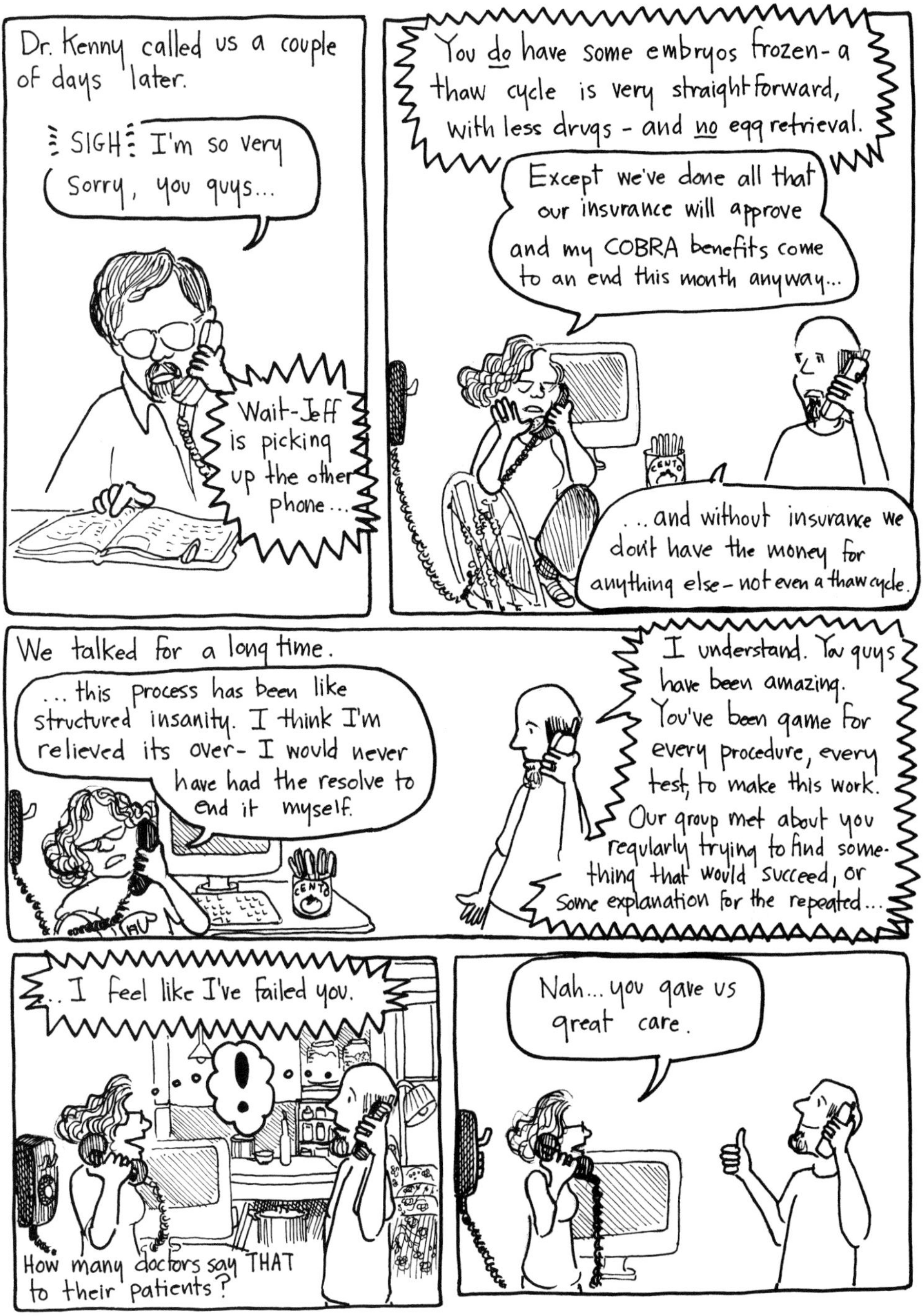
Dr. Kenny called us a couple of days later.
SIGH I'm so very sorry, you guys...
Wait-Jeff is picking up the other phone...
You do have some embryos frozen- a thaw cycle is very straightforward, with less drugs - and no egg retrieval.
Except we've done all that our insurance will approve and my COBRA benefits come to an end this month anyway...
...and without insurance we don't have the money for anything else- not even a thaw cycle.
We talked for a long time.
...this process has been like structured insanity. I think I'm relieved its over- I would never have had the resolve to end it myself.
I understand. You guys have been amazing. You've been game for every procedure, every test, to make this work. Our group met about you regularly trying to find something that would succeed, or some explanation for the repeated...
...I feel like I've failed you.
How many doctors say THAT to their patients?
Nah...you gave us great care.

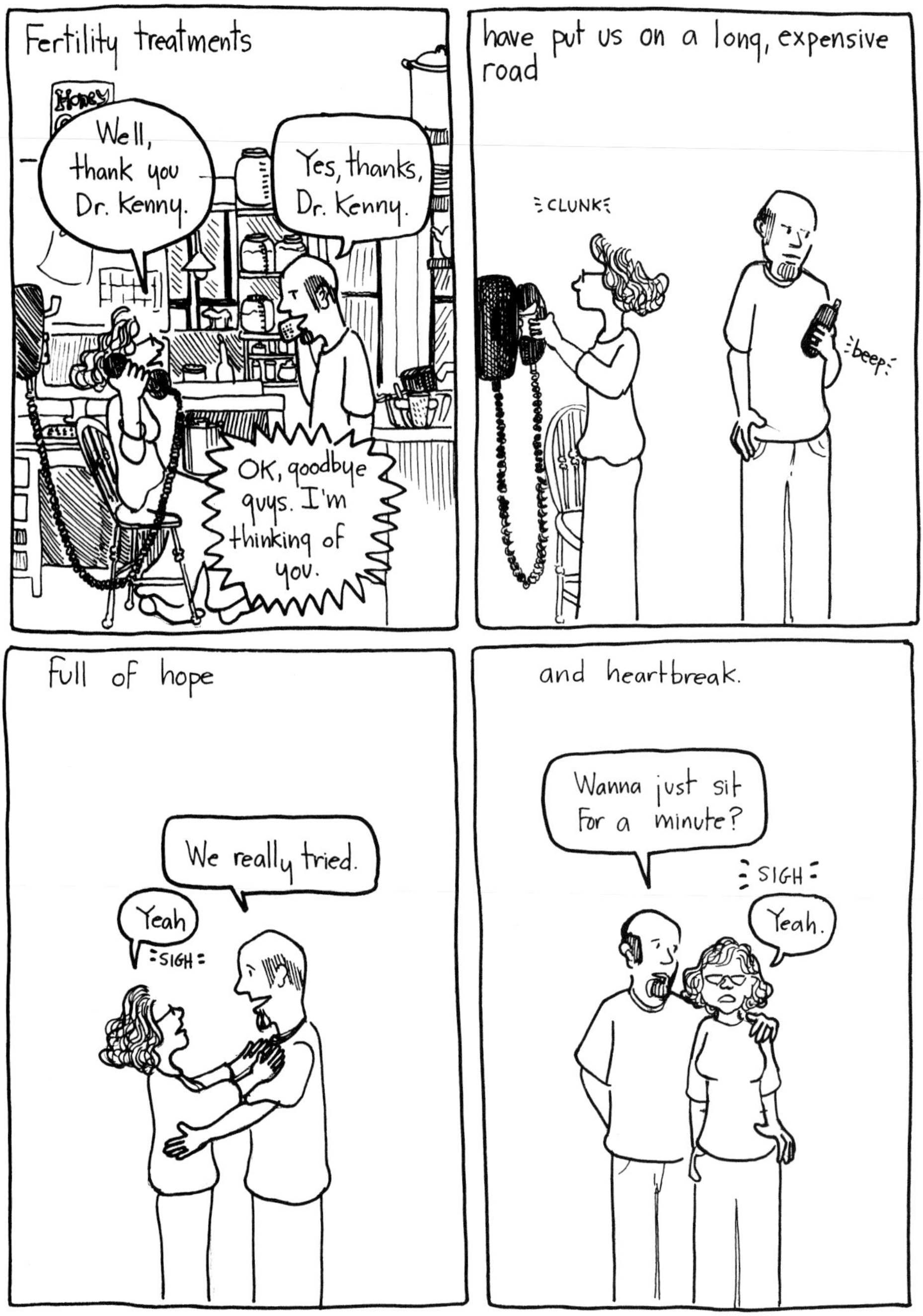
Fertility treatments
Honey
Well, thank you Dr. Kenny.
Yes, thanks, Dr. Kenny.
OK, goodbye guys. I'm thinking of you.
have put us on a long, expensive road
CLUNK
beep
full of hope
Yeah
SIGH
We really tried.
and heartbreak.
Wanna just sit for a minute?
SIGH
Yeah.

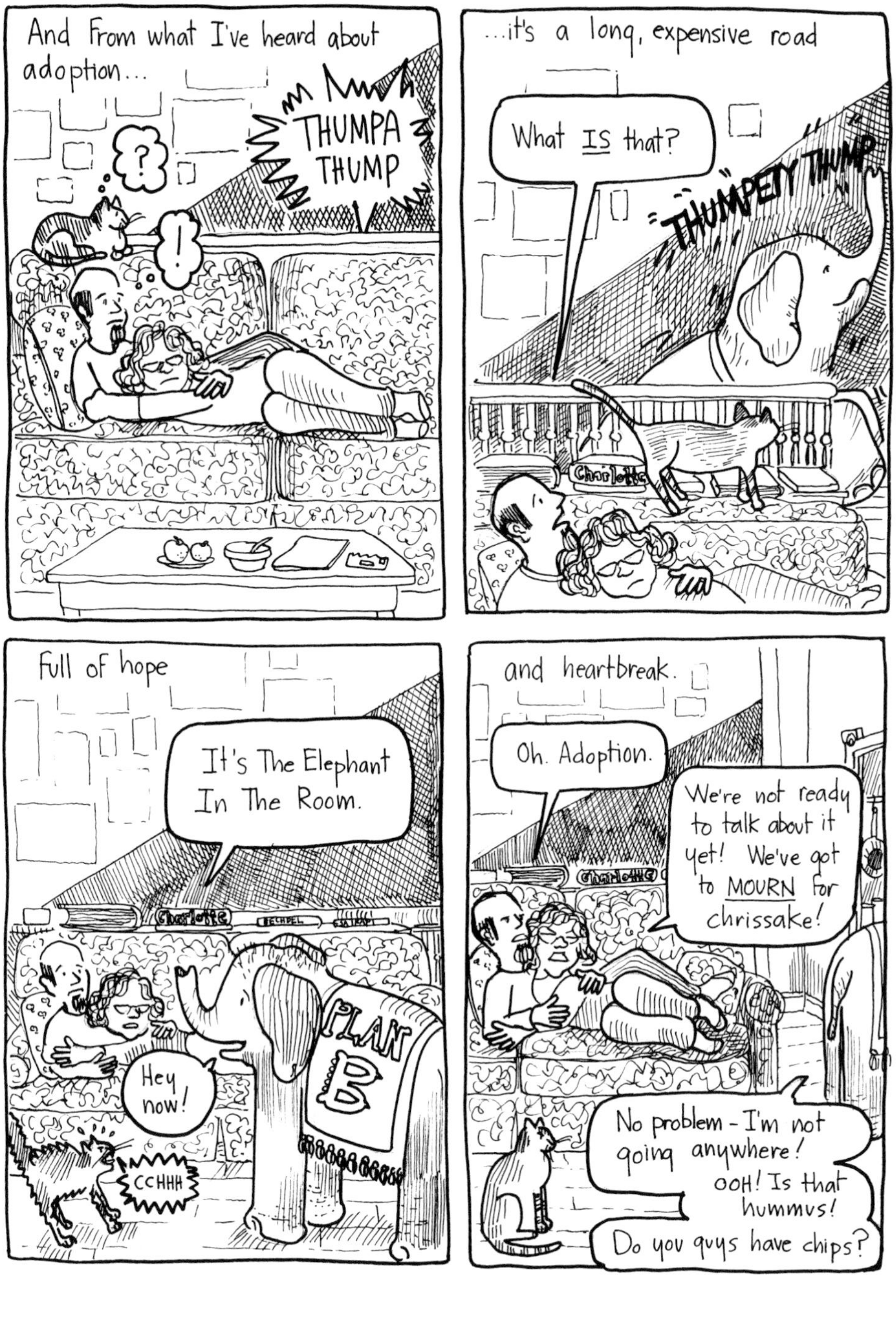
And from what I've heard about adoption...
?
!
THUMPA THUMP
...it's a long, expensive road
What IS that?
THUMPETY THUMP
Charlotte
Full of hope
It's The Elephant In The Room.
Charlotte
PLAN B
Hey now!
CCHHH
and heartbreak.
Oh. Adoption.
We're not ready to talk about it yet! We've got to MOURN for chrissake!
Charlotte
No problem - I'm not going anywhere!
OOH! Is that hummus!
Do you guys have chips?

But adoption has the highest success rate of getting folks like us a baby.

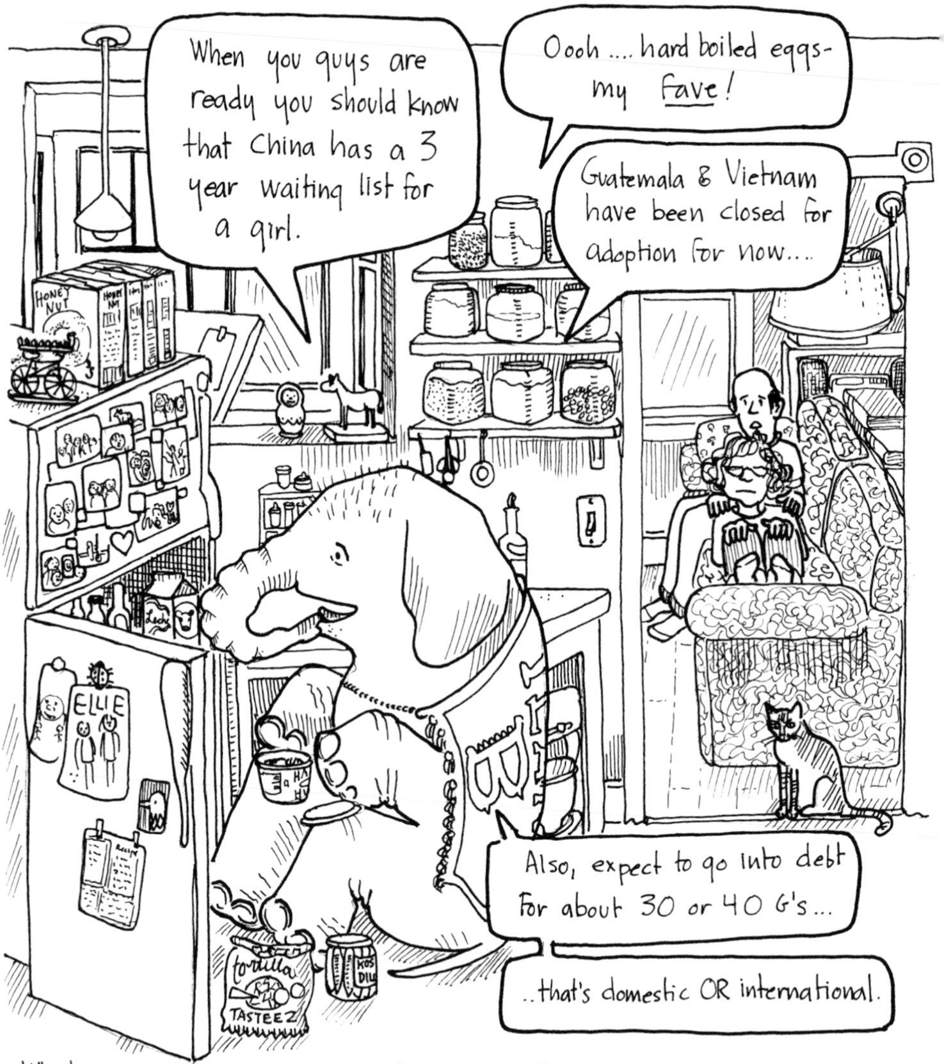
When you guys are ready you should know that China has a 3 year waiting list for a girl.
Oooh .... hard boiled eggs- my fave!
Guatemala & Vietnam have been closed for adoption for now....
HONEY NUT
ELLIE
Also, expect to go into debt for about 30 or 40 G's...
..that's domestic OR international.
TASTEEZ

Which means we can raise a family. We will become parents. Which by all accounts is another journey, long, expensive...

Full of hope...

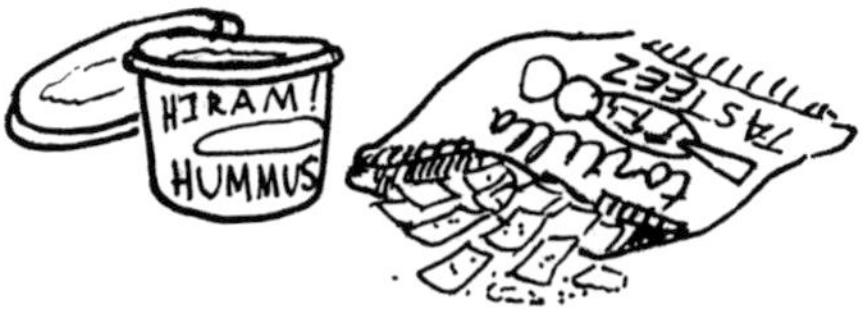
HIRAM!
HUMMUS

and heartbreak.

afterword

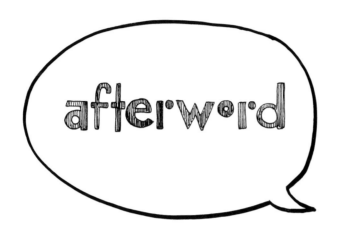

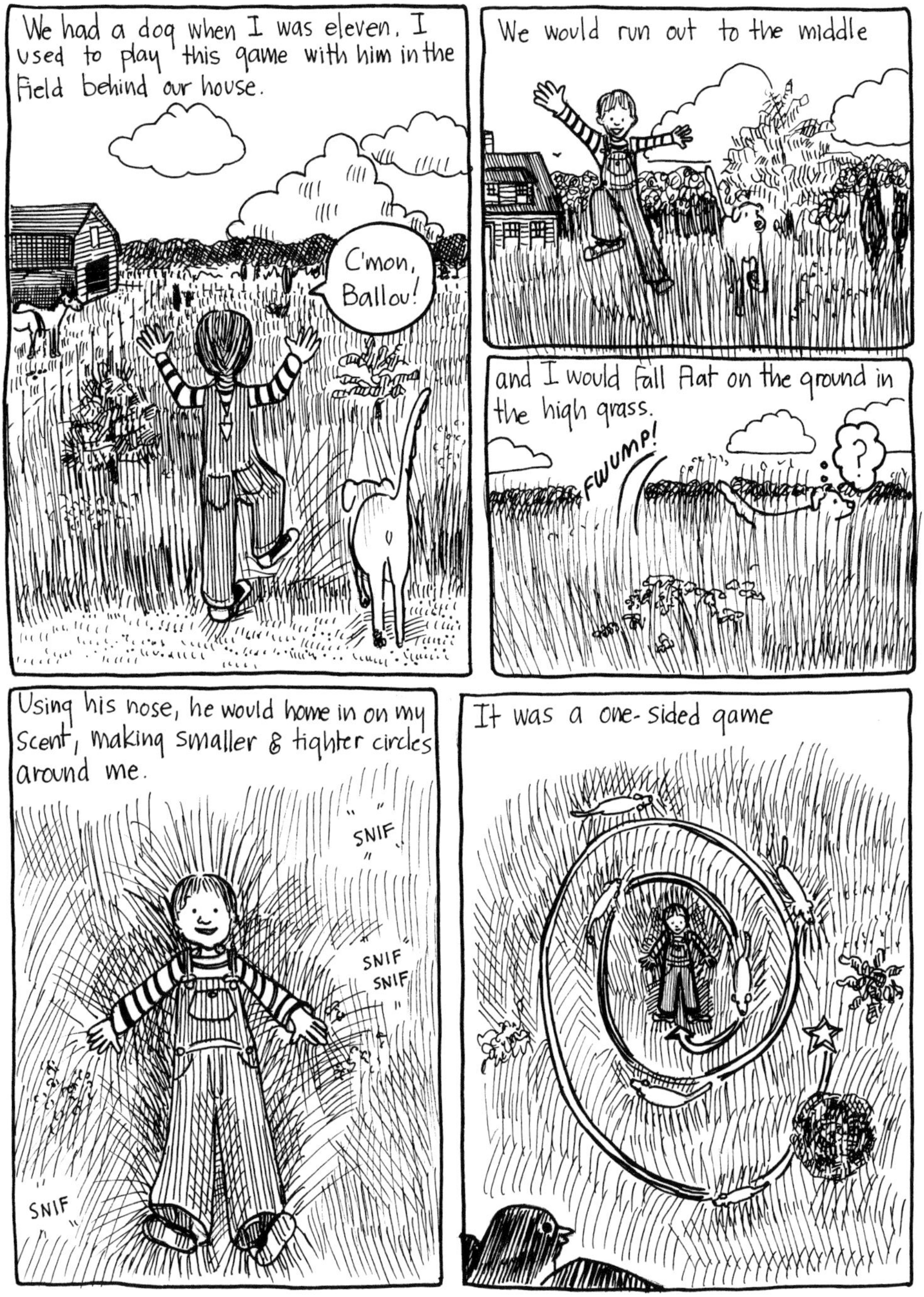
We had a dog when I was eleven. I used to play this game with him in the field behind our house.
C'mon, Ballou!
We would run out to the middle
and I would fall flat on the ground in the high grass.
FWUMP!
?
Using his nose, he would home in on my scent, making smaller & tighter circles around me.
SNIF
SNIF
SNIF
SNIF
It was a one-sided game

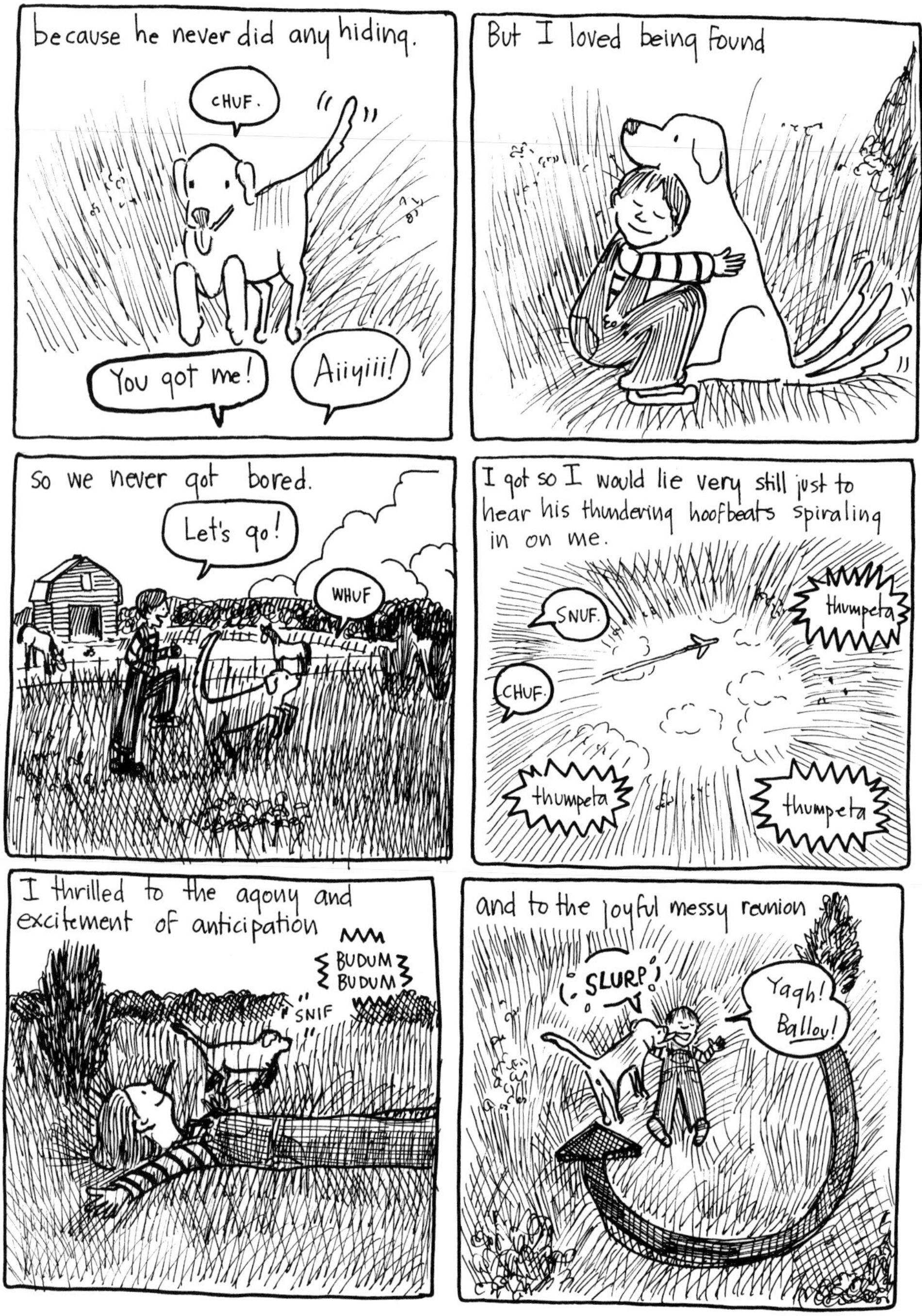
because he never did any hiding.
CHUF.
You got me!
Aiiyiii!
But I loved being found
So we never got bored.
Let's go!
WHUF
I got so I would lie very still just to hear his thundering hoofbeats spiraling in on me.
SNUF.
thumpeta
CHUF.
thumpeta
thumpeta
I thrilled to the agony and excitement of anticipation
BUDUM
BUDUM
SNIF
and to the joyful messy reunion
SLURP
Yagh! Ballou!

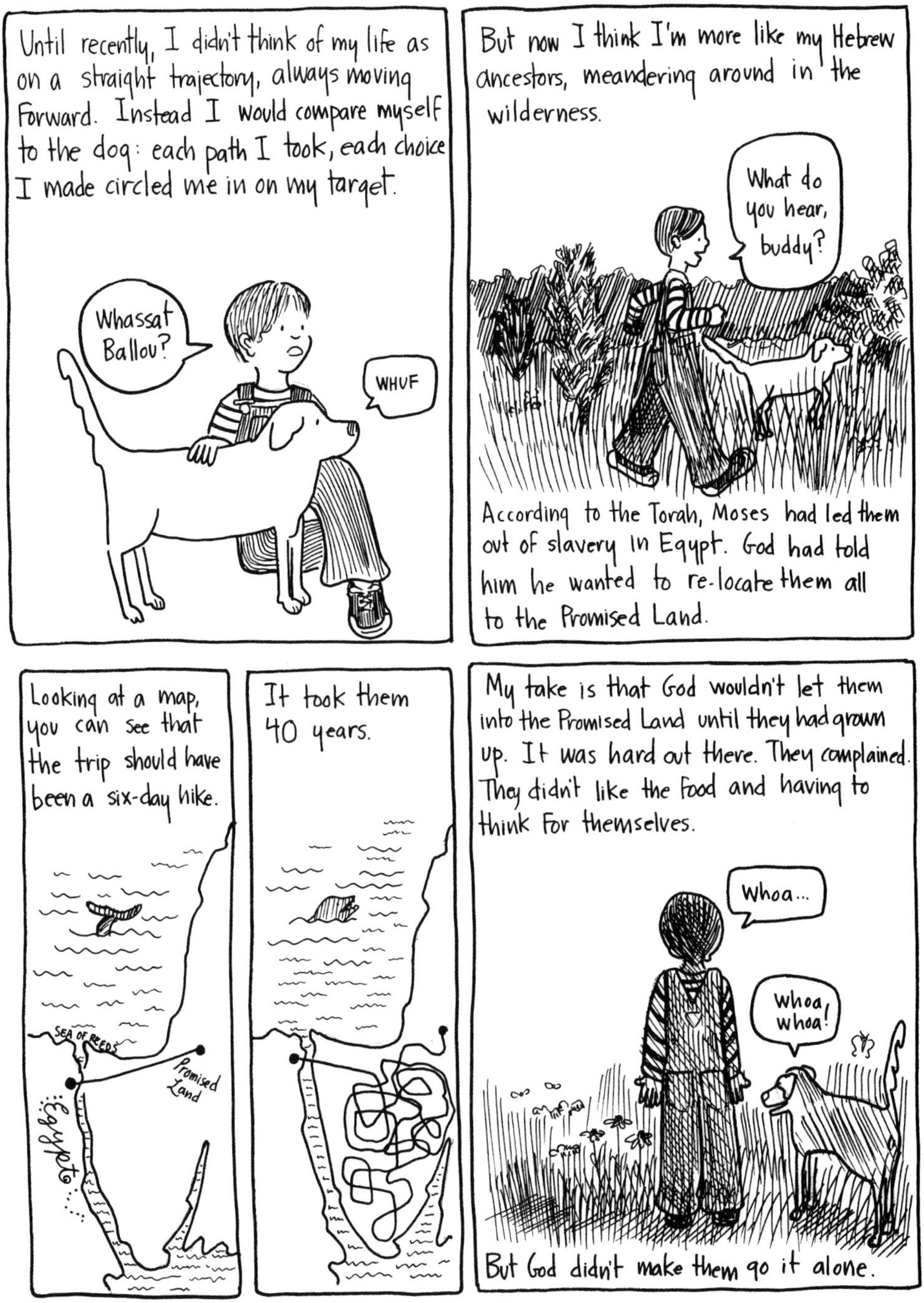
Until recently, I didn't think of my life as on a straight trajectory, always moving forward. Instead I would compare myself to the dog: each path I took, each choice I made circled me in on my target.
Whassat Ballou?
WHUF
But now I think I'm more like my Hebrew ancestors, meandering around in the wilderness.
What do you hear, buddy?
According to the Torah, Moses had led them out of slavery in Egypt. God had told him he wanted to re-locate them all to the Promised Land.
Looking at a map, you can see that the trip should have been a six-day hike.
SEA OF REEDS
Promised Land
Egypt
It took them 40 years.
My take is that God wouldn't let them into the Promised Land until they had grown up. It was hard out there. They complained. They didn't like the food and having to think for themselves.
Whoa...
Whoa, whoa!
But God didn't make them go it alone.

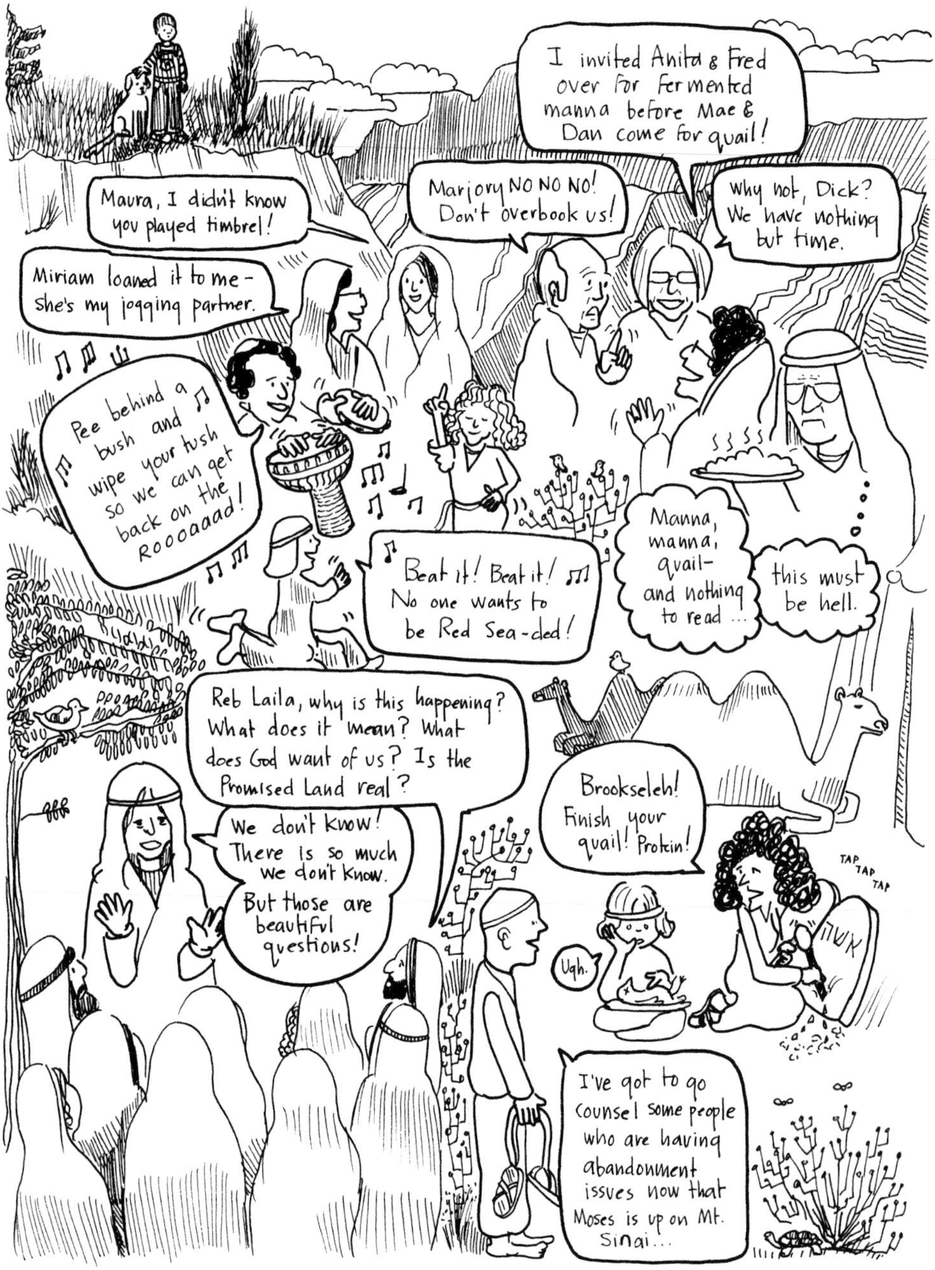

I invited Anita & Fred over for fermented manna before Mae & Dan come for quail!
Maura, I didn't know you played timbrel!
Marjory NO NO NO! Don't overbook us!
Why not, Dick? We have nothing but time.
Miriam loaned it to me - she's my jogging partner.
Pee behind a bush and wipe your tush so we can get back on the Roooaaad!
Beat it! Beat it! No one wants to be Red Sea-ded!
Manna, manna, quail- and nothing to read...
this must be hell.
Reb Laila, why is this happening? What does it mean? What does God want of us? Is the Promised Land real?
We don't know! There is so much we don't know.
But those are beautiful questions!
Brookseleh! Finish your quail! Protein!
TAP TAP TAP
Ugh.
I've got to go counsel some people who are having abandonment issues now that Moses is up on Mt. Sinai...

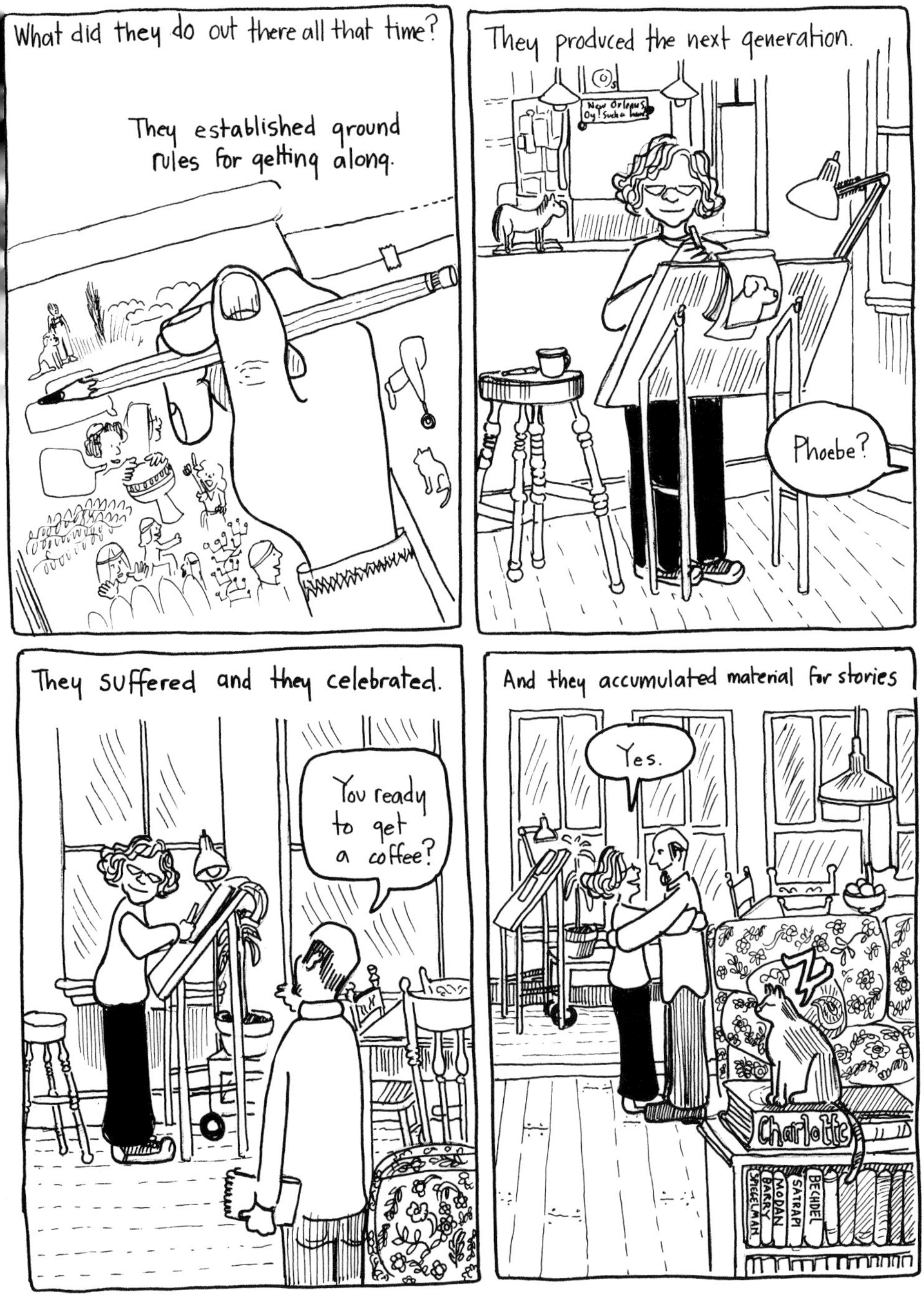

What did they do out there all that time?
They established ground rules for getting along.
They produced the next generation.
New Orleans
Phoebe?
They suffered and they celebrated.
You ready to get a coffee?
And they accumulated material for stories
Yes.
Charlotte
SPIEGELMAN
BARRY
MODAN
SATRAPI
BECHDEL

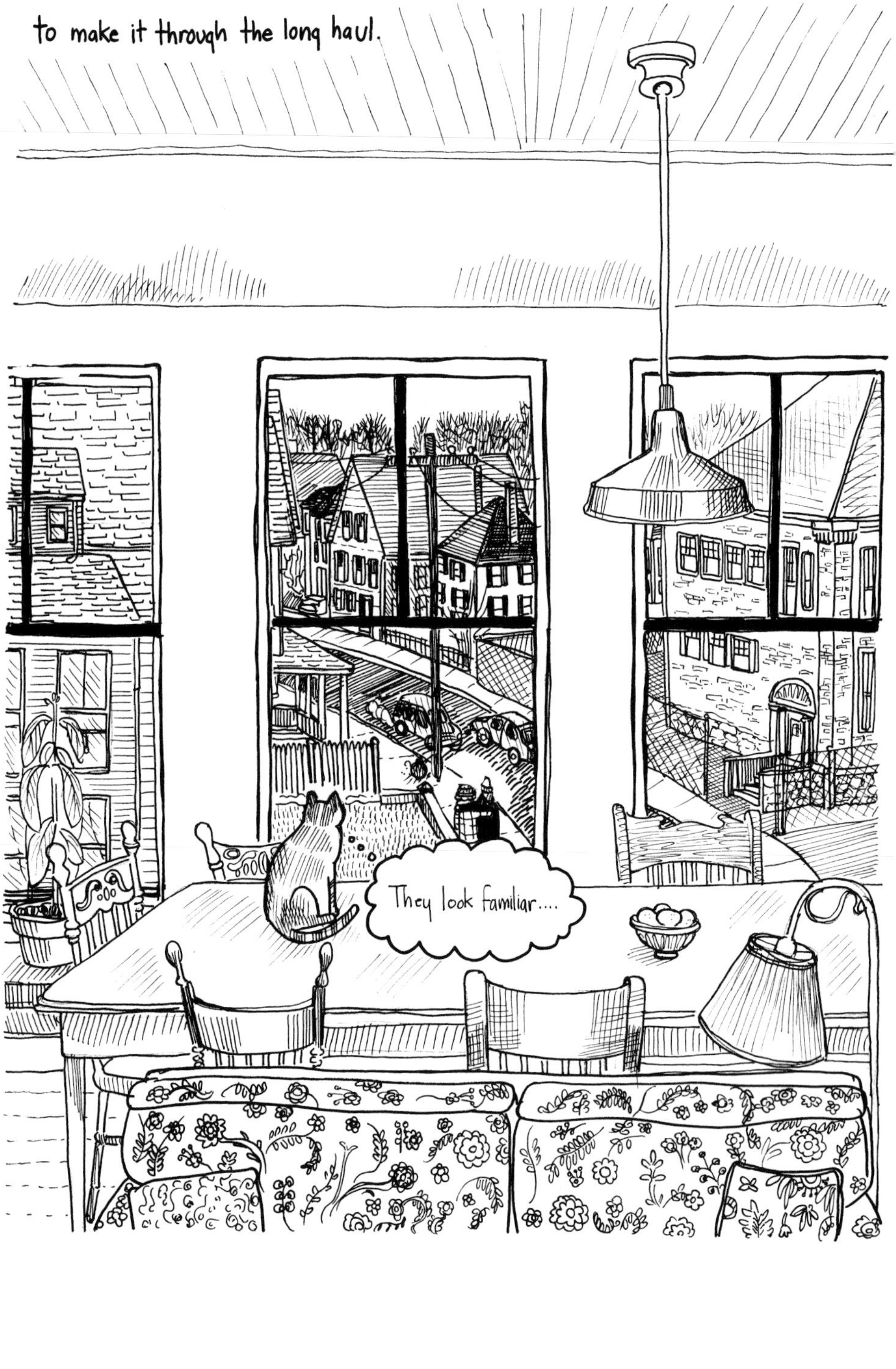
to make it through the long haul.
They look familiar....

IT TAKES A SHTETL☆ to make

a comic book. GOOD EGGS was not a glint in my eye until I got a mandate from comix guru PAUL KARASIK for 'five pages on fertility' and then gave me concrete advice at critical junctures in the process. Master Storyteller CHARLOTTE GORDON has consistently advised me in the wild wooly world of publishing, I'm deeply grateful for her knowledge, friendship & generous spirit. My fierce yet ebullient agent, BRETTNE BLOOM of Kneerim & Williams, championed this book from the beginning; I'm lucky to have her in my corner. That you hold a beautiful three-dimensional object in your hands is thanks in great part to the manuscript midwives of midtown: ELISABETH DYSSEGAARD encouraged me to make a multi-layered narrative, & then edited it with kindness & intelligence. ALLISON LORENTZEN saw the project through to completion with skill & grace. ARCHIE FERGUSON conceived the sock-o cover. TOM PITONIAK made quick work of the copy editing. JAY CROWLEY calmly & expertly made the drawing boards camera ready.

I owe a great debt of thanks to the families & staff of TEMPLE AHAVAT ACHIM, my little shul by the sea here in Gloucester. IF TAA is my spiritual home, then the LONE GULL COFFEE HOUSE is my place of worship. Every day Mary Ellen Borge and her happy crew keep me in latte's and polite society.

A very special thank you to HOWARD STERN of SiriusXM satellite radio for comedy candor and camaraderie every morning at 6 AM. my mother raised me in a box, like veal...

My muses are many. My Bees, my women, my art group: MARY KENNY, LESLIE SCHOMP, & CANDICE SMITH CORBY. Those Brooklyn Balabans, Maura, Nick, Annalivia & Leo & their excellent elders Mae & Dan. The Starkey Family, of course. Ginny & Steve Marshall !!! T & O and their beautiful progeny: The Juice, The Deuce & The Caboose. The Keating-Watson Family. Meg Monqin. Melanie DeForest Malloy, Shauna Hinchen-Joyal. Kathryn Hearn. Emi Rollins. David R. & Amanda L. Brooks Richon, Laila Goodman & Mark Konecky. My fellow artist farmers Lara Lepionka & Stevens Brosnihan. Reuben wranglers Trisha & Brian Cline Rabbi Jonah Pesner, Rabbi M. Geller. The Hughes-Margolis Family. Joanna Kreilick. The Erhan Tomases & the Gipstein Kabroskys. THANK YOU FOR YOUR WARM & CONSTANT SUPPORT, & FOR BEING SUCH GOOD EGGS.

☆ Yiddish for village, little ol' town

And finally,

thank you

to my intrepid and wonderful parents

marjory and robert potts

and to my favorite artist, my darling husband & my biggest fan

jeff marshall:

thank you for your vision, your smarts, your patience & your love.

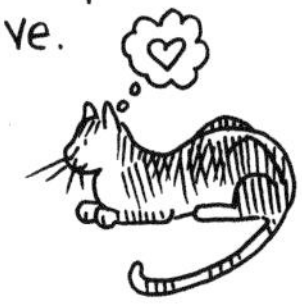